"**Captivating. . . .** You don't have to believe that the Giants stole the game to enjoy *The Echoing Green*. You don't even have to like baseball. That moment defined a generation."
—*The New York Times*

"**Compelling and thoughtful,** the book meditates on the meaning of that home run in the legacies changed forever by a single crack of the bat." —*The Miami Herald*

"**A seat along the first base line. . . .** Prager, like a good hurler with a command of many pitches, delivers nuance even when you're expecting a fastball." —*The Plain Dealer*

"Prager turns his **remarkable** powers of investigation on the men involved in the scheme. The result is **an absorbing critique** of the competitive ethic that too often rules not only America's playing fields but its boardrooms as well."
—*Sports Illustrated*

"The depth of Prager's research staggers the mind. . . . **A must-have for baseball mavens.**"
—*The Buffalo News*

"**You will not find a better-reported book** on any subject than *The Echoing Green*." —*New York Post*

JOSHUA PRAGER

THE ECHOING GREEN

Joshua Prager is a senior special writer at *The Wall Street Journal*. He lives in New York City.

www.joshuaprager.com

October 3, 1951

Giants	AB.	R.	H.	O.	A.	E.
Stanky, 2b	4	0	0	0	4	0
Dark, ss	4	1	1	2	2	0
Mueller, rf	4	0	1	0	0	0
‡Hartung	0	1	0	0	0	0
Irvin, lf	4	1	1	1	0	0
Lockman, 1b	3	1	2	11	1	0
Thomson, 3b	4	1	3	4	1	0
Mays, cf	3	0	0	1	0	0
Westrum, c	0	0	0	7	1	0
*Rigney	1	0	0	0	0	0
Noble, c	0	0	0	0	0	0
Maglie, p	2	0	0	1	2	0
†Thompson	1	0	0	0	0	0
Jansen, p	0	0	0	0	0	0
Totals	30	5	8	27	11	0

Dodgers	AB.	R.	H.	O.	A.	E
Furillo, rf	5	0	0	0	0	0
Reese, ss	4	2	1	2	5	0
Snider, cf	3	1	2	1	0	0
Robinson, 2b	2	1	1	3	2	0
Pafko, lf	4	0	1	4	1	0
Hodges, 1b	4	0	0	11	1	0
Cox, 3b	4	0	2	1	3	0
Walker, c	4	0	1	2	0	0
Newcombe, p	4	0	0	1	1	0
Branca, p	0	0	0	0	0	0
Totals	34	4	8	§25	13	0

*Struck out for Westrum in eighth.
†Grounded out for Maglie in eighth.
‡Ran for Mueller in ninth.
§One out when winning run scored.

Dodgers _____ 1 0 0　0 0 0　0 3 0—4
Giants _____ 0 0 0　0 0 0　1 0 4—5

Runs batted in—Robinson, Thomson (4), Pafko, Cox, Lockman. Two base hits—Thomson, Irvin, Lockman. Home run—Thomson. Sacrifice hit—Lockman. Double plays — Cox, Robinson and Hodges; Reese, Robinson and Hodges. Bases on balls—Off Maglie, 4 (Reese, Snider, Robinson 2); Newcombe, 2 (Westrum 2). Struck out—By Maglie, 6 (Furillo, Walker 2, Snider, Pafko, Reese); Newcombe, 2 (Mays, Rigney). Pitching records—Off Maglie 8 hits, 4 runs in 8 innings; Jansen 0 hits, 0 runs in 1; Newcombe, 7 hits, 4 runs in 8⅓ innings; Branca, 1 hit, 1 run in 0 innings (pitched to one batter in ninth). Left on base—Dodgers, 7; Giants, 3. Earned runs—Giants, 5; Dodgers, 4. Wild pitch—Maglie. Winner—Jansen (23 - 11). Loser—Branca (13-12). Umpires—Jorda at plate, Conlan, first base; Stewart, second base; Goetz, third base. Time—2:28. Attendance—34,320.

THE ECHOING GREEN

THE ECHOING GREEN

The Untold Story of
Bobby Thomson,
Ralph Branca
and the
Shot Heard Round the World

JOSHUA PRAGER

Vintage Books
A Division of Random House, Inc.
New York

The Library of Congress has cataloged the Pantheon edition as follows:
Prager, Joshua.
The echoing green : the untold story of Bobby Thomson, Ralph Branca, and the
shot heard round the world / Joshua Prager.
p. cm.
Includes bibliographical references and index.
1. New York Giants (Baseball team)—History. 2. Thomson, Bobby, 1923–.
3. Branca, Ralph, 1926–. 4. Baseball—New York (State)—New York—
History—20th century.
I. Title.
GV875.N42 P 796.357'64097471   dc—22 2006043157

Vintage ISBN: 978-0-375-71307-1

Book design by M. Kristen Bearse

Author photograph © Simon Eisinger

www.vintagebooks.com

Printed in the United States of America
10 9 8 7 6 5 4 3 2 1

To Bobby Thomson and Ralph Branca
And to Claire Gronich, my Bubster,
who always read aloud the name of the author

The Sun does arise,
And make happy the skies.
The merry bells ring
To welcome the Spring.
The sky-lark and thrush,
The birds of the bush,
Sing louder around,
To the bells chearful sound.
While our sports shall be seen
On the Ecchoing Green.

Old John with white hair
Does laugh away care,
Sitting under the oak,
Among the old folk,
They laugh at our play,
And soon they all say.
Such such were the joys.
When we all girls & boys,
In our youth-time were seen,
On the Ecchoing Green.

Till the little ones weary
No more can be merry
The sun does descend,
And our sports have an end:
Round the laps of their mothers,
Many sisters and brothers,
Like birds in their nest,
Are ready for rest;
And sport no more seen,
On the darkening Green.

"The Ecchoing Green,"
WILLIAM BLAKE, 1789

CONTENTS

PROLOGUE

ON OCTOBER 3, 1951, Milton Glassman sat on a brick stoop in Forest Hills tuned to a baseball game. His Philco radio wore him thin, the cabdriver and Giant fan listening as New York and Brooklyn—deadlocked after 156 games, seven innings and six months—at last diverged, his team down 4–1 in the eighth. But single, single, foul-pop and double, dared hope in the bottom of the ninth, in the final half-inning of a season. And when at 3:58 p.m. Bobby Thomson lifted a Ralph Branca fastball over a green wall for a 5–4 win, Glassman thrust his only child overhead and let go. Four days shy of his third birthday, the boy flew high.

His flight above 99th Street remains today a very first memory for Marc Glassman. And for millions more, the blast that sent him heavenward remains after fifty-five years as indelibly marked.

"Every American male over thirty can remember three things," wrote Wells Twombly in 1971. "(1) Where he was the day he proposed to his wife, (2) where he was the day he heard the news that President Kennedy was shot and (3) where he was when he heard Russ Hodges describe the greatest home run of the century." Anthropologist Marshall Sahlins compiled a different list: Thomson home run, Kennedy assassination, Pearl Harbor, the death of Franklin Roosevelt. Author Ray Robinson added to those four 9/11. And poet Jonathan Williams recounted his own life by telling where he was during the Cuban missile crisis, when Roosevelt died and when Thomson hit the home run, Thomson the only constant in the gauge of American memory.

That a home run was more than the ethereal cap of a pennant race was clear. And so over the years, it was christened "the Shot Heard Round the World" and honored with a stamp and voted by the *Sporting News* the greatest moment in baseball history. John Steinbeck, Jack Kerouac, Philip Roth and Don DeLillo saluted it on paper. Francis Ford Coppola, *M*A*S*H*, Woody Allen and *The Simpsons* paid homage on screen. The home run was a life marker—unfading whether miracle or trauma. Wrote Stephen Jay Gould: "I have never known a greater moment of pure joy." Wrote Larry King: "No day of my life since has brought me the pain of that day." Said Tallulah Bankhead: "Today was the happiest day of my life." Said Dick Schaap: "When Bobby Thomson hit the home run, my childhood ended."

Great as the wake of a home run was, it upended none more than Thomson and Branca. For one playoff pitch forever turned opponents to dyad, to hero and goat, each to hear tell of it a majority of their remaining days, each left to wonder for a lifetime why it meant so much to so many (and why, for example, the pennant-winning home run in the last inning of the 1950 season was quickly forgotten).

Of course, there were answers—books and poems and sermons and essays to explain that a home run flew in New York, that a rivalry was rabid, a radio call sublime, a national television feed historic. But the full effect of a home run on its co-protagonists went unexamined. For in all the exegeses of a singular moment, one crucial element went missing, unknown that autumn afternoon even to the nine Dodgers afield, the 34,320 spectators at the Polo Grounds, the millions who followed the flight of a ball on radio and television. On October 3, 1951, a Giant peered through a Wollensak telescope at the Dodger signs, the finger signals transmitted from catcher to pitcher that determine the pitch to be thrown. The most famous of 240,000 home runs had a secret. And the effect on Thomson—and later Branca—of keeping that secret was, in time, every bit as profound as the effectiveness of a scheme hatched one rainy day in Harlem in July of 1951.

PART ONE

Our Sports Shall Be Seen

ONE

Now do you understand serendipity?
—HORACE WALPOLE, letter to
Horace Mann, January 28, 1754

THE SKY ABOVE BROOKLYN darkened in seconds, a borough plunged into dusk five minutes after noon. It was July 18, 1951, and in offices downtown, people turned on lights and peered out windows. A squall in Brooklyn Heights toppled a tree on Willow Place onto three parked cars. A bolt of electricity cracked, hailstones big as marbles pelting Borough Hall. Gusts of wind rocked Sheepshead Bay, small boats radioing distress. The temperature freefell from a balmy 80 to 69 degrees and it began to pour, sheets of rain flooding Prospect Park, empty garbage cans afloat in Flatbush, eighteen inches of water cascading onto the tracks of the Grand Army Plaza subway station. Service halted.

The blitzkrieg stopped abruptly at 12:40 p.m. And born of a cold front in Canada, it all but sidestepped Manhattan, the IRT leading to the Polo Grounds just fine. Still, it was the second-to-smallest crowd of the season that wended this Wednesday to the Harlem field, just 3,538 folks come to watch Giants versus Cubs.

Turnout would no doubt have been smaller still were it not for Willie Howard Mays Jr. Mays was a rookie. The child of an Alabama railroad porter, he had joined the Giants just twenty years, eighteen days old, the youngest black ever called to the major leagues. And on that May day had all New York excited. For in thirty-five AAA games, the center fielder had hit a startling .477.

Harlem had pulsed with pride when Jackie Robinson turned Dodger, Larry Doby Indian, Monte Irvin Giant, Sam Jethroe Brave. But it was the great black ballplayers in Brooklyn to whom Harlem gave its 700,000 hearts. Wrote poet Langston Hughes in 1950:

On sunny summer Sunday afternoons in Harlem
when the air is one interminable ball game
and grandma cannot get her gospel hymns
from the Saints of God in Christ
on account of the Dodgers on the radio. . . .

It was however a black Giant who now bunked at the corner of St. Nicholas and 155th Street, Mays renting the first floor of a boarding house owned by a woman named Ann Goosby. And quickly did Harlem take to Mays as it had to no Giant before. For the pheenom brought to the north end of Sugar Hill not only three 34-ounce bats but humanity. Willie, not William, was his given name. He weighed just 170 pounds, stood two inches shy of six feet. His black wool cap flew off mid-gallop. He scolded his Rawlings mitt when it dropped a ball. One hitless night in Philly, well along an anemic 1-for-26 start at bat, Mays sobbed. But oh that first hit—a home run off Warren Spahn that left its mark on both the left-field roof of the Polo Grounds and Leo Durocher. Cooed the Giant manager, "I never saw a fucking ball get out of a fucking ball park so fucking fast in my fucking life." Harlem was in love.

Mays was the sure antidote to a proud organization's thirteen-year pennant drought. It seemed no coincidence that with his arrival, New York won three straight to slip above .500. And so a manager protected him, teammates marveled at him and fans adored him, bestowing by summer a nickname on he who greeted all with a chummy "Say hey!" Just one person in fact had reason not to celebrate the Say-Hey Kid—the man manning center field before the kid arrived.

Bobby Thomson was in his fifth full season. Twice an all-star, he possessed power at the plate and skill afield—fast enough to play shallow yet still cover the enormous expanse that was center field at the Polo Grounds. But Thomson had neither the arm of young Mays nor his preternatural glove. And the day Mays turned Giant, Durocher alerted the papers (even before his center fielder) that Thomson was shoving over to left.

"Every time a kid comes up and takes your job, you're not going to like it," says Mays. "But I never heard Bobby complain. Actually, Bobby and Al Dark helped me how to play the hitters." Dark went so far as to wag behind his back before most every *pitch* of the remaining 1951 season one or two fingers to alert the baby-face in center to what was upcoming.

Thomson, twenty-seven, received no such care. Batting just .229 when

Mays arrived, yielding his position further bled his confidence. Over the next month, Thomson hit but three home runs and lost his spot in the starting lineup, Durocher using him only as pinch-hitter and defensive replacement. And as baseball's June 15 trade deadline approached, the manager sought to unload him. Dangling Thomson and infielder Jack Lohrke, Durocher contacted Cub skipper Frankie Frisch to see if he might trade for Andy Pafko. Pafko was perfect, a left fielder who in 1950 had hit .304 with 36 home runs and a .591 slugging percentage. The slugger was off flying again with 12 home runs through 49 games. But when midnight struck on June 15, Pafko was a Brooklyn Dodger.

The deal was engineered by Emil Bavasi, a rookie general manager who had in the minors assembled five pennants. Just thirty-five, the wunderkind had wangled Pafko in person, flying to Chicago the day before to meet Cub general manager Wid Matthews at Wrigley Field. The trade was Bavasi's first for Brooklyn and most in baseball felt it assured the club the pennant. When it was completed—eight players and $25,000 changed hands—Brooklyn senior scout Ted McGrew telegrammed the young Catholic general manager all called Buzzie. Read his note: "And a little child shall lead them."

Desperate for help, Durocher picked up Earl Rapp, a minor league outfielder in Oakland. But in thirteen games in New York, the lefty contributed one single. Durocher would have to live and die with Thomson.

Thomson began July on a home run binge, belting six in eight games. But hitting just .231 at the all-star break, his .944 fielding percentage the worst of his young career, Thomson continued to sit more than he played. The fans did not seem to miss him—when in the ninth inning on July 15 he spelled Don Mueller in right, they booed.

And so now two days later at the Polo Grounds, Thomson was but a spectator, number 3,539 left this afternoon to watch Giants versus Cubs, to ooh when Mays hit a solo shot deep to left field, to aah when righty reliever George Spencer loaded the bases down 4–3 in the eighth.

It was a wonder Spencer, twenty-five, could pitch at all. For mid-game he had learned that wife Billie was in labor and rushed to the hospital. Cub pitcher Frank Hiller extended his lead off third and Spencer fired to Hank Thompson a pickoff throw. Hiller slid in ahead of the tag. Safe, his spikes pierced Thompson's right foot, a black shoe welling with blood. Eleven outs later the game ended: Chicago 6, New York 3.

As after every Giant loss, a maintenance worker named Henry Colletti raised high above the clubhouse in center field a red flag. And in the green concrete below him, Anthony Palermo sewed a stitch into Thompson's right big toe, the Giant doctor estimating the lefty hitter would sit at least ten days. New York needed another third baseman. And in Minneapolis, they had one.

Ray Dandridge was a minor league star. Property of New York, the bowlegged third baseman was batting in AAA .317 with 8 home runs and 53 runs batted in. He possessed a glittering glove besides. Dandridge in fact had but one drawback. He was black.

On February 28, a group of NAACP lawyers had walked into the federal district court at 424 South Kansas Avenue and on behalf of thirteen parents filed a class-action suit against the Board of Education of Topeka, Kansas. The parents wished for their twenty children entrance to a nonsegregated elementary school. As just one of the thirteen parents was a man, a black welder named Oliver Brown whose daughter Linda was eight, the suit bore his name. The trial of *Brown versus the Board of Education* began on June 25, and the national pastime, having wrestled with segregation, awaited its verdict.

Though four seasons had passed since Jackie Robinson trotted onto a diamond, the black major leaguer remained very much a statement, a conspicuous reflection of team policy. Just five of sixteen clubs had seen fit to employ a black player. And the major league owner who did, finger held to the wind of public opinion, remained careful to pussyfoot about the matter of race. He knew that many shook their heads when on July 7, in a Southwest International League game at Hidalgo Park in Mexicali, a man named Emmett Ashford was arbiter of foul and fair, the first black umpire in the twentieth century not in the Negro leagues. He knew that many bristled when on June 3, with two out in the second inning of a game at the Polo Grounds, Irvin, Mays and Thompson got aboard, white bases flush for the first time with black men. And he knew that many approved when on May 24, having called Mays up, New York at once sent down another black player, infielder Artie Wilson.

That unwritten quotas continued to hamstring black players was widely known. And it was certainly known by Dandridge. When in 1949 New York signed Dandridge, the son of a semipro catcher, it mattered not that in nine seasons in the Negro National League he had hit an estimated .315, an estimated .343 in an additional nine seasons in Mexico. It mattered not that his mitt was renowned, that he was en route to the Hall of Fame. He was black and thirty-five, and so off not to New York but Minneapolis. And when there in 1949 Dandridge promptly batted .362 with 6 home runs and 64 runs batted in, still New York did not call him up. And when the next season Dandridge was named his league's

Most Valuable Player, still New York did not call him up. And when he continued to shine after his roommate Mays was promoted in May 1951, still New York did not call him up.

That Mays would become the fourth black in five years to be named Rookie of the Year did not matter. Since signing its first black player, fastballer John Ford Smith, on January, 27, 1949, New York had been careful to field only so many Negroes.

But Hiller had now spiked Thompson. And owing a stitched toe, the New York Giants were at last on July 18, 1951, primed to overlook race—if only until Thompson mended.

Dandridge, though, was suddenly unavailable. Three days prior, before a doubleheader at Nicollet Park in Minneapolis, the third baseman had felt an acute pain in his side and been relieved in Asbury Hospital of his appendix. Dandridge would not play again until August 19.

Thus did a bloody digit and enflamed appendix now convene Durocher and Horace Stoneham in New York's center-field clubhouse. And minutes after their 6–3 loss, so desperate were Giant manager and owner to scrounge up a third baseman that they settled on Bobby Thomson.

Thomson had not played third base in five years, had not played *any* infield position since April of 1947. But serendipity had smiled on Thomson. And Stoneham and Durocher had now three pronouncements for the New York press: Thompson would be optioned to the Ottawa Giants of the International League, Ottawa pitcher Al Corwin would fill his roster spot, and Thomson would take over for Thompson at third.

The lineup, though, needed more than to add Corwin and shed a P. For the 1951 season was half gone and the orange and black trailed the Brooklyn blue by seven and a half games. Durocher was exasperated.

The fiery manager had come to New York from Brooklyn in July of 1948 and vowed to rebuild the team in his image. He had. Gone were sluggers Johnny Mize, Sid Gordon and Walker Cooper. In were scrappers Alvin Dark, Eddie Stanky and Wes Westrum.

The new Giant warp and woof had meshed under Durocher in little more than a season, the team running up baseball's best record in the second half of 1950. And on February 19, 1951, the very first day of the spring training that followed, Durocher chirped to the media that his boys would grab the pennant.

The press agreed, ninety-nine members of the Baseball Writers' Association of America fingering as pennant-winners New York. (Brooklyn, with sixty-nine votes, was runner-up.) "A new era has dawned," wrote Arthur Daley in the *New York Times* on April 20. "The hustling Leo

Durocher finally has assembled a team of hustlers, and hope actually is blazing in the lee of Coogan's Bluff."

The Giants lost 12 of their first 14 games.

The team righted itself—winning 21 of 33 to pull within 4 games of first-place Brooklyn on July third. But their loss to Chicago on July 18 was their ninth in 14 games. The team was heading south.

Facing reporters after the game, Durocher fumed. He ripped his team for its poor play, umpire Dusty Boggess for tossing second baseman Eddie Stanky, clubhouse-man Eddie Logan for not confiding that he had told Spencer that his wife, Billie, was in labor. Durocher then stamped from the clubhouse, a trail of Fabergé cologne behind.

With evening, the rains returned. They forced the DC-3 flying Corwin from Ottawa to Manhattan to land at 1:00 a.m. in Albany. They slicked Spencer's drive to Jewish Memorial Hospital, where Billie gave birth to a baby that was dead. And at 46 East 61st Street, they rapped the windows of Durocher's apartment where a terrier named Briney Marlin and a boxer named Slugger greeted the manager at his door. Durocher always went straight home after a loss, stepped onto the baseball diamond etched into his linoleum floor, put on silk pajamas and his RCA television. And always, as Perry Como or Milton Berle entertained, he scavenged for any edge to win the next damn game.

"As long as I've got one chance to beat you," Durocher later wrote in his autobiography, "I'm going to take it. I don't care if it's a zillion to one."

TWO

For de little stealin' dey gits you in jail soon or late. For de big stealin' dey makes you Emperor and puts you in de Hall o' Fame when you croaks.

—EUGENE O'NEILL, *The Emperor Jones,* 1920

L EO ERNEST DUROCHER WAS NO STRANGER to indiscretion, be it debt, infidelity, brawling, shady company or the like. And so now on July 19, 1951, the *Newark Star-Ledger* reported that the Catholic Youth Organization deemed his behavior in "complete contradiction to our moral teachings."

Once upon a time, however, Durocher had been an altar boy. Born on July 27, 1905, atop the kitchen table of his French-Catholic family in West Springfield, Massachusetts, Durocher had grown up with the church, serving mass on Sundays in a wee white surplice. But when at age seven he failed to recite the catechism in French, his priest excluded him from communion exercises and Durocher was left to root around for greener pastures. He found them on the sandlot.

The small boy with the blue eyes and light lashes was a wonder at baseball. Size mattered not in the game. And by the time Durocher had finished West Springfield Grammar School, he was as cocky as he was quick with the finger-glove he kept in his hip pocket.

Durocher was at home fielding baseballs for good reason. After his father, George, an engineer, suffered a heart attack, his mother, Clara, eked out extra money sewing figure-eight cowhide covers onto the Spalding baseballs produced in nearby Chicopee—108 waxed cotton-thread stitches per ball. The $1.50 souvenirs gathered about the Durocher home at 50 School Street.

Durocher soon left school. (He would later claim that he dropped out after a high school science teacher slapped him. But there are no records of his having been a student past the eighth grade.) The youngest of four sons, Durocher learned to shoot marbles then pool, learned also in the smoky comfort of local billiard halls to dress, to curse and to hustle. And all the while, he continued to play baseball.

Springfield boasted a league of teams sponsored by local companies. Boston and Albany Railroad was one and looked to scoop up the street urchin renowned on the town's pebbled sandlots, offering Durocher $30 a week to join its team. Durocher accepted. To make the deal kosher the kid needed a job, and so this summer of 1922 one was created for him: while two dozen men fashioned four-by-eight-foot wood blocks into railroad ties, Durocher sat and tallied their output. At night he played ball, all sure hands and pluck.

The Springfield league was rife with rivalry and Wico Electric Company decided it wanted Boston and Albany's shortstop. The battery manufacturer approached Durocher with a raise. The railroad counteroffered and a bidding war ensued, the price for Durocher rising nickel by nickel until Wico promised $57.50 a week. Durocher switched jerseys. Seventeen, he had money for the first time in his life.

Durocher, though, valued baseball even above his paycheck. And three springs later—grown to five feet nine, 160 pounds—he grabbed his glove and headed for Hartford, hoping to land a pay cut, a job with the class A Senators of the Eastern League good for $150 a month.

Durocher impressed, in the starting lineup when on April 22, 1925, Hartford opened its season. Two months later, Yankee scout Paul Krichell paid $7,000 for the sprig at short. And it was on October 2, 1925, in the eighth inning of a 10–0 loss in Philadelphia, that Durocher approached a major league plate, there to pinch-hit for pitcher Garland Braxton. Teammates Babe Ruth and Lou Gehrig looking on, Durocher flied to right.

Durocher spent the next two seasons with farm clubs in Georgia and Minnesota, and was still awaiting his second big league at-bat when in April of 1928, the Yankees deemed him ready for the Bronx, handing him a $5,000 contract and a starting job at second base. Durocher collected hits in each of his first seven games. Switched to shortstop on May 21, he continued to hit well, batting .312 after 37 games. It was afield, however, that he oozed potential. When on June 14 Durocher turned a Frank O'Rourke short-hop into a force-out at third, thousands marveled. "Durocher's play," gushed the *New York Times,* "was, for deft execution and quick thinking, one of the most brilliant performances we have seen on any field." Just twenty-two, Durocher was a big leaguer for good. And he intended to enjoy it.

It was the height of the Roaring Twenties, of jazz, flappers and Prohi-

bition, and Durocher suddenly found himself one of New York's gods—
a starter on the champion Yankees. Night baseball seven years off,
Durocher was free to spend his evenings as he liked.

After ballgames, Durocher retired to his room at the Piccadilly Hotel.
There on West 45th Street he prinked, dirty blond hair slicked back, nails
manicured, $5 argyle socks and $12 silk neckties and $25 pearl-buttoned
shirts slipped into, a wardrobe delivered always from Sulka. "Leo
Durocher," noted the *Los Angeles Times,* "is the only big leaguer with
nerve enough to wear spats and carry a cane." Thusly ablaze, the shortstop set off nightly, watched Jimmy Durante do his "Wood" number at
the Winter Garden, Bojangles Bill perform his soft-shoe routine at the
Cotton Club. He took in lots of showgirls—Florenz Ziegfeld's Follies,
George White's Scandals, Earl Carroll's Vanities. Always Durocher sat at
the best table and often, when the show ended, headed to Scabouche's, a
pool hall on 47th and Seventh where together with other hustlers he
chalked custom cues at 2:30 in the morning.

At each stop, Durocher mingled. And when the shortstop got off to
his quick start in 1928, a group of his friends organized "Leo Durocher
Day." The date was set for June 23 at Yankee Stadium, a promotional
brochure absurdly hailing Durocher "the freshest and gamest rookie ever
to make a big league debut."

The Yankees rolled their eyes. Durocher was obnoxious, would from
short instruct his pitcher to throw at opposing batters. ("Stick it in
his fucking ear!" he bellowed.) And so the great lineup dubbed Mur-
derer's Row in turn dubbed Durocher "Lippy," snickering when, come
Durocher Day, a slumping Durocher was out of the lineup. New York
lost two to Boston and in Pelham, New York, the Lip partied with a
demimonde that included a bootlegger, Mafioso and government snitch.

Durocher returned to the lineup, the Yankees to the World Series. And
though the shortstop had many debts—he owed, for example, the Hotel
Piccadilly $800—he used his post-season bonus, $5,831.91, to buy a
Packard.

On April 18, 1929, Yankee players slipped on numbered jerseys for
the first time. The numerals signaled each man's place in the batting
order, a navy blue "7" stitched to Durocher's back. Seven proved less
than lucky for the shortstop, his batting average dropping at season's end
to .246. Still, the Lip asked Yankee general manager Ed Barrow for a
raise. Barrow instead shipped Durocher to Cincinnati on February 4,
1930. "The Yanks," reported the *New York Sun,* "having been unable to
cut Leo's vocal cords, have cut the cables binding him to the club."

Likewise would other teams over the coming decades, Cincinnati dealing Durocher to St. Louis and St. Louis to Brooklyn. For though Durocher would anchor the Red defense, captain a grimy klatch of Cardinals to a championship and player-manage the proletarian Dodgers to a pennant, at every stop did the recklessness that brought him success afield trip him off it—a mess in Cincinnati involving a baby, divorce and alimony, in St. Louis great debts, in Brooklyn Durocher fleecing pitcher Kirby Higbe in card games.

But that Durocher was famous and talented helped him always to skirt repercussion. And 1946 saw the Lip manage Brooklyn to a seventh winning record in eight seasons.

In March of 1947, however, Durocher's luck ran out. It was then an associate justice on the U.S. Supreme Court named Frank Murphy telephoned baseball commissioner Albert Chandler. Murphy felt there no place in baseball for the heathen Durocher and suggested that unless he be excised from the game, the Catholic Youth Organization, millions strong, would steer clear of the turnstiles. (Father Vincent Powell of Brooklyn had recently upbraided the Lip for marrying freshly divorced starlet Laraine Day, twelve years his junior.) Chandler awaited Durocher's next slip.

It came on March 8. It was then, at an exhibition game in Havana, that Yankee general manager Larry MacPhail sat beside gamblers Memphis Engelberg and Connie Immerman. When Chandler did not reprimand MacPhail, Durocher bellyached that baseball had one standard for him and another for everybody else. Chandler had his man. On April 9, the former Kentucky governor, he who had signed thirty-four death warrants and was nicknamed "Happy," suspended the Dodger manager for the upcoming season "as a result of the accumulation of unpleasant incidents detrimental to baseball."

That night, Durocher bit his lip and, defiant, went to the St. George Hotel in Brooklyn for the annual dinner of the Knothole Club, a Dodger fan club. When he took his seat on the dais beside Ms. Day, his wife of four months beautiful in white gown and white cloth wrap, more than 1,500 diners applauded.

It was somewhat ironic that only now had a shady life tripped Durocher. For this spring had seen his noblest hour, a March night in Panama when the pajamaed manager rustled his team into a kitchen in the U.S. Army barracks at Fort Gulick. "I hear some of you fellows don't want to play with Robinson," spit the Lip, repeating what coach Clyde Sukeforth had told him. Indeed, Alabaman outfielder Dixie Walker had begun a growing petition stating the refusal to play alongside the black

Robinson. "Well, boys," continued Durocher, "you know what you can do with that petition. You can wipe your ass with it."

One day after suspending Durocher, Brooklyn signed Robinson. A black man would at last suit up alongside 399 white players. With the announcement on April 10, the baseball world all but forgot a suspension and Durocher headed home to Santa Monica to wait out a season. There at 668 East Channel Road he lived regally, shipping his soiled shirts three thousand miles to a trusted dry cleaner in Manhattan.

When Durocher returned to Flatbush for the 1948 season, Dodger GM Branch Rickey wrote on the face of an envelope twelve addendums to his manager's contract, absolving the club of liability in the event of more misconduct. Durocher was on tenterhooks, and few were surprised when on July 16, 1948, Brooklyn let him go. It shocked everybody however, that he ended up skipper of rival New York. Sacrilege!

"I'm through," a Giant fan named Charley Chefalo told the United Press. "I'll never enter the Polo Grounds again."

His was a view shared by many. For in all American sport, no rivalry was as fevered as that between Brooklyn Dodger and New York Giant.

Brooklyn and New York squared off on a diamond for perhaps the first time on October 21, 1845. The game took place at Elysian Fields in Hoboken, New Jersey, just four weeks after the newly formed twenty-eight-man Knickerbocker Baseball Club codified for the sport twenty inaugural rules. On this cold afternoon, the New York Base Ball Club bested the Brooklyn Club by 20 runs.

Within a few years, baseball was the country's preferred pastime, "the National game amongst Americans," wrote the *New York Clipper* newspaper on December 13, 1856. And Brooklyn had burnished its skills afield. Reported newspaper *Porter's Spirit of the Times* in 1857: "Verily, Brooklyn is fast earning the title of the 'City of Baseball Clubs.'" All about the city were starting nines, and the consequence most embraced of its newfound proficiency was the overtaking of New York. "If we are ahead of the big city in nothing else," wrote the *Brooklyn Eagle* in 1860, "we can beat her in baseball."

Numerous baseball teams from Brooklyn and New York battled over the next quarter-century, waging a sport's most heated contests. "No other games throughout the year," wrote the *Spirit* on August 13, 1870, of the New York Mutuals and Brooklyn Atlantics, "arouse the same amount of excitement. . . . The spectators feel as if they themselves were engaged in the strife and not merely lookers-on." On April 18, 1884, linked eleven months prior by the Brooklyn Bridge, the cities battled in an exhibition game for the first time as big league teams. New York of the National League beat Brooklyn of the American Association 8–0.

Before long, the teams were called the Giants and Dodgers (named after a tall lineup and trolley dodgers). And five years later they would finish atop their respective leagues and vie for the Dauvray Cup (precursor to the World Series). New York lost Game One 12–10. "Defeat from any other quarter would be bad enough," reported the *New York Times* on October 19, 1889, "but the stigma was intensified because Brooklyn made the mighty Giants lower their colors. The rivalry between New-York and Brooklyn as regards baseball is unparalleled in the history of the national game." In a series marred by games stalled and called on account of darkness, New York took the championship.

The next season there seemed even more on the line. For Brooklyn switched to the National League, twenty scheduled games suddenly worth more than a win, the regular-season showing against one club every bit as important as the annual pursuit of pennant. And so it was, against New York on June 12, 1890, that Darby O'Brien impersonated a New York base-runner, the Brooklyn captain and third base coach lending the 12–6 victory an ugly air. "Tactics were resorted to," reported the *Brooklyn Eagle,* "unworthy of fair and manly players."

In 1913, a fight between teammates turned the rivalry forever hostile.

The men were John McGraw and Wilbert Robinson. And on October 11, 1913, their Giants lost a third straight championship. What followed is unclear. Some claim a botched signal that sent a hobbled Fred Snodgrass to steal second triggered the fight, others that it was the alcohol-loosened lips of the two baseball lifers. Whichever, men who had for decades meshed afield—as teammates on the thrice-champion Baltimore Orioles, as manager and coach of the New York Giants—now came apart. Just thirty-six days after New York lost the 1913 World Series, Robinson left New York to manage Brooklyn.

Brooklyn had in 1898 joined New York, one of five boroughs. But with the divorce of Robinson from McGraw, the unified city split and a rivalry that for decades had simmered now boiled. Over the next twenty seasons, though New York won three rings and six pennants to Brooklyn's two pennants, head to head their records could scarcely have been closer: Giants 218, Dodgers 213, 7 ties.

McGraw and Robinson had recently bequeathed their animosities to skippers Bill Terry and Max Carey when on January 24, 1934, Terry, fresh off a championship, held with puffed chest a press conference in the lobby of New York's Hotel Roosevelt. A reporter asked Terry his thoughts on the Dodgers, they who in October had finished 26.5 games back of New York, and Terry answered question with question, wondering aloud if Brooklyn was "still in the league."

Just three of New York's nine dailies reported the comment. But Brooklyn business manager Bob Quinn spoke of it to the *Daily News* and, publicized, the quip cut to the quick, scraped raw the insecurity of millions. "What has kept the rivalry ripping through the years," wrote author Roger Kahn in 1958, "is the desire of Brooklynites to be taken seriously." Terry, clearly, did not.

The gods of baseball had what to work with. And with two days remaining in the 1934 season, New York sat tied with St. Louis atop the National League with just a pair to play in Harlem. That Brooklyn was in sixth place, 23.5 games back, mattered little. Here was its season—with the toppling of New York, stepchild Brooklyn would rejoice. Riffing off Terry's jab of eight months prior, fans prepared signs and taunts. And very much "still in the league," Brooklyn won both games, denying neighbor New York the pennant and its fans a winter of crow.

Dodger devotion was by now in Brooklyn ecclesiastical, the relationship between fan and club unique—of all big league teams past and future only the Dodgers neither of city nor state. The team was rather of borough. And that borough was a hearth where in Bensonhurst, James Agee observed "the plump blond boys who pitch ball quietly in the street," where in Brownsville, Alfred Kazin played ball on fields of goldenrod and goat-droppings, where "through the outer parts of Brooklyn," Walt Whitman had on "sun-down perambulations . . . observed several parties of youngsters playing 'base.' "

Still, those rooters could be indecent. "Dodger fans had every vulgarity but the vulgarity of wealth; Giant fans had no vulgarity at all," observed reporter Murray Kempton years later. "The old Dodger fans were the kind of people who picket. The old Giant fans would be embarrassed to do anything so conspicuous, but they were the kind of people who refuse to cross picket lines."

Fandom had turned undertaking, the defense of team a call to arms. And in October 1938, three months after a Dodger fan named Robert Joyce shot dead a Giant fan named Frank Krug, Brooklyn hired Durocher. Like a bellows to flame, the manager stoked the intra-city rivalry, initiating on July 2 a fistfight with New York first baseman Zeke Bonura. Days later Stoneham responded. "If Durocher keeps them hustling," he told the *Brooklyn Eagle*, "I feel they have a great chance for sixth place."

The owner, though, came quickly to admire the manager. For in eight-plus seasons, Durocher whipped Stoneham to the tune of 118 wins, 69 losses and 2 ties. On July 16, 1948, the horrified masses be damned, Stoneham hired Durocher. A rivalry frothed anew.

In New York, Durocher was true to form. The team improved greatly, the 1950 Giants winning 50 of their final 72 games. And scrapes perforated play. It was for example in April 1949 that a fan named Fred Boysen, hospitalized for abdominal contusions suffered in a melee after a game, claimed Durocher kicked him. In response, Giant management decreed that the fans who for decades had walked after games onto the field and out the park had now first to wait for players to reach the clubhouse. No longer forced to hustle from their boosters, players lolled from dugout to clubhouse, the tremendous minutes-hand on the Longines clock eighty feet above center field marking time.

Though the first half of the 1951 campaign had been a disappointment, Durocher awoke on the morning of July 19 feeling good, cooled since the loss to the Cubs the previous night. Sure, the Giants were seven and a half back of Brooklyn. But things were bound to improve. Thomson might actually work out at third. Corwin, up from Ottawa, might actually solidify the pitching staff. And inspiration had struck: Durocher would call a team meeting. It was time, time to discuss a plan that was set to motion nineteen days back when he picked up a journeyman infielder, a move that had garnered next to no attention.

THREE

The sailors come ashore
Out of their hollow ships,
Mild-looking middle-class boys
Who read the comic strips;
One baseball game is more
To them than fifty Troys.

—W. H. AUDEN,
"Fleet Visit," 1951

FROM THE MOMENT HANK SCHENZ finally cracked the majors at twenty-seven, he saw himself as he was: a middling infielder. Armed with an honest appraisal of his talent, saddled with a love of baseball, Schenz became practical. He was dispensable on the field and so made himself indispensable off it. Said Bill Meyer, who managed him in Pittsburgh, "Schenz can do everything but play regular."

It worked. Though Schenz batted just .247 in 538 career at-bats, though he walked a measly 27 times compiling an atrocious .291 onbase percentage, though he managed regularly to get caught stealing in spite of great speed, though he had below-average range afield and still committed 15 errors, and though he hit but two home runs en route to a paltry .310 slugging percentage, Schenz clung on for six seasons, a major leaguer until age thirty-two.

What's more, by the time Schenz retired, all the league knew his name. For Henry Leonard Schenz had turned baseball's greatest bench jockey, able to bellow louder and longer, conjure insults more disruptive and vitriolic, than any of his peers. Wrote Joe Garagiola, "the best one I ever saw."

Schenz's lungs were leathered from the start. When in 1937 Cincinnati scout Frank Lane spotted him playing second base for Ohio's New Richmond High School, he signed him, Lane told management, "because he could run and holler." And boy could Schenz run. He would one day be clocked rounding the bases in 13.5 seconds—.2 seconds off the big league record.

Schenz set off at eighteen for the Kitty League in Union City, Tennessee. A broken thumb ended his first season of pro ball before it began and Schenz returned home.

It was there in the summer of 1938 that ballplayer met bookkeeper. Betty Jane Claus worked for the Indiana Public Service. She was from Aurora, like New Richmond a hamlet on the Ohio River, and a year younger than Schenz. Her wavy brown hair and blue eyes stopped his heart. "It was love at first sight," remembers friend James Teaney.

After two seasons of Class D ball and another in the Piedmont League at hand, Hank and Betty decided to marry. On Saturday afternoon, March 8, 1941, Betty put on a skirt and jacket and, blue and pink, drove with Hank to the parsonage in Cochran, Indiana.

Schenz could not hit the curve. Picked up by the Cub organization, his 1942 season in Portsmouth, Virginia, was typical—a .243 batting average with one home run in 118 games. Forced to compensate for his play, Schenz began to hone what would prove his meal ticket, his taunts as loud as his bat was quiet.

"We used to call him 'Squeaky,' " remembers Edward Wodzicki, Portsmouth third baseman. "He had a squeaky voice that could irritate. He'd *kapitz* any time."

Schenz was cheerleader too, optimistic and tireless afield. When in 1942 a Portsmouth official composed an ode to each Cub, the tribute to Schenz ended with a telling couplet: "Never says 'can't' but uses common sense. Zealously keeps going, this Henry Schenz."

War meantime was raging in Europe and the zealous Schenz did not wait for his draft number to come up. On September 24, 1942, the baseball player enlisted in the United States Navy.

Boot camp lasted a month, Schenz given in Norfolk, Virginia, crew cut, camouflage and 20-millimeter machine gun. "Schenz did his job well," remembers fellow enlistee Phil Rizzuto, "in that he didn't take any guff." Told to put in for a job, Schenz, twenty-three, knew his wont.

Hank was the son of Henry, postmaster of New Richmond. The senior Schenz had for years battled the ceaselessly flooding Ohio River, the mailman taking to heart what was fast becoming his profession's unofficial credo: "Neither snow nor rain nor heat nor gloom of night stays these couriers from the swift completion of their appointed rounds." Those words, a recent translation of Herodotus describing Persian messengers, had in 1912 been etched by architect William Kendall into the entablature of the U.S. Post Office building in Manhattan, and postmaster Schenz often recited them verbatim to his family.

And so son now followed father, petty officer Schenz soon rated MAM 1C, mailman first class. Nicknamed "Stamp Schenz," he was a mail clerk.

Even so, Schenz spent little time in the Norfolk mailroom. Instead, says his son James, "He did what all the ballplayers did. He played ball."

Upwards of 4,000 minor leaguers and 500 major leaguers would exchange their jerseys for fatigues in World War II. Many of them, charged with boosting the morale of the 15 million men and women who served in the armed forces at home and abroad, were divvied into baseball teams and asked by Uncle Sam to engage in little more than the national pastime. Thus was Schenz. And nowhere did baseball turn military duty so seriously as at the Norfolk naval training station.

Norfolk earmarked annually an incredible $100,000 for its baseball team. It put the budget to use, seeing to a statistician, public-address announcer, groundskeeping, a yearbook, meat in the chow hall. Throngs of fans came to watch the team play, American servicemen who, far from home, cheered on familiar stars like Bob Feller and Rizzuto. They cheered for lesser lights too, for men like Schenz, who on May 19, 1943, trotted for the first time to second base as a navy man.

In 23 Norfolk at-bats, Schenz had five hits and scored four runs, mediocre as always. But he was playing ball for a living. And he was happy.

On March 23, 1944, Schenz's parents and sister were in a head-on car crash five miles from home. Mother Lucille died instantly, Henry fifteen minutes later when his ribs caved in on his chest. The crash was not his fault. "He drove like a postman," says Schenz's sister Gloria. "He drove slowly and as far off the road as you can get."

Next morning, Schenz flew home. Gloria had sustained a compound fracture in her leg and he visited her in the hospital. Schenz then went to the Lew White Funeral Home for the funeral of his parents.

Suddenly, Schenz shouldered alone the responsibility of family. He had a wife, a son of thirteen months, a sister seventeen. And he had to provide for them. He had a job but realized anew that it *was* a job, that it was not enough to slip on a jersey, jaw with the opposition and galumph around the bases. A new season had begun, and someone else, a fellow named George Meyer, was playing second base. That was *his* position.

Gloria saw the change in her brother. As she later told his son James, "If your dad says 'crows are white,' agree."

Schenz returned to Norfolk. And when he got in a game, he played with a vengeance. Base hit followed base hit. Soon he was a starter. Yet not even then did he relax. He screamed invective more distracting than he had before. He cared for his equipment, wearing three sets of spikes—one apiece for batting practice, infield practice, the game. And before games, in full view of the opposing team, he filed his spikes sharp as nails. By the close of the 1944 season, Schenz, the perennial runt, had led Norfolk to an 83–22–2 record, his transformation afield astonishing. In 409 at-bats he had rapped 151 hits, his average a team-best .369. In 107 games, he had scored 103 runs.

The coinciding of Schenz's tragedy and renaissance at the plate was too stark to go unnoticed. "How come this sudden development?" wondered Bill Diehl in the Norfolk *Ledger-Star*. "The reason for it may be something personal with Henry, a tragedy that could have ripped the very heart out of the youthful diamonder." Diehl continued, "It was early in the season and Schenz was working out with sailors with no particular thought in mind. He was just out there along with the rest.

"Someone handed him a telegram. He read it, blinked his eyes in utter amazement. No. No, it couldn't be true. His mother and father in Cincinnati had been killed in an automobile collision. Sometime later Schenz returned to the club. No mention was made of his misfortune. He just went back to work. His play improved, improved, then became sensational.

"Perhaps it's all for mother and dad. He may want to prove [to] them that he's a big leaguer."

No matter how his bat came to flower, this much Schenz knew: at last he did more than holler and run. And sure enough, when after the season the navy stocked its Hawaiian Fourteenth Naval District League with stars, Schenz got an invite, boarding on October 13 with Bill Dickey, Johnny Vander Meer, Pee Wee Reese and some thirty others the SS *Afoundria*, a retrofitted President Lines cargo ship bound from San Francisco to Honolulu.

Hawaii was two thousand miles closer to combat than was the mainland. And in the thirty-five months since the bombing of Pearl Harbor, the U.S. military had on the island built prisoner-of-war compounds, cordoned off land for military cemeteries, urged residents to lend their dogs to be trained as scouts, commissioned makers of leis to instead weave camouflage nets. Many feared the Japanese would return, and they did—a Japanese plane reconnoitering Pearl Harbor on October 17, 1943. Concerns of attack bubbled anew when President Roosevelt came to Hawaii in July to plot the Formosa and China offensive. And when the SS *Afoundria* docked in Pearl Harbor on October 21, 1944, a military curfew still demanded lights out across Hawaii at 2200 hours.

By the time Schenz reached the island, however, life was returning to normal. In January 1943, the military had okayed smoking during blackouts (except during air-raid alarms). In March of that year, "Restoration Day" trumpeted the return of governance to most local agencies. And four months later, the military gave word that unless they faced the sea, windows could stay open at night.

Eased restrictions had in fact made the Honolulu awaiting Schenz a relatively festive station. Servicemen could buy liquor until 7:30 p.m., eat in restaurants until eight. Prostitutes flitted about looking for sailors to comfort while the faithful contented themselves to pose for pictures with hula girls. The men in white and khaki could also go to Hotel Street where a Coney Island–style amusement park offered pinball, jungles stocked with miniature Japs to shoot at, and, best of all, a batting cage.

Schenz did not need batting practice. He spent his days playing second base and shortstop for Base 8 Hospital then Ship Repair Unit, two of ten teams in the Naval District League.

On September 19, 1945, Pearl Harbor Submarine Base won the league championship. The war was ending and so too now would the league, fifty-nine top players chosen and split into two squads for a last hurrah, a best-of-seven series. The National League led the American three games to two.

The islands were teeming with servicemen, by June an average of 450 ships docking daily in Pearl Harbor, some 253,000 troops stationed on Oahu alone. And on October 6, a crowd of some 22,000 servicemen mobbed Furlong Field in Honolulu for game six of the series. The game tied at two with two men on in the ninth, Schenz smacked a double against Ed Weiland, capping with a flourish navy wartime baseball.

On December 14, 1945, after thirty-eight months, twenty-one days and some 800 at-bats, Schenz left the service, honorably discharged. World War II had resurrected his career, and two months later the Cubs invited him to spring training to vie for a major league job.

Opening Day, however, saw Schenz in the Texas League, a Tulsa Oiler. Facing AA pitching, he displayed his wartime form, in 540 trips to the plate hitting .333 with 44 doubles and 23 strikeouts, fewest in the league. Schenz was a minor league star. Now when he played the prankster, mimicking managers, pouring water on sleeping teammates, hiding lit matches in shoes, men could only laugh. Voted MVP of all the league, Schenz won at last a call to the majors.

On September 18, 1946, the 2,116 fans at the Polo Grounds saw Schenz jog to third base in the bottom of the first inning. In the sixth they saw umpire George Barr collapse with a heart attack. And in the eighth, they saw a rookie named Bobby Thomson hit his first home run.

Schenz did not hit safely in four at-bats. But he did turn the one ball hit his way into a 5-4-3 double play, and the Cubs beat the last-place Giants 4–3. Schenz, number 17, walked the 500 feet back to the clubhouse a proud man.

Schenz finished the 1946 season with two hits in 11 at-bats. His stint in the majors the next season was even more fleeting—sent after a lone hit to Nashville in the Southern Association. There he hit .331, earning in 1948 a sustained go at the big leagues. The Cub enjoyed modest success, scoring 43 runs in 96 games. It was enough to see his signature branded into ash, Louisville Slugger tapering the handle of bat model S162, the better, said Schenz, to let go after a bunt.

The next season, Chicago swapped Schenz after 14 at-bats for Dodger Bob Ramazzotti, another spare part. And when Branch Rickey then exiled Schenz that same day to St. Paul in the American Association, again Schenz feasted on minor-league pitching, hitting .345, rated by New York scout Tom Sheehan best in all the league. Pittsburgh was also impressed, acquiring Schenz on November 4.

Back on major league soil, Schenz desperately set about rooting his 175 pounds in Forbes Field. "I can remember him sweeping out the dugout when it rained," says Garagiola, a teammate in 1951. But Schenz showed a profound inability to get on base, batting .222 in a season and a half, drawing zero walks in 162 at-bats. On June 30, 1951, Rickey let Schenz go a second time, the Pittsburgh general manager putting him on waivers.

The Giants snapped up Schenz that very day.

The league was full of men with anemic bats, and it was no coincidence that it was Schenz Durocher plucked from baseball's hoi polloi, the team footing his $10,000 waiver price. For above all the Lip wanted sass, and everybody knew that Schenz, a box of a man with a forty-eight-inch chest and sixty-eight-inch frame, could razz the bejesus out of the opposition. Durocher also prized belligerence. "Give me some scratchers and fighters," he would later remark. It was no secret that Schenz kept his spikes filed razor sharp.

Still, when Schenz arrived in New York, he was very much the twenty-fifth man. His teammates knew him only as an obnoxious opponent, and besides, the team already had a clutch of utility infielders including Lohrke, Bill Rigney, and John Jorgensen. And while Schenz had once shown promise as a pinch-runner, he was now thirty-two and slowed, thrown out in both of his attempted steals as a Pirate. And so, wrote the *New York Times,* "Schenz, in all likelihood, will be dispatched to the minors after the required thirty-day wait."

When on July 1 the Giants squared off in Boston against the Braves, Schenz was in uniform—on his back the number 10, on his head a black size 7⅛ cap topped with an orange button. But the man who had been dubbed in Tulsa "the Little Giant" did not play. And over the next few weeks, Durocher saw fit to use him only as a pinch-runner, not granting the righthander a single stroke.

Schenz minded not at all, that rare athlete content to stand in the shade of teammates. And so the redwoods came to appreciate him, to rely on Schenz for everything from the pitching of batting practice to the catching of tosses in the pen. Remembers Thomson with a wave of the arm, "He'd wash our backs in the shower."

Thus was Schenz, by the time he saw Thompson helped from the field on July 18 with a bloody toe, a dugout staple—a pinch-running, bench-jockeying, spikes-sharpening, batting-practice–pitching, warm-up–catching, dugout-sweeping, back-scrubbing Giant.

Schenz hoped to contribute in one more way.

Schenz had shared the dugout with Durocher for eighteen days, seen the skipper lose nine, win eight. Eighteen days was time enough for the utilitarian Schenz to talk, to tell Durocher of the afternoons he hid in the scoreboard at Wrigley Field, a spy with a telescope. Eighteen days was time enough to tell that he still had his Wollensak and that he had brought it to New York.

FOUR

The player on the home court stands at a tremendous advantage, specially if he has invented the rules of the game. He must rub this advantage in by every method at his command.

—STEPHEN POTTER, *The Theory and Practice of Gamesmanship: Or, the Art of Winning Games Without Actually Cheating,* 1947

AL CORWIN HAD NOT THOUGHT it would happen. After all, he was just 2–4, a loser in Saskatchewan. But on blessed July 18, 1951, Ottawa manager Hugh Poland told Corwin that a suit named Stoneham in New York had optioned a third baseman named Thompson and wanted him, Elmer Nathan Corwin, to pitch a game in the big leagues the very next day. He was going to the majors!

Hurriedly, Corwin said goodbye to teammates, handed the keys of his '47 Pontiac to shortstop Ziggy Jasinski, and crammed his shoes, jocks, undershirts and glove into a duffel bag. "That was about all I brought," remembers Corwin.

Corwin, twenty-four, had grown up in Newburgh, New York, a colonial town near West Point on the Hudson River. There he had dreamed not of ball but the navy, and in 1944 manned a turret on a ship in South America. But when during his sophomore year at Pasadena City College the Giants held an open tryout in nearby Monrovia, Corwin went on a lark then struck out batter after batter. A scout asked if he might like to play professional baseball. And so now three years later Corwin flew east.

Corwin had never been to Manhattan and wondered now if he would make it—lightning lit the wet night sky outside his window. The pilot announced that the propeller plane had to land in Albany, which it did.

Late the next morning, Corwin finally touched down in LaGuardia Airport after a rush hour slowed by the rain. He was exhausted and alone, and, when his duffel bag did not show with the rest of the luggage, all but ready to go home. He found a phone, inserted ten cents and dialed WAdsworth 6-8160—the only number of the city's nearly 3.5 million that he knew. Eddie Logan picked up the phone. It was almost 11 o'clock and, as always, he was already at the park.

Logan was born just blocks from the Polo Grounds in 1912, and had begun working there when he was seven. His father, Fred, was New York's clubhouse man, had been since 1896, and he made for his son a little wagon with which to wheel to the park from the family home on Amsterdam Avenue the players' towels which wife Julia washed at home. In 1921, when Logan was nine, he began operating the park's manual scoreboard for 25 cents a day. He finished elementary school the next year and never returned to the classroom, instead helping his father help the players. When the senior Logan died in 1947, the son took over as Giant clubhouse man, cigarette forever at his lips.

Along the way, Logan had welcomed arriving ballplayers. The first was the great Mel Ott who at age sixteen in 1925 Logan found on the Ninth Avenue El carrying his straw suitcase, lost on his way to the park. Now Logan set to calm another rookie. He assured Corwin that his luggage would turn up and told him to take a taxi to the Polo Grounds. Corwin hopped into a Checker cab, his fare ticking up from 20 cents. The team would foot the bill.

Gone were the days when Corwin, twenty-one and strapped for cash, drove the team bus of the Class C Reno Silver Sox for an extra $25 a month. If the pitcher stayed with the Giants the seventy-three days through season's end, he could expect half a season's starting salary— about $2,500. That beat the $500 a month he was making in Ottawa. And even that was good money. In 1951, the average American annual income was a shade under $3,500.

The cabbie readied 25 cents for the toll and drove onto the Triborough Bridge. Corwin looked out the window to his left. There for the first time he saw Gotham, its buildings wet and gray, Giant headquarters on 42nd Street, 1,046 feet beneath the steel needle of the Chrysler building.

The cab turned onto the Major Deegan Expressway. Driving north, two ballparks soon appeared astride the Harlem River—to the left the Polo Grounds snug below a 115-foot bluff, enormous Yankee Stadium to the right, its white façade high above River Avenue. The cabbie crossed the Macombs Dam Bridge onto 155th Street, turned right onto Eighth Avenue, drove north two blocks and dropped Corwin off in front of the green clubhouse door.

The pitcher had never been before to a major league park, and clubhouse security guard Tom Collins stopped him. "I'm Al Corwin," said the player. No response. "I'm here from Ottawa. Eddie Logan is expecting me. I'm a ballplayer." Corwin entered the clubhouse in search of a locker that bore his name.

The Giant clubhouse was a block of concrete. Built in 1923, it rose three stories above center field, 60 by 60 feet. And it was green.

"The Polo Grounds, painted bilious yellow last spring," noted the *Washington Post* on June 12, 1910, "made pitching easy work until a big section of background was made green." Its color changed, the center-field backdrop thus helped batters better see an approaching ball. And so it was green paint that little by little grew over the park like moss, the center-field bleachers going green in 1913, green wood affixed to the façade of the upper deck in 1922, the outfield fence, laden with advertisements, painted in 1948 green, just green, the same forest green that by 1951 coated everything at the Polo Grounds—its seats, its bullpen phones, its signs that read NO BETTING PERMITTED.

Green too were the concrete walls of the long and narrow Giant locker room where Corwin now walked. Here were the lockers of each player, wooden rectangular cubbies with wooden shelves and a metal rod for hangers. These were separated by wire mesh and open-faced (save a few with hinged mesh doors that could be locked). Atop each locker was a strip of adhesive tape upon which was written in black pen the player's name and uniform number.

To the left, an arched doorway opened into a trainer's room. There, extending under the left-center-field bleachers, were two whirlpool tubs, two massage tables, a handheld vibrating device to knead muscles, a Hbisch dryer, a heat lamp, a diathermy machine and a slew of metal trunks labeled in stenciled orange letters N. Y. GIANTS. Several of these Logan stocked with jockstraps, cups, road gear, old bats and, stuffed into leather bags, used balls. Another he filled with valuables, with a few dozen wooden boxes latch-locked and in beige cloth bags, each labeled in black pencil and holding a team member's jewelry and wristwatch wrapped around his wallet.

Up a flight of stairs toward Eighth Avenue were the commodes and sinks and a supply kept ready by Logan of Mennen hair cream, Aqua Velva after-shave, Gillette razors, tubes of Brylcreem, red-capped bottles of Vitalis, bars of Ivory soap, brushes, combs and white rubber shower shoes. Black rubber matting covered the concrete floor and extended down a hallway into a large open shower—a dozen-plus heads fixed into a wall. To the right were several large washing machines.

Four steep wooden steps up from the locker room was a large lounge on the second floor. In it were several round wooden card tables, a few dozen chairs, a pair of small wooden radios, a water fountain, two sand-filled stone tubs where players snuffed their cigarettes, a few black iron fans, several more metal trunks overturned and doubling as tables, and two waist-high Coca-Cola coolers filled with soda, Knickerbocker beer, cans of juice, ice and an ice pick. Pegged to the wall above the coolers was the Giant roster written on yellow paper. The players called it the "gyp sheet." When a man grabbed a drink, he check-marked his name and Logan knew who owed him what.

On the right side of the room was a large closet stockpiled by Logan from floor to ceiling with supplies—caps, gloves, bats and sweatshirts, hundreds of Spalding baseballs packed ten dozen per cardboard box, Coke bottles, Folger's coffee tins, paper bags of Red Man and Apple Jack tobacco, plain and almond Hershey chocolate bars, Juicy Fruit and Wrigley's Spearmint gum.

On the north side of this room, a green wooden door opened into Durocher's office. The office was directly aligned with home plate, its six windows running toward left field from just above the 483-foot mark on the center-field wall below. Durocher kept the office sparse, in it little more than a leather swivel chair, a glass-covered mahogany desk, two telephones, a bar stocked for newspapermen, a wooden coat tree, three dozen clipboards hooked to the wall, a closet filled with hanging suits, a second wooden desk, a beige-tiled bathroom, a shower and, flush against the windowed wall, a radiator. Through the wall behind Durocher's chair stood the visiting clubhouse, nothing more than locker room and lounge, its staircase landing afield just left of center.

Right of home, meantime, and up a flight, stood the press room—white-clothed tables and a bar to feed and water before games the newspapermen. Filling the rest of the third floor along a plush orange-and-black-carpeted hall were the offices of team ticket manager Peter Hoffmann, vice president Chub Feeney, farm-system secretary Jack Schwarz and Stoneham. There, past a receptionist at her switchboard, worked the owner, his office replete with desk, sofa, safe, bathroom, photographs of John McGraw and Mel Ott, and a wooden chest of father Charles's World Series trophies that bling-blinged in the light of four windows. These opened atop a Brobdingnagian butt (a prop in an advertisement for Chesterfield cigarettes), and looked out onto his ball-field forty-eight feet below. Gazing up at Stoneham from the warning track, the only hint of the owner and his signature dark suit was whether his white shades were drawn.

Fourteen more windows spanned the base of the clubhouse, seven on either side of a bronze plaque in dead center honoring manager McGraw. Five feet tall, their sills eleven feet above field, the single-hung windows were in play (though in five decades, no batted ball ever hit the face of the clubhouse). Each window had twelve panes and a shade. Each could be opened. And each was protected with thick wire mesh. The window farthest left fenestrated the visitors clubhouse, followed by the six in Durocher's office and the remaining seven in the Giant lounge.

Wandering through the clubhouse, Corwin finally found Logan and, again, clubhouse man calmed rookie. His luggage had been found and the team's doubleheader against the Cubs had been rained out—Corwin would not have to pitch. Sizing up the 73-inch, 165-pound Corwin, Logan handed him the smallest uniform he had. Still it sagged about his 31-inch waist.

It was late morning when Logan introduced Corwin to trainer Frank Bowman and then to the players, hellos offered up as they filed in one by one. Here were the men who would catch Corwin—starter Wes Westrum and backups Rafael Noble and Sal Yvars. Here were relievers Monte Kennedy and Dave Koslo who would live beside Corwin on West 57th Street in the Henry Hudson Hotel, here Eddie Stanky who would room with him on the road. Here were star pitchers Sal Maglie and Larry Jansen, captain Al Dark, rookie Mays, slugger Thomson, and Monte Irvin—legend of the Negro leagues. Here were a dozen more men who would stop traffic in New York. But Corwin, for whom professional ball was more paycheck than passion, did not recognize a single one, not even a name.

Corwin did, however, immediately recognize Durocher. For the little man was bigger than the sports page. He had in 1947 smiled on the cover of *Time* magazine. His wife was the beautiful heroine of the Doctor Kildare movies. His quip "Nice guys finish last" was en route to *Bartlett's Familiar Quotations*. And when Durocher, spry, balding and nattily dressed, called Corwin to his office, wishing him well, telling him he would get him innings, maybe use him in long relief, the skinny pitcher smelled the manager's woodhue cologne and, overwhelmed, knew that he was not in Ottawa anymore. He was in New York and could see, just out the windows of Durocher's office, the rubber he would toe while peering in for the sign.

The park out those windows had housed a string of fantastical events. There was in 1908 the base-running boner of Giant sophomore Fred Merkle, in 1920 the fractured skull and death by submarine-fastball of Cleveland shortstop Ray Chapman, in 1934 the striking out consecutively by Carl Hubbell of five legends, in 1941 the speech by President Roosevelt that halted play forty-five minutes. "When your enemy comes at you in a tank or a bombing plane," crackled the public-address system, "if you hold your fire until you see the whites of his eyes, you will never know what hit you." Neither did Bernard Doyle, the fan killed in 1950 in section 42, row 3, of the Polo Grounds by a stray bullet fired 400 yards away.

The Harlem green had also birthed baseball tradition. It was there in 1900 that vendors first hocked steamed dachshund sausages wrapped in Vienna bread, a delight sports cartoonist Tad Dorgan dubbed "hot dogs." In 1908, songwriter Jack Norworth wrote "Take Me Out to the Ball Game" after seeing a subway advertisement for Giant baseball. (He would not take himself out to his first ballgame for another thirty years.) In 1929, home plate ump Charles Rigler called balls and strikes at the Polo Grounds into a microphone in his mask, the first to amplify a game afield. And only after a controversial home run hit in 1939 at the ballfield did nets start appearing on foul poles.

Now, twelve years later, Corwin watched as rain slicked the historic park, nets and all. The Giants' doubleheader was rescheduled for August 27. Durocher wanted those games to mean something and so called a team meeting. The players gathered, each man sitting on the round, four-legged metal stool before his locker.

Durocher seldom called meetings. And so it was news when he did, as when exactly one year before he convened his players after a doubleheader lost to the Cardinals by the combined score of 28–7. Reported the *Daily News* the next day: "He told the boys to go out on the town and loosen up."

There was much in town to loosen a boy. There was fine food, for $16 pheasant served on the Upper East Side at Chambord. There was alcohol, spirits on tap at 331 Manhattan bars. There were drugs, dope for sale in midtown on the west side of Broadway and the east side of Seventh Avenue. And there were women—cabaret starlets in Manhattan, strippers in Union City, New Jersey, prostitutes in Harlem and on West 47th Street, where for $20 a slump was forgotten.

The meeting had proved the turning point of the 1950 season. After a night of bacchanalia, the Giants reeled off nine straight wins, eventually finishing in third place.

One year later the players were now in second, seven and a half games back of Brooklyn. And standing before them in slacks and a pastel sports shirt, Durocher began going through the team's signs.

It takes about two-fifths of a second for a ball to whirr from pitcher to catcher. And some twenty seconds pass between each of the 280-odd pitches in every game. In that window, players and coaches communicate strategy. Some of it, like where to position a fielder, is gesticulated for all to see, barked for all to hear. But most is dog-whistled, silent directives the opposition tries to detect then decipher. Among these are orders on everything from when to run to when to swing, when to bunt to what pitch to throw, secret instruction given ballplayers in a blur of filliped fingers, tugged earlobes, swiped cap-bills, adjusted pant legs and any other motion that may furtively convey the whim of a manager. These have included the blow of a nose, the covering of a crotch, the direction of spit saliva.

Signs often hinge on an "indicator"—a motion usually indicating that the next signal given will determine the play. The indicator and the ensuing signal can get quite complicated. Consider the system used by the Texas Rangers in the early 1970s. (In 1973, Joe Nossek, a business statistics major at Ohio University turned sign-stealing guru and then Milwaukee third base coach, learned of it when a Texas Ranger joined his club.)

The Texas batter peered at his third base coach, who mid-gesticulation swiped either his cap, his jersey or his legs. If he touched the cap, the very next sign he gave was the one to follow. If he touched the jersey, the second sign was the one. If he touched his legs, it was the third.

Now the batter looked for specific instruction. If the coach then went to his cap, the batter was to bunt. If he touched his face, the hit-and-run was on. If he touched his jersey, the runner was to steal. If he touched any place else on his body—a "dead spot" such as his elbow or belt—the batter was on his own.

Furthermore, each play had several variations. *Where* on his cap the coach touched determined what kind of a bunt was expected of the batter. If the coach touched the bill of his cap, the batter was to lay down a regular bunt. If he touched the front of the cap, the batter was to attempt a squeeze. If he touched the top of the cap, the batter was to try to bunt for a hit.

Given the subtle nature of signs, players occasionally do not spot them. And some players, though they do, "haven't the cerebral equipment," wrote *Baseball Digest* in 1944, "to grasp the fundamentals of their own manager's signals." Zeke Bonura, a slugging first baseman who came up with the White Sox in 1934, struggled with signs, his exasperated manager Jimmie Dykes yelling aloud at least once "Bunt, you meathead!"

Durocher had little tolerance for missed signals. And so, he now stood reviewing them before his team. Then, suddenly, he changed course. "Goddam it!" he yelled, remembers Corwin. "We can't get first, but we got to get second!" His words echoed like a thunderclap.

Durocher would later write, "Win any way you can as long as you can get away with it." And it was now the manager held an ace he resolved to play. Standing before all his team, Durocher said nothing of Schenz. Instead he spun a yarn. "He says a loyal Giant fan was in the navy, had a telescope," remembers catcher Yvars. "It could pick a crystal out of the water. I don't even know the son of a bitch." (Ever the protective manager, Durocher had turned sailor Schenz into a fan from the navy.) The Lip continued on, telling his players they had the perfect crow's nest from which to use that telescope, that from their clubhouse they could spy opposing catchers flashing signals to pitchers, that from their bullpen and dugout they could relay those signals—the DNA of every pitch be it fastball or off-speed—to the batter before it was thrown. And so, concluded Durocher, "We've got to start stealing signs."

Stealing signs, however, was already part of New York's game.

Like all baserunners, the Giant having reached base tried to spot the opposing catcher's signals and then relay them to a coach in the dugout. He had little time to do so. In 1949, Jules Loh and Bill Gilbert, two reporters at the *Washington Post,* calculated that the average span between the moment a pitcher received his catcher's signal and delivered his pitch was 11.3 seconds. In that window, the code the Giant baserunner typically used to relay a swiped sign was quite simple. The runner tugged on his belt if the catcher put down one finger, touched his chest for two fingers, his cap for three. The coach then jotted down the signal and set about decoding it—a cryptographer in a baseball dugout poring over ciphers.

"Everyone talks about getting the catcher's signs from second base," Stanky boasted to the *Sporting News* in 1962. "We got the signs while taking our lead off *first* base when the catcher was careless because he didn't think we could see his hands."

Once the Giants had deciphered an opponent's signals, base runners later in the game (and in future games until the opposition rejiggered its signs) relayed them directly to the batter. "The first-inning code might be 2-1-1," Stanky explained to the *Baltimore Scorebook* in 1980. "If we went to our cap twice and our shirt and pants once, that meant a fastball—and so on. Sometimes, it would be our feet or hand position at second base. A left foot crossed over the right leg might mean a curveball and the right foot over the left a fastball."

What Durocher was now proposing to his team, however, was entirely different. *Every* pitch would be spied. And instead of using the naked eye and smarts, the team would be using a telescope and buzzer wire.

Durocher began to walk about the Giant locker room. And as rain slicked the empty field outside, he asked aloud a simple question: "Who wants the signs?"

A batter has just .13 seconds to decide whether to swing at a pitch traveling ninety miles per hour. And so, in theory, knowing the incoming pitch gives the batter a huge edge. Much like a hitter ahead in the count, he can jump on the inevitable fastball, fully committing his swing. Or, he can comfortably wait on a curve. It is no surprise, then, that according to Stanky, every player but one, Whitey Lockman, wanted the teammate on second base to tip him the pitch.

But like Lockman, some batters do not want to know what's coming. "Suppose he calls a curveball and throws a fastball," says Westrum. "You could get ripped in two." Other batters say simply that to know the pitch before it is thrown is to disrupt their reaction to it. In a conversation with ESPN.com on October 9, 2001, Tony Gwynn, the great San Diego Padre, explained.

We were in Montreal one night, and Gary Carter's catching. I'm like three-for-three, and I come up, and he says, "You know what, Tony? We've had no luck trying to trick you, so I'm just gonna tell you what's coming." And Doug Harvey's behind the plate. So Gary Carter says, "OK, T, here comes a fastball—inner half." And I took it, because I didn't believe it. So that's strike one. And he smiles to himself.

I step back and I look at him and look at Doug, and I say, "Doug, he's not supposed to do that. He can't tell me what's coming." He says, "There's nothing in the rule book that says he can't." And I say, "I don't want to know what's coming! I just want to react to what I see." And Carter says, "Tony, breaking ball. We're gonna throw you a backdoor slider right here, you're going to have to stay on it to hit it." And I'm going, "He ain't gonna throw no backdoor slider." And it was, and Doug Harvey's yelling, "Steee-rike two!" I say, "Wait a minute, Doug, he cannot tell me what's coming. You can't do that." He says, "T, there's nothing in the rule book."

So, he's got me oh-and-two, and now he's telling me everything. Curveball, fastball, slider. So I decide to react to what I see, and I ground out to short, and as I go back to the dugout, Carter's horse-laughing. And Doug Harvey's got a chaw in, and he's kind of sniggling, too. There was nothing

I could say, but it was just horse-crap. They can't tell me what's coming. That's not fair, that's not baseball.

But it is. For the marrow of baseball—of all sport—is competition. And Carter volunteered pitches to Gwynn for the same reason Durocher wanted to steal them: to gain an edge. To win.

Durocher now approached Irvin, his star right fielder. "You want the signs, Monte?"

Irvin had left the Negro leagues for the Giants in July 1949, the sixth black man to play major league baseball. He was then thirty-two, possessor of one of baseball's sweetest swings. (It was estimated that over a decade in the Negro leagues, he batted .350.) But while throughout his career he had roamed the outfield and played a bit at third, in 1951 Durocher had penciled him in at first. The position frustrated Irvin—he made eight errors in 34 games—and he wilted at the plate, batting just .276 with 2 home runs in 116 at-bats. And so, on May 21, the day before Mays arrived, Durocher reinserted Irvin in right field. The move yielded immediate results, Irvin stroking three hits in his first game, a home run in his second, the outfielder batting by July 19 .301 with 12 home runs, a star fully realizing the final summer of his prime, his hands still lightning quick.

Those hands were the reason Irvin had never before wanted teammates—dancing off of second—to cop a sign and tip him a pitch. Why let expectation dictate a swing, why rely on the unfaithful peeks of others, why get distracted, when you already possessed the natural ability to react to whatever was thrown? See the ball. Hit the ball. That had always worked.

Irvin looked up at Durocher. He answered, "No thanks, coach."

Durocher had thought his question rhetorical. And as often happened when he angered, his voice rose in pitch and he kicked his legs. "You mean to tell me," snapped the manager at Irvin, "if a fat fastball is coming, you don't want to know?!"

The sweet results of a good sign-stealing scheme were widely known. The previous summer, on August 23, 1950, catcher Birdie Tebbetts had revealed to the *Boston Traveler* newspaper that a telescopic hunting sight saved the 1940 Detroit season. It was then, one summer afternoon, that Tiger Tommy Bridges had brought his new sight to the park and peered through it from the left-field stands. "He even tried to spot the good-looking girls," Tebbetts told the paper. Bridges soon eyed the catcher's fingers, and before long, the team stationed a pitcher in the stands with binoculars. "It really was wonderful," Tebbetts explained. Effective too. Hank Greenberg and Rudy York hit at least one home run between them in 17 straight September home games, the Tigers winning the 1940 pennant by one game.

Durocher continued around the room. Enough of the team *did* want to know the signs. Durocher calmed. His scheme was a go.

Outside, rain continued to pelt all the city, a Brooklyn grounds crew digging trenches behind the dugouts at Ebbets Field to prevent water from flooding two dressing rooms. The rain fell far from New York too, soaking towns in Oklahoma, Kansas and Missouri, canceling all major league games east of Cleveland. It was a hard rain, its toll on the Midwest devastating: forty lives lost, 200,000 homes evacuated.

In New York, however, the rain did little more than sodden the leads of thirteen daily papers, sportswriters sent off to retool their columns. Durocher, his mood light, helped out. "This rain is a great break for us," he told those reporters gathered come afternoon about his mahogany desk. "It gives the guys a day of rest and it gives me a chance to straighten out my pitching staff." Indeed, Durocher would not have to hand the ball to Corwin for five days. The *New York Post* had a story: "Rain Gives Lippy Chance to Reassemble Hill Staff."

Durocher did not, however, share with the press the most blessed consequence of the rain: it would give an electrician ample time to make possible a sign-stealing scheme.

FIVE

Early blue evening.
Lights ain't come on yet.
Looky yonder!
They come on now!
—LANGSTON HUGHES,
"Wonder," 1951

IN JANUARY OF 1898, Charles Hercules Ebbets became president
of the Brooklyn Dodgers, later boldly declaring "Baseball is in its
infancy." So was Abraham Chadwick, a baby boy thousands of miles
away in Russia who fifty-three years later would sway the fate of Ebbets'
team.

Chadwick's parents, Elke and Isaac, were first cousins. Married in
Poland, they moved to Russia. After the birth of Abraham, they moved
again, to England via Germany. And it was there in Manchester that
Isaac left Elke and Abraham for America.

Moored in Poughkeepsie, New York, Isaac sent for his wife and son,
who on December 6, 1899, boarded in Liverpool the two-masted SS
New England. The ship steamed into Boston nine days later and Elke
and Abraham, having lived the previous six months in western, not eastern, Europe, were spared disinfectant.

Still the two steerage passengers were processed, a combined twenty-
four years of life reduced to a string of facts: Jew. Russian. Unable to
read or write. In possession of $5. Wife. Boy of eleven months. Abraham
was in fact older, had turned one. But age was for the immigrant a yard-
stick as imprecise as any, and Elke and Isaac would pick indiscriminately
as a birthday for their son March 26, the parents sure only that Abraham
was born in spring sometime around the Jewish festival Purim.

Reunited, the family Chadwick made its way to New York, settling on
Hester Street in the Lower East Side. Isaac was a tailor and became a

pattern-cutter at the women's clothier Peck & Peck. Eager to shed his greenhorn skin, he anglicized his last name. (Likely it had been Czadwicz.) Elke also changed her first name to Anna, the couple leaving in Europe the Judaism of their forebears. As could be expected, the son further Americanized. Abraham spoke almost no Yiddish, was soon known only as Chick and became an impassioned fan of baseball.

With the ceremonial toss of an A. J. Reach ball by President William Taft on April 14, 1910, baseball would officially become the national pastime. But to immigrants like the Chadwicks, the sport had long been America incarnate: corporeal and carefree to the young, new-world foolishness to their parents.

"What value does a game like baseball have?" wrote a distraught father in 1903 to Abraham Cahan, publisher of the Yiddish newspaper the *Jewish Daily Forward*. "Nothing more than becoming crippled comes out of it." He continued, "I want my boy to grow up to be a mensch, not a wild American runner." Cahan responded: "Let your boys play baseball and even become outstanding players, as long as it does not interfere with their studies or make them keep bad company." Cahan added that it was important to raise children to be educated and decent but "they should also be healthy and agile youth who shouldn't feel inferior to others."

Chadwick was not a good ballplayer. But from the start, baseball was a boon to his self-confidence, his fandom proof of acculturation. For him the game was about allegiance. And in his neighborhood of a thousand landsmen, Chadwick bound his identity to the Brooklyn Dodgers. He had little to cheer. In 1905, Brooklyn finished in last place, 56.5 games out of first.

As Chadwick rose through PS 157, the Dodgers remained in the bowels of the league. But their losing only strengthened his devotion. The players, to be cast as "Bums" by cartoonist Willard Mullin, were lowbrow, blue-collar. So was Chadwick, living in a tenement at 120 Wallabout Street in Brooklyn.

On April 9, 1913, the Dodgers moved into Ebbets Field, the diamond at 55 Sullivan Place site of the former Pigtown garbage dump. Before long, Chadwick took in a game at the cozy park, happily occupying one of the 18,000 wooden seats that rose between Sullivan Place, Bedford Avenue, Franklin Avenue and Montgomery Street.

That same year, Chadwick became the starting shortstop on the Brooklyn Boys High baseball team. Afield he committed errors aplenty. At bat he steadily worked his way *down* the lineup, falling from sixth to eighth. But the next season Chadwick found himself the only student returning from the 1913 squad, and he was voted captain. The team went 2–6 and "Red and Black," the Boys High yearbook, reported that "Captain Chadwick was at all times an earnest spirited leader."

Chadwick was, however, less than spirited in the classroom. In fact, he rarely showed. And after the school's baseball season ended on May 19, truant Chadwick got kicked out of Boys High for playing hooky far too often.

Chadwick, sixteen, was fresh and street-smart, Runyonesque. He wore a fedora with the front brim flipped up. His favorite meal was meat and potatoes. He brushed his teeth with salt. And though he would never grow past 5′5″, he was stocky and quick to pick a fight with anyone who disparaged his Dodgers.

Chadwick's parents had little time to baby-sit their eldest. Anna had given birth to Ida, the last of seven children, in October 1913. And so, when Abraham—expelled from school—took up boxing, neither mom nor dad stood in his way.

As with baseball, Chadwick's ability in the ring was no match for his love of the sport. (In four years, he would not win a single bout at the Bronx gym where he fought.) But when in the fall of 1915 he got word of an amateur boxing tournament in San Francisco, he felt he was yet a contender and on October 29 took on, at a tryout at the Crescent Athletic Club in Brooklyn, a 115-pound-class fighter named Fabius Zellner. Zellner won.

Eighteen months later, Chadwick was a linotype operator living on Prospect Avenue in the Bronx when the United States declared war on Germany. Setting type seemed suddenly irrelevant. On July 6, 1918, Chadwick traveled to Fort Slocum, New York, and enlisted in the army.

Chadwick, twenty, did not go overseas. Assigned to a medical detachment, he instead bounced from New York to Virginia to Maryland where in suburban Baltimore he slept twenty-three nights among the psychiatric wards and prosthetic workshops of Fort McHenry. The private would later tell his daughters that along the way he "stuffed dead bodies" (victims, perhaps, of the influenza pandemic that had erupted in the fall). On June 18, 1919, the army honorably discharged Chadwick, serial number 396650, a private first class.

Away eleven months, Chadwick returned to live with his family at 647 Fox Street in the Bronx. He soon became a cabdriver, went back to boxing in his spare time and set out to look for a wife. And when in 1922 he and another man spotted simultaneously a young woman strolling along Prospect Avenue and 149th Street, the men agreed to meet back at that very spot that very night to settle the rights to her affection.

Chadwick, armed with a phalanx of friends and baseball bats, returned to the Bronx street at the designated hour. His foe returned as well and brought with him a gun. This Chadwick saw and turned to run. It was too late. A bullet caught him in the lower back. He collapsed.

Chadwick did not go to the hospital. How, he wondered, would he explain his wound? And so he went home, where on Fox Street the bleeding stopped and beneath a thickening scar a bullet remained.

Two years after Chadwick lost his duel, he met and fell in love with Miriam Marblestone. Miriam, seventeen, stood just one inch shorter than he, her posture perfect. She was more handsome than pretty, her build strong, her eyes and hair brown. But Miriam painted her nails and was everything Chadwick was not: she danced, loved parties, played cards, had dreams beyond the Bronx and was engaged to be married. No matter. Chadwick literally pursued Miriam, following her on dates. And when eventually he prevailed upon her for one of their own, he jump-started a parked car and took her out. Soon enough, Miriam, eight years his junior, broke off her engagement and started dating Chadwick.

Chadwick decided that no girlfriend of his should work, and driving a taxi left him enough money to give Miriam an allowance. Miriam was delighted. She lied to her parents—told them she had gotten a job as a stenographer—and was grateful to Chadwick for never telling her parents of their agreement. She liked that he could keep a secret. She also found it settling that he was traditional, that he did not drink or chase after women. And Chadwick was handsome with deep brown eyes, thick black hair and a cleft chin. On March 9, 1926, Miriam and Abraham married at Chateau de Luxe, the wedding hall at 670 Prospect Avenue soon to be converted into a garage. Nine months and two days later, daughter Helen was born.

A family man, Chadwick sat now behind the wheel of his cab every morning at seven, off at three. Arriving home at 480 Concord Avenue, tabloid tucked under his arm, he would kick off his Oxford lace shoes, lie down on his gray couch with the thin chartreuse crisscross and read about the Dodgers. (He preferred the *Daily News,* the *Daily Mirror* and the *New York Journal American.*) The news was rarely uplifting: from 1925 to 1929, the Dodgers finished sixth every season. The 1930 campaign began well. But after holding first for seventy-five days, Brooklyn finished fourth.

With the thirties came a daughter named Harriet, another Bronx address on Kossuth Avenue, and a new cab. Chadwick drove his Checker Model T with pride. The eight-cylinder taxi was manufactured just two years. And it was beautiful, the top half of its wood frame covered in canvas, the bottom in tin, vent slits marking the long nose of its hood, landau irons sloping over its back windows, front and rear doors opening opposite each other, running boards extending up over its Budd tires, a luggage grill behind the spare in back.

Chadwick was comfy in his leather bucket seat, happy to smoke cigars behind his eighteen-inch wheel, to watch from under his fedora the wind-up meter to his right tick off fares. His was a good job, solid pay through the Great Depression—20 cents the first quarter-mile, 5 cents each additional. And in September of 1937, two months after he went to work five miles from home for a dispatcher on Whitlock Avenue, he applied for Social Security, the federal program ten months old. Chadwick got a number, 123-03-3450, his future secure, he and Miriam comfortable enough to rent a bungalow summers in Rockaway.

All through the decade the Dodgers had continued to lose, the lone highlight come in 1938 with the introduction of night baseball in Brooklyn.

Baseball had first been played beneath the lights—36 of them—on September 2, 1880, at Nantasket Beach in Hull, Massachusetts. The lighting was poor, carbonized filaments of cotton emitting just 90,000 candlepower for 300 fans. Teams fielded by two department stores, Jordan Marsh and R. H. White, scored 16 runs apiece before boarding a steamboat to Boston. There were few night games over the next fifty years.

The first professional night game was played on April 28, 1930. It was then the Producers, a Class C team in Independence, Kansas, hosted the Muskogee Chiefs. One thousand fans watched the affair through squinting eyes—just ten foot-candles of light illuminated the outfield, twenty the infield. Still, lights increasingly went on at minor league ball fields all about the country as did a debate on the merits of night ball. Wrote the *Sporting News* on January 16, 1930:

> The night air is not like the day air; the man who goes to a baseball game after he has eaten a hearty meal is apt to have indigestion if he is nervous and excited; the disturbed and misanthropic fan will not sleep well after a night game. Who wants to go home in the dark when it is twice as pleasant to drive leisurely in the approaching twilight and sniff a good meal cooking on the range when the front door is opened and the aroma of a sputtering steak spreads through the house?

Nonetheless, the National League voted in the winter of 1934 to allow each team to host seven night games. And at 8:30 p.m. on May 24, 1935, lights shone down on Cincinnati's Crosley Field, a major league diamond lit for the first time.

The lighting system was state of the art, 616 1,500-watt lamps glowing three times brighter than did any minor league field. And the fans came in droves. The paying attendance, 20,422, was ten times the norm and spilled out into a cordoned-off section in the outfield. Cincinnati beat Philadelphia 2–1.

The Cincinnati fans maintained their excitement for night ball: 123,991 folks flocked to the Reds' seven 1935 night games. (Their 70 other home games drew just 324,256.) And so in 1938 night baseball spread to Brooklyn, off the next year to Philadelphia, Cleveland and Chicago, popular and lucrative at every stop. Wrote the *Sun* on November 15, 1939: "Night baseball is probably the finest thing that American labor has ever seen happen."

Beneath the lights, the Dodgers began to shine, finishing third in 1939 behind new skipper Leo Durocher. The next season, the team added Joe Medwick and finished second. And in 1941, as war raged in Europe, Brooklyn claimed its first pennant since 1920. Chadwick delighted. His team was again a winner.

Brooklyn's ascent happily coincided with the start of its radio broadcasts, Dodger games aired on WOR since spring training of 1939. Suddenly, behind the wheel of his cab, away from his wife and two daughters, Chadwick had company.

Walter Lanier Barber was born in Mississippi, raised in Florida and honed in Ohio—broadcasting Red games beginning with the very first major league game he ever saw. But it was behind a microphone in Brooklyn that the golden-throated announcer called Red found a home, introducing to the 300,000 Brooklynites who tuned in to him daily warm bucolic images. "The pea patch" was the diamond. A team "in the catbird seat" was a team in control. A speedy player ran "like a bunny with his tail on fire."

Before games, Chadwick often headed to the Bellmore, a café on Fourth Avenue. There he met a taxi driver and Giant fan named Willie Bly. "We used to bring our own chocolate syrup and make egg creams," remembers Bly. The shakes (home-brought Fox's U-bet mixed with milk stolen from the counter and seltzer ordered free), washed down talk of baseball and cabs, of tips, passengers and traffic. "We would tell hack stories," says Bly. Replenished, Chadwick hopped back into his cab and turned on the game. But even with Barber and his Bums as constant companions, Chadwick was tiring of driving a taxi. And he had something else in mind.

Chadwick idolized his younger brother Nat. Nat was smart and debonair. He was also an electrician and joined in December 1937 Local 3 of the International Brotherhood of Electrical Workers.

With the arrival the next spring of night baseball in Brooklyn, Local 3 represented electricians who worked for the Dodgers. Suddenly, the allure of night ball was for Chadwick greater than mere entertainment, novelty or convenience. The light stanchions above Ebbets Field beckoned him to a new career.

But Chadwick had no training as an electrician. And so in 1942, he tried to join the war effort. The army though rejected Chadwick, at forty-four too old to fight in World War II, and the cab driver stayed put, free to spend his afternoons at the ballpark. "He was very animated," remembers his nephew Bob Goldman. "His wife always complained about his screaming."

Nat, meantime, had climbed the union ladder, appointed in 1943 Local 3's business agent for northern Manhattan. Within a few years, Nat was as wired with connections as a power grid, and in May of 1947, finagled for his big brother a job repairing street lights. Chadwick sold his taxi medallion for $20.

Chadwick was thrilled. Suddenly, he spent his days outdoors, rising in ladder trucks, climbing the city's 250,000 light poles. Equally wonderful, he now spent his evenings at union meetings at the Knights of Columbus Hall, a fraternal organization on Roosevelt Avenue. Like his younger brothers Nat and Jack, Abe was at last 'Brother Chadwick,' a card-carrying union electrician. "This is to certify," read his union card with clenched-fist logo in its upper left corner, "that J516114 Abraham Chadwick is a member in good standing in this organization."

Membership meant steady employment. For Local 3 was abuzz with work, electrifying Brooklyn's gas-powered trolley cars, installing anti-fog lights on the runways at Idlewild Airport, wiring an NBC television studio, a Waterside power plant, housing for returning GI's. There was much to be done and Local 3 wanted to do it all. The union had little patience for independent contractors. Such electricians had to be dealt with.

And so it was, day and night, that Nat phoned his beefy brother Abe. "He would tell him where to go," remembers his daughter Helen. "They probably manhandled people in the shop to influence them to join the union." Chadwick did what was asked. Says his daughter Harriet, the union "was his life."

Meantime, the very month Chadwick had joined the union, Nat had wangled for him a second, part-time job. And it was glorious. Chadwick would operate the lights at a big league ballpark. The only problem was, the park was not Ebbets Field. It was the Polo Grounds. Chadwick took the job anyway.

Stoneham had long resisted night baseball. "Suppose Hubbell or Terry or Bartell was fooled by the lights and hit by the ball," the owner had said in 1934. "In one night my team would be ruined for the season." But five years of hefty receipts for night games at other parks converted Stoneham, and on November 14, 1939, the Giants finally announced that they would outfit their park with lights. The cost of installation, roughly $135,000, would be recouped in ticket sales to the seven scheduled 1940 night games.

Westinghouse Electric and Manufacturing Company oversaw the project and Harry Hays, Westinghouse chief engineer, translated the brilliance soon to illuminate Harlem into images the public could comprehend. The wattage at the Polo Grounds, he said, would be enough to light four thousand homes, to make all thirteen miles of Broadway five times as bright as Times Square on New Year's Eve, to make Municipal Airport (renamed LaGuardia Airport in 1947) visible to pilots flying over Harrisburg, and, if concentrated in a single unit, enough to make possible the reading of a newspaper eighteen miles away. The public was smitten.

Westinghouse fabricated the lighting equipment for the Polo Grounds in their Cleveland factory—steel lamps, copper fittings, glass bulbs, Pyrex covers—and, together with Belmont Iron Works, installed it in just three months. On May 24, 1940, lights shone down on the Polo Grounds a first time.

Leading up to first pitch at 8:45 p.m., it was abundantly clear that, though the Harlem park was the seventh major league venue equipped for night ball, baseball beneath the lights was still very much a novelty. The Giants, unsure of how to prepare for the contest, waited until four in the afternoon to eat lunch. Manager Bill Terry, uncertain if he should tweak his lineup, announced that he would use in the game only fastball pitchers. And the *Herald Tribune,* not knowing what to report, noted that when play began, the center fielder, pitcher, catcher and home-plate ump were the only men on the field to cast two shadows. Continued the paper, "It was so bright on the infield one could see the grasshoppers jumping."

The very brightness that inspired such tropes had worried the U.S. military. For come 1942, German submarines lurked in East Coast waters. And nervous that the nighttime glow of land-based lights would better frame in Nazi periscopes the silhouettes of Allied shipping vessels, U.S. government officials had banned nighttime baseball until January of 1944.

Three years later, high atop the Polo Grounds, it was Chadwick at the light switch. His was a simple job. Above the scoreboard in right field, just inside the foul pole, a concrete staircase rose from the orange metal railing of the upper grandstand. At the top of the staircase, behind the last row of fans sitting with their backs to 1,200 parking spaces, a wooden ladder, some twenty feet tall and screwed to the wall, led to a latch in the roof. There, before every night game (and whenever mid-game the umpire called for lights), Chadwick had only to climb the familiar rungs, step out onto the pebbled tar-and-asbestos roof, walk among the flagpoles to the park's circuit breakers, open the small asbestos-lined boxes and flip the light switches. "You had to have good thumbs," says Walter Carberry, a friend of Chadwick's from Local 3.

With the flip of those switches, 836 bulbs spangling eight steel towers 150 feet above the field throbbed with 1.25 million watts of light. All at once, the Polo Grounds' 8.7 acres shone with the luster of a spit-shined button. Chadwick, his work done, retreated to the stands to smoke cigars and watch baseball, a union emissary at the nexus of circuitry and the national pastime. Asked of his post, he liked to say, "Without me, no game." Months shy of fifty, Chadwick had found true joy.

There were other pleasures as well. Wednesday nights were for boxing, the former pug driving to Queens Boulevard with buddy Eddie Somers for the matches at Sunnyside Gardens. Saturday nights Chadwick and wife took in a movie and ate out Chinese. Sunday nights they talked politics, the registered Democrats walking two doors from their second-floor home at 1033 Elder Avenue to listen with the Lomrantzes to Walter Winchell on the radio. Often Chadwick set off five a.m. on weekends to fish City Island, the ever-practical electrician never packing lunch lest a friend get seasick. (Invariably Chadwick returned with a full stomach and a catch of tiny smelt Miriam fried whole in flour.) And periodic Sundays, when Miriam had over women to play mah-jongg, Chadwick played football, fathers versus sons in the empty lot on the corner of Elder and Eastern Boulevard. It was there one afternoon that Chadwick ran back an interception the wrong way, his romp in fedora and V-neck sweater captured in a silent home movie, Chick, as all called him, mistaking for cheers the implorations of teammates.

As the seasons that he worked at the Polo Grounds rolled by, it proved ever easier for Chadwick the Dodger fan to be in the Giants' employ. The

Giants were no threat to his Dodgers. For though a championship continued to elude Brooklyn, and the 1950 season ended in heartbreak—a pennant lost in its very last inning—Brooklyn finished comfortably ahead of New York a sixth straight year.

The baseball season over, Chadwick accompanied brother Nat to Miami Beach on union business. There, on October 17, 1950, as hurricane King began to gust outside the Sorrento Hotel, Chadwick sat down at 4:30 p.m. to write his first letter in twenty years. "Dear Miriam," he wrote. "I am in the best of health and believe it or not no cough in the morning." A cough had the previous year settled in Chadwick. "He coughed every morning," says daughter Harriet. "One of those real bad coughs."

Three weeks later, back in New York on November 9, the brothers Chadwick welcomed with the rest of Local 3 a visit from Vincent Impellitteri, the mayor careful to remember the union just two days after his election. Such was its sway.

Each spring, Chadwick had to secure his plum job anew. And each spring, brother Nat's influence helped him do so. That on the eve of more than one New Year Chadwick lighted the steel ball dropping into Times Square was no coincidence.

In 1951, Local 3 elected a business agent named Joe Jacobson, the union granting him jurisdiction over the Bronx and northern Manhattan. Jacobson, a crony of Nat's, had gotten to know Abe in the Bronx Acorn Club, a union-run Elks lodge of sorts where, thanks to Nat, Abe had become a board member the previous winter.

Like all of Local 3's business agents, in addition to seeing to it that contractors and electricians adhered to their contracts, Jacobson had the power to bestow not so much regular employment but the smattering of part-time jobs that, like the lighting of a ballgame or a midtown square, were the profession's lagniappes. "For these extras, the agent had privilege," says Jacobson, born the same month as Chadwick. He adds, "Naturally, I would favor members of the [Acorn] club." Chadwick was set for the 1951 season and its 14 scheduled night games.

Because Chadwick worked at night, the union paid him time-and-a-half, good for $4.80 per hour in 1951. By July 18, the overcast afternoon that blood pooled in Hank Thompson's shoe, Chadwick had earned $388.80.

Even better than the extra money, night games offered Chadwick the opportunity to illuminate his beloved Bums. The Giants and Dodgers squared off twenty-two times each season—one of every seven games. Of their eleven meetings at the Polo Grounds, two were at night. These were the special games for Chadwick, when beneath his pear-shaped lights the Dodgers glowed in road uniforms of royal-blue and gray. Chadwick would these nights climb the park's stone steps numbered in black paint, and sit at his familiar perch in the upper grandstand free to root for the visiting team. So far, it had been a good year. Heading into their double-header on July 19, the Giants were yet again—for the seventh consecutive season—well behind Brooklyn.

When rain washed out the doubleheader, Chadwick relaxed. Rainy days were stressful, circuit breakers apt to short, Chadwick left all through a wet game to peer up from the roof at the glass bulbs sixty-five feet above the brim of his fedora. Says Carberry, "He would watch the banks of lights to see that they didn't go out."

But this rainout brought work. For at some point before a first pitch the next night, Chadwick was told that the Giants wished to steal signs and that they needed his help. Yes, the New York Giants, they who had won fifteen pennants, needed *him*, Abraham Chadwick, né Czadwicz, a fifty-three-year-old street-light repairman.

Perhaps it was Durocher—he who years earlier had worked at Wico Electric—who thought to turn to an electrician. Regardless, it was a good idea. For Chadwick understood the task at hand.

The Giants needed to relay signals from clubhouse to batter. There were no lights in the park's scoreboards, so toggling a bulb was out of the question. But along the outfield walls, the bullpens, where pitchers warmed up, were in fair territory—the only pens in play in all the majors. And so, when a Giant batter stepped to the plate, he could look past the second baseman to his teammates on a bench in right-center field, shaded beneath a green metal awning "like cows sheltering beside a pasture shed in August," put in Roger Angell. Though they sat 449 to 455 feet away, they could motion signals to the batter unimpeded. So could players in the dugout, almost 400 feet closer to home.

And so, Chadwick's job was straightforward: devise a means, both instantaneous and inconspicuous, to relay a sign from behind a wire screen in center field to the bullpen and dugout.

Chadwick was an electrician of at best average ability. This he knew. He was a street-light repairman, of the union's J division. He loved his job, but among his peers, the "J" on his union card carried a stigma: tough but unskilled. Suddenly, though, he had an opportunity to prove his worth, to be creative. And he knew just what to do. He would install a bell-and-buzzer system in the clubhouse and run it to the wall-box phones in the bullpen and dugout, where, in recent years, telephone receivers had given way to handsets.

Carrying the few tools he needed, Chadwick walked into Durocher's center-field office. He scraped clean the ends of a few buzzer wires and led them through holes in the base plate of a push button. He fastened the wires under screw heads and, using a screw-joint base, mounted the push-button beside the fourth of the fourteen windows that looked out from the clubhouse onto the field.

The wires carried 90 volts A.C. They were small, anywhere from 22 to 18 gauge, and sheathed in fabric. Chadwick led them yard by yard out of the clubhouse and along the telephone and electric cables that ran below the stands to the bullpen and dugout. He unscrewed the bases of the two telephones and, with a twist and some tape, spliced the copper wires to the yellow wires that led to their bells. He then reattached the telephone bases and traced the two phone wires back to the clubhouse, fastening them under a second set of screw heads in the push-button on Durocher's wall. Just like that, he was finished.

The system was not ingenious—bells and buzzers were rudimentary, a staple of the profession. But he had thought to install it and had done so and it worked. Now, with the press of a button beside the fourth window in the clubhouse, two phones buzzed—one in the bullpen, one in the dugout. Chadwick had come through just in time for a four-game set against Cincinnati.

SIX

The best mirror is an old friend.
—GEORGE HERBERT,
"Jacula Prudentum," 1651

DUROCHER STOOD IN HIS OFFICE with Stoneham, mugging for the press. The National Exhibition Company, official corporation of the Giants, had offered him a new one-year contract and now, on Friday, July 20, as twilight blanketed the Polo Grounds, owner and manager signed it. Amidst congratulations, Stoneham noticed that the contract required a witness and so he asked Tom Watson, a photographer for the *Daily News* standing nearby, to sign it too. Watson obliged, and Stoneham locked the contract in his office safe. Durocher left the clubhouse, descended the fifteen steps to the field and, $50,000 richer, walked toward his dugout.

High overhead, Chadwick climbed his ladder, stepped out onto the tar roof in right field and flipped his lights. As the crowd of 14,205 settled into its seats, the manager below had time to think through one last time what would be his team's first stab at sign-stealing. The telescope, mounted on a tripod, was ready in the clubhouse. The buzzer in the clubhouse was connected to the phones in the bullpen and dugout. The players in the bullpen and dugout were ready with agreed-upon signs to relay to the batter. And just to be sure that everything went smoothly, Durocher stationed in his office the man he always turned to when he needed help: Herman Louis Franks.

Franks was born on January 4, 1914, in Price, Utah, to Edith Dozzi, a girl of eighteen from Colorado, and Celeste Franch, a photographer fourteen years her senior from Cloz, Italy. The family soon left coal country for the city in the valley by Great Salt Lake where, 105 miles northwest, Brigham Young had settled sixty-seven years before. The honeymoon was fleeting. In 1920, Celeste and Edith divorced. Celeste moved to Nevada, leaving his wife and son with only an anglicized surname.

No man at home, Edith encouraged her only child to play sports. This he did and always went quickly at Pioneer Park when the six-year-olds chose up sides. At fourteen, Franks began to play alongside grown men on teams sponsored by local mom and pops—Palace Laundry, Universal Film, Green Cab. That same year he started at East High, a lefty-hitting catcher by graduation a star. Read his 1931 yearbook: "Herman certainly needs no introduction in the athletic field since he is a first rate letterman in football, basketball, baseball and track." Recruiters from a Yankee scout to a Notre Dame football coach made offers. Franks, though, stayed home with his mother, enrolling come fall at the University of Utah.

Freshman Franks took up wrestling, a fifth sport. But the mat, like football, left him with a cauliflower ear, track did not come naturally, and as much as Franks loved basketball, baseball was his sport. And so just before the baseball season began, Bill Lane, who owned the AA Hollywood Stars, offered the freshman a contract. A smidge taller than five feet ten, weighing 187 pounds, Franks left the classroom, a professional ballplayer at eighteen.

Seven seasons of $3 per diems passed before Franks at last graduated the minor leagues, on April 27, 1939, the ninth native Utahan to wear a major league uniform. It was the bottom of the ninth when he stepped to the plate a first time, the score 4–4 with two on and two out. Patient, chewing gum, the Cardinal catcher worked a walk against Pirate Mace Brown. And when in the eleventh he grounded to second then hustled to first, Pep Young botched the ball, Don Padgett scored, St. Louis won and Franks, twenty-five, learned right off the bat to always take what the other team gives.

One hit later, Franks was back in the minors. But he had caught 13 big-league games and the eye of Larry MacPhail. And just before spring training the following season, Brooklyn's general manager pried the backup catcher from Branch Rickey for $25,000.

Franks provided a quick return on the investment. On April 30, 1940, he caught a no-hitter. It was Brooklyn's ninth straight win to open the season, tying a major league record, and the next morning, the *New York Times* ran a photo of Durocher, Brooklyn's beaming player-manager, hugging Franks and pitcher Tex Carleton.

Durocher immediately took to his new recruit. Franks could obviously call a game, had smarts and command of signals. ("I varied them so much," says Franks, "you could never tell what the hell they were.") He could also field. In 43 games behind the plate, Franks compiled a sparkling .990 fielding percentage.

Even better, Franks smoked cigars, played cards and played tough, driving the ball into the ribs of players sliding into home. "They were trying to kill you," says Franks. "I'd tag them pretty good."

Still, Franks batted just .183 for the year and, in the off-season, Brooklyn picked up Mickey Owen—the same Missouri farmer Franks had backed in St. Louis.

Behind Owen and Babe Phelps, Franks was a third-string catcher. And he was not surprised when, on April 17, Brooklyn optioned him to Montreal, Franks behind the plate that very night in a road game against the Newark Bears.

Providence, though, brought Franks back to the majors in a hurry. It was June 12, and at Penn Station, Brooklyn boarded a train for St. Louis. Phelps was missing. Durocher telephoned the catcher to no avail. "I've had the misery in my chest all spring," Phelps explained to a reporter. "And I've had bad pains in my head too." The stocky catcher had refused in spring training to travel with the team to Cuba and just that week had told Durocher he wished not to catch against Pittsburgh because he worried about his heart. The train left.

Two Brooklyn doctors examined Phelps. While he was physically fit, he suffered from neurasthenia, a mental disorder characterized by fatigue, memory loss and generalized aches. Durocher, apoplectic, was not buying it—the day before Phelps had batted cleanup. Durocher suspended Phelps, fined him $500 and, the very next day, recalled Franks from the minors.

Franks, meantime, was a Durocher dream. On June 23, he beat the Pirates with a pinch-hit home run. On July 22, he slapped a tag on the jaw of Reds shortstop Eddie Joost so hard it knocked him unconscious. And five days later, on Durocher's thirty-fifth birthday, Franks cursed out umpire Al Barlick over a called strike, good for a $25 fine. Franks, reporter Jim Minter later put it, "could cuss, chew tobacco, spit and scratch." Durocher loved it all and released Phelps, Franks his lone backup backstop.

Still, Franks seldom played. He was not nearly the hitter that Owen was, and sharp as he was defensively, Owen was even better. Beginning in September of 1940, Owen had made 476 consecutive plays without an error, then a league record for catchers. He ended the 1941 season with just three errors in 128 games and a team-record .995 fielding percentage. The Dodgers won 100 games for the first time in team history and grabbed the pennant. And as they readied on October 1, 1941, to face the Yankees in the World Series—the first of seven Subway Series between the clubs—New York was agog.

The crowd of 68,540 was the largest ever to attend a World Series game. And in keeping with baseball tradition begun the season prior, it rose now to sing the national anthem. It was still at attention when, in the bottom of the seventh, Durocher sent Franks in to catch. Franks coolly threw out the leadoff runner.

Trailing 3–2, Brooklyn came alive in the ninth. Ducky Medwick and Pee Wee Reese singled, and with one out and runners on first and second, Franks approached the plate. In 139 at-bats, he had hit just .201 with one home run. But with Owen spent and the neurasthenic Phelps cut, Franks had to bat for himself. Behind him Bill Dickey crouched with the sign, before him Red Ruffing gripped a baseball and beyond, in right-center field, Joe DiMaggio played him to pull. The titanic crowd rose. Somewhere in the stands, Edith Franks watched her son.

Franks wrapped his small hands around the handle of his 35-ounce, 35-inch bat, chewed hard on his gum and grounded sharply to second. The result: Joe Gordon to Phil Rizzuto to Johnny Sturm, a 4-6-3 game-ending double play.

The teams split the next two games, and on October 5, heading into the ninth inning of Game Four, the Dodgers led 4–3. On the mound stood Hugh Casey.

Casey was twenty-eight. He had first pitched in 1932 on the Atlanta Crackers of the Southern Association. He threw a curve as hard as he drank, whiskey his preference. He was a loner, had a bad temper and let fly enough beanballs to sate even Durocher. Dodger fans were glad he was theirs, and just three outs from tying the series, Ebbets Field thundered with cheers.

Casey induced Sturm to ground out to second to lead off the ninth. One out. Red Rolfe hit a tapper back to the mound. Two out. Tommy Henrich, "The Clutch," was next. Casey started him off with a ball followed by two quick called strikes. Franks and his teammates, on the edge of their bench, readied to celebrate.

It was 4:35 p.m. when Henrich fouled off a pitch. He watched another whiz far off the outside corner, then laid off a close one. Full count.

Casey had relieved in the fifth, had since allowed just two hits. His curve was breaking precipitously and now, even with three balls, Owen confidently called for the Uncle Charley. Casey slid his middle and index fingers across the ball's stitching and fired. For sixty feet the ball flew straight. Then, inches from Henrich, it broke sharply, diving low and off the inside portion of the plate. Ball four. But Henrich waved at it just the same. He missed, the crowd roared, umpire Larry Goetz raised his right arm to signal the out, millions across the country heard Bob Elson on the Mutual Broadcasting System say "He swung!" and uniformed police jumped out of the dugouts to keep fans off the field. The series was tied! But wait—Owen had not shifted his size-11½ feet. Out of position, he had reached for the ball a few inches off the ground and it had glanced off the heel of his glove, rolling quickly on a diagonal from behind his right foot. Owen dashed after it but Yankee coach Earle Combs shouted at Henrich to run to first, and he did. Henrich was safe.

"It's an error for the catcher," Elson explained to his audience. "Owen is charged with an error."

It was a record 89 degrees hot. And even ingesting salt tablets did little to stem the sweat that seeped through Casey's wool jersey, the pitcher shedding several of his 207 pounds. Owen tossed the ball back to his pitcher and, aghast, flipped on his mask. They had to secure a fourth out. DiMaggio singled, and on an 0–2 pitch, Charlie Keller doubled off the top of the fence in right. Just like that the Yankees led 5–4, 33,813 fans struck dumb. Durocher, too, sat stunned. The manager did not walk to the mound to settle Casey. He did not summon reliever Curt Davis who was warming up in the bullpen. And even as Casey completely lost his poise, allowing three hits, two walks and four runs, Durocher sat motionless in the dugout. The Yankees won 7–4, and the Dodgers trailed three games to one.

The longest nine-inning game in World Series history had taken its toll on Brooklyn. Mighty Casey was suddenly the first pitcher ever to lose successive World Series games, and as he dressed, reporter Bill Corum told his Mutual audience that "there's a redheaded, towheaded kid down [in the locker room] crying his eyes out and you can understand why." Owen meantime, lay naked on the rubbing table, a trainer dressing his bleeding legs. But it was his passed ball that hurt. Through bloodshot hazel eyes, Owen looked up at the reporters gathered about him. "It was a great breaking curve that I should have had," he said. "But I guess the ball hit the side of my glove."

Franks saw the suffering in Owen, his mild-mannered teammate. He saw the newspaper headlines that followed—"Series Goat," "Owen Shoulders Entire Blame for Blunder Which Opened Gates to Yanks," "Most Incredible Break in Baseball!" He saw, the next day, the winded

Dodgers lose the game and the series. And he saw Owen morph from an All Star into a whipping boy, into the given reason one borough lost to another, into the heir to the tortured legacy of Fred Merkle, bungler of the 1908 pennant. Losing was cruel.

Franks returned home to Utah and then returned, unsigned, his contract to the Dodgers. Surely he deserved more than a $50 raise. Surely he was worth more than $4,000. While the dickering over dollars continued, Franks, twenty-eight, applied for a commission in the Naval Aviation athletic program. The program accepted just one of every seven applicants, some 2,200 men. Franks was among them. And set now to join the military, he okayed his contract. Brooklyn sent him to Montreal, and on May 15, 1942, having batted .288 in 17 games, Franks entered the service, sworn in as an ensign in the Naval Reserve. The next day, he set off to Annapolis.

After a month's training, Franks was a physical training officer. And on June 14, before heading off to a naval base in Pensacola, Florida, he traveled to New York to play in a game at the Polo Grounds to benefit the war effort, visiting too the next day his former teammates at Ebbets Field. Bill Sullivan, a catcher from Detroit, had replaced him, but Durocher, eager to show Franks he missed him, offered him his private box. There Franks sat. And after watching Brooklyn lose to Chicago 6–0, he two-stepped to Florida and began training naval cadets.

One year later, Franks transferred to Norfolk. He became a lieutenant, junior grade. He was also player-manager of the naval air station team, batting .276, skippering eight wins and two ties in twenty-six meetings against the .369-hitting Schenz and his mates.

Franks left to Pearl Harbor in 1945. Again he caught and managed. And again he battled Schenz—yipping whenever the Ohioan dug into the batter's box before him. "Oh, they used to agitate each other!," remembers Wodzicki, who played alongside Schenz in Portsmouth and in Hawaii. "Hot-dog Franks," says Wodzicki, "was a squeaky bugger too." The foes turned mates in October, posing at Furlong Field in Honolulu with the navy National League All-Star team, their cross-legged knees touching.

Franks left the service the next month. And after spurning a large raise to play in the Mexican League, he rejoined the Bums in spring training.

Durocher was thrilled to have Franks back. But his aging catcher had been away from major league pitching for five seasons and so Durocher sent him now to Montreal to work his way back into shape. This Franks did, hitting .280 with 14 home runs in just 289 at-bats, compiling too a

.991 fielding percentage. Led by Franks and Jackie Robinson, Montreal won the International League championship.

Branch Rickey, who six years before had sold Franks to Brooklyn, was now Brooklyn's general manager and saw in him managerial potential. On January 10, 1947, Rickey appointed Franks, thirty-three, player-manager of the St. Paul Saints, the only player-manager in all AAA.

The St. Paul players liked Franks. He never badmouthed them to the press and always berated umpires who squeezed them on a call. American Association president Frank Lane was less impressed. When on May 27 Franks tongue-lashed the ump who called out on strikes outfielder Don Lund, Lane fined him $25 for "dilatory and other objectionable action." And when Franks got in his two cents on July 31 and August 1, Lane fined him $50 more for abusive language and for "charging" an umpire.

Weeks later, Connie Mack, owner and manager of the Philadelphia Athletics, let Rickey know he needed a backup catcher. And so Franks quit managing the sixth-place Saints, off on August 22 to play part-time in Philadelphia. It was a good move. Not only was the catcher now eligible for the pension plan Major League Baseball had instituted in 1946 but he met in Philadelphia Amneris Lorenzon, a woman eleven years his junior and as beautiful as the princess in the Verdi opera after whom she was named. The two married twelve months later.

Franks had not played in the major leagues in six years. But he was in good shape, 195 pounds. After batting .221 in 48 games over two seasons, he returned in October 1948 to Salt Lake City, there as every offseason to bowl, hunt, play gin rummy and plot with friends from the Italian-American Civic League against the local Mormon power brokers. It was now that Franks also bought forty-five acres in East Beach for $19,400. The land was obscure but high in the hills and Franks, a good catcher—the seer of baseball—saw in it vast potential. He subdivided the land and built water tanks.

That same winter Durocher phoned Franks. The Lip had taken over the Giants in July, was assembling a staff. And, no matter that Franks had batted .195 over his career, Durocher asked him to come to New York to be his bullpen coach. Franks was game and so was Ami. The fossilized Mack let Franks go. "It was very nice of him," says Franks. "I was getting old." On November 14, 1948, Franks signed with New York. After seven years apart, he and Durocher would again wear the same uniform.

The Giants limped along for much of 1949—heading into a doubleheader at the Polo Grounds on August 28, they were 60–61 with two ties, 14.5 games out of first. New York lost the opener 10–3 to Cincinnati. Durocher turned to Franks.

"Leo was disgusted," says Franks. "He said, 'how about catching and putting a little life in this team?' "

Durocher had activated Franks two days before. And he hoped now that Franks might show the greenhorns on his club how to really catch, to call a game, to mask signals, to greet a runner at the plate. Franks in his career had caught 141 games and allowed just five passed balls, his .985 fielding percentage solid. The thirty-five-year-old coach agreed to un-retire. Franks put on his gear.

The Sunday game began and, after an uneventful 15 outs, Franks came to bat in the third. He singled, delivering the first hit off Bud Lively. With one out, pitcher Monte Kennedy singled too and Franks headed for third. "He chugged down the line like a wheezy steam engine," wrote the *New York Times*. The relay throw from second baseman Jimmy Bloodworth smacked Franks on the back of his head as he slid. Safe. By the time Franks scored on a sacrifice fly, a welt throbbed beneath his cap and Durocher melted in appreciation.

Franks came to bat twice more, singling again in the penultimate at-bat of his career. His two hits put his lifetime batting average at .199. They also gave him a .667 slugging average for the year, making Franks the only player in baseball history to play six seasons and have his slugging percentage rise in each. (In 1994, Dann Howitt would become the second.)

Franks, in this his last game, also "exhibited plenty of zip behind the dish," reported the *Daily Mirror*. And when the game was called in the eighth on account of darkness, Kennedy and the Giants had won, 4–2. Franks, exhausted, collapsed into bed.

Six months later, New York opened camp in Phoenix and Durocher handed Franks another job. Franks was now the third base coach, back afield with the start of the 1950 season to wave runners home, send batters signals, holler at opposing players. He was intimidating, one of several Giants like Rigney and Dark sculpted in his manager's mold. "They were no-good bastards," Carl Furillo told author Peter Golenbock years later. "They all wanted to be like Durocher."

Franks, thirty-seven, was again coaching third in 1951, his seventeenth year in professional ball. The game he loved had proved a career. He had signed his first contract as a teen and now, on Opening Day, had a wife and seven-month-old son.

On July 3, as New York warmed up at the Polo Grounds, news reached Franks of a former teammate. At one a.m. that morning, Hugh Casey had sat on the edge of his bed in the Hotel Atlantan, held a 16-gauge shotgun to his neck and pulled the trigger. The particulars of the suicide were sordid—an estranged wife, a twenty-something groupie, a paternity suit, a court order to pay $20 weekly for care of a son, sworn last words: "I am completely innocent of those charges." But the fraternity of baseballers recalled also a precipitous curveball in the 1941 World Series, a catcher's misplay and the subsequent collapse of a pitcher.

"I should've called time and stopped the game," Owen told author Ray Robinson years later, "giving Casey and myself a chance to get over the shock."

Sixteen hours after Casey shot himself, the Giants beat the Phillies 9–8, overcoming five deficits in 13 innings. It was their best win of the year.

Ten days later, Frank Shellenback flew to Ottawa on a scouting trip. Down a man, Durocher turned, as always, to Franks, asking his pal of eleven years to fill in as pitching coach in the bullpen. Franks obliged and Durocher subbed at third. The Giants beat St. Louis 14–4.

No matter what Durocher had ever asked of Franks, Franks had done it. And on July 19, 1951, when Durocher needed to confide his latest plan, to talk beneath a red flag of sub-rosa signs, there was no doubt to whom he would turn. Durocher told Franks and Franks approved. And when the manager walked about the locker room asking who among his players wanted the stolen signals, the coach, they remember, walked about too, parroting the question.

After their meeting, Durocher had another question for Franks: would he leave the field to join Schenz beside a telescope in the clubhouse? Tapping Franks made sense. For not only was he Durocher's deputy, but a catcher. And who better than a catcher to make sense of catchers' signs?

With little exception, Franks would have only to educe if an upcoming pitch was a fastball, curve, pitchout or brushback. (In 1951, few pitchers threw sliders, and cutters, among other pitches, had yet to be conceived.) As there were but eight teams in each league (and no inter-league play), Franks would have to decode and set down just seven sets of signals, a baseball Rosetta stone. The coach, expert at gin rummy, had a fantastic memory. "Peanuts Lowrey, Herman Franks, Leo Durocher," testified infielder Joey Amalfitano in 1997, "Those guys could remember a card someone discarded five years ago." Franks answered Durocher yes. And he who had seen poor Owen and his bloodshot eyes, who saw what torment had done to Casey, had no qualms doing so. "We decoded the German signs, the Japanese signs in the war," offered the former lieutenant years later. "We weren't wrong for doing that."

And so it was that on the moonlit night of July 20, Durocher reached the dugout confident that all would go well with his sign-stealing plan. Holed up in his office, behind the green door, Franks would see to it.

SEVEN

Can't hear with bawk of bats.

—JAMES JOYCE,
Finnegans Wake, 1939

EWELL BLACKWELL TOOK THE MOUND in the bottom of the first inning. He was 6'6" tall and rail-thin, with long arms and big hands. He threw his pitches sidearm. His flailing motion, which Johnny Mize likened to that of "a man falling out of a tree," earned him the nickname "the Whip." His pitches burst upon batters, even his fastballs possessing a natural movement that bore down and in on right-handers. Blackwell had just made his sixth consecutive All-Star team.

Beneath the lights and a full yellow moon, second baseman Eddie Stanky dug now into the right side of the batter's box. Just 5'8" tall, he looked up at the Red giant atop the fifteen-inch mound.

The mound had not budged in the sixty years since Giant Amos Rusie first stood upon it on April 22, 1891. And the ground beneath it reached to the colonial roots of America.

It was a Dutch governor named Petrus Stuyvesant who in 1658 founded Nieuw Haarlem. (His countrymen had over decades appropriated the land from Indian tribes, including the Wickquaskeek, who maintained that the sale of Manhattan in 1626 for 60 guilders did not entirely relinquish their claim to this portion of the island.) Stuyvesant though was soon usurped, Colonel Richard Nicolls claiming Harlem for England in 1664. Nicolls quickly declared its riverfront communal property. Wrote Nicolls in 1667, it "doth and shall belong to the said Town."

The first to privately own the riverbanks were a German weaver named Pieter van Oblinus and a Harlem-born assessor named Barent Waldron. The marshland was apportioned to them in 1691, designated Lots 20 and 21 by four townspeople overseeing a "Division of the Common Lands."

The two lots meandered beneath and between the Harlem River and an avenue called Kingsbridge Road. Split by an inlet of the river, they extended north some 1,700 feet from what would later be 152nd Street and passed for decades among Oblinus and Waldron heirs until 1729, when a Waldron named Johannes relinquished the property to an emigrant of Westphalia named John Dykman. The land next belonged to a Jan Dykman who sold it to a Dutchman named Lawrence Low. In the Low family it largely stayed until 1767 when a shipping merchant from South Wales named John Watkins finished buying it up piece by piece.

Nine years later, Watkins set sail for Wales to tend to family property in Glamorganshire. And it was then, the Revolutionary War begun, that wife Lydia, mindful of a husband abroad, a Harlem in British hands and a son fighting for the rebel Whigs, left Harlem for New Jersey. There she soon welcomed to her home George Washington. "After leaving the falls of the Passaic, we passed through fertile country to a place called Paramus," wrote James McHenry, secretary to the general, on July 11, 1778. "We stopped at a Mrs. Watkins' . . . dined with Mrs. Watkins and her two charming daughters, who sang us pretty songs in a very agreeable manner."

War ended and the Watkins returned to Harlem, Lots 20 and 21 remaining in family hands until March 29, 1844, when Dr. Samuel Watkins sold them to a banker named Matthew Morgan for $16,731.82. Morgan in turn flipped the shoreline for $50,000 on December 11, 1850, to an English sugar refiner named Dennis Harris. Harris, though, invested in a fire insurance company that went belly up. And when a New York court foreclosed on the fourteen acres of his water and land that abutted the Harlem River, one William Lynch was their high bidder, the tea merchant from Ireland paying $21,500 on April 30, 1858.

Sarah Gardiner Lynch inherited her late husband's land. The mother of eight then ceded control of the property to her daughter Harriet, and Harriet, who would in 1897 officially acquire it from her mum for $2, entrusted its care to her husband, James Coogan.

Coogan and Lynch had wed in 1883. An upholsterer and lawyer, Coogan had eyes on political office. But when in 1888 his New York mayoral bid failed, he was left at age forty-three to focus instead on his married-into real estate concerns. "He was a practical business man who had no use for salt meadows and water courses," wrote Reginald Pelham Bolton in 1924, "so he caused the area in the valley to be filled in, and on the fill the Field and Polo Grounds that are so widely known in sporting circles, were constructed."

Come spring, the New York Giants found themselves homeless,

evicted by a city ready to extend 111th Street straight through their ballfield. After biding time in a park in Staten Island, the Giants turned to
Coogan in July, leasing the southern portion of his land just beneath a
viaduct on 155th Street. Giant owner John Day called his diamond the
New Polo Grounds, not letting go the name of the field where his team
had played previously and where polo matches had been held. By 1890,
the field went simply as the Polo Grounds.

It was then baseball was doubly good to Coogan, a new league in need
of diamonds leasing the northern half of his same field. And when the
upstart Players League promptly collapsed, the National Leaguers
skootched a few hundred feet north, Rusie and the Giants dropping to
Boston their 1891 opener.

New York's new park was beautiful, grass grown between the Harlem
River southeast and an outcropping of mica northwest. The promontory
offered onlookers a free view of a "narrow, tantalizing wedge of the
playing field," wrote Harpo Marx—shortstop, left field and center in
sight. Known as "Dead-Head Hill," it soon bore instead the name of a
landlord. When on Thanksgiving Day in 1893 the Princeton football
team defeated Yale 6–0, the *New York Times* noted that thousands of
resourceful fans "witnessed the game from Coogan's Bluff."

Down in the park (in what in time was called Coogan's Hollow), spectators parked horses in stables under the third-base deck and carriages
on a track beyond the center-field fence. In jackets and dresses, ties and
hats, they watched baseball from a roofed, two-tiered wooden grandstand that reached some twenty feet past both first and third base, room
enough for 16,000. In 1909, Giant owner John Brush extended his
stands to the lines drawn on the outfield fence where foul poles would
later rise. But in 1911 the stands burned to the ground.

That same ground that had for millennia lain in part beneath the
Harlem River cost Brush $40,000 in annual rent. And he now commis-
sioned a structure worthy of its lease.

New York's new park was a 1911 wonder, modern from concrete
footing to asbestos roof, from its telegraphs and telephones to its canvas
sun shields and double-decked steel grandstand, support for 25,065 fannies. It was opulent too. Blue and gold banners flew from thirty-foot
masts, Italian marble formed its boxes, and eagles spread wings atop a
gray-green frieze in which, eighty feet above ground, bas-relief human
figures held shields depicting the logos of the eight National League
teams. The Polo Grounds, wrote *Baseball* magazine, "was the mightiest
temple ever erected to the goddess of sport."

The temple was shaped like a horseshoe. While its foul pole in right rose just 257 feet, 8 inches from home, and the pole in left 22 feet farther, dead-center stood a ridiculous 483 feet away. "To a batter standing at home plate," wrote author Jonathan Eig, "center field at the Polo Grounds looked like it ended somewhere in the Hamptons." And so, when in 1923 the club added two tiers of additional seats reaching all the way to brand-new bleachers flanking the clubhouse in center, the horseshoe in Harlem had suddenly room for 43,000 fans. By 1951, capacity had risen to 54,500.

The stands at the Polo Grounds fully encircled its diamond, rising from home plate to left-center field on 159th Street, from left-center to right-center on Eighth Avenue, from right-center back home on the longitudinal equivalent of 157th Street, and behind home along the Harlem River Speedway. The wear of its forty years had turned Giant fans wistful in their green splintered seats. "The mere age and squalor of the Polo Grounds comforted its customers," wrote Murray Kempton. "You could as easily catch some bronchial disease in its dank recesses as you used to be able to catch malaria at night in the Roman Coliseum, and both contagions carried the romance of history."

On this July night, the crowd of 14,205 eyed Blackwell. He liked to start off batters with heat, and Red catcher Dixie Howell now obliged, extending an index finger toward the ground. Fastball.

A tenth of a mile away, steadied on a tripod and hidden in Durocher's locked office, a Wollensak trained on Howell's pink finger. Its view was unimpeded. For wire mesh had been clipped, a rectangle opened in the lower right corner of the fourth of the fourteen windows that looked out from the clubhouse onto the field. "Whoever cut that hole had a pair of wire-cutters," recalls Al Gettel, the Giant pitcher released that very week on July 27. "I knew about it. I heard it around the clubhouse from the coaches." Roughly the size of a shoe box, the peephole opened some two feet above a plaque honoring the late Christy Mathewson. THE GREATEST PITCHER OF HIS ERA AND ONE OF THE FINEST SPORTSMEN OF ALL TIME, read the tablet, bronze on green concrete. FOR HIS MODE OF LIFE AND CONDUCT AT ALL TIMES, HE STOOD FORTH AS AN EXAMPLE TO HIS FELLOW PLAYERS. (Mathewson had particularly scorned pinched signals. "All is fair in love, war, and baseball," he wrote in 1912, "except stealing signals dishonestly.")

Unlike most telescopes, Schenz's was designed for terrestrial viewing, extra lenses righting the viewed image. And it was perfectly suited to spying baseball signals.

The outside lens of the Wollensak measured 35 millimeters or 1.38 inches in diameter. An optically perfect telescope (one whose curvature, thickness and spacing of each lens fits the telescope's design) has a resolution of five divided by A arc seconds, where A is the aperture in inches. And so, from 500 feet, Schenz's telescope had a resolution of 3.6 arc seconds (five divided by 1.38) or .11 inch. (If less than optically perfect, the telescope provided a slightly less powerful resolution of, say, .2 inch.) Thus, Schenz could distinguish Howell's sign as long as the catcher's fingers flashed at least .2 inch apart. This, of course, they did.

Schenz knew his equipment. (The *Sporting News* listed photography as his lone hobby outside sports.) He had told Davey Williams, a backup infielder on the team, that if he pressed his eye too close to the telescope's black plastic eyepiece, the spied image was blurred. Now, holding his eye at the proper distance, he saw Howell's finger, recognized a sign and pressed the buzzer before him once. Fastball.

The electric current raced through the copper wires Chadwick had laid, and the green telephone fastened to the right-field wall in the Giant bullpen buzzed once. The buzz was so jarring that, although it was expected, Corwin, Yvars and all a bullpen fell clear off their steel-framed wooden bench. "It was so loud," says Corwin, "we all jumped."

The plan to relay the stolen sign from bullpen to batter had been simple. One player would sit on the end of the bench closest to center field, set off slightly from his teammates. After hearing the buzzer buzz, he would flash a sign—maybe toss a ball in the air to denote a curve or cross his legs or simply sit still. The method was based, says Corwin, on "what was easiest to see, what was the quickest." Batter Stanky peered discreetly beyond the right fielder to the bullpen. But he got no sign. The startled men had fallen from view.

For decades, the Polo Grounds had been sinking. Choked with clay and rock that had over time spilled from the palisade just northwest, its dirt was no longer porous. Grass struggled to grow, and each year, some half-inch of field oozed with the rain down the outfield drains. In October 1945, Stoneham paid Jimmy Slattery, a contractor from Woodside, Queens, $100,000 to uproot and resod the field. Slattery got to work, using 3,000 cubic yards of gravel, 1,500 cubic yards of topsoil and 160,000 square feet of sod—a hybrid of fescue, Kentucky blue and red top. Stoneham then asked the great Matty Schwab to care for his lawn.

Schwab was a third-generation groundskeeper. Grandfather John had first tended Cincinnati's Bank Street Grounds in 1883, father Mathias Crosley Field in 1894 and Schwab Ebbets Field in 1938. But Brooklyn had just denied him a raise. And so, come Opening Day 1946, a craggy Giant field was suddenly luxuriant.

The commute from Brooklyn to Harlem dragged. And when Schwab stumbled upon empty space beneath the Polo Grounds grandstand just foul of the foul pole in left, he asked Stoneham if he might build him an inside-the-park home. Park superintendent Joe Traynor okayed the plan and built with concrete blocks below Section 31 an apartment complete with kitchen, two bedrooms, living room, bathroom and three windows. (Stoneham said no to a fourth that would have been cut into the outfield wall.) A worker painted the kitchen pale yellow and the doorframes blue, and Matty, wife Rose and son Jerry moved in. The pad was rent-free.

Schwab was thrilled. He had only to step out the rolling green metal door some twenty feet from his kitchen and he was afield, there to work his four-acre backyard.

Schwab kept his tools in a small storage room behind the New York dugout. The room was discovered in 1946 when Giant skipper Mel Ott banged a fist against the concrete wall behind the dugout. The thud was hollow. Ott excavated and found a chamber, five feet by five feet, with a sloped floor and drain. The concrete room was some 15 degrees cooler than the dugout just paces away and on hot days, the manager stored his pitchers there. The players, though, soon used the room as a urinal. And so Schwab converted it into a storage area for sandbags, hoses, rakes and sprinklers.

After games, Schwab watered his field, attaching brass sprinklers to the nine rubber-capped pipes that peeked out all about the grass, careful through the night to rotate the heads every two hours. Sometimes little Jerry helped, a fourth-generation groundskeeper, four years old, grabbing a rake or turning with both hands the metal valves that shone red in the hall opposite his apartment, water sent whooshing underground.

Five years later, in 1951, the outfield grass at the Polo Grounds still undulated strangely. From the lip of dirt where it began at the edge of the infield, it sloped down 18 inches to drains some 20 feet into the turf. As it stretched on farther from home, the greensward rose 18 inches only to sink steadily again, the base of the outfield wall several feet below the infield. And so now, standing on the wooden planks of the dugout floor two steep steps below the diamond, Durocher could see only the top halves of his outfielders. And Stanky, standing at home plate, could barely make out his stunned teammates who scattered at the base of the 12-foot wall a few feet to the right of the 15-inch tin marker that read 455 FT.

But Chadwick's buzzer had also detonated in the dugout. And there too the players had set up a relay system. They would bark out a decided-upon code word for the fastball—sometimes it was the player's first name or any encouragement. (If the batter instead heard his last name or nothing at all, he knew the curve was coming.)

The player barked, Stanky took the pitch and Jocko Conlan, the bowtied Irish umpire behind home plate, screamed: "BAAALLL!"

Out in the bullpen, Corwin got up off the warning track, sat down, looked up anxiously at the fans and worried about his buzzing phone. "We thought the whole ballpark could hear," he says. The fans after all were little more than 10 feet above the bullpen awning, so close the players got to know them. There was heavyset Louis Kleppel who hawked novels in the bleachers, a cabbie who always brought pitching coach Shellenback cigars, a quartet of well-dressed women who sat every game beside the right-field foul pole, the Section 39 Solarium Club, and of course the Section 5 Club, a few hundred fans who sat in Section Five just above the bullpen and presented annually at a dinner in the Concourse Plaza Hotel an award to the Giant deemed by them most valuable. But no one seemed to notice. Not the fans above the pen, not the fans in the bleachers astride the clubhouse, not the fans atop the dugout, not Douglas MacArthur, the recently dismissed general, seated in a front-row box along first. Only Chadwick, watching from on high, was not oblivious.

Howell threw a first pitch back to Blackwell and again Stanky dug in. Nicknamed the Brat, Stanky was expert at getting on base. In 1950, his 144 walks had led the league, and once on the base paths, he was happy to kick a ball out of a glove. "He can't hit. He can't field. He can't throw. And he can't outrun his own grandmother," Branch Rickey had once said of Stanky. "But he's still a great ball player." Blackwell knew he would be taking the pitch and wanted simply to throw a strike. Blackwell and Schenz looked in to Howell for the sign.

Schenz had the clearer view.

Fully opened, Schenz's black-grain leather telescope was 26½ inches long. It had four stainless-steel extenders, each engraved with a corresponding magnification—15X, 20X, 30X, 40X. From 500 feet, the 40X setting made the catcher look as if he were only 12.5 feet away, roughly one-fifth the distance from pitcher to catcher. The 20X setting made him appear to be 25 feet away. The smaller the magnification, the brighter the image. Schenz picked a power suitable for a night game.

The glare of 836 bulbs did not hinder Schenz's view. Research into the transmission of light through lenses had led to the discovery during World War II that applying magnesium fluoride to a lens limited glare.

The Wollensak Optical Company in Rochester, New York, having started out in July of 1899 manufacturing photographic shutters, had then launched a line of telescopes complete with "Coated Optics," a boast etched into the sparkling chrome-plated base of Schenz's telescope.

Again Blackwell delivered, again Stanky abstained and again Conlan bellowed: "BAAALLL!"

Twice more the three-step routine—interception, buzz, relay—filled the dozen or so seconds between signal and pitch. Twice more Stanky, unable simply to look down at the wiggling fingers 30-odd inches below him—convention forbade a peek—waited for those signs to crisscross the park some 1,000 feet round-trip. Twice more Stanky's bat stayed still. Twice more Conlan called balls. Stanky jogged to first with a four-pitch walk.

Blackwell's right shoulder felt tight and he walked the next batter, Lockman, on four pitches too. He was frustrated, the Giants not swinging at balls out of the zone. Mueller, batting third, singled to right, scoring Stanky. Irvin lined out to shortstop Roy McMillan who then robbed Mays of a hit, fielding a hard grounder up the middle and forcing out Mueller at second. Dark and Thomson followed with sharp singles to left, Durocher waving in from third two more runs. Reds manager Luke Sewell had seen enough and brought in Harry Perkowski to relieve Blackwell. For just the third time in his seven-year career, the Whip had not survived a first inning.

The Giants rapped 12 hits and beat the Reds 11–5. And after 2 hours and 47 minutes, Schenz, 500 feet from home plate, collapsed his telescope to its 8¼ inches, slid the scope into its tan stitched leather case, popped shut a shiny silver snap engraved in tiny capital letters with the word WOLLENSAK, and walked with Franks to the locker room. High above them, as after every Giant win, maintenance man Colletti raised atop the clubhouse a blue flag while iron loudspeakers played the Giant Victory March:

We're calling all fans
All you Giant ball fans
Come watch the home team
Going places 'round those bases

Cheer for your favorites
Out at Coogan's Bluff
Come watch those Polo Grounders
Do their stuff.

Those Polo Grounders now shuffled into the locker room, first from the bullpen, then the dugout. Their scheme had worked! They would keep quiet, talk of sign-stealing restricted to the clubhouse. A sign later hung in the visitor's locker room in Milwaukee said it best: WHAT YOU HEAR HERE, WHAT YOU SEE HERE, AND WHAT YOU SAY HERE MUST STAY HERE.

Durocher showered and dressed, put on his Fabergé cologne and Patek Philippe watch, combed back what remained of his dirty-blond hair and met with the press. There was much to talk about—the manager had his new contract, Maglie his thirteenth win, the Giants another third baseman. Told two days before that he was to play third, Bobby Thomson had stared down at his shoes. "There's one thing it'll do," he told a clutch of reporters. "It'll put me nearer to the crowd so they can get a better chance to boo me."

But on this night, manning the hot corner for the first time since 1946, Thomson fielded a foul pop and a grounder without incident, hit three hard singles, and, for a change, was cheered by the fans.

EIGHT

The great American game of baseball is a fraud, a treachery and un-American. It offers a regrettable example to the nation's youth, is populated by cheats, thrives on sneaky tricks, and teaches Fagin values to thousands of Little Leaguers.

—SHIRLEY POVICH, *Washington Post,* October 20, 1972

IN THE SUMMER OF 1951, authorities sought to bleach scandal from sport. Judge Saul Streit sentenced fourteen students at City College of New York, Long Island University and New York University for conspiring to fix basketball games. The United States Military Academy at West Point expelled ninety cadets, among them thirty-seven members of the football team, for cheating in its classrooms. And on July 19, the very day Durocher exhorted his players to cheat afield, Pennsylvania governor John S. Fine signed into law Act No. 229. It stiffened the sentences for fixing athletic contests, for causing "to be lost any game or contest or match or race or sport," to up to $10,000 and ten years in prison.

None of that gave Durocher pause. Stealing signs was different.

Baseball has long been a subjective and unfixed game. Its official scorers are fickle. Its strike zone is often reinterpreted. Its outfield dimensions are not uniform. It has no clock. Play halts when an ump determines a shower has turned to downpour.

Teams, hungry for a leg up, push the elastic envelope. In 1923, the Yankees built their new stadium complete with a 294-foot porch in right to accommodate lefty slugger Babe Ruth. In 1942, Milwaukee minor league owner Bill Veeck, wanting more home runs, installed in Borchert Field a motorized wire fence that, when convenient, receded between innings from right field to foul territory. In 2002, the Colorado Rockies, wanting *fewer* home runs, stored baseballs in a room kept at 90 degrees and 40 percent humidity so that they might generate more friction in the thin air of Denver.

Ground crews have also long groomed the home field to advantage. In Chicago, all through the fifties, groundskeeper Gene Bossard sloped fair the Comiskey Park baselines, nudging into play the bunts of Nellie Fox and Luis Aparicio. The Shibe Park grounds crew did the same for Richie Ashburn, the 90 feet between home and third known by Philly opponents as "Ashburn's Ridge." And before dawn on October 1, 1962, San Francisco groundskeeper Schwab and son Jerry treated the topsoil off first and second base with sand, peat moss and water to help contain the speedy Maury Wills of the Dodgers. As Heywood Broun wrote in 1923: "The tradition of professional baseball is agreeably free of chivalry."

Some baseball tinkering goes beyond discourteous. Force equals mass times acceleration—the ideal bat has both a large hitting surface and can be swung quickly. And so batters have bulked their bodies with steroids and lightened their bats with cork. "If you bore a half-inch-diameter hole into the barrel of the bat and fill it with sawdust or cork (which is one-third the density of wood) the bat becomes an ounce lighter," explained Dan Gutman in *The Physics of Foul Play*. This Tiger Norm Cash did in 1961 when he batted .361 to lead the American League. And such was the bat Yankee third baseman Graig Nettles brought to the plate in the fifth inning of a game between New York and Detroit on September 8, 1974. When it split upon contact, six Super Balls shot onto the field.

Pitchers also cheat. On its way home, a pitch may rotate up to 16 times, or 30 times per second. The more revolutions, the sharper the break of the ball (which darts in the opposite direction of its spin). Hoping to grant baseballs unpredictable flight, pitchers rub them with spit, dirt, paraffin, licorice, talcum powder, moustache wax, soap, hair spray, pine tar and Vaseline, scuff them with emery boards and sandpaper, nick them with wedding rings, raised eyelets on their mitts, and, as Durocher did regularly while the Cardinal shortstop, a filed belt buckle. Each treatment alters the drag on the ball, fluctuates the coefficient "f" in physicist George Stokes's formulation of the acceleration of a sphere: $a = (18\mu\rho v / d^2) f + g$. "If the surface of the ball becomes irregular," explained Gutman, "the airflow around it is disrupted."

Cheating is not always easy. Few but catchers and coaches can consistently crack signals. Fewer still can cork a bat. And when pitcher Ken Brett tried just once in fourteen years to throw a spitball, it sailed against the backstop.

Nor is cheating always safe. A rash of ill effects may yet await the scores of players who have taken steroids. The misread stolen signal leaves the batter—expecting a curve but getting a fastball—in harm's way. And doctored bats and balls pose a constant if less grave risk too. Cork was never allowed in bats, the spitball was banned in 1920 and a suspicious umpire may at any moment confiscate a bat or toss a guilty pitcher. Baseball suspended pitcher Joe Niekro for ten days in 1987 after a knuckleball in an obvious tizzy led umpires to an emery board in his pocket. And it suspended catcher Angel Rodriguez for a full year in 1981 after he repeatedly identified upcoming pitches for rival Hispanic batters.

Baseball's disciplinarians, however, are not quite sure what to do with sign-*stealers*. It depends largely on the nature of the theft.

"Bootling information to the batter through a hidden observer equipped with field glasses is a dastardly deed," wrote Red Smith on August 5, 1950. "But the coach who can stand on the third base line and, using only his own eyes and intelligence, tap the enemy's line of communication, is justly admired for his acuteness."

There is much the acute coach, player and scout can tap. "Any difference in the manner of holding [the ball] will be quickly noticed by a clever batter," wrote John Montgomery Ward in his 1888 book *Baseball: How to Become a Player,* "and if for a particular curve it is always held in a certain way, he will be forewarned of the kind of ball to expect." Ward, a Giant pitcher turned shortstop, continued, "Some batters pay no attention to these little indications; but the majority are looking for them all the time, and once they detect any peculiarities, they will be able to face the pitcher with much greater confidence."

And so it was with great confidence that Yogi Berra batted against Connie Johnson. For with each at-bat against Johnson, the Yankee catcher stared at his right hand. Johnson, who pitched five seasons for the White Sox and Orioles, was black and, says Berra, "as long as you saw the white of his hand it was a fastball." (In 46 career at-bats against the righty, Berra batted .304 with five home runs.) On July 1, 1950, Red Sox first base coach Del Baker noticed that Whitey Ford, a southpaw on the Yankees making his major league debut, was tipping pitches with his left wrist. The wrist lay flat against his stomach before the fastball, bent before the curve. (Boston amassed seven hits, six walks and five runs in 4.2 innings.) And on April 30, 1961, Westrum, then the Giant third base coach, saw at County Stadium in Milwaukee that Brave catcher Charlie Lau crouched outside whenever a fastball was coming. Westrum signaled the pitches to the bullpen, where a player sat still for the fastball and waved a towel for the curve. (Mays hit four home runs.)

With such returns possible, teams have turned to skulduggery for as long as signs have been a part of baseball. And signs have long been part of the game.

It was in the early eighteenth century in England that folk games including stool-ball, trap-ball and tut-ball began to plait themselves into the warp and woof of baseball. The game spread. "There is nothing now heard of, in our liesure [sic] hours," wrote Bowdoin College student Henry Wadsworth Longfellow in 1824, "but ball, ball, ball." And in 1845, thanks at least in small part to a New York City bank teller named Alexander Cartwright Jr., baseball had in the United States its own set of rules. Much in the rules would never change—division between fair and foul territory, granting defense the ball, basepaths of 90 feet, scrapping the beaning of baserunners as a means to record outs. But Cartwright's game relied little on communication between pitcher and catcher, and so, at first, not at all on signs.

The pitcher of the 1840s stood some 15 paces from home plate. He had in his arsenal but one pitch—a straight, underhand toss. And as the location of each pitch mattered not at all—only a delivery swung at and missed was a strike—just speed distinguished in any real way one toss from another. The catcher, uninvolved in pitch selection, was similarly checked. Roughly 10 to 15 feet back of home, ready to catch bare-handed each pitch after it bounced, his value rested on an ability to cover ground (all foul balls first landing fair were in play), to throw out runners and to snare a third strike lest a strikeout be squandered. (A third strike caught on one bounce retired a batter.)

Thus were the first pitchers and catchers less difference-makers than facilitators.

But baseball soon changed. In 1858 the sport gave an ump license to call strikes, and in 1863, balls too. Location now mattered. Within two more seasons, pitchers like Candy Cummings, Phoney Martin and Ben Hannegan began to throw what became known as a curveball. And in 1884, pitchers had permission to throw overhand. Pitcher and catcher suddenly had arrows in their quiver. And with options came ever more the need to communicate, the need for signs.

Baseballers were hardly the first to use the signal. From the bang of Stone Age drum to the blow of Middle Eastern horn, the dispatch of Native American smoke signal, the strike of Oriental gong and the ring of European bell, man had long shared—instantaneously and without speech—information over distance.

Often the signal served as alarum. Beacon fires lit in Troy in 1200 BCE signaled to Mycenae the return of Agamemnon and his fleet. Six hundred years later, the prophet Jeremiah instructed the tribe of Benjamin to blow ram horns in Tekoa and light bonfires in Beth Hakerem to warn of invading Assyrians. On the island of Pharos, a 384-foot lighthouse completed in roughly 280 BCE guided ships by mirror and fire. And in 150 BCE, the Greek historian Polybius described two sets of five torches used to construct words of his twenty-four-letter alphabet. Such signaling continued through the next two thousand years, through April 18, 1775, when a sexton used lanterns in a Boston church tower—"one, if by land, and two, if by sea"—to warn Paul Revere and his fellow colonists that the British were coming. (A gun blast the next day would turn in Ralph Waldo Emerson's hand to "the shot heard round the world.")

Signal sets by now comprised complete languages too. In the early part of the tenth century, Benedictine monks vowed to silence in the Burgundy Abbey of Cluny formulated an extensive vocabulary of finger and eye gestures. A monk named Juan Pablo de Bonet published in Spain in 1620 a book of hand-shapes that formed a manual alphabet, forebear of sign language for the deaf. In 1738, a French naval officer named Mahé de la Bourdonnais created a maritime flag code, allocating different pennants to numbers zero through nine. In 1791, Claude Chappe, a French engineer and cleric, used three moveable wooden sticks atop a tower to signal letters, transmitting words over miles. Four decades later, a Massachusetts portrait painter named Samuel Morse invented an alphabet of sounds and rhythms, dots and dashes traveling via telegraph. And in 1860, an assistant U.S. Army surgeon named Albert James Myer created a system of flag and torch signals he called wig-wag. The army adopted the system, birthing in the Civil War the Signal Corps.

It was then signaling took to the baseball diamond too. When on July 7, 1860, the Excelsiors of Brooklyn defeated Flour City of Rochester 21–1, the press took special note of Joe Leggett. "The catcher was also proficient in his part," wrote the *Rochester Evening Express*, "and won encomiums for the manner in which he would telegraph advances to be gained, or the direction as to which one of the fielders should take a 'fly.'" Concurred the *Brooklyn Eagle* on July 13, 1864, "All pitchers should follow example of the Excelsior players in 1860. The pitcher and catcher of the Excelsiors had regular signals whereby the pitcher knew when to throw to the bases." (One year prior, the Brooklyn paper was perhaps the very first to use the word *signal* regarding baseball.) The use of signals spread. The *Daily Alta California* observed on September 26, 1869, that Douglas Allison, starting catcher on the Cincinnati Red Stockings, "indicates by signs to the pitcher and base-keepers the proper thing to do at the right moment."

Over the coming decades, as baseball tinkered with its rules, what was the proper thing to do changed. And with change continued the need for signs. In 1863 for example, worried that curveballs and called strikes would doom its batters, baseball sought to harness the pitcher, commanding him to pitch with both feet aground, to remain mid-delivery in the new pitcher's box and to throw hittable pitches. "Should the pitcher repeatedly fail to deliver to the striker fair balls," read the new rule, "the umpire, after warning him, shall call one ball." Pitcher and catcher had suddenly to rely more on control and change of pace than on speed. More than ever before was communication vital. "This is 1867, not 1860," explained the *Clipper* newspaper on May 18, 1867. "Sending in balls just as swift as you can, without any other object in view than mere speed, and without regard to what the cost of your delivery may be in passed and called balls, is a style of pitching which has become obsolete in first class nines." In 1871, another law passed, batters granted the right to request a high or low pitch, the umps forced to call two strike zones. But in 1884, it was the pitcher who rejoiced, at last allowed to throw overhand. Overnight, fastballs turned faster, curveballs severe, the difference in pitches great. And when three seasons later baseball no longer allowed the batter to request his strike zone, the possibilities of pitches grew greater still, pitcher and catcher needing be on the same page with each and every delivery.

With the passing of a few more rules—four balls per walk, pitching rubber set 60 feet, 6 inches from home, the infield fly rule—baseball was by 1895 much the game it is today. Thenceforth would its rules be less often changed wholesale than fine-tuned, baseball having long ago set games at nine innings, required fielders to catch a ball on the fly and found equilibrium afield, pleased that as now, good pitching beat good hitting. "The removal of certain restrictions upon the pitcher's motions," wrote New York Giant Ward in 1888, "the legalization of the underhand throw instead of the old straight-arm pitch, the introduction of 'curve' pitching, and, finally, the unrestricted overhand delivery, have kept the pitching always in the lead."

Signs helped too. "Every battery, by which is meant a pitcher and catcher," continued Ward, "must have a perfectly understood private code of signals." These insured that the batter had no inkling of what pitch was upcoming. And while the overhand fastball and curve were now his steady diet, a third pitch was regularly signaled for too. "Occasionally, say once an inning," wrote Ward, "a pitcher may make a round arm or underhand motion simply to mislead the batsman."

The use of signs in baseball was evolving, and some wondered as to their employ by umpires. The *New York Sunday Mercury* had years back on March 27, 1870, printed a letter from Cincinnati manager Harry Wright. "There is one thing I would like to see the umpire do at [a] big game," it began, "and that is, raise his hand when a man is out. You know what noise there is always when a fine play is made on the bases, and it being impossible to hear the umpire, it is always some little time before the player knows whether he is given out or not." At last, on October 20, 1886, an umpire named Ed Dundon did use signs. "He used the fingers of his right hand to indicate strikes," reported the *Clipper*, "the fingers of the left hand to call balls, a shake of the head decided a man 'not out,' and a wave of the hand meant 'out.' " A pitcher in Mobile on the Acid Iron Earths of the Gulf League, Dundon was deaf and mute.

The next season, signs spread farther, migrating from behind home plate up the foul lines, baseball mandating that "coachers" step afield to instruct baserunners. (The rule sprung from Baltimore, where the Orioles had taken to flagging runners. "They give signs instead of yelling directions," marveled the *Washington Post*.) At least one coacher made immediate use of signs, gesticulating every time William Ellsworth Hoy, a rookie outfielder on the Washington Nationals, stepped to the plate. "When he bats," explained D.C.'s *Evening Star* on April 7, 1888, "a man stands in the Captain's box near third base and signals to him decisions of the umpire on balls and strikes by raising his fingers." Like Dundon, Hoy, dubbed Dummy, was deaf and mute, disability again a prompt for communication afield.

Signals now flurried steadily on the diamond, every bit what Swiss linguist Ferdinand de Saussure, father of semiotics, would soon classify "a linguistic system." And that coaches flanked the field hastened what was an inevitable watershed in baseball: the practice of stealing signs. "The coacher," wrote Ward in his 1888 treatise on baseball, "standing at first or third, makes some remark with no apparent reference to the batter, but really previously agreed upon, to notify him what kind of ball is going to be pitched."

And so signals turned covert. While pitchers had for decades done most of the gesturing, "codes of this sort were too easily interpreted by the opposite side," explained *Everybody's Magazine* in 1906. "Catchers had to assume the task." Among the first to do so was Cincinnati Red Stocking Jim Keenan. "Jim would crouch down close to the ground in giving the sign, and would use two fingers," Brooklyn shortstop Germany Smith told the *Cincinnati Commercial–Gazette* in 1891. "The players on the baselines couldn't see him give it."

The top catcher was now not only adroit but keen. "Upon the

approach of a batter," wrote *Everybody's Magazine,* "the catcher must instantly recall the man's peculiarities." By 1888, nearly all did. "Now it is almost the universal practice for the catcher to give it to the pitcher," wrote Ward. "And if the latter doesn't want to pitch the ball asked for he changes the sign by a shake of the head."

Advances in equipment facilitated this shift from pitcher to catcher. On June 28, 1870, Red Stocking backstop Allison became perhaps the first to wear a baseball glove, a thin fingerless buckskin mitten on each hand. Seven years later, on April 12, 1877, Harvard College catcher James Tyng slipped on the sport's first mask—an oval of leather and iron—and scooted, whenever the count ran to two strikes, from his customary perch several feet back of home to a crouch just behind the batter. (As it was easier to catch a pitch on the fly than bounce, Tyng thus bettered his odds of snaring a strikeout.) Most catchers followed suit, by the mid-eighties masked, camped just back of home and mitted—large leather pillows on their hands. The number of stolen signals dwindled at once. "With the adoption of the huge catcher's mitten worn on the left hand," noted *Everybody's Magazine* in 1906, "signaling became comparatively easy. Shielded by the mitten on one side, by his right knee on the other, the back-stop now telegraphs with naked fingers, not only to the pitcher but to the outfielders." Clued to the upcoming pitch, the fielders stood ready. "When a right-handed pitcher delivers a low, curve ball to a left-handed batter, the probabilities are that the hit will be to right field," explained Chicago second baseman Fred Pfeffer in 1889. "If the first and second basemen know that such a ball is to be pitched, it gives them a special warning to be on the alert."

As further insurance against the theft of signs, rudimentary gestures now gave way to "combination" signals. But those on defense were half the time on offense, and knew what to look for. And so, signs were still pilfered.

"Some years ago," recalled Ward in 1888, "the Chicago club gave me the roughest kind of handling in several games, and [King] Kelly told me this winter that they knew every ball I intended to pitch, and he even still remembered the sign and told me what it was." The year was 1882. For the season, Ward was 19–12 with a 2.59 era. But in 35 innings versus Chicago, he surrendered 36 runs and lost three of four games, the very margin by which Chicago bested his Providence Grays for the pennant.

Seven years later, during the 1889 championship, Giant signals were again lifted. Brooklyn was this time the thief and, after plating 32 runs in 31 innings, led New York three games to one. Brooklyn, however, scored just 20 runs the rest of the way, New York taking five straight games and the best-of-nine series. "The Brooklyns would have beaten the New Yorks for the World's championship," asserted Brooklyn shortstop Smith to the Cincinnati press, "if [catcher Buck] Ewing hadn't discovered that we were on to his signs."

And so, baseball signals remained for many in the game tools of deceit, mere revelations of their use evidence of malfeasance. When four months before New York's championship, in the second game of a doubleheader on June 22, 1889, Pittsburgh second baseman Fred Dunlap discovered John Clarkson signaling from Boston's bench to teammate pitcher Bill Sowders, he called time and had the ump bounce Clarkson. Boston captain King Kelly in turn had Pittsburgh's entire bench vacated. In use a full three decades, baseball signals remained distrusted, the game yet to undertake a critical account of its hidden language.

That signs *could* be stolen clearly lay in part at the root of the discomfort. And yet, trickery had long been a valued component of the game. When on May 1, 1876, Everett Mills tagged out Joe Borden in the third inning of a Hartford–Boston contest, the pitcher-outfielder became Major League Baseball's first known victim of the hidden-ball trick. In 1884, Chicago superstar Cap Anson used a doctored bat, the lumber, reported the *Philadelphia Record,* "made of several separate pieces of ash, jointed and glewed together lengthwise, while in the center is inserted a rattan rod about one inch square." Catcher Connie Mack, in the game since 1886, liked to "push his big gloved hand under the bat," noted the *Sporting News,* "and lift the stick ever so slightly when the batter was trying to make a bunt or sacrifice hit." In 1889, pitcher Pud Galvin took an injection of animal testosterone, the aging ace hoping the elixir prescribed by French doctor Charles Edouard Brown-Sequard might give him a leg up. And common was the player who feigned gloving a trapped ball, who lifted his foot off the base ahead of the double-play throw, who framed the borderline pitch so as to get the strike call from the ump. Baseball and foul play went hand in glove.

More and more, the game also incorporated signs. In 1894, Baltimore dominated baseball with avant-garde plays like the squeeze, double steal, and hit and run, all of which hinged on signals. "If the batter fails to notice the sign," cautioned *Spalding's 1915 Official Base Ball Guide* of the hit and run, "it is likely to be disastrous to the runner." Added that same year the *American Physical Education Review* of the Orioles, "Inside baseball was their hobby. Now it is the general practice."

Indeed, on the eve of the 1896 season, new Giant manager Arthur Irwin published "his signal code in book form," reported *Sporting Life,* "so that his players may spend their leisure moments studying and learning them." Indianapolis Hoosiers manager William Watkins, noted *Sporting Life* in 1897, "believes in signs and his players are letter perfect in the code of signals which he employs to direct them from the bench." Boston manager Frank Selee went a step further. From the opening pitch of 1896, he insisted that while afield every Beaneater be signaled every *pitch* of their 132-game season.

Backlash was inevitable. "The signal system fails because of its very confusion-breeding complexity and elaborateness," Cleveland manager Patsy Tebeau told *Sporting Life* prior to the 1896 season. "Players should . . . be self-reliant and not mere machines." Spectator Walt Whitman lamented the overhand pitching that had borne signs in the first place. "The wolf, the snake, the cur, the sneak all seem entered into the modern sportsman," he wrote. Others opposed signals on simpler grounds. "The umpires objected to being overworked by the necessity of moving an arm to indicate a 'strike,'" reported the *Chicago Tribune.* "Consequently the public must continue to guess, until electric score boards are installed and perfected, and then miss some of the play while studying the score board." Gripers be damned, signal-happy Baltimore won its third straight ring in 1896. Signaling worked.

Little surprise then that in the winter of 1898, one in baseball set off to tackle the stealing of signals with as much industriousness as others had their use.

It was then, in the grandstand of a racetrack in New Orleans, that Pearce Nuget Chiles sat one morning peering through opera glasses at the ponies. Set to begin his major league career the following spring, Chiles, thirty-one, spotted a group of boys playing baseball nearby and trained his glasses on the catcher. It was with great excitement that the infielder-outfielder noticed he could discern the squatted boy's moving fingers.

Chiles returned north to Philadelphia. He shared his discovery with Philly catcher Morgan Murphy, and the club, Charles Dryden later reported in the *North American,* "invested in a double lens range glass of the finest make and costing something like sixty ace notes. By using this glass Murphy could see a freckle on the catcher's nose at five furlongs." Adept at reading signs, Murphy stationed himself by season's end in the eighth window on the top floor of a three-story tenement house beyond Baker Bowl's center-field wall, opera glasses in hand. Chiles, coaching third when not in the lineup, looked there to a newspaper in Murphy's hands. If Murphy held the paper horizontally, a fastball was upcoming, if vertically, a curve. Chiles then relayed the stolen sign to the batter with a coded shout. "Knowing that a curve was coming the batter could walk up on the ball before it broke and beat the life out of it," reported Dryden. "As the fast straight ball is liable to pop into the air it was allowed to pass unmolested, the batsman preferring to unbend the languid curve."

The Phillies finished the 1899 season 94–58, 16 games better than the previous year.

Success begat suspicion. By spring, rumors of a newspaper-holding spy in Philadelphia circulated throughout the league. There were reports too of a copycat mole in Pittsburgh. And so, cautioned *Sporting Life* on March 31, 1900, "Hereafter it will be the proper thing for a club to carry with it a sign discoverer."

Chiles however had no intention of being discovered. And by Opening Day of 1900, the utility man retrofitted his sign-stealing operation.

Chiles had once accidentally stepped on a live wire that, wrote Dryden, "imparted a genial glow to his bunions." Now, as he readied for his sophomore season, Chiles remembered his misstep and set about putting it to good use. What if, he thought, Murphy could relay the signals to the feet of the third-base coach using electric vibrations?

It was not long before Philadelphia installed a push-button beside Murphy's lookout and ran bell wire, along the left-field balcony, from the clubhouse to the bench to a buzzer buried below the coaching-box at third.

As the previous year, Chiles coached when he did not play. And in 1900, he coached in all but 33 games, feeling with his feet Murphy's coded vibrations and relaying them to the batter. A live wire, wrote Dryden, had "led to the introduction of electricity as an adjunct to the national pastime." It was an effective adjunct. Just 24–35 on the road, the Phillies began their season 36–20 at home.

On September 17, 1900, however, during a game against Cincinnati, Arlie Latham, the Red third base coach, noticed that Chiles was standing with one foot in the coaching box even though the sunken box was submerged in a puddle of rainwater. Latham grew suspicious and alerted Tommy Corcoran, the Cincinnati shortstop and captain. In the bottom of the third inning, Corcoran charged out of the visitor's dugout and began scraping madly with his spikes at the coaching box. Corcoran's cleat found a small wooden box. He opened it and out popped wires. An electric buzzer!

The eyes of 4,771 fans, two teams, a groundskeeper and a battalion of Philadelphia police all turned to umpire Tim Hurst.

"Back to the mines, men!" Hurst shouted. He continued: "Think on that eventful day in July, when Dewey went into Manila Bay, never giving a tinker's damn for all the mines concealed therein. Come on. Play Ball!"

They did, Philadelphia nonetheless topping Cincinnati 4–2 and 4–1. But while Philly had hit .336 through the first 13 games of its home stand, over the final ten, with its buzzer disabled, the team's batting fell by 44 points.

Reaction to the scandal was great. Ferdinand Abell, co-owner of the Brooklyn club, suggested that Philly's third-place finish (as well as the statistics of its batters) be declared invalid. Reporter Dryden recommended that all future games not begin until the ump be shown present every last player on the bench. Others weighed in on the as yet uncharted ethics of stealing signs. "The explanation that everything is fair in baseball will not suffice," wrote the *Sporting News*. "An advantage obtained by underhanded methods is unsportsmanlike." All agreed save Colonel John Rogers, hamstrung by allegiance. The Philadelphia co-owner claimed the buzzer in his field a relic of a traveling circus and declared binoculars no problem. "If it is fair to use your naked eyes to discover signals," he announced, "there can be no objection to the use of glasses."

Rogers' team was not punished. But a consensus had emerged: stealing signs with anything but the naked eye was wrong.

It was also, Murphy had made clear, part of the game. And so ball clubs continued to guard their signals, to change them too, careful not to mask them to the point of indecipherability. "The success of any system of signals," wrote Bates College student Royce Purinton in a 1906 graduate thesis, "depends on simplicity and the ability of a team to conceal them from their opponents." Added *Everybody's Magazine* that same fall, "Much depends upon the composite brain caliber."

Signals, bifurcated and multiplied, had come to dictate much the game's offense and defense—from the bunt to the pickoff throw. And at last, umpires were gesticulating too. "Two or three years ago Base Ball critics in the East and West began to agitate the question of signaling by the umpires to announce their decisions," explained the *Spalding 1909 Official Base Ball Guide*. "And now there is not an umpire but uses his arms to signal."

It was then another scam had the league vowing to clamp down on sign-stealing.

In 1908, the New York Highlanders finished 51–103. The next season the team went 74–77. The turnabout was spectacular, and in mid-1909, Joe Cantillon, manager of the Washington Senators, suspected the team of stealing signs. And so, when, on June 19, his club visited Hilltop Park on Broadway and 163rd Street, he decided together with catcher Gabby Street and pitcher Walter Johnson that Johnson should pitch using no signs at all. In spite of seven walks, a hit batsman and four wild pitches, Johnson, twenty-one, beat the Highlanders 7–4.

Detroit manager Hughie Jennings also suspected foul play. And when he and his Tigers arrived in New York, Jennings dispatched pitcher Bill Donovan to investigate. Donovan walked to the park's center-field wall but found nothing. Team trainer Harry Tuthill, however, ambled over the wall and discovered, in the fissure between it and an ad for Young's Hats, a man fleeing with field glasses.

"There was a handle which moved the crossbar in the 'H'," Tuthill told *Sporting Life* on October 30, 1909. And, explained the magazine, "If the catcher signaled for a fast, straight ball the cross bar would be turned to show white. If a curve was signaled for the bar would be black."

As after the hijinks in Philadelphia a decade before, the game did not punish New York. But that winter, Robert Hedges, president of the St. Louis club, drafted a resolution concerning sign-stealing. And on December 15 at the Hotel Wolcott on 31st Street in New York, the board of directors of the American League passed it at their annual meeting. It concluded:

> RESOLVED, That it is the sense of this Board that any manager or official found guilty of operating a sign tipping bureau should be barred from baseball for all time.

Ten days later, *Sporting Life* commented on the resolution. "There was no rule prohibiting such practices," wrote the magazine, "but there is no doubt that such a one will be adopted before the next season opens."

No rule was passed.

Still, there now hovered above the game at least an assumed ban on such theft. And when off and on again in 1910 that same "H" in the ad for Young's hats waggled, some like the *New York Sun* hoped aloud that New York manager George Stallings not be rehired. American League president Ban Johnson, however, wished to secure his young foothold in fertile New York (soon to go by "Yankees"), and it was little surprise that no one collected the $500 he offered to he who substantiated the rumors. The game, to hear itself tell it, had triumphed over impropriety, and soon, any lingering allegations of sign-stealing led not to reprimand but to yawns. "The annual charges of signal tipping," wrote *Leslie's Weekly*, "are one of the meanest forms of trying to cover up weak and slovenly batting." Added the *American Magazine* the following spring, "the practice of stealing signals by mechanical means . . . has been largely employed in the past but probably never will be again."

That a second set of eyes would soon patrol play—come 1912 an extra ump required afield—was of further comfort to baseball. But as the 1911 World Series approached, gossip had host Philadelphia somehow reading the signals of opponents. The visiting Giants were wary. "The reputation itself, if they never get a sign, is valuable," wrote Game One starter Mathewson in his 1912 book, *Pitching in a Pinch*. "If a prize-fighter is supposed to have a haymaking punch in his left hand, the other fellow is constantly looking out for that left." Distracted, New York lost in six games, repeatedly changing its signs as the series unfolded. It was a wasted exercise. For Philly second baseman Eddie Collins soon revealed in the *American Magazine* his club's secret and it was neither opera glasses nor buzzer wire. It was kinesics, the team skilled at reading the body language of opposing pitchers. "Chief Bender, Danny Murphy, Jack Coombs and Harry Davis," later reported the *Sporting News Official Guide*, "became so expert that they could call every pitch made by every pitcher in the league by watching the way he held the ball, the way he delivered it or other little eccentricities."

Teams had now to worry not only of the mechanical pickpocketing of signs but of the tipping of pitches. And the emergence of the latter helped further distill a divide in the judgment of stolen signs. "If a player is smart enough to solve the opposing system of signals he is given due credit," wrote Ty Cobb in the *New York Evening News*. But, he continued, "the use of field glasses, mirrors and so on, by persons stationed in the bleachers or outside the center field fence . . . is reprehensible and should be so regarded."

That signs, however, enhanced the nation's pastime was by now all but unanimously agreed upon. Frequent were the signaling tutorials in magazines like the *Youth's Companion* and *Leslie's Weekly*, while a 1916 short story in the *American Boy*, "Tipped Caps, Hitched Trousers," sought to convert any remaining agnostics. It told of a boy named Corky who welled with fondness for wig-wag after an obeyed signal and a daring double-delayed steal.

In February of 1920 there was suddenly one less sign to master. It was then that baseball forbade all pitchers (save a grandfathered group of seventeen) from throwing the spitball and other "freak deliveries." While the ban sought foremost to help hitters (and thereby attendance), it was not coincidental that it followed growing rumors of a fixed 1919 World Series. The game needed a cleanup.

Over the coming decades, signals continued to adapt to the changing game. As more players were traded, signals turned evermore mazy to guard against theft. As night baseball began, catchers increasingly forwent finger for bolder hand signals. And as the prototypical scoreboard evolved from simple slat to multi-floored structure, sign-stealing entered its golden age. "Every team with a scoreboard in center field has a spy inside at one time or another," wrote the great second baseman Rogers Hornsby in his book *My War with Baseball*. Continued Hornsby, who played from 1915 to 1937, "There's always a hole for the spy to peep out."

The holes in the center-field scoreboard at the Polo Grounds, for example, were 20 by 14 inches, as good for peeping as for the white numbered metal squares that filled them. There were lots of holes in the scoreboard at Chicago's Wrigley Field too, cavities filled with run tallies and player numbers. It was through one of those that late in the 1946 season a Cub rookie named Schenz began peeking with his telescope.

"Not a lot of guys knew that it was him," says Harold Manders, a right-hander who came to Chicago midseason and pitched just six innings. "But I did." Manders, who retired after the season to raise Hampshire hogs in Adel, Iowa, adds: "If it helped to win one game a year, it was worth it."

Durocher agreed. Just one win could make all the difference. And so, when Schenz brought his telescope to the Polo Grounds five years later, Durocher happily put it to use.

On July 21, 1951, the morning after Schenz first peered through his spyglass in the Giant clubhouse, Durocher awoke to a headline in the *New York World-Telegram and Sun:* "Life Lovely for Leo 'Neath Harlem Moon." Life *was* lovely. His sign-stealing system was in place. All he had to do was get an electrician to tone down his buzzer.

Bobby Thomson
(front row, looking down)
with his family in July 1926,
days after his mother and the
children left Scotland and joined
his father Jim in Staten Island.
The Thomson home was one
of reserve and propriety.
Jim instructed his children to
stay in the background and
to "do what's right."
Courtesy of Ruby Thomson Beatty.

Katherine and John Branca had seventeen children and raised them in a loud and warm home in Mt. Vernon, New York. Thirteen survived to adulthood. The Branca family gathers with spouses and children, an aunt and a brother-in-law on New Year's Day, 1950. Ralph is seated third from right. *Courtesy of Rosemary Leo.*

Robert Thompson
"Turkey"

Basketball Team 2; Baseball Team 2;
Marshal Squad 1; Class President 1;
Class Treasurer 1; Section Room
President 1; Section Room Treasurer 2;
Section Room Marshal 1.

Thomson (his name misspelled) in the 1942 Curtis High yearbook. Exceedingly shy, he didn't try out for baseball his first year, then missed the cut the next when he was the last to ask for a uniform. But he batted .327 as a junior and .346 as a senior, and starred on several local teams. *Courtesy of Joseph Streble.*

Branca *(back row, right)* in the 1943 A. B. Davis High yearbook. The senior pitcher dominated high school batters, winning seven straight games to lead his team to the Westchester Interscholastic title on June 4, 1943. "He used to say," remembers brother John, "'why did God give me this gift of being bigger and stronger?'" *Courtesy of Arthur Crawford, A. B. Davis High School.*

Thomson finished his first year
of pro ball with Class D
Rocky Mount, North Carolina.
And on September 11, 1942, in
the seventh and deciding game of
a playoff, the Rock third baseman
hit a home run to left field.
Courtesy of Bobby Thomson.

Branca was an overnight star, in 1947 winning twenty-one games at age
twenty-one. But he repeatedly lost the games that mattered most. Branca
is shown here after a Johnny Mize single ruined his eight masterly innings
in Game Three of the 1949 World Series. *Courtesy of Brooklyn Public Library,
Brooklyn Collection.*

By 1951 Leo Durocher well understood that Thomson responded to assurance, not brimstone.
From the New York Herald Tribune, *courtesy of Bobby Thomson.*

The Brooklyn brass believed in Branca. And, on the eve of the 1951 playoff, Charlie Dressen tapped him to start Game One. The manager and pitcher are shown here on September 30, 1951, en route to New York with owner Walter O'Malley and Ann Mulvey, who would marry Branca in twenty days. *Herb Scharfman, International News Service, courtesy of Pat Nuttycombe.*

Infielder Henry Schenz joined the Giants
on June 30, 1951, taking with him a Wollensak
telescope and a history of stealing signs.
*Courtesy of the Baseball Hall of Fame Library,
Cooperstown, N.Y.*

From a distance of five hundred feet, this thirty-five-millimeter
Wollensak telescope could distinguish a catcher's fingers spread
at least two-tenths of an inch apart.
Photograph by Donald Bowers.

On July 19, 1951, Leo Durocher set in motion a plan to steal signals.
His Giants won the pennant seventy-six days later—a feat that
would ultimately land Durocher in the Hall of Fame. Here he looks out a
window in the Polo Grounds clubhouse during a Mets game on August 26, 1962.
Wm. C. Greene, courtesy of the Baseball Hall of Fame Library, Cooperstown, N.Y.

Giant coach Herman Franks in the Polo Grounds clubhouse in 1951.
The former catcher was adept at reading signs. Asked in 1996 where
he was when Thomson hit the home run, he said "I was in the clubhouse doing something for Durocher." *Courtesy of Jerry Liebowitz.*

Catcher Sal Yvars rarely played in 1951,
marooned instead in the bullpen. Says Yvars,
"I was more valuable giving the goddamn signs."
Courtesy of Sal Yvars.

Abe Chadwick's
New York City
taxi license.
*Courtesy of Helen Smith
and Harriet Mesulam.*

Chadwick *(above right)* at the 1947 wedding of his daughter Helen. Chadwick loved
the Dodgers but worked for the Giants, installing a bell-and-buzzer system at the Polo
Grounds. "The electricians were proud of him," says Walter Carberry, a friend from
union meetings. "They never let it get around." *Courtesy of Helen Smith and Harriet Mesulam.*

Now There'll Be a Swarm of Counter-Spies

Baseball has vowed for more than a century to ban the stealing of signs by mechanical means. But as artist Amadee Wohlschlager illustrates here in the July 4th, 1956, edition of *The Sporting News*, the game has not done so. *Courtesy of* The Sporting News.

The 1951 Giants one day before the Thomson home run. Visible on the right side of the center window is the hole cut into the wire mesh through which the telescope spied.
William Jacobellis, International News Service.

NINE

For 'tis the sport to have the enginer
Hoist with his own petar.
—WILLIAM SHAKESPEARE,
Hamlet, 1600

MINUTES BEFORE 2 P.M. on July 21, Stanky peered toward right-center field, the Giant leadoff hitter looking a second straight game for a sign. He hoped for a tip on Howie Fox's first pitch. He got one. For unlike the night previous, a buzzer did not now send Corwin and his mates off the bullpen bench. Electrician Chadwick had quieted his buzzer.

"Whoever this guy was," says Corwin, "when we got out the next day, it was softer." New York beat Cincinnati 3–2.

Brooklyn also won 3–2. And on this very Saturday, the *Chicago Herald American* declared that the Dodgers would win the pennant by 20 games. "They bat the brains out of all comers," wrote Lawton Carver, "and when they don't thusly rearrange the intellect of the opposition, the Dodger pitchers let nobody get on base."

Back in the Bronx, Chadwick did not utter a peep to Miriam about buzzers and signs. His wife had a way of talking and besides, she would not understand. It was a baseball thing.

Still, Chadwick *had* to tell somebody, and he figured he could trust the men of Local 3. Some were friends from Harry Alexander, the electric company in Long Island City that contracted him to the Giants, some from Welsbach Electric, the street-lighting maintenance company in Queens where he worked, some from the Acorn Club and some from union meetings. Union brothers knew how to keep a secret. When Nat Chadwick slept around, no one breathed a word to wife Hannah.

Some weekends, Chadwick subwayed to the home of George Farrell, a colleague at Welsbach. There, across the street from LaGuardia Airport, he and a septet of electricians shared war stories over drinks, told tales of street-light repairs in the middle of hurricanes, of near-electrocutions, of emergency battery installations in antiaircraft machinery overseas.

Chadwick now had a doozy to tell. And gathered this weekend as always with his buddies in Farrell's finished basement, he preened that the New York Giants—the team of Mathewson, Hubbell and Ott—had decided to steal signs and had turned to *him* for help. He told them of his handiwork and the group, including Farrell's wide-eyed son George (who would become an electrician), was agape. "Abe was definitely involved in the bell-and-buzzer business," says George Jr., then eleven. He adds, "These guys were kind of my heroes."

Word of Chadwick's ingenuity spread quickly through Local 3. "The electricians were proud of him," says Walter Carberry, Chadwick's friend from union meetings. "They never let it get around."

And so when the Reds, after losing three of four, left the Polo Grounds on July 22, 1951, they knew nothing of a telescope.

The Giants took a train to Pittsburgh. There Schenz pinch-ran against his former club, Thomson stole home and Durocher earned his thousandth career victory. The team split a pair of games and headed to Cincinnati.

The next morning, July 26, Chadwick set off to Manhattan for the wake of Kathryn Van Arsdale, mother of union leader Harry Jr. Services ended at the Church of the Sacred Heart of Jesus on West 51st Street and Chadwick boarded the subway. But returning home on the Pelham Bay local, deep below the streets of New York, Chadwick grew faint. Recalls daughter Helen Smith, "He felt this weakness coming over him in the subway."

Chadwick left the subway and flagged a car. A stranger drove him to the emergency room at Lincoln Medical on 149th Street in the Bronx. Kept overnight, he told his doctors that he had not felt well since March. He was tired, often nauseated and had little appetite. It was probably ulcers, they said, and sent him home the next day.

But Chadwick still felt ill. And for just the second time in the four-plus years since he had joined the union, he skipped work. (A kidney stone passed in December 1948 had kept him home a week.) Chadwick stayed home the next day too and the day after that. And on July 29, an employee at Welsbach Electric penciled in lower-case print the word "sick" on Chadwick's time card and mailed the electrician a check for $67.20, payment for work he had done earlier that week.

Chadwick could stomach little food, his nausea worsened. His cough too persisted. And his home had turned to hubbub. For daughter Helen had in July moved in for the year with husband Gabe Smith, sending Harriet to the couch in the living room. And though Smith had since gone off to work in Camp Winadu, newborn Peter and his cries stayed, grandpa Chadwick often unnerved even as he proudly proclaimed the boy a fighter, lifting with glee his tiny fist.

It seemed only Dodger broadcasts soothed Chadwick, kept the attentions of a man that had otherwise started to slip. The team was his anodyne and closed out July with 10 straight wins.

It was August 3 when Shirley Marblestone drove brother-in-law Chadwick to Flower Fifth Avenue Hospital. He checked in, there on 105th Street examined by a general surgeon named Walter Mersheimer. The men were alike—short, bushy-browed, tough. The doctor had been adopted, gone to military academy in Vermont, been a combat surgeon for marines on Guadalcanal Island, won a Bronze Star for developing mobile combat medical units. "Nails" was his nickname. He was also a prolific writer, co-authoring just the previous month an article on primary bronchogenic carcinoma of the lung.

Mersheimer, forty, agreed with the folks at Lincoln. Chadwick likely had ulcers and they had to be operated on at once. But when that same day Mersheimer cut Chadwick open, he found not ulcers but tumors. Chadwick had stomach cancer, it was advanced and it had spread to his liver. Mersheimer happened to be a pioneer of liver-cancer surgery, one of the first in New York to perform a hepatic resection. But even he could do nothing. The doctor removed a portion of Chadwick's stomach and sewed him shut.

Chadwick slept at Flower Fifth directly across from the Conservatory Gardens in Central Park. It was a beautiful hospital, its limestone base and stucco walls topped with a round pavilion and burnt-tile roof. And it was within those walls that Dr. Mersheimer told Miriam that her husband had three months to live. Miriam told this to her two daughters and instructed them to lie to their father, to tell him that he had only ulcers. This they did.

But the next day, when Harriet, sixteen, stood beside her father in linen spiked heels and a sleeveless yellow dress, she could tell that he knew the truth. "God, you're all grown up," said Chadwick. Then he cried.

July had turned to August and the Giants were still on the road, playing out their longest trip of the season, a 17-game swing against the

Pirates, Reds, Cubs, Cardinals, and Dodgers. Heading into Brooklyn, Durocher's latest moves had clicked. Corwin had shut out Chicago for his first career win and since switching to third, Thomson was hitting .338 with five home runs. New York had won 9 of 14 games.

But the Dodgers were even hotter, their lead over the Giants having swelled to 9.5 games. The series in Brooklyn seemed less an opportunity for New York to gain ground than a chance to salvage respect.

They did neither. On August 8, after a day of rain, the Dodgers hit three home runs and beat the Giants 7–2. Hours later, they won 7–6, going up 11.5 games on New York. It was the largest lead any Brooklyn team had *ever* amassed, and the next day they added to it, winning 6–5. Brooklyn had beaten New York in 12 of 15 games.

An iron picket fence lined the dirt runway that led from Brooklyn bench to clubhouse, and after the game, euphoric fans reached through it to backslap their heroes. Manager Charlie Dressen and his Dodgers were giddy.

A wisp of a man, five foot five, 146 pounds, Dressen had spent much of his career in Durocher's shadow. As a backup infielder on Cincinnati in 1931, he got just one hit while Durocher started at short. From 1939 to 1946, he served as third base coach for Brooklyn while Durocher, seven years his junior, managed the club. He became Dodger manager, replacing Burt Shotton in 1951, only after Durocher was shooed to Harlem. Dressen alone had won pennants with all three New York teams—the Giants in 1933, the Dodgers in 1941, the Yankees in 1947—yet he earned this season half the $50,000 paid Durocher. Durocher was his white whale. "He was obsessed by a drive to show Leo and the world that he was the brains and always had been," said Dodger pitcher Carl Erskine in 1991. "Charlie Dressen was paranoid about beating Leo."

Dressen did not doubt he could. "Just stay close," he liked to say. "I'll think of something." The ego of the blue-eyed son of an Illinois German tavern-keeper was legendary. "If the letter 'I' were dropped from the alphabet," wrote Milton Gross weeks earlier in the *New York Post,* "Charlie would be denuded of half his conversational talent." Franks agreed. "Charlie's biggest problem was always I, I, I," he says. "I won it, you lost it."

As Dressen and his players now exulted in front of their open metal lockers, the Giants, miles behind in the standings, stood feet away in the visitor's clubhouse. All that separated the men was a brick wall. And fresh off a sweep of Durocher, Dressen approached.

"Leo," baited Dressen. "You in there?"

Durocher heard Dressen and steamed. He had thought a brick wall would be enough to muffle the man's voice.

Early in the season, New York had stumbled, losing to Brooklyn a fifth straight time on April 29. When after the game Dressen entered the Ebbets Field clubhouse, he walked right up to the wooden door adjoining the two locker rooms, a popinjay ready to serenade New York. Ralph Branca, Carl Erskine and Erv Palica stood nearby at their lockers. Dressen asked the pitchers to sing with him. Remembers Erskine, "He said, 'Come on, let's go!' "

"Palica and I didn't have any appetite to do that," says Erskine. "But Ralph went with him. Dressen pulled him in." Joined by Robinson, the men sang, Branca's bass belting into the visitor's lounge a parody of the Beer Barrel Polka: "Roll out the barrel! The Giants are dead!"

The Giant players had heard their nemeses loud and clear. "They were taunting," remembers Lockman. "It was Robinson and Branca." Adds Spencer, "I'll put it this way: it wasn't appreciated." Within days, the league had ordered a brick wall built. And months later, it had not sufficed.

New York was off on August 10. And the team was in no hurry to get back to the park. The players had gone 9–8 on their road trip and, certain the pennant was lost, at least a few Giants made plans now for the off-season. Mueller phoned his brother in St. Louis to schedule their annual fishing trip to Minnesota. Irvin and wife decided to head to San Francisco on October 2. And Durocher and wife quietly subletted their East Side apartment as of October 1.

The Dodgers meantime were in no hurry for their season to end, and the next day, August 11, two color television cameras set to capture their game against Boston. It was to be the first-ever colorized baseball broadcast and some ten thousand viewers within fifty miles of New York City tuned in to CBS sets equipped with color wheels. They found their heroes alight in fantastic hues. "The Dodgers and Boston Braves all came out as spectacularly beauteous critters," wrote Red Smith of the historic broadcast, "endowed with magnificently bronzed complexions." Smith made special note of Gil Hodges's arms, "encased in a pelt of somewhat lovelier tone—about the shade of medium roast beef—than Gil wears in real life." A polychromatic Branca defeated southpaw Spahn, 8–1.

Just over the Harlem River, back home at long last in their telescope-appointed park, the Giants hit rock bottom. Robin Roberts out-pitched Jim Hearn, and the Phillies beat the Giants 4–0. Philadelphia trailed New York by just 1.5 games.

The Dodgers learned of the loss in their rectangular clubhouse and delighted. They were 70–35, a juggernaut, perhaps the finest team in baseball since the 1929 Athletics. New York, meantime, was 59–51. With just 44 games left to play, New York had 16 more losses than Brooklyn, trailed them by a ridiculous 13.5 games. The bookies about town set the odds of a New York pennant at 100–1, laying $1,200 for a $12 bet. The season was surely over, and Brooklyn dressed with esprit for a second game against Boston.

The Braves beat the Dodgers 8–4. And as if the first out of a baseball game, Brooklyn's enormous lead over New York decreased by one-twenty-seventh.

After the twilight game, Chadwick lay in bed while Jews all about the city sat on synagogue floors reading the Book of Lamentations. It was Tisha B'av, the saddest day of the Jewish year, a fast day commemorating the destruction of the temple.

By morning, dark clouds filled the sky and Durocher put on a drab outfit—brown shoes, brown slacks, a brown and yellow striped and curlicued shirt. It was Wes Westrum Day at the park and the Giants were playing a doubleheader. Lights were needed and Harry Jacobsen, Chadwick's foreman, obliged. In game one, Maglie beat the Phillies 3–2. In game two, Thomson smacked a two-run double to give Corwin and the Giants a 2–1 win. The team won its third straight the next night, beating Philadelphia 5–2 behind Jansen.

One day later, the Dodgers came to town. Chadwick, lying in his hospital room, ached to be at the park. It was a night game—one of just two all year when he could shine his lights down on Jackie, Campy, Newk and the Duke. Jacobsen again filled in, his lights illuminating a 4–0 Giant lead into the eighth. Back-to-back home runs by Billy Cox and Duke Snider were for naught, New York winning 4–2 before 42,867.

The next afternoon, Mays made the finest fielding play of his young career. With one out and Cox on third, Carl Furillo hit a fly to medium right-center field. Mays caught the ball, pivoted on his left foot, spun left—so that, for a moment, he faced the center-field bleachers—and threw home. The ball smacked into Westrum's mitt on a fly. A disbelieving Cox was out. Westrum hit a two-run home run in the eighth off Branca and the Giants won 3–1.

Maglie and Don Newcombe, tied for the league lead in wins with 16 apiece, squared off on August 16. In a hot drizzle, New York won 2–1, Maglie allowing but four hits and no walks. The Giants had swept the Dodgers, were 9.5 back. Wrote Joseph Sheehan in the *New York Times*, "Maybe the National League is going to have a pennant race after all."

Next morning, two weeks after surgery, Chadwick returned home to Elder Avenue, climbed his stone stoop, opened his wooden door with its glass arch and walked the one flight to Miriam. Waiting for him atop a wheeled stand opposite his living room couch was a television set. Nat had bought his big brother a 12-inch Emerson. He hoped Abe might watch the Dodger games on WOR.

On this Friday afternoon, Brooklyn was in Boston for a doubleheader. And before Brave Max Surkont threw his first pitch, Miriam spread a sheet atop the gray-and-chartreuse couch, and propped a pillow against one armrest. Chadwick lay down, his long-sleeved broadcloth pajamas buttoned down the front. He was home. The game began and Miriam, as she would several times a day, poured into her Waring blender the powdered formula Flower Fifth hospital had given her husband. It was all he could digest. Miriam served her Chaddy a vanilla malted and Carl Erskine pitched a complete game. Brooklyn won 3–1.

That same afternoon the Giants traveled to Philadelphia for a night game and the team permanently replaced Chadwick with an electrician named Seymour Schmelzer.

TEN

He was but as the cuckoo is in June,
Heard, not regarded.

—WILLIAM SHAKESPEARE,
Henry IV, 1597

ALL SIX OF NEW YORK'S consecutive wins had come at home.
And through the streak, they had honed their sign-stealing rig-
marole. Franks, the retired catcher, had proven adept at decoding the signals and was now the staple spy (Schenz free to holler in the dugout).
Durocher permanently left the dugout and stationed himself on third.
The team largely stopped shouting signals from the bench, relaying them
instead from the far less conspicuous bullpen. The bullpen came to know
which Giant batters depended on signs. ("The guys who could hit the
long ball wanted to know," remembers Corwin. "Willie loved it.") And
relaying duties fell, as much as to anyone, to a third-string catcher who
passed most of his time in the pen.

Salvador Anthony Yvars was born on Houston Street in Manhattan
on February 20, 1924, eight years after an immigration officer misread
the surname of a Joaquin Ivars come to Ellis Island from Benissa, Spain.
Six months later, father, wife Lena, son and daughter Theresa moved to
Valhalla in nearby Westchester.

Valhalla fell into two camps. The well-to-do nestled atop the town
hill, the poor at its bottom. The poor also split into two camps: those
who worked at Kensico Floral Company, and those who worked at Kensico Cemetery. The Yvarses settled at 14 Leroy Avenue at the foot of the
gulch and Joaquin, known as Jack, went to work as a gravedigger.

The work was backbreaking and the salary meager—$14 a week.
When the children had grown, Lena worked too, a laundress from Calabria, Italy, earning in White Plains a dollar a day minus 20 cents for bus
fare.

Their pay was enough to get by, though amenities like running water were a pipe dream. The family bathed in the Kensico reservoir and, says Yvars, "you went outside to take a crap." To feed the furnace in the basement, little Sal collected the chunks of coal that flew from the trains chugging along the railroad tracks in town, and sawed, together with his grandfather Santo, branches from the oak, maple and elm trees that grew 20 yards from home. That was not allowed, but no one tattled.

The townspeople knew Yvars. For every Memorial Day at the cemetery, he planted flowers beside graves, the boy paid nickels and dimes he gave in turn to his folks. With no money for treats, when one afternoon his friends bought nickel cakes from Mr. Hutchinson's candy shop, Yvars, wanting to join them, stole a pastry.

Yvars was athletic—quick and with a cannon arm. And so, though he could afford no mitt, he starred in the Midget League at eight and at White Plains High at fifteen, a starter on the varsity basketball, football and baseball teams. The sophomore shortstop batted .416, baseball his best sport.

While playing fields showcased Yvars's athleticism, it was work that grew his muscles. Soon after entering high school, Yvars, like his father, began to dig. He dug, however, not graves but flower beds, working at the Dudyshyn nursery. "Begonias, petunias, geraniums, ivy, myrtle, pachysandra," remembers Yvars. "You name it. Every goddam flower." Using a trowel, earning a dime an hour, Yvars dug holes 9 hours Saturdays and 9 hours Sundays. The 18-hour weekends steeled his forearms. A second job, caddying at Knollwood Country Club, got him 50 cents a day, two strengthened legs and a rock-solid back.

Yvars, though, had a weak temper. When his sophomore year teammate Morton Grossman called him a "guinea," Yvars bloodied his face.

Suspended for a week, Yvars returned to school, then left voluntarily. He had brothers seven and ten years his junior and intended to help support the family.

But at White Plains High (which drew its student body from just five square miles), athletes like Yvars were unspeakably rare. And so Len Watters, Yvars's football and baseball coach, soon took to the Yvars home a proposal. If Yvars returned to school, an unmarked envelope holding $12 would be waiting for him every two weeks at the drugstore in White Plains. Yvars agreed. And indeed one was—the ballplayer walking semimonthly the next two years to White Plains then home, handing his mother an envelope filled with money. No questions were asked. "Somebody was paying me," he says, "and I don't know who."

Just seventeen, Yvars was fully grown, five feet ten inches tall, 160-plus pounds. Playing shortstop and a bit of catcher, he batted above .500. Yvars was a star. He was handsome too, with wide-set brown eyes, full lips and a pompadour, a "tall rugged specimen of masculine pulchritude," put it one paper. Yvars heard the pretty girls took typewriting and so did too. Sure enough, one row ahead of him in class, there he found Ann D'Aleo. As a matter of course, athlete and coquette started dating.

The next year, Yvars had a new coach. But his payments continued, Watters briefing Glenn Loucks on his arrangement with the young man called Sonny. Yvars responded afield, dominating play, declared in June a finalist for the annual award given by the *New York World-Telegram* newspaper to the top high-school player in New York City, Westchester, Long Island and New Jersey.

Yvars hoped to play college ball—Holy Cross had shown interest. But come graduation, he found himself a credit short and could not afford the cost of another class. Coach Loucks, desperate not to lose his captain for the upcoming basketball and football seasons, proposed to Yvars that he flunk a course. (Yvars would thus *have* to stay another semester and so be spared the cost of tuition.) And so it was that Yvars received an F in geography and a valuable lesson: bending the rules for the good of the team was just fine.

That same summer of 1942, Yvars played shortstop on a semipro municipal team. The right-hander won the Twilight League's batting title, slugging .550 in 14 games. He also caught the eye of Giant scout Nick Shinkoff. Hours after a game in Port Chester, New York, Shinkoff showed up at the ballplayer's home. "I got the okay to sign you to Class D," he told Yvars. Thrilled, Yvars signed on to play in Salisbury, North Carolina, for $85 a month. But when, months later, Yvars finished school, military duty loomed. Certain he would be drafted, Yvars enlisted in the air force on December 7, 1942, a year to the day after the bombing of Pearl Harbor.

Yvars hoped to be a fighter pilot and did his basic training in Miami. But when a doctor shone a light in his eyes during a physical exam, his left watered. Thus was Yvars deemed unfit for the cockpit. And so, stationed in Congaree, South Carolina, Yvars instead played baseball and became an Army Air Corps physical training instructor, ASN #12193301.

It was not long before Yvars volunteered for an extra job. The air force wished to know how many G's, should a plane dive, a pilot could endure without losing consciousness. Yvars became a test-dummy. "I took six and a half G's without any headgear," he says. Private first class Yvars spent three days in the hospital recovering. But he was proud,

proud to be eyed for clues, to do the dirty work so that others could fly. It was a role he would one day assume on the baseball field.

The next two years, Yvars taught calisthenics and played shortstop and catcher. He also bopped a sergeant for goofing off during jumping jacks. But the MVP of military teams in Georgia and Ohio was not court-martialed. And in January 1946, Yvars left the air force, honorably discharged.

The Giants quickly sent Yvars to their Class B team in Manchester, New Hampshire. His hopes were high. Watters, his high school coach, had seen Yvars play in the military and in February called him "the best prospect ever developed in Westchester." The protégé did not disappoint. After weathering simulated air disasters, minor league pitching seemed benign, the catcher in 220 at-bats batting .318 with eight home runs. In June, however, Yvars slugged Nashua manager Walt Alston. The league suspended Yvars for ten days and the *Union,* a Manchester paper, ran a photo of him above the caption "one of the most promising prospects in the New England League, and one of the fightingest."

Yvars began the next season a rung higher in Jersey City. Starting catcher Mickey Grasso was slumping and so was the team, 14 back of Montreal on July 6.

It was then the third place Little Giants took off, won 52 of 76 games. Along the way, Jersey City manager Bruno Betzel made Yvars, twenty-three, his starter. A 6–3 win over Baltimore on the last day of the 1947 season claimed the pennant over Montreal, and the parent clubs in New York and Brooklyn shook their heads.

On September 27, Yvars debuted in the major leagues at chilly Shibe Park, singling and catching the whole of a 10–7 loss to Philadelphia. On September 28, in a church in White Plains, he stood in a rented tuxedo and kissed his bride, Ann. And the following September of 1948, having batted .301 and thrown out 39 of 76 minor league runners, Yvars enjoyed 21 more days in the show, summoned to New York by new Giant skipper Durocher.

Five months later, Yvars flew to Phoenix, to spring training, hoping for a permanent big league job. All went well until March 28 when, with Hank Behrman on the mound, Yvars squatted to receive the first pitch of a game against a Mexican all-star team. It was a ball. So was the next one and the two after that. The batter jogged to first. The next batter walked too, and soon Behrman, readying for his fourth and final season, had gone 2–0 on the third batter as well.

"Goddammit, Yvars," barked Durocher. "Argue with that umpire!"

And so Yvars argued—with Durocher. "They're balls!" yelled the catcher. Durocher was livid that a kid of twenty-five with all of 43 major league at-bats would dare show him up and he summoned Westrum from the bullpen. Behrman, meantime, rattled further by the shouts of manager and catcher, threw his next pitch in the dirt short of home. Yvars blocked it and the ball broke the middle finger of his throwing hand. Westrum headed into the game.

Yvars entered the dugout. As he took off his equipment, Durocher cursed at him. Much as he had in high school, the catcher snapped. "I got the shin guard," Yvars says. "Threw it at his goddam head."

The players intervened. There was no fight. But Yvars yelled that he was through with the team (and that the only reason he had not gotten on the ump was because it was a meaningless charity game). That night, team secretary Eddie Brannick phoned Yvars in his hotel room to tell him that a plane ticket home was waiting for him.

The next morning, Durocher gave his pepper-pot a second chance. But as the days rolled by, Yvars wondered why. For Durocher was not playing him, was not speaking to him. Yvars passed his time at the ballpark sitting in the bullpen foul of third base.

It was there, during a game against Cleveland, that Yvars noticed catcher Jim Hegan tipping pitches. Hegan was closing his mitt for fastballs, opening it slightly for the curve. Yvars mentioned this to pitchers Koslo and Jansen, Jansen notified Durocher and Durocher told the team. The New York bats responded. Over the ensuing five games against Cleveland, against aces Bob Feller, Mike Garcia and Early Wynn, New York scored 54 runs.

Durocher did not approach Yvars about his observation. But when Opening Day 1949 rolled around, Westrum, remarkably, had been optioned and Yvars was with the club. And, though, three games into the season, Durocher sent Yvars, hitless in eight at-bats, to Minneapolis, the message was clear: salvation (and a $7,500 contract) had come through the stealing of signs.

Yvars did little to ingratiate himself to Minnesota. When in April a fan heckled the catcher after he got tossed for arguing a called ball, "he suddenly leaped into the box seats and commenced swinging," reported the *Minneapolis Tribune*. (Yvars loosened several teeth of one Alfred Koenig.) In May, when Yvars barked at an umpire, the league fined him $25 for abusive language. And in August, after Koenig filed an $11,000 suit against Yvars and his club (and Yvars refused to pay the latest in a string of fines for fights with umpires), manager Tom Heath suspended his catcher and proclaimed: "He'll never put a Minneapolis uniform [on] again as long as I'm here." Indeed, he did not. Yvars spent the rest of the 1949 season in New York and the 1950 campaign in Jersey City.

Up in the big leagues, Westrum was New York's starting catcher. And over the 1949 and 1950 seasons, catchers Ray Mueller, Walker Cooper, Sammy Calderone and Mickey Livingston backed him up. But heading into spring training in 1951, none of the four was still with the club and Yvars, veteran of just 65 major league at-bats, had a legitimate shot to make the team. This he did, together with Cuban catcher Ray Noble, a rookie at thirty-two.

Two years after their tiff, Yvars and Durocher were still at odds and rarely spoke. Come spring training, noted Ken Smith in the *Sporting News,* Yvars "was such a patsy that he was used as umpire for the intrasquad games." But every team needs a third-string catcher, a warm body to warm up pitchers in the bullpen. And that is where Yvars was on April 17 when New York blanked host Boston 4–0 to open its season. Yvars finished the month with zero at-bats.

Yvars's gig for the season was simple. Before each game, he had only to change into his uniform, take batting practice and walk to the bullpen with three baseballs. After the game, having warmed up Giant relievers, he was to return the balls to coach Shellenback.

It was during World War II that an initiative to ration balls began, fans asked to return those Spaldings hit their way so that the balls could be sent to servicemen in military camps. Some complied. Some did not, the Polo Grounds crowd for example at Branca's debut on June 12, 1944, surrendering just two balls.

Seven years later those same Giant fans knew that Yvars used but two of the three balls given him by Shellenback. And they knew that come the eighth inning, Yvars, seated just beneath the metal awning below, usually gave the third ball away. And so, throughout the game, while his teammates fended off brushbacks and one-hoppers, the catcher fielded all manner of enticements.

"Hey, Sal!" Yvars remembers one yelling. "You like salami?" He adds, "They'd give me cigars." Thus spent Yvars his afternoons, a scrub in the perennial shadows of the right-field bullpen jabbering with fans.

Occasionally too, Yvars got into a game. A pair of at-bats in May. Three in June. On July 7, he slipped into a tie against Boston in the tenth inning, and led off the eleventh with a home run to deep left-center off Spahn. The blast gave New York a 7–6 win, and afterward, Stoneham called Yvars into his office. Owner handed catcher a fistful of hundred-dollar bills. The money was appreciated. Four days before, Yvars had become the father of twin girls.

The catcher still, however, disliked his manager. And when Durocher's fawn boxer urinated one afternoon in June on his spikes, Yvars slapped Slugger on the ass. Little Chris Durocher started crying and his father summoned Yvars to his office. It was not long before the men needed to be separated.

Soon after, Durocher had an idea. Perhaps there was a way to tap the pugnaciousness of his bullpen catcher.

After a fantastic start, Maglie had struggled, the pitcher failing four straight outings to win his thirteenth game. Maglie was intimidating, dubbed the Barber for his perpetual scruff and chin-shaving fastballs, and Durocher now wondered if perhaps Westrum was too soft a catcher to call a game with Maglie on the mound. And so on July 20, as Maglie set to take a fifth stab at win number 13 (and New York readied to inaugurate its telescope), Durocher benched Westrum. "If Maglie makes the wrong pitch, I want him told off by the catcher," Durocher said before the game. "I think Yvars can do that."

And so it was Yvars who crouched behind home plate at 8:30 p.m., charged by his manager to yap at Maglie. The pit bull complied. As Lloyd Merriman, Cincinnati's leadoff man, dug in, Yvars yelled at his battery mate: "Come on! Bear down!"

Maglie did, and with each pitch, "I'd throw it back at him like a bullet," says Yvars. "It'd sting his fucking hand." Though the pitcher yelled at his catcher, his head was in the game, Maglie retiring the side—two flies, a double and a groundout. Hours later, aided by an Yvars home run, he had finally pushed his record to 13–4.

Yvars played the next two games as well, the first time in three years he had appeared in three straight. He got hits in each. And when, in Brooklyn on August 8, Yvars again caught Maglie, it was the tenth time in 20 games he had played. But that afternoon, the catcher made three subpar throws and New York lost 7–6. Durocher fumed. Yvars's playing time would not continue.

The next day, New York's 17-game road trip ended with a loss. And when the team returned to its park, Yvars headed to the bullpen, there to warm up pitchers, give spare baseballs to obsequious fans and relay to his teammates stolen signs. With Yvars out there, the team won six straight. By August 17, when New York again set out on the road, Durocher had found a permanent spot for his third-string catcher.

ELEVEN

we talked only about whether
the Dodgers would hold onto
their half-game lead
through September and whether
the new supervisor with the
great legs would turn out
to be a
bitch or a bastard.

—CHARLES BUKOWSKI,
"Dangling in the Tournefortia,"
1981

THE GIANT ROAD TRIP was short and easy, a weekend in Philadelphia against losers of five straight. They swept the three-game set.

It had been exactly one month since the team had begun stealing signs, and in that time it had gone 9–2 at home and 12–8 on the road. New York was eight games back of Brooklyn and on August 19, the team headed home on a train riding a winning streak of nine games.

That same afternoon, the eyes of the baseball world focused on St. Louis. "For the Browns," intoned public-address announcer Bernie Ebert, "number one-eighth, Eddie Gaedel, batting for Saucier." Thus introduced, a midget walked to home plate. In his delicate fingers he held a toy bat. But Gaedel, twenty-six, was legit—Browns manager Zack Taylor handed the ump, Ed Hurley, a contract signed by the tiny man good for $100 a game. Detroit lefty Bob Cain had no choice but to try to aim a Spalding into a strike zone barely bigger than the ball. After four tosses, Gaedel—an errand boy at the rancher newspaper the *Chicago Daily Drovers Journal*—trotted to first, removed immediately for a pinch-runner.

The stunt was the brainchild of Bill Veeck, new owner of the basement-dwelling Browns. (Perhaps he knew of Jerry Sullivan, a midget who batted once in 1905 for the Eastern League Buffalo Bisons.) Baseball was peeved, and the next day, American League president Will Harridge negated Gaedel's contract. Midgets could not play the game. But Gaedel already had, forging his mini mark in the annals of baseball: "Gaedel, Eddie-Edward Carl Bats R Throws L 3'7", 65 pounds."

The next afternoon, back in the Polo Grounds after a rainout, the Giants hit three home runs in the eighth and beat Cincinnati 7–4. They made it 11 straight wins the next day, topping Ewell Blackwell (he the first victim of a telescope back in July). And on August 24, after a day off that saw several Yankees accuse their Indian hosts of spying signs from their scoreboard, the Giants beat the Cardinals 6–5, their fourth consecutive come-from-behind victory and twelfth straight win. The streak remained intact the next day when a blessed rain washed out a game the Giants trailed 3–1 in the third.

For the first time all season, the scent of a pennant race tickled New York's nose, Giant players whiffing the cash bonus rewarded pennant winners. Brooklyn had been alone in first place since May 13 and still held a commanding seven-game lead. But on August 26, the Dodgers and Giants both set to play doubleheaders on consecutive days. And as the city prepared for just the tenth time in thirty-one years to host eight National League games in forty-eight hours, the muscles of its fans tensed.

Minutes before five p.m., both teams came to bat in their bottoms of the ninth. Thousands of fans at the ballparks in Flatbush and Harlem held radios to their ears, watching one game while listening to another. "PARKS INFESTED BY PORTABLE RADIOS" read a caption in the *Sporting News.* And so, when Pee Wee Reese flied out to give Pittsburgh a 12–11 win over Brooklyn, the Polo Grounds erupted in applause. The cheers crescendoed seconds later when Westrum homered to give New York a 5–4 win. Both teams won the nightcaps. The Brooklyn lead was six games.

It had been exactly one month since Chadwick had felt lightheaded on the subway. And his life was horribly changed. In lieu of all food, he sipped only vanilla malteds. He had lost some thirty pounds, down to 145. He was sallow and slept more and more. Of all his clothing, he wore only pajamas. There were no more nights at the Acorn Club, no more union meetings, no more stories at George Farrell's, no more weekends with Miriam at the bungalow in Rockaway Beach, no more movies at the Ward Theater on Westchester Avenue, no more after-dinner political discussions at the Lomrantzes two houses down. There was no more shimmying up light poles, no more climbing to the cantilevered roof of the Polo Grounds, no more lighting of the field. Only the Dodgers, it seemed, remained, there for Chadwick on his black-and-white television.

Branca started game one for Brooklyn the next afternoon. And in the third inning, opposing pitcher Mel Queen lined Pittsburgh's apparent first hit of the game to right. But Carl Furillo charged the ball, the Reading Rifle gunning a bullet to Gil Hodges at first. Incredibly, Queen was out. It proved a big play. As *Daily News* columnist Dick Young put it: "The fine Italian arms of Ralph Branca and Carl Furillo had a no-hitter going into the ninth inning."

Pete Castiglione walked to bat and Branca looked in for the sign. It was usually Roy Campanella behind the plate. But he had caught 18 innings the previous day and it was Rube Walker now calling for a curve. Branca shook Walker off—he wanted to throw his fastball. "Pitchers don't know a goddam thing," Campy once said. "That's why they have catchers." Castiglione lined Branca's fastball into center field for a base hit. Lost was the no-hitter. Branca settled for a shutout, his second in three days, the twelfth of his career. His earned run average dropped to 2.60, best among starters on the club.

"If the Dodgers blow what's left of their once proud lead to the crazy Giants," wrote Harold Burr of the *Brooklyn Eagle*, "it won't be the fault of Ralph Branca."

Meantime, 11.5 miles away, New York went to the bottom of the twelfth inning of its first game down a run. The streak, 14 games strong, was in jeopardy. But two walks, two singles and a sacrifice fly later, the team beat Chicago 5–4. Dispirited by the news, Brooklyn lost the second leg of its doubleheader. The Giants won theirs 6–3 as Corwin pitched a complete game. The rookie was 5–1.

When evening settled on August 27, New York had reeled off 16 wins in a row, baseball's longest streak in sixteen years. Thirteen of its victories had come at home, maintenance worker Colletti raising thirteen blue flags, the Giant Victory March played thirteen times. The Giants trailed the Dodgers by just five games.

Fans of both teams were more and more nervous. "QUICK, THE OXYGEN!" read a *Brooklyn Eagle* headline. "It's only a dream," reporter Red Smith cautioned New York. A month remained in the season.

As often happens mid-gallop, the Giant players, desperate to maintain their stride, gave in to superstition. Jansen refused to change the ink-stained sheet on his bed in the Henry Hudson Hotel. Thomson made sure before every game to slip on a pair of ants-patterned boxers and, before every *inning,* to kick the foul side of third base. Durocher carried with him at all times a picture of son Chris. Dark continued to use Rigney's glove which he had borrowed on a whim. And all the team insisted that Schenz and only Schenz pitch batting practice. "He's their lucky charm," wrote the *New York Post,* on August 21. "He has them talking pennant all over again despite the almost hopeless chore in front of them."

But superstition does not hit the cutoff man. The Giants were winning on the field. And while their batters knew what was coming, it was their pitchers who took off. During the streak, seven pitched, six got wins and nine complete games were tossed. In 147 innings, the staff surrendered but 35 walks, 1.38 fewer per game than the league average. They had allowed only nine base runners (walks plus hits), per nine innings, a whopping three fewer on average than they had before the streak. And the staff's earned run average plummeted from 3.86 before the streak to 2.39 during it.

Of course, a few of the bats improved too. Irvin, for one, batted .351 with 10 runs batted in. But overall, the team's hitting changed little. During their 16-game run, New York batted .263 and scored 72 runs. Prior to it, the team had batted .260 and scored, in an average 16-game stretch, 82 runs.

The bats did improve, however, when they had to. Four times in those 16 games, the Giants came back to win when trailing after the seventh inning. (Three more games they won having been tied after seven.) That was just one fewer late-inning comeback victory than the Giants had mounted in all their 110 games before the streak.

Watching from the shadows of the bullpen, Yvars felt he knew what was behind the late rallies. Sometimes, early in a game, he had no signs to relay—it took a few innings for Franks to decode them. And often, he says, the team would only turn to their telescope when they were in a pinch. "We get four runs ahead, we stop," Yvars explains. "Then the other team rallies. Now we go to the signs again."

For sixteen days, Yvars had relayed signs and watched fireworks ensue. And for sixteen days, aside from warming up pitchers, he had done little else, collecting but two sacrifices and no official at-bats during the streak. The victories were thrilling but still he wanted to play. On August 28, Durocher started Yvars for the first time in twenty days. New York lost to Pittsburgh 2–0.

The Dodgers exhaled. The Giants had lost! Several players began to sing in the shower and Pafko turned to a reporter: "Looks like the World Series in here." Meantime, general manager Bavasi chirped to columnist Dick Young that all those Giant wins would ultimately serve Brooklyn. "I'm glad they're winning now," he said. "It will put them to sleep. They think they'll have a better team than they actually do and they'll stand pat for next year."

But Chadwick had no next year. And he did not delight. The electrician knew what was happening, had watched for weeks the records of the Dodgers and Giants converge. And it was cruel. He could not bring himself to tell his wife or daughters the truth: after four years of flipping lights, a dutiful card-puncher, he had rigged a buzzer system on the eve of the very last home-stand he had worked. *He* had helped the Giants! Worse, he had hurt the Dodgers. Watching win after Giant win, it all seemed so conspicuous. How could nobody grow suspicious?

Three days later, a Dodger did.

It was the first of September, a cold northeast breeze presaging the end of summer. The World Series was a month away. And pushing its lead back to seven games, Brooklyn, after a day off, arrived at the Polo Grounds for the first of two battles. Starters Branca and Newcombe could all but finish off New York.

With two out in the bottom of the first, Mueller came to bat. Campanella, as always, had wrapped white tape on his black fingers to make them easy to spot, and he now wagged his index finger. Fastball. Branca delivered one low and outside. Ball. Three fastballs later, the count 2–2, Campy called for a curve. Branca threw one of medium height over the outside part of the plate and Mueller sent it to the upper deck in right. Home run. Thomson took Branca deep in the second, blasting into the wind a home run to left. In the third, Mueller again homered to right, just the twelfth home run Branca had given up all season. Seven, though, had been hit by New York, and the pitcher exited after four innings.

Mueller was not done. Beneath the lights, the right-fielder hit a third home run in the seventh, this one off the right-field roof to give the Giants an 8–1 lead. The crowd of 40,794 roared in happy disbelief.

Mueller was a slap hitter, a man dubbed Mandrake the Magician for his ability to navigate pitches into the clear. Heading into the season, he had hit but eight home runs in 662 career at-bats. And so at least one Dodger was incredulous. As Durocher love-tapped Mueller at third—the right-fielder on his third home run trot—Brooklyn bench-coach Cookie Lavagetto, filling in for Dressen home sick with the flu, shook his head. After the game, he spoke to the manager.

"Charlie," Lavagetto said, remembering the conversation to author Peter Golenbock, "you notice when we come here, we never fool anybody? We throw a guy a change of pace, he seems to know what's coming?"

Dressen vigilantly protected his team's signs. Often, he used one set for the first three batters in his lineup, another for the next three, a third for the bottom of the order. He was a renowned sign-stealer too, honing for thirty years a skill he picked up in 1922 from Mike Kelley, manager of the St. Paul Saints. "Charlie was great at stealing signs," says Franks. "His only problem was he wanted the world to know it." Sure enough, when in 1937 he coached the National League All-Star team in Cincinnati, just to wow his squad he instructed each player in his native signs.

Durocher too was a reputed master of wig-wag. On August 27, 1950, the *New York Post* had reported that an informal poll of major leaguers deemed Durocher and Boston coach Earle Combs the two "champion signal-stealers."

It was Dressen, though, a similar 1957 poll fingered alongside Durocher as expert thief. And Dressen considered himself keener than Durocher in this and all respects. "I know every thought he has," Dressen had said of Durocher in July to reporter Milton Gross. "I can sense every move he's going to make because I learned all about him in the years I was his coach in Brooklyn."

Indeed, as Dodger manager and coach, the men had become simpatico. And in their eight years together in Brooklyn, they reveled in a heightened ability to communicate signs. "His sense of timing was so perfect," wrote Durocher of Dressen in his autobiography, "that we had been able to develop a system of absolutely undetectable signs." As proof, Durocher proudly recounted in the book how, for sport, he once flashed a hit-and-run sign to Dressen with only a shift of his head and eyes, while Dodgers Billy Herman and Pee Wee Reese stood between them unable to detect the signal.

Now the student resolved to teach the teacher a lesson. On September 2, the day after Mueller's barrage, the day after Lavagetto voiced his suspicions, Dressen left his bed for the park and brought with him binoculars.

The last of Brooklyn's 11 scheduled games at the Polo Grounds began at 2:30. The sky was already dark. A cold drizzle fell. In the top of the first, the Dodgers went down—infield hit, double play, groundout. Newcombe walked to the mound and as Stanky came to bat, Lavagetto took out Dressen's binoculars.

Mistrustful managers had, from time to time, acted mid-game on suspicions of foul play. Two years earlier, on October 1, 1949, the Red Sox led the Yankees by one game when the teams squared off at Yankee Stadium on the penultimate day of the season. Late in the game, the score 4–4, New York came to bat. Yankee batboy Bert Padell knelt as always on a towel in the on-deck circle when Boston's skipper stopped play. "Joe McCarthy comes running out of the dugout like a madman," remembers Padell, "banging his hat and all this shit." McCarthy was sure Padell was somehow stealing Boston's signs and he told the umpire. "Take it easy," said big Bill Summers. "Take it easy." Ump Summers summoned Yankee manager Casey Stengel and explained the charge. "Bert," Stengel told his batboy, "sit by the dugout steps." Padell moved, McCarthy calmed and Boston lost 5–4.

Now, Lavagetto aimed Dressen's binoculars at the Giant clubhouse toward Franks, his roommate years earlier in Brooklyn. But as he tried to descry Durocher's scheme, umpire Al Barlick spotted him.

"He ran over and grabbed the damn binoculars," remembered Lavagetto to Golenbock. "There was nothing I could do. We were just trying to observe center field." The fourth window went undiscovered.

The game continued, and if Durocher was nervous, he did not show it. He sent his usual signals to Stanky, happy that Dressen eyed him suspiciously. Says Corwin: "Leo always wanted everyone to think that he was doing it on third base." The Brat walked, advanced to second on a groundout by Mueller, and scored, waved home by Durocher on a base hit by Irvin.

With two out and two on in the sixth, the Giants led 4–1. Mueller made it 7–1 with yet another home run to right. As Hearn, Stanky and Mueller trotted back to the dugout, Maglie, as he had all game, rode Newcombe, making choking gestures. So too did Schenz. He who had garnered a Good Conduct medal in the service now cursed like the sailor he was.

The score, Maglie and Schenz got to Newcombe. And when Irvin grounded to Billy Cox to end the inning, the pitcher seethed. He tossed a catcher's mask onto the field and got tossed in turn, off on the long, face-down walk of the departing pitcher at the Polo Grounds.

The entire Brooklyn team was frustrated. A great lead was slipping away. And on this afternoon, the team gave vent to months of pent-up nervousness, hollering no-nos from the bench. Five players were ejected and Dressen, bent on showing up ump Barlick (whom he felt had squeezed Reese on a called strike), ordered his remaining subs to leave the dugout for the clubhouse. The players, grateful for the sanctioned naughtiness, lollygagged their way to center field. And when Dressen called on Cal Abrams to pinch-hit in the seventh, Abrams took his sweet time returning to the diamond, set in the batter's box three minutes and three seconds after descending a staircase.

There was one out in the eighth and one strike on Mueller when Irvin, on-deck, called time. News had just reached the dugout that Mueller's wife, Genevieve, had given birth to a six-pound son. "It's a boy!" Irvin told Mueller. Mueller swung his 34.5 ounce bat at Phil Haugstad's next pitch, the ball landing over the exit gate beyond the 395-foot marker in right. The blast was his fifth in two games, tying a major league record, and over and over on his skip home Mueller repeated, "It's a boy! It's a boy!" Later that inning, Thomson homered over the black left-field roof and the Giants went ahead 11–1.

Throughout the slaughter, Brooklyn players banished by both Barlick and Dressen to the clubhouse carried on. Twice they opened the clubhouse door and twice Barlick bade the public address announcer to order it shut. (In direct line of sight of the batter, an open door stopped play.) And so the players, defiant, opened and shut and opened and shut and opened and shut the one clubhouse window in their locker room. The fans laughed.

All the while, even as thousands of eyes focused just three windows away, even as Bavasi sat beside Stoneham one flight above, Franks sat unnoticed beside his mounted telescope, behind his clipped wire screen. Bavasi and Stoneham were good friends, would more than once—as Stoneham drank a scotch and soda, as Bavasi charted a game in his scorecard—broker a deal right there in the Giant clubhouse. But on this day, as New York manhandled Brooklyn, the two barely spoke.

Brooklyn scored once in the ninth, 11–2 losers. The romp over, Stoneham turned to Bavasi. "Would you like a drink before you leave?" he asked. "Take your drink and stick it up your ass," answered Bavasi. Then he left.

Dressen had said nothing to Bavasi of sign-stealing. But had he mentioned his suspicions, the general manager would have been incredulous. For Bavasi had this afternoon noted anew the absurdity of catching a game from Stoneham's perch, of eyeing thumb-sized ballplayers gunning for a home plate 500 feet away. Says Bavasi, "It wasn't much fun sitting there."

Over 18 innings in two days, New York had amassed 21 hits and 19 runs (10 driven in by Mueller). And stripped of his binoculars, Lavagetto was left to ponder New York's success. "Whatever [Durocher] had out there," he told Golenbock, "he had a good system." The secret was safe. And it was unguarded from three little boys.

Eddie, Jerry and Chris were family. Eddie Jr. was ten, son of clubhouse-man Logan. Jerry was nine, son of groundskeeper Schwab. Chris was five, the son who (along with daughter Michele) Laraine Day and then Durocher had adopted. And ever since the end of school in June, the boys had ricocheted about the park.

The Polo Grounds was their playground. The three boys opened and closed (and opened and closed) the accordion gate of the clubhouse elevator door. They labeled everything in sight with Durocher's rubber stamp. They tore open the cases of baseball cards that in 1951 Topps Gum first printed and sent players, and launched from the upper deck the caramels that this year alone came in every pack. They climbed the wire screen that rose four feet above the outfield fence before the bleachers. They rode their Schwinn bikes down concrete hallways and up ramps. And they marinated in the five senses of the park—in the pungency of its police horse stable, in the vistas just up Chadwick's wooden ladder, in the tastes of hot dogs and peanuts to be had free in Harry Stevens's kitchen, in the clang of the metal sorting machines into which vendors poured their gelt, in the give of the catacombs where Schwab heaped fertilizer, dirt, clay and sand.

Before games, the boys readied for baseball, changing like the players into wool Tim McAuliffe uniforms, Chris donning dad's number 2, Eddie Jim Hearn's 21, Jerry Johnny Mize's 15. During games, each boy checked in on his father. It was from the far corner of the dugout that Chris saw his father manage, heard him bitch, the boy often sneaking out into the stands to swap ball for hot dog. Eddie stayed in the clubhouse, watched through glasses his namesake check inventory and sort jocks, the son believing a father's boast that he could tell each player by smell. And Jerry eyed his father in his wooden folding chair in left, watching on rainy days with pride the nonpareil groundskeeper roll out with his crew the dark gray canvas tarp without which play could not resume. After games, after even Eddie and Chris had gone home, the blond boy who lived under the left-field stands often camped on the emerald field for the night, a friend and 56,000 empty seats for company.

The Giants enjoyed the boys, offered them up the occasional tobacco leaf to chew. Some were family men happy for a touch of home at work. Some were kids themselves, closer in age to the half-pints than the veterans on the club. (Mays, for one, often roomed with Chris on the road.

"He went with me into the black neighborhoods," says Mays. "Ate what I ate.") And all were happy when the boys helped out with chores. For a dime, the trio would polish with saddle soap a pair of shoes. For a soda or sandwich, they would help Logan fold laundry. And for fun, they would whenever asked forge player signatures. (Logan requested that each player, every day, sign twenty-four virgin balls—currency for all manner of services.)

And so the players were comfortable among Eddie, Jerry and Chris, did not hesitate in their presence to kick water fountains or call someone a motherfucker or talk openly of a telescope. "There was always the talk of trying to steal signs," says Chris Durocher. "Even at that age, I knew what was going on."

It was the morning after umpire Barlick took binoculars from coach Lavagetto that Labor Day ended summer. School set to begin, Eddie and Jerry bid a Harlem green farewell. So did Brooklyn, sweeping at home a doubleheader versus Boston. New York, meantime, split a pair against Philadelphia and so trailed Brooklyn by six games.

Both Brooklyn and New York were off Tuesday and their beat writers zipped north to face off in a softball game at Bear Mountain. Among the crowd were Giant Franks and Dodger Branca who watched Dick Young lead the Brooklyn scribes to a 10–8 win. After lunch, golf and dinner, it was back to New York.

The pennant, though, would be won or lost *outside* New York. Sixteen of Brooklyn's remaining 23 games were on the road, while just three of the 21 games New York had left were scheduled for home.

Away from Chadwick's buzzer, the Giants swept three in Boston, split a pair in Brooklyn, and lost two of three in St. Louis. And when on September 14 they arrived in Chicago, they were still six back of Brooklyn. Only now, they had just 13 games left to play.

Driving to the game from New York was Kleppel the fan, prince of the Polo Grounds bleachers. And as big Bob Rush threw a game's first pitch at 1:30, Kleppel saw something he had not in nearly two months: Franks standing in the third base coaching box.

Durocher was recovering from the grippe and a fever of 101. And because his team was on the road, Franks was available to resume his coaching duties, Durocher free to rest on the bench. "I haven't felt well for some time now," Durocher told the *Daily News*, "and I put Franks out there to see if he couldn't bring us some luck." He added, "Maybe we can win them all from here on in with him out there."

The team got off to a bad start. With one out in the bottom of the first,

Chicago's Hank Sauer skied to left. As Irvin caught the fly and threw home, Frankie Baumholtz broke from third. Westrum caught Irvin's throw and blocked the plate. Baumholtz slid into home, Westrum tagged him out, umpire Al Barlick called him safe, Westrum flung his mask and screamed at Barlick, and Barlick ejected Westrum from the game. From the bullpen, Yvars watched the proceedings with an interested eye. With Westrum gone, Durocher had to send in another backstop.

Yvars had barely played of late, had in all September caught just the final two innings of a doubleheader in Boston on September 5. He had zero at-bats the entire month. He knew Durocher disliked him. But surely there was something more behind his lack of play, a reason he had gotten just 41 at-bats in spite of a .317 average. (In all the league, just six players with at least 40 at-bats would bat higher.) "I was more valuable giving the goddam signs," says the catcher. "[The players] were used to me."

Yvars moped. And though the team was on the road, he was not at all surprised when, after Westrum's ejection, Durocher tapped Noble and his .219 average. The Cuban catcher got two hits and New York beat Chicago 7–2.

The next morning, however, Durocher did turn to Yvars. The Giants were gathered in the clubhouse at Wrigley Field discussing Chicago's tall lefty Paul Minner when Logan disrupted the closed-door meeting. "What the fuck are you doing here?" Durocher snapped. "We're having a goddam meeting!" The clubhouse man apologized, explained that Durocher's friend, actor George Raft, was on the phone from California. "Tell that cocksucker I'll speak to him after the game," Durocher barked. Logan left with the message, only to return saying that Raft insisted on speaking to Leo right away. Durocher left the room.

Minutes later the manager returned. "He says he's got a horse running at Hawthorne who can't lose," Durocher told his players. The Lip was delighted, had padded his income with sure things ever since he was a kid with a cue in the pool halls of West Springfield. The only question was how to get a bet in. Minner would throw his first pitch in just a few hours—not long after an auburn gelding named Indian Gold would take off in the ninth at Hawthorne Race Course.

Schenz, veteran of four seasons in Chicago, knew a bookie. And so Durocher took out a yellow pad of paper, signed his name and put himself down for $100 on Indian Gold to win and another $100 on the horse to show. The pad went around the room. Yvars put $2 down on the horse to win, another $2 to show. Mueller pledged the same. By the time the pad had gone completely around the room, some $800 were bet on the horse.

Since first spying for Durocher, lap dog Schenz had done all that was asked of him, even watching at times Chris and Slugger, the boy and boxer left with him during games in the clubhouse. And he had all but stopped playing ball. Since pinch-running six times in eleven days in early July, he had stepped afield just twice—on July 24 at Pittsburgh and just two days before at St. Louis. And so Durocher now told Schenz to change out of his uniform. He would take the money to the bookie.

While Schenz changed, Durocher got nervous. "The Little Giant" was aptly nicknamed and $800 was a lot of money. Durocher scanned the room for someone to protect his courier. Franks, his usual stopgap, was busy coaching third. And so, he turned to Yvars. The catcher had a mouth on him and an eager fist. He would be sure to act up if anything happened. Durocher told Yvars to change out of his uniform.

Yvars was furious. Hours earlier, National League president Ford Frick had suspended Westrum three games for "pushing the umpire." Now, even down a catcher, Durocher wanted to send Yvars away on a babysitting mission?! "Do what the fuck I tell you," Durocher ordered. Yvars changed into his street clothes and hopped with Schenz into a cab outside Wrigley.

The ballplayers arrived at a smoke-filled lounge, tellers behind windows taking bets on races all about the country. Minutes before the ninth at Hawthorne, the odds were set: Indian Gold would pay $9.60 for a $2 bet. Schenz walked to a window, handed over the cash, took a white slip tallying his team's bets and sat down beside Yvars to listen to a live broadcast of the race on WMAQ.

Back at the ballpark, Franks was clearly rusty. As he waved instructions from the third base box, Stanky was thrown out at home in the second, Mays at second in the sixth, and in the ninth, Stanky, hoping to tag up, left too early on a fly to center field and was out on appeal at third. But the Giants won anyway, dispatching the Cubs 5–2 in just under two hours.

At 5:41 p.m., seventeen miles southwest of the ballpark in Cicero, Illinois, eight horses burst from the starting gate. Indian Gold, marooned in lane eight, fell straight into last place. The horse was still eighth after a quarter-mile. Same at the half-mile midway through the race. But soon after, Hall of Fame jockey John Adams began his move and by the three-quarter-mile mark, Indian Gold had passed Yardtown and Reigh's Comet. Adams quickly passed four more horses and on the final turn, with just an eighth of a mile to go, trailed only Royal Challa, a 6–1 long-shot. Adams slipped to the inside rail and Schenz and Yvars forgot the ballpark—surely this beat sitting in the dugout and bullpen. Unrecognized, the players stood up, WMAQ blaring as the horses flew down the homestretch: "And around the last turn it's Indian Gold . . . Indian Gold drawing away . . . Indian Gold's your winner!"

Raft's info had been good. For not only had Indian Gold won by two and a half lengths but just before the race a trainer named Milt Resseguet had paid $5,000 for the four-year-old. One minute, 38 and three-fifths seconds later, Resseguet was smiling.

So were Schenz and Yvars. The Giants brought their white slip to a window and the bookie ponied up, stuffing more than $3,000 in small bills into three paper bags. Giddy and nervous, the two reserves hopped in a cab without counting the money. It was all there. And long after a happy baseball team on a train bound for Pittsburgh ate well, Chub Feeney fed the press poppycock, the Giant veep telling reporter Fred Down that Durocher had bypassed Yvars because he so valued Noble's glove.

The next day, New York took both ends of a doubleheader from Pittsburgh. After a day off on September 17, the team beat Cincinnati 6–5 while Brooklyn lost 7–1. The Giants were just three games back.

More than anyone, Thomson was leading New York's charge. And the next day, the *Sporting News* ran an article about the converted center fielder. "He has been," Arch Murray wrote, "a tremendous tower of strength ever since the night of July 20 when Leo Durocher, in a sudden, inspired move, told him to take over at third base." Unknowingly, the paper had fingered as the turning point in Thomson's season the very date the Giants launched their sign-stealing scheme.

The statistics were stark. Before that night two months prior, Thomson had batted .237 with 16 home runs. He had since batted exactly 100 points higher with 13 home runs. "It's to be doubted," wrote Arthur Daley in the *New York Times*, "if there ever was such an about-face in baseball history." His newfound success was not limited to home games. Thomson had hit 11 of those 13 home runs on the road, far from a telescope but also from the long outs of an oblong field.

The *Sporting News* assumed Thomson's rebirth owed to more than regular playing time and a change in position. But to what then? "What turned Thomson," asked the *Sporting News,* "from a tame tabby up at the plate into a roaring tiger?" Thomson offered up an answer. He credited a new batting stance he had adopted, a semi-closed crouch suggested by Lockman, his roommate on the road. And so in turn would scribes forevermore finger as hinge of 1951 a crouch, no matter that in little time Thomson would instead claim to the *Boston Daily Globe* that it was the shaving down of his bat handle responsible for its flowering. "I don't think particularly that the new stance I picked up had anything to do with it," Thomson added to Jack Orr of *Sport* magazine. "Hitting is a matter of the mind anyway. Once you get that confidence you get your hits no matter how you're standing."

Chadwick read all the stories, the daily exegeses on how a rout had turned into a race. And though he never missed so much as an inning of a Dodgers game, increasingly he slept away his days, asleep more than he was awake. Once husky, he had lost some fifty pounds and now weighed less than his wife. His brown eyes were jaundiced, his skin a sickly yellow. The cancer spared only his thick black hair and more than once before the oval mirror in his bedroom, Chadwick exclaimed aloud, "What's happening to me?"

The Dodger players asked themselves as much. The team was slowly wilting. Brooklyn was 21–7 in July, 19–13 in August, and, through the first 18 days of September, 8–7. The reasons were obvious—a decline in both hitting and pitching.

While Brooklyn hit .312 in July with 99 extra-base hits and 163 runs batted in, it hit just .256 in August with 81 extra-base hits and 148 RBI. The slide continued through the first 18 days of September: .246, 37, 64.

The drop-off in pitching was equally severe. In July, Brooklyn's staff surrendered a combined 345 hits and walks and posted an earned run average of 3.49. In August, the number of runners allowed rose to 364, the ERA to 4.05. Midway through September, the numbers had improved only slightly: 174 runners allowed, a 391 ERA.

More than anyone, Snider and Branca embodied the team's dual fall. In July, Snider hit .308 with 14 extra-base hits, Branca 3–0 with a 1.97 ERA. In August, Snider hit .288 with 9 extra-base hits, Branca 4–3 with a 3.33 ERA. And when on the eighteenth of September Branca lost to St. Louis, surrendering three earned runs in 5.2 innings, the pitcher in five September starts had one win, four losses and an ERA of 5.02, Snider in 18 September days batting just .136 with two extra-base hits.

The next night, the wives of twenty-nine Dodger players and executives gathered at the Belle Harbor home of Brooklyn's secretary Harold Parrott to throw a surprise shower for Ann Mulvey. It was September 19 and Mulvey, daughter of Dodger owners Dearie and James, was engaged to Branca, the wedding set for October 20. The women gave gifts and listened to Red Barber and Connie Desmond describe on a Magnavox radio their husbands' 3–0 victory over St. Louis.

The Giants were off, spent the day playing golf. And while next afternoon they lost to the Reds, the Dodgers again beat the Cardinals. New York was 87–58. Brooklyn was 90–52. With seven games to play, New York trailed Brooklyn by six in the loss column. A *Sporting News* headline declared the Giants "'51 RUNNERS-UP."

The Dodgers were also certain the 1951 pennant was theirs, and that morning, at team headquarters at 215 Montague Street, fans snapped up 12,000 newly minted applications for World Series tickets. Bavasi, Brooklyn's general manager, gave Campanella $4,400 and Newcombe $3,600 when they asked for their World Series bonuses early. And the following night, September 22, Dressen stood at home plate on "Charlie Dressen Night," the manager accepting an oil portrait by Al Stone of Newark framed above a plaque that read, MANAGER OF THE BROOK-LYN DODGERS — 1951 NATIONAL LEAGUE CHAMPIONS! For the second straight night, Brooklyn lost to Philadelphia.

The Giants too were back home, a trophy given Thomson before the game by his fan club. And as Stanky walked to the plate to lead off the first, Durocher, not Franks, flashed him signals from the third base coaching box. The manager had told the *Daily News* that he hoped putting Franks at third would "bring us some luck," that he would keep him there as long as the team won. But though the Giants had won all four games played with Franks coaching third, he was not in the box on this night. For as Branch Rickey once said, "Luck is the residue of design," and Franks was needed in the center-field clubhouse. With him behind the fourth window, the Giants now swept three straight from the Braves.

On September 24, Brooklyn's once enormous lead was down to 2.5 games. Bill Corum wrote a humor piece for the *New York Journal American* titled "the Creeping Terror" about the foreboding gripping Brooklynites. But it was no joke. With six days left in the season, just as Welsbach Electric stopped penciling the word *sick* on Chadwick's time card, a sickening sense of the inevitability of the Giant march on the pennant overtook the Dodgers. It was "like waiting for the doctor to come back with real grave news about your health," explained Rube Walker years later to author Harvey Rosenfeld. "Your stomach muscles are always cramping. Your nerves are dangling right through your skin. When a book or other object drops, you jump and feel like you'll go through the ceiling. You lose your appetite. Your favorite food tastes lousy. You're tired but you can't sleep."

Still, with just six days left in the season, Brooklyn, as Barber liked to say, was in the catbird seat.

The next day, Brooklyn set to play a doubleheader in Boston. Branca took the mound in game one and gave up single, home run, single, walk—leaving the game having not retired even one batter. He had faced four Braves and all four had scored, his ERA for the month of September ballooning to 5.97. In 31.2 innings, Branca had given up 40 hits, 13 walks and 7 home runs. Boston, on a six-game skid, beat Brooklyn 6–3 and Branca's record for the month slipped to 1–5.

Between games in the Brooklyn clubhouse, the Dodgers learned that the Giants had beaten Philadelphia 5–1. Frazzled, they lost the nightcap 14–2. Brooklyn now led New York by just one game. And one thing was certain: with St. Louis 15 back in third place, Brooklyn and New York would finish one-two for just the third time in their sixty-one-year history.

Both teams won ballgames on the 26th. But only the Giants could relax. For quirk of schedule now provided them a forty-eight-hour break, time for aces Jansen and Maglie to rest up for the season's final two games. Brooklyn meantime set to play its fourteenth game in as many days. Preacher Roe would take his stupendous 22–3 record to the mound against Boston.

On the morning of September 27, Stoneham and Brooklyn ticket manager Jack Collins arrived at the National League office on 42nd Street to determine home-field advantage in the event of a tie and an ensuing three-game playoff. New commissioner Frick flipped a coin and Stoneham called "Heads." It landed tails. Brooklyn could choose to open the playoff home or away—the second and if necessary third games to be played at the other park. In baseball's only other best-of-three playoff, Durocher had in 1946 opened on the road only to watch his Brooklyn team lose to St. Louis in two straight. And so, though the possibility of two home games was alluring (New York had this season won just 2 of 11 in Brooklyn), Dressen instructed Collins over the phone to opt for opening the possible playoff at home.

Gathered before a television at the Kenmore Hotel in Boston, the Giants saw Dodger Campanella ejected for the first time in his career. Brooklyn then lost to Boston 4–3, the team the next evening tied at three after eight in Philadelphia. And when, at 10:42 p.m., Richie Ashburn's cleat touched home in the ninth, incredibly, incredulously, inconceivably, the Dodgers and Giants were deadlocked. A 13.5-game lead had evaporated in forty-eight days, both teams 94–58. Read the back page of the *Daily News*: "THEY'RE TIED!"

Indeed they were—though Brooklyn and New York did not have identical records. The Dodgers toted too a tie, midnight May 12 having found the team knotted at five with Boston's Braves. It had mattered not, then, that reliever Branca was an out shy of a fourteenth inning. Chapter 136, Section 21 of Massachusetts law stated that sports were not to be played outdoors on Sundays before 1:30 p.m. And so a contest that having swayed this way or that would have forever tipped a pennant race was instead stopped, a footnote lost to time.

The arc of the Giant season formed a near-perfect parabola. With two games left on its schedule, the team had a share of first place for the first time since Opening Day, 164 days past. No team had ever gone so long in one season between stops in first.

Both teams won the next day, and at two a.m. on Sunday, September 30, the last morning of the regular season, the clocks rolled back.

Thirteen hours later, a hepped-up Thomson still had not slept when New York took on Boston. Nonetheless he hit a home run in the second inning, a shot to left that tied the game at one and capped for him a prodigious month: in 90 September at-bats he had hit .433 with three doubles, four triples and seven home runs. His most recent blow gave him 30 for the year and a 12-game hitting streak besides. The game ended at 3:35 p.m., and over in Philadelphia, as third baseman Willie Jones dug in against Brooklyn's Carl Erskine, the Dodgers saw the slats in the scoreboard at Shibe Park fill with the final tally: NY 3 BOST 2. The Giants had won.

In August, Bavasi had decided that he wanted the Ebbets Field scoreboard to stop posting scores. It was a distraction to his players, reasoned the GM. (The opposite was true. In August and September, Brooklyn won just one of eight games it played when New York was idle.) But when Bavasi learned that the team, in its dugout, was listening anyway to the New York broadcasts, he let it go.

Since their team meeting months ago on a rainy July Wednesday, the Giants had gone 23–5 at home and 26–12 on the road. They had won 37 of their final 44 games (including the last seven). In the history of baseball, only four teams had ever won more games over such a stretch.

The Dodgers, meantime, had gone 23–21 in their last 44 games. And they trailed 8–5 in the bottom of the sixth.

It had been an ugly game. Dressen started Roe, his star lefty, on just two days' rest. Roe secured but five outs and gave up four runs. Branca relieved him and, in 1.1 innings, allowed two more runs, his ERA for the month rising to 6.27. Brooklyn was down 6–1 and, worse, saw Campanella pull his right hamstring running out a triple in the fourth. In the top of the fifth, Brooklyn pulled within a run at 6–5. But in the bottom of the inning, Philly went up 8–5 on pitchers Clyde King and Clem Labine. And it was in the sixth that the Dodgers learned the Giants had won. They had best win or their season was over.

The Giants, meantime, crowded about a radio in a steamy dressing room in Braves Field and listened to the Dodgers. For eighty minutes, they cheered and cursed. For eighty minutes, Durocher smoked and paced. And after Erskine held the Phillies scoreless in the seventh, they left by bus for their train, a police escort seeing they made it.

As Brooklyn came to bat in the eighth, Durocher boarded the Merchants Limited train in a blue houndstooth suit. His team filled the dining and club cars and, setting forth for Grand Central Station, played cards and ate steaks. New York had left Boston with Brooklyn down three, and six cases of champagne were now unpacked to toast a pennant. The men were giddy. "They were having a hell of a time," remembers Franks. "Cutting off each other's ties."

There was a phone on the train and Chub Feeney now called WMCA radio back in New York. As the train chugged south, the Giant executive relayed the action play by play. In the eighth, the Dodgers scored three, knotting the game. Several Giants began to pace. New York was encouraged when in the bottom of the inning a desperate Dressen brought in Newcombe less than twenty-four hours after he had thrown a shutout.

The game went to extra innings tied at eight. It was still 8–8 in the bottom of the twelfth when Philadelphia loaded the bases with one out. Suddenly, the WMCA broadcaster relaying the action to Feeney had to go on the air. He hung up and "the Giants sat there," observed reporter Fred Down aboard the train, "like a group of condemned men."

Newcombe was still pitching, Dressen not confident in Phil Haugstad, Bud Podbielan or Johnny Schmitz, the only men left in his pen. A hit, a walk, a balk, a wild pitch, a sac fly—anything!—and the Dodger season was over. The scenario was nearly identical to one Newcombe had faced 364 days earlier. It was then on the last day of the 1950 season, trailing Philadelphia by one game, that Brooklyn had met Philly. Tied at one in the tenth, Newcombe had faced Dick Sisler with one out and two on. Sisler had homered and Brooklyn lost the pennant. The home run resonated. When a young boy in Ernest Hemingway's 1952 novel *The Old Man and the Sea* asked the fisherman Santiago who will win the pennant, he answered "between Brooklyn and Philadelphia, I must take Brooklyn. But then I think of Dick Sisler and those great drives in the old park." Now, one day short of a year later, Newcombe struck out Del Ennis. Eddie Waitkus was next.

On June 14, 1949, a fan named Ruth Ann Steinhagen, nineteen, had shot Waitkus in the chest with a .22-caliber rifle in room 1297-A of the Edgewater Beach hotel in Chicago. (The incident inspired Bernard Malamud to write his 1952 novel *The Natural*.) Waitkus recovered and helped Philadelphia capture the 1950 pennant, singling off Newcombe in that final inning of 1950 just before Sisler's smash.

A season later Newcombe now again faced the first baseman. As he did, second baseman Jackie Robinson inched toward first, playing Waitkus, a lefty, to pull. Waitkus swung at a Newcombe fastball and met it solidly. The low line drive shot toward center field and Robin Roberts, leading off third, took off for home with the winning run. But Robinson planted his left cleat, raced right and then dove toward the bag, his left side outstretched and facing home. Backhanded he snared the ball, then landed, his face scraping dirt, his right shoulder driven into the ground. Waitkus was out. After flipping the ball to shortstop Pee Wee Reese, Robinson collapsed. His right elbow had jabbed his chest and he struggled to breathe. Brooklyn trainer Harold Wendler ran toward the second baseman, Robinson's wife, Rachel, began to cry and much of the crowd of 31,755 exploded in cheer.

Leaning on coach Jake Pitler, Robinson slunk to the dugout, where Wendler waved under his nostrils a cotton ball soaked in ammonia. Robinson revived and in the thirteenth trotted to his position. Podbielan relieved Newcombe, the seventh Dodger pitcher retiring Eddie Pellagrini to end the inning.

It was 5:45 p.m. when Reese walked to the plate to lead off the fourteenth. As the game was being played on a Sunday, Pennsylvania law decreed it had to conclude by seven p.m.

In 1794, legislators in the Pennsylvania Assembly passed "an Act for the prevention of vice and immorality, and of unlawful gaming, and to restrain disorderly sports and dissipation" on Sunday, the Sabbath. Not until November 1933, 139 years later, did the legislation known as the "Sunday Blue Laws" bend to allow Sunday baseball in Pennsylvania, last of the major league holdouts. In 1951 however, state law did require that baseball on Sunday stop at seven. The Dodgers and Phillies had but a few innings to plate a winning run.

Orthodox Jewish fans following the game back in New York faced an even more pressing deadline. Rosh Hashanah, the Jewish New Year, was to begin eighteen minutes before sundown. At 6:23 p.m., they would have to flip off their radios and televisions. Among them was my father. Showered and dressed in his Saturday best, standing beside his father in the living room of apartment 3C at 2705 Kings Highway in Flatbush,

Kenny Prager, eight, listened to Red Barber describe the action and prayed for the Dodgers to win and win quick before the year 5712 arrived.

Chadwick had never cared much for Jewish custom. But it was a part of him. A mezuzah adorned his front doorpost. When Miriam prepared his favorite dish, meat and potatoes, he called out to her not to flavor the food with butter and milk, the result of having been suckled in a kosher kitchen. Though he never joined his wife in synagogue on Rosh Hashanah or Yom Kippur, he marked them in his own way, the holy days the only days he stayed home from work and when, aside from at weddings and funerals, he wore a suit. And it was every Purim that he marked his birthday, Chadwick born close to the springtime festival that celebrated the hanging of a Persian minister on a gallows he himself built. It was a fate altogether analogous to what awaited poor Chadwick.

Chadwick was unable this Rosh Hashanah to don a suit. But at least he was home. As sunset now approached, he lay on his couch in his buttoned pajamas and watched the game.

Reese hit a foul pop to catcher Andy Seminick. Snider popped foul off third. With two outs, Robinson came to bat.

Roberts, Philadelphia's ace, had held the Dodgers scoreless since the eighth and now went 1–1 on Robinson. His third pitch was a fastball on the outside corner. Robinson swung and met the ball flush, a Spalding sent deep into the upper deck in left, soaring over the bleachers as high as it went far. Robinson knew the moment he swung that the ball would leave the park and, still bleary, slowly shuffled pigeon-toed about the bases. Philadelphia went down in the fourteenth, a 270-minute game ended. And on a train in Providence, Rhode Island, where reporter Fred Down got word over the phone of a score, a dining car full of Giants in clipped neckties sat in silence while a porter repacked six cases of champagne.

"A demented Hollywood script writer in the last throes of delirium tremens," wrote reporter Daley in the *New York Times*, "would not have dared pen anything so completely fantastic as the way this dizziest of pennant races finished." But New York and Brooklyn had, a vertiginous regular season come to a close, a playoff to begin in nineteen hours.

Robinson had fired what Arch Murray of the *New York Post* called "the shot that could be heard around the baseball world." And it certainly reverberated through the five boroughs of New York. In Brooklyn, my father and grandfather whooped in glee, flipped off their radio and walked to Kingsway Jewish Center. In Manhattan, the *New York Times* put word of the game on its front page: "BROOKS' VICTORY IN 14TH

LEAVES FANS LIMP." In the Bronx, Chadwick lay on his couch, his legs just short enough that they extended unbent, and blessed the courageous Robinson who had broken into the major leagues the very same day as he. In Queens, on oak-lined 177th Street in St. Albans, a joyous babysitter named Willette Bailey tried to explain to a little boy and girl that their daddy had saved the day. And in Staten Island, in a rented ranch home at 411 Flagg Place, Elizabeth Thomson prepared dinner and a bed for her ballplaying son who would now have to ready for a playoff.

TWELVE

Public opinion is a weak tyrant compared with our own private opinion.

HENRY DAVID THOREAU, *Walden*, 1854

THE MORNING OF OCTOBER 25, 1923, Elizabeth Thomson lay in her bed at 29 Tennant Street in the Townhead district of Glasgow and, at ten minutes after eight, gave birth to a boy named Robert Brown. Some forty-eight hours later, her husband, James, his visa number called, left her, little Bobby, their five older children and Scotland, boarding the steerage quarters of the double-masted *Columbia* and embarking for America down the Firth of Clyde.

James had left Elizabeth with an infant before.

On December 9, 1915, James Thomson had sworn his allegiance to His Majesty King George V, enlisting in Scotland's army. James felt compelled to volunteer—a chaplain's letter had in August informed him that his younger and closest brother Robert, an infantryman in Iraq, had been wounded in his left arm. And so James, the eldest of four sons (a twin brother had died as an infant and brother William was in the navy), headed off for training in Caterham, England, leaving Elizabeth home with children Jeanie and Jim, the boy seven days old.

James tried to do right. When in 1912 he got Elizabeth pregnant, he asked for her hand. They wed on March 24, 1913, four months before Elizabeth gave birth to Jeanie. James believed in propriety too. Never would he tell his children of his hurried marriage.

While in Caterham, James learned that on April 22, 1916, 2,725 miles southeast at the battle of Kut-al-Amara in Iraq, brother Robert had died at the hand of a Turk. James was distraught, writing to Robert's captain to learn the circumstances of his death. He hoped then to someday father another son and name him Robert.

Eighteen months later, on October 23, 1917, James headed to war, assigned to first battalion, Scots Guard, in Houlle, Belgium. In November, he moved to the front lines, a squat man in helmet and khaki tunic, five feet seven inches tall, his chest 34 inches fully expanded, ready with bayonet and Lee Enfield .303 rifle to avenge a brother's death. On the twenty-seventh of that month, at 6:20 a.m., hours after a snowstorm, James saw his first action, attacking the village of Fontaine Notre Dame just west of Cambrai. And at two in the morning on February 11, 1918, in the Belgian village of Arras, a German artillery shell packed with mustard gas found Guardsman Thomson hunkered underground. Yellow aerosol filled his trench.

Thomson's subsequent injuries were limited to a recurrently sprained left ankle. And on February 17, 1919, after serving his country one year and 317 days, soldier number 16700 returned to Elizabeth a hard-boiled man.

Glasgow was a crowded city, all tenement houses and factories. Many of its men mined iron ore and coal or built ships and cars. James was a cabinetmaker. Since May 8, 1908, he had worked at 108 North Wallace Street, home of Jas. B. Fraser & Co. Ltd., a timber importer. The pay was meager and James was increasingly hard-pressed to feed his family. Word was that in the United States (where in 1920, presidential candidate Warren Harding promised "less government in business and more business in government"), prosperity was quickly supplanting postwar depression. James decided to seek a better life across the Atlantic. And so, on October 16, 1923, Mr. Fraser composed a recommendation letter, describing James as "very able, industrious and conscientious," a worker whose "honesty and integrity cannot be challenged." James crossed the ocean at 16 knots in six days. And when on November 1, 1923, an Ellis Island immigration officer determined in the custom of the day that James Hay Thomson was neither polygamist nor anarchist, he was on his way, intent on growing the $45 in his pocket.

Thomson settled in Midland Beach, Staten Island, renting a room from the Quale family at 260 13th Street. There he found little work, earned scant money to send Elizabeth and quickly contemplated returning home. But in time, Thomson took to his blue-collar neighborhood, became a fan of baseball and the Brooklyn Dodgers, landed a steady job in construction and began sending dollars home. With one payment, James included a note to daughter Ruby, recently recovered from pneumonia. It read:

Dear Wee Ruby,
I almost put this piece of paper in blank, it was just to cover up the dollar bills but the instinct of the Scotsman being I suppose forever foremost within me it seemed gross waste of good paper sending it away blank.

If you were a little older and able to understand I guess you would think if this was all the reason that made me write you would not want the letter, which naturally would be good reasoning.

Mother says you are a big strong girl again which is good. Do you like to play in sand and splash about in water? if so you'll get plenty here we will get you a nice little bathing suit so that you can learn to swim and one day perhaps you will go over to merry England and attempt to swim their Channel.

With Love,
From Father

The note, black-inked script on white paper, betrayed its author. Thomson was self-conscious, loving of his family and above all practical, in sum a Scotsman as he saw fit, literally, to underline. He dreamed of great, even historic, athletic achievement. And there was more in the note. It held a confession, Thomson sure to explain to a toddler the spurious circumstance of its writing. It was "good reasoning," father told child, to "not want the letter," to not want something if it was of questionable origin.

Some 35 miles north of Thomson's home, at 9:30 p.m. on January 6, 1926, Katherine Branca delivered a black-haired baby boy. Ralph Theodore Branca, named after a grandfather and a U.S. president, was her fifteenth child.

Katherine Berger was born in 1885 in Sandorf, Hungary. Seventeen years later, on October 29, 1902, at Mount Carmel Church in Harlem, she married John Branca, the son of a railroad engineer born in 1880 in Lapana, Italy. Promptly the couple begat a boy named Raphael and a girl, Louise. But within two years the babies died of pneumonia and the heartbroken couple, together with John's parents, moved to Mount Vernon.

The town was crowded with immigrants, 30,919 Italians, Jews, blacks, Irish and Germans living in 4.21 square miles. The Brancas added generously to the glut, quickly filling the six bedrooms of their three-storied home at 522 South Ninth Avenue. Katherine gave birth to Antoinette in 1905, Annunziata in 1907, Anna in 1908 and Julius in 1910. Edward, Helen, Florence, Sylvia and Margaret followed, all born by 1920. Rosemary arrived in 1921, Suzanne in 1922 and John in 1924. By the time Ralph was born, birth in the Branca home was all but routine, an annual holiday like Easter or any other.

The Brancas absorbed their newest child into their home with practiced devotion, mom breast-feeding the boy, sisters changing his diapers, brothers working their two-man saw through that much more maple and oak for the furnace in the cellar below. Their nurturing had about it a wisp of self-interest—the sooner little Ralph got to his own two feet, the sooner would he help get going those siblings sure to follow (and the sooner would they emerge from the assembly line that had reared them). By the time Ralph was born, his two eldest sisters had married and flown the brown-shingled coop, and his paternal grandmother was buried in nearby New Rochelle.

Family chores had long been divvied up. Mother handled food and clothing, the girls floor and dishes, the boys wood and coal, father money and hair. John, a trolley-car conductor (he picked up his future wife in Harlem), had become too a barber and set in his basement a thick-wire barber chair complete with mirror and straight-edge razor. There, occasional Sunday mornings, the paterfamilias clipped the manes of his children, in summer even the girls snipped around the ears, their dark brown locks flittering to the concrete floor.

A flight up, the kitchen was always crowded. Its table, a large oak slab with drawers, grew porcelain appendages as grew the family. ("At first the table was an I," says John, "then an L, then a U.") Huge closets held huge pots and pans, and mornings, Katherine slid an enormous double-pot atop her gas range, filled its top with oats, its bottom with water, and served her litter HO Oats. Nights she fired up her coal stove, preparing vast doles of Hungarian, Italian and American cuisine, her kids sneaking tastes of wiener schnitzel and cabbage soup, pasta and roast turkey, beef and potatoes. On a typical day, the family consumed twelve quarts of milk, thirty-six eggs, ten loaves of bread, thirteen pounds of pot roast, five packages of Jell-o and whatever the yield of father's vegetable garden and Bing cherry tree out back.

The Branca brood slept two to a bed, head to head. They also shared clothing, hand-me-downs Katherine bought at Klein's On the Square on 14th Street and from Benny Heaps, a traveling salesman who twice a month rang the Branca bell inside the screened-in porch, bearing the socks, underwear, pants and shirts the Brancas put on and paid off little by little. They wore jackets, hats and dresses too when Sunday mornings the family (minus Katherine, who stayed home to cook) made its way to St. Francis of Assisi, the Roman Catholic church just around the corner on 10th Avenue and Seventh Street.

Music was shared by all. In the Branca kitchen, a Philco radio forever played the big bands like Tommy and Jimmy Dorsey, Vaughn Monroe and Benny Goodman. As the Brancas tidied after meals, they sang and danced, the lindy, the fox trot and the waltz family favorites. In the living room, a windup Victrola piano, given a crank, played music rolls that roused the family dogs Duke and Cindy, their white German shepherd and black cocker spaniel. Often Eddie took to the keys, playing standards like "I've Been Working on the Railroad," "K-K-K-Katie" and "Sweet Adeline," a choir of ten or so siblings belting them out. The home was loud, infants and teens mixing, food, church and music the family mortar. Remembers Rosemary, "it was a lovely life."

Like his siblings before him, Ralph spent his first few months in a wooden crib beside his parents' bed. And on the very first day of July 1926, as Ralph, six months old, set to graduate to a shared bed with his brother John in the attic, another boy two years his elder arrived 21 miles away at Ellis Island. Bobby Thomson was passenger number 13 on the SS *Caledonia*.

On this Thursday, the temperature in Manhattan hit 81 degrees. Still, the Thomson kin wore their wool finery, Elizabeth wanting them looking dapper for Pop.

Named after his late uncle, Bobby was unmistakably growing into his father. His light hair was beginning to darken, his nose nascent, his arms already long. And together with his five older siblings, the toddler inherited too the Thomson tartan, a twilled wool of aquamarine, red, yellow, black and white. But it had taken James Thomson thirty-two months to send for Elizabeth, Jean, Jim, Marion, Betty, Ruby and Bobby, and the father was a complete stranger to the younger of his children.

The eight Thomsons headed by railroad, ferry and foot to Prescott Avenue in Staten Island. Elizabeth approved of her new home, two rented stories with chocolate shingles, a cement stoop and chickens in the backyard. All about were Scots, the local families intermarrying.

The home's four bedrooms were easily divided. Jean bunked with Betty, Marion with Ruby, Jim with Bobby, mother with father. The chores were quickly divvied too. Little Bobby had but one, to collect Sunday mornings the shoes left outside four bedrooms and to carry them to the cellar for dad to buff for church. This Bobby did three days after arriving in America, the family Thomson walking in shiny shoes on Sunday, July Fourth to the New Dorp Moravian Church just up the street at 2205 Richmond Road.

James stayed home. Not that he did not hold religion dear. He had, through 682 days of military service, toted a 1,006-page bible. But at thirty-three, he had not the money to buy a suit he deemed befitting church. Nor would he ever.

Quickly, the Thomson children got to know their father. James was proud. James was stolid. James was quiet. James was a disciplinarian. James was strong. James was loyal. James was principled. And of all his principles, the Scot most valued reserve. "We were," says Bobby, "brought up to be seen and not heard."

And so it was that when Jean began voice lessons at the Third Street Music School Settlement on the Lower East Side, father James was explicit with instruction. "Stay in the background," he told his eldest. Jean did, a beautiful soprano never to solo.

James was equally clear with his second child. Mornings, when Jim tromped off to Stonybrook Prep School in Long Island, the last words he heard his father speak were "Do what's right. Do what's right." This the other children often heard too at partings.

Life was not all tuition. In the privacy of home, the Thomsons sang, gathering just like the Brancas Sunday nights. They harmonized old Scottish songs, "Mary of Argyle," "Loch Lomond," "There's a Wee Hoose 'Mang the Heather," Betty accompanying the family on the secondhand upright piano James had managed to buy. James finagled too lessons for Betty, sometimes paying two dollars, sometimes bartering his services in construction. But even home, restraint reigned and rather than sing, the youngest Thomson was silent. "I just didn't have the voice," he wrote years later, "or the talent."

Bobby did not join his siblings in the church choir either. He did, though, spend many hours at church, enduring Sunday school, frolicking in the Moravian Cemetery, praying, playing touch football and assorted parts in church plays. (Most memorable was his portrayal of Douglas Fairbanks in a Tom Thumb wedding.) And while dancing was not allowed in the Protestant congregation, boys and girls mingled on its grounds just the same. Church was fun.

It was baseball, though, Bobby adored.

Jim worked as a delivery boy at Sears Roebuck and one day in 1929 brought Bobby home a glove. Nine years apart, the brothers played catch in the backyard. Bobby, five, was hooked from his first toss and began to play stickball whenever possible. James soon took Bobby to watch his first game, a contest at Gillies Field just off New Dorp Lane, two local teams contending with houses in center field, coal silos in left. The game was intoxicating.

It was also free. This was important. Work was spotty for James and the family was poor. They had no car, could often afford no Christmas tree and ate soups Elizabeth filled with "the cheapest meat you could get," Ruby remembers, ground beef she called mince, her kids chiding, "Talk like an American, Mom!"

Elizabeth also cooked puddings and oatmeal, griddled soda scones, and boiled dumplings of suet, flour and sugar she wrapped in cloth— Scottish fare that listed toward the off-white and plain. Dessert was a bit more sprightly. Elizabeth had in Glasgow worked in her sister's bakery to earn a few extra pounds. And so she now baked shortbreads and pies with beautiful crusts. The family ate together, the children always reciting grace, leaving for their father any leftover dessert, six quiet Thomsons according James respect, holding him in, says Ruby, "a little bit of awe."

The year 1929 was a distressing one for James. In the spring, his last living sibling, brother William, died of a duodenal ulcer. And on October 24, the day before Bobby turned six, the New York stock market crashed. It was not long after Black Thursday that construction work grew sparser still and the children saw the hurt in their father. "He'd go down to the cellar and ponder," says Bobby. "He was a very proud man."

The Great Depression was less hard on John Branca. A barber and trolley-car conductor, he now also operated a lathe and sold chickens and rabbits from a lean-to he built and stocked next to the garage. But his elder children, grown, were able to help foot the family bills, Antoinette and Anna working as bookkeepers, Julius a meter reader at Con Ed, Eddie a dispatcher at Sylvestre Oil, the Branca family regulating itself, an ecosystem all its own. By 1929, Paul and Al, the last of seventeen children, had been born, while Sylvia, just ten, had died of rheumatic fever.

Ralph thrived in the Branca home. He was growing tall, believed in God and had a beautiful voice. He also had two older brothers, Julius and Ed, who passed for second fathers, and a strong right arm. In 1932, the boy of six started playing baseball. Ralph loved to pitch and most often threw to Julius in the gravel driveway.

Ralph developed asthma that same year, left to repeat the first grade after sixty-six missed days of school. But after scratch tests at Grasslands Hospital in Valhalla revealed an allergy to cats, Ralph inhaled stramonium smoke, stopped curling up beside Nellie, the gray-and-white family cat, and improved. By age eight, after skipping the third grade, he was back in school and settled on a dream: to play professional baseball.

The Branca family loved baseball. And it rooted for the Giants. Mother Katherine listened to games and kept score at home. Suzanne scored games too. Paul carved the name of Giant Zeke Bonura into the kitchen table. Ralph, like hundreds of thousands of others, settled on Mel Ott and Carl Hubbell as favorites. Near all the family, five or so times a year, pilgrimaged by bus and subway to the Polo Grounds. And the brothers Branca forever played ball, Al and Paul following Ralph, John, Julius and Edward into the driveway. "In this big family," says John, "there was always someone to have a catch with."

Ralph caught and played second base at PS 14, Longfellow Elementary School, while brother John pitched. The two also played for the Paramounts, a club run by the Mount Vernon Boys Club, and in the Midget League run by the town rec department. When John turned twelve, no longer an eligible midget, Ralph inherited the mound, a boy of ten in spikes, pants and T-shirt. He dominated. "I'd pitch five innings," he says. "Strike out eleven guys."

Always there to behold was Mrs. Branca, heading to Longfellow or Dyckman's Oval or Lions Playground or Vandies Field to root on her sons. After games, she led discussion of the boys' performances. "You sat down at the dinner table," says John. "You were like cross-examined on how you did in the game. And everyone kind of took pride in what you accomplished." Such was life with the Brancas—bills jointly paid, clothes handed down, successes by rights familial.

Confirmations were shared too. When Ralph was ten, he studied the catechism together with brothers Al, Paul and John. Father Peter Luciano of St. Francis anointed with crucifixes of oil their four foreheads in succession, the quartet confirmed and older brothers Edward and Julius turned godfathers. Ralph selected Joseph his patron saint—he wanted a name that resembled beloved brother John's.

Ralph Theodore Joseph Branca started at Washington Junior High. He walked to school each morning, a good student, math and science his strengths. Problems with homework were solved at home. Aunt Rose Marie Branca was a schoolteacher, the very first Italian-American teacher in all New York, she told her nieces and nephews. She was also single and spent most weekends with her brother's family. "My handwriting comes from copying her," says Ralph. "She'd write letters and I'd watch."

Ralph, thirteen, spent the summer of 1939 playing softball and baseball and working as a gofer for sister Ann's husband, Mike DeLeonardis, building gas stations in Shrub Oak, New York. He made $12 a week and gave it all to his mother. She asked little else, save that at the end of every day Ralph and his siblings wish her and their father a good night. If a child came home too late, she coughed aloud her disapproval. Her severest punishment was silence.

James Thomson believed in silence. And through much of the nineteen-thirties, he suffered stoically. Work was scarce and his heart grew weak and he started taking digitalis, an extract of purple foxglove a fellow Scot, Dr. William Withering, had first found to be a cardiotonic. James did land, in 1936, a job as a foreman at Rheinestein Construction Company on 40th Street in Manhattan, but much of the work was upstate and he often spent all but weekends away from his family. Even with semi-regular work, the 60-odd-dollar monthly rent on his house was a struggle to foot, and time and again James had to pack his tools and beat-up piano and move his family about Staten Island. "He built houses," remembers Ruby. "But we never owned a house. I never understood that."

Returning home Friday evenings, James caught up with his children. Jean continued to sing and held religion dear. Marion was a record-setting runner, Betty an organist for the church choir, Ruby musical too, singing duets with boyfriend Danny MacGrady in high school. Bobby had baseball and Cub Scouts, his pack meeting weekly at Brighton Heights Reformed Church. Jim still worked at Sears and ran track at Columbia College, his distance 1,000 yards.

The mechanical-engineering major invited his younger brother to a meet. The races thrilled and it was not long after Bobby graduated from PS 38 to PS 16 that he entered a batch of junior high Public School Athletic League track meets. He fared well. Thirteen, he had the build of a quarter-miler—thin with lanky limbs and a long neck. But his heart was not in it and the boy soon returned to his first love, his Sears glove, baseball.

Thomson, though, was as unsure of himself as he was gifted. And so Charlie Finkensifer, the baseball coach at PS 16, was careful to give the quiet seventh grader as much encouragement as fielding practice. But when Thomson left PS 16 for Curtis High, he left too his confidence afield and, in the spring of 1938, did not even try out for the baseball team.

James Thomson was nonetheless elated to have in his family a fan of the American game. He had become an American citizen on February 10, 1937, and had been a diehard baseball fan a full fifteen years. And so now, religiously, after Bobby finished Sunday school, father and son walked miles about town in search of a game.

This they did one Sunday afternoon in 1938, finding at Clove Lake, at the big field off Victory Boulevard in Sunnyside, Staten Island, a game under way between teams of twentysomethings. By chance, one lineup was down a man and so gave a boy a turn at bat. Bobby, fourteen, walked to the plate.

That same year, the entire Thomson family had gone to hear Ruby, at sixteen a soloist with the Third Street Music School, sing George Munro's "My Lovely Celia." After the concert, as the family walked from Town Hall on 43rd Street toward the subway, Jean turned to her quiet father. "She sang well, didn't she?" she asked. James answered yes. Jean continued, exasperated: "Couldn't you have told her!"

On this Sunday, home with his son after the game, James spoke up. Bobby had managed a squib through the right side of the infield and he now heard his father recount the hit. James was proud. This the son would never forget.

From that day on (much to his wife's dismay), James saw to it that their youngest skip church and instead play ball. James had bought a Willy's Knight Roadster for his trips upstate and now, Sunday mornings, readied the car for a drive to a game. There were many, Bobby playing in time for a number of local sandlot teams: the New Dorp Dairy, the Stapleton Darts, Ripley's Crescents, Moe Cohen's Tompkinsville Blue Jays, Sal Somma's American Legion team, teams sponsored by the Parks Department, the Catholic Youth Organization, the Police Athletic League and the funeral home directors Mssrs. Gugliuccio and Petrangello, their names stitched to the back of a jersey that hung beside the many others in Bobby's closet. Bobby was a talent. Lightning-fast and powerful, he usually played shortstop and batted third.

He was less productive in the classroom. Always he sat in the back and often studied just enough to pass. Not that Bobby was not capable. Daily, for example, he and friends picked three major leaguers and bet on them, tabulating quickly their cumulative production. But academics could hold no candle to sport. "I was just all baseball," says Thomson. "I remember carrying a newspaper to school, instead of books, to get the scores."

Thomson followed the Giants. And like Branca and most every other boy, he favored Mel Ott. But Thomson never made it to the Polo Grounds. His brother Jim was a Yankee fan and his father rooted on the Dodgers.

James did, though, once take Bobby to Ebbets Field. There, the son saw what mattered to his father. When outside the park Peter Coscarart, a weak-hitting second baseman on Brooklyn, walked past the Thomsons, James saw that he wore his white shirtsleeves rolled up. He approved. "There's a regular guy," James told his son. And when from their perch in the upper deck above third, father and son saw first baseman Dolph Camilli stride to bat, Bobby took special note. Brooklyn had picked up Camilli on March 6, 1938, and immediately he had turned hero to James. Here was the quiet slugger, a man who spoke softly and carried a big stick, a former boxer able to quell a fight with but a glance. James himself was the former lightweight boxing champion of his army regiment and that Camilli's brother had died fighting world heavyweight champion Max Baer only further burnished the first baseman. When now number 4 slugged a home run, Bobby watched James watch Camilli, the son agape. "He jumped out of his chair," remembers Bobby. "Arms went up in the air."

James's work meantime had at last steadied. For the immigrant had at Rheinestein become superintendent of all his construction jobs. But in 1939 his heart further weakened and James had to retire, had to stay home.

Wife and children now provided for father, Elizabeth working part-time as a nurse's assistant. Bobby alone did not pitch in. And when Marion questioned why the youngest Thomson was not doing his part, James made it clear that Bobby's Sundays were spoken for. Baseball took precedence.

James's increasing expectations and diminishing health weighed on Bobby. It seemed little coincidence that in his third semester at Curtis the son suddenly floundered, failing three classes. Thomson did summon the courage that spring to try out for the Curtis baseball team but, he says, "I was the last one to ask for a uniform and they said 'Sorry, son.' " Thomson did not make the team.

The next spring, he did. And from Bobby's first practice, Curtis coach Harry O'Brien swathed him in the encouragement absent at his home, starting the junior at third. Recalled Thomson to interviewer William Marshall: "Thomson, you got a lot of talent on the ballfield," coach told player. "But your trouble is your old man brought you up to be too polite." Thomson bought his first pair of spikes and, batting second, hit .327, scoring nine runs in 14 games.

James watched his son play every game. But he did not cheer. And, says Bobby, "never in front of me" did his father talk up his ballplaying exploits.

All the while, the father influenced his son. "[Bobby] was extremely quiet," says classmate Tommy Faucett, "extremely shy, straightforward and honest." Adds another friend, Ralph DiStasio, "If he was in a group of twenty men, if nobody spoke to him he wouldn't say anything for hours." And so Bobby never told his father that he wished to become a major league baseball player. And James never told his son that he dreamed he would.

On Wednesday, July 3, 1940, James stepped out of a bath, put on his robe and felt his heart stop. Elizabeth found her husband prostrate on their wooden floor, his brown wet hair flush against a foot of their bed. Scattered all about were white digitalis pills.

Bobby arrived home. His mother told him that his father was dead. James, who had left his youngest as an infant, had left him again.

Two days later, outside 102 Grand Avenue, Thomson lay on his porch in an open coffin before his wife and six children. He had lived quietly—forty-seven years, six months and sixteen days of deflected attentions. And when at 2 p.m., the Reverend J. H. Warnshuis eulogized him, it was suddenly apparent that Bobby did not know his father's birthday or where he had fought in Europe or what were the names of his late brothers. He knew instead only of the man's few enthusiasms, of his care to deliver food to a poor black family on Christmas, of his love of baseball, his pet proverbs, his inveterate reserve.

A hearse brought Thomson down the street to the Moravian Cemetery, the immigrant buried in plot 4399, seven feet below where his children had played. "There was none of the weeping and wailing," says Ruby. "It was quiet. Rather stoic." Adds Bobby, "You know, the Scots are very undemonstrative people."

Six months later, in January, Ralph Branca enrolled at A. B. Davis High School in Mount Vernon. He was a freshman. And Florence Exner was in his class. Florence had lived in Mount Vernon since her second day of life and Ralph had noticed her about town. She had dirty-blond hair and blue eyes, was very thin and tall—all legs. Now they spoke. While others at Davis called Branca "Googsie," she called him Ralph. Branca asked her out on a date. She said yes and out with Ralph tasted pizza for the first time. She loved it. Soon too she loved Ralph. "He had the most beautiful eyes," she says. "And he had such big hands." Ralph had his first girlfriend.

Florence lived at 324 Nuber Avenue with her mother and grandmother. Her father had died when she was two, and she was an only child. Home was painfully quiet. Florence craved hubbub. And so, when she and Ralph were not at the movies, they were at the Brancas'. "I loved going over there," she says. "It was so wonderful for me, so different."

Others, however, disparaged the Branca home. At 522 South Ninth Avenue, it stood well within the south side of Mount Vernon, the poor part of town. And as Mount Vernon's poorer children usually attended Davis for just two years, enrolled longer in junior high than high school, Branca's high school advisor Mrs. Burch had only to hear his name at the start of the school year before steering him onto a two-year track. Ralph resisted. He spoke of his brother John just one grade ahead, of wanting to be in school with his bedmate for as long as possible. Mrs. Burch relented. She did, however, instruct Ralph to pursue social studies, a less rigorous track than mathematics, his natural bent. The freshman had no choice. "I know your family," she told Branca, fourteen. "And you won't go to college."

Ralph sought out his mother. After seventeen births, after nearly thirteen years of pregnancy, Katherine had been many things for her many children—administrator, chef, motivator, psychologist. And now she soothed her son. One favorite adage had always proved helpful. "God has a long memory," she said. "And wrongs have a way of righting themselves over the years."

Thomson was a senior in high school, stood six feet, weighed 145 pounds. He had for a time played basketball, a forward at Curtis. But he had grown quickly and when severe growing pains gripped his knees, he heeded a doctor's order to leave the hardcourt. That left baseball.

Curtis coach O'Brien was a Staten Island institution. Corncob pipe in mouth, he now declared Thomson his cleanup hitter, shifting him also to short. Results were mixed. While the senior committed 14 errors in 17 games, he batted .346, good enough for first team on the Staten Island high school all-stars.

By the end of 1941, Ralph's world had grown smaller. Perhaps it was the war that spurred his siblings to matrimony, but within twelve months, six Brancas had wed—Julius, Edward and four of the girls. And at the end of the school year, Florence too moved away. Her mother had remarried and shooed her from the home, sending her to Southern Seminary Junior College, an all-girl prep school in Buena Vista, Virginia. Florence and Ralph wrote often to each other. She informed him that she now went by Fern.

Lonely, Ralph threw himself into sport. The sophomore started at center on the Davis basketball team, won a kicking-and-passing football contest sponsored by the town recreation department and pitched his high school over Roosevelt, 3–2, in the second game of the baseball season. But it was his big brother who starred. John opened Davis's season with a no-hitter at Gorton and finished it undefeated, starting all but two of Davis's games. Davis won the 1942 County Championship. And John, "Coach" to his teammates, was voted All-Metropolitan, named also by various papers the best pitcher in the New York metropolitan area and a finalist (along with Sal Yvars of nearby Valhalla), for an annual New York schoolboy MVP contest. Ralph meantime played second base and right field, pitching also those two games his brother did not.

Katherine was as proud of her two sons afield as she was of her ten sons and sons-in-law in the service, clipping all mentions of their athletic feats, fastidiously compiling scrapbooks. One gushing sister, Ann, in the spring of 1942, sent to New York's three major league teams word of her brothers. And when all three teams responded with invitations to try-outs, big brother Julius drove them to the first, an audition in early July at the Polo Grounds where some 300 boys hoped to turn Giants.

Ralph stood below Coogan's Bluff a gangly teen, 135 pounds, the only of nineteen Brancas to reach six feet. He often wondered of his special bequest. "He used to say," remembers John, " 'Why did God give me this gift of being bigger and stronger?' He used to say 'Why me?' quite often." If Ralph settled on an answer, it was that he was chosen to carry the responsibility of success for the rest of his family.

On this day, neither Ralph nor John brought the Brancas glory. John did not throw hard enough to wow the scouts. And the tryout ended before Ralph was handed a ball.

Some ten days later, the boys stood on the mound at Yankee Stadium. As he had in Harlem, Ralph wore his Paramounts jersey, the blue-gray top of his old Mount Vernon summer league team. Now he threw. And when Yankee scout Chief Bender asked if he had a curveball, the boy of sixteen threw a beaut. Bender jotted a note: "Too young. Get in touch with him next year."

August came and with it the Brooklyn tryout. Katherine Branca packed her boys sandwiches—peppers and eggs, ham and cheese the norm—and by 7 they were off, walking two blocks to the bus on Eleventh Avenue. They stepped off at 241st Street, subwayed for a nickel to Grand Central, took the shuttle to Times Square, the BMT to the last stop at Sheepshead Bay and walked to Celtic Oval Field, home to semi-pro ball and a right-field fence on wheels. At most, eighty aspirants made the trek and the hopeful pitchers began firing at Art Dede, a Brooklyn scout crouched and wearing no mask. Off to the side, scouts Joe Labate and Jimmy Ferrante observed. John threw, then Ralph. The taller Branca's fastball had sizzle the elder's did not and Labate asked Ralph what else he could throw. He answered a curveball and a drop. The latter he now pitched, an overhand curve that snapped from twelve to six o'clock. Labate invited Ralph to throw batting practice at Ebbets Field and brother John only smiled.

Over in Staten Island, another boy took pride in a younger brother. Since his father's death, Jim had slipped on James's shoes, parenting Bobby. And as had been James, he was rigid with the youngest Thomson. "His brother kept a tight rein on him," remembers Thomson's high school friend Danny Monahan. "Gave him a curfew." But Jim, unlike James, was vocal with encouragement, pushed Bobby to follow his dream of playing professional ball. And in the spring of 1942, that dream suddenly seemed possible.

It was then that Thomson's play on a semipro sandlot team got him noticed. The team was the Gulf Oilers, Thomson suiting up Sunday afternoons, a kid alongside men, the lot Gulf Oil employees. Playing shortstop in Staten Island's top industrial league, he shone. And when in May Giant scout George Mack saw Thomson play, he invited him to a New York workout. Thomson, eighteen, rejoiced and on the allotted day grabbed his mitt and took the bus to the ferry to the subway to the Polo Grounds.

Thomson had never before been to the ballpark. Now, officially a prospect, his spikes trod the same grass that did the immortal Mel Ott's. "Whoo!" says Thomson. "Big stuff!" He trotted to short and took ground balls, Giant coaches Dolf Luque and Pancho Snyder watching. Smooth. Next was a turn at bat, the high schooler granted five precious swings. "I hit the ball," says Thomson. A voice barked at him: "Haul ass, kid! Get the hell out of there!" It was veteran shortstop Dick Bartell. The kid had lost count of his cuts.

The Giants were not the only team interested in Thomson. The shortstop had also played that spring on the Dodger Rookies, an amateur club owned by the Brooklyn Dodgers. And now, soon after his morning audition at the Polo Grounds, Brooklyn invited him to a workout at Ebbets Field. Thomson arrived at the clubhouse to find the great Pee Wee Reese breezily playing cards. Glove on hand, earnest in his Rookies uniform, Thomson was appalled. What of preparation, sobriety? What would his father have thought?

The tryout went well. Brooklyn was keenly interested. Scouting director Mickey McConnell told Thomson that the Dodgers would better any offer he might receive. But Thomson dreamed only of playing for the Giants. And so he did not tell McConnell that he had another workout slated with New York the very next day. He did not tell McConnell that at that workout Luque turned to fellow Giant coaches Bill Jurges and Bubber Jonnard and said, "That boy good! Should be away some place play ball!" He did not even tell McConnell that New York so wanted him that Giant general manager Bill Terry had scout Mack travel to his home with an offer the very day he graduated Curtis High.

It was an offer Thomson would have been lost without. This, though, was not evident in the Curtis yearbook he received this same week. For there between the pearled Mabel Thiele and Ruth Thompson, gazed Robert Thompson—his look pensive, his tie tartan, his thick hair high off his forehead. And the type beneath his misspelled name betrayed that he had at Curtis taken turns as class secretary, treasurer and president.

But Thomson belittled those appointments. (Late in life, he would even forget he had held them.) What mattered instead to Thomson was his academic record. And struggles with school after his father grew sick had rendered him, in the spring on 1942, ineligible to play baseball, Thomson watching his classmates play, a semi-weekly ritual that left him humiliated. "That," says Thomson, "was a very embarrassing thing."

And so Thomson had been eager to be done with school, had spent as little time with classmates as he had studying, neither carousing with the boys nor dating the girls. This very week, he had even skipped his prom. Baseball was Thomson's sole aim.

It was now too his job. On Thursday June 25, 1942, a day after graduation, Thomson traveled alone to New York City, met Mack and accepted New York's offer, inking on the outside stone windowsill of a happened-upon building a contract for $100 a month. Still, somehow, Thomson remained acutely underwhelmed by his ability. "It's difficult to think back," he wrote forty-nine years later, "and know why the Giants signed me."

Branca had no such qualms. He deemed both his height and strength gifts from God and determined to put them to good use. This he did this same summer of 1942, a boy of sixteen throwing batting practice to major leaguers. "I got the ball over," says Branca. "I was walking two feet off the ground." Labate, Brooklyn's scout, liked what he saw.

Elizabeth and Marion Thomson accompanied Bobby to the bus depot in Manhattan. The baby of the house was off at eighteen to Bristol, Virginia, to play in the Class D Appalachian League. The trip was his first outside the metropolitan area, his first voyage since arriving from Scotland in 1926. And when at last Thomson reached Bristol, it was only thanks to a newspaperman who saw him wandering about town that he checked into a hotel.

Thomson was scared, scared as much of a leather-lunged lady in Bristol's stands as of playing. A letter from brother Jim found him just in time. More than instruction—Don't criticize your manager! Slide hard into second!—it offered solace. Jim signed his note "your severest critic but most ardent admirer," a phrase the younger Thomson would never forget.

Bristol manager Hal Gruber already had a capable man at third where Thomson was slated to play and so granted him just twelve at-bats in five games. Thomson shared, meantime, a boarding house with three other players. Away from the strictures of home, the Scot got drunk a very first time. Gruber caught his boys red-cheeked. The very next day, after a cold shower, Thomson packed for Rocky Mount, North Carolina, New York's affiliate in the Bi-State league. The move, though, had nothing to do with alcohol—George Ferrell, Rocky Mount manager, needed a third baseman and had asked for Thomson.

Thomson's new team, the Rocks, were mid–road trip and conveniently in state at Danville. There on July 20 Thomson joined them, in the lineup that first night. He went hitless, then drove with the team after the game to a nearby café. Thomson slipped off to the bathroom. When he returned to the counter alone with his soft drink and thoughts, a voice interrupted: "Bub, didn't you come in on that bus?" Thomson looked up to see a police officer and none of his teammates. The Rocks had rolled. Thomson was distraught, his team not having noticed him missing. And when the cop offered a ride and caught the bus with his patrol car after a few hilly miles of Virginia countryside, Thomson attempted a joke. "Gee," he said, "do you forget a guy just because he goes oh-for-four the first time out?"

Rocky Mount returned home on July 22 to take on the Sanford Spinners. Nine hundred fans showed, their first look at Thomson a good one. One month out of high school, facing Roddey Ligon in the third, Thomson hit the first pitch thrown him for a home run. He added a single in the seventh and the fans, led by local booster Ed Hattum, fell hard. So did Thomson, the Scot smitten with professional ball. No matter that as resident rookie he had to sit in the windowless back of a team bus chilly atop wet uniforms, or that his spartan living quarters had just two shower heads for five Rocks, or that manager Ferrell soon procured for the team another third baseman, one J. M. Long, rendering Thomson a part-timer. Thomson was a ballplayer. And after just one week in Rocky

Mount, above a photo of Thomson kissing a bat held to his mouth like a long cob of corn, the local *Rocky Mount Telegram* ran the headline, "THIS BAT IS ROCKS' INSURANCE."

Thomson did indeed perform well. In 29 games, he amassed 21 hits and drove in 18 runs. One swing shone above the rest. On September 11, 1942, Rocky Mount faced Wilson in the seventh and deciding game of a playoff. The Rocks had trailed the Tobs three games to none only to come back and even up the series. Leading off the bottom of the sixth inning, his team up 5–3, Thomson crushed a Bill Koy fastball over the house behind the left-field wall. Koy departed and the 3,600 fans packed into Rocky Mount Municipal Stadium exploded in cheer. Rocky Mount went on to win the game 11–4, as best anyone knew just the second time in the history of professional baseball that a team three games down came back to win a series. (Newark had pulled the trick in AA in 1937.) Rocks fans passed a hat for Thomson, handing their rookie $11.

Rocky Mount went on to beat Sanford in the finals, four games to one. The season over, Thomson returned home, turned nineteen and went to work with brother Jim as a riveter at the Grumman defense plant in Linden, New Jersey, readying sheet metal for use in F4F Wildcat fighter planes. It seemed just a matter of time until the draft found Thomson and so he enlisted, upping on November 5, 1942, after just 34 games a professional baseball player.

At his brother's suggestion, Thomson chose the Air Corps, heading off to Miami Beach for basic training. And on February 2, 1943, after three months of marching and pushups, of mess halls and latrines, Private Thomson, serial number 12193923, took a train to Sioux Falls, South Dakota, to attend Army Air Corps radio school.

The next month, the Air Corps drafted another New York ballplaying teen, John Branca. And it was one month later that brother Ralph again threw batting practice for the Dodgers.

Branca decided he would graduate Davis a semester early. If Brooklyn signed him, he could thus begin his baseball career immediately. And so the pitcher now doubled his course load and applied to New York University, resolving to attend college in baseball's off-seasons. Midway through the semester, on a cold day in April, Branca arrived at Ebbets Field.

Branca undressed, warmed by the electric heaters Brooklyn clubhouse man Dan Comerford set about. The pitcher had grown, six feet, two and a half inches tall. And while he weighed just 145 pounds, his fastball now reached 88 miles per hour. Comerford handed Branca a jersey and the pitcher again found the plate, throwing batting practice to major leaguers.

High school batters were no match for Branca. Pitching for Davis, he won seven straight games, leading his team at season's end on June 4, 1943, to the Westchester Interscholastic title. He also excelled in the classroom, scoring above 90 on all his regents exams save Latin, and graduating in June a member of the National Honor Society. Thus did a plan come to fruition. NYU admitted Branca and Brooklyn promptly bid for him.

Mom in tow, Branca traveled to meet Labate at 215 Montague Street, Dodger headquarters. The pitcher happily signed on to play for $90 a month and, as he was not yet eighteen, his mother signed the contract too. Labate handed Branca a glove and an athletic supporter. The teen asked what the triangular dish was for, Labate panegyrized the cup, and the threesome walked around the corner to Joe's Restaurant for lunch.

Marooned in Sioux Falls, South Dakota, Thomson mastered the dots and dashes of Morse code. And on May 1, 1943, the private first class left to ply his trade in Wisconsin. A train deposited him northeast of Madison at Truax Field, the airport activated the previous June as an army air base.

Thomson dutifully spun beeps into text, fending off boredom for country. Typing beside his radio, decoding with ease, he got faster and faster. "I got up to thirty-five words a minute," says Thomson. It was not long before others at Truax turned to Thomson for help. Allows Thomson, "I used to do their papers for them."

Jim Thomson, however, soon informed his younger brother that he was thinking of leaving the USS *Astoria*, where he worked as a gunman, to work on a PT boat. Suddenly radio work seemed to Bobby like the junior varsity. "I'm playing around taking code on a typewriter," Thomson remembers thinking. And when soon after a fighter plane swooped low over Thomson's base, his mind was made up: he would apply to become an air cadet. On August 31, 1943, Thomson returned by train to Miami for a second dose of basic training.

Branca could not wait to pitch. Just days before, he had been a high schooler—now he sat on an Erie train next to Billy DeMars, destination Olean, New York. DeMars, a shortstop born in Brooklyn, was also seventeen, set to earn $10 more a month than Branca. Labate was there too, a chaperone sent by Brooklyn's brass. The train chugged northwest through the night, Branca and DeMars retiring to the shared upper berth of a sleeper.

Pitcher and shortstop arrived in Olean. They were Class D Oilers, wee teens within hours bunking at the YMCA, eating at Welch's Soda Bar, playing ball at Bradner Stadium against the rest of the Pony League. (Save baseball's one season of Class E ball that very summer, Class D was pro ball's lowest rung.) Branca played well enough. In 14 games for manager Jake Pitler, a 65-inch Jew from New York, he went 5–5 with a 4.63 ERA, yielding 154 runners in 101 innings and picking up a new nickname, Hawk, a nod by DeMars to his nozzle. The pitcher wrote of his progress in letters to Fern. And when Labor Day arrived and the season ended, Branca returned to her in Mount Vernon.

Home, it was time for school. Denied the chance at Davis to pursue math, Branca now found himself unqualified to follow engineering as had been his wont. And so the pitcher went the predictable route of the student-jock, enrolling in six classes toward a degree in physical education. (Uninspired, Branca earned three B's, two C's and, in Observation, Conference and Student Teaching in Community Organizations, an F.) At least Branca's education cost him nothing. NYU had tendered him a full athletic scholarship.

Thomson finished his second tour of basic training in Miami on October 1, 1943, and hopped a train for Minnesota. He was off to St. John's University, a private Catholic college converted that March into an Army Air Force training center. There awaited C.T.D.—college training detachment—four months of instruction that would turn the private to cadet and, later, to pilot, navigator or bombardier.

Thomson and his fellow privates reached Collegeville's little gray station late the next night. They were half asleep and a pack of air cadets stood waiting. "They hazed us," remembers Thomson. "Got in your face. Hollered 'do this and do that.'" Thomson eventually made his way to the town of St. Cloud, and there to a bunk bed on the fourth floor of St. John's Benet Hall.

A bugle roused Thomson and the rest of class 43-C-12 at six the next morning. At 7:15, the men ate chow. At eight, class began. And every class, from first aid to physics, centered on flight. "You see this?" a teacher asked Thomson and his fellow trainees, pointing at an EB6 computer. "This can do everything but what your wife can do for you." The lecture ascended into a calculation of wind angles.

It was Thomson who of all the St. John's privates lowered the flag at the close of special events. Inspired, he daily stomached regulation from reveille at 0600 hours to taps at 2200 hours, keeping his face shaven, his walls bare, his tailored wool khaki uniform pressed, his radio off after lights out, his knife, fork and spoon silent. And too his mitt hidden.

Baseball was among St. John's forbidden fruits, its gear, discovered, levying demerits. Inspection could come at any time. But Thomson felt his Rawlings worth the risk. "His glove was just so important to him," remembers Daniel Reed, one of Thomson's three roommates. "He kept it all oiled up." Thomson was lucky. Reed happened also to be first sergeant of their class. And excused from standing at attention during inspections, he took it upon himself to hide his friend's glove, usually in the latrine.

For all its bluster, though, life at St. John's was almost mild. Priests outnumbered military officers, hours in the classroom surpassed those in flight 70 to 1, Franciscan nuns baked yummy breads every morning, a basketball court lay in wait and, most weekends, cadets were free from three Saturday afternoon until ten Sunday night.

It was then the bars of St. Cloud beckoned. Just six blocks away, the Pink Elephant, Hotel Saint Cloud and Bloody Bucket (where a brawl seemed always on tap) welcomed with open arms their town's carousel of underage cadets.

So did its women. For the women of Saint Cloud were young and lonely, their men off in Europe fighting a war. In February 1944, WIL-CO, the military supplement of the St. John's student paper, warned its incoming class: "It will be necessary for them to carry clubs in town to discourage amorous females."

Thomson and his fellow males were amorous too. And as they marched ad nauseam about the St. John's campus, a female student spotted adrift, say Lucy, had suddenly to contend with the barked verse of sixty pubescents.

Lucy is a friend of mine!
She will do it any time!
For a nickel or a dime!
Twenty cents for overtime!

The trochees of Flight 27 rose in the cold Minnesota air into the open windows of female dormitory Shoemaker Hall. There in room 207 lived Millie Geistfeld.

Geistfeld understood marching. Raised on a farm in Lewisville, Minnesota, the girl had been a tomboy, happiest climbing trees. And nineteen, she was now a physical-education major set to graduate and teach in 1946.

It was then, one evening in the fall of her sophomore year, that Geist-feld entered her dorm room. She had stopped by the USO and amidst the drone of music and card games and forked food, met a man. His name was Bobby Thomson. This Geistfeld told her roommate and LaVone Bergstrom delighted. "Bob was the epitome for all the girls," remembers Bergstrom. "He was so shy and he was so tall." And now too, he was so taken.

Thomson found comfort in Geistfeld. She was merry in spite of hardship, unbroken in the wake of a father who had one night fled his home. A Lutheran-Missouri Synod, she possessed reassuring belief. She was smart, bumped ahead a year in elementary school. And she laughed and teased, a middle child honest with others and comfortable with herself. Among the sparsely bosomed at St. John's, only Geistfeld it seemed did not pad her brassiere. "She said," remembers her roommate, "this is the way God made me and this is what you get."

Thomson approved. Geistfeld had brown eyes and brown hair, a round face and full lips. She was thin, dressed comfortably in slacks and tennis shoes, and stood seven inches shorter than Thomson. Weekends the couple shared, talking, clinking drinks, watching movies and strolling, the hours until curfew honeyed with caresses in Talahi Park along the Mississippi River.

Geistfeld had dated before. But never before Thomson had she fallen. Says Bergstrom, "She really loved him." As for Thomson, all was entirely new. "Other than when I was in grammar school carrying someone's books home, I didn't have anyone," he says. "It was my first situation where I went with a girl, where you think you're in love."

That same fall of 1943, Branca donned satin shorts and the number 16 and played basketball at NYU. Determined under the basket, the baseball player became a hardcourt star, a 178-pound starting center. In January 1944, however, he stepped from the court, traveling to the draft board on Whitehall Street.

Newly eighteen, Branca hoped to become a navy pilot. But a physical examination revealed an eardrum he did not know had been punctured, his asthma a second strike. The military rejected Branca, stamping him 4F.

With help in math from roommate Reed, Thomson made his way through the air cadet's seven hundred hours of class. Ten hours of flying lessons were required too and these he took in a Piper Cub, taking off from Whitney Field at St. Cloud Municipal Airport. And of course there was physical training—calisthenics, obstacle courses and myriad marching drills, Thomson high-stepping along with his class, in step come parades and exhibitions.

It was at one such event that Thomson waited at the starting line of St. John's' cinder track. His stay in Minnesota was near complete and on this winter day, Thomson stood the anchor of a four-man relay. Crouched in tan fatigues, he took the baton and bolted after fellow Pfc. Jim Shanley—a Scot and Irishman racing for country in brown U.S. Army boots. Shanley, nineteen and athletic, stood little chance. For Thomson was blindingly fast, would years later in a ballgame on September 6, 1952, dash from home to first in 3.3 seconds, fastest that season in all the major leagues. A few hundred students watched as Thomson cut inside Shanley around the far turn. Shanley fell and Thomson won the race. But the presiding military officers disqualified Thomson. "They said I jostled him," Thomson remembers. "It was foolish because I would've won the race anyway." The shame would remain for Thomson the clearest memory of his four months in Minnesota.

Days later, high above dairy farms and fields of wheat, the nose of Thomson's Piper Cub dipped. The young cadet did not maintain altitude to code. No pilot, he set to become a bombardier, completing C.T.D. on February 12, 1944.

Thomson and Millie exchanged photographs, Millie's clasped in leather. The couple vowed to keep in touch and kissed good-bye. Thomson boarded a train westbound for Santa Ana, California.

Life at Santa Ana was more severe than at St. John's. Here preflight training was exhausting, all calisthenics and physical competition. And here at the Army Air Corps base, cadets had better maintain the sheen of a belt buckle, the pitch of a cap's peaks, the sixteenth-of-an-inch length of a fingernail. And so Millie's letters to Thomson were bittersweet, posts recalling the drawl of Minnesota schooldays.

But then a magical opportunity arose.

Joe DiMaggio had the previous February enlisted in the army, landing on February 24, 1943, in Santa Ana. The base organized a team at once, playing against military, college, semipro and Pacific Coast League teams. Now, just weeks after Thomson's arrival, DiMaggio and his team readied for their second season. A tryout was scheduled.

Thomson had been apart from baseball for eighteen months. Save an occasional catch, he had not played the game since September 1942 in Rocky Mount. But he still deeply loved ball. When one night a fire woke him in his barracks, he grabbed but one thing. "We're all standing out there in our underwear," remembers Thomson, "and I've got my glove." But now that owing to DiMaggio he had an opportunity to use it, he balked. For Thomson told himself that his ability was limited. And far from the encouragement of familiar coaches, he who had been a professional ballplayer did not now even try out for Santa Ana's team. Says Thomson, "I didn't think I'd have a chance."

Branca took the mound. Just months after being deemed physically unfit, he opened NYU's season on April 22, shutting out CCNY 3–0 in one hour and forty-eight minutes. Four days later he tossed another shutout, then on April 29 extended to 23 his string of consecutive scoreless innings. NYU's Violets played Wednesdays and Saturdays, and when in June their season ended, Branca had pitched most every game and won seven straight. The freshman finished 9–3 having thrown 100 innings, struck out 77, and given up 63 hits, 36 walks and 28 runs. He had also since September gained 27 pounds, now a solid 205, and his fastball approached 90 miles an hour. NYU coach Bill McCarthy was giddy. In Branca, he had a real major league prospect.

Trouble was, Branca was no prospect. The pitcher was *already* property of Brooklyn, had played at Olean. This Branca had not told his coach for fear of losing his scholarship. But McCarthy now told Branca that his brother was Boston's team doctor and that the Red Sox were interested. Boston, McCarthy said, was in fact hoping Branca might travel north for a tryout, might accept a $10,000 signing bonus. And so, Branca confessed.

The Brancas powwowed. Julius, he who had caught Ralph in the driveway, was now on furlough from the service and set off to persuade GM Branch Rickey to excuse his little brother from his contract. The Mahatma was unswayed. "If you found a jewel," asked Rickey, "would you give it up?"

There was, though, good news: Brooklyn was ready with a major league contract. Ralph was to meet Rickey in his office the morning of June 6.

Thomson packed his photo of Millie and on May 25 left DiMaggio and the rest of the Santa Ana team, heading 60 miles northeast to bombardier school in Victorville, California.

The charge of the bombardier was simple—to determine when exactly midair to drop a bomb. The tool of the bombardier was complex. An Indonesian mechanical engineer named Carl Norden had in the early thirties developed a bomb sight, able often from 21,000 feet to drop a bomb to within 1,000 feet of its target.

The Norden Bomb Sight was a top U.S. military secret, bombardiers covering their sights while escorting them to and from planes before takeoff and after landing. This Thomson did, toting it together with parachute and maps at Victorville Army Airfield. Aloft, he peered through his sight's eyepiece. And weighing as he had learned the speed and drift of his plane, he released at the precise moment his bombs, sandbags aimed for targets dotting California's orange Death Valley and jade Pacific coast.

Thomson had also learned the bombardier's oath. It concluded: "I do here, in the presence of Almighty God, swear by the Bombardier's Code of Honor to keep inviolate the secrecy of any and all confidential information revealed to me, and further to uphold the honor and integrity of the Army Air Forces, if need be, with my life itself." Thus did Thomson learn to guard, at all costs, a secret. And as he readied to go to the South Pacific, he had a secret to guard.

Thomson was twenty years old and in peak physical condition. He stood six feet one and a half inches, weighed 178 pounds, his chest 39 inches, his waist 31, his pulse rate 72, his vision 20-20. He had been healthy since suffering the measles and mumps in early childhood, hospital-free since a tonsillectomy in 1932. But while at Victorville, he developed hemorrhoids. And daily, lugging his fifty-pound sight, they flared. But Thomson feared that any medical attention might separate him from his peers. "I'd lose my class," he explains. And so he said nothing, secretly soaking himself every night in a tub of hot water.

This Thomson did for months until the night he awoke in his two-story barrack "my whole face swollen," he says. Medics drove him to Victorville's hospital. Thomson had a severe earache. Drops of penicillin nursed him to health but by the time he left the hospital weeks later, his fellow bombardiers had shipped overseas without him.

Branca climbed into bed the night before his meeting with Branch Rickey and, a world away, 57,500 American boys stormed Normandy's Channel coastline. The soldiers ran into the surf and, while Branca slept, overtook beaches code-named Gold, Juno, Omaha, Sword and Utah, the culmination of three years of American military planning. Branca awoke on the morning of June 6, 1944, an Allied foothold in Europe achieved. And even as he learned the news, learned that this was D-Day, military jargon for an unknown date of attack, he could be forgiven for thinking of baseball. He packed his glove, jock, spikes and sweatshirt and headed to Brooklyn.

Branca shook Rickey's hand. It was 10:30 in the morning and the men stood over a large wooden desk on the fifth floor of 215 Montague Street. Rickey produced a contract and Branca signed. And though the GM was sure to tell the kid that nothing was assured, that still he had to make the team, Branca knew he was a Dodger, a big leaguer at eighteen set to earn $400 a month.

Branca subwayed to Ebbets Field, entering with Labate the park's Italian-marble rotunda. The rookie needed a jersey and scout led pitcher to clubhouse where waited Comerford. Sizing up Dodgers in his celluloid collar since the nineteenth century, he now again beheld Branca. Comerford tagged Branca a 46, then asked him a question. "Are you superstitious?"

Branca was not, had as a kid in Mount Vernon purposely walked under the ladder that reached for the marquee at the Loews theater on Gramatan Avenue, had made a point when playing ball at Davis to step onto the foul lines others avoided. "I was contrary," says Branca. "Joe Contrary." Thirteen in fact had been his number. Comerford now told Branca that as pitcher Kirby Higbe was in the service, that same number was available. Branca accepted.

The pitcher, though, had to wait to put on his jersey. For that morning, more than four thousand Allied boys had died in Europe, and Major League Baseball, for a second time owing to world events, had canceled its roster of games.

Come morning, baseball resumed. Branca slipped on his blue number 13, stepped into his Wilson pants and clasped about his neck a St. Christopher medallion, the silver necklace given him by his mother the night before. It seemed a suitable gift. For the third-century martyr was strong, had carried baby Jesus across a stream, able to shoulder the weight of the world. Philadelphia beat Brooklyn 6–5. The Dodgers were in seventh place, 19–24, 9.5 games back of St. Louis.

Over the next four days, Branca watched his team win four and lose one. But he did not pitch.

Sunday morning arrived and with it Branca's first road game. His family excited—the game was in nearby Harlem. Katherine and her eldest, Antoinette, headed to the Polo Grounds, avid Giant fans resolved to root on Brooklyn.

At the end of one inning, 37 minutes and 19 batters after it began, New York led 5–4 and Brooklyn had already gone to its bullpen. In the second, Durocher tapped a second reliever and from right field, mother and daughter Branca saw Ralph head to the pen. Just two weeks prior he had sat through a Memorial Day doubleheader, a Giant fan in one of the green seats now above him. But today, June 12, he was a player and the Giants the opposition. In the third, he began to warm.

A three-run, two-out home run by Phil Weintraub in the bottom of the third gave New York an 11–5 lead. And after Nap Reyes and Gus Mancuso followed with singles, Durocher summoned his rookie right-hander.

Off in left-center field, Branca lifted his blue wool jacket from the bullpen bench and turned to the pitcher's mound some 400 feet away. Down then up the undulating outfield grass he walked, his pants big and billowy. Just eighteen years, five months and six days old, he was nervous, set to become the third-youngest Dodger in team history. "I felt like I was walking on a treadmill," he says. Sweat began to wet his face.

Katherine, Antoinette and 10,042 fellow fans watched Branca warm. He finished his tosses. Runners were on the corners and the teen set to work from the stretch, peering in at veteran catcher Mickey Owen, goat of the 1941 World Series. Giant shortstop Buddy Kerr walked to the plate. Branca struck him out with a curve.

Brooklyn failed to score in the top of the fourth and Branca returned to the mound. Bill Voiselle went down on strikes. So did Johnny Rucker. Katherine was delirious. So too were the myriad other Brancas listening in on WINS radio. The great Mel Ott strode to the plate. Here was Branca's hero, he whose baseball cards he had saved, he who had debuted in 1926 when Branca was not yet four months old. On this afternoon, player-manager Ott had already clubbed a home run and double. Branca looked toward Owen. He fired an inside fastball and Ott swung, meekly foul-popping to first. Side retired.

Branca pitched 3.1 innings, giving up two hits and a run, a solo home run to Weintraub. He had struck out three and walked none. He had been superb.

The game ended: New York 15, Brooklyn 9. And neither Wes Flowers, whom Branca relieved, nor Jack Franklin, who relieved Branca, would ever pitch in the big leagues again.

Branca changed and met his mother and sister outside the clubhouse on Eighth Avenue. They hugged and kissed him, then together took the subway home, stops clicking by—Sedgwick Avenue, Anderson Avenue, 167th Street—all the while Branca atop the mound at the Polo Grounds popping up the great Mel Ott.

It was not long before Fern, Branca's high school sweetheart, returned home from Virginia for the summer. Her letters had sustained Branca in Olean. And now that he was a big leaguer, he delighted in her watching him pitch. Game in, game out, Fern headed to Ebbets Field, found her seat among the players' wives and cheered. She dressed to the nines for Ralph, sitting one afternoon beside Mrs. Pee Wee Reese, she remembers, wearing "a leopard hat and a scarf and a dress."

Fern, though, had just six weeks to cheer. For Branca faltered on the mound, wild and hit hard in eighteen appearances. And when on August 5 he allowed Boston two hits and a walk in .2 innings, Brooklyn dispatched him to Montreal. There he was effective, making eleven starts in thirty-three days. And after pitching 16.2 innings in four September outings over the last ten days of Montreal's season, Branca returned to Brooklyn. Back in the big leagues he allowed three runs in seven innings over three appearances, a nice close to his season. But all told, the rookie had in 44.2 innings compiled a 7.05 ERA, walked twice as many men, 32, as he had struck out, and in 21 outings finished with an 0–2 record and one save. (He had also been tossed from a game, ejected in July by Bill Stewart when Durocher barked at the ump then hid behind his kid pitcher.) It was a start.

Branca returned to NYU, to the classroom, to the basketball court, to sitting at the rail at Washington Square Park, he says, and "watching all the broads go by." Fern had gone. She was back in Virginia, in junior college. Soon their romance was over, a victim of distance.

On November 25, 1944, Thomson graduated bombardier school, no longer an aviation cadet. The army gave him wings for his uniform, a raise to $150 a month, a new serial number—T-9669—and ordered him to active duty in Lemoore, California. Flight Officer Thomson headed northwest, joining Squadron T-1 of the 461st Army Air Field Base Unit of the Fourth Air Force.

It was a fortuitous assignment. Captain Sam Molnar at Lemoore loved baseball, had organized on the base a team which he now urged Thomson to join. Lemoore's was just a local team, Thomson told himself, had no DiMaggio to measure up to, to disappoint. And so at last Thomson donned his glove and trotted to short. He starred. "He used to play the tunes off those fences," remembers teammate Al Cutruzzula. Jim Thomson came to watch his brother play. "His remark was 'Bob, you've really improved,' " says Thomson. "I remember that. Even though I hadn't played, he was impressed."

Leo Durocher was also impressed. It was early March 1945, and the manager gazed at the teenager throwing inside the field house at West Point some fifty miles north of Manhattan. Branca was throwing hard—92, 93, 94 miles per hour. Durocher turned to him with a question: "What did you *do* this winter?"

Branca had done little more in winter than pine for spring, for spring training. He still weighed close to the 205 pounds he had the previous fall but he now felt somehow different. In 1944, says Branca, "I was still a boy. Next spring training I became a man."

His development was unexpected. Earlier that month, at the baseball writers dinner, newspaperman Roscoe McGowen sang a parody of "Bless 'em All," the 1941 World War II anthem, suggesting that perhaps Brooklyn should part ways with number 13.

> Cal McLish, big Ralph Branca, Clyde King—
> Busy bees, but they hadn't a sting!
> The Cardinals whacked 'em and thwacked 'em and cracked 'em.
> 'Twas six in a row. Lose 'em all!

The Dodgers, though, kept Branca, signing him on February 9 for $450 a month. And on April 18, a day after Opening Day, the team sent him with high hopes and a 33-percent raise to the St. Paul Saints, their AA team in Minnesota. "I can recall Branca at any minute if I want him," manager Durocher told the press. "He's going to be [a] major league pitcher, no doubt of that."

Just two months later he was. Branca had, in 15 games in Minnesota, gone 6–5 with a 3.33 ERA, striking out 94 in 100 innings. And on July 18, after Dodger Tom Seats walked Cub first baseman Phil Cavaretta to load the bases with two out in the seventh inning of the second game of a doubleheader at Wrigley Field, Durocher summoned Branca to the mound just hours after he had recalled him to Brooklyn. Slugger Andy Pafko came to bat. The count went full. Pafko grounded to short, Branca got the save and, for the rest of the season, he was a starter.

Through 15 starts, Branca, so young, relied entirely on Brooklyn's catchers to call his pitches—save one or two a game. These Charlie Dressen handpicked, the third base coach raising to his lips his fingers, unleashing a shrill whistle that called for the curve. Dressen whistled only at critical turns of a game. He did so for the first time with Branca on the mound on August 14, 1945, as Whitey Kurowski of St. Louis readied for a 3–1 pitch with two outs in the ninth inning of a game Branca and Brooklyn led 1–0. Branca, who had allowed just two hits all game, threw a curve and Kurowski hit a two-run home run to left-center field. St. Louis won 2–1 and Branca damned Dressen and his whistle.

Still, Branca was excellent in 1945. In 109.2 innings, he compiled an ERA of 3.04 and tossed seven complete games. Branca returned to NYU.

Thomson had stood on the chow line in the Victorville mess hall when word had come last June of D-Day. He had stood at shortstop when word had come in May that the war was over. "I threw my glove up in the air," he says. And when now Lemoore's baseball season ended, so did his military career. It was on October 16, 1945, that the army informed officer Thomson he had until 0800 hours on October 19 to report to McClellan Field, a separation base in Sacramento. Discharge took three days. After squaring his ledger (Thomson paid $418.76), he was again a civilian.

Branca meantime wished for at least a sniff of military life. And so, when days later an opportunity arose to travel to the Pacific on a USO baseball tour skippered by Dodger coach Dressen, he took it. Branca withdrew from classes on November 1 and forty days later shoved off.

Thomson stayed on the West Coast. "Baseball people knew me," he says, "and got me a job." Thomson worked in a steel factory in Oakland and played ball for the Roma Vintners and Ben's Golden Glow, local semipro teams sponsored by a winery and brewery. He starred and scout Joe Devine, he who had signed such greats as DiMaggio and the Waner brothers, offered the stick at third a job with the San Francisco Seals of the Pacific Coast League. Thomson, twenty-two, did not know if he was free to sign and so Devine, fifty, contacted baseball commissioner Happy Chandler. The reply was unequivocal—Thomson belonged to New York.

Thomson stuffed his duffel into a car of homeward-bound soldiers and in late December headed east. Sharing the drive, he arrived just before Christmas at 20 Nightingale Street in Staten Island. Jim, Ruby and Elizabeth greeted him. But it was to be a melancholic holiday. While Thomson's four sisters had married, Ruby had also been widowed, left alone at twenty-three to care for her baby Barbara, goddaughter of uncle Bobby. Husband William Mackay, an army lieutenant on duty in the Philippines, had been killed in March in Mindanao.

Branca visited that very island that very month. It was his first trip abroad, he and his fourteen teammates having already played ball for troops in Hawaii and Guam. Branca returned to the U.S. on January 22, flying into San Francisco, and phoned home, HIllcrest 3-186J. Brother Paul told him his Dodger contract had arrived, Brooklyn again offering $3,300. Branca was furious and told Paul to return the contract unsigned.

Thomson was certain the Giant front office would send him directly to Class D in Bristol, Virginia. But when February 1946 arrived, the team instead asked Thomson and their other returned servicemen to head to Jacksonville, Florida, spring training home of the Jersey City Giants, members of the newly designated AAA league.

Elizabeth Thomson sent off the boy she called "wee Rab." And once manager Bruno Betzel shifted him from third to center in early April, his skills surfaced, he who had played no higher than D ball a shoo-in to make New York's top farm club. This, though, Thomson did not mention to his brother or mother. His father's son, he knew better than to speak of himself. Jim became frustrated. And so toward the end of his little brother's spring training, he trekked to the Jersey City public library and combed past papers for mentions of Bobby. What Jim read amazed him. "The young Staten Islander," wrote the *Jersey Journal* on April 11, 1946, "is the apple of Betzel's eye, and consequently Mel Ott's too." Jim went straight to his mother with his findings, a smile on his face.

Home from San Francisco, still steamed at Rickey and his lowball offer, Branca headed on January 31 to Dodger headquarters in Flatbush. His pique only grew. For next morning, as spring training arrived, no new offer came from the general manager.

Still, Branca remained confident. He was twenty, big and strong, the only Branca long of six feet. He knew what he was worth. And when a crony of Jimmy Powers, father of the *Daily News* sportswriters, asked why he was spending his days in the classroom rather than on the hill, Branca was happy to tell that in two and a half years Brooklyn had paid him $5,500. Powers branded Rickey "El Cheapo" and the February and March sports pages had good copy. "Branch Rickey," wrote Powers, "paid Branca, his white starting pitcher, less money than a colored bus boy collects each week in the lowliest Miami hotel."

Apart from his team, Branca worked out. Four or five days a week, he tossed a ball at Mount Vernon's YMCA and ran there too, wearing as he zipped along more than one sweater, the better to perspire and stay trim. On Friday, February 22, *Brooklyn Eagle* reporter Ben Gould found Branca at the Y panting after a run. "I'll hold out," Branca vowed, "if it takes all summer."

Branca was prepared for Gould, statistical ammo at the ready. He told the reporter that his 3.04 ERA was tops on the club, that his 5–6 record was misleading, that "two of those games went against me because of errors. With a break here and there," he said, "my record might have been about ten won and two lost."

Branch Rickey, though, was unswayed. And on March 4, the GM countered in the same newspaper, "Boys like Branca must realize that they can't receive star wages until they make good in the big leagues."

Days later, Branca caved. The pitcher phoned Rickey, took the train to Florida and, on March 12, met him in Daytona Beach. Branca asked for six thousand dollars and accepted five. Despite his raise, the pitcher brooded. "He let me sit and stew," says Branca. "I had just turned twenty, still in diapers for Christ's sake."

Branca's self-will had impressed his teammates. And it was not long before Brooklyn captain Pee Wee Reese fingered him the club rep. If the players wanted a toilet installed near the dugout, the kid still in diapers would be the one to ask for it.

The end of Grapefruit League play found Thomson a Jersey City Giant. And no matter that his daily commute from Staten Island was a haul—bus, bus, ferry, bus, mile walk—he delighted that he could again live home with Mother. On April 18, 1946, his first day in Jersey, Thomson arrived at Roosevelt Stadium late, the team mid-meeting and already dressed. "I was mesmerized by all these bright new uniforms," he says.

It was Opening Day, and 51,872 folks from New Jersey, New York, Pennsylvania, Maryland and beyond filled the steel-and-concrete stadium just west of the intersection of Danforth Avenue and Route 440. The horde came to witness history—Jack Roosevelt Robinson, a black man from Pasadena, California, was slated to play and bat second for the visiting Montreal Royals. This he did, grounding the sixth pitch thrown him to short. Out 6–3, Robinson returned to the visitor's dugout the first black man of his century to play organized professional baseball outside the Negro leagues. He would finish the day with a home run to left, a single to right, two bunt singles, two stolen bases, three runs driven in and four runs scored (two via the balks of pitchers rattled by his jukes). And though Thomson, batting third, collected two hits, Jersey City lost 14–1.

Branca had pitched just 15 exhibition innings when on April 22, 1946, he made his first start. Wearing number 20 (Higbe had reclaimed the number 13), he pitched into the seventh, yielding four runs. But a line drive in the top of the second off the bat of Whitey Wietelmann had struck Branca flush on the right elbow and by the time Brooklyn bested Boston 5–4 in 10 innings, he was sore and stiff. Branca missed his next start.

Coach Dressen asked Branca to toss batting practice and he did. Soon after, Dressen repeated the request. Branca, twenty, was frustrated. "You can't," he snipped, "make any money pitching batting practice, Charlie." Dressen walked away without a word. The young pitcher's sense of self, his talk of money, had upset a second superior.

When Branca did pitch again, relieving on April 28 in the second game of a lost doubleheader at the Polo Grounds, he faltered, surrendering two runs on two hits and two walks in two innings. He threw not again until May 9, when Durocher asked of him just one inning in relief. Two days later he started against Philadelphia, chased after just two outs by five singles and four runs. Branca felt alienated and confided only in brother John.

Thomson quickly got used to his commute. The 150 minutes en route to Roosevelt Stadium were tranquil, a time to think. And twenty-two, his enthusiasm for Millie Geistfeld suddenly waned. "I then stopped communication, which wasn't a nice thing to do," says Thomson. "I wasn't proud of myself. I just disappeared into thin air."

Mist and mosquitoes wafted from Newark Bay into Roosevelt Stadium. The field was large—330 feet down the lines, 397 to the alleys, 411 to center. No matter. From day one, Thomson, an interlocking J and C on his royal-blue woolen cap, clobbered the ball. "BOBBY THOMSON'S HITTING LONE FEATURE OF JERSEYS," read a *Jersey Journal* headline on July 27, 1946. "Each time Bobby steps to the plate," added the paper on August 5, "the chants and cheers arise." While Thomson endured occasional sliding and fielding problems, he finished his season tops on the club in hits, triples, runs batted in, stolen bases and home runs, his 26 drives shattering the club mark of 20 set by Jack Winsett in 1938. Thomson was a AAA star.

Early in the season, the third baseman and outfielder had received his very first autograph request, a mailed plea for a signed picture. Dutifully Thomson headed to a local photographer in Staten Island, mugged, signed his name across the black-and-white photo and mailed it. In case of future requests, the Scot bought a dozen prints of the photo at 25 cents each, a dozen envelopes at a nickel each and twelve 3-cent stamps.

The Giants were delighted. Thomson had spent scant time in the minors—185 games over two seasons. Prior to 1946 he had been away from organized ball for three years. And not one of his 1942 Rocky Mount mates had risen to the majors. Yet here he was at twenty-two, 190 pounds and just shy of six feet three, driving the ball with an easy swing, a natural power born of his legs and wrists. And so when on September 8, 1946, Jersey City's season ended, New York asked Thomson to join the big league club then en route to Philadelphia.

Thomson arrived the next morning at Shibe Park. Oh, how proud his father would have been! This Thomson thought of as he buttoned his major league jersey, number 23, the available number, his year of birth, given him at random by clubhouse man Fred Logan. James Thomson had loved baseball. Only baseball, a home run by Brooklyn Dodger Camilli, had roused him to jump in cheer. Only pride in his son's baseball ability had nudged him to the precipice of vainglory. This, somewhere, the son knew, and as he trotted out to third base on September 9, 1946, a steamy night in Philadelphia, he allowed himself a moment's excitement.

Thomson fielded no balls in the first, and in the second, he lofted a Charley Schanz pitch to center-fielder Johnny Wyrostek. But by game's end, a 5–4 loss, he had singled, doubled, scored a run, driven in two and marvelously scooped with his pint-sized Rawlings a throw from Sid Gordon in left field to nail Wyrostek at third. It mattered neither that Thomson's family was not there to take in his debut nor that New York, 56–80 and 30 games behind St. Louis, was playing out the string of a lost season, battling Philly for sixth place. Beneath the lights and 11,899 fans, Thomson had glowed.

Five days later, Branca stood atop the fifteen-inch mound at Ebbets Field warming up. Durocher had declared him Brooklyn's starter and now, as the Bulova clock atop the Con Edison scoreboard in right-center field read 2:30, so he appeared to be. But he was just a decoy. Unbeknownst to St. Louis leadoff man Red Schoendienst, Branca would face only him, to be replaced by southpaw Vic Lombardi after just one batter. It was an old trick—St. Louis having stocked its lineup with lefties in preparation for the right-handed Branca would thus be disadvantaged.

Durocher's willingness to squander Branca's arm infuriated the pitcher. He was no gimmick, no ploy. Since getting licked by the Phillies on May 11 he had pitched well, compiled a 4.26 ERA in 31.2 innings over four starts and ten stints in relief. Branca told himself that he deserved better and now, with each warm-up pitch fired at catcher Bruce Edwards, he cursed Durocher, grunting, "Sacrificial lamb my fucking ass!"

Schoendienst had no chance. He popped up Branca's fifth pitch to first.

Branca waited to be lifted. But as Harry Walker came to bat, Durocher stayed in the dugout. Branca popped up Walker, grounded out Stan Musial and left the mound. Durocher greeted his pitcher: "Keep thinking like that, kid, I'll keep you in." Branca pitched a three-hit shutout.

Whereas coach Dressen had turned his back on Branca, Durocher had channeled his brashness, and the pitcher sat now before his locker transformed. Something was suddenly very different. Years later it would seem to him that on this Saturday afternoon he was at age twenty tempered, steel fired then cooled. Already confident, he now went to sleep trusting his ability implicitly. Says Branca, "I believed in myself."

Thomson was nervous up in the big leagues. He jogged to his position and walked to the batter's box in front of tens of thousands of fans, and their daily shouts proved unsettling. It was not long before a recurring nightmare plagued the rookie's September nights, a dreamed female fan in a ballpark's front row screaming at the young third baseman: "Come on, kid! When you gonna get a hit?"

Thomson's commute to the park was longer when home than away, and after night games at the Polo Grounds he stayed at the King Edward Hotel at 120 West 44th Street. Still, he relished the half-hour ferryboat ride home. "Helps to get the noise of the ball park and the subways out of your ears," he told *Baseball* magazine.

Staten Island was for Thomson a balm to the bustle of ball. The borough was cloistered, Manhattan accessible only by ferry. Less than 200,000 people filled its fifty-seven square miles, one-tenth the population of Manhattan spread over two and a half times the acreage. It was beautiful land too, wooded and birded with salt marshes, a bog and—just down the road from Thomson in the Moravian Cemetery—Todt Hill, at 417 feet, the highest point between Maine and Florida overlooking the Atlantic. It was below on Staten Island's beach that Thomson retreated with his brother to work on his slide, newly planted Cape Cod beach grass growing all about.

Sliding had always been Thomson's greatest weakness. It was almost as if because of great speed he found himself upon his destination too soon. "At the last moment," he once explained to *Baseball* magazine, "my legs seem to freeze up and I wind up plowing into the bag head first." That Thomson was fast made his further inability to break up the double play and advance the extra base all the more frustrating.

Jim now arranged for his brother running lessons with Jack Brown, his old Columbia track coach. Thomson ran two miles on an outdoor wooden track, then took pointers from Brown on how to better turn a base using his arms.

These came in handy. In 18 games in 1946, Thomson four times chugged for doubles, once for a triple. And though he stole no bases, more than once was picked off first and botched three plays in 46 chances at third, he slugged two homers, batted .315 and made $600, silencing the screaming woman of his dreams.

Ralph Branca had had a good season too. After holding out for a better contract, he had made 23 appearances—nine of them starts—and gone 3–0 with three saves, two shutouts and a 3.62 ERA. Yes, there was obvious room for improvement: in 64.2 innings, he had walked exactly as many men, 39, as he had struck out. But undeniably was he starbound. And so the Minnesota apparel company Munsingwear, Inc., signed Branca to his first endorsement deal for a few hundred dollars, the resultant ad odd, a drawing of Branca, rear end in air, having just delivered a pitch. A tagline—"To pitch like Ralph Branca be sure to dress like this"—gave way to a second drawing of a man in elastic-waisted underwear, standing in a position identical to Branca's.

On October 1, 1946, Branca stepped into his Munsingwear ready to pitch the biggest game of his twenty years. While Thomson's Giants had gone 61–93, good for last place, Branca's Dodgers had finished 35 games ahead tied with the Cardinals for first. Brooklyn and St. Louis would play a best-of-three series, the first time in the seventy-five years of Major League Baseball that a playoff would decide the pennant.

Durocher named Branca his starter with confidence—the pitcher had dominated St. Louis two weeks prior, allowing no runs and three hits. "It'll be Ralph Branca," the manager told the *New York Times*. "And we'll win."

Jimmy Carroll was less sure. The St. Louis betting commissioner listed Branca a 3-to-2 underdog, favoring instead southpaw Howie Pollet and his 2.10 ERA. The Cardinal set down the first three Dodgers in order.

The air was cool, befitting this first week of professional football, and Branca walked to the mound in his blue-gray woolen jersey. Given the stage, the crowd of 26,012 was skimpy, 8,000 seats unfilled, the megaphone-toting ushers and sixty policemen on patrol not quite needed.

Still, the occasion frazzled Branca. Back home in Flatbush, where in freezing rain a queue of ten thousand formed for tickets, Branca's glove sat. He had left his Rawlings, a Mort Cooper model, in his locker. The pitcher had forgotten also his wallet, leaving it stuffed with $200 that morning under a pillow in his St. Louis hotel room. Branca did remember, however, that seventeen days before he had retired leadoff man Schoendienst and he now threw him a low fastball for strike three. Terry Moore followed with a single to left. But Branca froze Stan Musial and his .366 average with the same pitch he had Schoendienst. Two outs. Enos Slaughter singled to right and on four pitches Whitey Kurowski walked. Bases loaded. The next batter was Joe Garagiola, a local boy. Like Branca he was just twenty, the youngest catcher in all baseball. Garagiola ran the count full, then, true to his reputation, hit not more than a high-bouncing nub behind the mound. Branca, Lavagetto, Stanky and Reese converged on it, the shortstop finally firing a one-hopper to first. Too late. Though Durocher argued umpire Babe Pinelli's call, St. Louis led one–zip. A Harry Walker groundout to Reese ended the inning.

Brooklyn first baseman Howie Schultz sent Pollet's first pitch of the third inning 358 feet into the first row of the left-field bleachers to tie the game at one. But Kurowski untied it in the bottom of the inning when Brooklyn failed to turn two on his force-out to short. Garagiola then singled to center and Walker came to bat with runners on first and second. The lefty bounced right back to the box, a limp hopper any pitcher should glove. Big Branca, though, could not turn in time against his follow-through and Walker's bleeder trickled on, rolling off Stanky's glove into the shallowest of center field. St. Louis led 3–1. Branca was done.

After 168 minutes so too was Brooklyn, defeated this cloudless Tuesday 4–2. Branca, who had not lost since September 16, 1945, more than a year past, was collared with the defeat.

It was not just another loss. This Branca knew. Baseball's first-ever playoff had had all the trappings of a World Series game, luring to Sportsman's Park a dozen photographers, fifty writers, broadcasters from Cuba. Its outcome had even clamped the verbose Lip, Durocher clomping out of a shower in wooden clogs to yell "No comment!"

But as the long-faced pitcher mourned, saw his edgy teammates bicker through games of gin rummy on a train chugging east, he felt his fate unfair. Branca had been done in by bloops. "They got a lot of flub hits," he said years later. "They totaled three hundred feet."

Others were less sparing of Branca. For he had retired just half of the sixteen men he faced. "The 20-year-old righthander," wrote Joe Trimble of the *Daily News,* "was a boy doing a man's errand."

Press coverage of the playoff was great, a nation grateful that rid of war, its pastime was again whole. Among the millions hanging on every interview of Dodger and Cardinal was Thomson. And after St. Louis beat Brooklyn 8–4 on October 3 to advance to the World Series, he too was pumped for information, sent in this his first autumn a major leaguer a questionnaire by the National League Service Bureau. Thomson shared that he weighed 193 pounds, enjoyed golf, was born in Glasgow, felt brother Jim his greatest booster. There were other questions.

Q: "List outstanding performances of career to date (no-hit games, grand-slam home runs, big days at bat, etc.)"

The league provided more room for this answer than any other, a full three lines. Still, Thomson was stingy with his response.

A: "hit several grand slam home runs for Jersey City."
Q: "Do you have (or have you had) any other trade?"

Thomson returned the questionnaire to room 1909, 30 Rockefeller Plaza, this last question unanswered. He had no inkling of a second someday-vocation. And he carried within him a related ache, a dissatisfaction with his lack of higher education and what had been his struggles in the high school classroom. (All his life he would refuse to consider that it was only after his father turned ill that he had, at fifteen, failed classes.) And so now on October 7, 1946, Thomson, almost twenty-three, set out to ease what gnawed at him, enrolling at Saint Lawrence University in Canton, New York.

Thomson had not applied to the university. Rather, Hal Schumacher, Saint Lawrence alumnus and star Giant pitcher of the thirties, had sold Thomson on the coed liberal arts school and arranged for his acceptance. Four and a half years since he last attended school, Thomson was eager now to do so again. University, he explained the following fall to *Baseball* magazine, might someday "help me get the swing of things in returning to civilian life."

Thomson had a head start on his degree, Saint Lawrence granting the bombardier eight "war credits" and another sixteen from high school. He had also a roommate.

Victor Sacco slept in the twin bed to Thomson's right. He liked Thomson. "He had an easy way about him," remembers Sacco. "He was very quiet, slow-speaking." And in his third-floor dorm room, Thomson spoke little of himself. It was weeks before he told Sacco, a Detroit Tigers fan, that he *was* a New York Giant.

Clear though was that Thomson was an athlete. When playing touch football for the dorm team, his arm made waves. "Folks came to watch me throw," says Thomson.

Like Thomson, Sacco was an older freshman, an athlete, hailed from New York and had been a bombardier, flying sixty-two missions through North Africa and Europe. The roommates were also different. Sacco was social and naturally studious, an aspiring English major with a penchant for the Romantic poets. Thomson meantime—enrolled in a math, a history and an English course—was struggling. "He found studying rather hard," says Sacco. "His mind would wander and he'd go take a walk." Downtown Canton beckoned just two blocks away and there, amidst maples, elms, poplars and cedars, the baseball player strolled along the Grasse River frustrated by his lack of focus. "He wishes," explained his daughter Nancy years later, "he could read articles in the paper and remember exactly what he's read, give different people's viewpoints."

Thomson wondered if perhaps a quieter study space might help. And so in November he moved with Sacco into a bedroom at 1 University Avenue, home of John and Josephine Mentley, Saint Lawrence superintendent and librarian.

Study remained elusive. "I was starting to slip," says Thomson. "I was afraid of my studies. And then I got a letter from the Giants and that didn't help one bit."

The letter invited Thomson to join Johnny Mize, Walker Cooper, Bennie Warren and some other players at Buckhorn Mineral Baths, a motel beside hot springs in Mesa that had been a favorite of spring-training Giants since 1939. Thomson wished to accept. Jim, though, was furious at the prospect of his brother abandoning his education. "If you leave school," he told Bobby, "I'll never advise you on another thing."

Branca enjoyed the classroom but studied only when engrossed. (His 1944 fall semester grades had been telling: an A in Introduction to Physics, an F in Teaching Physical Education in Junior High School.) This mattered not at all. For as his third autumn at NYU filled now in 1946 with six classes, he was already a professional and, more, a success. Baseball had in October flown him to Cuba with a team of all-stars. Rickey had the season past given the pitcher his first car, a light tan Studebaker. And by the time Branca turned twenty-one on January 6, 1947, he had bought his parents a new home at 409 Seneca Avenue, brother Paul decorating the beige Tudor, a lavender glass vase set in the living room credenza.

That very day, Thomson left Saint Lawrence for a spa in Arizona, the registrar noting in his dossier that he withdrew "for baseball training." "That was a good excuse," says Thomson. Never again would he return to school.

Jim overcame his anger, the next month loading up with Bobby his old car and heading west. The older brother went to North American Aircraft Corporation in Los Angeles, the younger to Giant spring training in Phoenix.

Despite past work on the beach, Thomson appeared lost in the sliding pit—a box of sand with a base tethered by a belt to a stake. But running, he was a marvel. When manager Ott split his players into seven sextets and had each race sixty yards, pitted against New York's fastest—Buddy Blattner, Whitey Lockman, Jack Maguire, Al White and Lloyd Gearhart— Thomson won his dash by a full yard, the fastest man on all his team.

Ott auditioned Thomson at third, rotating him with Sid Gordon and Jack Lohrke. There Thomson played well. The manager wanted him on his club and had New York give Thomson an $8,000 contract—$3,000 above the league minimum. Second baseman Blattner meantime faltered. And so, just before season's start, on a private train heading back to New York, Ott asked Thomson if he might try second. Thomson said yes.

The Cleveland Indians had trained near New York in Tucson. The team happened to be on the same train and Indian second baseman Joe Gordon happened to be a friend of Ott's. And so, steaming east, Ott now asked Gordon to help Thomson, to tutor his young Scot on the position. Gordon agreed and when the two teams, en route home, stopped to barnstorm, to perform afield in a few sleepy towns, Gordon coached Thomson on how best to turn the double play.

There was much though Thomson had yet to learn. This was apparent on April 15, 1947, when in the sixth inning of Opening Day, Thomson, starting at second in Philadelphia, failed to get down on a grounder hit by Del Ennis. The ball skittered through him and New York lost 4–3. Thomson, though, had homered off Schoolboy Rowe in the second, his shot to left the very first home run of 1947 in all the league.

This same Tuesday, minutes before two, Jackie Robinson stood on a white baseline in Brooklyn, the first black major leaguer since Moses and Welday Walker played for the Toledo Blue Stockings in 1884. As on every Opening Day, two rosters now extended perpendicularly from home plate. And it was no coincidence that just to the right of Robinson stood Branca. "It didn't bother me being next to him," says Branca. "Growing up, it was a league of nations on my block." Reaching base on a bunt-induced error, Robinson scored the lead run in a 5–3 win.

Three days later Brooklyn set to take on New York at the Polo Grounds. The temperature was a lovely sixty degrees and Branca made his way to Harlem from Mount Vernon, Thomson from Staten Island. For the first time in their lives, the men would suit up in the same game.

Thomson walked in the Giant dugout—six curved metal cleats heading on wood toward a batboy and his racked bats. "What's your name, Bub?" asked Thomson. It was Garth Garreau and this, the Giant home opener, his first game as batboy for the home team. Thomson's greeting relaxed him. "How about a bat for me?" continued Thomson. "Give me the one with the hits in it."

Schumacher, the Saint Lawrence alum, had recently gone to work for McLaughlin-Millard, Inc., maker of Adirondack bats. And so, even as most of the league used Louisville Sluggers, New York filled its bat rack with Schumacher's lumber. Garreau, eighteen, handed Thomson a thirty-four-ounce Adirondack and together they stepped from dugout to on-deck circle. Player and batboy knelt.

Big Willard Marshall took an outside fastball. Ball one. The bottom of the second was under way and Thomson reached for Garreau's hand, crossing his middle and index fingers. "Keep them that way when I'm up there," he said. Marshall grounded out to second and as Thomson walked to the plate, Garreau handed Lohrke, up next, a bat, then ran back to the on-deck circle, his fingers crossed.

Dodger Vic Lombardi's sixth pitch to Thomson was an inside fastball and Thomson turned on it, the ball soaring high toward left-center field and from there, farther still beyond the bullpen. It landed in the upper deck, a home run. Thomson stepped on home plate, then shook Garreau's hand. "Nice going, Bub!" he told the batboy. Long after Thomson added another home run and two singles, after New York triumphed 10–4, after Garreau returned home to Teaneck, New Jersey, after the 1947 baseball season ended and the next season too, Garreau held on to that moment. "Bobby Thomson," he wrote two years later, "had stopped to shake my hand!" The shy ballplayer had grown famous, his simple gesture the high point of a young man's day.

On a single Friday afternoon, Thomson had matched his home run total of the previous year. Still one thing bothered him—none of his family had seen him do it. "I thought the place was sold out for today's game," he explained to reporter Leonard Cohen, "and never thought of asking anyone for some tickets."

Elizabeth Thomson settled the next afternoon in her green, shallow seat. For the first time this young season, she would see her son play. Mrs. Branca was present too. The season's fourth contest, it was to be her fifth son's first outing and as always on days he set to pitch at home, she was present, scorecard in hand. When in the bottom of the first, Branca walked Lloyd Gearhart on five straight fastballs, she jotted "BB." And when Johnny Mize hit an outside fastball to right for a home run, she drew four dashes.

It was still 2–0 in the second when Thomson took a bat from Garreau and walked to the plate. Team doctor Anthony Palermo had before the game vaccinated the Giants for smallpox. Inoculated, Thomson set now to face Branca for the first time, the thirty-five miles that had separated their childhoods shrunk to sixty feet, six inches.

Branca, two years Thomson's junior, was the veteran ballplayer, this his sixty-second outing. Thomson meantime readied for just his sixty-fifth official major league at-bat.

Pitcher and batter wore different numbers than they had the previous season—Branca reunited with 13, Thomson wearing 19, his 23 given to the hyped Clint Hartung. Branca, 212 pounds, wound and fired. The pitch was low and inside and Allan Roth, Brooklyn's statistician among the 37,546 on hand, annotated the ball in his scorecard. A curve not swung at evened the count, followed by a high inside fastball fouled off and a high inside curve taken for ball two. The count did not go full. Thomson skyed Branca's next pitch, a fastball down the middle, to center, where Snider put it away for the first out of the inning.

Thomson did not fare better in the third, grounding a low inside curve to third for a 5–4 force-out at second. And by the time Thomson came to bat again in the fifth, Branca had departed, pulled by manager Burt Shotton after yielding eight hits, three walks and four runs in 4.1 innings. New York went on to win 4–3, Branca hung with the loss.

Thomson and the Giants lost their next five games. Their fielding was particularly shoddy, among the weak gloves, Lloyd Gearhart, Al White and Joe Lafata in center field, and Thomson at second where in nine games he had committed five errors. And so among the changes manager Ott announced on Monday April 28, 1947, was the shift of Thomson from second to center.

There the young Scot flourished. The position showcased his great speed—all the more apparent on his vast home field. And while occasionally Thomson threw to the wrong base and sometimes even off the wrong foot, in little time was he sure of his glove, his shallow positioning, his break on the ball. Thomson had, through 50 games, more assists, three, than errors. And by year's end, his range would surpass the average National League center fielder's by .5 balls a game, 2.69 to 2.19.

Comfortable afield, Thomson lost nothing at the plate, batting .295 with 12 home runs and 40 runs batted in at the all-star break. He was happy too, good friends with two other quiet and talented Giants—Whitey Lockman and Larry Jansen. Often after games the men would drive upstate to a cottage Thomson rented for his mother in Greenwood Lake, there to canoe and swim and eat and talk baseball. When heading into the break on July 6 Jansen beat Philadelphia 4–3, New York trailed Brooklyn by just 1.5 games.

That same day, Branca pitched Brooklyn over Boston 4–0. The shutout was his fifth straight win, lifting his record to 12–6, lowering his ERA to 2.67. Though a lowball pitcher, his fastball more and more rose in the zone and by all rights, he was an all-star. Eddie Dyer agreed, the genteel Louisianan, manager of the National League squad, inviting Branca to Chicago along with pitchers Ewell Blackwell, Harry Brecheen, Red Munger, Schoolboy Rowe, Johnny Sain and Warren Spahn.

Dyer did not pitch Branca at windy Wrigley. The young Dodger instead watched from the dugout his all-star mates lose 2–1 on a run-scoring single by Stan Spence in the seventh. But two days later, a fully rested Branca pitched 11 innings to win both ends of doubleheader, coming in in relief to close out the Cubs in the nightcap, his mother among 35,876 rooters screaming in appreciation.

Branca had won seven games in a row—not to mention his team's last three, the second-to-last starting pitcher ever to do so. (Sam Jones did it in 1959.) He was now a robust 14–6 and each of his siblings from Al, nineteen and pitching Class B ball in Stamford, Connecticut, to Antoinette, forty-two and running a physician's message service in Tuckahoe, New York, rooted on their relation, three, four, five Brancas at each of his starts. "Each pitch we were on tenterhooks," says John. "It was fantastic."

And so it was with pleasure that Paul Branca, enrolled at Parsons School of Design, handled Ralph's fan mail, scything his way through the adulation mailed his famous brother. "He would prepare the mail, clip it to envelopes," says Ralph. "He made it easy for me." Ralph had only to sign his name.

Young Branca was the talk of Brooklyn and of all Mount Vernon too. And on August 13, 1947, Mount Vernon mayor William Hussey and Brooklyn borough president James Cashmore stood before 31,684 fans at Ebbets Field to praise him and his 17 wins. It was "Mount Vernon Day" at the ballpark, the men also honoring Boston relief pitcher Andy Karl, Mount Vernonite Karl in town with his Braves to take on the Dodgers.

The affair drew 1,500 fans in twenty buses. Near 5 percent of the crowd, they came to the ballgame to exult, and this they did orgiastically, madly applauding every microphoned hosanna and offering, from the scroll of thanks signed by 5,000 Mount Vernon children to the his-and-his portable radios, bronze plaques and $1,000 bonds they themselves had footed, each paying $3 for a $1.75 ticket.

"There will be other great days," wrote Guido Cribari in Mount Vernon's hometown *Daily Argus,* "but it is doubtful if any will surpass the spine-tingling demonstrations of civic pride and spirit displayed by the 1,500 proud people of Mount Vernon."

Brooklyn triumphed 10–5, Branca smiling all the while, a hero at twenty-one.

Thomson readied for a similar fête. The rookie center fielder had been magnificent—in 129 games scoring 100 runs, driving in 81, hitting .284 with 26 home runs. And on September 20, Staten Island wished to say thank you, fans gathering this Saturday at the Polo Grounds for a Giant–Phillie contest hailed as "Bobby Thomson Day."

One by one, borough representatives presented Thomson gifts at home plate. There was a plaque, a camera, a radio, two pen-and-pencil sets, a car—a black Buick convertible bought by Staten Islanders and wheeled into the Polo Grounds that morning. The uniformed ballplayer accepted each with a handshake and smile. Then he stepped to the microphone.

Thomson had worried that at this moment he might forget his thoughts. And so, he says, "my brother made up a speech for me." The typewritten notes of thanks lay tucked in Thomson's cap, which he now doffed. Scared, grateful and humble, he spoke, peering down at words he had rehearsed the night before. Some 4,500 members of the Police Athletic League come to cheer their alum now stood, more than a third the small crowd. So did Thomson's mom—she given flowers in a first-base box. Her son, gushing, waved his cap above his head. His speech fluttered in the breeze. Perilously close to wafting free, it caught the eyes of his teammates. The players giggled, the crowd quieted and Thomson resumed his thanks. The crowd again cheered, Thomson again doffed his cap, notes again fluttering, again holding on, a lineup again laughing. Thus did the center fielder, oblivious, continue on, Thomson tipping his black cap in thanks six times, a team of mighty Giants wheezing in laughter.

New York beat Philadelphia 5–3, a solo shot by Thomson one of three Giant home runs. The team's power was historic. When eight days later their season ended, Giant batters had slugged a record 221 home runs, shattering with their Adirondack bats the previous mark of 182. Thomson himself finished with 29, good for fifth-most in the league. (A thirtieth off Harry Brecheen was lost to a rainout.) The Scot added 85 runs driven in, 105 scored, 60 extra-base hits and a .283 average.

Thomson had wowed the baseball world. "Of the newcomers of 1947 in our circuit," Mize told the *Sporting News*, "he has the best chance to make the Hall of Fame." Thomson was powerful, whistling fast and, once in center, a very good fielder. (In 127 games, he committed just seven errors.) And so, no matter that he was ostensibly a rookie or that he had fanned 78 times (in all the league only Bill Nicholson and Ralph Kiner struck out more), many comparisons were made between the quiet center fielder and the great Joe DiMaggio, their wide stances and mild miens too similar to ignore. Asked a *New York World-Telegram and Sun* headline on September 22, 1947, "JUNIOR THOMSON A NEW DIMAG?"

At least one pitcher, though, gave him fits. In 10 at-bats against Branca, Thomson managed but one single, fanning twice.

Few in 1947 had fared much better against the big right-hander.

Branca had led Brooklyn to the pennant, starting an incredible 36 games, most in all the league. He had thrown 280 innings, 15 complete games, four shutouts. Pitching so much (he threw an additional seven times in relief), it was not surprising that he had surrendered 22 home runs, second-most in the league, or more base runners than any other National League pitcher, allowing 251 hits and 98 walks. But his ERA was an excellent 2.67, he had fanned 148 batters, controlled the inside of the plate (he led the league with six hit batsmen), and halved his walks-per-nine-innings from 6.48 in 1945 to 3.15. And so it was that Branca won 21 games and saved another, at twenty-one the youngest Dodger ever to win 20 games in a season. Just seven other pitchers in all the century had done so by age twenty-one—Christy Mathewson, Joe Wood, Al Mamaux, Babe Ruth, Pete Schneider, Wes Ferrell and Bob Feller who had pulled the feat twice. Branca was an ace.

It surprised no one when on September 30, 1947, after Brooklyn finished its season in first place five games ahead of St. Louis, Shotton named Branca starter of Game One of the World Series.

An enormous crowd of 73,365, the largest ever to attend a World Series game, congealed all about Branca, there at Yankee Stadium to behold the start of a Subway Series. Such a multitude swelled receipts. On this temperate Tuesday, the players' take was a cool $166,172.64, the pot to be divvied later. Branca hoped for a winner's share. All season he had earned just $6,500.

Branca felt strong. He weighed 221 pounds, had put on nine pounds since Opening Day. And he was rested, had not pitched in five days. A Dixie Walker first-inning single put him up 1–0 and Branca now took the mound, on this last day of September a baseball prince. Eminence had come quickly, he the very youngest pitcher ever to start the first game of a World Series. (He remains so at this writing.) Just five years prior, he had toed the same rubber auditioning for a job. Yankee scout Bender had never, as promised, called the kid of sixteen back. And now, in the bottom of the first inning, his organization readied to face the man. The fastballer cut through the top of the Yankee lineup in order—Snuffy Stirnweiss, Tommy Henrich, Yogi Berra.

Inning after inning, Brooklyn failed to pad its lead, rookie righty Spec Shea yielding just two singles through five innings. But Branca was even better. Heading to the bottom of the fifth, 12 Yankees had come up and 12 gone down, Branca just the sixth pitcher in 252 World Series games perfect into the fifth. He set to face Joe DiMaggio and far off in the upper left-field stands so did Branca's parents and six of his siblings.

DiMaggio smacked a Branca inside fastball deep into the hole at short. Pee Wee Reese ranged far to his right and gloved the ball. But his throw was late and the center fielder was on. First baseman George McQuinn came to bat and for the first time all game, Branca forwent his windup for the stretch (the better to hold DiMaggio at first). Then, in seconds it seemed, a masterpiece spoiled—McQuinn walked, third baseman Bill Johnson plunked on the left arm, left-fielder Johnny Lindell depositing a ball atop the foul line in left to score two.

"There are times when I say to myself," Branca confided later to the *New York Sun*, " 'Why did I ever have to be a ballplayer? Why couldn't I do something else?' " Now was such a moment, Branca suddenly aware of the stage, of the 150,000 eyes upon him, of his magisterial opponents, owners of 10 championships, winners that season of 19 straight, scorers of 5.12 runs a game. His tempo had slowed, grown arrhythmic, his control lost with his poise. And Yankee third-base coach Charlie Dressen, he who had managed Branca in Asia and coached him the previous fall in Brooklyn, was now razzing the pitcher unstintingly.

Hundreds of feet from play, John Branca wished to grow wings, to fly to the mound and settle his kid brother. But he could not. And not one of Branca's teammates approached the mound, Dodgers only watching together with John, when Branca, overthrowing, walked Rizzuto to load the bases, then threw two pitches wide of home to go 2–0 on pinch-hitter Bobby Brown.

Shotton lifted Branca. The crowd cheered kindly and reliever Hank Behrman completed the walk of Brown.

After retiring 12 straight, Branca had allowed 6 consecutive batters to reach base. The Yankees scored five runs, a confident Babe Ruth left the park in the seventh and the home team won 5–3.

"Suddenly, as if frightened by howling goblins," wrote Rud Rennie in the *New York Herald Tribune*, "Ralph Branca, Brooklyn's fine young pitcher, went to pieces." Rogers Hornsby, reported the *Sporting News*, "said that Branca blew up as if he were a high school lad who was upset by sideline cheering." Added DiMaggio to the *Washington Post*, "I was amazed at the way Branca blew. He was so good at first you couldn't see what he was throwing." Sniped the *Los Angeles Times*, "How Ralph Branca ever won twenty-one games during the regular season beats us, unless they were using asparagus tips for bats."

Reporters found Branca hunched on the stool before his locker. "Do you feel that you can go against them again?" one asked. Branca straightened his back, looked into the eyes of his inquisitor. No matter that the pitcher had lost the biggest game of his career, undone by an infield single. Branca had confidence and blamed not himself. "I don't see why not," pitcher answered reporter, his black hair sweated. "I didn't see any infielders getting killed out there today."

Though Branca had given up just two hits while striking out five, and though he had taken 21 wins with him to the mound, his wilt in the post-season limelight scared the Brooklyn brass. He would not get another start. (He did relieve in Games Three and Six, picking up a win despite surrendering in 4.1 innings 10 hits, 3 runs and the first pinch-hit home run in postseason history). The Yankees won the World Series.

Left to ponder his performance, Branca took on semipros, joining in October an exhibition team called the World Series Stars. That he *was* a star, a major league pitcher, eased his postseason troubles. For when back at NYU an oblivious professor asked Branca where he had been and he answered "Working," a classroom roared in delight.

It was now in fact more than ever before that the glint of fame illumined Branca, and Thomson too. Strangers recognized them, wanted autographs. For the first time (excluding a Dodger-issued team set), they appeared on baseball cards, black-and-white cardboard rectangles slipped into bags of homogenized Bond Bread, Branca in Tip Top Bread too. And for the first time, each was now the subject of a feature article in a national publication.

The periodical was *Baseball* magazine, Branca and Thomson spot-lighted in the very same October 1947 issue. There Roscoe McGowen declared Branca "one of the most remarkable pitchers to have come up in the major leagues in years." Fifteen pages on, John Drebinger pro-claimed Thomson "one of the outstanding 'finds' of the post-war era." Readers learned of Branca's large family and minor league grooming, of Thomson's Gaelic roots and sliding woes.

Thomson's choppy slides and headfirst dives had taken a toll. By late season, a bone spur and calcium deposits had hobbled his left knee. And so on November 19 he went under the knife at Harkness Pavilion in Washington Heights, his spur shaved and deposits removed.

Nine days later, before 1,300 fans at Mount Vernon's armory, Branca returned to the hardcourt, a forward on the semipro Westchester Whirl-winds. The team topped the New York Gothams 52–47, Branca also to play basketball this off-season with a team he and John dubbed the Branca Travelers.

Branca struggled, however, to summon vim in the classroom. A base-ball star at twenty-two, he found himself halfway to a degree that had never excited him. And so in early 1948, Branca left NYU to teach at a baseball clinic opened by his Dodger roommate Stanky in Mobile, Alabama. Seventy-three credits shy of a degree, Branca would never to return to college.

Nonetheless, Branca was, as his hometown *Daily Argus* put it, "Mount Vernon's pride." And on February 13, the town held at its armory "Branca Night," presenting the pitcher a set of golf clubs. It had been a good week. Seven days earlier, Brooklyn had awarded Branca a $12,500 contract, roughly double his 1947 salary.

Thomson meantime was at odds with New York over his contract. The previous May, New York had upped his pay from $5,000 to $8,000. Now in early 1948 he wanted $7,000 more. His request seemed reasonable. He had slugged 29 home runs, played a beautiful center field and been likened unceasingly by scribes to DiMaggio. Had Thomson not had 54 at-bats the previous season, he very likely would have been voted Rookie of the Year. (It was not until 1957 that baseball declared players entering a season with up to 75 at-bats eligible for the award.) Stoneham offered $12,000. Thomson balked.

In 1948, however, the unsigned player held little clout. Baseball's reserve clause gave clubs exclusive rights to a player even once his contract expired. In 1922, the Supreme Court exempted baseball from federal antitrust laws, enabling it to enforce the clause.

Still, two years earlier, five Pasquel brothers began offering big contracts to big leaguers to play in Mexico. And though Major League Baseball promised to ban for five years all who crossed the border, widespread player disgruntlement convinced Boston labor lawyer Robert Murphy that the time was right to form a players' union. This he did on April 18, 1946, registering the American Baseball Guild. Among much else, Murphy sought to abolish the reserve clause and institute a $7,500-minimum player salary. But on June 7 a vote among Pittsburgh Pirates to sit out a game against New York came up four votes shy. Unfortunately for Thomson, by the spring of 1948 Murphy's union was near collapse.

And so, though New York had scoffed in December when Cincinnati offered to trade for Thomson star southpaw Johnny Vander Meer, the Scot was nonetheless over a barrel. And when manager Ott now barred him from the team's opening practice, the eager player, already in Phoenix, moped.

On March 3, Thomson ended his holdout after just forty-eight hours, signing for $1,000 less than hoped for. "The spectacle of his mates out there in the sun," explained the *New York Times*, "apparently proved too much for the Staten Islander."

That same day an airplane landed Branca in Ciudad Trujillo, *beisbol-*

crazed capital of the Dominican Republic. The pitcher had tried unsuccessfully to make the trip six days earlier, his boat grounded by fog in Mobile, Alabama. Now, on this sunny Tuesday, he reached Dodger spring training just one workout missed.

All about strutted Branca's teammates, happy to see their ace. Pee Wee Reese worked out bare-chested. Johnny Van Cuyk introduced to all his younger brother Chris, a six-foot-six lefty. Preacher Roe explained that he had gained back twenty-three of the twenty-four pounds lost along with his tonsils in November. Pete Reiser drove a Paul Minner pitch 425 feet to right, the ball skipping on one bounce over the fence. Branca, twenty-two, took it all in. The pitcher was pleased to be back in camp and, months later, could not help but share an old refrain. "There are six boys," he told the *New York Sun*. "We almost all wanted to be ballplayers. I look at the rest of them. They're five-feet-ten or five-feet-ten and a half. I say to myself: 'How come I was the one to be six feet three? Why should I be the one who can throw fast? Why should I be so lucky?' "

It was a different question about the pitcher that this spring lingered in the minds of millions. The *Sporting News* set it to print: "What will happen to Ralph Branca in 1948?"

A bunt in October travels farther than a home run in April. And after a glorious six months, Branca had folded in the World Series—"probably the most outstanding dereliction by a hurler who had been a great pitcher during the regular season," wrote reporter Stan Baumgartner. The flop cast Branca's future into question. "Will the blowups of the big righthander in the World's Series," wondered Baumgartner, "ruin him for all time as a winning pitcher for the Dodgers? Did Charlie Dressen prove to the baseball world that Branca can't take it?"

Over and over, Thomson slid in the sliding pit, coaches Tom Sheehan and Red Kress, mindful of the crescent scar on his kneecap, tutoring the center fielder. Thomson's leg felt fine, and through mid-April he was as hot as the nearby Mojave Desert, batting .406 in the Cactus Belt, driving in 24 runs in 27 games.

It was then, one 1948 spring training day, that Thomson looked off into the Arizona distance and swung his Adirondack, his follow-through captured on film. The shot, notable only for the windbreakered arms peeking out beneath Thomson's short-sleeved jersey, became Card 47 of the Bowman Gum Company's forty-eight-card set, the tiny cardboard Thomson forevermore flipped, traded and collected by worshipful little fingers.

Spring training ended and Thomson and Branca burst from the starting gate, each picking up in April where he had left off the previous September. By season's midpoint, Thomson was hitting .286 with 10 home runs and 37 runs batted in, Branca 11–7 with a 3.22 ERA. It was no surprise when both men were invited to St. Louis to play on July 13 in the All-Star Game, given gold Lord Elgin wristwatches besides.

Branca started the game, allowing two runs in three innings. Thomson almost finished it, striking out as a pinch-hitter to lead off the ninth. Manager Durocher and the National League lost 5–2.

Never again would Durocher hand Branca the ball. For skippered to a 5–3 win over Cincinnati on July 15, Brooklyn let go its manager. The club had itched to lose the Lip from the moment of his 1947 suspension and now did, blessing his jump to New York. Ott was out, thrown a sinecure beside farm director Carl Hubbell in the front office.

The next morning, even as it retired in perpetuity Ott's number 4, New York flew Durocher by chartered plane to Pittsburgh. There on July 17, gathered in the Forbes Field clubhouse, sat silently Durocher's new team.

Brooklyn was the enemy. In his near two years in baseball, Thomson, twenty-four, had spoken to just one Dodger, muttering hello to Gil Hodges, the first baseman held in such esteem. And so as Durocher sat before his team on this Saturday and said, "All that counts now is Giants"—swiping for effect his hand several times across the chest of the uniform he borrowed from coach Kress—it was for his players shocking. And it was, for at least one Giant, upsetting too. The previous morning, Durocher had told the press what he thought of his new club, singling out just one player for criticism. "Thomson," he told reporter James P. Dawson, "never has impressed me as an outfielder, certainly not as a center fielder."

It was the maligned Thomson who won for Durocher his debut, a pinch-single with two out in the eighth giving New York a 6–5 win.

New York would win 40 more games and finish fifth. And along the way, the players found there was fun to be had in a Durocher clubhouse. They excited when celebrities Tony Martin, Cyd Charisse and Groucho Marx stopped by, and applauded when the manager told trainer Willie Schaeffer to no longer check that they were in their rooms by midnight. But the Lip was also gruff, all bile and billingsgate. And he did not yet know his team. He had from day one questioned the ability of Thomson, sapped of confidence he who did not respond well to criticism. Moved to left, the Scot finished the 1948 season with 16 home runs, 63 runs batted in, a .248 average, and a dreadful .296 on-base percentage.

Branca's second-half swoon was as precipitous. Suddenly his arm was sore—"hurts every time I throw hard," he told the *Sporting News*. And two days after beating Boston 4–2 on August 15 for his thirteenth win, Branca's left ankle swelled. It was infected, the delayed result of an errant throw by Tommy Brown in practice more than two months prior. Branca checked into Swedish Hospital. A Dr. Dominic Rossi lanced the ankle and gave Branca shots of penicillin. Recovery was slow, Branca resting with shin guard until August 31, winning just once more the rest of the season. On October 3, Branca emptied his locker.

That same day, after an 11–1 embarrassment at home versus Boston, Thomson walked through the green door of Durocher's office a first time. He wore on his right pinkie a reminder of better days, a fourteen-karat "221," record home-run total of the previous season. "I'd really rather play center field," said Thomson. Manager assured player that come spring he would and wondered aloud why Thomson had not mentioned his frustration before.

The end of a baseball season—its concluding pitch, final dash to first, last umpiring call—is for many ballplayers emancipating. Others panic, not wishing to lay down bat and glove for the long winter months. Thus did Dick Sisler. And so, when Del Ennis fouled out to first to end Philly's season, first baseman Sisler set to take a group of major leaguers west and play ball.

For decades, hodgepodges of major leaguers had headed at the close of baseball seasons to towns too small to regularly see them play. There, against whomever rural America pitched at them, they had played ball for just enough money to cover gas fare and beer. If no opponent presented itself, they took on one another. The exhibition play, called barnstorming, ended by November having shaved one month off the interminable wait for spring.

It had been easy for Sisler to cobble together a club. He had simply, as the season wound down, inquired of opponents afield if they wished to join him. Many did, including Bobby Thomson. And when in Illinois, on October 11, 1948, barnstormer Russ Meyer left club for classroom, Sisler invited Branca west too.

Branca had been home for eight days, the lackluster close of his season fresh in memory. He had no plans this off-season and so welcomed the opportunity to barnstorm, boarding at once a flight to Cleveland.

There was time to pick Branca up—the club had no games scheduled for four days. Perusing the roster for a transport compatible with Branca revealed just one who was young, single, a New Yorker, an all-star and with nice wheels to boot. And so Bobby Thomson set aside his Dodger loathing and headed for Cleveland, driving alone his black Buick convertible some 400 miles east along U.S. 6 and Expressway 20.

Branca and Thomson recognized each other not only from the 44 games played in opposite dugouts over two seasons but from the St. Louis locker room of an all-star game in July. But it was now that they met, "thrown together" in Cleveland, remembers Branca, "because we were close in age and two New Yorkers." Batter and pitcher said hello and drove off.

The men wore slacks and sport shirts, baseballers sleek as Thomson's car with its wheel skirts and chrome grille. The open sky above, a V-windscreen preceding them, their seven-hour drive passed with talk of what they knew and loved—of pitches and swings and wins and losses, of contracts and fans and fame and family, of baseball.

The men shared youth too, its testosterone and metabolism. Both lived with their moms, were veterans of but one romance and little else. And as they zipped through Indiana, Branca, whom brother Julius had in the fall of 1946 taught to drive, marveled at the yellow strip of paint in the middle of the highway. He had not seen one before. It stretched on and on, running nearly all the way to Springfield's Fitzpatrick Stadium, where, at eight p.m. on October fifteenth, a game began, Branca taking the mound in the bottom of the first inning against Dutch Leonard's Local All-Stars.

Sisler, twenty-seven, eyed the crowd. It seemed of a few thousand, the locals having gone for tickets to Alvey's Cigar Store, Machino's Tavern, Rose's Eat Shop. General admission was 50 cents, the grandstand 74 cents, boxes a buck. Late in the game, Sisler would count and divvy the receipts, each player pocketing on average some 25 dollars. Tonight seemed promising. Springfield-native Robin Roberts, fresh off a strong rookie season in Philly, would start opposite Branca.

Roberts, twenty-two, pitched well, striking out six, one run yielded in five innings. Branca struck out seven, no runs allowed in six. And in what would be the only game he ever played behind Branca, Thomson added a single and a triple. Together afield just this once, Branca, Thomson and the National Leaguers won 12–1.

Two days later, on a Sunday afternoon in Johnson City, Tennessee, the barnstormers delighted the crowd at Cardinal Park with "shadow ball"—practice pantomimed with no ball. The team then split in two. Facing Tennessean Clyde Shoun, Thomson slugged home runs in the fifth, seventh and eighth innings.

The team headed west toward Missouri, all about President Harry Truman's home-state reelection campaign in full swing. The players stopped in Walker Cooper's hometown of Buckner, gathering in his backyard the night before a ballgame to drink beer. Coop was a hunter and soon, remembers Thomson, the ballplayers were "throwing beer cans in the air and firing at them." Thomson felt sick. Ribbed for being a lightweight, he went to sleep in his fellow Giant's home, awoke the next day and shared more beer with his mates. A sharp pain soon raked his midsection. Cooper called a doctor who, hours later in Independence, removed Thomson's appendix. Done barnstorming, Thomson spent weeks in the hospital. And after celebrating his twenty-fifth birthday in the care of Cooper and his wife, Doris, the Scot headed to Newport, Vermont, where a camp run by his high school coach O'Brien promised to nurse him to health.

October begat November then December, baseball's hot stove league warming with every off-season trade and signing. There were many—Dutch Leonard, Eddie Waitkus, Pete Reiser and dozens more flicked to and fro at baseball's Chicago winter meetings like so many marbles.

Thomson and Branca, coming off down seasons, were on the block too. And it was little surprise when New York offered Boston Thomson and Walker Cooper for Warren Spahn, or when Brooklyn offered Pittsburgh Branca for outfielder Wally Westlake and $150,000 in cash. But Boston and Pittsburgh declined. And so it was that in the third week of December 1948, on the third floor of the Palmer House hotel in Chicago, rival approached rival, Brooklyn GM Branch Rickey wondering blithely to Durocher if he might perchance land Thomson. The Lip pondered. He wanted in return just one player. "When Leo Durocher demanded Ralph Branca in exchange," reported Harold Burr in the *Sporting News,* "Rickey retreated." And so Thomson and Branca stayed put, oblivious to what had almost been brokered.

On January 24, 1949, as New York re-signed catchers Westrum and Yvars, Branca stood backstage at the Oxford Theater in Plainfield, New Jersey, waiting on a Monday afternoon to begin his professional singing career.

Branca had in December been the "mystery voice" on Jackie Robinson's fifteen-minute WMCA radio program, the bass singing a parody of a Frank Loesser song. Bitten by the stage bug, Branca began to take voice lessons from Fred Steele, a blond baritone with a piano in a soundproof office at 1650 Broadway. The pitcher had promise. He had name recognition too, and PR man Ted Warner had had little trouble booking for the Dodger a seven-day singing tour. Now, as polite applause escorted from the stage an acrobat troupe, Branca watched MC Don Cummings walk to the mike. Cummings told a joke, then continued: "And now, I would like to present Ralph Branca of the Brooklyn Dodgers."

Branca, newly twenty-three, walked onstage. He wore a suit and beads of sweat, nervous before the matinee crowd as it paused from its popcorn. Cummings popped a question: "How will the Dodgers do this year?" They will win, answered Branca. Some cheered and some booed and Branca spoke. "I'd like to sing you 'A Slow Boat to China,' " he said.

This Branca did, performing with accompaniment Loesser's sad song, a crooner not even once touching the microphone before him.

Branca did, however, continue to sweat. And when he finished, he confided in his audience. "This is the first time I've ever been onstage," said Branca. He then volunteered a story, told of another nervous day. "I feel like I did the day Leo Durocher put me in my first big league game," he said. "It was at the Polo Grounds and that bullpen is four hundred and thirty-five feet from the pitcher's box. It took ten days to walk it." Unburdened, Branca sang another song. There was applause and he told another story and a joke and sang an encore and surrendered the stage to a dog act.

Branca was happy. He relished performing and in the last week of January serenaded audiences in towns from Long Branch, New Jersey, to Saratoga Springs, New York. But it was baseball that remained a love and livelihood. The next week, on February 7, Branca agreed to return to Brooklyn, signing for $15,000.

Thomson saw his pay cut to $10,500, then set off in February to Phoenix, Arizona. There he returned to center field, to the number 23 and to stardom, batting by mid-season .314 with 100 hits, 11 home runs and 50 runs batted in.

On July 11, Giant Thomson tripled off Dodger Joe Hatten at Yankee Stadium. And having raised this Monday $40,000 for treatment of cancer, heart disease and polio, the three New York teams mugged afield, Thomson and Branca fourteen men apart.

The two men met again the next afternoon in the home dugout at Ebbets Field. Each had been voted an all-star. Branca had burst from the gate an incredible 7–0. It seemed Branca's year: when on June 25 he surrendered 10 runs, Brooklyn scored 17 and he won to go 9–1, his record 10–3 at the all-star break. His ERA, however, was 5.12 and a tweaked elbow had twice forced him in July to forego starts. Billy Southworth, managing the NL All-Stars, did not pitch Branca and the senior circuit lost 11–7.

Days later, Branca's phone rang. It was Wolfe Cribari, brother of his friend Guido, inviting him to a dinner dance at the Westchester Country Club. "I needed a date," says Branca. "I didn't know who to ask."

Branca had met Ann Mulvey four years earlier in Bear Mountain, New York. She was then just fourteen and, like Branca, upstate for spring training, schlepped along by parents James and Dearie Mulvey who owned 25 percent of Brooklyn's club. In the summers since, Branca had seen her at Ebbets Field near every week, Ann whiling away games in Box 117 in the first row behind home plate. The two had often chitchatted, a screen and five years separating them. Ann had grown. She was now eighteen and beautiful, five feet six with blond hair and green eyes. Branca invited her to the dance and she said yes.

Branca put on a suit and on this Saturday night drove toward work. Five blocks from Ebbets Field, at 39 Maple Street, he parked his green Pontiac. Ann emerged in a dress of blue flowers and polka dots, a matching shawl atop her bare shoulders, her sun-bleached hair parted to the side. Branca gaped. "She looked a lot like Katharine Hepburn," he says. By 10 p.m. she was home, Branca given a kiss on the cheek. By August 1, when Branca shut out Pittsburgh to run his record to 12–3, Ann was his girlfriend.

Thomson had never played so well. When on October 2 against Boston he made four putouts and no errors, he finished the season with a .982 fielding percentage. He had starred on defense all season, collecting 10 assists and fielding on average an incredible .94 more balls per game than other center fielders. Thomson had sparkled offensively too, among the league leaders in nearly every offensive category. His 156 games played were second-most, his 198 hits, 332 total bases and 641 at-bats third-most, his 27 home runs and 71 extra-base hits fourth, .518 slugging percentage fifth, .309 average and 109 runs batted in sixth, 99 runs scored and 10 stolen bases seventh, 9 triples eighth, .873 OPS (on-base percentage plus slugging percentage) ninth, and 244 times on base tenth. He had also walked far more than he had the previous season and struck out far less—just once every 14.2 at-bats. And so, it was little wonder when one day after season's end New York gave Thomson a huge raise, more than doubling his salary to $23,000.

Thomson was a big star in a big city. His name carried, and he became a pitchman for Adirondack Bats. "When it comes to really BELTING the ball, the bat you use is mighty important," read a 1949 ad. "That's why Bob always swings a power-packed Adirondack."

Despite Thomson, New York finished fifth, 73–81. Losing for Thomson was routine. In his three full seasons, the Giants had finished no higher than fourth.

Branca, meantime, was used to winning. In his four full seasons, Brooklyn had won a pennant, lost another in a playoff and twice finished third. And on October 2, 1949, after beating Philadelphia 9–7, Brooklyn won the pennant again.

Branca, though, had won just three games the second half of the season, starting 10 and relieving half as many. But he had been solid down the stretch, allowing just five earned runs in his final 22.1 innings, his ERA dipping to a respectable 4.39. What's more, in 14 appearances at home he had not lost once. And so on October 7, 1949, manager Shotton started Branca in Game Three of the World Series, the first at Ebbets Field.

Brooklyn and New York had split 1–0 games to open the series and went now to the ninth inning of Game Three tied at one. Branca was still on the mound. Through eight innings he had surrendered just two hits—a single and a double—his six-year career at last culminating in near perfection. Branca's ninth started well, Robinson gloving a whistling grounder hit by Henrich between first and second. One out. Berra walked to snap a string of 14 straight retired by Branca but DiMaggio (already down twice on strikes for just the second time all season), popped out. Two out. Branca had given his eight allotted tickets to his family, and now, together with girlfriend Ann, the claque, behind third, cheered him. So did 32,780 strangers. Bobby Brown quieted the crowd with a single to right. Gene Woodling walked. The bases were loaded. Coach Clyde Sukeforth walked to the mound, Reese, Robinson and Campy gathering about Branca too. Branca wished to stay in the game. Shotton allowed it and Yankee manager Casey Stengel pinch-hit Johnny Mize for Cliff Mapes. Mize, the former Giant, lined Branca's 127th pitch for a single to right, driving in two and Branca from the game. New York scored again then won 4–3, two solo home runs by Brooklyn in the bottom of the ninth not enough.

A silence overtook Brooklyn's locker room. Winless in four World Series, the team was down again. And Branca, wrote Jack Lang of the *Long Island Press,* was "most disconsolate of all the Dodgers." For good reason. He who had lost the opening games of the 1946 playoffs and 1947 World Series had now lost another important game, had now surrendered 12 runs in 17 World Series innings.

While his teammates showered and dressed, Branca sat alone at his locker, head down. "Just one more out," said the pitcher, staring at the base of his cubby. "Just one more damn pitch. Just one more out. Just one more out." Branca was muttering to himself.

Branca had thrown Mize a chest-high inside fastball, a good pitch.

And this, he who had pitched valiantly, he who had lost at home for the first time all season, wanted people to know. "That's just the way we're supposed to pitch to him," Branca told reporter Dana Mozley. "I got the ball just where I wanted it." The pitcher, noted Mozley, "was certain that one vital delivery to Johnny Mize was a pardonable sin."

Most agreed. And on this Friday afternoon, player after player and reporter after reporter did not resuscitate the specter of Branca post-seasons past. Instead they praised him. Said Rex Barney of his roommate: he was "overpowering the Yankees." He had "terrific stuff," added Campanella. Reporter Daley came closest to aspersing the big pitcher. "There generally is something about Branca's pitching which is quite baffling," read his *New York Times* column the next morning. "He'll move along beautifully for the longest while and—boom! He's gone."

Brooklyn lost the next two games and the World Series.

October failures did not much linger with Branca. "[They] never stuck in my craw," he says. Ann made sure her boyfriend's most recent setback was no exception. She whose grandfather Stephen McKeever had with his brother Ed built Ebbets Field knew the game, knew of the evanescence of its fortune. "Her family was steeped in baseball," says Branca. "She understood." And so, when the pitcher was not playing basketball Monday nights in the Brooklyn Paramount Theater with a quartet of Dodgers, he was with Ann, the Marymount College freshman heading home from Tarrytown about twice a month, the couple going out to dinner, to the movies, to the Knights of Columbus, to the family cabana in Breezy Point. James and Dearie Mulvey liked Branca and, on January 26, 1950, signed him too, together with their fellow owners, apportioning him $15,000 for the 1950 season.

Another World Series start, though a disappointment, had only added to Branca's renown. And at twenty-four, he was enjoying all the appurtenances of celebrity. There was representation, Branca among the very first clients of the very first sports agent, Frank Scott. There were endorsements, a lipsticked Branca hocking cereal and cigarettes. ("He's eaten Wheaties for 15 years!" read one ad. "Chesterfields are tops with me," read another.) There was a record, the pitcher recording in June with Palica and Furillo a dance number in F major entitled the "Brooklyn Dodgers Jump." There was a tour, a week of warbling in November at the Chez Maurice nightclub in Montreal. And there was a modeling gig, the pitcher posing for *Sport* magazine in March of 1950. "If Ralph Branca looks like a song-and-dance man," read the caption beneath a photograph of Branca in straw sennit hat (Knox, $6), "it's because he is one!" The six-photo spread had the pitcher holding towel, sunglasses and pipe, bedecked from white linen cap to tan crepe moccasins. The next month, a bit more dowdy, Branca reappeared in the national press endorsing Buster Brown, "Official Boy Scout Shoes."

That same month, Thomson also appeared in a magazine ad. "My Gillette super speed razor makes shaving easier," read a word bubble above a cartooned Thomson, "and far more refreshing than any razor I've ever owned!" The soft-spoken spokesman had spent the winter pitching Adirondack bats at the minor league winter meetings in Minnesota and, more regularly, sports equipment in Davega's Sports Shop in the Hotel Commodore at 111 East 42nd Street. He was increasingly rented for the dais, introduced this off-season at the Staten Island Varsity Club dinner and at a dinner for third baseman Heeney Majeski. He was good to reporters, telling *Sport* magazine in May of his Fred Waring records and of the Western films his roommate Dave Koslo favored. And always he dutifully replied to fan mail, answering each of the twenty-five-odd letters he received weekly in the off-season and quadruple that number once the season began, so much mail that the cost of his response dwindled significantly, the sensible son of a cabinetmaker able to buy stationery and photos in bulk, 1,000 prints just $40.

"Bobby's a Scotsman," says Ted Rosen. "He saved his money." Rosen was a friend from Saint Lawrence who after college decided on law, then jumped to Lehman Brothers after failing a legal ethics class in law school. Buddy Thomson was a client come spring, his money put in stocks. Says Rosen, "I handled money for him for years."

Spring training began, an eager Thomson overstepping first base on his first home run jog of 1950. When twelve days later the regular season opened on April 18, Thomson and his pinkie ring were near all that were left of New York's home run record of three seasons past. Durocher had exiled boppers Johnny Mize, Walker Cooper and Sid Gordon, a purge that put increased pressure on Thomson to produce. When in April the manager declared him second only to Musial among National League outfielders, Thomson pressed, batting at the all-star break just .247 with 11 home runs and 44 runs batted in.

Branca too was floundering. In 62.1 innings he had served up a staggering 16 home runs. His ERA, 6.06, had risen to heights unseen since his 1944 rookie season. After nine starts and nine stints in relief, he was only lucky that his 2–5 record was not worse.

Still, Branca had not pitched poorly out of the pen. In 16 innings, his ERA was 3.38. And so Shotton now used Branca far more frequently in relief. The pitcher responded—in 25 second-half appearances heading into Brooklyn's final game on October 1 against Philadelphia, his ERA was 3.50. While Branca the starter had surrendered 21 home runs in 94 innings, in 48 innings of relief he had yielded just 3.

Brooklyn trailed Philly by one game. A win would force a playoff. Shotton sent Don Newcombe to the mound one win shy of 20. Newk pitched heroically, yielding one run through nine on a sweltering Sunday afternoon at Ebbets Field. And no matter that Branca stood waiting foul of the foul line in right, a rested reliever having thrown just 10.2 innings in ten days. After Phillie center-fielder Richie Ashburn threw out Cal Abrams at home in the bottom of the ninth, it was number 36 who in 88-degree heat returned to the mound at 4:25 p.m. to start the tenth. The lights at Ebbets Field went on and Newcombe surrendered successive singles. Shotton, though, did not summon Branca and with two on and one out, the stuttering Dick Sisler whistled Newcombe's 127th pitch to left for a home run. The game and pennant were lost.

Newcombe sat in a clubhouse whimpering before Branca and all his teammates. But Shotton spoke to his crestfallen club and the pitcher pepped up. For he and the team had played beautiful ball, had won 14 of 17 to reach the precipice. Shotton and Brooklyn were proud of their team and in the days that followed, any second-guessing involved only third-base coach Milt Stock who had waved Abrams home in the ninth.

Thomson and the Giants had experienced no such drama. When on September 8 Warren Spahn beat them 4–3, they trailed Philly by 9.5 games. The loss was the low point in a low season for Thomson, the slugger leaving five men on base, failing to bat a ball out of the infield and dropping his average to .228. Durocher fumed. "I never saw anything like it," he told reporter Bill Roeder. "Wouldn't you think he'd try something just on the chance he might do it right even by accident? Drop his hands maybe or move around in the box or use a different bat once in a while?"

Thomson relented. He would tweak his stance. And so, while his teammates showered, the center fielder stepped into the batter's box and swung for an hour, the Polo Grounds empty in the gloaming save retired slugger Mel Ott on the mound. Thomson's boyhood hero had him shift his 190 pounds to his back foot. Thomson hit .393 the remaining 24 games of the season, finishing at .252 with 25 home runs, 85 runs batted in and a new nickname, "Hoot Mon," Alvin Dark conferring what his father called his fellow Scots.

The next month, in early November, Branca again drove to 39 Maple

Street in Flatbush. His performance in the second half of the season had all but ensured that Brooklyn would retain him for 1951. But the pitcher now spoke not of baseball. He told Brooklyn's minority owners that he wished to marry their daughter. They offered their blessing and Branca drove his green sedan to Canal Street where a family friend, Carmine Lauricella, waited with a blue-white diamond. Days later, Branca slipped the ring into a blazer's breast pocket and asked his girlfriend of sixteen months to peer inside. News of their engagement made the papers. The wedding was set for October 20, 1951—a date safe even in the event of playoff, World Series and rainout. Branca breathed free, the next month undergoing an operation to clear his sinuses (and lessen his nose).

It was then, on December 22, 1950, that the *New York Times* christened Thomson "Staten Island's most eligible bachelor." The outfielder had just signed on with fountain pen to return in 1951 to New York, again for $23,000. And he had no girlfriend.

Eleven days later, as the first afternoon of 1951 turned to dusk, Thomson drove to South Plainfield, New Jersey, to a New Year's party at the home of Roberta Hamilton, a friend from Saint Lawrence University. Thomson removed his long khaki storm coat with belt and buttons and lamb's-wool lining and said hello to Vic Sacco. The college roommates caught up. Sacco was a graduate student in theology at Saint Lawrence. Thomson had spent the fall barnstorming with a basketball team run by his high school coach O'Brien.

The men said hello to Roberta and her sister Patricia. Patty had also gone to Saint Lawrence and fallen there for Thomson. The ballplayer had had no clue. "I was too naïve to see it," he says. And so, Patty had instead gone out with Vic. Patty, Vic and Thomson now headed outside with a fourth, Elaine Coley, a friend Patty had invited to the party. "Here we go running across the ice," remembers Thomson, "and Patty grabbed me." The foursome paired up.

Night fell and Thomson readied to return home to Staten Island. But back inside the Hamilton's mauve manse he beheld Elaine anew. She was beautiful, demure, with short wavy brown hair and dark brown eyes. Emboldened by alcohol, Thomson said hello. Her head at his shoulder, they chatted. She went by Winkie. She was twenty-two. She had graduated from North Plainfield High School. She had modeled. She now worked at Muhlenberg Hospital in the social service department. She had one sibling, Nancy, three years older and married with two sons. Elaine smiled and laughed a lot. Thomson liked her. "Can I call you?" he asked. "Yes," she answered, and went home.

Winkie was well accustomed to the attention of men. But she had never truly been interested until now. "Bill was stuffy," remembers her sister, Nancy. "Herb was too old and self-important. When she met Bob, that was it."

Thomson was equally struck. "This gal," he says. "Whoo! She just took a hold of me." But Thomson was shy and did not phone on January 2, 1951. Nor did he call the next day, or the next. Or the next day or the next. Winkie was hurt. But when at last Thomson did phone a few weeks later and ask her out, she mistook his shyness for insouciance and, impressed, said nothing but yes. Thomson drove his black Buick convertible to the white Cape Cod house with aqua shutters on Locust Place in North Plainfield where Winkie lived. The couple shared a wonderful dinner, and this time Thomson did not wait to phone. For the first time in seven years, he had a girlfriend.

Even so, Thomson was eager to return to baseball. His 1950 season had disappointed—the biggest fall-off in all of baseball, according to the *Sporting News*—and so he had asked Stoneham for permission to report early to spring training. This he now did, arriving in St. Petersburg, Florida, eleven days before the other position players. In shape quickly, Thomson played every inning of New York's first 15 spring training games, leading the team in both extra-base hits and stolen bases. Durocher pronounced his center fielder the fastest man in all of baseball, which he may well have been, and the fleetest Giant finished the spring at .363.

This was expected of Thomson. Scribes had noted his on-again, off-again ways, an excellent 1947 giving way to a poor 1948, a fantastic 1949 and a frustrating 1950. It was time now again, in the spring of 1951, to shine, and Winkie delighted to find pint-sized versions of her Giant dotting everything from Bowman baseball card number 126 to the face of a Stadium Pin to an Exhibit Supply Company card won from vending machines by lucky kids at carnivals.

Branca was also in Exhibit's set. Readying for his eighth season, he found himself on cards by Bowman, Topps and Fischer Baking Company too, the last beautiful, the pitcher drawn mid-delivery against a pink backdrop.

A promotional staple, Branca was also popular with his teammates. He dated the owner's daughter, was color-blind (an unabashed friend to Robinson from the start), and had smarts, the college boy Brooklyn's player representative since 1946. His first duty as club rep in 1951 came on May 23. It was then, hours before Brooklyn disposed of Pittsburgh to go 20–13 on the young season, that the team decided it wished for every bullpen to have two mounds and for St. Louis to provide a better batting cage. This Branca had now to inform the league, the pitcher left also to explain to *New York Times* reporter Roscoe McGowen that his team, alone in first place, had yet to decide whether to invest its anticipated World Series share in a pension fund or to simply divvy it after the series— the better to buy the latest in 1951 technology like air-conditioning, power steering and a doohickey called a credit card.

Branca helped his teammates afield too. From the start of the season, new Dodger manager Dressen had used him only in relief. And after recovering from a bout of pneumonia in spring training, the big right-hander had pitched marvelously. When on May 26 he tossed two shutout innings against Boston, striking out four and walking none, his ERA dropped to 1.40. In 19.1 innings over nine relief appearances, Branca had given up three earned runs.

Still, Branca saw himself a starter and was happy when two days later Dressen gave him the nod against Philadelphia's Ken Heintzelman. Though rain delayed play twenty-five minutes in the middle of the eighth, Branca returned to the mound to finish what he had started. Branca and Brooklyn won 4–3 and eight starts later at the all-star break, Branca was again king of the hill, 7–2 with a 2.27 ERA.

Thomson, meantime, was struggling. So high in spring training, north he had gone south, batting in New York at the end of April .194 with three home runs. Thomson felt weak and quickly learned why: he had a stomach ailment, and his blood count had dropped. A Dr. Stern on Fifth Avenue prescribed for him a bland diet but even so Thomson drooped through May and June. The diagnosis this time was clearer: Willie Mays, seven and a half years Thomson's junior, had bumped him from center field and bled his confidence. Durocher soon benched Thomson, batting him just nine times in a 10-game stretch ending June 27. Winkie, at many games, was a balm to Thomson. But still he moped.

On June 28, New York led Branca and Brooklyn 5–4 when, in the top of the ninth inning, Durocher told a benched Thomson to replace Mueller in left. On this day it mattered little to Thomson that New York won. He felt like a bit player and was, batting .220 with 9 home runs and 32 runs batted in. And so, after the game on a train bound for Boston, Whitey Lockman badgered his roommate to shorten his batting stance just as he had the previous season, to plant his feet some eighteen inches apart. Desperate to produce afield, Thomson agreed.

Durocher began to play Thomson. And Thomson began to produce, by July 15 batting .237 with 16 home runs. It was four days later that Durocher told his Giants they would begin to steal signs with telescope and buzzer. Thomson, owing an injury to Thompson, would also begin to play third base. And it was after that team meeting on that rainy Thursday that Durocher and Thomson then walked outside, manager fungoing player some twenty ground balls at third. Thomson fielded the wet hardballs impeccably and, forty-two years later, remembered aloud to researcher Tom Harris the exact words his manager had called out to no one in particular. "Hey!" Durocher yelled. "You can't play third any better than that! Don't worry about him. He's all right."

The second half of a baseball season followed, the fortunes of two men and two teams about-facing—Branca and the Dodgers high then low, Thomson and the Giants low then high. On October 1, 1951, they stood in an exact tie.

THIRTEEN

Thy hour and thy harpoon are at hand!
—HERMAN MELVILLE,
Moby-Dick, 1851

POOR VINCENT IMPELLITTERI. New York City's mayor was in his birthplace of Isnello, Sicily, eating roast lamb, fried eggplant and susciameli, a hometown dish of chocolate and almonds, when for the first and last time all three of his city's baseball teams finished a season in first place. Acting mayor Joseph T. Sharkey, running for City Council president, was quick to grab the spotlight. On October 1, as a playoff set to pressure-cook the Big Apple, Sharkey declared it "Baseball Week in the World's Greatest City" and called on New Yorkers to display American flags.

Thanks to a coin flip and Dressen's druthers, the action kicked off at Ebbets Field. Before noon, the Dodgers, in their home white and royal blue, stretched, tossed balls, fungoed and took batting practice. The Giants followed, NEW YORK stitched across their chests in black with orange trim. The limbering ballplayers were the league's best—a remarkable ten all-stars spangled the two lineups. Three were Giants: shortstop Dark and pitchers Maglie and Jansen. Seven were Dodgers: center-fielder Snider, four-fifths of the Brooklyn infield—Campanella, Hodges, Robinson and Reese (who had backed up Dark in the All-Star game)—and pitchers Newcombe and Roe. The two teams also boasted the league's eventual Most Valuable Player (Campy), Rookie of the Year (Mays), leader in runs batted in (Irvin), leaders in wins (Maglie and Jansen), and co-strikeout king (Newcombe tied with Spahn).

It was Branca though who at 1:30 p.m. threw the playoff's first pitch. And it was a fastball seen by more sets of eyes than had ever before beheld a ball's flight.

American Telephone and Telegraph Company had in 1948 begun outfitting the country for the transmission of live television, running below-ground from New York to St. Louis insulated copper wire known as coaxial cable. From there to the West Coast, radio transmitters and receivers were affixed to the tops of metal towers. The undertaking took almost four years, completed in August 1951. And on September 4, television viewers witnessed live for the first time an event unfolding time zones away—an address by President Truman at a United Nations–sponsored peace conference in San Francisco. Picture quality was clear and that 14,670,000 people tuned in left the television world aglow. The telecast, wrote *Variety* magazine, was "almost awesome in its potentials."

Slated to begin October 2, the 1951 World Series was to have been the first sporting event to utilize the new technology. When, however, the baseball season ended in a tie, the pioneering broadcast became instead game one of the playoff.

It was a game so unexpected that Durocher had, as of this day, sublet his apartment. (A gracious tenant allowed him to stay.) And not until the midnight previous had owner Walter O'Malley hocked to CBS the game's TV rights. CBS in turn had no time to secure an in-game corporate sponsor, American Tobacco for one deciding there were not enough hours to publicize sponsorship. Nor was there time for CBS to tap its broadcast into WOR, local television home of home Dodger games. And so, last minute, CBS had turned to rival ABC, whose local affiliate WJZ shared a Manhattan studio with WOR. ABC generously tapped into WOR, then relayed its signal to AT&T whence it went to CBS.

Unforeseen or not, the game this Monday afternoon began. And Branca, who in August had started the first baseball game ever broadcast in color, now threw another historic pitch—the first with a live national television audience.

Exactly how many folks watched on CBS Stanky take Branca's fastball for a strike is not known. (Surveyors were caught unprepared too.) But all assumed it was an unprecedented crowd. For seven months prior, a courtroom drama starring Tennessee senator Estes Kefauver had brought to light the limitless reach of unscripted live television.

Kefauver was then chair of a senate committee investigating organized crime. And having set off about the country in May of 1950 to oversee a string of public hearings on crime, everywhere had he found corruption. (He estimated illegal U.S. gambling at 20 billion dollars annually.) On March 12, 1951, Kefauver and Co. arrived at the Foley Square courthouse in lower Manhattan, their hearings to be broadcast live on WPIX.

Frank Costello asked that he not be televised. The cameras obliged, training only on the mafioso's hands. And as lawyer Rudolph Halley grilled Costello—Halley: "What did you do in 1946 to earn fifteen thousand dollars?" Costello: "Practically nothing."—the telecast turned theater, the hands of a don from Calabria fidgeting, fidgeting, fidgeting beside a sweating pitcher of water. Thousands tuned to WPIX, then thousands more. WPIX fed one station, then another. Within days, the hearing was television's top show. "It has everything," noted *Variety* magazine on March 21. "It's a panel show, a quiz show, a whodunit and an amateur hour. . . . There are dirty dishes in the sink, and no shopping, too, as the folks hug the television sets at home, in restaurants, pubs and clubs." Added *Life* magazine, "In eerie half-light, looking at millions of small frosty screens, people sat as if charmed. . . . Never before had the attention of the nation been riveted so completely on a single matter." It seemed no coincidence that on March 18, NBC inked Milton Berle to a thirty-year contract at $200,000 a year. Television was a phenomenon. Only on TV could politics be every bit the star as entertainment. And now, with Branca on the mound, so too could sport, its inauguration on live national television watched on the 16 million sets dotting the country, clusters of fans in bars, in living rooms, outside storefronts. After a foul pop, a fly ball and a groundout, Branca was out of the inning.

Chadwick watched the action on Channel 9, papers by his side. "It will not solve your personal troubles," Jimmy Cannon wrote that day of baseball, "give you health if you are sick, reward you with money if you are poor, or diminish your grief. But it might grant you the gift of hope."

So it did Chadwick in the second inning, Pafko, Bavasi's mid-season pickup, homering off surprise starter Jim Hearn. Branca and Brooklyn led 1–0.

The lead was short-lived.

Branca had pitched 54 innings in August—18 more than in July. In the month since, his right arm and his season had slackened. Branca seemed a boxer on the ropes. And in the fourth inning with two out and one on, Thomson came to bat, a batter rising since July digging in against a pitcher falling since August. Branca delivered, the ball smacked into Campanella's mitt and Allan Roth, sitting in the press box, jotted two symbols in pencil: a print capital B, and, just above and to the left, a tiny arc, as if an arched eyebrow. Thusly recorded (a curve, high and inside, taken for a ball), Roth's notation of Branca's pitch fell neatly into place on his twelve-by-nineteen-inch piece of yellow graph paper.

Again Branca threw and this time Roth put down "S_". (Fast ball, low and away, swung at and missed.) Roth charted the next three pitches too—high and inside fastball fouled off, low and away fastball taken for a ball, high and inside fastball hit for a home run. As Thomson jogged around the bases, Schenz left the dugout, the first to greet number 23, and Roth wrote two words in a column on the far right of his paper: BRASS RAIL. Thomson had deposited Branca's fifth pitch over the Brass Rail Restaurants sign in left-center field. New York led 2–1 and Roth readied his pencil for Branca's next delivery. He had not missed a Brooklyn pitch in five seasons.

Roth, thirty-four, was Brooklyn's statistician. He saw baseball, as the saying went, as a game of inches. And more than had anyone before, he set out to chart its quantitative underpinnings.

Roth had always loved numbers. As a boy of three growing up in Montreal, he took to counting backward by twos from 100. He also loved sports, later becoming the star running back at Strathcona Academy high school. His two passions converged when, in 1930, he embraced baseball statistics.

It was then Roth, thirteen, began to compile stats on Brooklyn's farm club, the Montreal Royals, as well as on the entire International League. Four years later, he turned his eye to Major League Baseball. And on December 16, 1940, Roth, newly married and packing neckties in his uncle's factory, sent Dodger president Larry MacPhail samples of his baseball analysis. "I didn't know what the hell he was doing," says Esther Roth, his widow.

But MacPhail did. And he was wowed. Roth's work was like nothing he had ever seen. Roth had, for example, parsed Montreal outfielder George Staller's performance by opponent, ballpark, time of game (day, twilight or night), month, day of week, batting position and fielding position (right field or left), and mined the numbers for telling patterns. "It was fascinating what the figures told him," says Esther. They told him, for example, that walks mattered greatly, that on-base percentage was king, findings that Branch Rickey would report in *Life* magazine in 1954. Big league baseball, concluded Rickey, "will accept this new interpretation of baseball statistics eventually."

Brooklyn meantime already did. And so in the early forties, MacPhail met Roth at the Mont-Royal Hotel in Montreal where he was on business. There, the pioneering statistician shared more of his work (including a chart of every pitch of the 1941 World Series).

Lingering visa problems, a petit mal condition and two years in the Canadian army kept Roth from his dream. But at last, on April 14, 1947, Branch Rickey hired Roth and anointed him team statistician, the title good for $100 a week. Roth and Esther moved south to Empire Boulevard, a few blocks from Ebbets Field.

The season began the very next day and Roth, thirty, went to work. "Back then, my system was unique," he explained to author Lee Heiman in 1991, a year before he died. "I would record types of pitches and location. I even had averages for players when they were ahead or behind on the count. My system showed a record for a hitter against a pitcher for the year and over his career. I even had breakdowns on where opposing batters hit the ball." Roth overlooked nothing, noting, for example, which advertisement on the outfield fence at Ebbets Field each home run cleared.

After games, Roth updated his files. "I had one for each team," he explained, "and would offer it to the manager before each new series."

Burt Shotton, who became Brooklyn's manager in 1947, was thrilled. While others advised on whim, Roth leaned on fact. During games, when Roth wanted to alert Shotton to a glaring statistic (say, what a potential pinch-hitter batted against lefties), he would scribble it onto an index card and, from his seat just to the left of the Dodger dugout, pass it to the manager. He did so on the road too, toting to every ballpark his brown leather briefcase chock-full of information. "At that time," recalls Esther, "they wanted to keep him quite secretive and he roomed alone."

Brooklyn won the pennant.

The team finished third in 1948, won another pennant in 1949 and fell to Philadelphia on the last day of the season in 1950. Roth never missed a pitch, had mid-game, wrote C. David Stephan, "never even gone to the men's room!"

In October of 1950, Rickey, who had hired Roth and was his biggest booster, left Brooklyn for Pittsburgh. O'Malley became team president. "When Walter took over the club," remembers general manager Bavasi, "there were two men he wanted to get rid of—Harold Parrott and Allan Roth. They were Rickey men."

Dressen did not want Roth around either. While Shotton had appreciated the statistician, Dressen, who confessed to never having read a book, was wary of his copious notes. And so when Dressen became Dodger manager in 1951, he asked Bavasi to relocate Roth from his seat alongside the dugout to the broadcast booth. This he did. "Charlie won't pay attention to you," Bavasi told the statistician, "but the radio booth will." Roth moved upstairs, feeding statistics to appreciative members of the press.

It was there during Game One of the playoff that Roth now recorded

Thomson's latest home run and waited for Branca's next pitch. It came, a belt-high curveball on the outside part of the plate. Mays popped it to short and Roth penciled a "6" followed by another tiny arc midway up the numeral. Branca was out of the top of the fourth.

Buoyed by three double plays, Hearn finished the seventh up 2–1. In the eighth he went up 3–1, Irvin homering a curve to left. Branca finished the inning and left the game having thrown 133 pitches, each documented by Roth. Branca had pitched adequately, Giant batters unable to get on top of his pitches. (Discounting two sacrifice bunts, in 36 trips to the plate they grounded out just once.) But neither team scored in the ninth, and five years to the day after he had lost baseball's first playoff game, Branca lost again. "I was only twenty then," noted the pitcher to reporter Ben Epstein after the game. "Today, I feel twenty years older."

All Brooklyn had tuned in to the 3–1 loss, cell-blocks in city prison lent portable radios, televisions installed at military recruiting posts and the municipal blood center. And the borough was glum. After taking 9 of 11 home games from New York in the regular season, its team had lost the one that mattered most. New York, meantime, had now won 8 straight and 13 of 14, a single victory from the World Series. Hours after the game, the *Daily Mirror* had its headline: "1 GAME TO GO FOR GIANT MIRACLE."

Angelo Ambrosio arrived at the Polo Grounds at eight the next morning. Just sixteen, he was Logan's clubhouse assistant. And he had work to do.

After winning the previous afternoon, the Giant players, as always after road games, had stuffed their equipment and uniforms into numbered fiberboard boxes. The boxes were then packed—four to a trunk— and transported back to the clubhouse. Ambrosio and Logan now unpacked the boxes, assistant polishing to a shine with saddle soap more than 100 shoes, sliding each pair into its appropriate locker. Next he lay in each locker the proper glove, and hung for every player a fresh towel. Finally, he carried to a tailor two blocks away under the El any clothing the players had left hanging in their lockers with instructions to have dry-cleaned and pressed. Ambrosio loved his job.

Normally Ambrosio had also to serve as batboy for the visiting team. But as the opponent was Brooklyn, the only team to tote its own batboy to the Polo Grounds, Ambrosio had no need to change into his numberless uniform. He was free until after the game.

Ambrosio decided to head out to the stands. Come game time, he could return to the clubhouse and sit just about anywhere—anywhere, that is, but in Durocher's office. Ambrosio knew Franks would be there with the telescope. "I heard it around," says Ambrosio. "The office was off limits." And besides, Franks was no fun. "He was someone you feared," says Ambrosio. "He'd holler at you if you did something wrong." Ambrosio headed outside, his work done.

It was then Billy Leonard's work began. Leonard, seventeen, was the Giant batboy. His father, Arthur, a diehard fan in the Section 5 Club, had secured the gig for his son (not long before alcohol drove him from home). The job fit neatly into the boy's life. Leonard had only to take on game days the B-35 bus from Manhattan Prep in Riverdale to his home on Summit Avenue, walk the four blocks to 161st Street, cross on foot the trestle bridge over the Harlem River and enter Eden four blocks south. After games, he returned home with broken bats and stories unknown (like the one he told friend Ed Goin about Herman Franks once having to hide with his telescope in a clubhouse locker). School-work, meantime, was made up by Leonard during Giant road trips. Thus did the skinny, freckled, auburn-haired boy become the envy of all. Says friend Jim Beattie, "He was our big celebrity."

The celebrity worked hard. There were blocks of rosin to bang into powder and then pour into socks to be bounced on the sweaty palms of pitchers. There were mid-doubleheader dashes to Spotless Dry Cleaners on 164th Street and Ogden Avenue, arms loaded with dirty jerseys. There were gloves to mend, spikes to repair, sandwich runs to make, the cease-less pregame queries of players. (Lockman: "Red, where's the gum?" Mays: "Red, where's my lucky glove?" Dark: "Red, did you throw away that old bat with the nick in it?") And most exhausting, there was the transporting of bats from clubhouse to dugout.

This was a big job. Each trunk held ninety bats and Leonard, having this morning arrived as usual at the clubhouse by 10:30, now dragged two of them by their leather handles onto a rubber-tired dolly. He then rolled them the hundreds of feet to the dugout where he opened the trunks and stocked the bat rack, a wooden box with slats on top and two deep shelves below for fungo bats. Next he returned to the clubhouse for the catching gear, the players now trickling in.

The Giants dressed, then walked to the field. Cued by a quorum of pho-tographers, they filled three rows of bleachers erected deep on the center-field grass. It was time for the team photo. And so twenty-five players, two coaches, manager, trainer and batboy, eyed William Jacobellis.

Jacobellis, thirty-one, knew the men well. He had shot them March through October, turned Giants four-by-five in his studio off Third Avenue where rumbled the El, last of the city overhead railways. And he who had once considered the priesthood was devoutly scrupulous. "His caption read like a short story," says colleague Vern Shibla. Adds friend Paul Bereswill, "He was more talented than the equipment." Newspapers, Bowman Gum Company and a Giant rag called *Grandstand Manager* agreed, for years turning to the olive-skinned Italian for shots of Redmen, Globetrotters, Rangers, Yankees, Dodgers and Giants.

Jacobellis raised his Speed Graphic to his glasses. He focused—thirty men framed beneath seven clubhouse windows—then pressed down his right index finger, the spirit of a team preserved. Here was Mays, the only player holding his glove, the Rawlings Mort Cooper slipped between jersey and forearm. Here were Durocher and Franks side by side and unsmiling. And here, six feet above the cap of Davey Williams, was a window within a window, a rectangular hole in wire mesh fittingly present in team portrait. Unknowingly, a freelance photographer had documented the secret of a team.

The players disbanded. And after ninety minutes of batting practice (an extra fifteen this morning for the slumping Mays), they lumbered back to the clubhouse, changed their shirts and dried off. Leonard, in cap, jersey, pants, stockings and spikes, gathered and re-racked the bats while the Dodgers batted for thirty minutes. He then readied, at the far end of the dugout, a water cooler, a box of Wrigley's gum and a bucket of ice enlivened with an ammoniac spritz. Overheated players would dip a towel into the bucket and wipe their necks with what they called "Florida Water." Says George Spencer, "You'd inhale those fumes and it kept you going."

At 1:30 p.m. it was game time, time again for opposing sides to court Lady Luck. Here, four Dodger wives and Branca's fiancée, Ann Mulvey, crossed nail-polished fingers. There, Schenz asked starting pitcher Sheldon Jones if he wanted for his pocket a lucky half-dollar. Jones declined (he had already some charms), then walked to the mound followed by television cameras, millions of fans heading indoors to tune in. Wrote the *New York Times,* "Times Square assumed a Sabbathlike calm."

NBC was broadcasting the game nationally and, unlike CBS in Game One, had locked up a corporate sponsor. If a Giant hit a home run, broadcasters Ernie Harwell and Russ Hodges would be sure to announce that 600 Chesterfield cigarettes were on their way to the boys in the hospital.

The game began: a fly ball by Furillo, a single by Reese, a strikeout by Snider. And up in the press box, within earshot of reporter Dan Parker, a dispirited fan now wondered "why Dressen isn't stealing any signals lately."

Dressen, though, was on the ball. And the moment Snider whiffed, he suspected foul play. Only a spitball, he reasoned, could drop so precipitously. "Jones is spitting on his fingers," he screamed from the dugout at home plate umpire Larry Goetz. "That wasn't a spitter," Goetz responded. "It was a spinner." As Dressen barked obscenities at Goetz, Robinson pulled the next pitch thrown him deep to left field for a two-run homer.

In the bottom of the inning, Clement Walter Labine walked to the pitcher's mound. He had not pitched a lick in eleven days.

Back on September 21, Labine was roughed up by Philadelphia. The big blow was a first-inning grand slam by Willie Jones. Dressen was furious that Labine had pitched to Jones from the stretch and not the windup as he had ordered, and when Labine left the game having given up six runs in 1.1 innings, he found himself squarely in Dressen's doghouse. No matter that before the incident, Labine had thrown four straight complete-game victories. No matter that he had given up just four runs in those 36 innings, an ERA of 1.00. The manager was angry and as the season dwindled, he refused to pitch Labine. "He was a very vindictive person," says Labine, "and he liked to make points."

Over the last three days of the regular season, rather than pitch Labine, Dressen had trotted out Erskine, Newcombe and Roe each on two days' rest. His blockheadedness had tired his staff. And now, with the season on the line, it left him no choice but to throw the rookie.

It was, ironically, Dressen who had brought Labine to Brooklyn. In 1943, a Boston scout named George Army had watched Labine throw in the parking lot of a racetrack in Pascoag, Rhode Island. He liked what he saw and told Labine, seventeen, to come to Boston for a tryout. A few weeks later Labine did. But when he arrived at Braves Field a few hours before Boston faced Brooklyn, the clubhouse door was locked. Brooklyn coach Dressen saw the kid knocking. That very night, he and Rickey signed Labine to a contract.

Eight years had passed and now, armed with a 2–0 lead, the man called Clem took the mound for the biggest game of his young career. He retired the Giants quickly in the first and in the second survived a double by Thomson and a single by Mays.

Labine and Walker returned to the dugout (the catcher subbing for Campanella, whose right hamstring, injured two days before, was still sore). Dressen told them he was sure Thomson, standing on second, had spied a signal and relayed it to Mays. And so the battery switched its signs. The count on the batter would dictate which sign Labine was to follow.

Labine was again in trouble in the third. An error, a single and a walk had, with two outs, loaded the bases for Thomson. The count went full. As there were three balls on Thomson, Labine now looked for Walker's third sign. The catcher had the temerity to call for a curveball. Labine nodded.

Nine years earlier, a high school football pass had snapped a tendon in Labine's right index finger. The finger mended curiously, its top knuckle bent, and it was not long before Labine noticed that he no longer needed his thumb to steady a ball pre-pitch but could instead grip it with just his middle and index fingers. What's more, his bent forefinger, a linchpin of sorts, lent his curve movement. "It gave me so much pressure on the ball that I could give it great spin," explains Labine. Folks called it a cunnythumb curve.

As good a pitch as it was, the rookie at times tipped off when he would throw it. And so Dressen often reminded Labine to turn his glove over his pitching hand with each delivery, come spring the manager going so far as to write in black ink on four fingers of Labine's mitt T, U, R, N. This worked, an idea born perhaps in the poetry scrawled by Jerome David Salinger in green ink on the lefty mitt of Allie Caulfield, *The Catcher in the Rye* published just seventy-seven days earlier.

Now, facing Thomson, Labine did not tip his curve. Gripping the baseball within his glove, the pitcher dug the calloused and angled tip of his right forefinger into its stitching, his middle finger below and to the right. He kicked and fired. The ball flew straight, then veered wildly from the strike zone, as low as it was outside. Thomson waved at the cunnythumb. He missed badly.

Thomson had looked foolish. Had Franks, off in the clubhouse, been fouled up by the changed signs? "If the ball's at [a batter's] ankles," says Corwin, "and he has a hell of a cut, both benches knew." After the game, Thomson spoke of the at-bat to Ben Epstein of the *Daily Mirror*. "I was expecting him to hang one in there," he said. "But he tossed me a curve, a good pitch."

Thomson had swung and so did the series. Brooklyn had life.

The Dodgers scored in the fifth and again in the sixth, waiting out a forty-one-minute rain delay to plate three runs and take a 6–0 lead. They scored twice in the seventh and twice more in the ninth to go up 10–zip. Hodges, Pafko, Walker and Robinson hit home runs. Spencer and Corwin surrendered eight runs in relief. Official scorer Jack Lang ruled a quintet of Giant miscues errors, five times the first "E" in the Chesterfield ad high above Franks lighting in center field.

In the bottom of the ninth, Westrum worked a meaningless walk to lead off the inning. Schenz jogged to first to run for the catcher.

Schenz had not appeared in a home game in seventy-nine days. And yet, the New York World-Telegram and Sun (hungry for extra playoff copy) had that very morning devoted ten paragraphs to the obscure pinch-runner. "It's just enough," Schenz told columnist Lou Miller, "if I can be there with the team and help in any way." A photograph showed Schenz smiling, crossing four fingers for luck.

When Schenz reached first, he found reserve Davey Williams already there. The men looked to Durocher, who pointed to Williams. Embarrassed, Schenz retreated to the bench.

Labine was in complete control. His slow sinkers and off-speed curves induced soft grounder after easy pop-up seriatim. The Giants had managed just six hits and two fly balls to the outfield when, at 4:55 p.m., a playoff series knotted at 1–1. "As far as I can see," Jackie Robinson told the press in the clubhouse, "it's just as if the season were beginning. No lead. No nothing." Durocher, meantime, praised a rookie. "Labine pitched a great game," he said. He had pitched an even greater game than Durocher let on. It had mattered not a wink that the Giant batters knew what was coming.

"Many times, in baseball," wrote catcher Moe Berg in 1941, "a club knows every pitch thrown and still loses." Indeed, over the years, numerous lineups had been unable in big spots to capitalize on inside information. On October 8, 1940, for example, in the seventh and deciding game of the World Series, Detroit batters knew exactly what Cincinnati ace Paul Derringer was going to throw before each and every pitch. Reds catcher Jimmie Wilson was holding his right hand too low, his signaling fingers peeking out beneath his thighs in view of their bench. (Wilson, a forty-year-old coach, could be excused. Starter Ernie Lombardi had sprained his ankle and backup Willard Hershberger had committed suicide, forcing Wilson into duty.) Even so, Detroit managed just seven hits off Derringer and lost 2–1.

Clem Labine had also won, blanking New York. And if, heading into the game, Dressen had still harbored suspicions of sign-stealing, Labine's shutout surely snuffed them out. For the Giants' system was undetectable, an effective scrim unfurled over the second half of their season. Down the stretch, the men behind it had left no fingerprints. And they were men forgotten. Yvars last batted on August 30. Chadwick last went to work on July 23. Schenz last appeared in a home game on July 14. Durocher last managed from his home dugout on July 18. And that same day, Franks had last manned his coaching box at the Polo Grounds. Ever since, no one had bothered to wonder where he was.

The second playoff game was over. Roth updated his files, Ambrosio and Logan tidied the clubhouse, Leonard put away the bats, Schwab readied his sprinklers, Colletti raised a red flag, and the players and coaches headed home to their families—Yvars to Allen Street in Valhalla, Schenz to the Henry Hudson Hotel, Durocher to East 61st Street and Franks to West 85th. On Elder Avenue in the Bronx, Chadwick shuffled to bed and went to sleep.

New York and Brooklyn had played 24 games against each other, 265 versus the rest of the league. And after a combined 289 contests and 2,817.1 innings, they were tied. One final game would decide the pennant.

FOURTEEN

No steel can enter the human heart as icily as a full stop at the right moment.

—ISAAC BABEL, *Guy de Maupassant*, 1932
(translated by Gregory Freidin)

OCTOBER 3, WEDNESDAY

John Steinbeck wrote the date in mini, cursive letters. Settled in a blue wing-back chair four flights above East 72nd Street, he started his morning with a note to Pascal Covici, just as he had every workday since beginning his novel *East of Eden* on February 12. The letters to his editor, Steinbeck said, were a way of "getting my mental arm in shape to pitch a good game." And so it seemed fitting that on this day, months shy of fifty, Steinbeck began with baseball. "Today," he wrote, "Giants and Dodgers play off their tie."

Chadwick, supine on his couch, needed no reminding. Still, when Miriam returned three cents poorer from Sadie's Candy Store with the *Daily Mirror*, he took the tabloid and read of the game. "This is it, boys and girls," wrote Dan Parker. "And it's about time because a few more days of the nerve-shattering suspense that has the town in a frenzy would fill all the hospitals, booby-hatches and hoosegows, and provoke a civil war."

Chadwick's face was wan from months spent indoors. His body was gaunt, dwindled to 130 pounds. His cough lingered and he did not even have the strength to walk to the phone in the foyer when well-wishers called. Still, though butterflies fluttered in his sutured stomach, he was emboldened—the great Newcombe was taking his 20–9 record to the hill. And though Newcombe had shed six pounds pitching in humid Philadelphia on Saturday and Sunday, the Dodger was still 109 pounds more solid than he.

Newcombe left his home in Colonia, New Jersey, just before 10 a.m.

He paid a 50-cent toll, drove through the Holland Tunnel, up the West Side Highway, onto the Henry Hudson Parkway, across 125th Street and north on Seventh Avenue to the Polo Grounds. He parked in the lot behind right field and filed past Collins, the genial, white-haired guard standing sentry at the clubhouse. A bundle of teammates soon followed—they had boarded a bus in front of the St. George Hotel on Clark Street in downtown Brooklyn.

The Giants arrived now too, walking piecemeal into their locker room and changing into uniforms. Sewn to each man's left sleeve was a patch. White, sky blue and red, it depicted a ball in a glove on a diamond, commemoration of the league's seventy-fifth anniversary. In all those years, just eight times had a Giant or Dodger regular season gone 157 games as both did now.

Dressen and Durocher spoke to the sportswriters, then posted their lineup cards in the dugouts (a Campanella hamstring again activating Walker). Home team, then away, took batting practice, the park's loudspeakers serenading each with a carefully chosen song: "It's the Loveliest Night of the Year" for New York, "Enjoy Yourself. It's Later Than You Think" for Brooklyn. Then it was back to the clubhouse for a change into dry jerseys, infusions of pep from the managers and a rundown on how to pitch the men powwowing one room over. (Dressen to Newcombe: pitch Mueller inside. Durocher to Maglie: pitch Hodges outside.)

Jackie Gleason and Frank Sinatra threw back a pre-noon nip. The men, both thirty-five, were at Toots Shor's, Gleason planning to drink in at the midtown saloon a Dodger victory. But Sinatra offered tickets to the game, Shor called a ride, and the trio, feet already light on the oak-plank floor, stepped from 51 West 51st Street into a liquor-stocked limo.

The men were of similar stock. Suckled on the streets of Brooklyn, Philly and Hoboken, the actor had been a barker, restaurateur a bouncer, singer a copy boy arrested at twenty-three for seduction and adultery. Sinatra had since with velvet voice seduced millions, and it was adultery, an affair with Ava Gardner, that would in twenty-six days allow him to legally leave wife Nancy for the actress.

Gleason also set to honeymoon, to up, in forty-eight hours, with a housewife named Alice. For it was this coming Friday, in a live six-minute sketch on his TV show *Cavalcade of Stars,* that loudmouthed Jackie Gleason would turn loudmouthed Ralph Kramden. Now, though, the bus driver was in a limo. "Jackie guzzled booze all the way to the Polo Grounds," remembered Sinatra to author James Bacon, "and ate most of the food."

That Shor, the son of immigrants, found himself rubbing elbows with

Sinatra and Gleason was unsurprising. For a circular bar had turned the rotund Toots every bit the celebrity at forty-eight that were his patrons, this very day the connected saloonkeeper lending a Hemingway a hand. Wrote Jack Hemingway, "I took advantage of Papa's friendship with Toots Shor to get tickets."

Papa was off in San Francisco de Paula, home at his Finca Vigía, a farm just east of Havana. February had seen completion of a novella titled *The Old Man and the Sea,* and what would become *Islands in the Stream* was on this Wednesday well underway. But suddenly was Hemingway halted. For yesterday had come wired word that Pauline Pfeiffer (whom the author had divorced in 1940) was dead of a brain tumor. Still, Hemingway did not set off for the funeral. "I wonder," says son Pat, "whether he was sufficiently upset to have missed the game."

Gleason, Sinatra and Shor arrived at the Polo Grounds. Flush with drink, the trio strode through a vomitory into green seats given Sinatra by pal Durocher. Only Gleason would pull for Brooklyn.

At last it was time for ball, and each man went to his station. Yvars sat down beneath the bullpen awning in right. Franks entered Durocher's office. (Back in Utah, people would wonder where was their hometown boy.) Durocher smiled at his wife and daughter seated beside Danny Kaye in Section 19, then descended into the dugout. Schenz waved to his cousin Robert sitting just behind Laraine Day and then too stepped down from view. And Chadwick lay before his twelve-inch set, Miriam beside him on her favorite Queen Anne chair.

The sky was leaden, the air damp, a stiff wind blowing to right. But the day was mild. As the crowd fanned into waiting seats, the temperature was 71 degrees.

The fans, divided in their loyalties, antagonized each other. Here a Brooklynite with a packet of napkins offered "crying towels" to Giant fans. There a quartet of Giant boosters with another prop, a hose, promised all Dodger fans free gas.

A devout few had huddled outside the park overnight, seen the sun rise over Harlem at 5:35 a.m. and been first on line for tickets—$3 for box seats, $2 for reserve grandstand, $1.25 for general admission, 60 cents for bleachers. There had though been no need to camp out. Strangely, as the crowd finished singing the national anthem, some twenty thousand seats were unoccupied, the green wings of the upper deck empty.

The previous game had not sold out either, the *Daily News* and the *New York Times* putting forth the best guess as to why. "ASSUMED SELL-OUT CUTS SIZE OF CROWD," read a headline. Strangely, this was plausible. On September 28, the Giants had announced that they would accept no more applications for World Series tickets and the next day, a headline in the *New York Herald Tribune* had screamed: "GIANTS HAVE NO TICKETS! SERIES OVERSUBSCRIBED." The fans, it seems, assumed the playoff was sold out as well.

And so the crowd numbered just 34,320. The tally pushed Major League Baseball's 1951 attendance to 16.1 million. That number was down 7.7 percent from the previous season.

Leading up to the playoff, only 986,610 of the more than four million tickets to New York's seventy-seven home games had sold. And though only Brooklyn and its bandbox had drawn more fans, New York's attendance was disappointing. (On August 28, for example, just 8,803 folks went to the Polo Grounds to watch the Giants gun for their seventeenth straight win.) The Giants had enjoyed their best season in fourteen years. And yet, hosting two playoff games, they drew just 50,000 more fans to their park than in 1950.

Attendance had stagnated during the war. In 1941, 9.7 million fans attended games, 8.8 million in 1944. After the defeat of Hitler, however, attendance soared, jumping from 10.8 million in 1945 to 20.9 million in 1948. But then, again, attendance cooled. Not until expansion in 1962 would as many people turn out for games.

Some would-be ballpark-goers were likely sidetracked not by waning enthusiasm but by postwar gravitations toward suburbs and television. For in 1951, baseball was king. Herbert Hoover would in November declare the sport second only to religion in influence for good on American life. Fans the year prior had spent 55.4 million dollars on tickets to baseball games—more money than on all other pro sports combined. And including the Negro leagues, there were a total of thirty big league baseball clubs in the United States, two more than all the country's football, basketball and hockey teams combined, just boxing and horse racing competing at all for public attention. (Heavyweight Joe Louis, in Manhattan this October morning to promote a fight, hustled from press conference to ballpark so as to not miss a pitch.)

The future of the national pastime was as bright. "Baseball is a thousand leagues," testified Larry MacPhail earlier in the year to a House subcommittee. Indeed, millions of kids across the country played the game and the many others it had spawned—kickball, stickball, punchball, stoopball, wallball. And so on this Wednesday, eight separate broadcasts set to air the Giant–Dodger playoff game to all forty-eight states, baseball to be carried by every last one of the nation's 96 million radios and 16 million television sets.

In the New York area, those sets were now turning to baseball. While at 1:00 p.m. the pre-game programs on WNBT and WPIX had roughly half the combined viewers of the other four shows on air, by 1:15 they were even.

Maglie warmed up "as nonchalantly as if this were just a World Series," joked Bill Roeder in the *New York World-Telegram and Sun,* and Gordon McClendon leaned into his microphone. "Twenty years from now, the fans will be talking about this afternoon's hero as yet unknown," McClendon told his audience. "If there is a goat, his name will echo down the corridor of time."

McClendon's deep voice echoed over the Liberty Broadcasting Network. Just thirty, the Yale graduate owned the Texas-based network, had launched it in 1947. It aired mainly re-creations of baseball games, broadcasts that lagged ten minutes behind live action and relied on telegraph wire, Morse code and a vivid imagination. New commissioner Ford Frick would in months ban such unauthorized re-creations, forcing McClendon to fold his network. But on October 3, 1951, McClendon was wildly popular. The Oklahoman was on 431 stations.

On this afternoon, McClendon was in very good company. Six of the eventual first thirteen recipients of the Baseball Hall of Fame's Ford Frick Award (given annually to a top broadcaster) peppered the press box beside him.

The press box clung to the curved bottom of the upper deck, a boomerang jutting some ten feet toward play. At one end, above third, sat Dodger announcers Barber and Desmond, sharing today the WMGM moving-coil mike. (Second-year Brooklyn broadcaster Vin Scully was on hand but not working.) In the booth to their right was McClendon and beside him Al Helfer, whose Mutual Broadcasting System was the largest in the land. Buck Canel and Felo Ramirez were next, calling the game in Spanish for all Latin America. Then came the newspapermen, fifty or so reporters straddling home plate. The men—and they were all men—sat behind chicken-wire in a long row, hunched shoulder to shoulder over portable Olivetti typewriters.

Heading toward first, clustered with their equipment, stood the photographers and cameramen unenclosed. They looked like marksmen, the enormous black lenses of their Graflex cameras, painted with the names of New York newspapers, aimed like rifles at the field. The newsreel cameras were ready to shoot too—the handheld spring-loaded Eymos and the gargantuan Mitchells balanced on tripods, their enormous 600-foot magazines elapsing twenty-four frames per second with a steady hum.

Next door was the tin-ceilinged TV booth where Harwell called the action for Channel 11, one of fifty-two NBC stations across the country. A wooden door to his right led to the WMCA radio booth where sat his partner Hodges in a short-sleeved yellow shirt and, a few feet over, behind a hanging blanket, Harry Caray, pipeline to the Midwest. (Bob Prince, announcer for Pittsburgh and Hodges's guest, sat quietly beside them.) And some 250 miles southwest, in a studio on Tenth Street in Arlington, Virginia, Nat Allbright set to air the game's eighth broadcast on WEAM 1390. His would be a re-creation of the game fed by Western Union's ticker and staged roughly two batters behind the live action.

At long last, 1:30 p.m. arrived. The men behind the mikes gave the lineups in dulcet voice, Carl Furillo walked to the plate and, as Westrum flashed Maglie his sign, four umpires readied for a first pitch. They were a formidable crew: Jocko Conlan at first, Bill Stewart at second, Larry Goetz at third, Lou Jorda at home. The quartet had cumulatively called ten All-Star games and nine World Series. And they were famous. Conlan would land in the Baseball Hall of Fame. Stewart would be inducted into *hockey's* U.S. Hall of Fame, the Massachusetts native not only a former NHL referee but coach of the 1938 Stanley Cup champion Chicago Blackhawks. And a Norman Rockwell painting of Jorda and Goetz scanning a rainy sky (together with ump Beans Reardon) had graced the April 23, 1949, cover of the *Saturday Evening Post*.

"First pitch of a historic game," McClendon told his audience. Jorda was unimpressed with the delivery and this McClendon reported: "Sidearmer raked outside for ball one." The game was underway.

Furillo took Maglie's first four pitches. The count was 2–2 when he finally swung, fouling one off. Maglie's next pitch froze Furillo and Jorda punched him out. It was strikeout number 141 on the year for Maglie, fourth-most in the league.

Salvatore Anthony Maglie was a superstar. He had won a combined 41 games in 1950 and 1951, and his composite 2.84 ERA over those seasons was tops in all baseball. He had beaten Brooklyn five times in 1951, and with him on the hill and the Giants at home, the betting line in Reno had New York 13–10 favorites to take the game and the pennant.

Maglie had not always been an ace. The Niagara Falls native had posted a losing record in the minors and was twenty-eight before he appeared in a big league game. Though in 1945 he had a solid rookie season, 5–4 with a 2.35 ERA, he was overlooked the following spring training and so headed south of the border to pitch 7,100 feet above sea level for the Puebla Angeles of the Mexican League.

Maglie's curve did not snap in the thin Puebla air. And so his manager, Adolfo Domingo De Guzman Luque (a Cuban-native known as Dolf who won 194 games over twenty seasons in the majors), taught Maglie to tighten the spin on his curve, to throw it harder and to spot his pitches. Maglie flourished. Still, he was blackballed for having played in Mexico and did not return to the majors until 1950. When finally he did pitch again in Manhattan (a city just 265.05 feet above sea level at its highest point), he was dominant, throwing 45 consecutive scoreless innings and a league-high 5 shutouts.

Maglie was not to have a shutout on this day. He walked Reese and Snider—the first time in twenty days he had walked consecutive batters—then gave up to Robinson a single to left. Reese scored, Jansen began to warm in the right-field pen and, within the facing of the upper deck in left, foul of the foul pole, Henry Colletti yanked with his 137 pounds a cable that lifted a twelve-inch number "1"—white paint on black metal filling a scoreboard cavity. At the end of one inning, Brooklyn led 1–0. And tens of millions tuned in on radio and television knew the score, in New York alone, the number of TV sets tuned to ball now outnumbering all others roughly five to one.

Millions more suddenly knew the score too. For it was now that the first of what would be inning-by-inning updates of the game appeared on Dow Jones's stock ticker, echoed between races at Belmont Park, greeted all who phoned the New York Telephone Company wondering only as to the time of day. Brooklyn led New York one to nothing.

In the second, Maglie retired the Dodgers in order, and with one out in the bottom of the inning, Lockman singled off Newcombe. From his perch in the fourth window of the clubhouse, Franks watched a tiny Thomson walk to the plate. He knew that Thomson was squarely in the wanting-the-signs camp. And as Newcombe peered in for his sign, so did Thomson, looking beyond second baseman Robinson toward the bullpen. Says Thomson, "I don't know why I wouldn't have."

Thomson took ball one, then lashed a single to left. In the press box, an amplifier carried the voice of Willie Goodrich: "Thomson has now hit safely in fifteen consecutive games." Running hard out of the box, Thomson rounded first head down. Pafko fielded the ball cleanly and Durocher, raising his arms, held Lockman at second. Pafko threw to Reese, who turned to find what 34,320 already saw—Lockman standing on second and Thomson, oblivious, running to join him. The base was already occupied. When Thomson finally looked up, Reese tossed the ball to Hodges, who waited for Thomson to retreat to first, then tagged him out.

Up above, the press box was glutted. And so, higher still, the first rows of the upper deck behind home plate were cordoned off for the overflow, among it Arch Murray of the *New York Post*, Dodger press agent Irving Rudd, seven members of the International News Service and the great Grantland Rice. Twenty-seven Octobers past, watching the Notre Dame backfield run wild on the very same field before him now, Rice had typed the most famous of all sentences in the history of sports journalism: "Outlined against a blue-gray October sky, the Four Horsemen rode again." Now, a few seats over, statistician Roth, eager to clarify Thomson's base-running gaffe, wrote on his yellow graph paper a sentence somewhat more prosaic: "5 went for 2nd on hit evidently thinking 3 went to 3rd and 5 out xtracking to 1st." The rally quashed, Mays lined to Pafko and the inning ended.

Lying on his living room couch, looking over his feet, Chadwick watched Furillo walk to the plate to lead off the third. It was 2:04 p.m.— Roth noted the time—and Chadwick saw suddenly the 6 on Furillo's back brighten. Chadwick had known that Schmelzer would soon flip the lights, the gray of an afternoon visible through the two curtained windows behind his television.

The Dodgers went down quickly—groundout, pop-up, strikeout. And throughout the park, a dig resounded: "Now maybe Thomson can see where he's going."

Discussion of Thomson's blunder carried into the bottom of the inning. "We may have had a famous repetition of the Fred Merkle incident here today," McClendon told his audience, invoking the goat of 1908 as Newcombe threw ball three to Westrum to run the count full. "It might be this afternoon that Bobby Thomson's play . . . would be joined alongside that." Westrum, the leadoff man, walked. But a sacrifice bunt by Maglie failed to advance the catcher and the third inning ended with Brooklyn still ahead 1–0. Durocher left the coaching box off of third and Dressen took his place. (He too often coached afield.)

The lines of the twenty-by-ten-foot coaching box, neatly laid in chalk by Schwab before the game, were long since erased. As was his routine, Durocher had kicked them clean in the bottom of the first so as to be able to creep toward home and more effectively bark at the ump (and, seasons past, peek at catcher signals). Now, after Robinson grounded out to Stanky to lead off the top of the fourth and the count went to 2–2 on Pafko, Dressen also inched down the line. Westrum was alert. As Maglie looked in for the signal, his catcher, noted McClendon, was "shielding his signs from Chuck Dressen, a good sign-stealer at third." Pafko struck out swinging, Hodges grounded weakly to Thomson and the inning ended. Maglie had retired eleven in a row.

It was still 1–0 Brooklyn in the bottom of the fifth when Thomson hit a one-out double to left, beating Pafko's throw with a head-first dive. Mays then struck out, and as Newcombe set about walking Westrum intentionally, Robinson called time and notified third-base umpire Goetz that Durocher was straying from his coaching box. Goetz ordered Durocher back to his borderless box, and across the outfield grass, big Branca now rose in the Brooklyn pen.

Five hours earlier, Branca had arrived at the park, his right arm stiff. Trainer Wendler had then rubbed the arm with Capsulin, an oil that he called a counterirritant. "It burned so much," explains Branca, "you forgot you had pain in your arm."

Branca's pain had flared in his right triceps—the muscles had ached ever since his consecutive shutouts in late August. And sure enough, the Capsulin, a hot goo produced from chili peppers, had lessened its hurt. But after batting practice, though Branca was careful to keep his arm in the heavy blue wool sleeve of his sweatshirt, still the muscles felt tight, and now in the fifth inning he rose and lobbed a ball to Clyde Sukeforth. He would toss, just toss, to try and get loose.

Sukeforth, two months shy of fifty, was the bullpen coach. And as a retired catcher, scout and, fleetingly, manager, he knew baseball to its cork core.

Sukey, as the players called him, had caught ten seasons for Cincinnati and Brooklyn, then become a scout. It was he, in 1945, whom Branch Rickey had dispatched to Chicago to vet one Jack Roosevelt Robinson, shortstop of the Negro league Kansas City Monarchs. Robinson was injured but Sukeforth saw in him enough (off the field) to recommend he be hired. He was. And when on April 15, 1947, Robinson made history, so too did Sukeforth, the first in the twentieth century to write the surname of a black man onto a major league lineup card. (Durocher had been suspended four days prior and Sukeforth managed the club for two games.)

Now, four and a half years later, Sukeforth stood on the warning track in left field at the Polo Grounds having a catch with one of his pitchers. With each toss, the lighter felt the five-ounce ball Branca flung to his coach.

Still, it did not appear that Branca would soon be needed. Newcombe got Maglie to ground out to Reese and the fifth inning ended. The Dodgers still led 1–0. And despite two hits, Thomson was still very much the game's goat.

With four innings left in the season and down a run, Durocher ordered his starters to replace his relievers in the bullpen. If Maglie needed help, he reasoned, he wanted his best on the mound. And so, by the time Maglie struck out Reese to start the sixth, a quintet of pitchers had switched places: Corwin, Kennedy and Koslo to the dugout, Jansen and Hearn to the bullpen, there to sit alongside coach Shellenback and catchers Yvars and Noble.

After a scoreless sixth, announcers Harwell and Hodges switched places too—Harwell to the NBC booth, Hodges to finish calling the game on WMCA radio. Hodges preferred the radio. It allowed for little dead air and, simply put, he liked to talk. Though Hodges had a cold, was up late the night before gargling Listerine, his voice was fine, smoky after six innings of Chesterfield cigarettes. And, just in case, his mike had a cough switch.

Hodges had first sat behind a microphone in 1928 as a sophomore at the University of Kentucky, helping a clueless program director at Louisville's WHAS radio broadcast the second half of a college football game. Three years later, having enrolled in law school, he earned $20 a week hosting at dawn a hillbilly music program. Hodges soon segued into sports, assisted the great Yankee broadcaster Mel Allen, announced on Wednesday nights the CBS TV Pabst Blue Ribbon bouts and became in 1949 the first-string broadcaster of the Giants. Hodges was a natural, his salary two years later $75,000.

But now, Hodges was disheartened. Newcombe had thrown 22.1 consecutive scoreless innings. And with just three innings left in the game, Brooklyn's 1–0 lead was safe.

So too, for now, was Newcombe's money, the $3,600 Bavasi had given him back in August against his inevitable World Series share.

Pennant winners had been pocketing extra money since 1903 when Boston defeated Pittsburgh in eight games in the first World Series. (It was then Pirates owner Barney Dreyfuss donated to his players his share of the receipts, for the first and last time the losing player collecting more money than the winner.) After long fluctuating, the calculus of World Series shares had stabilized in 1947 when owners earmarked a minimum of $250,000 for pennant-winning players, roughly $5,000 per man. In 1950, for example, when the Yankees swept the Phillies, $5,737.95 went to each winning player, $4,081.34 to each loser.

Each such check was a windfall. (Labine's salary, for example, was $5,000 for the whole of 1951.) And so, while the Dodgers and Giants burned during the playoff with a pure will to beat the other, it is not wrong to say that money added incentive.

The Longines clock above center field struck three and at 18 Broad Street, trading on the New York Stock Exchange stopped. It had been a good day. Driven by metals, oils, rails, rubbers and films, the Dow Jones Industrial Average had risen 1.53 points to 275.87, save one session in September its highest close since 1930. Hodges fouled off Maglie's second pitch in the seventh to even the count at 1–1 and McClendon spoke. "Boy," he said, "the wondrous terms of endearment that must be going on between these two teams down there on the field with five thousand dollars riding on the line for each player."

Playoff or not, no barb was off limits when Brooklyn faced New York. Robinson, though a gentleman, cracked about Laraine Day. Durocher, though a friend of integration, screamed racial obscenities. Outfielder Earl Rapp remembered to author Harvey Rosenfeld a talk Durocher gave his black players before facing Brooklyn on August 14. "If the game gets close and tense," Durocher told them, "I may be shouting 'nigger' and 'watermelon' at guys on the other side like Jackie Robinson. But I want you guys to understand that you are on my team."

Newcombe, the second black man ever to pitch in the major leagues, had heard it all before. And as he came to bat with two out and one on in the seventh, he did now. Number 36 swung at a first-pitch strike, grounding to Stanky. As it was time again to pitch, Newcombe did not bother running down the line.

Branca's arm had begun to loosen, and now so too did the nervous crowd, nodding to tradition with a mid-inning stretch. By the time Brooklyn's nine walked to their positions in the bottom of the seventh, Branca was throwing in earnest and more than once did Dressen lift the handset of the dugout phone to check up on his reliever. Sukeforth was pleased.

Irvin drove Newcombe's second pitch solidly to left and slid into second with a double. The bullpen phone rang again. "How's he throwing?" asked Dressen. Sukeforth reported that Branca was throwing hard.

Lockman was next to face Newcombe. The two men looked up for instruction: Lockman to Durocher doing his St. Vitus' dance off third, Newcombe to Dressen gesticulating in the dugout. Newcombe fired. Pitchout. Irvin was not running. Ball one. Point Durocher. Lockman bunted on the next pitch and it rolled but a few feet toward the mound. Walker pounced on the ball cleanly and fired to Cox at third. Safe. Runners were on the corners, no one out, and up stepped Thomson, "dangerous," cautioned McClendon, "as a Great Dane behind a meat counter." All that was needed to score Irvin, to tie the game (and exonerate Thomson) was a semi-deep fly. After a called strike and three foul balls, he delivered—a drive to center gloved by a retreating Snider. The game was tied and Thomson, the Staten Island Scot, moseyed southwest toward his cheering dugout. Mays grounded into a double play, 6-4-3, and a season was reduced to two innings.

Newcombe returned to the dugout. He had thrown 9 innings on September 26, 9 more three days later, the next day another 5.2, and thus far on this day 7 more. Says Newcombe, "He worked the shit out of me, Dressen did." The pitcher was spent and he turned to his manager. "Don told Dressen, in front of the entire ball club," Robinson shared three days later on a WNBC broadcast, "that his arm was dead." Dressen left it to Newcombe to decide whether he would stay in the game.

Above the dugout in the press box, the newspapermen split into two camps—those who wrote for morning papers like the *Daily News* and so had to recount the narrative of the game, and those who wrote for afternoon papers like the *New York World-Telegram and Sun* and so instead crafted articles that did not hinge on a score. Some twenty-five reporters in the latter camp rose with the start of the eighth and set off for the clubhouse. There they would file their features by phone after the game.

Two hundred miles southwest, in another press room, Frank Bourgholtzer turned on a television set in the West Wing of the White House. He flipped to the game. The set was mounted above the desk of Robert Nixon of the International News Service, but Bourgholtzer, NBC's White House correspondent, did not consult Nixon or any of his colleagues. Instead, he says, "I insisted that we watch it because the guy who inherited my electric trains was playing in the game."

That guy was Bobby Thomson.

Weeks shy of thirty-two, Bourgholtzer had, from the age of six months, grown up in Thomson's hometown of New Dorp. His father Crawford had taught Sunday school alongside Thomson's sister Jean at St. Andrews Episcopal Church. And when Bourgholtzer outgrew his Lionel trains they found their way to young Bobby. Ever since, Bourgholtzer, otherwise a Yankee fan, had rooted for his beneficiary.

But no sooner did Truman's press corps glue to the 1–1 game than Genevieve Zeren appeared at their doorway. "Press!" she yelled. Zeren was secretary to press secretary Joseph Short, and her call meant that Short was set to hold a press conference. It was, however, a familiar gag to bid the men come when their attentions were elsewhere and, transfixed by a game, they ignored her shout. But Zeren insisted. "I'm serious," she said. "You'd better come." And so at 3:20 p.m. they did. The television stayed on.

Even as the men scurried out, government bowed to ball. It was in the Capitol just southeast that as Washington Republican Harry Cain held forth on the Korean War, a majority of senators took to televisions and radios in four chambers abutting the Senate floor. And it was in Gatlinburg, Tennessee, that the forty-six of forty-eight U.S. governors come south to hammer out social security and law enforcement hung now instead on an eighth inning. "Compared with that," wrote *Newsweek,* "even the big question of November '52, Who will be the next President of the United States? for the moment seemed inconsequential."

Facing the north lawn of the White House, seated behind his large wooden desk, press secretary Short began: "This won't take long." White House official reporter Jack Romagna recorded the four words in Gregg shorthand and the press—Bourgholtzer, Nixon, John Adams of CBS, Ernest Vaccaro of the Associated Press, Edwin Darby of *Time* magazine, Merriman Smith of the United Press Association and some others—readied their notepads. Short turned to Zeren. "What about the rest of the people?" he asked. "Is this all we have got? Is this the works, Genny?" It was and he continued.

"This is a statement by me: Another atomic bomb has recently been—"

"Wait!" interrupted a reporter. "Wait a second!"

"—exploded," Short continued.

"Wait a second!"

". . . within the Soviet Union."

The reporter called out: "Just a minute, Charlie!" Frazzled, he had called Short by the wrong name.

Months earlier, on December 5, 1950, Short's predecessor, Charlie Ross, had sat behind that same desk and collapsed a few feet from Bourgholtzer, dead of a heart attack. Three days later, Short, a White House correspondent for the *Baltimore Sun,* took over—a photograph of Ross hung on a pale green wall of his office. Unfazed, Short now continued. "In spite of Soviet pretensions that their—"

"Just a minute, Joe. Please!"

Another interruption: " 'Their,' possessive?"

"Right," answered Short.

"—atomic energy program is being directed exclusively toward peaceful purposes, this event confirms again that the Soviet Union is continuing to make atomic weapons. In accordance with the policy of the president to keep the American people informed—"

"Just a minute!"

"—to the fullest extent consistent with our national security, the president has directed me to make this statement and to stress again the necessity—"

"Wait a second!"

"—for that effective, enforceable international control of atomic energy which the United States and the large majority of the members of the United Nations support. Further details cannot be given without adversely affecting our national security interests."

The whole conference had taken little more than one minute, President Truman, three rooms over in the Oval Office, readying now to discuss meat control with J. Edgar Hoover and five others. Bourgholtzer and his colleagues darted back to their desks and in suit and tie composed their reports, the AP first on the wire at 3:27 p.m. And as whispers of Russia's second atomic explosion mushroomed about the country—the bomb six kilotons of plutonium—Furillo sauntered to bat, the television above Robert Nixon's desk humming all the while, a national pastime ambient in the West Wing of the White House.

Back north, it enveloped a city. Literally near all New York took in the game, the share of its TV broadcast well above 90 when Maglie let fly a baseball to start the eighth. He held it a second later—Furillo lining back to the box—and in the Giant pen, Yvars crouched and began to warm Jansen. Reese and then Snider followed with singles to right, where the line of newspapermen now made their way. Having reached Section One at the far end of the upper grandstand, the men half descended the stone ramp that opened onto Eighth Avenue, stopping at the iron gate that led to the clubhouse. With a flash of credentials, they were in.

Robinson walked to the plate. Durocher figured that with a man on third, Dressen might have Snider steal—daring Westrum to throw to second—and so he had Maglie pitchout. But Dressen held his runners. Ball one. Point Dressen. Maglie's next pitch, a curve, broke in the dirt short of home and skittered through Westrum's wickets. Reese scored and Snider raced to third. Brooklyn led 2–1. With Pafko due to bat next, Durocher ordered Robinson intentionally walked to set up the double play.

Pafko was incredibly slow. He had been thrown out in four of his season's five attempted steals and dubbed "Pruschka" by Charlie Grimm, his manager in Chicago—from *hruška*, Slovakian for "pear." (Pafko was Slovak, his parents born in the foothills of the Tatra mountains.) Pafko also had hypertension and his blood pressure, as always when he gripped his bat, now rose.

Maglie walked Robinson and Pruschka hit on cue a sharp grounder to third. But Thomson missed the ball—it kicked off his glove into foul territory—and Snider scored to make it 3–1. After Hodges popped out, another ball found Thomson, a smash by Cox that buzzed on one bounce past his ear. Robinson scored and Brooklyn led 4–1. Walker grounded out to end the rally and Thomson again was the goat.

In the bottom of the eighth, Newcombe mowed down New York on ten pitches: strikeout, groundout, pop-up. One inning remained and Adrienne Dark, Bernice Koslo, Antoinette Yvars and other Giant wives left their seats in Section 19 for the ladies lounge beneath the stands. Says Yvars, "The Brooklyn fans were heckling us."

High above home, Yogi Berra and four Yankee teammates rose disappointed from upper-deck seats. The Polo Grounds held nearly twice as many fans as did Ebbets Field and so a Giant win meant larger World Series shares. New York, though, was down 4–1, and so, resigned to a Brooklyn win, the men headed for the parking lot. "We wanted to beat the crowd," says Berra. "Newcombe was pitching good. I thought it was over."

So did the two dozen writers now in the clubhouse. And so the men squeezed into the Dodger lounge in wait for the winning team. A few jostled for position by the lone window but there was little room— Brooklyn clubhouse man John Griffin was not budging. "He was sitting there on a chair in front of the window and we couldn't see," says Jack Lang, a reporter for the *Long Island Press*. "He was three hundred pounds."

As the ninth inning set to begin, Maglie was done. He had thrown 109 pitches on the afternoon, 298 innings on the season. In all the league, only Spahn and Roberts had pitched more. His last inning had been costly. Just three outs from the pennant, Brooklyn led by three. Durocher summoned Jansen, and Lang and his colleagues set to content themselves with Red Barber's radio broadcast.

As Jansen walked to the pitcher's mound, Labine left Brooklyn's pen for the clubhouse. He was off to smoke a cigarette.

The rookie had not smoked before coming to the majors. But when he had arrived in April, he heard that there was money in endorsing cigarettes and was soon pitching, along with his cunnythumb curve, Old Gold cigarettes. In exchange for his endorsement—"Not a Cough in a Carload"—Lorillard Company of Greensboro, North Carolina, sent Labine not only $500, a tenth his salary, but hundreds of cartons of the unfiltered cigarettes each month. Labine dutifully passed them to friends until the afternoon he opened one of the cream-and-wine-colored cases himself and lit his first smoke.

Below the Chesterfield sign in center, Labine now climbed the clubhouse stairs, entered the locker room, took a match and cigarette from his locker, sat on a wooden step and, safely from view, took a drag. "You didn't smoke in uniform," he says. The nicotine and Turkish tobacco calmed Labine even as he caught sight of the champagne cases and TV cameras now before him.

Newcombe was Brooklyn's leadoff batter in the ninth, and he watched Jansen warm up. Jansen had impeccable control, had averaged all season just 1.8 walks per nine innings. "You could catch him in a rocking chair," says Yvars. True to form, Jansen threw nine pitches in the ninth, eight of them strikes. Brooklyn went down in order.

Three outs remained in the season and Labine hurried back to Brooklyn's pen. There in left field he found Erskine up and throwing alongside Branca. The routine was synchronized: after catching each pitch from Branca, Sukeforth threw it back, then watched Erskine's pitch snap into the glove of Steve Lembo squatted beside him. Having spent the season in Mobile in the Southern Association, Lembo had joined the parent club on September 5. He was delighted. For Brooklyn was home, the catcher born there, living there and due to marry there on October 20, the very same day as Branca.

With both rubbers occupied, Labine sat on the wooden bullpen bench and waited for Newk to close out the game.

Dark walked to the batter's box and Robinson walked to the mound. Robinson, pride of Cairo, Georgia, extended his arm to Newcombe. Their handshake seemed to Schenz, watching from the dugout, an affront, and he screamed at them: "Don't shake yet! It isn't over!" A few seats over, Lohrke disagreed. "Piss on the fire and I'll call the dogs," he mumbled to fellow infielder Williams. "I think the hunt's over."

Indeed, it at all but was. Not once in baseball's 278 preceding playoff and World Series games had a team overcome a three-run deficit in a ninth inning. (Nor, at this writing, has any team in the 879 subsequent such games.)

Still, the fan defers not to logic, and Giant rooters, desperate, disconsolate, turned now to last resorts. Thomas Fitzgibbon, thirteen and listening to Russ Hodges in a living room in St. Albans, Queens, beseeched his mother for help. Mary Fitzgibbon went to her bedroom, returned with Catholicism's patron saint of hopeless causes resplendent in a green robe, set the plaster statue on their large console radio and spoke to her son: "You must have faith in St. Jude." In the Holbert home on St. John's Avenue in Staten Island, brothers Chick and Roy—a retired cop and a retired butcher—decided it might help the home team if they ran counterclockwise about the dining room table. And so together with friends they did. And at the Polo Grounds, midway between third base and home, Morty Rothschild rose from his box seat, hurried to his Buick sedan parked behind home, turned the key in the ignition and headed north on the Speedway. Since driving in August to visit his daughter Diane at Camp Navajo in Honesdale, Pennsylvania, he had noticed that his beloved Giants never lost with him behind the wheel and so now, though it meant leaving his friend and the ninth inning of a deciding playoff game, that is where he sat.

Back at the Polo Grounds, Yvars sat too, set off from his teammates on the center-field end of the right-field bullpen bench, a human signpost. As Newcombe went into his windup, Yvars sat still. A fastball was upcoming. Dark took it for strike one. The captain then fouled off two pitches before slapping with his black bat Newcombe's fourth delivery along the ground toward right. Hodges and Robinson converged on the ball. It glanced off Hodges's glove, trickling along the infield dirt toward second for a single.

Dressen again phoned Sukeforth. "Who's ready?" he asked.

Branca surely was. His right arm, rubbed with oil, swaddled in wool, tenderized with four innings of activity, was loose and strong. It occurred to Sukeforth that, this game in hand, Branca was auditioning for the World Series. "Branca was showing off," Sukeforth told reporter Paul Green years later. "He wanted to pitch tomorrow in Yankee Stadium. He was really humming." Erskine too looked good. This Sukeforth told his boss.

Dark stepped off the canvas bag and Newcombe shortened his delivery. The pitcher would forego the windup for the stretch, sacrifice a few miles-per-hour on his fastball for the shortening of Dark's lead off first.

Up three runs, the adjustment sufficed. It stood to reason that Dressen would not order the extra step of holding the runner, of having Hodges guard the bag. Dark's run, after all, meant nothing and so reason dictated that Hodges would play some ten paces behind the runner to better guard against a hit. But Dressen gave Hodges the order to hold Dark close. And so as Newcombe pitched to Mueller from the stretch, the first baseman planted his black left cleat some five feet diagonally from the bag.

Mueller, of all his team best at directing a pitched ball into the gaps afield, did so now, Mandrake the Magician sending a fastball on the ground toward right. Hodges dove to his right but the Spalding shot under his glove. Runners were on first and second, none was out and Dressen called for time.

Watching his little Emerson, Chadwick saw Dressen walk to the mound. So did Art Suskind, assistant director of the NBC broadcast, and he told the production booth downstairs to cut to the Dodger bullpen. It did. The image on Chadwick's set changed and Harwell, eyeing his monitor, spoke into his Western Electric microphone, model 632C. "That's Carl Erskine on the outside," he said, "and Ralph Branca, Monday's starter and loser, on the inside."

NBC had just two cameras working the game. They were large and mounted on turrets, an NBC lightning-bolt logo on either side. One camera sat just behind home plate, a second high above. The cameras, RCA model TK11, boasted three lenses—a wide-angle, telephoto and normal view—that the cameramen rotated with a large metal handle. While one man racked, the other filmed. Still, filming play was tricky. "Of course you don't get everything," noted Stan Musial that morning in the *New York World-Telegram and Sun*. "There were four home runs yesterday but Robinson's was the only one I saw all the way."

Filling in the blanks for the national television audience was Harwell. The native Georgian had in 1948 been the voice of the Atlanta Crackers when Brooklyn's Red Barber collapsed from ulcers. Barber would miss six weeks behind the mike and so Brooklyn contacted Atlanta owner Earl Mann about obtaining Harwell. Mann demanded compensation. And so it was that he traded Harwell, twenty-seven, a 5'9", 155-pound right-handed announcer, for Cliff Dapper, twenty-eight, a 6'2", 190-pound catcher. Brooklyn got the better deal. Dapper lasted in the major leagues one 1942 month, Harwell fifty-five years.

Harwell had since left Brooklyn to share the broadcast booth with Hodges in New York. And he now watched, together with his audience, Dressen and the Brooklyn infield—Walker, Hodges, Robinson, Reese and Cox—confer with Newcombe on the mound. Newcombe wanted to remain in the game. "I'm okay," he told his manager. Dressen acquiesced and the uniformed klatch dispersed. Newcombe set to face Irvin, the league's top run-producer.

Durocher turned to umpire Goetz at third. "Now, a belt," he said. "A home run right now." Irvin popped out to Hodges in foul territory and Dressen looked like a genius.

Lockman stepped up and Billy Leonard approached the bat rack. After 156 home games, the batboy was but two outs from retiring, set to leave the Giants for an unencumbered senior year at Manhattan Prep. Girlfriend Pat Kannar, fifteen and seated with the Giant wives, watched Leonard hand Thomson his stick, Adirondack model 302. The bat weighed thirty-four ounces. Northern white ash, it was lacquered Giant orange, the top of its barrel branded with a Bob Thomson signature. Farther down the bat, just below its sweet spot, was carved FLEXIBLE WHIP ACTION, script letters filled with black paint.

Thomson gripped his bat and left the dugout for the on-deck circle.

The pennant was two outs away and an announcement echoed through the press box: "Attention, press: World Series credentials for Ebbets Field can be picked up at six o'clock tonight at the Biltmore Hotel."

The Hotel Towers was also abuzz with baseball. For there on Clark Street in Brooklyn the Dodger team would bunk through the World Series, and manager John Webber had arranged a four-day fête, chef Walter Misbach cooking now a battalion of turkeys. The cost: $20,000.

It was 3:50 p.m. and minutes earlier, in the Polo Grounds clubhouse, Stoneham had left nephew Chub Feeney, scout Tom Sheehan, farm director Carl Hubbell and others in his office, and headed downstairs to console Maglie. He found the pitcher drinking a beer on his way into the shower. The owner smiled.

Newcombe checked the runners and fired. Lockman fouled off the pitch and the announcement for Ebbets Field credentials repeated. Since homering on July 5, 1945, in his first-ever major league at-bat, Lockman had strolled 2,477 official times to the plate and not one at-bat had been as big as this. The lefty made it count, lashing Newcombe's next pitch to the green left-field wall on two bounces. Pafko ran after it, Dark raced home, Mueller headed for third and Lockman for second. A double. The score was 4–2, the crowd erupting in paroxysms of fear and hope.

Mueller had not slid. Turning as he ran to watch Pafko throw the ball to Robinson, the right fielder had stepped awkwardly on third, twisting his left ankle. Tendons tore and he lay now in pain at Durocher's feet. The Lip knelt and touched the swelling ankle, then waved his arms hurriedly for help. Schenz, Rigney, team doctor Palermo and trainer Doc Bowman hustled to third. Batboy Leonard fetched a stretcher from the First-Aid station behind home and Schenz and Rigney carried Mueller to the clubhouse, his backside bowing canvas.

Durocher needed a pinch-runner. He had all season pinch-run five men—Davey Williams ten times, Schenz eight, Jack Maguire seven, Rigney three, Clint Hartung once. With Schenz now halfway to center field,

Rigney ineligible (having struck out in the eighth) and Maguire off the team, Durocher curiously forwent Williams for Hartung.

Once upon a time, Hartung had made scouts drool. No one could pitch like him. No one could hit like him. Clinton Clarence Hartung was the young Babe Ruth reincarnate, only at 6'5" and 210 pounds better sculpted. In 1939, the freshman pitched and hit his Hondo Owls to a high school state championship and Hondo, Texas, all corn, cotton and cattle, onto the map. Three years later, Hartung, the "Hondo Hurricane," set off to play for the Minneapolis Millers.

Hartung transferred to Eau Claire, Wisconsin, and, after a lusty season, joined the army. On December 17, 1945, during his fifty-three-month military stint, New York snapped him up. He had cost $25,000 and four players, but hey, the blond, blue-eyed son of a German carpenter was an übermensch. A team "could get $100,000 for him easy as falling off a log," baseball scout Ted McGrew told newspaper *PM*. "He has a chance to become one of the all-time greats of baseball."

Poor control on the mound and strikeouts at the plate had by 1951 reduced the Hurricane to a zephyr, to a part-timer with all of eight singles and a double in this his fifth big league season. The weight of failed expectation saddled Hartung and as public-address announcer Jim Gorey announced now his number 26, he jogged to third an almost apologetic sub.

Dressen lifted the handset beside him and asked yet again who in the bullpen was ready. "He sounded frantic," remembered Sukeforth years later. Labine heard Sukeforth's reply: "Erskine just bounced a curve but Branca's fast and loose."

Erskine's seeming wildness was not necessarily a bad thing. His best pitch was an overhand curve, a pitch he held across the seams and threw, much like the great Spahn, with a straight downward motion. When effective, the bottom fell out of the ball, just as it had now before Sukeforth. "I never had a problem burying that curveball in the dirt with Campy," says Erskine. "I bet Dressen thought 'This is no place for a wild pitch.' "

A wild pitch would indeed be catastrophic, would score a run and move the tying run to third with but one out. And though catcher Walker had a good glove, he was painfully slow, the prospect of him chasing a ball in the seventy-four feet behind home terrifying. Dressen walked to the mound.

As he did, Schenz and Rigney, jackets covering their numbered jerseys, disappeared into the clubhouse carrying the lame Mueller. Coach Freddie Fitzsimmons counseled Lockman at second, who removed and then put on a shoe. And the entire Brooklyn infield again gathered about Newcombe.

Newcombe had been economical—it was his hundredth pitch that Lockman drove to the wall. But he was utterly exhausted. Over eight days, he had thrown an incredible 32 innings. No Major League Baseball pitcher would *ever* again throw so much in so little time.

Newcombe turned to his manager. "This is too important a game," Robinson would in three days remember Newcombe saying, "to take a chance on my arm." Announcer Hodges relayed the scene. "The Dodgers have another conference out there," he reported. "And Chuck Dressen is making up his mind whether to bring in powerhouse Ralph Branca, Carl Erskine or Clem Labine."

Of the two pitchers now warmed, it was obvious whom Dressen should call. Off Branca, Thomson had in 49 at-bats hit .265 with nine singles, a double, triple, two home runs, four walks and five strikeouts. Off Erskine, Thomson had in 22 at-bats hit .545 with seven singles, two doubles, a triple, two home runs, two walks and two strikeouts. Erskine could scarcely have fared worse.

There were, however, six other pitchers Dressen could now have warmed in his stead. Thomson had faced each. He had a home run in three at-bats against Phil Haugstad, a double in five at-bats against Labine, a single in six at-bats against Clyde King, two singles in eight at-bats against Bud Podbielan, five singles and two doubles in twelve at-bats against Johnny Schmitz and in fifty at-bats against Preacher Roe, seven singles, a double, triple and two home runs, his average just .220. That Roe was well rested, having thrown just 1.2 innings in five days, begged further to question why he was not now up in the pen.

First-base umpire Conlan walked to the mound. "Who are you bringing in?" he asked. Dressen answered Branca and the bow-tied ump barked a last name, summoning Branca with a wave.

Off in left field, Sukeforth patted Branca on his back. The pitcher slipped on his wool jacket, took his Rawlings glove in his right hand and headed for the mound. And as Rigney settled in center to watch play from the Giant lounge, "Hank Schenz returns to the bench," Hodges told his radio audience, "and Ralph Branca makes the long walk from the bullpen." The announcer recapped the Newcombe ninth, then continued: "So don't go anywhere. Light up that Chesterfield. Stay right with us and we'll see how Ralph Branca will fare against Bobby Thomson and then Willie Mays to follow."

Harold Burr, seated in the press box, had a pretty good notion of how

Branca might fare. Awaiting the pitcher, the *Brooklyn Eagle* reporter turned to writer Tom Meany. "I don't want to see this," he said. And so as Branca left the pen, Burr left the press box.

Allan Roth was no less skeptical. And it was now, just above Burr in the supplemental press box, that the statistician manifestly shook his head. Sure, Branca's 3.22 ERA was ninth in the league. And yes, he was fourth in both fewest hits allowed and strikeouts per nine innings. But Roth's notes also told of those such as Roe with superior numbers against Thomson. They told that Thomson, long average versus Branca, was *this* year 4-for-12 against him with two walks, a triple, two home runs, four runs batted in and just one strikeout. And they told that Branca simply pitched poorly against New York. He had in 1951 given up 10 home runs to the club, three more than he had surrendered to the rest of the league *combined*. New York had handed him five of his 11 losses.

As always, Roth had compiled a sheaf of notes on New York. And as always, "Dressen didn't want to see it," Roth told author Lee Heiman. "He made little or no use of the information I provided. The man didn't want help from anybody. He thought he could do it all by himself. It's always been that way with the big ego managers. They couldn't believe a statistician sitting in the stands could give them information they didn't know themselves. So Charlie ignored me."

Branca walked farther and farther from the bench in left field between the 447- and 455-foot markers. Seven years earlier, those tin plates had lodged in his memory. For on June 12, 1944, Durocher, then managing Brooklyn, had phoned his bullpen and called upon Branca to mop up the third inning of an 11–5 debacle. Branca, eighteen, had grabbed his jacket from that same bench and headed to the mound for the very first time a major leaguer. It was a trek he would never forget. "It took ten days to walk it," he told the *Long Island Press*.

Branca now walked in his own footsteps. He reached Pafko and the gentle slugger slapped him on his back. "Go get 'em, Ralph," he said.

Branca was happy to get the call, eager to end a personal five-game schneid. Sure, he had struggled of late, had surrendered since the first of September nine home runs, the same number he had allowed in all April, May, June, July and August combined. And, since the first of September, his ERA was 5.71. But while he had been overworked in August and September, he was now finally rested having thrown just 9.1 innings all the previous week.

Branca continued on, walking down then up the "turtleback" slope of

Schwab's outfield grass. "Go get 'em," said Robinson. "Go get 'em," said Reese.

Stepping onto the topsoil that was shortstop, Branca slipped his left hand into his glove and greeted Newcombe with a half embrace, slapping three times his back, his number 36. Newcombe patted Branca too and the pitchers' leather gloves touched between their stomachs. "Don't worry about it, big fella," Branca told Newcombe. "I'll take care of everything." Newcombe had reason to believe he would. Three times Branca had relieved Newcombe. Three times Newcombe had won.

Newcombe walked slowly off to center field, happy Giant fans waving at him handkerchiefs. Branca removed his jacket. Stitched to his back, that which Branca had claimed on D-Day—a royal-blue 13—faced the clubhouse.

Dodger batboy Stanley Strull ran to the mound and took now Branca's jacket. "Let's go get 'em," the boy said. He ran off, leaving on the mound Dressen and Walker and Branca.

Dressen had a decision to make. He could have Branca pitch to Thomson. Or he could walk Thomson and pitch to Mays. As Roth's files attested, in 19 at-bats against Branca, Mays had just one single and a double, his .105 average coupled with two walks, four strikeouts and zero runs batted in. That was a matchup a manager craved. What's more, Mays had wilted down the stretch, hitting two home runs in August and one in September. The rookie had batted .266 since August 1, .250 since August 15, .233 since September 1, .222 since September 15, and .100 in the playoff, a single in 10 at-bats.

But walking Thomson would violate the baseball axiom "never put the potential winning run on base." Four years earlier, Dressen had as Yankee coach watched manager Bucky Harris intentionally walk Pete Reiser in the ninth inning of Game Four of the 1947 World Series only to be burned. And all this season, Dressen had done so in the ninth inning of a game only once. (It had worked. On July 28, Brooklyn led St. Louis 3–2 with two out and Red Schoendienst on second when Dressen had Erskine walk Musial. Hal Rice fouled out to Hodges to end the game.) Dressen decided now to pitch to Thomson.

Dressen normally chatted up his newly summoned pitcher, reviewed strategy. But now, looking up at Branca ten inches taller than himself, manager offered reliever but the simplest of instruction. Said Dressen: "Get him out." The skipper turned and walked back to the dugout, in his pocket jangling 18 cents of Korean *won*. The coins were given Dressen in spring for luck by the mother of a soldier abroad.

Some sixty feet away, Durocher had little more instruction for Thomson. When Mueller's ankle turned, Thomson had run from the on-deck circle toward third. While his friend lay waiting for a stretcher, he had stood beside the bag quietly, bat in hand. The injury distracted Thomson and as Branca took the mound and Hartung did knee-bends at third, Thomson walked slowly back toward home. "During that ninety feet, I was talking to myself, psyching myself up," says Thomson. "I called myself a son of a bitch. I'd never done that before."

Now, some ten feet from home plate, Durocher walked up to Thomson. "Boy," he told his leading home-run hitter, "if you ever hit one, hit one now." With that, Durocher slapped with his right hand Thomson's rear and retreated to his coaching box alongside Hartung.

Hodges watched Thomson walk to the plate. His voice was hoarse and his throat hurt but still he leaned into the white call letters on his metal microphone. "He'll be up there against big Ralph Branca swinging," the announcer told his WMCA audience. "A home run would win it for the Giants and win the championship. A single to the outfield would more than likely tie up the ballgame and keep the inning going."

On the mound, Branca and Walker prepped for Thomson, reviewing that which Dressen and his coaches had laid out before the game. "We had said," remembers Erskine, "keep the ball up. Thomson was a low fastball hitter. His power was low." Now Walker told Branca to try and get ahead of Thomson with a fastball. If he did so, they would then bust him up and in, thus setting up the curve low and away. Branca, who had overruled Walker thirty-eight days before only to see a no-hitter broken up, agreed. Then he asked, "What signs are we using?"

Walker was partial to the "count system." The number of signals flashed would determine the pitch to be thrown. Such was the system Branca normally used with Walker. The pitcher nodded.

Walker trotted back to home and squatted in front of umpire Jorda. The catcher was for Branca not an unfamiliar target. He had pitched to him already six times this season and with great success. In 36.1 innings, the battery had yielded just six earned runs, its ERA 1.49. Branca reared and fired his first warm-up pitch, a BB. "Probably the best I felt since the second shutout in August," he says.

Branca was comfortable coming out of the pen. Over the previous two seasons, he had relieved in 42 games, exactly the number of games he had started. And out of the bullpen he had fared fairly well. Over that two-season span, Branca was 17–15 as a starter with a 3.92 ERA and 375 base runners allowed in 270.2 innings. As a reliever, he was 3–5 with a 3.35 ERA and 96 runners allowed in 75.1 innings.

Branca hurled another warm-up pitch. And as St. Christopher danced about his neck, the pitcher was eager for redemption. For in the history of the major leagues, just five playoff games had been waged and he had lost two of them. The baseball gods had been unfair. "Why is it," Branca's brother John had asked him the night before, "the team scores ten runs for Labine and one for you?"

A dozen rows behind the Brooklyn dugout, Al Branca rose in his seat. The youngest of seventeen, he was off to the army in just days, set to begin basic training in Fort Lee, Virginia. Unfettered, he was on this weekday the only Branca at the park, the only with a rectangular ticket—section, row and seat printed in red—to cheer on his relation. Brother Ralph set to pitch and Al walked toward him, kneeling now in the stone aisle beside Ann Mulvey, an orange "NY" figural prettying her armrest.

Seated with her parents in a box just behind the Brooklyn dugout, Mulvey watched her fiancé finish his eight practice throws. She turned to owner O'Malley. "Isn't it nice of Dressen," she said, "to call in Ralphie to nail down the pennant?"

Thomson positioned his 10½-D black shoes in the inner half of the batter's box. "My cleats fit like a glove," he remembered years later. Branca stepped to the third-base side of the rubber, his 11-D black shoes two sizes too small. The pitcher liked his spikes tight. Branca wiped his brow, and pitcher and batter, both nicknamed Hawk, eyed each other. Mueller's injury had distracted Thomson and only now did he notice Newcombe's relief. "Branca!" thought Thomson. "Where did he come from?"

Pitcher and hitter had both awakened that morning at 7:30 in the home of parents. Both had eaten eggs prepared by his mother, Thomson with a side of bacon, Branca a side of ham. Both had left a New York suburb for the Polo Grounds minutes before 10, Thomson in his blue Mercury, Branca his blue Oldsmobile. Six hours later—it was now 3:57 p.m.—one held a bat and one a ball. And a batter faced the pitcher Durocher had once sought to swap him for.

Unseen in the overhang in left, Colletti, thirty-nine, kept up by pulley his scoreboard: A.B. 23, OUTS 1, BKLYN 100000030, N.Y. 00000010. Another run already in, Colletti would wait for the end of the inning to fill the ninth New York slat.

It was now that Durocher had infielder Lohrke run toward the Giant pen in right to warm up. In the event the game went extra innings, Thomson would replace Mueller in right and Lohrke would move to third. Brooklyn's infield inched back and, as planned, Walker called for a fastball. Lockman, lurking off second, saw the catcher's fingers move. They were bare, not taped like Campy's. "I didn't recognize the sequence," says Lockman. The first baseman touched his belt buckle to let Thomson know he could not read the sign.

But Franks could. Through the season, the Giants had played Brooklyn two outs short of 25 games—just the sixth time teams had in one season squared off so much. The coach knew Brooklyn and its signals inside-out. Walker had called for a fastball. Of this Franks was certain and he pressed his push-button once. The current coursed along Chadwick's yellow and slate wires and the ringer on the green phone in the bullpen buzzed.

The previous inning, Yvars had warmed up pitcher Larry Jansen. But the catcher was now in the hot seat, now at the far end of the right-field bullpen bench set off under cover of shadow from coach Shellenback, pitcher Hearn, catcher Noble and third baseman Lohrke. When the metal buzzer sounded just once, the former test dummy knew what to do. "If I did nothing, it was a fastball," he says. "I did nothing."

Off in center field, Newcombe stepped into a shower. And as big Ralph went into his windup—five ounces in the grip of 220 pounds—the posse of writers squinched into the Brooklyn players lounge listened to Red Barber's call: "Branca pitches and Thomson takes a strike."

Franks was right. Branca had thrown a fastball.

The pitch, a little low and a little inside but squarely over the pentagonal plate, seemed an eminently hittable one for Thomson. And far off in the Brooklyn pen, Erskine and Labine, the latter now warming up too, paused momentarily from their tossing to holler at their brother-in-arm. "Oh, no!" shouted Erskine. "Ralph, not down there! Good-night! Not down there!"

Lying beneath a naked lightbulb on a trainer's table in the clubhouse, Mueller missed the pitch. He was in pain but at the moment ignored. "Nobody was tending to me," he says. Logan did share his room. But he was far away. The bespectacled clubhouse man had learned mid-game that his sister Marie had died of cancer, had had her last rites. So as to be able to hurry after ball to her home across the river on Merriam Avenue, he had packed the team trunks and stood now by a wire-mesh window, his back to the injured right fielder.

Walker tossed the ball back to Branca. And as Colletti inserted at the far left of the left-field scoreboard a "1" in white paint, statistician Roth noted the called strike too, a capital letter "C" drawn in pencil in the first-pitch column on his blue score sheet. Branca was pleased. He had gotten ahead of Thomson.

A season hung in the balance and everywhere did people turn to God. Jews observing an annual fast for a governor of Judea murdered 2,537 years before recited this afternoon a silent Hebrew prayer: "Answer us, God, answer us, on this day of our fast, for we are in great distress." This Nota Schiller would, in his Brownsville tenement, read in minutes. But his current distress had less to do with a fast than a fastball just thrown, the yarmulke'd boy of thirteen, home early from yeshiva, hanging now on the every word of Red Barber. Just below Barber, a girl of twenty wearing the blue-white diamond ring the pitcher had given her in November began to move her lips in prayer, to ask that above all Ralph Theodore Joseph Branca emerge unscathed from this contest seventeen days before his wedding: "Hail Mary, full of grace, the Lord is with thee. Blessed art thou amongst women and blessed is the fruit of thy womb Jesus. Holy Mary, Mother of God, pray for us sinners, now and at the hour of our death. Amen." General manager Bavasi invoked the virgin mother too, mumbling in the ear of gossipmonger Walter Winchell seated one row ahead. So did Carl Bayuk, a sandy-haired boy of thirteen beseeching intervention not on behalf of Brooklyn but New York. Middle son of gentile and Jew, Bayuk balanced now on hands and knees on a Persian carpet in New Jersey. And having communicated with Mary, he spoke now to Thomson, the player tiny in his living room RCA television: "If you hit a home run, I will do anything the good Lord wants me to do." Bayuk's idol Willie Mays, a boy of twenty genuflecting in the on-deck circle at the Polo Grounds, prayed too. "Please don't let it be me," mouthed Mays. "Don't make me come to bat now, God."

As much as anyone, the rookie had Jack Carter to thank he was not in Thomson's spikes.

Carter, twenty-four, loved statistics. Born Jack Cohen in the Bronx, he was a statistician at Standard Oil, his first job since graduating City College in 1948. But less keen on barrels of oil than bats, the Giant fan had from his apartment on Walton Avenue devised in 1950 two baseball statistics: "Equivalent Batting Average" and "Equivalent Batting Average Allowed." These weighted the effectiveness of hitter and pitcher (a single advancing a runner to third, for example, more valuable than one hit with no one on base). And in the spring of 1951, having for months foisted voluminous tables of EBA and EBAA upon his Phi Delta Pi fraternity brothers, Carter had shopped his analysis to baseball.

Giant vice president Feeney had been interested. For stats were the future. (While the just published *Official Encyclopedia of Baseball* took a first statistical stab at baseball history, the U.S. Census Bureau had in

June put to use the brand-new UNIVAC, the world's first commercial computer.) Feeney had pitched Carter to Durocher. The manager was game and so off to the clubhouse went Carter, tall, fair and giddy. "He was very excited to meet Durocher in the nude," remembers Estelle Kraysler, then his wife. "He didn't know whether to extend his hand." Carter did and New York offered him a job, $2,000 for a season of stats.

Carter was diligent, once sending in his stead to a game his wife with grids at the ready. "He had to teach me what his system was," remembers Kraysler. "I went to the game pregnant." By May, Carter had set for Durocher what he called a "Most Productive Batting Order."

What Carter gave New York was not quite what Allan Roth gave Brooklyn. But unlike Dressen, Durocher welcomed the input, altering his lineup at Carter's behest, the statistician later wrote, "when the Giants started their stretch drive." Remembers Kraysler, "Durocher changed the batting order many times because of some of the things my husband told him."

Though the press would never learn of Carter, Durocher had indeed endlessly shuffled his lineup through the season, using Thomson, for example, in every slot in the batting order save leadoff and second. Now, for the fourth game in a row, Thomson was batting sixth.

That morning, driving in his Mercury, zipping alone along the West Side Highway, Thomson had decided that if he could somehow collect three hits in the game, the team would likely win. Three hits. As he now crouched and cocked his orange bat above his right shoulder, two hits already claimed, this thought came to mind.

Another thought, another memory of morning, wafted now to Branca. Robinson had in the clubhouse before the game declared that anyone who did not feel butterflies in his gut was not human. Branca then confessed to Robinson and Reese that he did feel butterflies. The men had laughed. And now, as Branca adjusted his belt, cap and sleeve, rubbed a ball and flipped a white cotton bag holding three ounces of yellow rosin, he thought of butterflies.

Walker's fingers wigwagged. He wanted a fastball and Branca agreed to throw one. Perched in the press box above first base, Hodges painted the scene: "Hartung down the line at third not taking any chances. Lockman without too big of a lead at second but he'll be running like the wind if Thomson hits one."

The wind was blowing southward, the American flag high in center field riffling to right. Some ninety feet below, Franks sat behind the fourth window in the clubhouse, brown eye held to a telescope. About him were pictures framed: a team portrait, actor George Raft, Franklin Roosevelt smoking a cigar, beautiful Laraine and the kids. The room was dark, sunlight glinting off the silver ridges of a radiator peeking up and over the sill before him. The window was open some six inches, the shade drawn even with the lowered wooden frame. And it was through the aperture cut months ago in the wire grid beneath that frame that Franks, all but hidden in Durocher's locked office, now peered. Again, the coach pressed the push-button once. Again, Yvars was still, unaware that he sat within the eye of a newsreel camera off in the press box.

Thomson crouched, in his mouth half a stick of gum. He knew Franks was off spying in center field. "Of course!" says Thomson. And he knew Walker's sign was there to be gotten in the person of Yvars far beyond Robinson. From the batter's box, says Thomson, "you could almost just do it with your eyes."

Branca withdrew with his large right hand a baseball from his mitt. It was a hand befitting his surname, *Branca* Latin for "paw." As the starting center at New York University, he had palmed a basketball with ease and so now, a baseball, nine inches in circumference, all but disappeared in his fingers. Branca raised the ball above his head together with his gloved hand, leaned back on his right leg, kicked his left and brought down his arms, elbows bent inward to his chest. Ball in hand, he reached his right arm far behind his head, elbow pointing toward first, then took with his left leg a giant step toward home, his right leg leaving the ground. Branca whipped his right arm forward and, twenty-three seconds after a first pitch, again let go of the ball. Hodges spoke: "Branca throws."

Thomson watched Branca and like all good hitters slowed his rival's delivery. He saw the pitch unfurl, saw the momentum of a windup thrust Branca's right side past his left, saw the ball leave his right hand, rolling off at last touch his long middle finger. It was all very clear: a buttery sun had in the sixth inning joined Chadwick's eighteen-inch lights to illuminate play.

Atop the concrete outfield wall, astride both staircases that led to the clubhouse, five canvas panels stood side by side, each 17 feet high and 20 feet wide. Batters appreciatively referred to them as "the eyes"; dark green, they helped the hitter pick up a pitched ball homeward bound. This they now did Thomson, Branca's second pitch a white ball with red stitching whooshing brightly through the air against a green backdrop.

The ball was fast moving, traveling some ninety-three miles per hour. As it approached, Thomson slightly lifted then returned to earth his left foot. Walker raised his glove to receive the pitch: it was high, at the level of Thomson's triceps, and set to pass over the inner portion of the plate. The approaching ball some ten feet away, Thomson began his swing, an uppercut, his torso coiling, his right shoulder moving toward first, his arms struggling to extend yet still direct his clenched bat into the path of the inside pitch. Thomson's bat struck the ball before it reached home plate.

Branca's right leg landed, his body following his pitching arm down. Thomson's right wrist turned over, his body following his swinging bat up. The men were moving in opposite directions.

The ball shot toward third base and Branca whipped his head right to watch its flight. Still in the batter's box, so too did Thomson. He took a step toward first, letting go his bat with his left then right hand.

There loomed the possibility of an extra-base hit, and Branca should now have stepped toward the plate, run to back up Walker in the event of a throw home. But the pitcher stayed cleated to the mound, imploring a baseball: "Sink!" Reese was also unmoving, the shortstop not running toward left for a possible cutoff, only screaming where he stood: "Drop!" Cox at third spoke too to a ball as it flew overhead: "Get down!"

The ball continued uninfluenced toward left field, a Ford Frick signature soaring with topspin. Durocher called to Hartung to tag up off third. And at 3:58 p.m. on WMCA radio, Hodges yelled: "There's a long drive!"

Pafko, Pruschka, raced sideways in left toward Schwab and his hidden apartment. Snider in center barely moved, forgetting a possible carom. Batboy Leonard reached for a warm bat.

"It's going to be!" Hodges screamed. "I believe!"

The ball reached as high as the façade of the upper deck, then, dipping slightly, careened leftward toward a seventeen-foot wall. Pafko backpedaled—back, back, back—his blood pressure rising, the hypertensive outfielder stopping a step to the right of the tin 315 FT. marker, his right side touching green concrete. He looked up. The ball disappeared overhead. Umpire Goetz signaled home run and, after five distracted strides, Thomson, running toward first, leapt into the air.

So did Hodges. And lifting to his mouth his cast-metal microphone, the announcer shouted: "The Giants win the pennant! The Giants win the pennant! The Giants win the pennant! The Giants win the pennant!"

All about Hodges, men roared over mikes. "Going, going, gone!" yelled McClendon. "It is a home run!" yelled Barber. "*Los Gigantes son los campeones!*" yelled Felo Ramirez. Simultaneous also were the calls of Caray and Helfer and Harwell, the last, his audience watching with him, declaiming but two words: "It's gone!"

The ball landed some two rows deep in Section 35. Not hit particularly far, it was, however, hit extremely hard. All season, 204 home runs had been hit at the Polo Grounds and Thomson's was just the fifth to land in the lower deck in left. The upper deck extended twenty-one feet over left field and so, with little exception, for a ball to find its way into the lower deck it had to be smoked, to fly on a beeline with nary an arc.

Thus had Thomson's shot. "The ball was hit so hard," says Pafko, "it didn't have a chance to dip." And so in the supplemental press box above, Roth jotted a small capital "L" beside the diagonal line rising right to left that was his notation of the line drive. It was there too that Charles Einstein turned now to Benny Schorr to dictate a lead. "The Giants," declared the INS baseball writer. "Exclamation point. Exclamation point." Schorr punched his keyboard as told, and from a teletype on the eleventh floor of 235 East 45th Street, a bulletin emerged one block from the new white marble United Nations, tissue paper to be wired around the world.

Just below Schorr, one man who had double-dated with pitcher and one with batter sat now in live radio booths. The first groaned. "Oh my God," said announcer Scully, covering his face with both hands. "Poor Ralph." The second set pen to paper. Clay Felker was statistician for WMCA and, twenty-six, he had now the presence of mind to tabulate a buddy's stats and whisper them to Hodges palpitating beside him: Thomson had knocked in six of the eight Giant playoff runs, raised his RBI total to 101.

Three miles away, on the second floor of a red-brick home at 1033 Elder Avenue in the Bronx, an electrician's heart broke. Chadwick lay on his gray couch stonefaced. Miriam, seeing the home run and then her husband, screamed. Daughter Harriet, fifteen, ran from kitchen to living room to find her parents pale.

Frank Bourgholtzer stood in the White House some 100 feet from the President of the United States. And forgetting for a moment Russia's atomic blast, he marveled at Thomson's. "That's my boy!" he shouted. "That's my boy!" In St. Albans, Queens, as St. Jude, his work done, looked on, Thomas Fitzgibbon screamed and tossed a tan couch pillow into the air, then another and another while his father danced an Irish jig. In Staten Island, the brothers Holbert running counterclockwise about a table now changed course, jumping and screaming and hugging wildly in a dining room on St. John's Avenue. And behind the wheel of his Buick, Morty Rothschild, miles from the ballpark in an abandoned grassy lot just south of Dyckman Street, hollered deliriously, the used-car salesman as responsible as any for New York's pennant.

Thomson leaped and loped his way down the line. He began to hyperventilate, and when he reached first, his right Wilson cleat atop a canvas bag, coach Fitzsimmons screamed at him to be sure to touch second, then hurled his wool cap into the air.

Hodges, his voice high, hysterical, continued to scream. "Bobby Thomson hits into the lower deck of the left-field stands! The Giants win the pennant! And they're going crazy! They're going crazy!"

No one could say anything just once. As Thomson hit first, Stanky shot from the dugout toward Durocher, the second baseman calling out, "We did it! We did it! We did it!" Pafko, confetti flittering down about him, spoke to a wall that had given no carom: "It can't be! It can't be! It can't be!" Behind the Brooklyn dugout, a girl of eighteen in tears named Terry O'Malley turned to her father, owner of the Dodgers: "Oh, Pop! Oh Pop! Oh Pop!" And Chadwick, supine before his wife and daughter, repeated over and over: "I can't believe it. I can't believe it. I can't believe it." He began to sob and Miriam turned off the television.

Plucked from the bench a moment earlier, Hartung now gamboled home. A sad career had finally bestowed a frisson of joy, a kiss, and as he neared the plate, the Hurricane began to wave his arms in large backward circles, a tap dancer performing wings—one, two, three, four, five, six. Hartung touched home followed by Lockman, the tying run. Watching it all, Hodges capped his call with an ecstatic cry: "Ohhh-ohhh!"

Never before was the cruel superfluity of baseball's home run trot so apparent, and eight of the Brooklyn nine turned their backs on Thomson. Only Jackie Robinson watched. Standing in short center field, hands on hips, the second baseman would be certain to spot if Thomson missed a base.

Thomson half-ran for second, arms swinging, feet jumping. He was a step from the white bag when Branca, sixty feet off and facing him, bent to grasp a rosin bag that had not helped. The pitcher picked it up then hurled it down. Poof. The white cotton bag skittered toward short and a cloud of yellow burst then settled on the green grass like the spores of a puffball. Branca stuffed his mitt into his hip pocket and set off for the clubhouse, his head stooped, his brown eyes affixed to the first of some two hundred slow and piercing paces.

Yvars and his bullpen-mates dashed in the opposite direction, the five men running to join the mosh pit that awaited Thomson at home.

Thomson stepped on second then made for third. So did Stanky. The Brat got there first, slapping Durocher on the back, jumping upon him from behind as his manager jumped too. Thomson rounded third, passing the two men with a balletic stride. For a moment, all six of their feet were off the ground. Stanky climbed down off Durocher, spun about so they were face to face, and hugged him. Pressed together, the two short men danced and hopped, Durocher pulling his cap from his bald head and pirouetting free.

Thomson loped for home, chuffing and smiling broadly. Some ten feet from the plate, he leapt. The Giant was mid-air, his right leg forward, when Irvin, foul of the foul line, slapped his back with his left hand. Flashbulbs popped and Thomson's right foot returned to earth. Umpire Jorda checked to see that it landed on the rubber plate. It did. After 148 minutes of ball, New York won 5–4. The pennant lost, Robinson turned to take baseball's longest walk.

Outside the park, millions hushed and millions hurrahed, millions withered and millions enlivened. A home run had quickened hearts, widened pupils, warmed skin, whooshed dopamine, constricted and dilated vessels—blood flushing and draining from millions of lips and ears and cheeks and hearts.

It was now that two of 34,320 hearts at the Polo Grounds stopped beating. And it was now that a ballfield quickly clotted with players and ushers and cops and reporters and fans. "Mature people," wrote INS reporter Bob Considine, "broke through the guards and ran about basepaths in wholly deranged manner." A textile printer from Rye, New York, named Bernard Davies dashed afield and swiped Thomson's cap from off his head. A man and woman seated past first spilled over a metal rail onto dirt and pulled down his underpants. And a herd of Giants lifted Thomson and held him high, Lockman's left shoulder and long neck straining beneath the bouncing weight of a leg. But no matter. Here was Caesar—Schenz and Spencer, Yvars and Jones, Fitzsimmons, Mays, Kennedy, Lohrke, Thompson, Corwin, Hartung, Irvin, batboy Leonard and the rest whooping and parading, pennant winners all, thousands of dollars richer besides.

Only little Chris Durocher remained in the dugout, his mommy just above in Section 19, a Mormon movie star, the baseball wife of wives, cheering and crying and screaming and chewing gum all at once. Then Laraine Day saw Branca. The pitcher was shuffling slowly away, had not yet reached the outfield, the size 46 jersey on his broad back bearing a number that suddenly seemed a cheap joke. Day quieted. "I know the great sorrow I felt for him," she says. "I felt more for Branca than I did for Thomson." Across the diamond, one row above the opposite dugout, Ann Mulvey began to cry.

Brooklyn had lost the pennant and slowly, some thirty feet left of their victors, a string of numbered players—39, 27, 38, 29, 18, 32, 7—snaked its way off the field. Up ahead, number 1 spoke to himself. "It can't happen like this," muttered Reese. "We have to get another chance." Their blue caps were bowed, bloodshot eyes spared the caravan of champagne and reporters and television cameras that now fled their clubhouse for New York's. Newcombe heard the stampede and stepped naked from his shower to inquire. "Home run," offered clubhouse man Griffin. Newcombe stepped back under water.

Off in Arlington, Virginia, Nat Allbright read the ticker report of Thomson's home run. And turning now to his WEAM microphone, he smacked his lips, the crack of the bat simulated. "It may go!" he cried to the nation's capital. "It is gone!" With that, Thomson set off again around the bases, his romp eternal.

The Giants danced and pushed for center field, not yet in their clubhouse save Maglie, Rigney, Mueller and Franks. "I was," Franks explained forty-five years later to the *Salt Lake Tribune,* "in the clubhouse doing something for Durocher."

He had done that something well, and outside, many sets of hands held Thomson high while Branca walked alone. A moment had irrevocably cast two lifetimes, a fifty-fourth career face-off apportioned batter and pitcher opposite fates. Yet, it had also soldered the two men together. For the rest of their long lives, Thomson and Branca would comprise two sides of a coin, their names never more than a hairsbreadth apart.

PART TWO

The Darkening Green

FIFTEEN

No matter where you sit in New York you feel the vibrations of
great times and tall deeds.
　　　　　　　　—E. B. WHITE, *Here Is New York*, 1949

THE IMMEDIATE EFFECT of a home run was physical. As always,
recoil followed gunshot, and Thomson's graying mother, Elizabeth,
dropped to the wooden floor beneath her television, unconscious. Rose
Krobot fainted too, a widow of fifty-nine motionless on the kitchen floor
of a brownstone on Bergen Street in Brooklyn. And when Dodger fan
Philip Arbiter heard Thomson's blast at the launderette he operated at
21-06 Cornaga Avenue in Queens, his heart stopped beating. The Pole
flumped to the floor of Far Rockaway Laundermat dead at fifty-five of a
coronary occlusion.

Those folks left standing were jolted just the same. The blow, as if a
gigantic reflex hammer struck against the patellar tendons of millions,
jerked its witnesses and all about the country, objects, clutched, took to
the air.

Fred Fields, a boy of twelve in Chatham, New Jersey, saw the ball
leave Branca's hand and then the peanut-buttered slice of bread in his do
the same, heading for his twelve-inch RCA television screen. It stuck.
Atop a stairwell in Brooklyn's Thomas Jefferson High School, a group
of boys fresh from Ms. McPherson's biology class heard Red Barber
describe Bobby's shot, then the crash of a handheld radio a flight below.
Freshman Bobby Siegel had dropped his red Emerson. In Riverdale, New
York, Russ Hodges told Gerry Kremenko whose husband, Barney, covered the Giants for the *New York Journal American* that the ballplayer
she was closest to had won the pennant. She jumped from her lounge
chair and baby and bottle slipped free, little Myra jangling in a bedroom
on Netherland Avenue. On West 121st Street in Manhattan, George Carlin sat in his bedroom beside his Crosley radio, a boy of fourteen squeez-

ing his black kitten. The moment Thomson's home run landed, Ezzard took off, thrown unwittingly toward an open window. The kitten clawed a curtain, clung on even as he swung out three stories above a concrete courtyard, and lived. Fedoras and straw hats flew too, thrown in glee and disgust in Grand Central Terminal where housewife Pauline Plimpton, forty-nine and unsure of the hubbub, watched, never to forget. Thirty-five hundred miles away, her son paused from his literature studies at Cambridge University to listen to the game and play bridge. Thomson swung and George Plimpton toppled over in his chair, a Giant fan of twenty-four letting go his hand, playing cards fluttering through the air.

Everywhere, the dip of a ball behind a wall triggered shock. Giant fan Bob Berggren, twenty-eight, a mailman sorting parcels in Branca's hometown post office, heard Hodges's call and jumped, his blond head smacking into an air vent. At the front end of a railroad apartment on Driggs Avenue in Brooklyn, a boy of twelve sat unmoving, Larry Groff unable to rise from the maroon armchair before his Philco for a full four hours. In the press box at the Polo Grounds, John Drebinger lost track of limb, the deaf *New York Times* reporter pounding the hat of a scribe before him down to his ears. Dodger fan Doris Kearns, eight, could not record in the red scorebook on her lap the home run she saw on a 10-inch table console in Rockville Centre, New York. And circling a basepath, he who hit the home run began to hyperventilate, a hero wheezing, "Gee whiz! Gee whiz!"

The home run was a hazard. One thousand feet over Lubbock, Texas, Ron Littlefair sat at the stick of his T-6 trainer shuttling between a baseball broadcast and a control tower. Thomson's shot shook the cadet and at once the Brooklyn fan radioed Reese Air Force Base: "Making final landing." In an empty barn on Long Island, a paper boy named Paul Knatz counting copies of the *Nassau Daily Review Star* heard Thomson's homer then watched a keyed-up colleague dart blindly into Brower Avenue. A shiny black Buick struck him flush in the hip. In a Waldorf-Astoria suite, Thomson sent ice skater Geary Steffen over a chair. He who had long leapt beside Sonja Henie landed hard, spraining an ankle. And behind a meat counter at Mike's Luncheonette on 65th Street in Bensonhurst, Fred Wilpon, a Dodger fan bled by the blast, sliced along with a ham his left pinkie.

The shot unleashed tears. In a Brooklyn basement on Crown Street, contagious sobs convulsed an intermediate Girl Scout troop, Grace Lichtenstein among a score of fifth-grade girls camped about a radio in green uniforms and yellow ties. Inside Coward's Shoes, on the second floor of the Empire State Building, Red Barber broke the news to a black janitor named Joe Hill and a white cashier named Ann Hoen. Together, in front of their customers, they started to cry. So did Katherine Branca, the terror-stricken mother seated in her living room before the DuMont TV son Ralph had bought her to watch him pitch. In a radio studio in Guantanamo Bay, Cuba, a naval petty officer in white fatigues named Ron Bloom wept, beside him WGBY sports programmer George Balamaci untrained to help. Winners wept too, Giants Stanky, Franks and Brannick—player, coach and secretary—breaking down in a victorious locker room in Harlem.

On this afternoon at 3:58 p.m. Eastern Standard Time, Warren Buffett found himself sitting in a waiting room outside Phil Gilmore's office in Omaha. Set to recommend Government Employees Insurance stock, Buffett, twenty-one, readied his pitch when he heard Branca's swatted to left. Pafko backpedaled and Cub fan John Paul Stevens paused from his months-long investigation of Major League Baseball's reserve clause. The bow-tied associate counsel to a House subcommittee sat hushed over a radio just around the corner from his future chambers in the U.S. Supreme Court. Thomson's rope cleared the left-field wall and Harold Bloom halted, the Yankee fan and Yale graduate student busily writing an essay on philosopher David Hartley. Seated at his parents' kitchen table on 170th Street, Bloom put down his pen. Branca threw down his rosin bag and at 247 Park Avenue, Alan Greenspan, a Dodger fan and junior employee at the National Industrial Conference Board tuning in to the game at work, ached for the pitcher exactly two months older than he. As eight broadcasters raved, a ninth, freshman Red Sox announcer Curt Gowdy, pulled over his blue Chrysler on a highway somewhere between Boston and Springfield to listen in. Inside a pool hall in Mobile, Alabama, Hank Aaron, seventeen and playing hooky, ran for home as did Thomson, imagining all the way that he was the Flying Scot to be carried off the field. And as a Harlem crowd roared, word of Thomson's heroics reached Gerald Ford. Out on the hustings in Michigan, the Cub and Tiger fan, campaigning for reelection to the House, paused quietly to marvel.

Most of all, Thomson's home run set off screams. On the Q36 bus heading toward Floral Park, New York, a Dodger fan and high school sophomore named Guy Cogan shrieked. So too did much of the busload, and the nervous driver, stopped at a light on the Jericho Turnpike in Bellerose, Long Island, stayed put even after the light turned green. Five stories up 6 West 57th Street, the shouts of stunned New Yorkers reached the writers of the NBC television program *Your Show of Shows*—Sid Caesar, Carl Reiner, Mel Brooks, Neil Simon, Joe Stein and others rushing open their windows to listen. Twenty-seven blocks north, in his eight-room apartment on Madison Avenue, Milton Berle yelped, his Cuban Larranaga cigar slipping from his mouth as he fell backward onto his couch. In the nation's capital, the roar of a pride of truant senators forced Harry Cain, the Washington republican on the Senate floor, to pause a full three minutes from talk of the Korean War. A boy of twelve and a girl of thirteen, holding hands and jumping on Westminster Road in Brooklyn, squealed yays and yippees, Donald Millus sure the only other time neighbor Fredi Lieberman had danced in front of her home was when Israel declared its independence three years before. And in an office two stories above Broadway on 46th Street, where three lit and smoking cigars filled an ashtray, Kermit Bloomgarden bellowed.

Bloomgarden, an accountant and producer of plays, had recently staged *Death of a Salesman,* and at this moment, its author found himself in an elevator rising toward a scream. Arthur Miller, twelve days shy of thirty-six, had long stopped reading box scores. But as he stepped out of the elevator, saw his producer and learned of Thomson's heroics, the playwright was struck. Bloomgarden, "a very quiet if not lugubrious personality," Miller recalled in a letter fifty-one years later, "was screaming at two or three people in the office and red in the face between laughter and tears.

"I was not any longer a baseball fan," wrote Miller, "but when I heard what had happened I felt the axis of the world had shifted slightly and we must all be happy for at least five minutes."

Such was the instant legacy of the home run, reaction to it so extraordinary that millions for whom the shot held no obvious meaning were vivified just the same, their coordinates at its firing remembered for all time. Reflex had given way to meaning. Branca's offering had in an instant joined the national trust, a shared experience, an orientation. And thus a question was born: "Where were you when Thomson hit the home run?"

Two minutes had passed since the blow—it was now exactly 4:00 p.m.—and Thomson and Branca approached the Polo Grounds clubhouse, agony of defeat stage left, thrill of victory stage right. Theirs was an unrehearsed drama. Girded not for their roles, the men were left now to lean instead on what the accretion of a combined fifty-three years had irreversibly made them. And as bursts of flashbulb lit their sweated faces—one brazened, one blanched—back on Flagg Place in Staten Island, Elizabeth Thomson revived, stood and ran next door.

The Polo Grounds on October 2, 1951, one day before the Thomson home run.
Gordon Rynders, courtesy of the New York Daily News.

The oblong park featured the only bullpens in baseball located in fair territory,
as well as a clubhouse aligned with home plate. It was suited to the stealing of signs.
The field on September 29, 1954. *From the author's collection.*

Giant owner Horace Stoneham watching a game from the clubhouse above center field, 1957. Beginning on July 20, 1951, manager Leo Durocher stationed coach Herman Franks one flight below, there to spy on the signals of the opposing teams' catchers.
Photograph by Arthur Daley.

The right-field bullpen at the Polo Grounds August 20, 1957. Here Giant pitchers warmed up and here, in 1951, Giant batters looked to catcher Sal Yvars for the sign.
Photograph by Arthur Daley.

Looking for the sign from batter's box to bullpen was discreet. The pen is in view here as Willie Mays bats on September 29, 1957—the last game the New York Giants played at the Polo Grounds. *Richard Meek, courtesy of* Sports Illustrated.

Before Thomson came to bat, Don Mueller injured his left ankle stepping on third base. He is shown here being carried off the field. The disruption focused Thomson. "I was like a mechanical doll," he says. "I wasn't aware of anyone else in the ballpark but me." *Frank Rino, courtesy of the Harry Ransom Humanities Research Center, the University of Texas at Austin.*

The ball in flight. This photo remains the most famous image of the home run.
But just once, in the May 1952 edition of *Sylvania News*, did photographer Rudy Mancuso receive for it credit.

Rudy Mancuso, courtesy of Bobby Thomson.

Herman Franks

Leo
Durocher

Andy Pafko

Clint Hartung

Billy Cox

Pee Wee
Reese

Bobby Thomson

Rube Walker

Ralph
Branco

Whitey
Lockman

Willie Mays

Duke Snider

Jackie
Robinson

Freddie Fitzsimmons

Unpublished for fifty-five years, this photo of the ball in flight extends to center field,
where a faint shadow can be seen in the fourth clubhouse window (*see inset*).
Atop the clubhouse, a clock documents the moment the home run flew.
Frank Rino, courtesy of the Harry Ransom Humanities Research Center, the University of Texas at Austin.

Dodger leftfielder Andy Pafko stands impotent as the home run enters Section 35. An arrow points to the vicinity of the ball, but who gloved it remains a mystery.
Hank Olen, courtesy of the New York Daily News.

Jackie Robinson, number 42, watches what Branca cannot: the Giants mobbing Thomson at home plate.
Courtesy of Getty Images.

Thomson acknowledging what *The New York Times* termed
"the most frenzied 'curtain calls' ever accorded a ballplayer."
Seymour Wally, courtesy of the New York Daily News.

Thomson celebrating hours after the home run at
Tavern on the Green, a restaurant in Staten Island.
Dick McEvilly, International News Service, courtesy of Bobby Thomson.

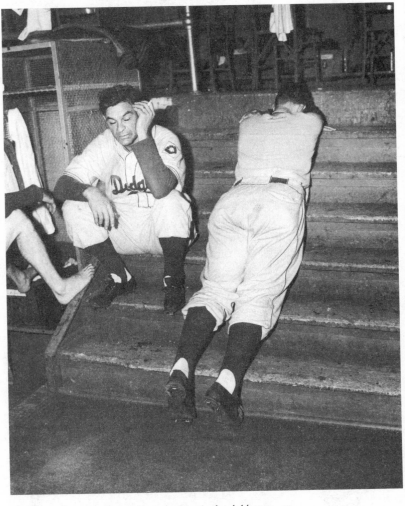

Branca crying in the clubhouse.
Sitting next to him is bench coach Cookie Lavagetto
and beside him bullpen coach Clyde Sukeforth, who along with
manager Charlie Dressen sent him in to face Thomson.
Branca saw photographer Barney Stein but didn't ask him to leave.
Barney Stein, courtesy of Bonnie Crosby.

SIXTEEN

Man as the spectator and manager of history imagines himself to be freer of the drama he beholds than he really is; and man as the creature of history is too simply reduced to the status of a creature of nature. . . .

—REINHOLD NIEBUHR, *The Irony of American History,* 1952

IT MIGHT WELL HAVE BEEN Carl Erskine on the mound. But he had bounced a curve, been passed over for Branca and stood now safely at his locker looking about, an Indianan of twenty-four aware suddenly of a moment's weight and wanting to remember its trifles. Here Hodges lightly rested his glove. There Robinson slammed his. And everywhere skittered buttons, their tails of cream thread flying from the size-42 jersey Dressen, pathetic Dressen, now tore open on his own 146-pound body.

None spoke. But for the clack of cleats and susurration of self-admonishments, the Brooklyn Dodgers were silent, incredulous as the last bottles of bubbly whisked now next door.

Ralph Branca walked on, his flesh numb, his mind blank. The pitcher found himself at the foot of a staircase, grass giving way to wood, then atop fifteen steps, through the arch of a doorpost and before a cubby on the lower of two planes in a one-windowed room. He pitched his sweated blue cap into his locker and turned his head about. "There was nowhere to hide," he says. And so Branca sat where he stood, his feet cleated to the worn wooden floor, his rear on the third of seven splintered steps. Silent, the pitcher rested his elbows on bent knees, touched before his shins the five fingertips of one hand against the other and let drop his chin to his chest, sequins of sweat streaking his face. The silver chain of a good-luck medallion glistened across the nape of his exposed neck, St. Christopher captive to a wet undershirt.

Just five minutes had passed since Thomson long-jumped to home, since Hodges yelled into his microphone "I don't believe it! I don't believe it! I do *not* believe it!," since Barber sat silent over his mike a full fifty-nine seconds, since a row of stunned newspapermen elbow to elbow in the press box yanked and crumpled in unison the prose rising from their Olivetti typewriters, front-page news turned fish-and-chip paper. Not a syllable was salvageable.

This Joe King did not know. A few miles south, the reporter had approached a Western Union branch ready to wire an article to the *New York World-Telegram and Sun*. Brooklyn, wrote King, had beaten New York 4–1. But as King neared 40th Street and Broadway, he heard screams. "The screams became alarming," King later wrote. "In a matter of two paces or several seconds of my progress, literally, people, males and females, tumbled out of office fronts, out of restaurants, out of parked cars, out of the little cigar joints." King learned of a home run. And the most startling upset since Truman defeated Dewey did not, like that contest three years prior, go misreported.

It nearly did. On the third floor of 24 Johnson Street in Brooklyn Heights, an editor and clerk at the *Brooklyn Eagle* stood astride a stone slab laden with warm metal type. NIW SЯƎ⅁⅁Oꓷ read the headline, upside-down and backward. At two minutes to four, however, an anonymous voice called out that no, the Dodgers did not win, and the clerk, an aspiring sportswriter of twenty-two named Dave Anderson, watched what was not taught him at Holy Cross, dead lead lifted letter by letter.

At the Polo Grounds, Anderson's future colleagues scanned through chicken wire the serried stands and chaotic field for words to fill their blank sheets of paper. The storyline was beyond schmaltz. Two teams, the fiercest of rivals and once 13.5 games apart, had conjoined in a regular season's last inning. Three days later, in the bottom of the ninth inning of a final playoff game, one team had been down three. And then what? (It beckoned review.) A hit glanced off a glove, a managerial misstep, an injury, stretcher bearers, a number 13 on in relief, a home run, a goat turned hero. It was too much. A reporter could fiddle with quote and color, sidestep cliché and pleonasm, make documentary of melodrama, limn a moment, probe it for meaning and still would his lead read "Once upon a time. . . ."

Walter Smith sat among the men. The second child of a Green Bay grocer, he had upon graduation from Notre Dame in 1927 covered metro news for the *Milwaukee Sentinel*. He shifted the next year to the *St. Louis Star* and to sports, and by 1945, the man known as Red was, among sportswriters, second only to Grantland Rice in renown, his column for the *New York Herald Tribune* syndicated in ninety newspapers.

Smith wrote spare prose, wry and understated. It seemed a fitting tribute when in 1950 Ernest Hemingway wrote of a semiautobiographical character named Colonel Cantwell that "he was reading Red Smith, and he liked him very much."

Smith, forty-six, eyed a drunk tussling with a group of ushers. He began to type.

Buzzie Bavasi had planned after the game to toast the pennant and his mother's sixtieth birthday. But Susan Bavasi, devout Catholic and Branca fan, canceled her shindig at Mama Leone's restaurant to instead pray for the pitcher at Saint Patrick's cathedral. Her son the general manager now stood before his squad forlorn. Just once before had a baseball team two years in a row lost the pennant on the last day of the season. Brooklyn had now done so in the last *inning* of consecutive seasons, and in suit, bow tie and fedora, Bavasi mustered but a few words: "We're a good club. We'll win it next year." Manager Dressen, suffering from a cold, told his players the same. Owner O'Malley attempted to kid Cox about his black underwear.

Their words were empty, optimisms and levity lost in the miasma of Brooklyn's dressing room. And they went unrecorded. Reese, Dodger captain, could not hold back tears and had Brooklyn's redoubt closed to the press.

Just one man stood outside that door, Barney Stein begging Charlie DiGiovanna to let him in. The Dodger clubhouse boy went off to ask permission of Dressen.

Stein was a small man with a big camera—five feet tall and a Speed Graphic in hand. The youngest of eleven children, born in Russia in September of 1908, he had arrived at Ellis Island the following October and begun his career in 1929, a photographer for the *Brooklyn Times Union* newspaper.

Strolling with his camera eight years later in Prospect Park in Brooklyn, Stein saw a woman riding a horse. He asked to take her picture. The woman agreed and introduced herself as Dearie Mulvey. And when in time Dearie saw the photo, she who owned a baseball team offered Stein a job as "Official Brooklyn Dodger Photographer," a post he held by spring training.

Fifteen team portraits later, Stein, a photographer for the *New York Post,* awaited word from a heartbroken Dressen. And he too was heartbroken. Through years of scotch and conversation at the Mulvey home, Stein had come to call Jim and Dearie friends and to love their team. It was no surprise that though this Wednesday he had risen before dawn in his Flatbush frame-house on East Seventh Street, his shift starting at 4 a.m., off duty he had headed straight for the ballpark.

DiGiovanna returned. Dressen had said okay.

Stein entered the locker room and looked about. Here was a charnel house. All present were hunched. And the lintel of loss weighed heaviest on Ralph Branca. Stein beheld the pitcher, he whose wedding he would shoot in seventeen days. Still he sat on his step head down, staring through sweated forearms at the brown floor. He appeared a wraith. And he was sobbing. "I never saw such a lonely figure," says Pafko. Newcombe, toweling dry, also saw his relief and forgot his own tears of a year and two days before. "I'm never going to let baseball do that to me," he pledged to himself.

Stein raised his camera with its flashbulb, two shutters and three viewfinders, focused on Branca and snapped. It was 4:11 p.m. Thirteen minutes after a home run, Stein reversed the four-by-five-inch film sheet on the back of his Speed Graphic, ready to shoot again.

Baseball had many times before trained its lens upon Branca. The pitcher had in 1946 been the first to throw a playoff game, in 1947 the youngest to start a World Series. He had pitched Game Three of the 1949 Series and just two days prior the opener of the 1951 playoff. But always these games had spoiled. Somehow, some way, in big spots Branca was always the loser as he was now again.

And yet this blow was like no other. So traumatized was Branca that never would he recall his slow walk from infield to clubhouse, some two hundred paces lost to disassociative amnesia.

But as he cried, cognition returned to Branca. Here, the pitcher told himself, was Barney Stein shooting his photograph. "I didn't give a shit," says Branca. "I really didn't care." The pitcher removed his jersey, rolled onto his stomach and hid his long wet face in the cotton sleeves of arms folded atop top step, toe-tips touching the floor six stairs below. Seated beside him, coach Lavagetto endeavored to comfort the prone pitcher, a smoking cigarette steadied just off his temple.

The New York Giants were in a frenzy. Grabbed and de-capped by a delirious crowd gaining like a feeding mosquito size and gall, the team had shrugged Thomson from off its shoulders and hightailed to center field, one by one charging through a clubhouse door with joy let loose. Thomson whooshed in too, at once backslapped and bear-hugged and yelled at and goddamned and spritzed with alcohol by any and all who found the hero within arm's length. Bobby Thomson had won the pennant.

No Giant could believe it. None could believe the pennant was actually theirs, King Tantalus having suddenly seized the choice fruit he had so long reached for with outstretched arm. And so there was only to swig and sweat and swear, to chest-thump and shout attestations of conquest and love, to make heard louder and louder above the din of the clubhouse one name: BOBBY THOMSON!

He whose name they shouted was no less unbelieving. For Thomson had hit 130 major league home runs before and not one had ended a game. Shot 131 had and ended much more—a playoff series, a six-month race, a fourteen-year pennant drought, the seesaw of a sixty-one-year National League rivalry. And so the clubhouse phone rang, a giddy Buddy Kerr (the first ever to face Branca) belly-laughing congratulations to his former teammate. And so a lackey from the Perry Como television show offered Thomson $500 for fifteen minutes, then double that when the third baseman declined. And so, fed their first pennant since 1937, thousands of fans hungry for a curtain call stood now outside a green clubhouse chanting, "We want Thomson! We want Thomson!"

Thomson could not hear them, a scrum of reporters, photographers, newsreel crews, league honchos, team officials and friends shouting questions pell-mell. Sam Aro spotted Herman Franks amidst the chaos. Entrusted with the WMCA microphone until announcers Hodges and Harwell reached the clubhouse, Aro shot Franks a question: "What do you have to say?"

He who minutes before had peered through a telescope at Rube Walker's white fingers now held in his own a paper cup brimming with scotch. Franks was drunk. "I'm too upset to"—the coach paused, his words slurred. "I, I just don't know what the." Aro moved on and the intoxicated Franks, noted Ed Sinclair of the *New York Herald Tribune,* "sagged against a pillar and sobbed unrestrainedly." Bill Rigney approached his coach. "Why are you crying, Herman?" he asked. "Damned if I know," answered Franks.

Yvars was aglow. The catcher had now, a *second* time in five years, roared from 13-plus games back to overtake a Brooklyn club. And that minor league stud had turned big league backup, asked only at season's summit to sit still on a bullpen bench, mattered not. For a home run by Thomson was the blessed down payment on a house Yvars so needed— his twin girls, Debbie and Donna, on this day three months old. At twenty-seven, the son of a gravedigger would join the rich atop Valhalla's hill.

Durocher clasped Thomson's left shoulder, nuzzling ear and cheek against his hot neck. Cameras clicked, the embrace to run on the front pages of the *New York Times, Daily News* and *Herald Tribune,* a ballplayer Durocher had sought to unload forevermore his greatest glory. Announcer Hodges found the manager. "We want you to say hello!" he demanded. Cued, the Lip spoke: "This is the greatest ball club that I've ever managed."

The microphone beckoned also Henry Schenz. And addressing live the WMCA audience, he whose telescope had spied a playoff's last pitch spoke for many. "This is," said the pinch-runner, "the happiest moment of my life."

The same was true for Thomson. And asked now by Hodges a question, "Did you fall down coming around third or was—," the Scot did not as was his nature mull his response but instead cut Hodges off. "Did I fall down?" he shouted back. Thomson was hyperventilating, his voice high as helium. "I wasn't even—I didn't touch the ground once around there!"

Thomson had not touched the ground in the fifteen minutes since. Nor would he ever return to earth. He had hit a home run and life had changed irrevocably, the champagne uncorked—Hank Thompson drinking now his share, he who would struggle with alcoholism giving Mays his maiden nip, the rookie sick at once and carried into a shower. Eyeing a row of champagne bottles beside glassed beer and magnums of liquor, Thomson too felt suddenly nauseous.

It was then word reached Thomson that he was wanted outside, that only a curtain call might dissipate the stubborn throng chanting the surname stitched in red thread to his neckline and waist. And so out Thomson went, wading through the packed clubhouse to its top outdoor step.

A roar rose at first sight of the great Scot. It burst from above where men leaning dangerously over a bleacher's metal rail reached for Thomson, outstretched fingertips inches from his thick brown hair. And it thundered from below where thousands more larded the rectangular patch of grass between the two clubhouse staircases, hundreds of arms, though a touch was impossible, craning upward. It was a delirious crowd chanting en masse one man's name and Deputy Inspector Cornelius Lyons and his detail of cops struggled to safeguard the staircase of concrete and green wood that led to the afternoon's hero.

Thomson waved and waved, waving as did many of the screaming who reached for him with two upraised arms. The cheers were deafening, "the most frenzied 'curtain calls,' " wrote Drebinger in the *New York Times,* "ever accorded a ballplayer." They were anesthetizing too. After a dozen or so swells, Thomson ducked back into the clubhouse, his queasiness forgotten.

Branca, however, remained sick—still recumbent, still crying into folded arms. Months after he had sung through a clubhouse wall "the Giants are dead!," those same Giants were very much alive, cruel comeuppance, a cluster now succeeding Thomson to bow and bask in singsong cheer, Durocher throwing kisses, then his cap, to the crowd.

"Why me?" Branca muttered to himself. "Why me? Why me?" It was a question he had posed and answered years before, wondering as to his physical gifts, concluding that they were given him to help shoulder for his family the burden of provision. But now he wondered as to his misfortune and Duke Snider, overhearing Branca as he shuffled by, offered no reply.

Easier for the center fielder was to bid, next door, his defeater luck, which he now did together with a cast of automatous well-wishers—Robinson, Reese, Roe, Campy, Dressen, O'Malley, Labine. Labine offered Thomson a handshake. "Nice going, Bobby," he said. "Good luck in the Series." Thomson did not recognize the crew-cut blond. "I pitched against you yesterday," said Labine. With that, the righty left.

Branca peeled himself from off wooden stairs, stepped to a water fountain, bowed, drank, straightened. Nowhere was there refuge, the thrum of celebrating Giants ambient, everywhere a silent Dodger on a three-legged stool. The pitcher meandered, pounding a fist against whatever passed—a concrete wall, a run of wooden lockers—then returned to a step and to sobbing.

It was now, denied entrance some fifteen minutes, that the press finally swooped in on Brooklyn's green crypt to scavenge for quotes, the mortar of any good story.

No one spoke to Branca. And Branca, brown eyes cast down, spoke to no one, reporters loitering just feet from the pitcher so as to catch whatever would be his first words. Minutes passed, five then ten, Branca hearing well with his large ears the ovations outside. The pitcher stopped crying and spoke. "I guess," he said, a passel of pencils sprung to life, "I'm too lucky in love to be lucky at anything else."

Here was a first stab at understanding. No matter that Branca had long mocked Lady Luck, had walked beneath ladders, stepped on foul lines, worn the number 13. Desperation breeds faith, the pitcher in need of a logic to his suffering. And so he found one, found comfort. Ann would still love him. He would, in seventeen days, still marry. Among the scribbling reporters, Les Biederman of the *Pittsburgh Press* found himself moved, a go at peace of mind poignant.

Will Grimsley was unstirred. The AP reporter wanted more, wanted a goat's take on what had transpired afield. And so, no matter how down-trodden was Branca and no matter his betrothal to the owner's daughter, the redhead from Monterey, Tennessee, spoke up. "What happened?" asked Grimsley. Branca said nothing and Grimsley repeated his question. "Leave me alone," said Branca. "Just leave me alone." But Grimsley did not and in his prodding there was for the pitcher value. For where in thirty devastating minutes there had been for Branca no precedent, there was now, the pitcher as countless times before subject to the drill of the interview. He had lost a game, a big game, perhaps the biggest. But it remained a game and there were questions to answer and he had been here before.

Branca turned to an 0–1 fastball. "It wasn't a bad pitch," he offered in low voice. "I didn't think he hit it too well. It was sinking when it went into the stands." The pitcher continued. "I guess we weren't meant to win it," he told Roscoe McGowen of the *New York Times*. "The ball was high and inside, not a good pitch [to hit], and it only cleared the wall by this much." Branca held his large hands inches apart, indicating his margin of loss.

Thus did Branca confront a home run. Thus did he yank tight a tourniquet to stanch the bleeding. Yes he had failed afield. But he had as always performed admirably. The home run was not his fault.

One room away, a horde looked to Thomson for *his* take—press, poohbahs and players hungry to know how the quiet third baseman had come to hit a home run.

"If I was a good hitter I'd have taken that one," Thomson told James Dawson of the *New York Times*. "It was high and inside, the kind they've been getting me out on all season." Thomson was shouting, his voice high and hoarsening, his unbuttoned jersey exposing an undershirt, off-white with black sleeves. The hero told United Press reporter Milton Richman of floating on a cloud and turned to a stringer for his hometown *Staten Island Advance*. "Honest," Thomson said, "a better hitter would have let Branca's pitch go by for a ball." Thomson's teammates cut in, hoisting him onto their shoulders, carrying him above the champagne-basted floor. Set down, the Giant continued, back in little time to his same self-disparaging point. "It was a pitch," he assured Jim McCulley of the *Daily News*, "that Musial or any other good hitter would have taken. It was high and inside. I didn't deserve to do a thing like that."

Thus did the undeserving Thomson persist with his leitmotif, together with Branca the only to qualify in any way what he had done. That he had gone 5-for-10 in the playoff, driven in six of eight Giant runs, hit the first home run in baseball history to end a playoff or World Series, mattered little. Half an hour had passed since the Scot turned hero, sufficient time for a swing to filter through his system. And for the record, Thomson let it be known that he had been foolish to swing at Branca's second pitch.

And so it was that Branca and Thomson came together. He who had lost stated he had done his job well. He who had won stated he had done his job poorly. In the aftermath of a home run, pitcher and hitter, by dint of disposition and fortuity, were strangely in step.

But the downplaying of two men could not contain their collaboration. Its ejecta were already airborne. In Staten Island, factory, ferry and tugboat whistles sounded, the beaming borough celebrating its finest hour since Giovanni da Verrazano happened upon it 427 springs past. In Manhattan, Angelo Lomangino heaved into an incinerator bushels of Dodger World Series programs, the foreman at Blanchard Printing Press saving from fire two of 10,000 phantom booklets. In Queens, detective Salvatore Secino rushed to the corner of Hobart Street and 31st Avenue where the body reported dangling from a lamppost was a stuffed Dodger. In Brooklyn, hundreds phoned in curses to a grandmother, Dodger operator Grace Therkildsen left to answer MAin 4-5091. And in Bronxville, in the maternity ward of Lawrence Hospital, Branca's sister Margaret lay miserable. Her daughter, Sylvia Rose, hours old, was a healthy pink. But one bed over lay a sassy Giant fan. "She rode her," remembers Margaret's husband, Bill. "It wasn't a happy day."

Brooklyn was broken. The most populous of boroughs needed a drink. Like the Giants who now poured warm champagne over Mueller's busted ankle in a trainer's room at the Polo Grounds, Brooklyn turned to alcohol as a balm to its suffering. Taverns jammed, eyes to redden until last call at 4 a.m. On the corner of Seventh Avenue and 11th Street, a high school dropout at Rattigan's Bar ordered a draft beer and looked about. "Big, grown men were in tears," Pete Hamill told author Ray Robinson years later, "getting wrecked, drunk."

One fan forlorn over a beer at the end of a bar on Flatbush Avenue hit bottom. "I don't think I've ever felt more depressed in my life," wrote Willie Sutton two years later. Sutton, fifty, was on the lam, having escaped in February of 1947 Philadelphia County Prison. It had been his sixth prison break, and on March 20, 1950, the FBI put Sutton, a bank robber with a pencil moustache and an appetite for fine dress, on its list of Ten Most Wanted Fugitives. Sutton knew well that Brooklyn police headquarters was just a block away on Bergen Street and Sixth Avenue, and after Branca's doomed pitch, freedom was hollow. "I felt like going into headquarters," wrote Sutton, "and giving myself up."

The Dodgers, meantime, *did* surrender, yielding to their annual wait till next year. And they tabled more than hopes of a pennant. "New cars, television sets, payments on the mortgage had blown up in their faces," wrote Milt Dunnell in the *Toronto Star*. Each family had suddenly some 5,000 fewer dollars—a sizeable salary in its own right—Branca, Brooklyn's player representative, squandering in an instant far more than he had in years negotiated.

Still, a few players now approached the pitcher set on his stool. Erskine and Labine, whom fate might have stood in Branca's MacGregor spikes, told him he was a victim of circumstance. And he who had once known unspeakable loneliness and whom Branca had then befriended, tried to comfort him too. "If it wasn't for you," Robinson told Branca, "we wouldn't even have been here."

Stoneham approached Logan. The owner handed the keeper of his clubhouse $18,000 in tickets. And it was then Logan knew that the divvying of box seats and the transport of gear to Yankee Stadium would prevent his saying good-bye to Marie. Said Logan, "I never did get to see my sister."

Elsewhere in the clubhouse, a television camera found Laraine Day. She who had played on the silver screen the prim nurse Mary Lamont had since turned First Lady of baseball. And overcome, she spoke now of her father, Clarence Johnson, a religious Mormon who early in the season had assured her that New York would win the pennant. "He told me," said Day, tears rolling down her cheeks, "that he was praying for the Giants."

Antoinette Yvars, a happy wife in a happy dress, sat in the passenger seat of a green Pontiac in a parking lot south of right field. Waiting for husband Sal, she noticed now a woman in the pale-blue Oldsmobile beside her. "I was right next to Ann [Mulvey] of all people," remembers Yvars. "She was in her car with the windows rolled up. She was alone. . . . I just saw her wiping her eyes, her tears away. I wanted to go to her but I didn't know her."

Thomson undressed. His line drive had turned his gear to gold—his Adirondack bat, thirty-four ounces of lacquered white ash, and his Wilson shoes, black six-eyeleted leather cleats, to be encased in glass. The hero showered, then shaved, given as he did by a drunken Hank Thompson an invigorating kiss on the lips. He dressed, slipping a dark blazer over a white shirt with a plaid collar, a thin strip of tartan extending to his sternum. And after posing for one last photo—cigar in mouth, arm around a Burns security officer—Thomson stepped out into night, instructed his friend Al Corbin to drive home his Mercury and hopped a cab with Maglie for CBS's studio. His family could wait. For that thousand dollars, he would talk to Perry Como.

Herman Franks, meantime, phoned John Mooney. Three days prior, before the start of the playoff, the coach had agreed to call after each game his hometown paper. Now he did, his amanuensis, a sports reporter at the *Salt Lake Tribune*, ready to spin to prose the observations of a coach.

Franks had no need to share anything but pablum. And so, seated at Durocher's desk, he told Mooney that the manager rallied his team, that the Giants never gave up, that in the bottom of the ninth the players spoke as one: "We'll get the Bums."

But hours after Franks had set down scotch and spyglass came suddenly an admission. "Branca had a good fastball," said the coach. "But Bobby Thomson saw the fastball coming as Branca tried to sneak a second strike past him and he was ready." Franks volunteered a final sentence to what would comprise the eighth paragraph of a short story on page 29 of a Utah newspaper. "Maybe," he said, "we caught the sign for the fastball."

Franks headed home, the players and press and fans gone too, a blue flag raised, a victory march sung, a field dark, Chadwick's replacement Seymour Schmelzer extinguishing for the night 836 bulbs. In all the Polo Grounds it seemed just one man remained, bent atop a stool. Branca uncinched the leather belt about his thirty-eight-inch waist, undressed and walked into a concrete shower naked but for his medallion. The pitcher stood under cold water, "to cool my body down," says Branca. He showered a long while—fingertips turned raisins—toweled dry, put on a blue suit and tie, and stepped down onto the empty field. To his left, beneath the midpoint of fourteen clubhouse windows, rested perspective, a bronze plaque commemorating Eddie Grant, the Giant killed in the Argonne Forest thirty-one years before.

Branca turned toward right field. Confetti underfoot, he walked past the Giant bullpen, treading in size-13 shoes the same path that did Chadwick's wire. On through an upward-sliding metal gate he continued beneath the stands and into the parking lot, unable even as he opened the driver's door of his Olds to recall clearly what hours before had happened. Ann sat in the backseat in tears, her father's second cousin Francis Rowley, a Jesuit priest, come to console her. Rowley turned to Branca.

"Forget it, Ralph," he said, Roman collar about his neck. "It could have happened to anyone. You did your best."

Branca's mind cleared. He had lost the pennant.

A need to make sense of his lot welled again in Branca. He had once been a great pitcher. And at twenty-five, he remained a good man. He did not smoke, did not cheat and, save an occasional highball, did not drink. And so he answered Rowley, a man of the cloth, with a desperate and familiar question. "Yes, Father," he said, "but why did it have to be me? Why me?"

Father Rowley, he whose brother James would later head the U.S. Secret Service, understood what it meant to safeguard a public figure. And head of campus ministries at Fordham University, he did not hesitate with his answer. "The reason God picked you to throw that pitch," he said, "was because He knew that your faith was strong enough to withstand the agonies that would follow. That you would know it was His will and you had done your best and no one could ask more of any man."

Branca listened. Here in a sedan in an empty parking lot in Harlem was an answer that made sense, that jibed with scripture and his world view and his sense of self, an answer elastic enough to accommodate all that was sure to follow. Here was a reply tantamount to reprieve. The home run was a crucible. Fiancée at his side, Branca drove off.

It was high time to settle bets won and lost. The Nevada Turf Club had pronounced the Giants 13–10 favorites, Thomson redeeming with one uppercut the oddsmakers and Philip Eiss. Eiss had agreed to flip on the game in his Boro Park yeshiva classroom with one proviso—that each of his twenty-plus students wager a dime on its outcome. The yarmulked boys, devout Brooklyn fans, agreed. Thomson swung and Eiss passed around a blue and white metal pushka, the heartbroken sixth-graders surrendering their kitty to the planting of trees in Israel. In Palo Alto, Ralph Feichtmeir waited with dread for Jack Snell to show. The men together drank, watched Stanford football, bet. And when a TV at 449 Emerson Street told Feichtmeir, thirty-one, that he had lost their largest-ever wager, had lost to Snell $500 and bragging rights, the barber dropped mid-cut his shears, circling twice the block as Al Talboy waited in his chair. Jack Bader walked too, leading on a Brooklyn perp walk, up then down Flatbush Avenue, curvy Alice Hall. The girl of eighteen, in heels, bathing suit and leash, had bet on Brooklyn. Patsy Esposito would find Gerald Eskenazi nearby on Sutter Avenue, would jerk his right arm behind his back, bone bowing, a boy crying. Eskenazi, fifteen, had bet $3 he did not have, mother Adella to foot the bill. And in upper Manhattan, on the stoop of 184 Nagle Avenue, a ponytailed girl of thirteen named Arlene Brey squealed with joy. Back in August she had asked for a puppy. Her father, not wanting one, had said yes—providing the Giants win the pennant. Russ Hodges had now testified again and again that a father's great hedge was for naught, that a shaggy black-and-white mutt named Rags would join the Breys in Inwood to live with Arlene for thirteen years.

Even where bets had not been made, few victorious fans could now bite their tongues. In Greenwich Village, Muriel Gloster ran from a dressing room to a sidewalk to hoot and cheer—no matter that the housewife of 29 was naked save slip. In midtown Manhattan, the PEnnsylvania telephone exchange glutted with calls. It had to be shuttered. The *New York Herald Tribune* switchboard was for sixty minutes stalled with calls of "I told you so." And, besieged, the Dodger fan had only to hide. At 3807 Oceanic Avenue in Brooklyn, Bobby Cantor and Bobby Ringel called for Jerry Stern to step outside. Sixteen and crying, the boy did not. "It was," says Stern, "the worst event of my life." In Rockville Centre, New York, Doris Kearns, eight, resolved to cross Brower Avenue to and from school, sidestepping butchers Max Kropf and Joe Schmitt. And in Rochelle Park, New Jersey, where Jim Bouton, twelve, knocked ten full minutes on the door of friend Robert Iriana, it was his mother who emerged from the shades-drawn house. Said Mrs. Iriana, "Robert's not feeling well."

Neither was Anne Prince. The heartbroken housewife had shut her television after the home run, had retreated from son Carl and daughter Marcia to a closed bedroom on the second floor of a tenement at 39 Eckert Avenue in Newark. Husband Phillip returned home to find his wife of forty-two unable to leave her room, and the plumbing-parts salesman now prepared dinner a first time in twenty years of marriage, four cans of spaghetti and meatballs heated, three bottles of Royal Crown Cola opened.

Branca and Ann had long stopped crying when they parked on Courtlandt Avenue and entered Paul Daube's restaurant. Here the couple set to meet Rube and Millie Walker, pitcher intent on keeping the pregame engagement he had made with his catcher in spite of their last luckless communication.

Inside the steakhouse, all eyes fell on Branca. News of his pitch already filled the afternoon papers, a rebroadcast of the game on WMGM just begun. Branca steeled himself. But before he sat, a room stood, applause echoing some 2,000 yards from where his fastball flew. Remembered Walker the next spring, "Branca ate all right."

So too did Giant fans. A boy of eleven named Joseph Grange found in three South Bronx shops doughnuts, ice cream and pizza suddenly free. Shannon's Café at 1162 Third Avenue served up two rounds on the house. And at the 21 Club, just tables away from John Steinbeck, wife, Elaine, publisher Harold Guinzburg and son Tom, a party of four Durochers, three doctors, two toy makers and a housewife shared a feast on West 52nd Street.

Two blocks away at Studio 52, Thomson consented to applications of blush. The gussied hero could barely sit still, introduced live by Perry Como to his CBS audience at 7:45 p.m.

Across town in the Commodore Hotel on East 42nd Street another broadcast was ongoing, a succession of slaphappy sponsors, writers, league presidents and announcers slavering on Mutual radio over a home run. It was a gay broadcast and so a gay Frank White, president of Mutual, who now introduced baseball's commissioner. Frick began:

"Thank you very much, Frank. It's very difficult to know what to say at a time like this. I suppose I'm expected to speak for baseball. But it seems to me that baseball in the last five days has spoken very loudly for itself. I think it needs no expression of mine."

But the rookie commissioner continued—incongruous and somber and defensive:

If there has ever been in the minds of any of the public any doubt as to the honesty and the fairness of baseball competition, it seems to me that has been answered forever. And I hope that none of you fans will start writing me letters in the face of this about the fact that baseball is not on the level. We have had the evidence beyond all reason. There's nothing much I can say to you as commissioner of baseball. I'm a freshman—it would be presumptuous indeed for me to talk about things that I might do or think or feel. Baseball is in fine hands. And I don't refer to the commissioner—I refer to those men who own the ball clubs. It is not necessary that baseball have a commissioner to keep baseball men honest. Baseball men are fair and decent and real sportsmen.

Abraham Chadwick did not hear the commissioner. Nor did he tune in Perry Como, no matter that the fifteen-minute show was his favorite. For a Scorpio had stung a Capricorn beneath a Libra sun, batter vanquishing star-crossed pitcher with one apocalyptic swing. And so on the second floor of a red-brick home in the Bronx, a sallow electrician in buttoned broadcloth had no appetite for vanilla malteds, much less radio or television. Chadwick shuffled from gray couch to bed, his little Emerson turned off.

High above Elder Avenue, a waxing crescent glimmered three nights grown. Chadwick, his cancer spread, would not see such a moon again. And it was in the satellite that Tallulah Bankhead in Bedford Village, New York, saw now the end of days. "There was," wrote the actress, "blood on the moon."

A trio of men looking heavenward this same night in Kadena, Okinawa, reported seeing a UFO. In upstate New York, residents testified to seeing some 400 feet over the Saint Regis Indian reservation a "fantastic flying ball." And a matinee extraterrestrial named Klaatu had five days before landed a spaceship in Washington, D.C. But it was another celestial sphere that soared now on movie screens all about the country. Set atop a black-and-white aerial photograph of the Polo Grounds, the newsreel began with a three-tier headline: "MIRACLE TEAM, GIANTS ENTER SERIES, WITH HOMER IN NINTH." Block letters gave way to footage of a Branca pitch and a Thomson swing, the dramatic voice of Ed Herlihy narrating: "With one blast of his bat, Bobby Thomson, the Flying Scot, brings the pennant race to a swift stunning close." To the music of John Philip Sousa and the rat-a-tat of film through a projector, Thomson set off on his diamond dance.

It was now in a two-family Flatbush home at 1020 East 12th Street that Larry Goldberg discovered Russ Hodges screaming (the transportive call to supplant Sousa in perpetuity as Thomson's escort about the bases). Hours earlier, Goldberg, a Giant fan and trip planner for the Automobile Association of America, had readied beside his radio a Webcor recorder. Mother Sylvia had as instructed pressed RECORD, and home from work her son now listened: "The Giants win the pennant! The Giants win the pennant!" Goldberg, twenty-six, mailed the reel to WMCA care of Hodges.

A fusillade of camera clicks had further documented in black and white the home run. And fished now from tanks of dektol were enough snapshots to fill the reel of a Mutoscope—a swing, a ball whirring northeast, Branca turning to watch, Pafko impotent in left, Thomson frisking about first, Robinson unmoving behind second, Durocher jigging at third, Branca descending the mound, Thomson leaping for home, a fan swiping his cap, a team lifting his body, the hero dashing toward center, Branca walking head down, sitting head down, lying facedown, Thomson hugging teammates, waving at fans, kissing his bat as he did nine seasons prior in North Carolina, his first in professional ball.

For all the dozens of photographs, however, just two would ever be shown to have captured the home run and its protagonists in their entirety, two snapshots clicked a second or so apart high above the crest of a ball in flight.

Rudy Mancuso's shutter closed first. Mancuso, a die cutter who weekly studied photography in night school, had this morning brought to his seat in the upper deck at the Polo Grounds his Busch Press camera. High above the right side of play, just fair of home, the Giant fan, thirty-one, spent the first of his two exposures on Hank Bauer (the Yankee seated close by), and by hunch, his final camera click on Branca's second pitch. "When I heard the crack of the bat," says Mancuso, "I snapped my picture."

A few rows lower and to the right, a smidge foul of home, stood Frank Rino, about his neck an octagonal photographer pass. Since joining the *New York Journal American* in 1934, the heavyset photographer had pursued what he called "the supreme moment action shot." Rino, forty-one, had already this Wednesday attempted dozens when, Thomson at bat, he snapped again—his Speed Graphic steadied atop a tripod in the packed press box jutting from the underbelly of the upper deck.

The portrait revealed itself to Mancuso in a darkroom on East 79th Street. Here like insects in amber were sixteen men and a white ball, the smote Spalding some forty feet from Thomson. None afield had yet time to react, catcher Walker, glove held high, waiting for a pitch that would never come.

Walker had since lowered his leather in the photograph Rino now hung to dry in a fifth-floor darkroom on South Street, the catcher gazing with Branca and Thomson at a baseball careering in left. Rino's photograph extended too toward right, capturing five more men afield than had Mancuso's—Snider in center, Robinson at second, Fitzsimmons at first, batboy Leonard, and a kneeling Mays on deck. Captured too were the distant dark windows of a center-field clubhouse beneath a clock frozen at 3:58 p.m., the faintest of figures silhouetted in the fourth window between sill and lifted frame.

A few miles north at 220 East 42nd Street, a galley proof of six photographs lay on a seventh-floor desk beneath the glare of Pete Coutros. The photos, of a home run and its celebration, comprised what would be tomorrow's *Daily News* centerfold and it fell to Coutros, twenty-eight, to give them a caption.

Coutros had joined the tabloid in 1942, a clerk. Then a literature major at Long Island University, he had from seven at night until three in the morning put photos in a chute to be whisked from art on the seventh floor to photo-engraving on the sixth. The work was tedious, and after taxes good for just $15.84 a week. But the polymathic clerk was free to help prune the meandering caption. And when in 1944 a drunk and broken writer named Bob Jeans put his head in an oven, it was Coutros who turned head caption writer.

A tie forever dangling over his Royal typewriter, Coutros had only to stare at a photograph and a caption leapt to mind. (Thus, for example, did American soldiers cooling their feet while marching German POWs turn "Hot Dogs and Sour Krauts.") The wit now stared down at Thomson, waiting for a catchphrase to come.

Willard Mullin already had his phrase. Since joining in 1934 the *New York World-Telegram,* the celebrated cartoonist had always, it seemed, known just how to capture, with pen, ink and conté crayon, the marrow of sport. In his hand did Dodger famously turn "Bum," an everyman. And after New York had won the opening game of this playoff, Mullin drew a Giant galoot carrying in his pocket the movie script of a magical season. The fairy tale had come true. And so, at his desk at 125 Barclay Street, Mullin now leaned over a rectangle of coquille board, his jolly Giant again toting "The Little Miracle of Coogan's Bluff."

Fern Hack sat down to write a letter. She had not been in touch with Branca in five years and there was much to share—a home in Florida, a daughter of nineteen months, a husband named Art, he a silver salesman now away on business. But on this horrible night, she wished only to tell her first love that she cared for him and that good could come of bad. This Fern wrote and stamped and sent on its way.

Millie Martin would send Thomson a telegram. This she decided at first word of her wartime-love turned hero. But Millie's husband of four years asked kindly that she not, and home in Pelican Rapids, Minnesota, Millie obeyed.

Winkie Coley, meantime, had stolen away midgame down a stairwell to a television in the all-male interns lounge at Muhlenberg Hospital. It was there in the ninth inning the social worker had promised champagne to a roomful of young doctors if the man she loved hit a home run. She was now in their debt.

Thomson sang on air a Chesterfield jingle and, the Perry Como show ended, hopped a cab down the West Side highway to the ferry, off at 9 for a nickel across New York Bay. There, for some twenty-three minutes, the hero sat alone on an upper deck. Setting foot on Staten Island, he evaded a crush of fans, then headed straight for his brother, taxiing unrecognized down Bay Street past the Coast Guard and post office to Engine 154, the red brick building on Hannah Street. A fireman fetched Jim.

"Bob," Jim asked his little brother, "do you realize what you did?" Thomson found the question silly, answered that he had hit a home run to beat Brooklyn. "No," said Jim. "You don't see it. That might never happen again." And so a hero took true note of his heroics, understood suddenly five hours after a swing that life would never be the same, the ballplayer like pilot Chuck Yeager who in 1947 realized only after peering down at an instrument meter that he had broken the sound barrier. The brothers Thomson, supersonic, climbed into a station wagon and headed for dinner.

Elizabeth Thomson arrived in a yellow dress at Tavern on the Green in New Dorp, on her breast an orchid, in her silver hair a rose. She who at fifty-seven was not yet naturalized was suddenly mother to America's most famous son. And waiting now with daughters Jean and Marion for her boys, she accepted wine and ginger ale and a newspaper with the massive headline "GIANT HR IN 9TH WINS." Robert Brown arrived at 10, scores of friends, family, fans and press ready with a uniformed police band to cheer and toast him too.

Thomson acknowledged the crowd. The home run was a great thrill, he said. "No matter what I ever do again, I'll never live up to it."

Nor would any player. For after eighty years, 85,000 major league games and 5.8 million at-bats, the national pastime had at last produced perfection.

And so it was fitting that there were those who would never again watch the game. Antonio Masse, born in Sorrento in 1873 and living on Kermit Place in Flatbush, had hours ago thrown his Rheingold beer *into* his television set, cursed Branca and forswore the sport he loved—the Dodger fan in short order to cancel his subscription to the *Brooklyn Eagle,* shun the World Series and die before spring training. And Ed Lucas, an ecstatic boy of twelve in Jersey City who this afternoon had watched Thomson romp home, then played ball on a blacktop outside the Lafayette Gardens housing project, been hit between the eyes by a line drive and seen his vision grow cloudy, would by Opening Day be blind.

Thomson ate a steak and salt-speckled fries. He drank too, careful before the snap of each photo to hand his glass of wine to friend Al Corbin. With Game One of the World Series hours away, it would not do to see the playoff paladin enjoying a drink.

It was now on West 57th Street that Voice of America piped to Latin America word of Thomson. The Spanish bulletin finished at 10:56 p.m. and, down the block at the Henry Hudson Hotel, Schenz, Spencer and Koslo turned in. Thomson did too. "We got a ballgame tomorrow," he told his townsfolk from atop a chair. Thomson, mother and brother returned to their six-room home.

A ringing phone awaited. Hero picked up. "We just got in," Thomson told Lou Miller, reporter for the *New York World-Telegram and Sun.* Thomson assured a readership that his team was not overawed by the Yankees, then offered Miller the polite hope that he would find sleep. Home in a twin bed on Flagg Place, he did.

Home in a full bed on Dexter Avenue in Malden, Neil Romano lay down with his wife, Mary. The Giant fan, 28, had moved with his bride before the baseball season from New Jersey to Massachusetts. Separated from his fellow rooters, he now celebrated an orgasmic pennant as best he could, son Chuck, born 38 weeks later.

Another life dimmed. Back in New York, Jim Borax had watched the home run one flight above Central Park West. The Dodger fan, 14, was distraught. "I wanted to kill myself," he says. "I wanted to end my life."

Branca parked at 39 Maple Street. And on this night, when seventeen parking meters first dotted the boulevards of Brooklyn, he did not linger. The pitcher kissed his fiancée goodnight then drove for Mount Vernon.

The temperature had fallen eight degrees since Branca's last pitch, a cool 63 at midnight. And buffered by bride and priest, the pitcher put to bed the day just ended. "I knew I had done my best," wrote Branca months later, "and I made up my mind right then and there that I wouldn't let the thought of Thomson's hit haunt me." But resolute, Branca entered his beige Tudor to find that a volley of phone calls and telegrams had already bloodied his family. "Why," asked a woman of Katherine Branca, "don't you teach your son how to pitch?" Hundreds were more direct. "Most of them said just about the same thing," recalled Branca. "Drop dead."

SEVENTEEN

The task of an American writer is not to describe the misgivings of a woman taken in adultery as she looks out of a window at the rain but to describe 400 people under the lights reaching for a foul ball.
—JOHN CHEEVER, *The Journals of John Cheever*, 1963

ERNEST THAYER SET THE great game to verse. "The score stood four to two with but one inning more to play," he wrote. There were, he continued, runners on second and third, the leading slugger of the home team due to bat. Thayer, twenty-four, wrote also a fourteener of the game's final pitch: "And now the pitcher holds the ball, and now he lets it go."

The Harvard graduate finished his poem and mailed it to a friend at the *Daily Examiner* of San Francisco. And it was then on June 3, 1888, that William Randolph Hearst ran "Casey at the Bat."

Sixty-three years later, Thayer's iambic ballad resonated anew, blueprint for the greatest of all baseball games. But on an 0-1 fastball, life broke from art. While Casey, mighty Casey, had struck out, while in just months novelist Bernard Malamud would in *The Natural* strike out Roy Hobbs too, Thomson had hit a home run. Never did the serious dramatist send his leading actor loping about the bases. The sophisticate would not buy it. It did not happen.

But now it had. And so in the clubhouse at the Polo Grounds minutes after Thomson's home run, McCulley of the *Daily News* had turned to Rigney with a question: "How in the hell do you write this story?"

The newspapermen were not long at a loss for words. For a simple realization drove their fingers to type: an echoing green *mattered*. Thomson's home run had imposed itself on a nation. And, cynosure of 300 million American eyes, it sent hundreds of writers scrambling at deadline for precedent.

"First came the most tumultuous blowing of automobile horns throughout the metropolitan area since V-E Day," wrote the AP. "Even when Pearl Harbor was bombed," wrote reporter Irving Marsh, who heard the ballgame at the *New York Herald Tribune,* "there wasn't as much excitement in the city room." The comeback, wrote the *Los Angeles Times,* was a "modern day version of Custer's Last Stand." Giant fans, wrote the UP, enjoyed "as riotous a night of celebration as any since the repeal of prohibition." Dodger fans, wrote the *Newark Star Ledger,* suffered "the greatest bubble bursting since Wall Street went to pieces in 1929." Added the *Daily News* with a nod to Thayer, "There Is No Joy in Flatbush."

The army of baseball writers turned also to a pair of military blasts, the first fired on April 19, 1775. It was then a bullet begat the Revolutionary War, a gunshot described in 1837 by Ralph Waldo Emerson as "the shot heard 'round the world." The shot of a uniformed man had again bookended battle and so, wrote the *New York Times,* Thomson hit "a home run heard round the world." The *Long Island Star Journal* concurred, calling it "the shot heard round the country," while the *New York Journal American* hailed "Thomson's shot heard round the baseball world." So did two articles in the *Staten Island Advance,* the home run both "a shot that was heard around the world" and "the blow heard 'round the baseball world." Coutros, caption guru of the *Daily News,* had settled on Emerson too. And on this day of a thousand headlines, it was owing *his* atop a centerfold that six words would spread like kudzu. Read the two-page fifteen-inch banner: "THE SHOT HEARD 'ROUND THE BASEBALL WORLD."

Word from the White House that Russia had exploded an atom bomb proved for journalists a second and more immediate muse.

"The Giants exploded a bomb, too," began a *New York Times* editorial. The home run, wrote Grantland Rice in the *New York Herald Tribune,* was an "atomic crash." Brooklyn fans, wrote Bennett Schiff of the *New York Post,* "wore the kind of expressions that children wore in the war after a bombing." Read a *Post* editorial headline: "JOSEPH STALIN'S BOMB, BOBBY THOMSON'S BLAST."

The latter was louder. "Any repercussions of the atomic disclosure," wrote the *Post,* "were firmly overshadowed by a thunderous noise that . . . was registered at 3:58 p.m." And so, while the banner headline "RUSSIA EXPLODES 2D A-BOMB" spanned the front page of the *Newark Star Ledger,* a second headline ran *above* it: "GIANTS DO IT, 5–4!" While the *Call Bulletin* in San Francisco ran in 72-point type across its front page the headline "RUSS EXPLODE 2D ATOMIC BOMB," a second headline in 144-point type stood taller: "GIANT HOMER WINS FLAG!" Nearly all a nation's papers, in fact—from the *New York Times* to the *Fargo Forum*—trumpeted news of Thomson's home run with at least as much oomph as they did word of a second Russian nuclear test.

Gordon Dean was delighted. Chairman of the Atomic Energy Commission, he had the previous afternoon met in Washington, D.C., with James Lay, executive secretary of the National Security Council, to discuss how best to break to the nation that at 9:19 a.m. on September 24 Russia had detonated a plutonium bomb atop a tower in Semipalatinsk, "confirming the end to the American nuclear monopoly," put it Jules Tygiel. Thomson's home run, manna from heaven, had diffused the news and the Day After, Dean now jotted in his journal his good fortune. "Did not receive," he wrote, "as large a headline in the evening paper as the play-off for the world series games."

Thomson had been writ large. And his bio tilled anew, all manner of claims were now lain to him. "He's Our Uncle Bobby" read the front-page of the *Cleveland Press* above a photo of Ruby Jakosh and her three children. "ALL ISLAND JUBILANT AS BOBBY WINS GAME" reported page one of the *Staten Island Advance*. "TIS A BRAW, BRICHT NICHT AS THOMSONVILLE BLOWS CORK" read a UP headline. Thus did relatives, neighbors, countrymen, dip a toe into celebrity.

With each printed word were the ravages to Branca laid bare. It was he now limp on the entire back page of the *New York Post*, the staggering photograph of a head in hands earning Stein a $100 bonus. The pitcher was pitiable. But he was culpable too. For the twenty-seven white-ink dashes atop Rino's photograph on page 25 of the second edition of the *New York Journal American* traced the trajectory of what would forever be an imminent home run, of what had sunk 150,000 Dodger dollars and the spirit of millions. "There were those," wrote the *Daily Mirror,* "who thought of ending it all in a long leap from the Brooklyn Bridge or a deep dive into the Gowanus."

For once, hyperbole was understatement. This the normally understated Red Smith understood, his autopsy of the home run best of all its inspirations. "Now it is done," began his column in the *New York Herald Tribune.* "Now the story ends. And there is no way to tell it. The art of fiction is dead. Reality has strangled invention. Only the utterly impossible, the inexpressibly fantastic, can ever be plausible again." A fleet of trucks set out from West 40th Street to deliver Smith's prose to all a city.

Coverage of the game carried well beyond both his readership and Manhattan's 22.3 square miles. New York, the *Jewish Daily Forward*: "דעם סענסאַצי״אנעלסטען אין דער גאַנצער געשיכטע פֿון לעיסאָל." Canada, the *Montreal Star*: "The finish was super colossal." Mexico, *El Universal*: "Branca Apenas Pudo Hablar." Cuba, *Diario de la Marina*: "Los fanáticos, increíbles, estupendos 'Gigantes.'" Japan, *Nikkan Sports*: "最終回の猛逆襲、トンプソン劇的3ラン." It was atop Filipino swimming, volleyball and jai-alai results that the *Manila Times* trumpeted word of a Giant pennant. And in. he *Scottish Daily Record*, Frank Oliver set out to introduce the great Glaswegian to his homefolk. Thomson, wrote Oliver, "is America's most eligible bachelor. He gets $30,000 a year and last night his mother cooked him a Scotch dumpling."

Steinbeck awoke in an East Side New York brownstone ready before dawn to write of the game. The author walked the flight from bedroom to office, sat at his wooden drafting table with its black calculator and meerschaum pipe, opened a blue-ruled notebook and fished from a plastic tray atop the green blotter before him a Mongol pencil. Set now at 5:30 a.m. to begin chapter 46 of *East of Eden,* he began in his black notebook a letter to editor Covici. "Baseball yesterday," he wrote. "Probably the best game I or anyone ever saw."

The ballgame swayed Jack Kerouac too. The Beat poet loved baseball, had as a boy in Lowell, Massachusetts, created a fantasy league of six clubs complete with standings and newsletter. And when this past April he had, high on coffee and in just twenty days, typed a revised version of a novel titled *On the Road,* his references to baseball were several. "So we quickly find out," he wrote, "what happened to Bobby Thomson when we left him thirty seconds ago with a man on third." With a man on third and second too, Thomson had now homered and Kerouac, twenty-nine, exulted. "When Bobby Thompson [*sic*] hit that home run in 1951," Kerouac later wrote, "I trembled with joy and couldn't get over it for days and wrote poems about how it is possible for the human spirit to win after all!"

The home run made clear too that it was possible for the human spirit to lose. And in an eight-by-twelve-by-nine-foot cell in Ossining, New York, this Julius Rosenberg mourned.

Rosenberg, thirty-three, had in March been convicted along with wife Ethel of passing on to the USSR information about U.S. atomic weapons. A federal court had sentenced the parents of two to death and their hopes rested now on an appeal that would reach the Supreme Court in October 1952.

Prospects were slim that the nine justices (among them Harold Burton, careful the evening previous to note in his diary the Giant 5–4 decision), would spare the Rosenbergs the 2,000-volt electric chair down the concrete hall from Julius. Fears of growing Soviet influence had in the name of country, snuffed due process, given rise to loyalty tests in government employment, jump-started a blind hunt for closeted Communists, fed an inchoate McCarthyism, sold millions of books by Mickey Spillane, sent schoolchildren under their desks. A red scare was oozing over the planet. That just three days prior Pope Pius XII warned of World War III did not aid Rosenberg.

But as Sing Sing inmate 110-649 sat now behind twelve steel bars to write Ethel a letter, he made no mention of courtroom. Rosenberg was on this day a despondent Dodger fan. And what mattered most was not a bomb dropped in Kazakhstan or a press conference in Washington, D.C., but a home run hit in New York.

"Gloom of glooms," wrote Rosenberg in a neat script. "The dear Dodgers lost the penant [sic]."

EIGHTEEN

Toss'd and retoss'd, the ball incessant flies.
—HOMER, *The Odyssey*
(translated by Alexander Pope)

T HE WAR IN KOREA WAS leeching the American pastime. Voted by club owners baseball commissioner, Emmett O'Donnell remained instead (under order of President Truman) Far East Air Force bomber commander. Ted Williams, Whitey Ford, Curt Simmons and others had left for the peninsula in 1951. And baseball would forfeit more stars, Willie Mays soon drafted, Don Newcombe unaware that an 0–1 pitch thrown Lockman was to be his last until 1954.

The U.S. had planned in the event of war little more than SAS-SAFRAS—code name for the evacuation from Korea of U.S. nationals. But when in June 1950 North Korea invaded South, America suddenly minded the oversea seep of Communism, massing there by October 1951 228,000 soldiers.

And so when Thomson hit his home run, Red Barber sought perspective in Korea, offering up to his Brooklyn audience the abattoir.

This the U.S. 24th Infantry Division did not yet know. For only now—fourteen hours later in a time zone fourteen hours ahead—did Maglie's first pitch fly on Armed Forces Radio from New York to California to Japan to Korea where south of Kumsong some thousand foot soldiers in foxholes heard via loudspeaker Furillo take ball one.

A continent westward, another young American listened rapt to an AFR rebroadcast of the game. Eugene Istomin had come to southern France from the West Side of Manhattan to play the piano, invited by Pablo Casals to perform Mozart's Concerto no. 14 in E-flat Major at a summer festival in Perpignan. Istomin had done so and sparkled. And now, months later and in the middle of a European tour, he visited Casals at his wood-paneled home in Prades.

Istomin loved the Dodgers. And he loved Casals. The men had met in 1950 when, seventy-three and world famous, the Catalan cellist conducted Istomin at his hometown Bach Festival, the pianist at twenty-four its youngest-ever soloist. Two autumns later, they sat now together at a square writing table some fifteen miles from Spain listening to Al Helfer deliver a penultimate pitch, Bobby Thomson taking strike one from Ralph Branca. Then Thomson swung.

"When the holocaust struck," Istomin later wrote, "I jumped out of my seat, and stood transfixed before the nonplussed Casals." The great cellist started. "What happened, my boy?" asked Casals. "A most catastrophic and magnificent thing," answered Istomin. The young pianist fell silent, imagining, in the foothills of the Pyrenees, the final flight of a ball from Branca to Thomson to lucky, lucky fan in Section 35 of the Polo Grounds.

In the seventeen hours since his home run, Thomson had not wondered as to its landing. But as he stepped now before Game One of the World Series from his blue Mercury in the Yankee Stadium parking lot, a stranger approached. Fan told ballplayer that he had caught his blast and that for tickets to the game, the Spalding was his. Thomson rushed into the Giant locker room. But there clubhouse man Logan revealed a stash of baseballs hand-delivered with the same claim and the hero resigned to fate. Provenance was impossible.

Calls for the ball would nonetheless issue forth forevermore—days later Jimmy Powers reporting that Thomson wished it given to Cooperstown, in 2004 auction house Lelands.com offering for it one million dollars. And too would scores of fans aver ownership. (The most recent to do so was Bill Moore, a retired budget director of a Connecticut bank who in 2005 sold for $47,824 a ball given him by a colleague of his father. Written on the Spalding in faded blue ink is BOB THOMSON HOME RUN LAST OF 9TH LF.) None, however, would muster evidence of title the least bit compelling. And free of fact, fiction would have at it, author Thomas Kiernan splintering a struck seat, screenwriter Michael Sloane landing the ball in the grip of a black girl of nine named Pauline Watkins, professor Bob Mitchell placing it in the left hand of carpenter Solomon Stein, novelist Don DeLillo describing its carom off a green pillar, its rolling onto a mound of clothing and then, below a seat, the wresting of the souvenir by a turnstile-jumping black boy of fourteen from Harlem named Cotter Martin.

Martin happened to fit the testimony of a Baptist minister named John Lee Smith. Photos place Smith on October 3, 1951, in the front row of Section 35 at the Polo Grounds, a Yale divinity student of twenty-three standing some twelve feet above Dodger left-fielder Pafko. Smith credibly claims to have watched Thomson's shot land in the mitt of a capped preteen standing in the aisle just to his right, a black boy who cheered Monte Irvin all game long and then, homer gloved, scuttled from sight. Clearly visible in a photo by *Daily News* photographer Hank Olen are two black youths standing beside the incoming ball.

That ball, wrote Michael Santa Maria and James Costello, had marked "the birth of the pitcher as scapegoat." And nowhere was it worse to wear horns than in Brooklyn.

Baseball in Brooklyn was "religion, a cause, a mania and a disease," wrote the *Sporting News* in 1938. It was there the perennial pain of second fiddle turned rooters to drink, to cry, to shut in at home, frustration metastasizing every fall through 80.95 square and dejected miles. It was there the previous afternoon that at the corner of Court and Montague Streets benumbed loyalists had gathered outside Dodger headquarters as if for a wake. It was there on East 94th Street that a redhead with red eyes kicked neighbor Naomi Schwartz for her Giant taunts, Todd Merer driven to a precinct on Empire Boulevard where officer Schultz sent the boy of eleven home. It was there center-fielder Snider saw swaying from light and telephone poles a school of stuffed Brancas wearing in effigy the number 13. And it was there this morning on Seneca Avenue that telegrams continued to wish Branca dead.

A few tender telegrams were also sent Branca and these brought him now to tears. "There were still some nice people in this world," he says. There remained also family. And home, where mother Katherine had bronzed in scrapbooks every pitch of a career, adages of God's memory and of wrongs righted were now dusted off, the Brancas swaddling their relation—thirty-five nieces, nephews, siblings, parents and fiancée an eiderdown on which to lie.

It was at home on Seneca Avenue that a decision was now reached. Branca was the only pitcher in baseball to wear the number 13. He did so with gall, posing with a black cat for the *Brooklyn Eagle* on Friday, April 13, 1951, driving since 1948 a car with the vanity plate 13-RB. But fate had called his bluff. And in the wake of disaster, he who had now lost three of the six playoff games in the four score years of baseball turned triskaidekaphobe. The pitcher would shed his number. He would lose his license plate. The Brancas approved. Wrote Ralph in the spring, "They had wanted me to change it for some time."

Across the Bronx and Harlem and Hudson rivers, two men wearing .38 caliber revolvers mounted stools at the counter of Joe's Elbow Room in Cliffside Park, New Jersey, and ordered 80 cents of orange juice, coffee and cake. Two more gunmen arrived at the restaurant minutes later. The foursome moved to a table to wait for Quarico Moretti.

Moretti, fifty-seven, was well connected, paisans including everyone from Frank Sinatra to childhood chum Frank Costello. When in 1933 Mob boss Costello slunk from bootlegging to betting, Moretti found himself prince of gambling in northern New Jersey, an underboss called Willie feeding on cards, dice and sports.

Moretti was not a cautious man. When the previous December the Senate Crime Investigating Committee requisitioned him to testify, he prattled on. And though some ascribed his loose lips to syphilis, there were a passel of mafiosi who wished him offed. Costello, however, did not and on Moretti lived, a funny, churchgoing father of three growing rich on bookmaking.

But nineteen hours prior, a home run, it seems, had cost Moretti. For in his Jersey gambling dens, chief among them the Marine Room, a swish casino beside the George Washington Bridge, the Giants, 13–10 favorites, had drawn heavy money.

Moretti parked his cream Packard convertible at 793 Palisade Avenue. It was near 11:20 a.m. A friendly face emerged from Joe's Elbow Room, a hand slapping Moretti on the back of his brown suit, and the men walked to a waiting table for breakfast. All was well, five men joking in Italian, waitress Dorothy Novack disappearing to the kitchen to get a menu.

One bullet ripped through Moretti's left ear and out his right cheek. Another pierced the top of his head, the underboss falling dead to the linoleum floor at 11:28 a.m. The hit was ordered by Vito Genovese but bound to another, to a home run. "The pudgy, partly bald victim," wrote the *New York Times*, "might have 'welshed' on baseball bets after reportedly losing a huge sum yesterday on the outcome of the Dodgers-Giants game."

That Reno now offered $15.50 for a $10 bet on the Giants in the World Series mattered not a wink to Harlem's underdogs. For just once before had a team at least 10 games below .500 come back to win the pennant and that New York had done so in fantabulous fashion rendered anything left of this 1951 season pure gravy. Thomson's home run, after all, "was a climax built on top of a climax," wrote reporter Daley in the *New York Times*. And so the World Series turned anticlimactic. "World Series?" wrote Al Buck in the *New York Post*. "So what."

The series, however, mattered to the Yankees. New York measured seasons not in mere pennants but in rings. And they were primed for a third straight. Berra anchored the offense, Rizzuto the defense, Vic Raschi, Ed Lopat and Allie Reynolds the pitching. Manager Casey Stengel had guided the team to 98 wins even as rookie Gil McDougald was the lone regular to bat .300. And without rival, the Bombers were indifferent to foe. So were their fans. It was no coincidence that as Thomson went yard the previous afternoon, Don DeLillo sat openmouthed for Dr. Fish, a boy of fourteen agape on Crotona Avenue. "The Yankees had already clinched," says DeLillo. "That's why I was at the dentist. I was aloof from the playoff game. It didn't involve me viscerally."

Thomson's shot though had called a nation to attention. And at 1:00 p.m., panjandrums J. Edgar Hoover, Herbert Hoover, Douglas MacArthur and Margaret Truman among the crowd of 65,673, America tuned in en masse, some 140 million people to follow on radio or TV at least one game of the Series.

Over the coming days, they beheld excitements. Irvin stole home. DiMaggio sent to left the final home run of a golden career. Mays, Irvin and Thompson comprised a first all-black outfield. Mantle and DiMaggio converged on a ball one last time (ligaments tearing in the rookie's right knee).

There were happenings off the field too. At Mount Carmel Mercy Hospital in Detroit, James and Louise Thompson named a blue-eyed boy after a Giant hero. At Mount Ararat Cemetery in North Lindenhurst, New York, Belle, Harold and Rhoda Arbiter buried in range J, plot 33, he who had died pulling for a Dodger goat. Wary of a center field crowded with press and officials, the Giants did not use a telescope for the first time in 30 home games. ("They're roaming around during the game in the clubhouse," explains Yvars. "And once you get in the World Series, what do you care?") And parceling their pennant dollars, the Giant regulars saw fit to vote Schenz more money than eight other reserves (no matter that in 100 days, the scapegrace had *zero* at-bats).

The Giants lost two of three at home. And on October 10, down 3–2 in the series, the team suited up across the Harlem River one loss from elimination.

Ralph Branca decided to attend Game Six of the World Series. Seven days after Armageddon, he would confront and be done with.

In dark tie and light overcoat, Branca settled into a box behind the Giant dugout with Ann and her parents (the Mulveys never wanting for tickets). Herb Scharfman spotted the pitcher. Here was a photo op. The International News Service photographer fetched Thomson and called to

Branca, the smiling goat ambling afield, reports of his death greatly exaggerated. Heads turned. "I thought it was pretty big of him to show up," says Thomson. Scharfman suggested that pitcher place large hands about batter's neck. Branca did. "I was being a good guy," he says. And so vanquished strangled victor, Branca and Thomson kibitzing beneath the glare of popping flashbulbs.

That Branca wished to be seen was testament to his constitution, Thomson gracious, the price of battle won. But on this Wednesday morning, theirs was a *pose* preserved, revenge and smiles choreographed, contrived. The whisking past of grief was peculiar—Newcombe had not joshed with Sisler after their theater the previous fall. It was causative too. For what is scraped in fresh cement sets to stone. And just one week after fate had paired numbers 23 and 13, after the *Daily News* had headlined "THOMSON THE HERO, BRANCA THE GOAT," a reunion augured the assumption of lifelong roles.

Play began, Branca watching unfold precisely what had the week before. Again the Giants went to the ninth inning of an elimination game down 4–1, again they rallied, again landing men on second and third, one out, again the score 4–2, again Thomson readying to face a reliever, a weaker hitter again on deck.

Thomson had had a mediocre series—five hits, five walks, one run scored, one driven in. And while his 27 plays at third were a record for a six-game series, all that mattered now was an at-bat against Bob Kuzava.

Second-guessers had all week had at manager Dressen for both calling on Branca and choosing not to walk Thomson. Still, Stengel now did what had Dressen, instructing his pitcher not to walk the potential winning run.

Yankee Stadium tensed, déjà vu disquieting. The third pitch thrown Thomson was a fastball and he swung, Gene Woodling racing back to glove the deep fly in left-center field. Thomson had hit the ball well, driven in his second run of the series, cut the Yankee lead to 4–3. But the Wednesday previous expectations of Thomson had changed and he returned now to the dugout having not delivered what millions half-expected he would. Says Thomson, "I wasn't very happy with myself."

One out remained in the Giant season, midnight at hand for Cinderella. Durocher called time. Wishing to bat right-hander against left, he would pinch-hit for Hank Thompson. Durocher turned from coaching box to bullpen and called to play Yvars. "He engineered a mad dash from the bullpen," observed reporter Joe Diehl, "sorted out a couple pieces of lumber, discarded one, and set himself at the plate." Unused at bat for forty days, spitfire Yvars had broken all six of his Louisville Sluggers.

The Giants had in 1951 more often than not won close games, 34–21 in 55 one-run contests. And with Lockman on second, they were a base hit from life. Berra asked for a fastball and got one, the Kuzava pitch outside and at the waist. Yvars swung. The ball rocketed on a low line to right. Bauer charged then slid, Mantle's replacement gloving the ball inches above the ground.

Yvars and the 1951 Giants were out. And sky-high above Gate Seven in the last row of the upper deck, Philip Hamburger of the *New Yorker* magazine watched a sad woman swig from a flask. "Come on, Branca!" she yelled, World Series deferring instantaneously to playoff. A larrup to left long landed lingered as if a rumble of surf out a beachfront window and Branca, unforgiven, headed home to read of his having strangled Thomson. Wrote Louis Effrat in the *New York Times,* "Wonder if he was posing."

Thomson walked from dugout to clubhouse, his brown eyes welling with tears. Never before had the Scot cried over baseball. And never again would he return to the postseason.

Yvars reached the clubhouse irate. The catcher picked up a bottle of beer and hurled it at the wall above the head of his manager. Noted infielder Pete Castiglione (later an Yvars teammate), "Sal was just never meant to be a hero."

Neither was Schenz. The sub had pinch-run in Game Two. But he had been stranded at first and stepped now from the Yankee Stadium dugout, like DiMaggio, never to wear a major league uniform again.

As he had each afternoon since the start of the playoff, Franks now phoned John Mooney at the *Salt Lake Tribune* to dictate a column. The coach confided he would in days be back in Salt Lake, home at 1559 Cherokee Circle to hunt.

Leo and wife headed for the 21 Club, a last New York supper. And the day after next, they flew west with Michele and Chris to a homecoming bash postponed a week by Bobby Thomson.

In the nine days since Brooklyn had lost the pennant, Abe Chadwick had done little more than sleep. Miriam and malteds were no longer enough to keep the Dodger fan alive. And so, as she had in August, Shirley Marblestone drove her black Pontiac to 1033 Elder Avenue, ready this October 12 to shepherd her brother-in-law to the hospital. Helped from his gray couch, toiletries and slippers rounded, Chadwick slowly descended his wooden steps and stone stoop, never to return. The Russian Jew would make just one more trip and soon, to Maspeth, Long Island, there to lie alongside father Isaac and mother Anna just left of path seven on Gate Road in Mount Zion cemetery.

None on this Friday were disappointed in the disappointed Thomson. For two days after a lost World Series, only the playoff remained, a ceaseless stream of telephoned kudos forcing the hero to disconnect his number, DOngan Hills 6-3196, a tsunami of mail overtaking him too, the wave beginning minutes after his home run with the wiring of a seven-word telegram from Cornelius Hall, proud borough president: "The people of Staten Island love you." So in these letters did bobby soxers falling for Bobby, Thomsons wondering if they might be relatives, charities and shysters hungry for a headliner.

But answering his mail would have to wait. Before a home run had turned him superstar, Thomson had agreed to barnstorm through New England with catcher Birdie Tebbetts. The ballplayer hopped in his blue Mercury and drove to Hartford.

The fallout of another postseason in New York was typical. The Yankees ordered from jeweler L. G. Balfour Company a pile of diamond rings. The Dodgers returned to fans $190,000 in undeposited checks along with a typewritten plea. ("We have no alibis. Your loyalty, particularly at this time, is deeply appreciated.") And Giant fan Robert Wagner relented to a crew-cut, for years the lot of losing borough presidents.

Though the Giants had lost a ninth World Series in 13 tries, fans now bought up 930 season box seats, most in team history. A miracle pennant clearly sufficed, and management slathered its players with gifts—a team portrait painted on tile, baseball cufflinks of gold, a cigarette box wrapped in green leather, a 78 record of Hodges in rapture, and money too, $156,957.46 of World Series receipts theirs to share.

Five days later, Ann Mulvey stood in white—white lace, white satin, white pearls, white orchids. Her green eyes shone and when William Scully asked bride if she took groom to be her wedded husband for better and for worse, she might have answered that she already had. Seventeen days had usurped years of glory, and yet here she stood beside Ralph Branca on an altar in the St. Francis of Assisi Roman Catholic Church. "I do," said Mulvey. In herringbone ascot and tails, Branca told bishop the same. "It was," says Branca, "the happiest day of my life."

Ann clutched with her left hand the bend of her husband's right elbow and craned her neck upward. The couple kissed. It was a kiss preserved, among the guests a newsreel crew and photographers Barney Stein and Fabian and Bradford Bachrach. It was also a kiss that in just months would sell facial soap. "The kiss a Woodbury bride deserves," read an ad in *Family Circle* magazine. "On her exquisite satiny complexion, Anne [sic] loves Woodbury's rich, mild lather."

Never again would Ann endorse product. She was now Mrs. Branca, and to let private turn public was to return catcall with favor. The newlyweds stepped out onto Nostrand Avenue and hours later into their Olds, motoring to the Warwick Hotel in Philadelphia, slipping from a city that would this very month welcome James Dean, Frank O'Hara, Ayn Rand and, at imaginary 623 East Sixty-eighth Street, Lucy and Ricky Ricardo.

At 5:00 a.m. on November 3, one month after a home run, Abraham Chadwick died in room 348 of Flower Fifth Avenue Hospital. He was fifty-three years old, yellow skin loose on 130 pounds, a bullet in his back. That he died an accidental quisling, a Dodger fan complicit in robbing Brooklyn of the pennant, was Chadwick's last lament.

In keeping with Jewish tradition, Chadwick was buried the next day. It was men from Local 3 who dug his grave at Mount Zion, who lowered into the earth a pine coffin holding the light body of Brother Chadwick, J516114. And it was into the eternal company of Jewish men and women descendant from Brainsk, a small town in the Grodne province along what was then the Russian-Polish border, that Chadwick came to rest. "He was a strong man," says daughter Helen. "He died with all his black hair." No one from the Giant organization was present.

NINETEEN

That day she put our heads together,
Fate had her imagination about her,
Your head so much concerned with outer,
Mine with inner, weather.

—ROBERT FROST,
"Tree at My Window," 1928

THIRTY-TWO YEARS AFTER eight bribed White Sox tanked the 1919 World Series, the black eye coloring the most famous of the octet had begun to fade. Joe Jackson was now a liquor store owner with a weak heart, and on February 21, 1951, the South Carolina House of Representatives introduced a resolution to reinstate "Shoeless Joe" into the good graces of baseball. The senate concurred and Ed Sullivan asked Jackson, sixty-three, onto his December 16 show. But on December 5, a heart attack killed Jackson, his death the coda to a year of scandal in sport.

Americans did not take lightly the disgraces of 1951. No sooner was point-shaving at City College exposed than students were sentenced and a movie made, *The Basketball Fix* opening in September. And when photographs snapped on October 20 at Oklahoma A&M showed a white defensive tackle breaking the jaw of a black running back, racism in football was declared laid bare and a Pulitzer Prize awarded. The national pastime, though, went unsullied. For in the months since Thomson's home run, Franks's opaque admission to a Utah newspaper the day of the blast remained the only public whisper of a stolen sign—in October the *Sporting News* innocently cropping from its pages the clipped clubhouse window atop photographer Jacobellis's team portrait, in December New York's many papers, oblivious, breathing no word of a Wollensak when the Giants shipped Schenz to the AAA Oakland Oaks, in January a ballroom in Chicago only charmed when Durocher quipped, "All I had to do was give Bobby Thomson the signal for a home run."

Thomson returned from barnstorming, a thousand letters and telegrams in wait. The Giant had come to see the baseball fan more clearly. (When days before he lined a two-run double to win a game in Massachusetts, asked only was why he had not homered.) Still, Thomson felt it right to answer every last note and set off at his buried desk to do so, composing in longhand some thirty-five letters per five hours, enclosing with each a signed photo. The hero, though, could not keep up with his mail and on December 10 issued via the press a three-paragraph statement, thanking all, explaining that so manic had life post-playoff become that he had often been forced to unplug his phone.

Jean and Jim meantime triaged requests of brother Bobby—yes, yes and yes to Ed Sullivan, the Heisman Trophy dinner, the March of Dimes, yes to engagements aplenty. And so Thomson schlepped to shindigs from Boston to Minneapolis, Buffalo to Chicago, there the Illinois Saint Andrew Society honoring their fellow Scot on a Saturday night in December with haggis, bagpipes and a gold watch. Home had at him too, the Police Athletic League in New Dorp honoring Thomson with a dinner, Curtis High bestowing at a school assembly an honorary cloth "C," Staten Island borough president Cornelius Hall declaring the sixth of December Bobby Thomson Day.

Word of the holiday spread about Richmond. And when the appointed Thursday arrived, Thomson rolled in an open convertible through town, his pinkie ring sparkling with each wave, Frank Merriwell come to life. As in dime novels, the cheers for the athletic hero were unceasing, thousands of proud and happy islanders come to hoot on Hoot Mon. A twelve-car caravan led Thomson to Borough Hall, where at 3 o'clock he accepted gifts—a tie from PS 16, a suitcase from the merchants' association, a homemade cheer from a class of sixth-grade girls. Thomson gave thanks, shook a thousand hands, patted someone's pet Dalmatian, told the crowd he had lived just yonder on Van Duzer Street.

It was after Thomson danced the Highland Fling, a sort of Scottish can-can, that on to a dinner dance at the New Dorp Rolladium moved much of the throng—the 1,400 homefolk who paid $7.50 for tickets, the twenty-seven dignitaries dotting the dais, a Rabbi Millner whose benediction put to words the *nachas* born of a hometown hero. Giants spoke too, Irvin, Westrum, Yvars, Durocher and Thomson, the hero announcing that he would donate to charity his evening's gift of $8,000. A borough swooned.

One man scheduled to speak, however, did not, no matter his name in capital letters on the program. Branca had in November returned from a honeymoon in Sea Island, Georgia, to a city that had not forgotten. He and Ann needed to find in that city a home. And while that very month a suburb called Levittown opened in Long Island—Cape Cods and ranches available for just $60 per month—the newlyweds paid $87.50 for a Fleetwood shoebox, for two and a half rooms at 300 Hayward Avenue.

Branca took two jobs, a pitching instructor at the American Baseball Academy in Manhattan, a haberdasher at swank American Shops in Newark selling with tape measure overcoats and slacks. But eight seasons and 1,250 innings suddenly deferred in memory to one sour pitch, and every kid in every class and every customer at 800 Broad Street had for Branca just one question: "How about that Thomson homer?"

"How do you go on," *Sports Illustrated* asked years later of another goat, "when every time you walk into a liquor store or a gas station, there is someone pointing at you, reminding you of your worst moment?"

Branca, twenty-five, braved the comments. And though suddenly fame was more burden than blessing, he who had mugged with Thomson at the World Series continued not to hide, showing up in November at the Roger Smith Hotel in White Plains to praise (of all people!) fellow Westchester native Yvars. But there too Thomson was on hand. And that the hard-luck pitcher did not in his address mention a certain home run spoke louder than his words, an awkward elision the gracious Thomson saw fit to repeat.

And so it was now that Branca, summoned to Staten Island to toast his nemesis on Bobby Thomson Day, did not even show, big Newcombe filling in last minute, turning in his stead to gooseflesh when a holy half-inning was rebroadcast.

That weeks later the *Sporting News* would name Hodges announcer of the year was a matter of course. For of the three playoff broadcasts preserved on tape—the *sprechstimme* of McClendon, Barber and Hodges—only his testament was worthy of the miracle (posterity lucky the announcer had not yet settled on the phrase "bye-bye baby" to escort from ballparks long flies).

"It's such a spontaneous and resonant response to a moment," says announcer Bob Costas, "that captures not only the excitement of it but the sheer unbelievability of it." And, points out Costas, Hodges went blooey at no expense to detail, in seconds imparting to his audience what at first he had not—that a ball flew to left field. The call was complete.

It was also spreading. WMCA engineer Lou Weber had turned Hodges vinyl and, just days after the broadcast, the radio station had contracted Gotham Recording Corporation on Fifth Avenue to make copies, the record a gift for clients. Liggett & Myers Tobacco Company had records made too, distributing them to members of its Chesterfield 3 to 1 Club. The LP was a hit. And so in time would producer Bud Greenspan introduce Hodges to Columbia Records, package his call with everyone from Tunney to Tchaikovsky, sell more than a million copies. And so in time would Gillette hock with razors a million more, would the call be superimposed onto newsreel, would "talking" baseball cards play it at 33⅓ rpm, Hodges caterwauling always five times in 13 seconds that the Giants won the pennant, the Giants won the pennant, a mantra embedded now in the minds of millions, among them parkfuls of fans to swear that it was Hodges they heard holler of a homer, though in truth they had on October 3, 1951, tuned in beyond the reach of 570 AM.

It was after Bobby Thomson Day that Greenspan phoned Branca. The producer wished to include on an album of great sports moments what the pitcher had whimpered on a clubhouse step minutes after the home run. Only, Branca's tears had not been recorded. Greenspan now proposed that pitcher and producer meet over a microphone. Branca agreed, and days later at Toots Shor's took direction from Greenspan. "He said 'make believe it's after the game,' " says Branca. "I became an actor."

"Let me alone. Let me alone. Let me be. Will ya? You saw what happened." Branca paused, the patter of patrons passing on a recording for the mumblings of despondent Dodgers. His voice was tender, his manner forlorn, his recall of an exchange with AP reporter Grimsley comprehensive. "Things are tough enough. Yah, I knew it was gone all the way. All I kept saying was 'sink, sink, sink.' I knew he hit the ball. He uppercut it, he hit the ball with over-spin. It was like a curveball. It was sinking down. All I remember is seeing Pafko up against the wall and then I was walking to the clubhouse. All I kept saying was 'Why me? Why me? Why did it have to be me?' " Greenspan delighted.

December ended and with it 1951. But on fueled the octane of an October home run. In Santa Monica, Jean Curry turned to clothing the bolts of fabric patterned with a smiling Scot that were sent to neighbor Durocher. ("We had Bobby Thomson pants, shirts, nightgowns," says Michele Durocher.) In New York, with "unanimity such as the United Nations never dreamed of," wrote Red Smith, scribes voted the homer the AP "Thrill of the Year." And everywhere, on stoops and buses and bar stools, fans rehashed the drive every passing day of the off-season.

"They talked over and over again about Bobby Thomson's home run," wrote Pete Hamill of the regulars at Parkview, a bar on Prospect Park in Brooklyn, "and how it had destroyed more than the Dodgers, it had wrecked *them.*" Mel Heimer, a reporter for the Pennsylvania *Bedford Gazette*, found the same in Bermuda. "The town loafers in St. Georges still are having a high old time talking of Bobby Thomson's home run," he wrote. "Aside from that, they do not appear to talk." On the first floor of 1901 Hall at Princeton University, freshmen Ralph Nader and Bill Shafer tabled their rooting for Red Sox and Reds to discuss a Giant home run. "We massaged that event endlessly," remembered Shafer to author Justin Martin. And at 1636 Lexington Avenue in East Harlem, Joe Treceno captured for *Sport* magazine an imagined discussion of the home run, the cartoonist and Dodger fan drawing with crow-quill pen and black ink a man supine on a couch talking to a shrink. Read his caption: "And then, Bobby Thomson came to bat."

Squeezed from the conversation were those poor souls who had somehow missed the shot. Reinhold Niebuhr was one. The Protestant theologian had been seated sky high at the Polo Grounds between third and home when, his team down 4–1, he set to make peace with second place. "God, give us grace to accept with serenity the things that cannot be changed," Niebuhr had written in 1943. That the pennant was surely lost could not be changed. And so it was that when Thomson homered, Niebuhr and daughter Elisabeth had long since subwayed home to Union Theological Seminary. Forty-nine years later it still pained Isaac Jaffe, a character on the ABC television show *Sports Night,* to recall that he had been washing his hands in a Polo Grounds restroom when Thomson went deep. In Rochester, Minnesota, teacher Russell Hanson would have caught Thomson's shot had fifth-grader Rob Adams not stuck a paper clip into an outlet and shorted his radio. And it was back at the ballpark as Ralph Branca hurled that Jackie Gleason ralphed, the actor throwing up on Frank Sinatra, Ol' Blue Eyes looking down, seeing not a home run but regurgitated hot dog and beer. "Here is one of the all-time classic games," lamented Sinatra years later to author James Bacon, "and I don't see Bobby Thomson hit that home run. I just heard the Giant fans going wild around us. Only Gleason, a Brooklyn fan, would get sick at a time like that."

Three months later, he who had sat beside Gleason and Sinatra welcomed to his saloon Thomson and Branca. Toots Shor was hosting the premiere of filmmaker Lew Fonseca's annual ode to the World Series, the players among some four hundred invited guests.

The film began with the end of a playoff, with a home run. It would by year's end show some 70,000 times to some 15 million viewers, 30 million eyes to again see Thomson win and Branca lose. Pitcher gamely proclaimed it a fine film. And Thomson told the *Sporting News,* "I believe Branca has been criticized much too harshly for the pitch I drove into the stands."

Dressen deflected none of that criticism. The manager had instead right off the bat covered his bases, chirping to any and all that it was bullpen coach Sukeforth responsible for the summoning of Branca, adding years later that he himself had tried just before the pitch to whistle for the curve but had not done so in time. The alibis were absurd. Sukeforth had simply done his job. As for his whistle, Dressen had had ample time to discuss with Branca pitch selection during his visit to the mound but had instead said only "get him out," limited instruction which if anything left Branca and Walker unsettled.

Of course, had Brooklyn not hemorrhaged its lead over New York, Branca would not even have faced Thomson. And, of course, more than any other was Dressen responsible that it had, the manager among other September blunders overworking Newcombe as absurdly as he underused Labine. This was apparent to O'Malley, the owner letting slip in the locker room minutes after Thomson's home run, "We fired Shotton for less." But because he had canned manager Shotton in 1950, he spared Dressen in 1951, O'Malley not wishing to develop a reputation. And so instead of losing a job, Dressen claimed an award, voted by the baseball press on January 8, 1952, "Most Courteous and Cooperative."

Every squandered lead demands a scalp, and the very next day Sukeforth's was handed to Brooklyn, the coach offered as scapegoat unto 2,716,347 jilted souls. It mattered not that he had been in the organization twelve years, nor that he had scouted Jackie Robinson, nor that in the final inning of the 1951 season he had done zero wrong, nor that Branca had had in fact far better numbers versus Thomson than had Erskine. Thomson had hit a home run, bitterest pill of the 1,255 games played between rivals over sixty-one years. And so owing to a mayday in October—a call to the bullpen—did Sukey now resign, the coach giving way to Billy Herman. "Sukeforth," reported the AP, "commenting on published speculations, said it was true he had told Dressen that Ralph Branca was 'ready' to step in and pitch to Bobby Thomson."

The same proximity to the home run that seared Sukeforth and singed Dressen made Durocher glow. For it was a comeback *he* had captained that the home run made complete, made relevant, Durocher the very first manager to lead a team that lost 11 straight games to as many consecutive wins that same season. And so a lost World Series did not bite the Lip. The AP voted him "Manager of the Year" and the *Sporting News*

"Man of the Year." Already tops, Durocher now turned, wrote Lewis Burton in *Sport* magazine, "absolutely perfect master-mind, superior to radar and Einstein." No one recalled that the mastermind had three winters back tried to pawn Thomson for, of all people, Branca.

But that lo it was Thomson who had beatified Durocher, the skipper would not soon forget. As Boston's writers presented Thomson a Roman-numeraled clock on the last night of January, indebted manager asked tuxedoed hero if he was as yet signed for the 1952 season. Hero explained that on account of an insult—Stoneham offering just a *two*-thousand-dollar raise—he was not. And so, no matter that baseball's reserve clause still bound the unsigned player to his team (the courts to shoot down lawsuits filed this very spring by two indentured pitchers and a third baseman), an unsigned hero now held the cards. "What do you want?" Durocher asked Thomson. Thomson got his want two days later, a *twelve*-thousand-dollar hike. And that the hero in woolen suit signed for $35,000 was not because he had hit 32 home runs (another off Al Brazle washed out in August) but because he had hit just one, Thomson's Adirondack, cap and spikes already enshrined in the Hall of Fame.

The rosin bag Branca had cast down on October 3, 1951, was also in Cooperstown. And Branca as ur-loser was on display elsewhere too, Stein's photograph of the head-bent pitcher (to win first prize in the New York Press Photographers' Sports Class) hanging now in the Museum of the City of New York, Branca himself trotted out in the grand ballroom of the Waldorf-Astoria four months to the day after the home run.

Thrown by the New York arm of the Baseball Writers' Association of America, the Waldorf banquet, complete with revue, was, for twenty-eight years running, "the premier social occasion of the baseball world," wrote Leonard Koppett. On this Sunday evening the show would include props, costumes, parodies and sketches, for one month the city scribes having rehearsed with mimeographed scripts and jazz pianist Cliff Burwell. Branch Rickey would be lampooned as penny-pincher, Dressen as egomaniac, Durocher as target of the IRS. But it was the playoff that would stir, sportswriter Arthur Mann pouring the blameworthiness of a home run into the mold of the 1940 tune "Because of You"—Dodger bankroller George McLoughlin pointing a finger at O'Malley, O'Malley at Dressen, Dressen at Branca, Branca at Thomson, Thomson in turn giving credit the pitcher.

The writers hoped the players might play themselves, Thomson aboard, he told them, only if Branca was game. And so, reported Dan Daniel in the *Sporting News*, "It was with some hesitation that the baseball writers approached Branca." Happy for any chance to sing, the basso profundo consented. And as Burwell, former pianist for Rudy Vallee, began now to play, pitcher stood backstage alongside the tenor Thomson.

The audience looked to the stage, to large portraits of Mann's quintet resting on easels. Posing as McLaughlin, O'Malley and Dressen, writers stepped out from behind a curtain to address in turn their cardboard nemeses, three verses fetching laughter and knowing nods of allusions not missed.

Thomson's turn came. Clutching a bat, he emerged onstage from behind the curtain, a Giant in uniform, cap and rouge turning to serenade a two-dimensional Dodger.

> *Because of you, there's a song in my heart.*
> *Because of you, my technique is an art.*
> *Because of you, a fastball high*
> *Became a dinky, Chinky fly,*
> *Now Leo and me-o won't part.*

Too shy as a child to join in song even his family at home, it was with restraint that Thomson now sang of his triumph belittled—Chinese flies the unfortunate label in 1951 given short home runs. A quatrain and high E-flat remained, and on he scaled the ten-note melody.

> *My fame is sure, thanks to your Sunday pitch.*
> *Up high or low, I don't know which is which.*
> *But come next spring, keep throwing me that thing*
> *And I will swing, because of you.*

Applause burst from ballroom and balconies, a crowd grateful for its paladin, happy that come spring and evermore would Thomson, as now he did, swing at that same Branca delivery and never ever miss.

Burwell played on, and in backward cap Branca stepped into the spotlight. Gesticulating toward his foil, he began to sing.

> *Because of you, I should never been born.*
> *Because of you, Dodger fans are forlorn.*
> *Because of you, they yell "Drop dead!"*
> *Several million want my head,*
> *To sever forever in scorn.*

The deep and velvet voice and vibrato of Branca caught his audience off guard. Some tittered when the pitcher sang that life was misfortune. But when he spit out "drop dead!"—words ascribed to *them*—recognition and shame clutched at 1,400 people, the public and press as responsible as any for Branca's jeremiad. He continued.

One lonely bird had a word for my ear.
The only girl, what a pearl, of good cheer.
I lost the game but wound up with the dame.
She took my name in spite of you.

Branca finished, a minstrel no longer. And having bared himself publicly for the first time since crying on a clubhouse step, the pitcher found his audience in tears, National League president Warren Giles crying unashamedly. "A great many eyes," noted AP reporter Gayle Talbot, "were no more dry than those of Giles." A room rose in ovation, Talbot recording the "floor-stomping applause."

While the crowd had leapt to cheer Thomson too, it was, reported the *Sporting News*, "even more vociferous during the Branca chanty and he got three encores." For as one in the crowd put it to reporter Red Smith, here before them stood "the good winner and the great loser." Who four months before was hung in effigy was now embraced.

"Baseball is one place where it is acceptable and even admirable to side with failure," wrote Nicholas Dawidoff years later. "Baseball is no different from Shakespeare and Chekhov, in that the most appealing stories are always tragic. Othello and Gene Mauch are far more compelling than Henry V and Derek Jeter. Not only that, they are more virtuous."

And so on this night was Branca admired, a virtuous failure. And if pitcher had before been extricable from batter, he was no longer. For having fully drunk of Thomson and Branca, it was now apparent to all that alone, one was a winner and one a loser but together the men a passion play. And at last assuming the roles long longed for them— months ago the fingers of one coaxed about the neck of the other— Thomson and Branca stood together on this night the salvation of a ballroom in tears.

The singing of a few more ditties drew the Waldorf dinner to a close. But well into morning did one song carry, the sports pages on the laps of commuters proof that pathos paid, that a first true embrace had pocketed batter and pitcher $500 and Branca much, much more. Wrote the *New York Times*, "Branca's pitch, this time, was perfect."

Still, it was as stoic that the losing pitcher won. And so Branca had now to greet with impassivity the reports again spooling out of his ruin. "The world ended for Ralph Branca in the late afternoon of Oct. 3, 1951," reporter Daley began his column two days later. "Bobby Thomson had just hit THE home run and life no longer was worth living for the broken-hearted youngster from Mount Vernon. His sensitive soul was whipped by the fires of regret and despair."

Branca and wife headed to Goldsboro, North Carolina, there en route to spring training to bunk with Clyde King. The pitchers had been good friends since 1944, two of just three college men then Dodgers. And it was as they rehashed an off-season that Norma King now answered the telephone. It was Ed Sullivan and he wished to speak to Branca, TV host inviting pitcher to sing with Thomson on his show that same Arthur Hammerstein song that had made the papers. And so the duo was together in makeup a second straight Sunday night, *Toast of the Town* on air at eight, Audrey Hepburn and Michael Evans and Roberta Peters introduced to some 13.6 million people, CBS cuing newsreel of a home run, then the piano and the portraits and the elegy and the $500 given each man, the second in a lifetime of joint checks. Thomson and Branca—humble hero and unbowed pitcher—were an act.

Strange this was for the two men. For before a home run were they but acquaintances, unattached save 53 at-bats, two all-star teams, a seven-hour drive, a week of barnstorming, an August fundraiser and one known photo, the pair shot at that 1949 ballgame benefit fourteen men apart.

Sullivan had showcased the men before, Branca on air in 1949 to sing "That Lucky Old Sun," Thomson a guest with Maglie, Stanky, Rizzuto and Reynolds after Game Three of the World Series just passed. Applause had been loudest for the playoff hero, a nationally telecast home run turned him sensation. "MOVE OVER BERLE, HOPALONG ET AL," read a cartoon in the *Boston Daily Globe* the day after his homer. "HERE'S TV'S BIGGEST STAR!" The Giant had since only grown, Thomson now A-list, his mere chipping of golf balls fodder for news.

"The Giants were pleasantly discovering," reported Arch Murray in the *Sporting News,* "that they had a national idol who was capturing the imagination of the hinterlands. Everywhere Bobby Thomson goes, he is subject of idolatrous adulation, the result of his homer on that fabled afternoon of last October. Crowds gather at the station just for a glimpse of him." One peek did not often suffice. "A girl's voice squealed," observed Murray as Thomson stepped from a train in Denver. " 'There he is.' Suddenly there was a surge in his direction to get a closer glimpse of this new national hero.

"No longer can Bobby have his quiet breakfast in the hotel restaurants with his long-time roommate, Whitey Lockman. Always there's somebody coming up for an autograph or just to shake the hand that swung the mighty bat. Or there's a page booming through the loudspeaker or photographers or reporters seeking pictures and interviews. The peace of anonymity is gone."

The spotlight, though, was warm, and for now Thomson phototropic, the hero, as Branca once had, modeling for *Sport* magazine, handsome in a rayon robe, a sharkskin suit, a crewneck sweater. It was clear that he who had been raised to be seen and not heard was happy to have hit the shot heard 'round the world. "I have to admit it," Thomson told Murray. "I eat up this adulation. It does something to me. It makes me feel good when I wake up in the morning. It makes me want to step right up and hit that ball so that it will never stop. I never want to hear those boos again."

So that he would not, so that come spring the praise he went without as a child would continue, Thomson had begun to train for the new season with the new year, forgoing come January near every dais. His regimen was simple: rise at seven, hike woods with boxer Major, eat bacon and eggs, row choppy Great Kills Harbor.

Sport magazine now asked Thomson if they might run a story on the slugger. They wanted it first person; reporter Joe King would ghostwrite. Thomson agreed. But disliking the finished product—it was not *him*— Thomson asked if he might write the story himself. This he did. "Ever since I came up to the Giants in the latter part of 1946," began Thomson, "sportswriters and fans have predicted great things for me." The Scot averred (in sixteen penciled pages) that he had not met those expectations but that his home run was at least a start.

It was also, wrote Thomson, a confidence boost. When on February 20 he hopped in trench coat an American Airlines flight for spring training, he just knew that at last his capricious career would see a second straight good season, just knew that he would in 1952 pick up where he left off, a season's final swing lowering to 5.1 his ratio of at-bats to runs batted in, raising to .293 his average, tenth-best in league. Hungry for news on Thomson, the *New York Times* covered his shoving off, charmed that a big leaguer took to Phoenix not only his MacGregor mitt but the mom he called Liz.

That same Wednesday in the *Washington Post,* Branca answered questions about answering questions about a home run. "I got hardened to it after a while," testified the pitcher, spring training just begun. "I don't think it will have any effect on me." That he had sung alongside Thomson was offered up as proof of salubriousness. And, his job secure, Branca given his first raise in three years, there remained for the newly-wed a future in baseball. "Of all the young pitchers now in the game," proclaimed Giant publicist Garry Schumacher in January, "he has the best chance to win 300 games."

Asthma benched Branca for the last two weeks of Dodger camp at Vero Beach. But come Opening Day he was on the roster, a fifth starter hoping four days later on April 19, 1952, to beat New York.

Branca had lost five straight to New York. The team he had cheered as a boy had tormented him all his career, handing him 12 of his 56 defeats, 6 in 1951 alone—one off the record for single-season losses to one team. It was Giants who had hit 39 of the 120 home runs Branca had surrendered in the big leagues, Giants who had hit off him the only 2 to end games. The clock read 1:30 and Branca stared in at Davey Williams.

Many in the Brooklyn crowd now booed their own, remembering to a pitcher his last pitch. And after Williams flied to center and Dark walked, the crowd of 21,301 booed again, borough-beating Thomson stepping in gabardine jersey to bat.

In the six months since the men last faced off, all had changed—batter earning near-double his pay, pitcher wearing a new number, a red 12 stitched across his abdomen. And so now before a first pitch did Giant distaste for Dodger about-face into pity, a gladiator disarmed, alpha pitcher turned almsman. Were Thomson to no more than bunt it would affront, insult added to injury. "The last thing I wanted to do was to hit a home run," allowed Thomson in print thirty-nine years later. He did not, in five goes at Branca, Thomson not so much as batting a ball out of the *infield*.

Though Branca gave up a quartet of home runs, Brooklyn beat New York 11–6. The pitcher was a winner.

Branca now fully understood, though, that baseball would never have its fill of one October loss. "Big Ralph threw the pitch which Bobby Thomson hit for Giants' pennant-winning home run," read the back of 1952 Bowman baseball card 96. "Undisputed champ for Hard Luck honors had to go to Brooklyn's Ralph Branca," read page 12 of the 1952 Dodger yearbook. His *own* baseball card and yearbook page proclaiming his defeat, there was only to succumb, to appropriate the torment, to pick up where a song left off. Branca, twenty-six, would tell his tale.

"I'd be kidding myself if I tried to minimize the crushing effect that moment had on me," pitcher confessed to *Sport* magazine. "No one knows how I felt—the humiliation, the crushing disappointment, the feeling of utter helplessness. I don't think words can describe the experience." Still Branca tried, telling reporter John Ross all, of a sign, a pitch, amnesia, money, telegrams, the number 13 and marriage, of butterflies, bullpens and goats. "I've been told," added Branca, "that no matter what I do from now on in the major leagues, only that pitch to Thomson will be remembered."

Branca allowed himself exculpatory mention of both the injuries that had pocked his career and the 2.38 fewer runs plated for him per nine 1951 innings than for other Dodger starters. But no matter his yen for absolution, the desire to explain away a home run, pitcher had come to see in just one winter that unalterably was Thomson's shot, as John Updike wrote of another, "in the books while it was still in the sky."

Branca pitched on, through June his season good enough: ten appearances, six starts, four wins, two losses, an ERA of 4.02. But hours after tossing 81 pitches in Brooklyn on the first of July, his right shoulder and lower back stiffened and Branca remembered anew a tumble in spring training, a metal folding chair giving way, pitcher landing coccyx on Coke bottle, a crescent cut a centimeter deep. It was not an extravagant spill—Dodger wives Jo Lembo and Rosemarie Romano would in time forget having witnessed it. Nor did it seem to damage, Branca declared fit in morning by team trainer Wendler. But even as the right-hander continued to throw pain-free, his speed dropped. Branca turned to Ralph Capalbo, the chiropractor finding his pelvis inclined to the left, realigning it with a pop. After facing Philly, though, Branca turned rigid. On the advice of team orthopedist Eugene Zorn, the pitcher hobbled in late July onto the thirty-day disabled list having thrown just 52 innings.

"Whatever the trouble," wrote the *Sporting News* on July 30, "whether in his back, shoulder or arm, it is definite that he is unable to pitch." Others felt the trouble in his head, Branca suffering what the *Sporting News* would in December call "mental miseries." And so was an injury to Branca no longer assumed just an injury, all a life refracted through one playoff loss.

With one out in the ninth, Thomson stepped in against Willard Schmidt, New York down three with three men on. It was June 17 and, hitless in 17 at-bats, his average stood at .265. Here was a first pitch from the Cardinal rookie and Thomson swung, a ball sent northeast in a Harlem sky, a game-ending home run to left, runs 46, 47, 48 and 49 batted in. Thomson had done it *again,* and thousands marveled, all a life refracted through one playoff win. "This is an act which cannot be improved," wrote Joe King in the *Sporting News.* "DeMille can have Samson and Delilah; Giant fans will take Thomson in the Ninth."

And so Thomson was hero once more, his grand slam turning him 9 Down in the Wednesday *New York Times* crossword puzzle, pitchman too of Rheingold Beer. ("I'm glad I did it again this season," aw-shucked a new ad.) Thomson was now in fact Madison Avenue darling, endorser of Red Man Chewing Tobacco, Armstrong Tires, Grub Stopper Lawn Care (for the "shot heard 'round your lawn"), Bromo-Seltzer, Coca-Cola, Adirondack Bats and *Sport* magazine, his cardboard mug shilling the weekly atop cash registers and in storefronts. Thomson was even the star of a comic book, a square-jawed mastodon in Fawcett Publications' *Thrilling True Story of the Baseball GIANTS.* "KER-RACK!" read one rectangular frame, green block letters above bat on ball. "It was a homer, a story-book homer!"

This same summer in an Oakland bar, Schenz sat down with team-mate John Jorgensen. The Oaks had been Giants, the men together comprising a full 1951 New York season, Jorgensen playing his final game the very June day Schenz arrived. It was obvious Schenz had seen a season's better half. But only now over alcohol did the infielder called Spider learn of its secret, of signs sussed from center field. "He said he had that telescope, that he could see the spots on the moon," remembered Jorgensen years later. The Wollensak—above minor league peeping—lay now unused in a leather sleeve in a drawer in a chifforobe in a bedroom in Deer Park, Ohio.

Where Schenz's telescope had last espied, the mesh of a fourth clubhouse window remained clipped and the wires of the late Chadwick were still live. But the Giants were not this season stealing signs. Says Corwin, "the nucleus of the club then just didn't want them." And so Franks returned to the dugout and New York sought to unload the suddenly dispensable Yvars, a deal for cash and Chicago rookie George Wilson falling through on May 6.

It was a kid pitcher from the Texas League named Joe Landrum Jr. who replaced Branca on the roster. And it was Erskine who now replaced the inactive pitcher as club rep. But as his shoulder and back mended, so also continued to his psyche, the sidelined loser with time to court perspective, to audition what would be his daily retorts and propoundments. Many were his findings. Humor could only ingratiate. The fist of newborn daughter Patricia Ann could kayo all disappointments. And introduced by Aunt Rose to Julius Caesar, it was Shakespeare Branca could now loose on the critic. "The evil that men do lives after them," rejoined the pitcher over and again. "The good is oft interrèd with their bones. So let it be with Caesar. So let it be with Branca."

Branca stepped from the disabled list on August 25 knowing he might soon have at his ghost. For Brooklyn was a shoo-in for the pennant and Branca, off the disabled list, had only to be activated by the end of August to be eligible for World Series play. Handed the ball by Dressen eight days later, Branca yielded one run in three innings against Philly. The fans cheered.

The fans booed. It was August 15 and in the eight at-bats of a doubleheader, Thomson had but a single, his average dipping to .263. No matter that he had also 17 home runs and 78 runs batted in. No matter that 1,172,244 fans had voted Thomson to start the All-Star game at third. His October blast echoed—a record replayed in the Giant midtown office, a photo rerun on page 36 of the Giant yearbook—and expectations were sky-high. "Although Bobby is loathe to admit it," *Sport* magazine would later note, "his miracle of 1951 is still haunting him. . . . They will settle for a lesser hit, but they want and half-expect him to come through every time up." Of this Thomson was forgiving. "I can't blame the fans for expecting more from me after I hit the homer," he told *Sport*. Thomson finished 1952 with stellar numbers: a .270 average, 24 home runs, 108 runs batted in and 14 triples, best in league.

Branca pitched four more times in September, the reliever sharp, allowing one run in six innings, finishing 1952 with a 3.84 ERA (his ERA just 2.79 since the first of May).

Dressen, though, did not trust Branca. Worse, pitcher reminded manager of his own epic failing. And so though Branca was now healthy and effective, Dressen had not added him to the roster until the first of September—until hours *after* the deadline for World Series eligibility.

National League president Warren Giles intervened. He who had wept in February watching Branca sing now ruled that because the pitcher had been on the Brooklyn roster all season, he was eligible to play in the World Series. Everyone, it seemed—save Dressen—was pulling hard for hard-luck Branca. The pitcher would have his shot at redemption.

Branca was as yet unused when on the first anniversary of what comedian Phil Foster would call D-Day—"Dat Day"—Brooklyn went up two games to one on New York. And when four days later on October 7 the Series went to a seventh and final game, Dressen still had not pitched the pitcher.

Dressen had in fact used just six pitchers in the six games, among them rookies Ken Lehman, Johnny Rutherford and Joe Black. And having started Black just twice all season, the manager now started the reliever a third time in seven days. "Charlie wanted Black over Ralph—that was it," says general manager Bavasi. He adds, "Rutherford and Lehman were good pitchers but not as good as Ralph."

It was during the sixth inning of this seventh game that Black allowed a third run, Branca watching Dressen summon Preacher Roe a second straight day. Roe yielded a run in the seventh. His team down 4–2, Branca then saw Dressen call for Erskine in the eighth, number 17 having thrown 11 innings two days prior. Passed over yet again, Branca now left a season on his own terms, home plate ump Larry Goetz thumbing the pitcher for heckling with one out in the bottom of the eighth, Branca just the third ballplayer ever ejected from a World Series in which he did not play. Brooklyn lost the game.

All through the Series, rumors had buzzed of Thomson being traded for either pitcher Gerry Staley or pitcher Bob Rush. It was, after all, for lack of arms that New York had finished 4.5 games back of Brooklyn. Still, Durocher held on to his star Scot, Thomson at last the architect of consecutive good seasons, powerful at bat and superlative in center, where in 63 games he had this season committed just one error.

Thomson rumors filled the gossip columns too. It was Durocher who in spring had floated word of the bachelor hip-deep in Barbara Benson, a singer in the Sammy Kaye orchestra. In truth, Thomson had neither met Benson nor wished to, the ballplayer long in love with Elaine Coley.

Winkie was beautiful and proper and cosmopolitan, partial to an occasional Salem cigarette. The social worker was in love with Thomson too, saw in the quiet ballplayer more than introversion. "His shyness," says daughter Nancy, "came across as sophistication." Both had strict fathers, were insecure over educations that had stopped with high school, and loved outdoor sports, together golfing in Connecticut and swimming in Jersey. When the Giants were home, the couple bunked weekends in Staten Island—in separate rooms—Winkie watching her beau Saturdays and Sundays at the Polo Grounds.

It was a speeding ticket handed Thomson at 2:00 a.m. in Jersey that nudged him toward matrimony. "I decided it'd be easier to get married than making this trip," he says. And so in November Thomson proposed, asking all at once permission of parents and marriage of daughter. The three Coleys said yes, and on November 14, one day after word of their engagement made the papers, the affianced couple and a two-karat diamond boarded the ocean liner *Uruguay* bound for Caracas.

Branca cashed his $4,200 World Series check, then sent baseball $200 right back, punishment for heckling umpire Goetz. But just as the pitcher would deny that he had in April 1951 taunted the Giants with song, he disavowed now that it was he who rode Goetz, fingering instead teammate Rocky Nelson. The sidestep snapped back at Branca. "What escapes me is where Branca, of all people, had the nerve to bellow to Goetz or at anyone else," wrote Dick Young (allowing that Branca was not the lone heckler). "In his position as purely excess baggage, Branca should have sat silently on the bench, and, between innings, uttered an inward prayer of thanks that he was considered part of this Series, a very inactive part." The lesson was clear, flip side to a pardon given Branca by a public let feed on his suffering: the pitcher had best not ever pin his greatest defeat on anyone but himself.

It was this winter that Branca, again selling suits in Newark, took a first true look at a second career. No job entirely appealed. Sales were unfulfilling, phys-ed pay low, an engineering degree years away, the professional singer seldom home. And so he who had still to answer daily for a home run enrolled now at the Flennenheirmer School of Insurance in Manhattan, a calling perhaps born of torment. Forevermore would Branca cover his bases. Durocher tried now, at the December meetings in Phoenix, to land the insurance agent. He had always liked Branca and, in desperate need of pitching, offered Brooklyn $25,000 for his right arm. Brooklyn declined. Thomson and Branca would not be teammates. And so, come Christmas, it was only Thomson whom Durocher mailed the compote his wife, Laraine, had jarred.

Two days later Thomson pinned freesia to lapel, pearl to black tie. His wedding, set for January, had been pushed up owing to the tax concerns of college friend Rosen, and the mother of the bride had seen to last-minute holiday trimmings—poinsettias, gladiolas and carnations dressing the white wood of New Dorp Moravian Church, evergreen sprays and pine cones the altar, on either side seven red candles and an untrimmed pine.

The Saturday ceremony began twenty minutes late, groom affirming to Reverend Allen Schattschneider at 1:50 p.m. that he wished to marry bride. Schattschneider turned to Elaine Coley. Phosphorescent in satin and seed pearls, brown eyes bright behind an illusion veil, she spoke. "The bride's response," noted the *Staten Island Advance,* "was almost a whisper." Yes. Mendelssohn then motorcade escorted husband and wife to the Richmond County Country Club where, after honeymooning in Florida, the couple rented a four-room cottage some 100 yards from a first tee. Remembers Thomson, "You'd hear the golf clubs clanking."

Thomson was at twenty-nine a man in full, 190 pounds after feasting a month in Bel Air Beach. Again would he earn $35,000 for a year of ball. He remained a pitchman and headliner. Honors and gifts still abounded—a televised dance with Kathryn Murray, Libbey glasses from Scottish war veterans. And now by his side was wedding-ringed Winkie.

That Branca, meantime, was on the downswing was undeniable, his Dodger pay cut this winter to $15,000. Worse, his infamy was unstinting, a 1951 fastball horning in on the opening of Ralph Branca & Company. ("From his local office," wrote the *Mount Vernon Daily Argus,* "Branca will be able to insure you against anything—except a home run by Bobby Thomson.") Still Branca set about thawing his right arm for a tenth season, throwing occasionally to the nearest big league catcher. Five towns north, Yvars had whiled away the winter playing pinochle at the Italian American Club on lower Main Street in White Plains. "I was king shit of that place," he says. As a Giant, however, he was expendable, sold to St. Louis in June months after reporting to the *Sporting News* that Branca was "throwing as hard as ever."

Branca, though, was soon stiff again. And after Brooklyn beat Pittsburgh 8–5 on Opening Day 1953, the pitcher headed to 71 Broadway to see Kenneth Riland, an osteopath. "He told me I was swayback," remembers Branca. "My left side was up an inch and a half. He popped me back in." Relief was temporary. When come mid-May Branca had yet to pitch—beset also by asthma, toe fungus, a liner in practice off his right arm—suspicions arose as to whether he had instead run aground on the shoals of a playoff loss.

"Ailments, some real and others believed to be imaginary, have made him a very infrequent starter," wrote Oscar Fraley in the *New York Herald Tribune.* Particularly suspect was the harm to his back. Wrote Fraley: "The validity of the injury undoubtedly is questioned by manager Chuck Dressen. The little leader of the Dodgers has taken no pains to conceal his disdain at Branca's continued reluctance to fire the ball at the plate. His unspoken indictment is that Branca, in his mind, always will be throwing that fatal home run ball every time he steps to the mound, thus accounting for an unconscious unwillingness to pitch."

Clear, however, was that Branca was increasingly at ease with his lot. Eighteen months healed, it was now he again wore number 13, now he returned the number to his license plate, now he made public a priest in a parking lot—Branca writing in the *Daily Argus* of Father Rowley, of words that had made sense of a home run and still did.

Thomson was tough, overcoming in March the fracture by fastball of the fifth metacarpal bone in his right hand. Thomson was good, turning an Opening Day pitch from Robin Roberts into the first big league home run of 1953. Thomson was textbook, offering on a red wax Columbia record tips on batting stance, weight shift and conditioning. Thomson was consistent, en route to a third-straight 100-RBI season. Yet somehow he remained for many a disappointment, done in by expectation born both of a home run and a likeness to DiMaggio. "Baseball people sigh when they think of the Thomson that might have been," wrote Jack Orr in June in *Sport* magazine. Agreed a general manager, "Temperamentally, I think he's not equipped to be a great one."

The trade deadline near, rumors again had Thomson swapped for pitching, for Herm Wehmeier or Warren Hacker. Only pitching, it seemed, could lift New York from fifth place.

In first place was Brooklyn. But no thanks to Branca. Dressen had used the rehabilitated reliever in just three lopsided losses, number 13 yielding two runs in five innings. Branca griped publicly, and it was little surprise that come mid-June he was on the trading block. Like Thomson, however, Branca stayed put. "It could be thought," wrote John Lardner, "that he kept his job as a semi-useless pitcher because of his connections." Eighteen days after wife Ann bore two Dodger owners a third granddaughter, Branca set to mop up another blowout, Brooklyn trailing New York 11–2 on July 5.

Branca left the Polo Grounds pen, summoned now to where he had not pitched since October 3, 1951. St. Christopher draped from his neck, he reached the rubber where his life had turned. Branca walked Mueller to lead off the home fifth, served up singles to Westrum and Maglie, walks to Dark and Lockman, a home run to Hank Thompson. Six runs were in, no one out—the worst outing of a career and Dressen summoning no help. Ill at ease, Thomson waited on deck. He was this season superb, batting .321 with 52 runs batted in and 12 home runs, the most recent struck in the third inning. Irvin popped to second and Thomson approached. The Scot had in 54 career at-bats versus Branca been solid, nine runs batted in, five walks, eight singles, one double, one triple, four home runs. But since that last here in Harlem, Thomson had yet in five trips versus Branca to drive a ball to the outfield. He did now, down two strikes flying to Furillo.

Brooklyn trailed 20–6 when in the eighth inning ump Frank Secory ejected Jackie Robinson for heckling. Robinson left bench for clubhouse. Branca did too. The pitcher simply felt now like leaving—leaving, with a friend, this ballfield forever. This he did, off on a long walk to center field, to a wooden staircase, number 13 slipping a last time behind the green door. Never again would Branca pitch at the Polo Grounds. Never again would he face Thomson.

Two days later, Brooklyn put Branca on waivers. And when no NL team claimed him, they let him go, content for $10,000 to see a goat switch leagues. This Branca did, on July 10 picked up by Detroit. Though he had been battered by New York and had in 11 1953 innings surrendered 12 runs, Branca now had a new home.

Hours after turning Tiger, Branca arrived at Ebbets Field. The ten-year vet wore civvies, come with his wife this Friday night to the runway behind home plate to say good-bye. Players and wives gathered. Ann cried, a housewife grown up in Box 117. But while as child of Mulvey she owned Dodger stock, as wife of Branca she suffered Dodger defeat. And so, though Brooklyn was family, though the team was in first and Detroit in last, though Branca had for a decade worn royal blue, that he would not tonight in a 6–1 Brooklyn loss he counted a blessing.

So too did baseball. Convinced that a home run had felled one of their own, teammate and rival saw in the move rebirth. "This is the greatest thing that could happen to Ralph," Dodger pitcher Roe told the *United Press*. "The memory of that Thomson home run stuck with him more than anybody realized." Added the *Sporting News*, "the Giant players think he has a chance to make a real comeback with Detroit. They are all rooting for him, too."

Thus did Giant come to cheer on Dodger, curious upshot of the Shot Heard Round the World. But if an upending of the status quo, it was too an affirmation of human nature, "of the curious inclination of the baseball public, and maybe of publics in general," noted *Newsweek* magazine, "to cherish people whose lives have been blighted."

Settled in Detroit, Branca quickly befriended Ted Gray. "Our lockers were together," remembers Branca. "There was an immediate rapport. Class act. Good priorities. A pitcher. He was number thirty-four. I was number thirty-five." Says Gray of Branca, "He was a helluva nice guy. A lot of humility."

It was hard for Branca not to be humble. On July 12, 1953, the first batter he faced in Briggs Stadium homered to left, three Browns later homering to right. And, no matter the inclination to cherish the blighted, boos rained down. Says Gray, "The whole world got on him."

The world had once gotten on Gray too, the Tiger surrendering in the fourteenth inning of the 1950 All Star game a home run to Red Schoendienst. NL 4, AL 3. Thus was an afternoon for Gray like what were years for Branca.

Branca settled, no more runs yielded through five. And in little more time did the pitcher, on the field and off, take to Detroit. His next start, he allowed just two earned runs—his first nine-inning, complete-game win in fifteen months. His back felt better, trainer Jack Homel massaging it daily. And come his first road trip in late July, he roomed with Gray, the fastballers fast friends happy to speak of more than a game, both once player reps, both husbands, both dads. Oh, to have left Brooklyn! Testified Branca on August 9, "It was almost like being dead and coming alive."

The previous afternoon, Dodger Dressen had declared, "The Giants is dead." And indeed at 53–51 they was, the club to finish 35 games back of Brooklyn. Sorry Detroit, meantime, would finish 40.5 games behind the Yankees. But Branca was happy. For sometimes it is less important to win than contribute, and this the pitcher did, throwing in five September days two masterpieces, three runs yielded in 20 innings. Though Branca would lose his last two starts to finish 4–7, his 4.15 ERA was lowest on all the staff, half also what it had been this season in Brooklyn, cynics left to snicker of a lower back magically healed.

Branca returned to his wife and daughters in Fleetwood. And on October 9, four days after his former teammates lost another World Series to the Yanks (and after they voted the departed pitcher a quarter-share), Branca arrived in Baltimore to barnstorm with a team put together by Jackie Robinson. Distractions soon beset both men—Branca benched in Birmingham by a city ordinance against mixed-race baseball, Robinson subject to irreverent rumors trading him for of all people Bobby Thomson.

Thomson was at last expendable, a prize to be bartered for pitching. For though he had in 1953 finished in the league's top 10 in at-bats, hits, total bases and runs batted in, Willie Mays was due back from Korea.

Thomson, though, had heard the rumors before and was confident of staying put. He had already put down the $200 deposit on a Phoenix cottage for Giant spring training. And it was in Staten Island Hospital that daughter Nancy, seven pounds, ten ounces, was this October born.

On the first of February, Thomson returned home, sweated from a hike with Major, to a phone message from Chub Feeney. And on the second of February, word of their conversation hit page one of the *New York Times*. Thomson was off to Milwaukee, traded with reserve catcher Sam Calderone for $50,000 and four players, among them southpaw Johnny Antonelli. Owner Stoneham, who minutes after a miracle had told Thomson "I'll never forget you," had peddled the Giant in the same Waldorf ballroom where two years before Thomson had sung a song.

That a hero had proved dispensable more than shocked; it disillusioned. Suddenly, it seemed foolish to savor a home run, naïve to remember that in 1942 Thomson had so wanted to be a Giant that he had given Brooklyn no chance to sign him.

Still, the newest Brave could only buck up, smile for the AP photographer come to shoot, thank Milwaukee GM John Quinn for his $35,000 offer, answer the man who had wired him good wishes. "Best of luck to you and Laraine, and the Giants," Thomson wrote Durocher. "And take care of my boy, Lockman." Within weeks Thomson was gone, the Staten Island Scot moved west.

Shock had dissipated by the first cuts of spring training. And Thomson was not unhappy. Both his contract and the Braves were good, and he would bat cleanup, snug between sluggers Eddie Mathews and Pafko (he who had chased to a green wall his playoff home run). Thomson opened Grapefruit League play with a single, a triple and a home run. All a team excited.

One week later, in St. Petersburg on March 13, 1954, Thomson stood on first and Mathews on second, Milwaukee down 3–1 with none out in the eighth. Pafko grounded to Yankee pitcher Bob Wiesler, who threw to shortstop Woodie Held. Thomson slid, the better to break up the double play. But long his bugaboo, the slide went awry, the spikes of his right shoe catching in a clod of dirt short of second. Pain shot up his leg. "It was a fool thing to do," Thomson later told the press of his sliding, "as I had no chance of beating the throw."

Thomson had suffered the first severe injury of his career, a triple fracture of his right ankle. And as he worked with therapist Pearl Brockman from crutches to cane to ace bandage, a boy of twenty up from the South Atlantic League got his chance. Thomson, who had given way to Willie Mays, now ceded his job to Henry Aaron.

Branca and Gray limbered their arms. The pitchers had long relied on the strikeout, each among the current top 10 in career whiffs per nine innings, Branca at 5.08, Gray at 5.63. It felt good to be back in Florida, back to the provisions of baseball. Life outside the game was less fun. Gray had sold Chryslers this off-season to support a wife and three kids.

Gray had also this winter touched base with an old friend named Earl Rapp. The Michigan natives had met in Buffalo as AAA Bisons in 1946. Right-fielder Rapp had since played three big league seasons with five teams, among them New York, where in July 1951 his was the lefty bat Durocher acquired in search of the oomph a slumping Thomson had once provided.

Rapp had that summer been a Giant for two months. And this winter, as Schenz had Jorgensen, he had told Gray of a telescope and signals, a secret slowly revealing like a ballfield beneath a receding tarp. "We were having a couple of beers," remembers Gray. "He told me they were stealing signs right through the home run pitch."

That Gray knew well the man who threw that pitch, that Gray roomed with Ralph Branca, Rapp was unaware.

PART THREE

Such Were the Joys

TWENTY

Then he filled up the hole, and went away, at peace with himself until a reed sprouted from the bank and whispered the secret to all who passed.

—MIDAS, *The Greek Myths* (translated by Robert Graves)

THREE SPRINGS AFTER THE three-second flight of a home run, it could be stated indubitably that Branca had gotten on with life. The pitcher had married, fathered kids, found a second ball club, a second profession. And though famous as loser, he had come to coexist both with Thomson and his lot. "I'll always be one of the all-time goats of baseball," Branca remarked the summer previous. "It's rough. But gee, I guess that's baseball."

Here then was a happy enough ending. Here was acceptance, rapprochement, perspective. Branca had put a fastball to bed.

The pitcher began 1954 in the bullpen, eight scoreless innings thrown in twenty days. He was sharp. But awarded a start, then two more, Branca faltered, eight runs yielded in eight innings. Another fine outing in relief landed Branca two more starts. But again he sputtered, seven runs let score in 10.2 innings. Banished again to the pen, even relief was now a struggle, ten men scoring in 7.1 innings, Branca tagged with three straight losses. That a career was winding down was by June obvious. Branca was twenty-eight years old.

Ted Gray, twenty-nine, was also on the decline, had one more year in him. And in a hotel room on the road, the southpaw now remembered a secret. Perhaps, he wagered, talk of a telescope might soothe his roommate, a vaccine against future pain. "I thought it was something he should know," says Gray. "He was downhearted." Gray turned to Branca.

"We got to bed," remembers Branca. "He just came out, 'I'm not supposed to tell you this but—' "

Branca lay quiet as Gray spoke of signs, buzzer wire, a spyglass and bullpen, struck dumb as Gray recounted what Rapp had avowed: on October 3, 1951, the Giants copped the finger signals to both Branca fastballs. "It was a shock," says Branca. "I had to just ponder it." Remembers Gray: "I think he just kind of shook his head in sorrow."

That the 1951 Giants had stolen signs en route to a pennant, players would from time to time bring up to Thomson. "Guys gave you the needle," he says. This was hard. For a father's admonition to "do what's right" lingered in Thomson. And not only had the 1951 shot turned him hero, but his having benefited from a buzzer was so demonstrable. (Thomson led all baseball in batting the second half of 1951, his .358 mark after July 14 127 points higher than before.) And so the taunts found their mark. "I know this," says Thomson. "Whenever it came up, I wanted to get away from it."

Strangely, it was a fellow Brave most eager to zing Thomson. His name was Danny O'Connell. "He was a chirpy Irishman," remembers the Scot, "whose best talent was singing in the shower. Our wives became very good friends." The wives did not know, however, that O'Connell, an infielder of twenty-seven shipped in December to Wisconsin, made sport of a seamy rumor. "He'd bring it up," says Thomson. "For some reason he was aware of it. I didn't enjoy hearing it."

It was O'Connell who made way for Thomson on July 12, 1954, Thomson pinch-hitting for the infielder in the fifth inning of a Toledo exhibition game, the hero at last returned to action. His ankle had shed screws and stitches and cast, and Thomson wore on his right foot a high-top shoe, the better to bear the weight of expectation. For Milwaukee, 41–41, trailed New York by 15 games. And leading the Giants was, of all people, Antonelli—he who was traded for Thomson now best in league, 13–3 with a 2.33 ERA. It was with relief that on this Monday Thomson drove more than 400 feet to center field the very first pitch thrown him. Home run.

Two days later, in his Brave debut, Thomson walked to great applause. He would pinch-hit until fully healed, and it was after two pinch-singles in three at-bats that on July 23 he faced his former team, Thomson lifting his Adirondack with two out in the ninth of a 2–2 game, man on second. Durocher left Hoyt Wilhelm on the hill and Thomson ripped a fastball to left. Jim Pendleton scored, Milwaukee won and the largest-ever crowd at County Stadium erupted. Thomson had done it again, his single, wrote the *Sporting News*, "the most dramatic hit in the modern major league history of this community." A bat in his hands, Thomson—somehow—had always a knack for theater.

Branca had long viewed his lot as more unfair than unfortunate. He had as Tiger told reporter Will Grimsley that his doomed fastball to Thomson "was a *perfect* pitch." He had recently shared again with his hometown paper the favorite family saw: "wrongs have a way of righting themselves over the years." And so the revelation of a roommate bore out for Branca an injustice he had persisted in seeing all along. Lying now in a hotel bedroom, two thoughts seized the pitcher: the miracle Giants had done something despicable, and an unendurable Dodger loss was in no way his fault.

Branca returned to the ranch house he and Ann rented on Stawell Street from Gordie and Colleen Howe, a secret already confided in his wife and brother John. The Tiger wanted confirmation, and so phoned now the one 1951 Giant he called friend. "He said," remembers Yvars, " 'Sal, did this really happen?' He said, 'You never told me?' "

Indeed Yvars had not, an omerta unbroken even as pitcher had toasted catcher on a Westchester dais in the fall of 1951, even as catcher had warmed up pitcher in the spring of 1953. But given now again the opportunity to come clean, "I did," says Yvars, "from A to Z."

It did not matter that Yvars repeated now the canard of the Giant fan with the naval telescope. Nor did it matter that Yvars knew not of Schenz, of Chadwick, of when exactly a fenestrated clubhouse had first been put to use. For the catcher did know of when it was *last* put to use and told Branca not only of Franks but of his own post in right field. "I said," remembers Yvars, " 'Ralph, I was the messenger.' "

That a goat had tapped the horse's mouth was an irony that left Yvars unbothered. "I didn't feel guilty about anything," says Yvars. "I was just doing my job." And so, looking back, a bullpen catcher saw in his sitting still not the assassination of competition but an order followed. Perspective lost to the cult of expertise, Branca left the news alone. Says Yvars, "He didn't say too much about it."

Nor would he. Branca had come to see that his slings left only himself muddied. He saw too what had prompted them. "It was my competitiveness," the pitcher later reflected. "I was hurting. I could see my career going down the tube." And so even as a deus ex machina had swooped down to absolve Branca of his greatest defeat, the pitcher was now at last mum, resolved to await a whistleblower. "I made a decision not to speak about it," says Branca. "I think I matured. I didn't want to be a crybaby. Anything I would say about that situation they would label me a sore loser."

A day before the July break, the Tiger brass mulled its sinking season. Detroit was in fourth place, 34–44. Branca had just three of those wins and worse, a 5.80 ERA, highest on all his team. It was the home run that did him in, 10 yielded in 45.1 innings. And after Detroit beat Baltimore 2–1 on July 11, 1954, general manager Muddy Ruel told Branca that he wished for him to bone up in Buffalo. The ten-year vet, though, had veto power and refused his dispatch to the International League. And so on this Sunday, a year and a day after picking Branca up, Detroit let him go.

Back home, Branca did not wait to unpack to begin throwing at Mount Vernon Memorial Field to Frank Merola and John Brescia, childhood chums who had played minor league ball. "I threw every day for a week," says Branca. "My arm got strong." Ready for a tryout, Branca eyed the schedules of the three local teams. The Dodgers and Giants were on road trips through July 25, the Yankees home for 13 games. And so, says Branca, "I called up Casey Stengel and asked if I can come work out."

Manager Stengel had led New York to an unprecedented five consecutive rings. A sixth was in reach: on July 20 the Yankees were 62–29, tied with Cleveland for first. Stengel invited Branca to Yankee Stadium, and a crouched Mickey Mantle warmed the righthander. Branca threw batting practice. Pitching coach Jim Turner approved and on July 22, needy after a 15–3 loss, Stengel had Ralph Houk converted from catcher to coach to make room on the roster. Branca was a Yankee, number 24.

Five days later, Branca threw a scoreless frame in Chicago. The pitcher was again a major leaguer, again based in New York, soon also again a starter, allowing on August 1 just one run in four innings. Best of all, Branca once again had a shot at the postseason.

Bobby Thomson pulled aside his catcher. It was August 6, and for the first time since returning from injury, the Brave was a visitor at the Polo Grounds. "Even then, I didn't talk about stealing signs," says Thomson. "But I did tell Del Crandall, 'Hey, be careful.' " Crandall understood. New York was in first place, 69–38. And sure enough, for the first time since 1951, the home team had this season pressed the long-dormant push-button of Chadwick, had spied signals from its clubhouse. "As the year progressed and we felt we had a decent ball club," says pitcher Corwin, "it was there for those who wanted them." (Since moving alone into first place on June 15, New York was 25–7 at home.) Cautioned by Thomson, catcher Crandall safeguarded his signs, New York scoring just nine runs in three games. Milwaukee swept the series, 7.5 games back.

Milwaukee was still 7.5 back of New York when, two weeks later, Thomson was at last able to start, inserted in left field. Having rapped five hits in 15 pinch at-bats, the Scot on this Tuesday collected two more. But no sooner was Thomson back than Aaron departed, on September 5 the rookie also breaking an ankle mid-slide. Milwaukee was done.

The Yankees remained alive, heading into play this Sunday 3.5 back of Cleveland. Branca had been fantastic, two runs yielded in 12 innings. But given the start today in Washington, he faltered. And before three Senators were out, Stengel lifted Branca—for the rest of the season. New York lost and, despite 103 wins, finished second to Cleveland, failing to reach the World Series just this once in ten years, another go at redemption snuffed for the luckless Branca.

Thomson had bad luck this season too. For exacerbating his weakened ankle and .232 average was the league-best 2.30 ERA of the pitcher traded for him. When on October 2 Antonelli popped up Indian Dale Mitchell, the New York Giants were champs. And Thomson was not.

Weeks later the Yankees let Branca go, their first cut. Released three times in fifteen months, the pitcher found himself at twenty-eight unemployed—his insurance company folding this same month, several clients not repaying the premiums advanced them by partner Jim DiMarzo. Aggravating matters was a new mortgage, the Brancas moving now into three bedrooms at 17 Wilshire Drive in White Plains. And so on December 6, back from a baseball tour combating juvenile delinquency, Branca loitered in the lobby of the Hotel Commodore, there at the winter meetings to be seen by all.

Durocher and the Giants bit. And no matter bygones or signals or a skimpy contract—New York offering Branca roughly half the $15,000 he earned in 1954—the pitcher signed with his undoing. Branca would start 1955 in the minor leagues, intent on leaving Minneapolis before long.

Thomson did not wish to leave the Midwest. Milwaukeeans loved their Braves, gave them free gasoline and ice cream and laundering of clothes. And, starstruck, they took to Thomson in spite of an unlucky season. For he moved with his wife and daughter to the banks of Lake Michigan, traded in his kelly-green Cadillac for a Ford, was sick over whether to destroy his dying boxer, took a job at the local publicity house on North Water Street, turned spokesman for Schlitz beer, and spoke at the local Optimist Club. Wrote the *Sporting News*, Thomson "is proving to be about the best 'mouthpiece' in the Milwaukee organization."

Branca spoke too, addressing in December a swarm of Connecticut Little Leaguers, months later a guest on KEYD TV in Minneapolis. It was, as always, the home run that intrigued and from these pulpits the pitcher vouched for his fastball. But the television spot disheartened him. For welcomed alongside Branca was pitcher Charley Root, he who in 1932 had served Babe Ruth his "called shot." Root now testified (as he always did) that no, Ruth had not pointed yonder before his swing. Left to listen to a proud pitcher, Branca in turn made no mention of signals.

But discretion had its price. Leashed, a secret raced round and round in Branca, overtook the baby steps turned strides that had in three years brought peace. "It changed my personality," observes Branca. "I was quick to criticize. I was always looking for reasons to be skeptical. I think I became an angry man after that." More and more did Branca come to see the home run as misbegotten, to see Thomson as a fraud. "Guys who get credit for being something they're not," says Branca, "those things annoy me."

If pitcher now perseverated about signs, batter all but let them slip from memory. "I put it out of my mind because it wasn't a plus," says Thomson. "I've thought about this later and I feel bad about it. I guess it didn't sound good. Why would I want to be connected to that?" So as not to be, Thomson would never tell wife Winkie or brother Jim of a spy-glass. And what he would tell *himself* of a stolen sign, Thomson had not yet made clear.

This winter, however, there was no need for introspection. Thomson had another plum contract and a beautiful home on a great lake. And motivated by a raft of stories that had Milwaukee rooked in its trade for him, he biked and rowed and played handball with a monomania that alchemized all he ate this off-season to 12 firm pounds, Thomson a taut 192 come 1955. Still, he entered a tenth season tender—Brave doctor Albert Schmidt left to treat a sore elbow, an aching shoulder, and a reha-bilitated ankle still prone to swell.

Branca, meantime, was healthy. From the start of spring training he was also lights out, AAA batsmen scoreless his first 15 innings. And so Branca left Florida for Minnesota expecting to soon join a third big league New York club. But eight of the first 19 hits he surrendered in Minneapolis were home runs, and a loudmouthed fan in Omaha got his goat. Branca yelled back. A kerfuffle was sad, the pitcher manacled to a moment. Minutes later, teammates Alex Konikowski and Al Worthing-ton, former Giants, told Branca of a telescope. But lo, this goat already knew. On July 22, the Millers let Branca and his 3–3 record go.

This same summer, off on a Milwaukee road trip, Andy Pafko turned to his roommate to talk of the Thomson home run. It was Pafko who had stood beneath the magical ball before it slipped into lore. And, sent by Brooklyn to Milwaukee in 1953, the Slovak shared now, two years later, a room with the Scot who had hit it. Thomson demurred. "Andy," he said. "That's history."

Less and less did Thomson rehash what in 1951 had drawn him out, had warmed him to the dais, the mike, the endorsement. For the self-doubt of a diffident man will reemerge at first stumble. And fresh off an amputated season, injured and demoted to left field, Thomson was timid. When on April 29, 1955, *New York Times* reporter Drebinger asked what he thought were his chances of helping the club to a pennant, it did not matter that Thomson was leading the league in runs batted in, 21 driven home by May. "That's a tough question," said the Scot, "because it assumes I'll have a lot to do with it. Maybe so. But there are a lot of other fine players on this club even more important. I think *their* chances of winning are excellent."

That Thomson lacked confidence was by now well known. He was not, noted *Sport* magazine this May, "by nature, well suited to carry off the valorous role that was suddenly his in the fall of 1951. He has little of the chesty self-assurance . . . of which most of our heroes, both real and fictional, are composed." Thomson did not disagree. "I suppose I have been too timid," he told *Sport* reporter Jack Newcombe. "There never was much tiger, or whatever you want to call it, in me. My brother Jim was always building fires under me, even when I was first starting out in the minors. Let's face it, I've never had a great season."

Newcombe marveled at his subject. "Not many .280 hitters," he wrote, "who have hit 25 home runs a year, have driven in 100 or more runs in four of seven complete major-league seasons, have played exceptionally well in the infield and the outfield and who can cover ground like a thoroughbred, have felt compelled to apologize for their work."

Thomson's bat soon cooled, slapping three singles in his first twenty May at-bats. And after a sore right shoulder then sat him down 11 games, his right calf and ankle flared, a gimpy Thomson batting just .250 when on June 24 he swung with the bases loaded at strike three, the first of 2,396 to strike out against newbie Sandy Koufax. By July 1, Milwaukee was 13 back of Brooklyn, its left fielder kayoed by injury a second straight season. Benched 53 games, Thomson managed still to knock in 56 runs.

The end of the 1955 season saw Brooklyn win its first World Series and an old Giant quartet break from the game. Durocher left dugout for NBC broadcast booth. Franks, who had long midwifed Leo, resigned from the club to manage Utah real estate. Yvars, cut from St. Louis and then Buffalo of the International League, became in July an investment broker in White Plains. And, bounced recently from Oakland and Sacramento, Schenz was let go in September from Tulsa, cut for good just forty-one days shy of a major league pension.

Branca, meantime, was unsure of a next step. "I was thinking of retiring," he says. And so even as the pitcher sold insurance and dabbled in PR (promoting a horse-racing contest to name a chestnut colt), he kept an eye out for jobs in sport. "A radio-TV announcer or writer," suggested Branca to the *Sporting News*. "I'd take a managing job in the minors, too, so long as I could make some money with it."

Given that Thomson had batted just 442 times in two seasons, his new $30,000 contract was fair. But it remained a first pay cut in seven years. And eager to prove to a loyal club (and himself) that he had not slowed, Thomson was not above adjustment. In March he readopted his open stance of seasons back. In April, after a 6-for-33 start, he swapped his number 34 for 25 on the advice of a numerologist.

It was this spring of 1956 that Branca considered purchasing a sporting goods store on Fourth Avenue in Mount Vernon. He knew equipment, had come a long way since looking blankly at the jock handed him in 1943. But out of pro ball a first season in thirteen, Branca wished in truth only to pitch again. And not long after NBC aired a 90-minute ode to seasons past—and above all to his albatross—Branca passed on the store, instead asking Brooklyn if he might again throw batting practice. This he did in August, aiming most often at catcher Dixie Howell, a grateful Dodger lineup finishing the month just 2.5 games out of first.

It had been two years since a revealed secret exhumed for Branca a fastball. And still it was hard to let go, to let lie the thought of a spyglass. Says Branca, "I fantasized that we'd changed the signs." Disquieted, the pitcher was left yet again to try to append a happy ending to a sad career.

Branca had thrown a month of batting practice when, on September 3, catcher Howell talked him up to manager Walter Alston. Alston needed arms, Brooklyn bracing this Monday afternoon for a third doubleheader in as many days. Manager beseeched general manager, Bavasi signing Branca before even nine innings had passed, the pitcher again a Dodger, his salary some eightfold the $400 a month he had earned a dozen years prior. "He was a local boy," says Bavasi. "I just wanted him to retire a Dodger." The signing stunned. "Scribes who thought they were being kidded," wrote the *Sporting News*, "had to be convinced when they saw Ralph running down to the Brooklyn bull pen [*sic*] as the second game started." A desire to play on was no joke.

And so those same scribes reminisced of a home run even before Alston summoned Branca. "On the morning of Oct. 3, 1951, Ralph Branca was a powerfully built 25-year-old," wrote reporter Daley. "By nightfall, he almost looked as though he'd been whisked mystically from Shangri-La to the outer world where he'd aged several hundred years." The lineaments in his long face had only deepened when on September 7 Branca warmed—the relief pitcher Ogden Nash would write of in spring:

> How the muscles bulge in his sweatshirt,
> How his heart with hope is full,
> When the manager beckons the bull pen
> To send him another bull!
> How he mutters a silent prayer,
> Lord, let me be that bull!

This afternoon, Branca was. And though the home team trailed New York six-love, "I was more nervous pitching those two innings," says Branca, "than I was when I walked on the field at eighteen." One of just eighteen 1944 big leaguers still active, he pitched well, no runs yielded, Bill Sarni and Willie Mays struck out besides. A nostalgic crowd applauded lustily. A career continued on.

There was for Thomson both bad and good this 1956 season. He continued his Milwaukee slump but was at last healthy. He amassed just 106 hits but drove in .69 runs per hit, best in his career. He gave up playing time to rookie Wes Covington but was at last again a contender, Milwaukee .5 games ahead of Brooklyn with just two to play. Thomson contributed three hits and two runs in the final pair, finishing his season with 451 at-bats, 20 home runs, 74 runs batted in, and a .235 average. But winners in St. Louis of just one of two, Milwaukee lost the pennant to Brooklyn by a single game.

Since signing Branca, Brooklyn had gone 15–8, had overtaken Cincinnati and Milwaukee. But in those four weeks, Alston had not pitched Branca even a second time. And because the right-hander had joined the team in September, he was (unless tapped to replace an injured Dodger) ineligible for the World Series. And so it was from blue box seats that Branca watched Yankee Don Larsen throw his perfect game, that he watched Brooklyn lose Game Seven of the World Series, the pitcher yet again denied a go at postseason salvation.

Three days later, Branca stood on a mound in Maui—a stopover before traveling with Brooklyn to Japan where manager Alston pitched him again. But Branca had not warmed and his right arm soon ached. By December 14, when Branca and wife returned to New York aboard the *Queen Mary*, the pitcher could not lift a comb to his hair let alone shoulder the avoirdupois of a ball.

Thomson left Staten Island for Jersey, left country club for his in-laws. The Coleys owned some 150 acres in Pluckemin, grazing pasture for their ponies Sparky and Pepper. They had too an unused wing of a fieldstone farmhouse, a fireplace in every room, which they now offered to Thomson and his wife together with a proposition for the aging ballplayer.

Henry Justice Coley was a strong and self-sufficient man, a builder and electrician who at fifty-five drove a Willys jeep, kept up a working well and barn, wore flannel and khaki, was expert with rifle and rod. He was also smart, a Presbyterian who had run a tavern during the Depression. Coley had since turned to real estate, to land bought and developed, and this winter asked Thomson if he wished to buy into property in Basking Ridge, New Jersey. The left fielder agreed. "We were going to build houses," says Thomson. "We cleared the ground and put in sewers." Seeing his son-in-law lay down bat for axe pleased Coley. Says Thomson's daughter Nancy, "He didn't care about any of the baseball stuff."

Branca arrived in Florida, the once puissant pitcher to nibble for strikes with a new, slow screwball. Cortisone had calmed his deltoid, and at thirty-one, Branca hoped for one more spring. But on March 19, a septet of Kansas City batters scored five—Branca serving up walk, home run, double, triple, hit batsman, groundout, error.

Perhaps it meant something to the 2,580 on hand that an aging pitcher, perspiring in the West Palm Beach sun, recouped now in an exhibition game to throw two scoreless frames. But to Brooklyn management it mattered not at all. Nine days after surrendering the mound to southpaw Koufax, Branca lost his job.

The pitcher had been a major leaguer for 12 seasons. He had been durable, completed 71 of 188 games started. He had been flexible, 134 games relieved, 19 saved. He had been powerful, 829 batters struck out in 1,484 innings. He had been effective, his ERA 3.79. And he had won. Between the Giants bookending his career—Buddy Kerr struck out in 1944, Daryl Spencer tapped to the mound in 1956—Branca won 88 games, 20 more than he lost. His record as Dodger was even better. Of the 357 pitchers in Brooklyn's sixty-six years, just nine with at least 100 decisions trumped his .580 winning percentage.

Yet Branca craved absolution. And not from the basic chaff of a career—the 31 hit batsmen, 44 wild pitches, 68 losses, 149 home runs, 663 walks, 702 runs, 1,372 hits. It was the *almosts* that haunted, the big games on the precipices of glories in which Branca had failed, pummeled in 1946, 1947, 1949, 1951, a fighter stumbling from his corner round after round despite a 5.90 ERA in 10.2 playoff innings, despite a 6.35 ERA in 17 World Series innings, despite an uppercut on October 3, 1951, so severe that the minutes following it were still lost to amnesia.

On March 28, 1957, the fight stopped. Told by Brooklyn to leave the parent club for the Pacific Coast League, Branca declined. He would instead go home. He would retire. He would sell insurance. "I'd like to have pitched once more," Branca told the press. "It's tough to come back with a club like the Dodgers. The club has a terrific roster problem and I'm not bitter."

Opening Day saw Thomson go hitless in Chicago. By May 7 his average was .156. And so number 25 sat, unused by manager Grimm for 10 games, the longest a healthy Thomson had ridden the bench in all his career. When at last he batted again on May 19, Milwaukee was 18–9. And so it made sense that on this same Sunday, rumors surfaced that Thomson, thirty-three, was back on the block.

Perhaps it was relief that finally sprung Thomson. For it was on the eve of the 1957 trade deadline that the Scot, happy to still be a Brave, stole a base, drove in two runs and had four singles—as many hits as he had gotten in any of his 326 previous games in Milwaukee.

The Braves were unswayed. In 148 at-bats, Thomson had just four home runs, a .236 average and 23 runs batted in. Hours later, as June 15 turned to dusk, they returned Thomson to New York.

Thomson was crushed, far more upset at being traded to the Giants than from them. He and the missus had loved Milwaukee, voted by scribes "happiest" couple on the team. He had enjoyed his teammates, been elected alternate team-rep. What's more, the Braves were in first place, at 32–21 nine games up on the Giants and a shot at World Series money. That in exchange for Red Schoendienst Milwaukee now sent not only Thomson and pitcher Ray Crone to New York but also O'Connell— he who took repeated pleasure in airing a Giant secret—was a final frustration. Thomson hardened. "All the luster had gone out of it," he told researcher Tom Harris years later. "It was just baseball."

And baseball was business—a realpolitik venture that, having since 1953 uprooted the Braves, Browns and Athletics, dognapped now the Dodgers and Giants. Both New York teams were vamoosing to California. "When we go to San Francisco, we'll make money," owner Stoneham told his stockholders on August 7. "If we don't get out of New York we're going to lose money and all the good cities will be gone."

Thomson stood in Harlem once again a Giant, on his back in left field the number 21. It was toward the green wall behind him that 105 days later he pointed, recalling with a forefinger on September 29, 1957, where once had flown a glorious home run. Thomson was not alone in his look back, his homer heavy in the nostalgic air. "All I could think of as I rounded the bases," said Hank Aaron after his walk-off won the pennant days before, "was Bobby Thomson's home run in 1951." And published this same month was an E. B. White story about the widow of a fatalistic Giant fan, the author imagining a home run hit by Thomson with one out in the ninth.

As had befallen Thomson in 1954, the club that had let him go had won the pennant. His new club, meantime, had lost 14 of 17, had on this final September morning of New York Giant baseball long since quit on manager Rigney. Thomson had not, had driven home 38 runs in 212 at-bats. And when at 4:35 p.m. a toss from shortstop Dick Groat to Frank Thomas finished off Dusty Rhodes and a 9–1 Pittsburgh win, Thomson sprinted for a clubhouse, leading on a dash to center field—one step ahead of rampaging fans—a suddenly extinct club.

After the Giants had emptied their wooden cubbies, after clubhouse man Logan had tagged his metal trunks SEALS STADIUM, SIXTEENTH AND BRYANT, SAN FRANCISCO, after maintenance man Colletti had raised a final red flag (mood ring of millions), after fans had stolen bases, ripped free bullpen phones and whittled nubs of rubber from the pitching mound, Thomson stepped onto what remained of center field, onto turf shredded by sixty-six years of Giant ball. Off in the home dugout sat his wife and daughter. Thomson approached and snapped their picture and little Nancy ran around the bases. It was then before exiting the Polo Grounds one last time that he aimed a camera back at center field, the splintered steps and mesh windows and green doors of a Harlem clubhouse preserved.

TWENTY-ONE

Sweet it is to remember labors.
—FRANCESCO PETRARCA,
Bucolicum Carmen, 1346
(translated by Denis Feeney)

I F THERE WAS TO BE FOUND any sense in the overnight loss of two baseball teams, it was that they had deserted New York together. For it was the hissing between Giant and Dodger that defined both, the 1,387 games played in sixty-seven seasons. Were a New York April to greet one and not the other, the crisis would be existential.

But that it was *two* teams dissolved meant also of course two pools of fans now bereft. Wrote Roger Angell in 1964: "What does depress us about the decease of the bony, misshapen old playground is the attendant irrevocable deprivation of habit—the amputation of so many private, repeated, and easily renewable small familiarities."

And so a great lacuna hollowed the city. And memory alone left of the two teams, it was memory the jilted millions now summoned as surrogate, as stopgap, decades soon distilled to a single swing, to one and the same moment both most precious and most painful. The Thomson home run was the avatar of an era.

For looked back upon, the shot was from every angle ideal. To begin with, it was baseball that for a century had crowned the world of American sport. Moreover, the home run flew in New York which, with its three major league teams, was the great sport's hub. As sealant of Giant-Dodger fate, Thomson's swing sizzled with baseball's greatest rivalry. As baseball play, the walk-off home run knew no equal. And as denouement of a months-long comeback—not followed by even one pitch—the shot was scripted like a schoolboy's imagined scenario. "The beauty of it was," observed reporter Newcombe in *Sport* magazine, "it was an all-conclusive hit."

And not only had Thomson struck his blow at just the right time and in just the right place. But baseball's perfect storm had been bottled in perfect fashion. There was its radio call, Russ Hodges conveying sublimely the ineffable. There was its newsreel, silent footage of a ball seen launched but never landed. There was its TV broadcast, which though not taped had carried the great shot unprecedented distance, vanguard of live nationally televised sport, what tens of millions had watched *together*. There was its write-up, a home run channeled through the classical Red Smith. There was its preferred photograph, a ball stilled on its way to left. There were its nicknames, the "Miracle of Coogan's Bluff," the "Shot Heard Round the World" (time trimming from each an extraneous word). And of course there were its twin protagonists, Thomson and Branca astride a home run. Thus preserved, the shot turned what Henri Cartier-Bresson defined a "decisive moment." Wrote the photographer in 1952: "It is the simultaneous recognition, in a fraction of a second, of the significance of an event as well as a precise organisation of forms, which give that event its proper expression."

The home run in fact seemed only to be lacking itself, a ball. And that a Spalding remained at large only further consecrated its flight—a keepsake not of one but of all. "If we knew who had that baseball," author DeLillo told the *New York Times,* "it's possible I never would have begun work on the novel." But we did not and so he did, the ball in *Underworld* "a holy relic of memory," wrote David Firestone in the *New York Times,* "a talisman of history," added David Remnick in the *New Yorker.* "The ball is a kind of grail."

It was also now, in the eye of a bereft city, the crystallization of a time no longer. For what lingered most of a home run was the carnival it begat. "Maybe it was the last time people spontaneously went out of their houses for something," wrote DeLillo in *Underworld.* "Some wonder, some amazement. Like a footnote to the end of the war." Added Luc Sante in the *New York Review of Books,* "[It] might have been the last innocent expression of community."

Indeed, since a home run had life disillusioned, had crusades upended and breakthroughs blurred. Six years had turned cigarettes suspect, the Pill imminent, Puritanism passé. Robert Oppenheimer was now defendant, Joseph McCarthy conspiracist, George Jorgensen Christine, transsexual celebrity of Massapequa. Barriers had been smashed—DNA mapped, polio tamed, school desegregated, the four-minute mile bested, Everest mounted, Earth this very month orbited by *Sputnik.* Since 1951 had Hugh Hefner and Alfred Kinsey exposed body and behavior, had

Margaret Sanger birthed Planned Parenthood, had housewife Betty Friedan begun to discern the dissatisfaction of women, had Estragon and Vladimir stood in uncertain wait of Godot. Sociologist C. Wright Mills saw in the comfy mass migrations from city to suburb a loss of purpose, and it was likewise American affluence John Steinbeck fingered as having cooked TV quiz show *Twenty-One.* "If I wanted to destroy a nation I would give it too much," wrote Steinbeck to Adlai Stevenson. "On all levels, American society is rigged."

And so of a bygone epoch, a home run lingered all the more pure. It was, wrote philosophy professor Joseph Grange, "an experience of beauty had all at once and truthfully." And, sacrosanct, it would outlive the city's loss of two teams just as it had its own dismantling—by spring, all seven Giants who comprised a miracle ninth moved on, Dark who singled and Lockman who doubled dealt to the Cardinals, Mueller who singled sold to the White Sox, Irvin who popped up traded to the Cubs, Hartung who pinch-ran released, Thomson sent to the Braves, Durocher taken hiatus. Wrote Sante in the *New York Review of Books,* the home run "can be retrospectively seen as marking the division between edenic and fallen worlds."

Thus was home run hinge of history. And evermore resonant, its emotional and cultural valence unique in the history of American sport, it was safe now in 1957 to answer what had been posed six years earlier. "As we weigh the momentous events of Oct. 3, 1951," asked the *New York Post* that same day, "the great question remained unanswered: will it be remembered by our children as the day of Durocher's biggest triumph or of Stalin's atomic windfall?"

Time had made clear its answer. Stalin usurped, the empirical and nostalgic alike would marvel at a home run. "It is an icon of the eternal," wrote Lee Congdon in *World & I* magazine. "Through it we catch a glimpse, however small, of permanent things." Wrote David Cort in the *Commonweal* magazine, "Bobby Thomson's home run was a triumph for faith and heroism. . . . Life, it was said, is not like that." Wrote J. H. Hexter in the *Encyclopedia of the Social Sciences,* the shot is "the equivalent (in its sphere), of the defeat of the Armada, the battle of Stalingrad, the Normandy landings."

As in those battles, it was a culmination that historicized a baseball season—the last-gasp winning of a pennant all but lost. "Here was a reversal of the order of things, a structural change that qualifies Bobby Thomson's home run as a historic event, even as it qualified him as a hero, a history-maker," wrote anthropologist Marshall Sahlins. "And it is from this revolutionary denouement, working backward, that we discover and rhetorically motivate the tempos, turning points, and agents of our history. The structural reversal in the story is the determining principle of historical value and relevance, a *telos* that rules the organization of the account."

"So is it truly chutzpah," wrote Sahlins, "to put 'the shot Heard round the world' on the same plane as the Peloponnesian War or the 2000 U.S. presidential election?" Or, as the Center for Defense Information did in a film on foreign policy, put it alongside the Truman defeat of Dewey and the postwar rebirths of Germany and Japan? Or, as author Russell Baker did, alongside the defeat of Dewey and the 1962 attack of China on India? Wrote DeLillo: "Isn't it possible that this midcentury moment enters the skin more lastingly than the vast shaping strategies of eminent leaders, generals steely in their sunglasses—the mapped visions that pierce our dreams?"

If it was teleology that made relevant the flight of a ball, it was pathos that lifted it together with player and fan where even *Sputnik* had not flown. "A sporting event had reached the zenith of tragedy and sublimity, as in a great work of art," wrote pianist Eugene Istomin. "I learned to weep for winners as well as losers after that game." Added historian Jacques Barzun, "The wonderful purging of the passions that we all experienced in the fall of '51, the despair groaned over the fate of the Dodgers, from whom the pennant was snatched at the last minute, give us some idea of what Greek tragedy was like."

Indeed was this drama *tragic* to its root, τραγωδια (*tragoidia*) Greek for "goat song." For while in ancient Greece it was a goat awarded for the winning play, a prize to be eaten by chorus and company, it was all of America that now feasted on Branca, on a scapegoat offering his song. And that Thomson sang beside him was apt. For only *together* were pitcher and batter tragic hero—one suffering unfairly, one weighted by guilt. And while as in all Greek tragedy moral failing had led to catastrophe, to denouement inevitable and ruinous, redemption, requisite, had not yet come.

The Shot Heard 'Round the Baseball World

The New York *Daily News*, October 4, 1951.
This headline—the work of caption writer Pete Coutros—
was most responsible for the honorific accorded the home run.
Courtesy of Eric Fettmann.

The front page of *The New York Times*, October 4, 1951. Newspapers across the country trumpeted the Thomson home run at least as loudly as word of a second Russian nuclear test. A delighted Gordon Dean, chairman of the Atomic Energy Commission, noted this in his diary. *Courtesy of* The New York Times.

Among the reporters seen here in the Polo Grounds press box in 1957 are Bill Roeder *(with pipe)* and John Drebinger *(standing, in overcoat and hat, to Roeder's left)*. It was behind this same chicken wire that Red Smith wrote of the Thomson home run: "Now the story ends. And there is no way to tell it. The art of fiction is dead. Reality has strangled invention." *Photograph by Arthur Daley.*

Branca pitched, Thomson swung and announcer Russ Hodges screamed five times "The Giants win the pennant!" WMCA engineer Lou Weber recorded the classic call, and among its many incarnations was this 1951 record made by Liggett & Myers Tobacco Company. *From the author's collection.*

Four months after the home run, Thomson and Branca sang together at the annual
dinner of the Baseball Writers' Association of America. Their performance of *Because
of You* elicited tears and turned the men into an act. Among a lifetime of collaborations
was a 1974 PBS television program advertised on subways with this painting by
Richard Hess. *From the author's collection.*

When Thomson retired in 1960, he knew that he wanted a job outside of baseball. Career aptitude tests pointed to sales, and the baseball hero became a paper-bag salesman. "One of the great satisfactions of my life," Thomson remarked, "that I learned the meaning of work." *Courtesy of Bobby Thomson.*

Branca hoped baseball might provide a second career, but he received no viable job offers when he retired in 1956. He turned to insurance, his notoriety an asset. Says Branca, "that would get me in the door." *Courtesy of Ralph Branca.*

Thomson and Branca at the former site of the Polo Grounds on March 23, 2006.
Courtesy of Susan Meiselas/Magnum Photos.

TWENTY-TWO

So set, before its echoes fade,
The fleet foot on the sill of shade,
And hold to the low lintel up,
The still-defended challenge-cup.

—A. E. HOUSMAN,
"To an Athlete Dying Young," 1896

THE 1957 WORLD SERIES outed inside baseball. New York PR firm Hill and Knowlton had settled on the wave of hands to drumbeat series-sponsor Gillette and so the announcers alerted 80 million eyes to the signaling of coaches, the writers ranked Dressen top signstealer and Durocher fourth, the fans riffled a wig-wag flip-book, and the papers printed primers on cheating—exhuming a buzzer in Philadelphia but leaving another in Harlem unsounded. A Giant secret remained untold.

Thomson arrived at an Arizona spa, sent for in February by manager Rigney to sweat off pounds before a first season in San Francisco. But on April 3, the Giant turned Cub—number 9 singling twice that same afternoon against his former team.

Baseball, profane, will given time disrespect every player, even the great Jackie Robinson dealt two Decembers past for cash and a Giant lefty named Dick Littlefield. While Robinson had then retired, turned coffee spokesman for Chock full o'Nuts, it was Mutual Benefit Life Insurance that in May had landed Branca.

That Branca left baseball as baseball left New York eased his exit. For all the city was in withdrawal, Dodger and Giant fans bereaved. (Even Yankee fans were discombobulated, attendance in the Bronx to somehow drop this same 1958 season.)

Branca had thus far pitched insurance well, sold from June through December one million dollars of policy, good for some $21,000 in salary.

And at thirty-two, he had at last his weekends free, the Brancas often dining Friday nights with their friends the Lavines and Villantes, tending Saturdays to a lawn and tomatoes, Sunday mornings reserved for church, their 13-RB license plate parked always on Mamaroneck Avenue, four Brancas stepping through the red wooden door of Our Lady of Sorrows.

Chicago took quickly to Thomson. For while in autumn the team had finished last, it claimed first on the first of May. And he who was gotten for no more than reserve Bob Speake and cash (and who in January took a third straight pay cut, down to $22,000 a year) was smack in the middle of things—Thomson batting fifth and manning center field.

Thomson delighted to be back in center. His ankle healed, he fielded .5 more balls per game on average than other center fielders and played in more games than every NL outfielder save Aaron, Ashburn and Mays. His bat reawakened too, an Adirondack hitting .283 with 21 home runs, 5 triples, 27 doubles and 82 runs driven in—tenth most in the league. His was a grand comeback, Thomson at age thirty-four again accorded respect, walked intentionally three times by Philadelphia on June 4. And though a loss the next afternoon sunk Chicago to sixth place—one rung below where it would finish the season—Thomson, come dinner-time was, as *every* night, home in Northbrook. For in Chicago, the Cubs played only at midday, Thomson free evenings to loll with wife and daughter in suburbia, to enjoy barbecues, a pool next door and a yard so large he had someone else mow it.

Thomson remained a draw, booked the off-season past by a Little League, a Lions Club, a tire company. Such talks, like the royalties of a bestseller, had over the years been good for at least $10,000, endorsements ongoing too, Thomson this 1958 season hocking Mennen products, gracing a baseball card put out by Hires Root Beer. Read card number 46: "Bobby will always be known as the fellow who hit the 'home run heard around the world.' "

Back in New York the city was a palimpsest, another pinstriped pennant brush-stroked atop the orange and blue of bygone teams. But that the Yankees now won, and that Giants and Dodgers time zones away finished third and seventh, mattered not at all to the fleeced fans—among them Queens housewife Harriet Mesulam, left to tell her newborn son of the two phantom teams his namesake, Abraham Chadwick, had once worked for and rooted on so feverishly.

It was this winter of 1959 that Thomson and wife saw plainly the need to leave her parents. "We decided," says Thomson, "hey, we've got to get our own place."

Thomson had recently bought land in Arizona on the advice of Cubs owner Philip Wrigley. "I could see real estate as a good investment," says Thomson. And so even as he now cut business ties with Henry Coley (baseball left insufficient time for land development), and passed also on his offer to buy a lot on the family farm, he and Winkie paid $48,000 for a ranch house on dead-end Sunlit Drive in Watchung, New Jersey. On the eve of a fourteenth season, Thomson at last owned his first home. He would live in it for forty-six years.

Eleven stories above Grand Central Terminal, Branca the broker continued to sell protection insurance and estate planning. In August, he offered up to John Q. Public entertainment too, opening with his brother Paul Stratford Bowling in Connecticut—thirty-six lanes and a restaurant besides. It was also in August that Branca accepted an invitation to pitch at Yankee Stadium. On August 8, Old-Timer Branca, thirty-three, retired Wally Pipp, sixty-six, on a fly to right.

The gravitas of a famed comeback and the moral nuisance of an unknown buzzer had in eight years elicited from a team of Giants varied behaviors. Yvars was more and more comfortable to speak of stolen signs. Thomson was less and less keen to reminisce of a home run. ("Talking about it now," he told the *New York Times* in March, "makes me feel like a has-been.") Lockman, straightest arrow on all a club, was sweated semimonthly by a nightmare that had him grounding into a double play before Thomson came to bat. And it was now on September 16, 1959, that Rigney, successor to Durocher, decided to cheat.

Rigney was, along with Mays, the only Giant left of a miracle team. And gathering now his starting lineup, the manager proposed a simpler plan than had been used in 1951. A spy would stand with looking glass behind two slats in the center-field scoreboard. He would close the right slat to denote a fastball, the left a curve. First place at stake—Milwaukee just two back and in town for a pair of games—the team decided the scheme a go.

A first run was unsuccessful, San Francisco blanked by Lew Burdette 2–0. But a second invigorated, the team blasting Milwaukee 13–6, the great Warren Spahn chased after just 18 pitches, not a single batter retired. With just eight games remaining, the Giants led the Braves and Dodgers by two. They eyed the World Series.

It was then Al Worthington learned of a telescope. And the Giant pitcher, thirty, disapproved.

The June previous (together with a woman in an iron lung and 696,524 others), Worthington and wife had headed to the Cow Palace to hear tell of the Holy Trinity. "Its work is to convict you of your sins," boomed Billy Graham in the San Francisco dome. "And only when it has can you find the eternal life."

The message had lingered in the pitcher and housewife who days later returned to a cement bleacher to again take in Graham. And when on that June night the evangelist asked his audience to open itself to the Holy Spirit, hundreds cried and a young couple ascended an altar to pledge two lives to Christ. "My heart had pounded," says Worthington. "I stood there and told God I'd come to live for him."

Fifteen months later, Worthington stood before Rigney a Baptist. He had been a Methodist when in 1954 the Giants last pinched signs, the pitcher not yet saved. And so it was now a first time that religion and baseball clashed. Though ball gave Worthington worth—665 innings thrown in six seasons—Christ gave him ballast. "If we continue to cheat," pitcher told manager, "I am going to have to leave the team."

Rigney acquiesced, the Giants scored six runs in 27 innings, lost three straight to Los Angeles, finished the season in third and, come spring, traded Worthington.

That Chicago finished fifth was no surprise. Nonetheless, an aging Thomson was content, in 122 games manning all three outfield positions, batting .259, plating 52 runs including the thousandth of a career.

Two months later, Thomson shipped off a fourth time, traded to the Red Sox for not more than minor league pitcher Al Schroll. A career was nearing its end. Older than all but ten players in his new league, Thomson would at thirty-six back the oldest, forty-one-year-old Boston left-fielder Ted Williams.

Ebbets Field, meantime, was weeks shy of forty-seven when, on February 23, 1960, Branca stood in camel-hair coat beside its home plate. The last and first to crouch behind that home were also present this winter morning, Campanella and Otto Miller among the few Dodgers come to pay last respects. On this Tuesday a wrecking ball would wreck a ballfield, sacred park to turn housing project for 1,317 families. And so some 200 folks sang now of an auld acquaintance to be forgot. "Ladies and gentlemen," said Tex Rickard, the public address announcer announcing a last time, "now coming in to pitch for the Dodgers, Number fourteen, Ralph Branca." No matter a wrong number, the insurance salesman and bowling proprietor stepped forward to a polite cheer. Two tons of iron dropped atop a visiting dugout, the phone to the bullpen knocked loose.

Spring arrived, Red Sock Thomson spelling the great Williams in left for 12 games, playing also center and right (and, for nine innings, first base). At bat he was efficient, 30 hits and 20 runs driven home in 114 goes, 5 home runs besides. The last of these flew deep to left on June 8, scaling in Boston a different green wall than had his first fifteen years prior, Thomson off on the last of 264 diamond jogs, brown eyes fixed as always straight ahead in deference to pitcher.

Nineteen days later, Boston released Thomson. Baltimore picked him up. But after six hitless at-bats the club let him go, a final pitch on July 17 from Early Wynn skyed to center.

Offers to play on came at Thomson from the Pacific Coast to Japan. And Winkie was amenable. But home in New Jersey on July 23 with wife and daughter and French poodle Nina, Thomson, thirty-six, saw plainly that he had no need for comebacks, half-starts, minor leagues. For despite a championship never won, persistent yips of potential unmet and a hard-wired inability to self-congratulate, looking back on a career brought contentment. With singular speed and good glove had he played outfield and infield. With power and consistency had he batted, averaging in the seven full seasons before a career turned on a broken ankle 26 home runs, 7 triples, 26 doubles, 88 runs, 94 runs batted in, a .485 slugging percentage. Just 23 of the 9,415 major leaguers since 1871 had hit more home runs. Thomson had hit his 264 off 136 pitchers—10 off Herm Wehmeier, 9 off Jim Konstanty, 9 off Warren Spahn. And it was the last of four off Branca that had Thomson retiring now a hero.

The hero was unsure of a next step. Reflected Thomson years later to his local *Daily Record*: "I had to look at myself as a person and say, 'Would you be satisfied to coach third base and wave people around or do you want to get out and use your head?'"

Thomson, though, belittled that head. A second career could not require more than a high school education, and this remained for Thomson a source of shame. "He would give up a lot of what he has in his life," observed daughter Nancy years later, "for what he calls a sharp mind, a college education."

Thomson decided together with Winkie that an aptitude test might help. And so the hero paid the New Jersey Stevens Institute of Technology $150 for fifteen hours of counseling and testing. Multiple-choice analogies and diagrams laid bare the desiderata of a salesman. The earnest Thomson set off for a job in sales.

Interviews at companies from American Cyanamid to Canada Dry led nowhere, and Thomson set off on September 29, 1960, to 299 Park Avenue. It was there in suit and garter socks that he applied with blue ballpoint for a job in sales at West Virginia Pulp and Paper Company, "the established and successful type of firm," wrote Thomson, "with which to embark on a new career after 15 years of pro. baseball." The company, founded in 1852 by Scottish immigrant William Luke, wished to know more of the Scot and sent for word from the Stevens Institute.

It was in a six-page report that Ph.D.'s William Hirschman and Donald Livingston wrote of Thomson's sociability, objectivity, creativity, humility and high intelligence (including for good measure his IQ score). They recapped as well his shortcomings: "lack of business experience, a somewhat undisciplined mind, and some difficulty (though correctable) in quickly and efficiently grasping written materials." It was one trait in particular, though, the doctors flagged again and again and again:

"[Thomson] responds most eagerly when he is called upon to engage in activities which he feels are useful and worthwhile in a moral sense," wrote Hirschman and Livingston. "He wants to do the 'right' thing, that is to say, and he will seek out tasks which have some positive moral or economic value. He would not put his heart into work which he considers parasitical, for economic gain alone, or which requires him to offer an inferior product."

On November 14, 1960, West Virginia Pulp and Paper Company hired Thomson. He would sell paper bags, his salary $10,500. Who once had made a living with a bat of ash now did with pulp of oak, sweet gum and loblolly pine.

This same fall, Patti Branca began third grade at Our Lady of Sorrows, a girl of eight in plaid skirt, white blouse and blue bow tie. And it was in a classroom of yellow cinder blocks that she heard now from little Carl Brocci a first bad word of her father. "He told me," says Patti, "my father was a bum and that my father cost a lot of people a lot of money." This a confused Patti repeated to her mother, then father, daddy left to tell of fans and Dodgers and Giants, of a playoff, a home run and a man named Bobby Thomson, a bequeathal from father to daughter as real as her brown eyes.

On the eve of its tenth anniversary, however, a blown playoff had a sterling silver lining, Branca turning fastball to sales pitch. "That pitch gave me notoriety," says Branca. "That would get me in the door." This fellow insurance agent Cy Block observed. "For at least two years after he was shell-shocked," the former Cub infielder told the *New York Times*. "Now he's played it to his own advantage. He'll tell a guy the inside poop on the pitch and then he sells him a policy."

Indeed, Branca sold in 1960 more than $1.5 million of policy—boast of just one in twenty Mutual Benefit brokers and good for $25,000 in salary. And so when this May of 1961 NYU offered him the job of base-ball coach, Branca declined. And when competition in Stratford shut-tered his bowling alley, Branca simply entered a league with Ann, rolling Friday nights his sixteen-pound ball. Insurance was a good living, Branca earning eleven stories above Grand Central Terminal far more than ever he had on the mound.

Two stories higher and six blocks north, another salesman sat in a suit behind a desk. Selling industrial paper—bags strong enough to hold cement, fertilizer, seed, salt and chemicals—the baseball hero did not employ baseball, seeing to it that the name on his business card read not Bobby but Robert B. Thomson. His was a new stage of life. "Paper bags," reflected Thomson to *Sport* magazine. "I get up at seven. I ride subways with all the working stiffs. No more breakfasts at noon in hotels, taxis to ballparks. And I love it. This is fun. I'm part of the real world. I'm producing."

But Thomson, thirty-seven, was also earning 30 percent of what he had at twenty-nine. His salary his lowest in thirteen years, the salesman developed ulcers, forced nightly to sip Mylanta. Winkie, meantime, had years prior endured an ectopic pregnancy. Unable since to conceive, the couple decided now to give their baby furniture to Elma and Kenny Freile, neighbors set to adopt. And so was a wife depressed and a hus-band stressed.

Thomson's ulcers were done no favor by the allegations of sign-stealing fizzing as usual through baseball. In May of 1961, the Cubs accused the Cardinals of stealing the pitches of Don Cardwell from their scoreboard. In September, the Braves accused the Cubs of stealing the pitches of Carl Willey from *their* scoreboard, Milwaukee filing a protest for good measure. And in March of 1962, Washington infielder Danny O'Connell spoke to reporter Joe Reichler. In exchange for a promise that his name be kept mum, he who had long chafed Thomson would at last air a Giant secret.

TWENTY-THREE

I have only one eye—I have a right to be blind sometimes. I really
do not see the signal.

—HORATIO NELSON to Thomas Foley at the
Battle of Copenhagen, April 2, 1801

JOE REICHLER PACKED his Buick and, as every February, drove
south with his wife, Ricky, and son Paul. Since 1943, the AP sportswriter had mined for gold dust the tedium of spring training. And in
twenty years he had come to know where in baseball's streambed to
dredge. When, for example, on March 22 Reichler took in Senators versus Athletics, though O'Connell sat out the 6–3 loss, it was to the Washington infielder that Reichler wisely turned. "Danny," wrote once the
Sporting News, "is outspoken and articulate. He doesn't duck questions
and he'll respond on any subject you want to kick around."

Perhaps Reichler knew it was O'Connell who in Milwaukee and then
New York had upset Thomson with talk of a telescope. Perhaps O'Connell knew that come October he would lose his soapbox, this his tenth
and final big league spring. Regardless, it was now in Pompano Beach
that a ballplayer from New Jersey revealed to a writer from New York
the arcanum of a miracle. "You might say," O'Connell told Reichler,
"that the shot heard round the world was set off by a buzzer."

That his scoop came secondhand (O'Connell not a Giant in 1951) did
not faze Reichler. Nor did he care that his source was vague. For this
once, it sufficed to report only the what, where, why and approximate
when, to report that the Giants had over the last three months of the
1951 season hornswoggled at home in pursuit of pennant. Reichler
would leave unmolested the whos—who had spied and who relayed,
who had brought forth a telescope and who a buzzer.

The reporter did not doubt O'Connell. For it was demonstrable that
not only had O'Connell needled Thomson in seasons past but also that

he had seen a spyglass firsthand, the Senator having been a Giant when in 1959 born-again Worthington issued his ultimatum. And so while Reichler did not seek comment from Thomson, he did from Ford Frick. "If such a charge were substantiated," promised the baseball commissioner, "I would forfeit the game. But I would have to have evidence."

That Frick threatened forfeiture of baseball's greatest game made clear that a Reichler dispatch was not just another allegation. It was the Shot Heard Round the World now slandered. And baseball wished its Hope Diamond unscratched.

For all his bluster, however, the commissioner had slung an empty threat. For Frick was careful to note that he "certainly would not be guided by rumor." And the AP story was nothing more. Its four hundred words did not name a single player—save Thomson by implication. Its alleged cheating had no verifiable beginning. And most important, its source was anonymous.

On the morning of March 23, 1962, Thomson was blindsided. Here, in hundreds of papers, was word that a magical home run ought be viewed through the lens of a telescope.

It was Protestant propriety that had reared Thomson, the boy told always "Do what's right." And it was his decorum above all that decades later swayed his counselors at Stevens. Suddenly, though, that which defined Thomson and always would—"the meaty portion of the first sentence of his obituary," put it Roger Angell—was seen as to some degree fraudulent. And so on this Friday morning, the Scot sat behind his desk distraught.

Thomson had a decade past acted no worse than his teammates. And that he had in 1951 benefited from a manager's plan—that signals were for him not a distraction—was unsurprising, Thomson having helped in 1943 his fellow Air Corps privates with Morse code. But because it was he who had hit a home run, who had turned hero, it was he forced now, ten years later, to answer a ringing phone. The AP wanted comment.

Just across town on West 67th Street sat Branca beside Howard Cosell. The sportscaster had in January invited him to co-host *Speaking of Sports*, a radio program that would recap game by game the travails of the expansion Mets. Though the job paid $50 for thirty minutes (and cost far more in insurance not sold), Branca accepted, had commuted since spring training from Mutual to mike, broadcasting from either a padded room in Cosell's Stamford home or a soundproofed Manhattan studio. It was there, beside Café des Artistes, that Branca now sat with Cosell. And as they prepared to chew over on WABC a 4–3 Met win in

Vero Beach, producer Larry Goodman ripped a story from the wires. "Larry came in to Cosell's office," says Branca, "and read the AP report."

Branca listened. And he thrilled. At last, on a breezy Friday in March, a secret was out. Millions knew what he knew. The revelation, Branca told himself, would surely lasso and hog-tie his legacy as loser. He told himself too that it would show him to be a man. For the backlash of his finger-pointing past had learned the pitcher. ("It was so ingrained to not be accusatory," he says.) And when the public would ask him about a secret, he would grudgingly acknowledge that while years ago it had been whispered to him, he had never felt it his place to profane a miracle.

And so, when asked now for comment by Cosell, Branca demurred. "I said I knew about it but I didn't want to talk about it," says Branca. Calls followed from the wires, the pitcher turning Solomonic, condemning a pennant as stolen but pardoning a home run. "Thomson didn't get advance notice of that pitch," Branca told UPI. He insinuated to the AP, however, the opposite. "I tried to brush him back a bit but I didn't get the ball in tight enough," said Branca, able suddenly after ten Octobers to label a pitch imperfect. "I always figured he just outguessed me."

Thirteen stories above Park Avenue, Thomson was quick with his response. "It positively isn't so," he told Reichler. "That's the most ridiculous thing I ever heard of. If I'd been getting signals, why wouldn't I have hit the first pitch? It was a fat one right down the middle." Hero, like goat, then vacillated, moving beyond a denial. "There are some things, I think, which are the private business of the ball clubs," said Thomson. "They shouldn't get beyond the playing fields. But there are always some malcontents who want to kick up a fuss." Thomson had a message for the malcontent in question. "Show some character," he chided. "Come out in the open and reveal yourself." In time O'Connell would, the father of four fessing up privately to Thomson before a heart attack behind the wheel killed him in 1969.

The interview over, another began, Met announcer Ralph Kiner asking Thomson about a telescope. Put on air, the honest salesman lied publicly for the first time in his thirty-nine years. "I said," recalls Thomson, " 'You mean Leo Durocher would steal signs?' I didn't admit it. I didn't admit it to anyone."

Neither on this day did Mays, Lockman, Westrum, Jansen, Dark or Stoneham, the Giants, artful dodgers all, seconding from a ballpark in Mesa the denial of their former skipper. "No, no, no," said Durocher in Vero Beach, the Lip a Los Angeles coach. "There was no buzzer. There was no information for Bobby to go on. He used his own judgment."

Baseball, meantime, beyond the threat of Frick, was unsure how to respond. For regarding the theft of its signs, the game had in recent years continued to give off mixed signals.

On June 23, 1956, American League president Will Harridge (in response to a protest filed by Baltimore manager Paul Richards) had ruled that stealing signs was not illegal, "even if they are stolen," *Sports Illustrated* put it, "by a man in a long black beard carrying a brass telescope." Five seasons later, however, in a letter about scoreboard spies, his successor Joe Cronin had warned several clubs that "this office cannot stress too strongly the objections to this practice and the severe penalty that might be involved."

And so now again did the blaspheming of a Holy of Holies reveal baseball as schizophrenic. For while, despite the Cronin memo, there remained in March of 1962 nothing in its rule book against the stealing of signs, baseball wished action be taken. In short order would pitcher Spahn propose that offending owners be fined, manager Tebbetts that offending skippers be suspended without pay, and commissioner Frick that a rule on spies be written to render "the practice illegal in strong language."

Nine days after the Reichler story, sportswriter Dick Young reported that baseball had in fact instituted just such a rule the winter previous. The rule, according to an unnamed National League official, was blunt: "Should a team be proven to have employed mechanical means to steal signs during a ball game, the game shall be declared forfeited."

Young, however, was wrong. For just as baseball had not enacted the sign-stealing ban put forward after the shenanigans of 1909, this latest rule had not found its way into the rule book. Neither would what Frick was now proposing. Baseball would yet again spurn legislation it itself had drafted.

The Reichler report had nonetheless spurred a hidebound national pastime to look anew upon the Thomson home run. And so now did Branca allow himself hope that he too might get a second glance, prepping his daughters just hours after the AP story with a first word of crooked Giants. "Lying and stealing to us—they were horrible people," says Patti, then nine and in Catholic school. "And here's Bobby Thomson and he's the hero. It was very confusing."

It was confusing to Branca too. For in the coming days and weeks, he found a scarlet letter unfaded. Passersby still yipped, a fastball still sold insurance, Cosell still wondered on air how Branca had felt after a homer. ("It was a question Cosell never tired of asking," wrote the *Washington Post.*) When on April 13 the Mets opened play at the Polo

Grounds, their interim home, "Ralph Branca was there, with an abject grin," wrote Murray Kempton, "to be photographed pointing to the fatal spot in left field." It was, in short, life as usual, a published rumor if anything peeving the public. Wrote the hometown *San Francisco News–Call Bulletin:* "No responsible wire service should dredge up a yarn."

Months passed. And on July 14, lineups of retired Dodgers and Giants readied for their annual bath in nostalgia. Branca was among the Old-Timers invited to play at the Polo Grounds. He would pitch, then talk on WABC of the Met game to follow.

Little Patti Branca sat beside her father on the drive to the park, a birthday girl of ten dressed in peach. She was eager to watch her daddy pitch. And when at 11 o'clock he entered a clubhouse then jogged afield, Patti took a seat above the home dugout, flowers of tan and white pretty-tying her sleeveless shirt.

All about were happy reunions—Durocher with Franks, Casey Stengel with Zack Wheat, Thomson with Yvars, Mueller, Irvin and Stanky, Branca with Hodges, Snider, Robinson and King. But Branca reacquainted now also with the fans, hundreds pecking at him like so much carrion. "I heard 'bum, disgrace,' " says Patti. "They were tearing my dad apart."

The taunts found their mark. For as painful to Branca as a home run had been traumatic and a secret shocking, was that the laying bare of a telescope had not one iota changed his lot, the helicopter come to his rescue departing without him. And when now his daughter Patti began to cry, the exasperated pitcher set off to whisk her away. Reporter Dick Young, however, stopped Branca in the dugout, he who in 1952 had chided the pitcher for heckling an ump, speaking of pride. Pitcher stepped back afield, Young into the stands to console a child.

There remained, however, the unfortunate matter of Branca v Thomson. That an encore neither wanted would nonetheless be staged was a surety, the men long ago sacrificed to the needs of a public like sanbenitos at an auto-da-fé. As Branca now warmed for his reprisal, a photographer approached. Thomson agreed to a photo. Branca did not. "I'm not going to pose with that ——," *Sports Illustrated,* censoring, quoted the pitcher. "I'm human. It's taken years to live down that hurt. If you want a picture, take one of the guy with the binoculars who was stealing our signs that day. There's your picture."

Eight years after learning a secret, Branca had finally snapped.

Thomson stood nearby, his hair grayed, his uniform yellowed. It had been easy in March to laugh off an AP report over the phone, to defend publicly his legacy. But on this summer Saturday it was not, Thomson discomforted as he had only been a decade earlier in the five at-bats versus Branca after the home run. For it was in the presence of his doppelgänger that a home run reminded both that never since did Branca shine. And it was in the presence of his doppelgänger that the mention of a telescope was a shot to the sternum. "Uncomfortable," recalls Thomson. "Uncomfortable." Thomson shrugged and said nothing, batter and pitcher unable to speak of a secret that plagued them both.

Harder and harder Branca threw to a Duke named Snider and a King named Clyde, warming now for the one-inning game. The Polo Grounds slowly filled, and Branca found the ear of reporter Howard Tuckner. "Nobody remembers that at twenty-one I won twenty-one games," he said. "Nobody remembers that at twenty-five I had seventy-five wins. All they remember is the homer. It was a good pitch. It was a cheap home run. But the good that men do is oft interred with their bones and the evil lives on. Shakespeare. Julius Caesar. I went to college."

It was 2:00 p.m. when Jack Doscher, at eighty-two the oldest living Dodger, tossed a first pitch. More Dodger than Giant fans were about, and player introductions saw Thomson booed and Branca cheered.

Brooklyn went quickly in the top of the first, New York down to a last out in the bottom of the inning when Irvin set to face King. But, yuck-yuck, Durocher and Dressen replaced them with Thomson and Branca. Wrote Tuckner in the *New York Times,* Branca "seemed sad as he appeared on the field."

A light rain began to fall and Robinson ran to the mound with a word for Branca. The old friends laughed. But the pitcher quickly sobered. This Irvin told Thomson, the Scot answering in jest that a brushback pitch would not surprise. Durocher pointed to left field, Thomson dug in, and Branca looked to Herman Franks, unaware that eleven years prior it was his catcher who had stolen a sign. Branca fired. His fastball drilled Thomson in the foot.

It is likely that never before had Old-Timer hit Old-Timer, likely even that never had such a pitcher thrown so hard. Thomson, though, did not take first base. "I just stayed up there," he says, all left to assume that a pitch had hit dirt. Thomson let pass for strike one a replica of the fastball he had years ago tomahawked, then swung at strike two. A fourth fastball brushed him back, no exhibition this, Branca slavering if not for revenge then for an undoing of his lot—of eleven years a goat, of the inconsequence of revelations, of a crying daughter. After a foul ball, Thomson managed a high fly to short center field.

But Branca did not win. He could not win. For no sooner did Snider glove a ball than thousands, even those who had this afternoon cheered Branca, let ring one theme: "*Now* you get him out!" And when Snider heaved a ball over an upper deck behind third, Branca rued that he had been made a spectacle, that word of a blowup—of a photo with Thomson not taken—would surely make a national magazine, a blot on only his escutcheon. Little Patti began again to cry, and Branca headed for the green door of the clubhouse, a carapace hardening about him. Thomson hustled to center field too. "I was happy to get out of there," he says. "I was tired of this Branca-Thomson thing."

TWENTY-FOUR

There are, it is true, those who lie consciously, coldly falsifying reality itself, but more numerous are those who weigh anchor, move off, momentarily or forever, from genuine memories, and fabricate for themselves a convenient reality.

—PRIMO LEVI, *The Drowned and the Saved*, 1986
(translated by Raymond Rosenthal)

RALPH BRANCA STOOD BEFORE a buzzer and thirty numbered squares, a contestant on the game show *Concentration*. He had watched the show from its 1958 inception, matched with ease what lay behind those squares, solved the picture-puzzles revealed with each remembered pair. So much better was Branca than the contestants host Hugh Downs enriched weekdays that in 1961 he had called NBC, aced an audition and won seventeen straight games, then the most ever on the program.

Two years later, on Friday, September 13, 1963, Branca led Arthur Levine in a face-off of former champs when Levine insisted in a Rockefeller Center studio that his answer to a third rebus had beaten the buzzer. Fearful of a lawsuit, NBC awarded Levine the game. Branca did not win another, he who in 1946 had lost the first baseball playoff game losing come Monday the second game-show playoff.

Branca, though, had won—both a raft of prizes (a swimming pool, diamond ring, china) and the admiration of the public. And, taken with his memory, the public continued to call upon Branca to use it, to reminisce daily—at work, at home, on the street—of his brush with Thomson. "I have a running gag," Branca told reporter Gerald Eskenazi. "After two questions, I ask, 'Isn't somebody going to ask me how I felt when . . . ? It's always the third question.' "

His answer was always the same, he who had held a fated ball belittling *its* hold on him. "An hour after the game, the Thomson home run was killing me," Branca would soon tell *Sport* magazine. "I felt rotten. Then I got over it, then it was something in the past. It never bothered me after that. It was a blessing in disguise. That's what it was, a blessing in disguise."

Thus did Branca, thirty-seven, counter what he had in anger let slip at the 1962 Old-Timers' Day game—that it had "taken years to live down that hurt"—settling instead on hurt that had lasted one hour and then turned to blessing. It was a comfortable narrative.

It was also akin to the retellings of *all* who might be held accountable for the home run. Catcher Walker would tell daughter Deborah that manager Dressen had called the pitch. Dressen would allege that he had tried to whistle for the curve. Pitcher Newcombe would maintain that he had wanted to remain in the game. Even umpire Conlan would write that he had questioned Dressen about his relief. "Branca? A *fastball* pitcher?"

Branca, meantime, had not only to play down the degree of his burn but to coat it with aloe, to pin his decline on a 1952 pratfall. "That home run didn't crush me," he would tell *Sport* magazine. "My back injury, that was the whole thing. If it hadn't been for that, I'd be pitching today." (Branca had not mentioned the spill when, just months after he fell coccyx-on-Coke, he ran down his injuries in an article he wrote for *Sport*.)

If there was what to blame for a diminished career, it may have been overuse in August of 1951. For having thrown 1,548 pitches through May, June and July—a comfortable 516 per month—Branca then threw, at the behest of Dressen, 808 in August, the most he had in any one month since June of 1948. (In 10 subsequent 1951 outings, his ERA, 2.60 until then, was 5.93. And Branca would never fully return to form.)

That Thomson, meantime, *had* been done in by injury was glaringly clear, his career felled in 1954 by a broken ankle. But, wary of alibis and embarrassed by a slide, he never mentioned this.

It was another episode that left Thomson unsure of what to say and even of what had happened. And as the discomforting question of a stolen sign was so seldom put to him, he did not force himself to reminiscence in search of an answer.

Endlessly, though, Thomson told of the home run. And within his soliloquy that took shape over years, within his telling of the injury to Mueller (just before the home run), there evolved an intimated out. Thomson in 1955: "The delay really helped me. . . . I was concerned only with getting a hit." Thomson in 1959: "I was worrying about [Mueller] instead of me." Thomson in 1986: "I didn't pay that much attention to the pitching change. I was watching them work on Mueller." Thomson in 1991: "People have asked me if the crowd noise affected me. Well, to tell the truth, I felt like I was the only guy in the ballpark." Thomson in 1996: "Well, I was in the ballpark all by myself. I wasn't aware of the crowd." Thomson in 2000: "I was like a mechanical doll. . . . I wasn't aware of anyone else in the ballpark but me."

Here then—conscious or not—was the only plausible explanation that a stolen sign had gone unnoticed. For barring a trance, a daze, how else to imagine Thomson not glancing toward right field where Yvars offered information? To know that a teammate sits just a shift of the eyes away and yet not take note is near impossible.

The memory did more than parry a telescope. It enabled the anhedonic Scot to take pleasure in a home run. "I take credit," Thomson oft concluded his soliloquy, "for sitting back and waiting for the ball."

Despite a baseball career that even a friend could only call frustrating, Branca did not struggle to tout it, ready always with a point of pride, with his 21 wins at age twenty-one. But to recollect his career meant also to reconcile, with a mulish sense of self, the failures of a dozen seasons. And as we all do, Branca confabulated. The *Concentration* king did not recall taunting the Giants with song in April 1951. He did not recall being benched in the 1952 World Series (remembering instead that he was *ineligible* to play). And counter to what he himself had written in 1952, Branca did not recall that it was *his* decision to drop the number 13. "The team management had changed my number to twelve," Branca told Ira Berkow in 1981. "I was livid."

Looking back demanded further that the goat be ready with recriminations. He was. On losing in the limelight: "Every postseason game I started, I got one run." On retirement: "That idiot Alston pitched me without a warm-up and hurt my [biceps] tendon." On the Thomson drive: "It would not have been a home run in any other park."

This last claim is likely true. The home run landed roughly two rows over the 315-foot sign of a 17-foot wall. Two photos of the ball in flight, coupled with its dip beneath an overhang 21 feet over left field, put its approximate projected distance at 340 to 355 feet. (The landing point squares with radio broadcasts which reveal the ball airborne some three-plus seconds.) Thomson's shot would therefore in most of the thirteen other ballparks have been caught where it landed, some six degrees to the right of the left-field foul line. Had it flown in Fenway Park, it would have caromed off the wall for a hit. And had it flown in Braves Field or Ebbets Field, it *may* have done the same.

Branca, of course, held true one more contention. And the secret out, he would in time tell any and all—from teammate Cal Abrams to baseball memorabilia king Barry Halper—that the Giants had cheated. The accepted view of the home run, however, would not change. And Thomson spoke for many when he lamented to the *New York Journal American* that a homer had "ruined the baseball career of a fine young man."

A telescope, in fact, went entirely unmentioned in the ever-more-frequent autopsies of 1951. As Arnold Hano wrote in 1966: "Down the stretch . . . they roared, ignited by Monte Irvin's hitting, Dark's hitting, Thomson's play, Maglie's and Jansen's pitching and Westrum's catching, steadied by Dark and Stanky's work around second, by Lockman's daily improvement at first (in the beginning he didn't know which foot to use on the bag, and pop flies were a source of puzzlement) by Mueller's stroked base hits to all fields—but inspired mainly by the presence of Willie Mays. How else did it happen?"

The Giants knew how else. And so, in 1963, the team asked Henry Colletti to jury-rig in San Francisco a better mousetrap, the maintenance man wiring a pine box with lightbulbs and push-buttons. Put in center field, the box was in use when, on the last day of the season, Herman Franks took over as Giant manager, in use as four straight seasons under Franks the club finished second.

As 1964 neared, Branca stewed. For while the hurts of a home run and telescope had dulled since 1951 and 1954, the half-life of a third trauma—the fruitless airing of a secret—had begun to elapse only in 1962. And so, though more and more Branca made peace with a home run, he did not with Thomson, the result a modified routine, Branca happy to sing his goat song but only alone. This he did, "Because of You" soloed this spring to both the New York writers and Dodger brass.

Branca had in winter left TV station WOR, let lapse both his job with Cosell and *Branca's Bullpen,* a Met pregame show he had hosted in 1963. ("Not enough money in it," he says.) And outside the eight days Branca spent this August in Windham Center, Connecticut, head instructor of a baseball camp he had begun in 1962, it was only insurance that high over 42nd Street filled his workweek.

Little more than a homer away, another salesman sat suspended over Manhattan. Thomson, forty, would earn this year $13,000, *half* his final baseball salary four years past. And yet he had double the mouths to feed, Bobby Jr. born the February past, Megan this March (father taking back the baby gear he had long ago given the neighbors).

On April 10, 1964, demolition of the Polo Grounds began. "Very well built," noted Harry Avirom, veep of the Wrecking Corporation of America. "It could have lasted forever." But it did not. Forty-nine years after the eponymous Coogan had died, onlookers atop his bluff watched the vital parts of a ballfield resected in preparation for transplant—oodles of chairs and piping and sod to live on in other parks. Off to Closter, New Jersey, went seventy of Chadwick's lamps. Off to Cooperstown went a canvas base, a metal turnstile, a wooden plank, a cotton pennant. And already preserved on celluloid was the very room where coach Franks had encamped with telescope, Lucille Ball and Victor Mature walking about a clubhouse in the 1949 film *Easy Living*, the wire mesh of a fourth window not yet clipped.

Still, a ballpark disappeared in short order, 120 red brick stories to rise in its bathtub-shaped footprint. "We are stabbed by the realization," eulogized Roger Angell, "that we may not possess the score cards and record books to help us remember who we are and what we have seen and loved." Indeed, the only trace of the diamond that had preceded the housing project was a bronze plaque listing six Giant championships. Affixed to a support, it read: APPROXIMATE LOCATION OF HOME PLATE.

Thomson found time in 1964 to reminisce of the lost park, paid by Schaefer beer $100 a pop at some fifteen gigs. He endorsed Viceroy cigarettes too, a TV spot ("Not too strong. Not too light . . ."), hooking at once he who had never smoked, a decade passing before a pack-a-day habit gave way to a pipe. It was further income from Lehman stocks and Arizona land that helped Thomson purchase now a Cape Cod on the Jersey shore. There in Beach Haven he would unwind two weeks in August, cocktails at six, dinner by candlelight, pie crusts homemade, Winkie in her platinum wedding ring and Ferragamo shoes insistent on ambience, on weaning her husband from the simple and frugal ways of his father and mother.

Come December, Elizabeth Thomson succumbed to liver cancer, about her neck a gold "23." The following winter, her orphaned son, five years retired, turned eligible for the Hall of Fame. Needing 75 percent of the vote, he got just four—12 of 302 ballots swayed by a home run. A very good career was in no way as great as an autumn afternoon, and Thomson would never get more than 13 votes, would never join his bat in upstate New York. No matter. The salesman had moved beyond ball. Read his performance review in November 1966, "Bob Thomson is one of the hardest working men in the New York District."

Branca was no longer mere blocks away. Tired of his commute, he left Mutual this same year to sell pension plans for Guardian Life Insurance Company in Scarsdale, New York. And as goat wished less and less to affiliate with hero (declining a recent offer to pitch Schaefer beer), their meetings were reduced to polite collaborations—handprints in cement at the 1964 World's Fair, a photo at a 1965 Old-Timers' Day game, seats on a 1966 dais among trucking executives. Anything more would discomfort, Branca bristling when in May of 1967 his old bête noire sat just across the aisle on a flight to Toronto. "I was not very pleasant to him," says Branca. "I didn't say anything. I was pissed." Thomson recalls the trip differently. "We talked," he says. "I would remember that as friendly."

And so, decades later, Branca believed that he had acted in anger knowing Thomson had publicly denied a spyglass. Thomson believed that there was no anger in Branca across the aisle. One was apt to remember the fallout of a stolen sign and one to forget.

Branca and Thomson landed. They who more than once since a home run had sung a song and posed mid-strangle and battled afield as retirees headed now in jackets and ties to the Royal York Hotel to headline a dinner in support of sandlot ball. "Branca revealed," noted the *Globe and Mail*, "it was the first time he and Thomson had appeared together as guest speakers."

Branca spoke first, 388 fans hearing tell of a bad back and the wresting away of his number 13. Thomson followed, promising to omit "a few of the things I usually say about Ralph." A room laughed and Thomson told of a home run hit not off Branca but Elmer Riddle, a rolling ball he said was lost under a bullpen bench. It did not matter that the *New York Times* had described the 1949 homer as a "tremendous smash in deep left." Thomson had found a story suitable to the occasion. For it was really to Branca that he spoke, and to him that spoke Branca. And so it was in Toronto that five years after the airing of a secret, goat and hero again found, if not friendship, détente, poised—one with moxie, one with humility—to meet together the years ahead. There remained only the matter of confronting what had nearly torn them apart.

TWENTY-FIVE

Can two walk together, except they be agreed?
—AMOS 3:3, King James Bible

THOMSON HAD LONG STOPPED plugging rotgut and smokes when, in August 1967, he assumed the office of a Watchung councilman skipped town. Debates in Borough Hall left him sweated but still he ran to complete the term, edging opponent James Murphy by *five* votes then slipping from office, able come 1969 to focus at newly named Westvaco Corporation on his promotion to national accounts sales representative of multi-wall bags.

Branca had new work too, joining in 1970 Security Mutual. But he missed ball. And so a second spring he drove weekends from White Plains to Rye, throwing on a high school diamond to Greg O'Brien, Fairfield University catcher and friend to his daughters. Branca even tossed a few afternoons of Met batting practice, a gig he hoped might lead to a job. But outside that offer in 1961 to coach at NYU, "nobody asked me to work in baseball," the old pitcher confided now to the *Sporting News.* Come October 1971, twentieth anniversary of an imperfect pitch, Branca still had gotten no offers. He never would. And so it was that as Thomson eschewed baseball, baseball eschewed Branca.

The men, though, no longer eschewed each other, their relationship having thawed in Toronto. They sang their song for cartoonists, mugged for a society of Jews, coached actors in a game of ball and played ball themselves—Old-Timer Thomson for a change pitching to Branca, pitcher skying to center field at Shea. "They're a more famous team," wrote Bob Addie in the *Sporting News,* "than Martin and Rowan or Nixon and Kissinger." But built on a fault line, their relationship was imbalanced. When this fall of 1971 Thomson readied for a celebrity tennis tournament, he lamented that Branca would not be on hand. "Maybe [Pancho] Gonzales should have invited him," Thomson told reporter

Willie Klein, "and he would have the chance to even things." This hero wished for near as much as goat.

On October 13, 1972, Richard Nixon welcomed the pair to Washington. The ballplayers would in twenty-five days vote for the president a second time. But the budding scandal dubbed Watergate displeased even Republican Thomson and, steps from the Oval Office, he turned now to a presidential aide. "I said, 'I don't like reading all this stuff in the paper,' " recalls Thomson. "I said why don't they do something about it, get it off the paper and get rid of it as a story? He said the president is making his own study of it. I wasn't satisfied with that. . . . Get it out, get it off the table, admit it. Why kid yourself?"

Fifty-six days after Nixon resigned his office, Thomson, fifty, chose to keep quiet a heist. It was October 3, 1974—anniversary of a home run— and for weeks, large posters of Thomson and Branca painted in primitive American style had advertised in subway stations the PBS television program on which they now appeared alongside Durocher, Snider, Mays, Newcombe and announcer Harwell. Natty in tweed and turtleneck, sideburn and afro, the men peddled myth twenty-three years after a sublime season. Thomson said the Thomsons and Brancas were good friends. Branca denied he had taunted Giants. Newcombe denied he had wanted out of a game. Snider said he had run after a ball. PBS passed off as genuine the tape of Branca whimpering to producer Greenspan. Harwell said it was only owing to fan Larry Goldberg that the Hodges call had survived.

Time had burnished the gravelly call, surefire portal to an October afternoon. A Cub fan named Joel Schuster would, upon hearing Hodges, cry so regularly that the recording turned cure for hiccups. A brother and sister in Flatbush named Meir and Miriam Feder would mimic the call when they wished to zing mother Judy who, heartbroken at ten, had tuned in in Danville, Virginia. A professor of education named Marc Glassman, who had been tossed as toddler while his father listened to WMCA, says, "Every time I hear that, I have this sense of being thrown." A Dodger fan named Jerry Stern who received a copy of the LP from an impudent stepfather broke and buried it in his Sea Gate, Brooklyn, backyard.

That same sepulchral record played in the summer of 1976 as Old-Timer Branca jogged onto fields in Texas and California. A fellow retiree spoke up. "Hey, Ralph," said Ralph Kiner, Branca remembering his words to author Golenbock. "What are you doing? You don't need this crap." Indeed, the annual exhibitions had only flayed, Branca booed when hit by Mike McCormick and DiMaggio, discomforted even when

Thomson went deep off Van Lingle Mungo. And so it was that Branca, fifty, would not again play in such a game for twenty-one years.

The calendar turned to October 3, old lovers of New York and Brooklyn commemorating a silver anniversary with habits that had in twenty-five years become ritual. In Alexandria, Virginia, Betsy Engelken wished husband Albert a happy anniversary though the Giant fan had married her in August. In Far Rockaway, New York, Dodger fan Emil Lucev aimed a dart at a photo of Thomson he had years before mounted on a woodblock in his living room for an annual toss.

That the joy and pain of a New York minute had in twenty-five years not lessened was clear. The home run was "an unhealed wound," wrote author Larry Freundlich. But he who opened the wound had ever since admitted only to his well-being. "That home run never bothered me at all," Branca told the *Sporting News* in 1969. "It was one of the best things to happen to me." Twenty years later he would again vow as much, telling the magazine that it had taken him but one hour to recover from Thomson's blow. But if Branca was able (in any measure of time) to let the home run lie as he had let lie a secret, the airing of that secret and the musings of humble but human Thomson, he grappled still with a public that since 1951 had greeted his every signature on a credit card slip with derision.

Even his peers, in fact, did not leave be the peace Branca had made with an 0–1 pitch. When these years later Branca told Maglie that his fastball to Thomson was meant to set up a curve, the Giant pitcher snapped: "Dago, if you wanted him to hit the curve, why didn't you throw him a fucking curve?"

Suddenly, Branca had had his fill of a second generation of second-guesses. The silver of an anniversary was for Branca only tarnish.

"For twenty-five years, I'd have to say I tolerated going through that ordeal," Branca later told the *New York Times*. He no longer could. "I had had it," he said. "I was tired of being introduced as being the guy who threw the home run pitch." Branca sought to express the interminableness of his lot. "A guy commits murder and he gets pardoned after twenty years," he told reporter Malcolm Moran. "I didn't get pardoned."

Other goats did. "Sisler hit a home run off Newcombe and won a pennant for Philadelphia, and Mazeroski hit a home run off Ralph Terry to win the World Series, and Bench hit a home run off somebody to win the pennant in a playoff game," Branca told author Golenbock. "You never hear about those things."

A pardon had yet to be granted when by decade's end Branca and wife moved to the very same country club where a 1949 dinner dance had been their first date. For the popular memory of Ralph Branca had almost literally come to consist of but one pitch. Read a question submitted by one Robert Cline of Phoenix to the *Sporting News* on January 5, 1980: "Is it true Ralph Branca never pitched another game in the major leagues after giving up the winning home run to Bobby Thomson in the 1951 National League playoff?"

Cline had barely gotten his answer when, on Opening Day 1980, the Mets trotted out the pitcher head-bent and crying—a full-page photo in a play for fans. "This is dedicated," read the ad by Jerry Della Femina, "to the guys who cried when Thomson connected with Branca's 0 and 1 pitch." Branca seethed.

For as long as fans had turned the knife, Branca had turned his cheek. When a merchant at Sherry-Lehmann, for example, signed the invoices sent to the pitcher "Bobby Thomson," Branca simply shopped for wine elsewhere. But the Mets were baseball. And, disrespected, the old goat combed New York Civil Rights Law with help from an attorney, Section 50 classifying as misdemeanor the misuse of a name. Ann Branca prevailed on her husband not to sue, Branca contenting himself with word from new owner Wilpon that an ad would cease and desist. It did.

But the pull of a home run would never cease, Octobers an annual undertow dragging the goat back to the counterclockwise dance of a hero. Branca spoke of the anniversary on October 3, 1981. "I've lived with this thing for thirty years," he told reporter Ira Berkow. "And, really, I think it's about time it died."

But on it lived. For the home run had in three decades ribboned through American culture. Novels *Goodbye, Bobby Thomson! Goodbye, John Wayne!* and *The Orange Air* used the men as metaphor. Episode number 200 of the TV show *M*A*S*H* starred the homer as McGuffin while in the movie *The Godfather* it was a spritz of Americana, director Francis Ford Coppola cuing the ballgame on a car radio mid-murder of Sonny Corleone. Wrote Coppola, "it did seem to work perfectly and so it made its way into the sound track."

Art and literature would continue to pay homage. A cartooned broadcaster on television's *The Simpsons* would wail, Hodges-like, "The Isotopes win a game! The Isotopes win a game!" Men of letters, business and science would go weak-kneed, Roger Angell to declare the homer "the grand exclamation point in the history of the pastime," Michael Steinhardt to relay his happy tears, Abraham Pais to assert (with definitiveness unbecoming a theoretical physicist) that all other home runs were "never, repeat *never*, as dramatic as Thomson's." And among the many to render the shot in acrylic and song and verse were an impressionistic LeRoy Neiman, balladeer Terry Cashman and Joseph Pacheco, his poem titled "Where were you on October 3, 1951?"

Thirty years on, Thomson and Branca had ripened to reference, the men used by ministers and teachers and historians to make real everyone from humble apostle Peter to overshadowed Johann Ludwig Bach to one-time wonder Harry Blackmun to the eternal youths in Keats's Grecian urn. Each had also turned figure of speech. Shamed philosopher J. L. Austin suffered, wrote the *New York Times,* "the philosophical equivalent of the Ralph Branca syndrome." The *Washington Post* quoted the caveat of a defense lawyer on what seemed a lost case: "Don't forget Bobby Thomson." And the public continued to employ the men as parable, journalist Dorothy Rabinowitz seeing self-determination in the stroke of a Giant, that "there is always a future if you will it," Rudolph Giuliani alerting beaten attorneys to he who had best utilized defeat. "Had Ralph Branca not thrown that pitch," said Giuliani, become this same year associate attorney general, "he would not have his place in history." This Branca knew. And this after thirty years he rued, the pitcher shanghaied by the Shot Heard Round the World. "I really wish," he allowed at last, "it never happened."

Thomson, meantime, had long been ambivalent about where the homer had landed *him.* "I sometimes wish I hadn't done it," the hitter told the *New York Journal American* in 1961. "Everything I've done since has fallen short." Secure a decade later in a second career, Thomson was only a bit less sorry. "Honestly it was the only thing I did in my lifetime," he told folks at the Brooklyn Chamber of Commerce in 1970, "but I don't play that record for my kids before they go to bed each night." Another decade hence, Thomson put word on his résumé of his former glory, hailing himself the "Perpetrator of the 'Miracle of Coogan's Bluff.' "

That rumors continued to profane the miracle nettled Thomson. "It's reared its ugly head every once in a while," he says. And it was now, on its thirtieth anniversary, that a phone call from another reporter had the perpetrator again swearing to its sanctity. "No," Thomson told the *Los Angeles Times.* "I had no help from any illegal sign-stealing on the homer." Branca in turn told reporter Earl Gustkey that he had no desire to speak of the playoff, that over the years he had "talked about that day so much it was like the water was up to my nostrils." But goat then stepped from the gangplank. "The Giants cheated and stole the pennant in 1951," said Branca, "and that's the truth." And so page 11 of the *Times* carried word of a buzzer, word that just as Thomson had pulled a fast one—lining to left a fastball—so had a miracle team.

Thomson, meantime, had punctuated his denial with a familiar refrain. "If I was tipped to the pitches that day," he told Gustkey, "I wouldn't have taken that first pitch. It was a fastball right down the pike."

This would seem a fair point. Statistician Roth had charted every pitch thrown Thomson by Dodger arms in 1951, and evident is that Thomson became more aggressive after July 20. While he had swung at a first pitch just twice in 15 home at-bats versus Brooklyn before the inauguration of a scheme, he did so in 13 of 26 at-bats afterward. And while pre-telescope he had let pass the first *two* pitches of such at-bats 7 of 15 times, post-telescope he did so just 6 of 26 times—usually swinging instead, as he had against Branca on October 3.

All the while, Thomson took pride in his steady sales of industrial packaging, the former straphanger happy that since 1978 a commute had shrunk to the eleven steps to his basement.

It was in winter of 1983 that a Baptist reverend named Ronald Durham changed forever the relationship of hero and goat. Durham owned a New Jersey sports promotion firm. And when it now occurred to him that they who together had ruined his 1951 could pack a room, he asked each if he might for three hours sit beside the other and sign memorabilia.

Baseball cards and autographs had turned adult pursuits, and Thomson, crush of the forty-something, had done some shows. Branca had not. "I didn't quite know how much I should ask from [Durham]," the pitcher told reporter Bill Madden in February. "But to tell you the truth, it was kind of nice just to be asked."

On December 27, 1983, Branca and Thomson signed on for a thousand dollars each. Eighty-eight days later, atop a table in the ballroom of a New Jersey Sheraton, they signed and signed more, an endless queue of aging men tugged to Hasbrouck Heights by nostalgia and worship and schadenfreude and investment. "Guys had suitcases," says Branca. "Thirty-three items."

The twin signatures were clear, Thomson at sixty still "Bobby," Branca setting apart the capital "R" of a first name as had done his aunt Rose. Signing together a first time, the men found a rhythm, alternating as they would forevermore who signed on top and who on bottom. Partners but not quite friends, Thomson and Branca spoke little. "They didn't have a meaningful conversation," says Durham, the reverend seated this spring Saturday between them. "It was very polite."

More shows followed, the most famous winner-loser tandem in American sport for rent. Branca turned to Thomson: "I said, 'Bob, these guys are making a lot of money. Maybe we ought to get more.' " And so the men upped their fee to two grand each, signing and hearing tell where thousands were when, the collateral damage of a home run revealed piecemeal—Thomson told by a sorry fan that at 3:58 p.m. on October 3, 1951, he had slipped in a bathtub and broken his wrist, Branca by another that he had at last been situated to lose his virginity when the consummatory shot intervened.

Hero and goat were headlining by 1986 some five shows a year. And hours side by side, the men found common ground—from their dogs Licorice and Grumpy to their daughters in dental hygiene to their staunch support of both the integration of baseball and the Vietnam War. The fan found in them common ground too, hard to tell who had won and who had lost, a pair together treating (as Rudyard Kipling had implored) those two impostors Triumph and Disaster just the same.

And so as two signatures overlapped time and again, the relationship of a hero and goat steadily warmed—and a secret grew ever harder to broach.

The regular reliving of a loss, meantime, was for Branca double-edged. "He was always sensitive," says Thomson. "Someone would say something and Ralph would holler at him. I felt uncomfortable being around him." Says Branca, "I got tired of man's inhumanity to man. . . . You don't bring up something a man doesn't want to be remembered for." Observed reporter Mike Lupica this same year: "Branca looks at you and what he really says is, 'Listen to me, I was more than one lousy fastball.' "

But why if not for one fastball did a generation wait on line to meet Branca? Branca was booked *because* he lost a game. And that the goat glad-handed beside the hero was what in turn elevated the hero over the humdrum great, over, say, Steve Garvey or Whitey Ford. "It's not about Thomson hitting the homer," wrote DeLillo in *Underworld*. "It's about Branca making the pitch. It's all about losing."

If doubt lingered as to whether it was an unrecoverable loss that had spurred the goat to sell insurance, there was consensus as to why he now turned president of the Baseball Assistance Team. BAT, formed in August of 1986, would support the indigent former big leaguer, and Branca (elected by a panel of retired players) would oversee the annual uplift of fallen stars. "[BAT] subconsciously might be helping me," Branca told reporter Malcolm Moran. "I know there are a lot of guys that are a lot worse off than I am."

Thus did upset mature anew into perspective. And he who had long been only as high and low as the wake of one loss reached out now to those whose hurt hit home—to infielder Bill Buckner who this fall saw a ball roll between his legs, to footballer Scott Norwood who come 1991 would miss a kick wide right, to manager (and son-in-law) Bobby Valentine who come 1992 would be fired—each to learn what author Michael Mandelbaum wrote, that the professional athlete's "frequent and inevitable failures will be personal ones, responsibility for which cannot be shirked, will be universally known, and will be recorded forever."

Recorded as indelibly, of course, were the heroes and, among them, the Bobby Thomsons. "In *social memory*," wrote anthropologist Marshall Sahlins, "such one-time heroes may enjoy more than their allotted fifteen minutes of fame—something like fifteen minutes of immortality." Thus did aging men request to simply meet the immortal whose stance they had mimicked as boys, Thomson to greet in this his fourth score judge Harold Enten at the Manhattan Harvard Club, doctor Pete Paganussi at his Watchung home, transit executive Albert Engelken off exit 10 of the New Jersey Turnpike. "If you have the chance in life to make somebody this happy," the *Wall Street Journal* reported Thomson telling Engelken in October 1989, "you have an obligation to do it."

Seven months later, Thomson and Branca set with Bob Costas to rehash a home run at Runyon's Bar on Second Avenue. Talk turned to reminiscing fans. "Two people came up to me, people I hadn't met before," began Thomson on air. "And you know, 'Hey, can I tell you where I *was*?' And ah, hey, kind of fun you know? Let's face it, because I've got to get up and go to work tomorrow. So you know, I'll, we get a, we get a kick—well, I get a kick out of it. Ralph doesn't. Ralph's had enough of it. Let's face it. But hey, here we are, Ralph." Indeed, here they were their different selves—Thomson desultory and sweet, Branca sensitive and headstrong, one letting the record speak for itself, one not, pitcher compelled to tell of a back injury, of the mismanagement of a rotation, of a short porch in left. But a pas de deux was peaceful. When Branca announced now on air that the homer Thomson hit off him in Game One of the playoff landed "in the first row—and I do mean the *first* row," hero only laughed. "Dressen must've thought an awful lot of him to"—Thomson paused—"to, to work him the way he did." Branca spoke: "Thank you, sir."

It had been thirty-six years since Yvars confirmed for Branca that New York had spied his final fastballs of 1951. In all that time, the backup catcher had not gone public, instead dishing his indictment on the dinner circuit. But on August 27, 1990, at a benefit for spinal-cord-injury research, a reporter was among his audience. "Leo sent Herman Franks to sit up by one of the windows in that center-field clubhouse in the Polo Grounds with a telescope," Phil Mushnick quoted Yvars. "He'd buzz me the signal, then I'd signal our batter." Thus came word in the *New York Post* that, like the 1988 Olympic sprint when Ben Johnson used stanozolol, and the 1980 Boston Marathon when Rosie Ruiz Sholtcart, and the 1965 bridge championship when two in Buenos Aires used finger codes, a pennant was suspect. And thus was a very first 1951 Giant on record about a secret.

It was little coincidence that the canary was Yvars. For not only chirpy, he had been one of the four men *involved*. Says Yvars, "I wanted to tell the truth." He adds, "No one believed it. Who would believe it?"

Who indeed? (Not Mushnick, says the reporter.) For a pennant was sacred and a catcher profane. And those three men who in 1951 had assisted Yvars would not now corroborate the tale. Chadwick had told of a buzzer to but a few electricians in Local 3 when in 1951 he died. Schenz had told of a telescope to few but sons James and Jerald and teammate Jorgensen when in 1988 a heart attack killed *him*. And since retiring from baseball in 1980 to the hills above Salt Lake City, Franks had been mum about his center-field perch. "I have never discussed it," he would later assert at age eighty-six. "If I'm ever asked about it, I'm denying everything."

Yvars soon came clean again, a guest of Ed Randall on cable television in 1991. His teammates boiled. "I saw him," says Thomson. "I said, 'tell me, Sal, do you think there's another guy on this ball club who would have done what you've done talking about signs?'" Another soon would, Mays confessing to Erskine at a golf tournament in Indiana. ("He pulled me over," says the Dodger pitcher. "'You know, Carl, we stole your signs.'") But Yvars had gone public. And so he who four years prior at a TriBeCa dinner had been the lone teammate to celebrate a homer with Thomson was now only rat, pariah of the 1951 Giants.

The public, though, paid Yvars little mind. And it was now an offer came at Thomson to put to print the narrative of his home run and of his life too.

The homer had for years inspired prose. Observed author Daniel Okrent: "Grab a poet who was once a 12-year-old listening to his Emerson the day Bobby Thomson hit his home run . . . and suddenly great stretches of Canadian pulpwood forest are imperiled by the omnivorous publishing industry." The industry now gave Thomson $16,000 for his story. But the hero aggravated his autobiographers. "It was like pulling teeth," says Bill Gutman, coauthor of *The Giants Win the Pennant! The Giants Win the Pennant!* When, for example, Thomson, the old bombardier who had been taught to above all keep a secret, did not once bring up a telescope, Gutman had on his own to lance the boil Yvars had recently inflamed. "There has been speculation about Durocher and the spyglass for years," wrote Gutman. "Leo probably stole signs any way he could." Thomson did not read the book. And despite the fortieth anniversary of a home run, it sold poorly. "The book died because of him," said co-author Lee Heiman. "He was just unable to publicize himself. I don't know why. He was a little lost sheep."

That the man so often beside him was a milquetoast suited Branca fine. "Ralph appreciated that I didn't rub it in," Thomson told *Sports Collectors Digest*, "and we just sat back and enjoyed being remembered." They also enjoyed their checks, hero and goat paid $10,000 each this fortieth anniversary to hawk balls and photos for 120 minutes on the Home Shopping Network. And that the home run had turned meal ticket was another reason to let the secret lie, two men content to sign, sign, sign, to recite not more than pro forma spiels and a timeless goat song.

It was on this same ruby anniversary that Gore Vidal celebrated a sixty-sixth birthday oblivious to a home run. The author of twenty-seven novels knew not of Thomson or Branca or the shot that forty birthdays past had rung out eighty-five miles south of his Barrytown, New York, home. For baseball had once been the be-all of his schoolmate and deepest love, of pitching prospect Jimmie Trimble, who in 1943 spurned the New York Giants for the Washington Senators. And when a grenade in Iwo Jima killed Trimble—"the half of me that never lived to grow up," wrote Vidal—a sport died too.

That baseball evoked the men who played it—and the men who played it the games they played—was apparent four days later. On October 7, 1991, Durocher died. And left of the baseball lifer dead at eighty-six were not only a thicket of broken relationships (Day the only of four exes to attend his funeral) and a lineup of epigones gone on to manage (among them pallbearer Franks) but 2,008 wins, the most luminous of which would land Durocher in the Hall of Fame and had all remembering on this Monday where they were when, when the natty and brilliant and foul Lip pulled off his mid-century miracle.

The miracle, meantime, continued to inspire testimonials. "The '51 Giants were the one genuine miracle of my lifetime," wrote Woody Allen in the movie *Deconstructing Harry.* "When he hit that home run, that was the only hint I've ever had that there may be a God." "The Jerusalem Giants win the pennant! The Jerusalem Giants win the pennant!" wrote Philip Roth in the novel *The Counterlife,* a character leaping against the Western Wall to glove an imagined clout. "Messiah is on his way!" Eschatological class notes recalled the echo of the blast at Brown, UTEP and Yeshiva Etz Chaim, where Brooklyn sixth-grader Jack Berger had been certain that a home run heralded the End of Days. And in October 1992, there appeared in *Harper's* magazine a celestial story that would turn to *Underworld,* author DeLillo to roll a ball through history, through 827 pages, the home run, he later put it, "some unrepeatable social phenomenon."

Neither Thomson nor Branca would read *Underworld.* The two men had no need to see in their collision the spark of flint on steel, to see import and unrepeatability, each content to hopscotch as invited celebrity from screening to reading to cruise to fantasy camp to tournament to dinner, content with the honors of cameo appearance, first pitch, induction, board membership, honorary degree, *stamp*—post office and plebiscite to price a homer at thirty-three cents—content with an eponymous baseball field, society chapter and racehorse, content to shake hands with Sinatra, Rosa Parks, DeLillo, Condoleezza Rice, content with the tributes of Congress and Madison Avenue and Carnegie Hall, hero and goat listening always to the Shot Heard Round the World—the apposite phrase, in *Merriam-Webster's Dictionary of Allusions,* emphasizing not a blast but its echo.

But that these were for the men fulfilling years owed to more than an echo, what with their jobs and causes and churches and families, the pitcher at peace talking to Ann from the mahogany rocking chair given him by baseball, the hitter happy in the den with Winkie nursing an old fashioned on ice come 6:00 p.m.

It was in January 1993—months after a husband at last imported a wife to Scotland, weeks after he set gold about her wrist to mark a fortieth anniversary—that back pain sent the couple to the hospital. A CAT scan revealed an abdominal mass. Winkie, sixty-four, had uterine cancer. Four months later she was dead, her ashes buried in the garden of a church one mile from the ranch house where her widower now lived alone.

An August Red Cross fundraiser had Thomson and Branca at the Wykagyl Country Club in Westchester when Rod Gilbert spotted them on the seventh tee. "You know who's here?" the hockey star remembers telling his toadies. "The guy who threw the famous pitch."

Branca had long ago settled on the ammo with which to repel the fresh fan, telling when taunted that he was among the few to win twenty-one at twenty-one, pitcher safe then in his annus mirabilis, shoulder to shoulder with Mathewson, Ruth and Feller. But the pet nugget did not always suffice. "Maybe once in fifty times I'll get mad," Branca told reporter John Devaney in 1966. "I jump him."

And so now Branca did on a par three, reacting in anger to a familiar Montreal accent, to a dig, to a lifetime of digs, the telegrams long ago wishing him dead every bit the fatwa that would in eleven months see soccer goat Andres Escobar shot in Colombia. Remembers Gilbert, "He says to me in front of my people, 'Rod Gilbert, you're an asshole!' " Gilbert cautioned Branca not to speak thusly, Thomson and a clique of rich duffers aghast and aware that all was his doing.

The exchange lingered. "He's supposed to be a friend of mine," said Branca eleven years later of Gilbert. "He brings that fucking thing up. He's not supposed to bring up the worst fucking event of my life!"

A man can easier speak the truth when filled with anger, and Branca had slipped, had acknowledged as the nadir of his life a lost pennant. But a freshet of hurt quickly emptied into the sea that for so long had lapped perspective against the man, had turned his rough edges smooth. And in his Westchester office, the insurance broker was quick now to tell of a priest in a parking lot, Branca true to a narrative.

It was in 1996 that Thomson retired from a second career, able at seventy-three to spend time with a "lady friend." Paper bags had been very, very good to him. "One of the great satisfactions of my life," Thomson told researcher Norman Macht, "that I learned the meaning of work."

There remained also meaning in life, his three children married, the last of six grandkids soon to be born. "I had to keep house," says Thomson. "I had to keep living." And so he did, answering fan mail, playing golf, lending his name to an arthritis appeal, fixing a staple meal—American cheese, ham, mayo, lettuce and tomato on white bread, skim milk on ice, chocolate chip cookies from daughter Megan. Buoyed by the pensions of two careers and the rising rent of his name (hardnosed Branca upping to three, then four thousand dollars his fee per show), Thomson was financially secure. And standing in the garden at Wilson Memorial Union Church, grass underfoot, he regularly talked it all through with his late wife.

It was in August 2000, one year after the *Sporting News* voted a homer pinnacle of a pastime, that hero and goat landed their biggest check, each paid some $240,000 to up with Steiner Sports Marketing, to attend twenty-four events through the jubilee of a home run. "We had to sign thousands of things," says Branca, "different-sized pictures, jerseys, bats and balls." This they did over and again in a corporate office in New Rochelle, two men signing in lockstep, one on top, one on bottom, one on top, one on bottom, one on top, one on bottom.

TWENTY-SIX

These theories were based on the hypothesis that all matter in the
universe was created in one big bang at a particular time in the
remote past. It now turns out that in some respect or other all
such theories are in conflict with the observational requirements.
And to a degree that can hardly be ignored.
—FRED HOYLE, BBC *Third Programme*, March 28, 1949

IN SEPTEMBER OF 2000, Barry Halper regaled me with stories from
a life in baseball, with tales as tall as a Giant telescope. There I stopped
him. Was it true?

It had been a year since I raised a paddle at Sotheby's, since I let the
king of sports memorabilia know that one of his 2,481 auctioned treasures had found a proper home. Halper had answered my note with a
phone call, asking me before long to name the only player to catch two
perfect games. (I fanned. Answer: Ron Hassey.) More calls followed,
Halper telling me this September afternoon that no, he did not think the
Giant rumor true. For not only had allegations of a telescope gone
unproved in half a century but they had been told him by Branca.

Still, Halper was uncertain. And so I procured a list of the twenty-one
living players and one coach who, if only for a day, had been 1951
Giants and asked each, from captain Dark and rookie Mays to forgotten
Francis Hardy and Artie Wilson, of espionage and the weight of harbor-
ing a secret. "I have carried that for forty-nine years," infielder Williams
told me. "I'm not going to go into that now."

With canoodling, some of the ballplayers were compliant, if not forthcoming. And as their memories piggybacked flecks of history, this much
became certain: Durocher called a meeting. Schenz produced a telescope.
Chadwick installed a buzzer. Franks turned spy, Yvars messenger. And
on July 19, 1951, shortly before the Giants went on their historic tear,
the team set into motion an elaborate system to steal the finger signals of
opposing catchers.

After two months of research, I was ready to call Bobby Thomson. And after five decades of silence, he was ready to talk.

"The word 'stealing' isn't a very nice word," Thomson told me over the phone when I explained that I knew the 1951 Giants had stolen signals, that I had spoken to each of his surviving teammates. "Obviously it's something I've never been proud of. Let me say this. I've got nothing to hide." We arranged to meet that Sunday at his hometown church.

On November 19, 2000, I stood in the lobby of Wilson Memorial Union Church and waited for an American hero. "I'm tall and thin and I wear glasses," Thomson had told me.

Thomson, seventy-seven, entered the Watchung church where he had worshipped Sundays off and on since 1958. A parishioner greeted him: "Hey, Long Ball!" The old ballplayer smiled politely, grasped a nametag from the wall and pinned it to his lapel. It read BOB THOMSON.

Thomson wore loafers, a tweed jacket, steel-rimmed glasses, silver hair. His head stooped but his slight frame appeared every bit the six feet and two inches accredited him in the *Baseball Encyclopedia*.

Thomson and I exchanged hellos, then walked to a pew in the rear. His gait was slow but graceful, Thomson months removed from surgeries for an aneurysm and a worn left knee, hampered also by an arthritic right ankle. We took our seats, and almost immediately he made it known that he had given our lone conversation thought. "I guess we were brought up to know the difference between right and wrong," said Thomson of himself and his five siblings. "And I'm far from perfect. Put that down."

The chiming of bells signaled the start of the service. Thomson took my right hand, then joined in singing beneath the ambient chords of an organ "We Gather Together," a tenor quiet and on key. The music stopped and all read aloud the "Prayer of Confession and Assurance." Benedictions were recited, scripture parsed, announcements made about caroling and poinsettias. And it was then, her lectern bathed in splotches of refracted and colored light, that the reverend began a sermon about contentment. "Suppose for a moment," said Barbara Peters, "all the things you have around you were taken away."

Thomson clasped his hands and, staring ahead, seemed to do just that, a Protestant hero retracing life to an afternoon choreographed in baseball's welkin. "We can be content whether we are abased," continued Reverend Peters. Church over, Thomson returned the mile home, walking from den to kitchen to living room to chintz loveseat, crossing loafer over knee before *The Book of Virtues* and picture histories of Scotland and baseball erect on the marble table before him. He spoke at once of stolen signs.

"I realized," said Thomson, " 'Why should I be so sensitive about this?' " He recalled aloud that the Giants had not scored at the Polo Grounds the day before his home run, then continued. "I asked myself, 'Bob, you know who you are and who you were. You shouldn't let this bother you.' " Thomson paused, his left foot bouncing. "But I must admit," he continued, "it kind of takes something away from it." Thomson added one more thought. "So many people," he said, "are happy to meet me. They make me—gee, they make me seem important almost."

Thomson told me that on October 3, 1951, he knew Franks was in center field and that in his first three at-bats, he likely availed himself of stolen signs. I asked whether he glanced at the signal before his home run. His reflex pricked, a monologue spilled forth, Thomson telling of the Mueller injury, of standing distracted at third base, of prodding himself with curses the ninety feet home, of being unaware of anyone in the ballpark but himself. "I was like a mechanical doll," he said.

I asked Thomson again if he got the sign. "I'd have to say more no than yes," he answered.

Suddenly, Thomson uncrossed his legs, squared his feet with his shoulders and put his fists together, right over left, as if gripping a bat. He hunched forward his torso, turned his head toward his left shoulder and looked out of unblinking eyes into his fireplace. Did he take the sign? From the batter's box, said Thomson, "you could almost just do it with your eyes."

His hands relaxed and his arms dropped to his sides. Thomson was back again in tweed and tie. "It's all rationalizing," he said. "So it's silly. I don't like to think of something taking away from it. I've never taken credit for a heck of a lot in my life. But what I've given myself credit for in my heart is giving myself a chance to hit. I think I've got a right to take credit for that."

The notion, though, of credit made Thomson uncomfortable. And he grappled now with what had been his lifelong lot. "I've not thought I've deserved all the attention I've gotten because of that one home run," he said. He added: "I'd have been more successful if I had more arrogance . . . more confidence. I'm just not as smart as I'd like to have been."

It was now that something Winkie had once observed of her husband came to his mind. Thomson was unsure what exactly it was, but, he said, it was somewhere in his autobiography and his autobiography was somewhere in his house. He looked for the book he had neither written nor read in the small office where the only visible signs of a celebrated career laid low: a facsimile of his commemorative stamp, a small replica of the Polo Grounds, a signed copy of *Underworld* translated into Greek. Thomson did not find it. Intent, he retreated to his basement, to a fusty clutter where the Shot Heard Round the World echoed below a dead end in Jersey. Here was hero oak-tagged and stained-glassed and yellowed, Thomson the essay subject of a child since middle-aged. Here was a pile of photographs signed only by Branca. Here were hardened mitts, stale uniforms, dinged plaques, clippings and portraits furled. Here was his autobiography.

Back on his loveseat, Thomson quickly found his way to an epigraph on page 13. I read it aloud. "He's sensitive and humble to a fault with a tendency to play himself down," Winkie had said. "I sometimes think this has been the monkey on Bob's back, his thing to handle in life."

Thomson followed the words, the brown eyes of a widower welling with tears. "Why didn't I do better than that?" he asked. "You can only play yourself down so much and then it gets dumb. I'm seventy-seven."

Thomson turned to another page and asked to be read aloud another epigraph, his sister Jean telling how their father, James, did not let her solo in music school. "And remember," Jean concluded, "Bob was brought up the same way." The youngest Thomson listened, he who still recalled the pride of his father after a first sandlot hit, crying noiselessly.

It was not only restraint but propriety that had formed his upbringing. And so it was not only the scraps of praise but the shames of a life that above all Thomson had never let go—high school classes failed, a military footrace lost to disqualification, a Giant scheme. Clear now was that regardless of whether hero had received a stolen sign, it was, of all a miracle team, in *him*—in the superego of he who was already prone to abnegate the rightful boasts of a career—that the soiling of a home run found fertile ground.

December arrived and I phoned Branca. He did not speak to me long, intent only on pointing out both a back injury in 1952 and that when talk of a Giant spy came and went ten years later, he had pledged to keep mum. "I didn't want to look like I was crying over spilled milk," he explained. And so now, days shy of seventy-five, he spoke of a New York scheme only off the record. For attribution was that, helped or not, Thomson hit the pitch. Added Branca, "Bobby and I are really, really good friends."

One month later, Thomson and Branca put on tuxedos and met in Manhattan, there at the Marriott Marquis to headline a BAT benefit on January 23, 2001. Introduced by emcee Dick Schaap, the men bandied the praise and sidesteps that like the recurrent themes of a fugue had marked their collaborations for fifty years. A piano began to play. And cued, the senior citizens performed their goat song, a ball again aloft in Harlem, an aging audience filing from a ballroom with misted eyes.

Thomson and Branca had this evening been in fine fettle, hero telling all that "it helps to be lucky," goat that he was fortunate for a partner he "could love and really cherish." But in truth, neither man savored his time with the other. "I didn't enjoy being in his company," Thomson told me flatly of his five decades beside Branca, "because people would bring up *the* subject. I've been a burden to Ralph."

Indeed, theirs was a union predicated on an imbalance, Branca on this night levying at Thomson a charge he knew well: "Because of you, I should never been born."

Ralph in turn was a burden to Bobby. For beyond the Branca bravado that dovetailed with his humility, it was most of all cognitive dissonance that had sustained a marriage—Thomson forced in 1962 to accommodate the reality that Branca knew of a telescope. Reconciling left no room to speak of it. And so even as Thomson co-signed the sweet spots of baseball after baseball, not once had he offered up to Branca a confession. "I guess I've been a jerk in a way," he said. "That I don't want to face the music. . . . Maybe I've felt too sensitive, embarrassed maybe."

Neither had Branca ever broached the taboo. "I wasn't going to cry over spilled milk," repeated Branca. "I don't know if it was a macho thing." There was more. The pitcher had grown accustomed to a grievance, had come in fifty years to lean on an alibi best left undisturbed. And neither man wished to upend a status quo. "We've been together enough," said Thomson. "We need each other."

Three days later, I phoned Thomson. "I was just being too honest and too fair," he told me of our conversation. "I could easily have said, 'No, I didn't take the sign.' "

Thomson seemed uncertain whether he had. "You got me thinking serious about this, which I had never done," he said. "I've told this same story for years about Mueller sliding and me walking to home plate—I'm in another world, getting back to fundamentals, swearing at myself." The story itself had become memory. And so now in the jubilee of a home run, Thomson reasoned with it. "It didn't make sense for me," he explained of his at-bat, "to think beyond Branca throwing the fastball."

I asked Thomson again if he took the sign. "It would take a little away from me in my mind if I felt I got help on the pitch," he said. But *did* he take the sign? "My answer is no," Thomson said. He added: "I was always proud of that swing."

Thus concluded on January 31, 2001, my article in the *Wall Street Journal,* postscript to a home run in its fiftieth year.

Branca sat in his rocking chair and eyed an oval face drawn in miniature—his own half smile and empty follicles dotted into page one, column one, of the *Journal.* He began to read. He knew already of Yvars and Franks. But here in the back story of a home run came a first word of the July day that had gotten a ball rolling, a first word of Durocher and Chadwick and Schenz and the Wollensak that had peered at his pitch (the scope now, he read, on the desk of a Schenz grandson in Westford, Massachusetts). Here also was the hero grappling a first time with a question he had always before derided, with the memory of a fastball pitched 18,018 days past. Just as important, here was the goat all but absent, no tattletale he. Rumor at last real, the wrong a Branca adage had insisted upon at last righted, Branca lifted his phone and dialed the man he had let be in 1954, 1962 and ever since. Said Branca the next day, "I just called him to see how he was feeling." Thomson picked up and Branca asked if he had seen the article. He had.

The ease with which the men now spoke of a secret begged why they had not done so sooner, hero and goat conversing with a freedom unshared since they were boys cutting in a convertible through a Midwest dusk in October 1948. "I guess you feel exonerated," said Thomson. "No," said Branca. "But my tongue is loosened."

Indeed it was. For unlike the past resuscitations of a rumor that had quickly expired, the *Journal* had breathed life into a discussion respiring now on television where Branca and Thomson testified on CNN, on radio where Noah Adams contextualized a scheme on NPR, on the Internet where the Society for American Baseball Research considered the statistical fallout of a secret, in print where disquisitions on fair play filled scores of papers. Read the *Staten Island Advance:* "It's about as larcenous an act as reading a paper over someone's shoulder." Countered the lead editorial of the *Chicago Tribune:* "It's as if the Nazis secretly made the D-Day invasion easier than it looked. As if the first moon landing was faked at some desert in New Mexico. As if Picasso clandestinely paid his landlady to sketch his best stuff. One of the most admired sagas in the history of sports turns out to be, to an unspecified extent, a fraud."

Branca and Thomson took in the debate. And after Dodger again phoned Giant the next morning, he spoke on air of their conversation. "Today I had a long talk with him," Branca told host Christopher Russo on New York sports radio station WFAN. "Rightfully so, he feels that, you know, he hit a hell of a pitch and he executed [at] the proper time.

And he doesn't think he should take any slack over it and I don't either."
Added Branca, "I have reservations that he took the sign." Thus did goat
at last take what he had long aspired to—the high road, there above an
outed scheme not to indict but to simply speak of a signal. "I can now
talk about it," he told Russo. "And that might be good for me."

Hours later Thomson followed Branca, Russo asking if a telescope
had aided the 1951 team. "Obviously it had to help us," Giant told
Giant fan. "Sure. No question about it." Asked whether it facilitated
also his home run, a familiar answer emerged in the negative space of a
story about Mueller (Thomson adding as before that had he eyed a
stolen signal, he would surely have swung at a first fastball). The hero
then stepped closer to the unequivocal. "Signs at that moment?" he
asked. "No. And that's honestly the way I feel."

It was what Thomson had long evaded, however, that he most wished
now to discuss. "It's been brought up before and I've always been glad
where it quieted down," he said on air. "But you know, that's foolish. . . .
Getting it all out is the best thing. I feel almost like I just got out of
prison."

Thus was an accounting a *catharsis*—the word put forth by Branca
this same day in the *Daily News*. Thus were batter and pitcher at last
redeemed in the golden anniversary of a goat song. For in confessing,
as he did now on radio, that "I didn't feel good about what we were
doing," Thomson palliated the ulcer that had long panged his gut. That
coming clean lifted also the yoke from off the goat by his side, tilted the
interdependent balance of two men toward equipoise, relieved the hero
of an even greater burden. "Ralph, uh, you know, it, it kind of helped
him get off the hook a little bit," observed Thomson on air. "We all like
to get off hooks."

The interview ended and public deliberation resumed. Most praised
Branca—the heroic goat who had kept quiet about a buzzer lest he
demean a home run. Most defended Thomson—the humble hero who
still had to hit a pitch and whose alleged offense was not illegal. And
while Branca condemned a team but not Thomson, Thomson condemned a home-field advantage but not a home run.

It was three days later at an annual banquet of New Jersey writers that
Branca approached Thomson in a busy ballroom. "Hiya, Hoot!" The
men shook hands, Thomson suggesting they slip from the horde come on
this fourth of February to toast a golden home run. This they did, two
men in an empty corner of the Edison Pines Manor undivided by a secret
a first time in fifty years. They spoke alone, then turned to a reporter.

"It's been a cleansing for both of us," said Branca to Ben Walker of the AP. "He knew that I knew. It's better this way." Added Thomson: "Ralph has been vindicated and I feel the same way about myself. My conscience is clear."

The men walked to a dais, joshed with a thousand people, signed autographs and left for New York, hours later together again with another guild of writers in another hotel at another celebration of the Shot Heard Round the World. A piano introduced a ten-note melody and Bobby Thomson and Ralph Branca began to sing.

EPILOGUE

WHEN JOURNALIST MARTIN ARNOLD sought at the start of the new millennium to convey the power of alternative history, of the envisioning of might-have-beens, he proposed three hypotheticals: What if in 1863 Ulysses Grant had been seriously injured when he fell from his horse? What if in 1933 assassin Giuseppe Zangara had, as intended, murdered Franklin Roosevelt (and not Chicago mayor Anton Cermak)? What if in 1951 Thomson had struck out?

Had Thomson failed, he would likely have been lost to self-recrimination and Branca to vanity. But *still* he had not. A revelation did not change history. The opening of a green door did little more than better bring to light the effects of a home run and a secret on two men.

It was primarily, however, the influence of a spyglass on posterity and play that was now reexamined. Two Georges quickly framed the discussion. "No one except perhaps the most die-hard Brooklyn fan, would ever question what Thomson did," wrote George Plimpton, die-hard Giant fan. "Anyone who has watched batting practice can see how rarely even a fat pitch is hit out of the park." Wrote Cub fan George Will: "The importance of protecting the integrity of competition from the threat of advantages obtained illicitly is underscored by the sense of melancholy, of loss, that baseball fans now feel about the no longer quite so luminous season of 1951."

Those nostalgists who recalled a home run in the alpenglow of the fifties wished only to airbrush away a cloud. And so they took heart in what Dave Smith soon presented to the Society for American Baseball Research and Stan Jacoby to the *New York Times,* in statistics illuminating that it was Giant pitching, not hitting, that had markedly improved after July 20, 1951. To them it did not matter that unknowable, as ESPN.com writer Rob Neyer pointed out, is how the miracle team would have performed without knowledge of the upcoming pitch. It did not matter that a home run was true to the track records of two men—Branca losing on center stage before, Thomson homering (as minor leaguer) in the only other deciding playoff game he had ever played. It did not matter that the measure of behavior is not in its result but in its doing.

The disillusioned were equally partisan. To them, a found telescope explained away a fifty-year ache, the glittering 1951 season turned Potemkin village. To them, a Wollensak was a peripeteia that inverted hero and goat—Thomson turned dodger and Branca giant, batter waffling in the *Wall Street Journal,* pitcher resisting an alibi. Some wished action be taken. Brooklyn fan Joel Kramer felt baseball (presented the "evidence" commissioner Frick had sought in 1962) ought now affix an asterisk to the pennant. *Washington Post* reporter Thomas Boswell suggested that Durocher be removed from the Hall of Fame. Baseball said nothing.

The sport, in fact, had been silent on the issue of sign-stealing since the previous March when, after several coaches in press boxes used walkie-talkies to position their players, it sent a memo to all thirty teams. "Such equipment may not be used for the purpose of stealing signs or conveying information designed to give a club an advantage," wrote Sandy Alderson, then executive vice president of baseball operations. Bud Selig, baseball commissioner since 1992, would state in 2005 that no team had ever complained to him about mechanical sign-stealing and that there was therefore no need to legislate its ban. Were a team to use a telescope, he said, "they would be dealt with." Ken Singleton, baseball player turned analyst, said in 2005 that he did not foresee a team using a spyglass ever again. "It's impossible to do today," said Singleton (who happened to grow up in Branca's boyhood home). "There are too many cameras."

The public, though, had strong opinions on a telescope already used. These followed home both Thomson and Branca. A son-in-law wrote for Thomson a four-hundred-word defense. ("So did I know what Branca was throwing at me that fateful afternoon?" it concluded. "The answer is 'NO!'") A brother wrote for Branca a twenty-five-page manifesto. ("Ralph Branca," it concluded, "is the hero in this messy baseball betrayal.") And as the fiftieth anniversary of the home run drew near, pressure to deny even a soupçon of culpability—whether for wrongdoing or loss—weighed equally upon hero and goat.

It was Branca who shucked diplomacy first. "If you watch him swing at it, he attacks the ball," the pitcher told HBO in spring. "He leaps like a tiger pouncing on some wounded antelope." "The evidence is irrefutable," he told the *Daily News* in summer. "I'm proud to say I played the game *fairly*," he told ESPN.com in fall. Unmuzzled, a goat thus bleated on, Branca time and again calling the Giant scheme "the most despicable act in the history of the game."

Thomson in turn denied with newfound gusto talk of a ninth-inning sign. ("It's laughable," he told HBO.) But he did not bite back at Branca. For goat had long refused scapegoat, had in five decades publicly fingered an unfair fact not more than five times. The hero lamented now only that a relationship had cooled. "We've come apart a bit, and that hurts me," Thomson told *USA Today* in late September. "We're just too damned old for this. . . . We did steal signs and I did take some, and I don't feel good about it. But I didn't get the sign on that pitch. Ralph says I did, and if that eases the burden of what he's carried around all these years, I'm glad for that."

On the very eve of a fiftieth anniversary, however, Thomson *did* bite back. Branca had days before told the *New York Times*, "Bobby has had to live with a lie." And on air now with Branca and Bryant Gumbel, the TV host thrice brought up that which Thomson said upset him, panting after a quarrel like a tabby after catnip. "To say I've got to live with a lie," responded Thomson. "A lie! Hey, Ralph, come on. Think a little bit!" To denigrate a home run was one thing, to diagnose a man quite another. Thomson was upset.

But he was also freed. For what had bothered him most of all these fifty years was feeling a burden to Branca—the hitter unable since a homer to swing at the pitcher with bat or barb. And clear as day was that a home run did not now burden the goat. It was Branca, not Thomson, who would shill the homer for an online ranking of baseball moments. It was Branca, not Thomson, who would make the Mancuso photograph his computer's screen saver (Thomson to auction off his original copy of the same snapshot). It was Branca, not Thomson, whose 13-RB license plate recalled a career (Thomson long ago discarding the RT tag the Giants put on his 1947 Buick). It was Branca, not Thomson, raring always for their next signing, a Dodger-blue Sharpie forever on his person. "Now he doesn't see himself as the goat," says daughter Patti. "He's more of the hero. He kept his mouth closed."

He who had forever played down a home run meantime could at last *open* his, could speak almost pridefully, dare say what he had not been able to amidst even the rapture of a winning clubhouse. "They'll never take away what happened that time at bat," Thomson now told Branca and Gumbel. "Uh, you know, I, I happen to win that time at bat and I happen to win two days before that. . . . I've never said that much about it. But I've always been feeling good about myself that I gave myself a chance to hit." Thus did hero assert that half a century earlier he had given himself what he had so often lacked—confidence.

Come morning, celebration was subdued. Just twenty-two days since 9/11, the men visited firehouses and Ground Zero, a San Francisco fête postponed. And just ninety-nine days since Robert Brown Thomson, Jr., died of a slightly enlarged heart, his mourning namesake was left now to visit a late wife and son together. Come July 2006, Thomson would leave the home he had lived in since 1959 for a house near daughter Nancy in Skidaway Island, Georgia.

Still, October 3, 2001, was a golden anniversary. And the tintinnabulation of the Stock Exchange bell that Thomson and Branca now clanged in New York carried clear to Edinburgh where twenty-six months later, the Scottish Sports Hall of Fame inducted the Flying Scot. "What I picked up in the museum earlier today," said Scottish parliament member Frank McAveety of Thomson, "was his modesty still many years after that remarkable achievement. And sometimes that is a great Scottish trait but sometimes it's also quite infuriating because we should be speaking from the rooftops about [our] achievements."

This, increasingly, the unprepossessing hero understood. And in time, Thomson like Branca was as comfortable to discuss with me the glory of a home run as he was the tincture of a telescope.

If it was a book that more and more meshed the pasts of two men, it was above all money that conjoined their presents—hero and goat signing nine straight weekends in spring 2003 (in spring 2005 suing and settling with Steiner Sports after Branca found them unforthcoming about a baseball-card deal). Side by side, the two men again found a genuine comfort with each other. Again Branca told any and all that he had been married to Thomson seventeen days longer than to Ann. And when in earshot of his better half Branca added word of a telescope, Thomson was sure to remind Branca and fan that walking to the plate one afternoon long ago, he had given himself a talking-to and hit a home run.

And so it was the grievance of a goat now eighty that enabled a hero now eighty-two to at last take unreserved pride in a triumph. "Right now I'm more aware that I hit the home run than ever," said Thomson, home alone on a winter Tuesday in 2005, folding leftover ham and cheese in a crinkle of plastic wrap. "To sit back and realize and get some enjoyment from the fact that people want to say hello to me."

AUTHOR'S NOTE

IN 1993, ROGER KAHN WARNED writers to leave be the Thomson home run. "Summarizing the 1951 race is akin to summarizing King Lear," he wrote. "Before anything else, your effort will diminish majesty." J.H. Hexter, though, invited the effort. In a 1968 essay on historiography, the Yale history professor posed a question with which to illustrate the task of the historian: "How did the New York Giants happen to play in the World Series in 1951?" he wrote. "How to explain the overwhelming superiority of New York in the last forty-odd games?" Hexter asserted that the sufficient answer—good historiography, that is—would offer "confrontation with the riches of the event itself, a sense of vicarious participation in a great happening, the satisfaction of understanding what those great moments were like for the ordinarily cool Russ Hodges. . . . for those who saw what he saw and those who heard him."

It was with Kahn and Hexter in mind that I wrote my book, that I tried to offer the reader "vicarious participation" in a great moment and thereby not diminish it.

Some felt, however, that I had *already* demeaned a home run in newsprint. (The emcee at the 2001 national baseball writers dinner declared my article "scandalous.") To them I say that what I reported was fact. I say that in these pages I took pains to place a telescope in the larger context of baseball thievery and to recognize those writers who long before me nibbled at a rumor. I say that I have intended to *honor* a home run, to make clear why for millions it remains a memory so unshakeable that one doctor used it to describe the limits of Wernicke-Korsakoff syndrome. And I say that as regards the stealing of signs, my book is not about the debatable effects of a telescope on play but about the undeniable effects of a secret on two men.

These effects the two men shared with me. "You loosened my tongue," Branca told me the day after my story ran. "I might have to be disgustingly honest," Thomson later echoed over the phone. And so they were with me, pitcher and hitter—one with informed asides, one with words like "whoops" and "silly" and "heck"—relating their combined 163 years.

To convey in turn to the reader the vicariousness that Hexter wrote of required mountains of detail. For if the reader were to follow with craned neck a Harlem home run, he ought first, it seemed, to sit in a green and narrow chair of eight wooden slats. And so I set off to learn all I could of a ballpark, an electrician, signs, a corps of Giants, Branca, Thomson and a home run, set off on a quest that over five years snaked through some 2,000 interviews with 500 people, some 3,000 e-mails, 3,000 articles, 250 photographs, 200 books, and 50 broadcasts, through scores of academic, employment, military, baseball, family, municipal and land records, through dozens of letters, lectures, poems and paintings, through mounds of memorabilia.

I began this book having already excavated the bare bones of a Giant scheme. But there remained much to flesh out. There were people to find. Who wrote the caption "The Shot Heard Round the Baseball World?" Who in 1962 was the anonymous source of a rumored telescope? Who on October 3, 1951, crouched beside Sukeforth in the Brooklyn bullpen? Who operated the scoreboard at the Polo Grounds? Who defeated Branca on *Concentration*? Who dated Thomson during the war? (The *Daily News*, the AP, the Dodgers, the Giants, Branca and Thomson did not remember.) There were documents and data to find. Where was Thomson born? Which boat brought Chadwick to this country? Who first owned the land beneath the Polo Grounds? How did spied signals affect the Giant bats? Did another team ever overcome a three-run deficit in the ninth inning of a playoff? Where did each of the 204 home runs hit in 1951 at the Polo Grounds land? There were hunches to confirm. Did someone die listening to Branca lose the game? Did someone name a newborn after Thomson when he won it? Did the home run echo through the White House? The Mafia? Korea? And there was an unceasing hunt for documentation. Was there a photo that pinpointed which clubhouse window was the Giant lookout? A photo that showed the view from batter's box to bullpen? A photo or footage that revealed spy Franks and signpost Yvars at the very moment the home run flew?

With tremendous help, I located the above. But I did not find all I wanted, for example, a Muslim fan who prayed alongside Jew and Christian on October 3, 1951, or past which Thomson ear the Billy Cox liner zipped in the eighth. Not all those I contacted were helpful, baseball fan Fidel Castro not caring to share if he recollected the game, Brooklynite Bobby Fischer willing to reminisce only for $200,000. Even some central to my book, like Ann Branca and Franks, were tightlipped, the otherwise gracious coach not so much as acknowledging to me a telescope. "I don't know anything about it," he said. Wife Ami laughed: "Oh, Herman!"

The more I interviewed and read, the clearer it was that lore clung to a home run, that in fifty-five years its protagonists time and again contradicted their own rehashings, that a consequence of its tremendous spawn of copy was misinformation. Accuracy could be no less assumed than comprehensiveness short-cut. And so I set for myself steadfast if obvious rules: Defer always to the primary source and the earliest record. Vet all recollection and accepted fact. Discard what could not be corroborated.

As a result, I often veered from what is in print. I found, for example, that Branca had better numbers versus Thomson than did Erskine, that the home run was hit *hard*, that Eugene Istomin did not hear Russ Hodges call the homer, that J. Edgar Hoover was in the Oval Office (and not the ballpark) when it flew, that Dodger fan Antonio Masse did not die watching it, that Carl Prince did not eat Spaghetti-Os after the game. I could not report, as have others, that the nineteenth-century Hartford Dark Blues stole signs, that pitcher Dale Mohorcic swallowed sandpaper on the mound, that a Boston marine high on the homer triggered a gunfight in Korea, that the Dodgers had Branca ditch his number 13, that Thomson first attributed his summer resurgence to a batting stance, that in 1951 Dressen declared "the Giants is dead," that in 1962 baseball outlawed sign-stealing. (These last two I regurgitated in my 2001 *Journal* article. I hope this can pass for a correction.) I found, in fact, that for almost every note and quote I *could* verify, there was one I could not (author Thomas Kiernan for one unsure of whence had come word that Albert Einstein handicapped the 1951 race, archives from Princeton to Jerusalem yielding nothing).

That I have had the opportunity to tell this story, I consider an honor. There are, after all, but a handful of moments that linger in millions.

I know, however, that to write of the Shot Heard Round the World is to be subject to the expertise of those millions. And I hope that they in whom the home run still echoes, still rouses atavistic pleasure or pain, will not only send me stories of October 3, 1951, but alert me to any missteps in these pages. As Herman Melville wrote, "This whole book is but a draught—nay, but the draught of a draught."

NEW YORK CITY
JUNE 2006

ACKNOWLEDGEMENTS

I COULD NOT HAVE WRITTEN THIS BOOK without the help of hundreds.

Thanks to Barry Halper who started the ball rolling. Thanks to Jonathan Kaufman and John Blanton who helped me turn his aside into a story, to Robin Haynes, Dan Hertzberg, Mike Miller, Kevin Salwen and everyone else at the Wall Street Journal who gave me the opportunities that led to a job I love, and to Melinda Beck who shepherded me along when it took me months to write an orphan. With patience and warmth, Melinda, you taught me near all I know about writing.

Thank you to my agent David McCormick. You took me on when I had an idea that promised little and you helped me to write a proposal when another came along. Thank you to my editor Dan Frank. I had no idea how lucky I was when Pantheon bought this book. Each of your suggestions made these pages better. And my god, you are a patient man! I very much hope we work together again. Thanks to Fran Bigman for a lot of little things, to Jenna, Lydia, Kristen and Stuart, for dotting every I and crossing every T, and to Altie, Janice, Elisabeth, Archie and everyone else at Pantheon who worked so hard on my behalf.

Thank you to Bobby Thomson and Ralph Branca for opening your lives to me, for letting me tag along from Westchester to Scotland. You are good men and I will forever be honored to have called you friends. I hope that I have done right by you. Thank you to the many, many Thomson and Branca relatives for trusting me with your brother, father, etc. Special thanks to Ruby, Rosemary, John, Patti and Nancy.

Thank you to Herman Franks. I know you'd rather have left well enough alone. But still you were good to me. I admire you for that. Thank you to Sal Yvars for the truth. (Everyone assumes you were my Deep Throat but we both know that way back when, you slammed a door in my face.) Thank you to the Schenz family for letting me peer through a Wollensak, to the Durocher family for remembering the details, to the Chadwick family for transcending a ballfield. Helen, Harriet, I never met your father. But I came to care for him a great deal.

Thank you to the rest of the 1951 Giants, to Al Corwin, Alvin Dark, Al Gettel, Clint Hartung, Monte Irvin, Larry Jansen, Spider Jorgensen, Whitey Lockman, Jack Lohrke, Jack Maguire, Willie Mays, Don Mueller, Bill Rigney, George Spencer, Wes Westrum, Davey Williams and Artie Wilson. You brought a clubhouse to life. Thank you also to all the other ballplayers who looked back including Hank Aaron, Hank Bauer, Yogi Berra, Buddy Blattner, Jim Bouton, Rocky Bridges, Mace Brown, Carl Erskine, Eddie Fisher, Joe Garagiola, Ted Gray, Ralph Kiner, Clyde King, Bob Kuzava, Clem Labine, Hal Manders, Eddie Miksis, Don Newcombe, Andy Pafko, Phil Rizzuto, Eddie Robinson, Frank Saucier, Andy Seminick, Ken Singleton, Duke Snider, Eugene Thompson, Del Wilbur and Al Worthington.

Thank you to Bill Francis at the Hall of Fame and to Dave Smith at Retrosheet. Tirelessly, you found and confirmed for me hundreds of loose facts and figures, and did so with enthusiasm and speed. Minus your input, this book would have tanked—kind of like the 1948 Braves without Spahn and Sain.

Thank you to Russell Adams, Trenton Daniel, Jonathan Kaplan, Rebecca Myers and Valerie Thomas. No matter how absurd or obscure my question or hunch, you searched and found. Your fingerprints are on every page.

Thank you to Ted O'Callahan, Michael Prospero, David Stegon, Julie Tate and Mike Train. You helped me put the damn book to bed. A tremendous thank you to Jodi Brandon. You are fast and fastidious. Had you not come to my rescue, I'd have disappeared in a blizzard of endnotes.

Thank you to the members of SABR who helped me sieve a sea of minutiae for ejections, hidden balls, hypothetical clouts, et al. They include Phil Birnbaum, Warren Corbett, Bill Deane, Jane Finnan Dorward, Lloyd Johnson, Jane Leavy, Skip McAfee, Peter Morris, Alan Nathan, Ray Nemec, Doug Pappas, John Pastier, Greg Rhodes, Glenn Stout, John Thorn, Stew Thornley, Frank Vaccaro and David Vincent.

Thank you to Freddy Berowski, Bill Burdick, Dave Jones, Sue MacKay and everyone else at the Hall of Fame who found articles and photographs for me and even weighed a magical bat.

Thank you to the collectors who lent or described or sold to me relevant treasures. They include Tim Cammett, Charlie Greinsky, Mike Heffner, Andrew Leeming, Jerry Liebowitz, Bill Mastro, J. Fred MacDonald, John Miley, Pat Nuttycombe, John Rogers, Michael Santo and Marc Schafler, Henry Yee.

Thank you to the many reporters and authors who remembered a home run or lent expertise on everything from cryptography to poor hitting. They include Dave Anderson, Roger Angell, James Bacon, Jacques Barzun, David Block, Harold Bloom, Hal Bock, Jimmy Breslin, Jim Costello, Robert Creamer, Kit Crissey, Paul Dickson, Joe Dittmar, Roy Doliner, Bob Edwards, Charles Einstein, Gerald Eskenazi, Charlie Feeney, Ron Fimrite, Red Foley, Larry Freundlich, Betty Friedan, Peter Golenbock, Christopher Gray, Bill Gutman, Pete Hamill, Arnold Hano, Lee Heiman, Noel Hynd, Stan Isaacs, David Kahn, Roger Kahn, Thomas Kiernan, Leonard Koppett, Phil Lowry, David McCullough, Arthur Miller, Phil Mushnick, Al Pepper, Carl Prince, Dorothy Rabinowitz, Lawrence Ritter, Ray Robinson, Charlie Rosen, Harvey Rosenfeld, Philip Roth, Michael Santa Maria, Curt Smith, Fred Stein, Gay Talese, Studs Terkel, Calvin Trillin, Jules Tygiel, Gore Vidal, Craig Wolf, Daniel Wyatt and Vic Ziegel.

Thank you to the hundreds of people at libraries, newspapers, museums, societies, schools, archives and institutes, and the hundreds more unaffiliated, who helped me to learn about everything from Sing Sing to game shows, about everyone from midget Eddie Gaedel to Giant batboy Billy Leonard, who put me in touch or had good suggestions or reminisced of a homer or helped me find stuff. They include Roger Abrams, Michael Henry Adams, Rob Adams, Nat Allbright, Sandy Alderson, Michael Angelich, Bill Aqualino, Andrew Arbiter, Megan Thomson Armstrong, Buddy Arnold, Ernest Baker, George Balamaci, Jack Balletti, Patti Barnes, Ted and Hal Barker, Tom Barthel, Gil Bassetti, Jim Beattie, Debbie Beatty,

Ruby Thomson Beatty, Geoff Belifante, Paul Bereswill, Peter Bileckyj, Henry Bischoff, Peggy Black, John Blackadar, Phylis Blackadar, John Bloomgarden, Norman Blumenthal, Willie Bly, Bill Bonanno, Larry Booher, Jean Boone, Jim Borax, Debbie Bosanek, Frank Bourgholtzer, John Bowen, Rosella Boyle, Molly Bracigliano, Al Branca, John Branca, Julius Branca, Marie Branca, Arlene Brey, Scott Bruce, Ronny Buchman, Warren Buffett, Linda Bunch, Alain Burgisser, Sid Caesar, Gordon Calhoun, Roy Campanella Jr., Walter Carberry, Benedict Carey, George Carlin, Pat Carlin, Karen Carpenter, Joseph Carr, Steve Carter, Jim Cartwright, Dominic Cavello, Ina Chadwick, Sid Chadwick, Dave Chase, Benjamin Cheever, David Clark, Guy Cogan, Deborah Cogliano, David Colchamiro, Craig Cole, Tommy Colletti, David Coogan, John Cooley, Francis Ford Coppola, Bob Costas, Pete Coutros, Robert Crockett, Bonnie Crosby, Ellen Cummings, Bob Cutter, Clifton Daniel, Margaret Truman Daniel, Michael Davies, Ronald DeChant, John Decker, Robert DeMott, Henry Deppe, Jim Dervin, Megan Desnoyers, Ralph DiStasio, Hugh Downs, Ronald Durham, Chris Durocher, Michele Durocher, Jim Edgemon, Robert Ehasz, Susan Ehasz, Osborn Ellliott, Albert Engelkin, Harold Enten, Robert Fagles, George Farrell Jr., Tommy Faucet, Katie Feeney, Andrew Fegyveresi, William Feldman, Clay Felker, Eric Fettmann, Fred Fields, Carolyn Filippi, Brian Fisher, Thomas Fitzgibbon, Helen Foley, Gerald Ford, Pearlene Foster, Amnerus Franks, Francine Franks, Gene Frederickson, Ken Frydman, Jesse Furman, Bill Gallo, Sarah Gehring, Richard Gelbke, William Gienapp, Rod Gilbert, Rudy Giuliani, Ed Goin, Larry Goldberg, Bob Goldman, Evan Goldsmith, Joe Goldstein, Bill Gorman, Melinda Gottlieb, Curt Gowdy, Cyril Greenhouse, Alan Greenspan, Bud Greenspan, John Greenwood, Frank Grossman, Estelle Gucik, Tom Guinzberg, Lauren Gurgiolo, Todd Gustavson, Mark Hacala, Fern Hack, David Hardy, Ted Hathaway, Mark Havens, Beatrice Hay, Sylvia Hebb, David Helfand, Pat Hemingway, Cheryl Brown Henderson, Greg Henderson, Mark Hess, Jack Hicks, Jim Hicks, Walter Hill, Ken Hirdt, Irene Hochberg, Sheldon Hochheiser, Pat Hodges, Milt Hoffman, Tot Holmes, Jerome Holtzman, George Hoover, Benny Huffman, Timothy Hughes, Irwin Hundert, Nancy Huseby, Karen Hyde, John Hyslop, Neil Isaacs, Joe Jacobsen, Andy Jurinko, Sylvia Kaiser, Earl Kallemeyn, Jessica Kaplan, Douglas Kass, Nathaniel Kiernan, Rich Klein, Tom Kleinschmidt, Nathaniel Kleppel, David Klingeman, Gloria Knapp, Richard Knies, Bob Knight, Estelle Kraysler, Gerry Kremenko, Charles Krobot, Bowie Kuhn, Sally Kuisel, Tara Lambert, Mark Langill, Dan Leary, Marty Lederhandler, Ronald Lee, Stuart Leeds, Rosemary Leo, Pat Leonard, Al Leoncini, Earl Leppo, Jerry Levine, Grace Lichtenstein, Josie Limbo, Marie Lippolis, Ron Littlefair, Nick Lomangino, Bernard and Paul Lomrantz, Leonard and Philip Lopate, Ed Lucas, Norman Macht, Rudy Mancuso, Shirley Marblestone, Len Marini, Michael Marletta, Anna McAuliffe, Roberta McConochie, John McCormack, G. Richard McKelvey, Jean Ann McMurrin, Patrick McVicar, Barbara Meek, Michael Meeropol, Leon Metzger, Missy Mikulecky, Arthur Miller, Calvin Miller, Jim Miller, Michael Laurence Miller, Sunny Mindel, Chuck Mitchell, Nancy Mitchell, Simon Mitton, Bergie Moffatt, Paul Mogren, Danny Monahan, Bill Moore, Noel Moran, Nelson Morgan, Mike Murphy, Suzie Narron, Harold Nelson, Lynn H. Nelson, Charlene Neuwiller, Joe Nossek, Greg O'Brien, Jim O'Connell, John O'Connell, Fred Opper, Erin Overbey, Charlie Owen, Bert Padell, Michael Paoli, Donald Papp, Ev Parker, Nick

Paumgarten, Tom Pendergast, Anthony Perrone, George Plimpton, Jack Pokress, Arty Pomerantz, Nancy Pope, Mike Porter, George Potterton, Samantha Power, Jeanene Prince, Seth Purdy, Felo Ramirez, Ed Randall, Del Reddy, Seth Redniss, Daniel Reed, Carl Reiner, Marianne Reynolds, Paul Rice, Jay Ricks, Joni Roan, Rachel Robinson, Werner Roeder, Fred Roos, Jerry Rosen, Ted Rosen, Faigi Rosenthal, Esther Roth, James Roth, Michael Roth, Marty Rothschild, George Roy, Art Russ Jr., Victor Sacco, Liz Saffly, Marshall Sahlins, Steve Samtur, Dorothy Sawatski, Rudie Schaffer, Jerry Schenz, Jim Schenz, Robert Schenz, Mordechai Schiller, Nota Schiller, Edith Schmeiser, Myrl Schnell, Alan Schuster, Joel Schuster, Allen Schwartz, David Schwartz, Bud Selig, Bill Shafer, Sheila Shale, Marion Shanely, Terry Seidler, Vern Shibla, Susan Shillinglaw, Elisabeth Sifton, Wilda Simonton, Stacy Slaughter, Michael Sloane, John Lee Smith, Billie Spencer, Bob Staake, Elaine Steele, Elaine Steinbeck, Brandon Steiner, Michael Steinhardt, C. David Stephan, Jerry Stern, John Paul Stevens, Joseph Stoldt, Brett Stolle, Stanley Strull, Seth Swirsky, Al Talboy, James Teaney, Margaret Tenney, Nancy Thommes, Jeff Thompson, Robert William Thompson, Glenn Thomson, Harley Tison, Jim Tobin, Matt Tyrnauer, Mary Valentine, Mike Veeck, Tom Villante, Brad Wadlow, Mary Wagner, Ben Walker, Josie Walters-Johnston, Jules Warzybok, Don Weber, Bobby Weinstein, Bill Weiss, Harry Wendelstedt, Shirley Wershba, Harlan Whatley, Fred Wilpon, Antoinette Yvars, David Yvars, Jack Yvars, Dorothy Zaiser, Dave Zenner, Genevieve Zeren and Agatha Zinnanti.

Thank you to Don DeLillo for sharing your research and thoughts. You uplifted me. Thanks to David Jurist who always had in mind the best interest of Bobby and Ralph, to Gerald Finkel who introduced me to Abe Chadwick, to Spider Jorgensen who fingered Hank Schenz, to Roger Sinnott who explained a telescope, to Rob Neyer who kept an eye out for writing that might be of help, to Glenn Codere and Kevin Gorman who unearthed records in Glasgow, to Yoichi Nagata who uncovered headlines in Japan, to David Wolitz who translated them, to Lauren Redniss whose special contributions extend from cover to penultimate sentence. Thanks to Susannah E. Brooks whom I turned to those few times I came up empty. There is nothing you can't find. Thanks to buddies Charlie Honig and Eric Columbus who answered a steady drip of questions. (Eric would like all to know that Dave Winfield was born on October 3, 1951. There. It's in the book. Here's the *other* tired bit of 10/3/51 trivia: Bill Sharman, future basketball great, was on the Brooklyn bench when Thomson hit the homer.) Thanks to Meir Feder for seventy-five minutes. Thanks to Sean Forman for baseball-reference.com. It is indispensable. Thanks to Angelo Ambrosio, Buzzie Bavasi, Laraine Day, Steve Gietschier, Pearl Gill, Michel Grilikhes, Jane Klain, Jack Lang, Eddie Logan Jr., Roger Logan, Jerry Schwab and Tom Shieber for many answers. Thanks to Ernie Harwell, the nicest man I encountered on this trip, to Jack Smalling for his booklet, to Nick Littlefield, Sandra Levinson and Sæmundur Pálsson for trying. Thanks to family and friends who helped me up those inclines that steepened this twenty-six-chapter marathon to Columbus Bakery, which fed me these past five years, and to my right index finger and thumb for typing this entire book.

Most of all, thank you, Mom. No passage was complete until it had your ear. I'm off to the Cape.

NOTES

A FEW NOTES ON THESE NOTES. I chose not to source the simple play-by-play of games or the more basic statistics. I chose not to source my many interviews that simply corroborated prior sources. Six times, rather than cite a string of sources particularly recurrent in a stretch of text, I wrote a summary of attribution (though I did cite separately all quotes). I absentmindedly did not date a small number of my interviews. And less than one percent of these near 4,000 notes are incomplete, missing a page number or date. (The gaps are often the result of having found a stray article belonging to a newspaper edition not transferred to microfilm.)

EPIGRAPH

ix The Ecchoing Green: Blake, "The Ecchoing Green," p. 8.

PROLOGUE

xiii Milton Glassman sat: Milton Glassman, interview, July 20, 2005.
xiii "Every American male": Twombly, "Arguments Rage," p. 7.
xiii Marshall Sahlins compiled: Sahlins, *Apologies to Thucydides*, p. 135.
xiii Ray Robinson added: Gelman, "Historic Baseball," p. 20.
xiii Jonathan Williams recounted: Williams, "Paying Respects," p. BR7.
xiii voted by the *Sporting News*: Falls, "Thomson HR No. 1," p. 35.
xiii "I have never known": Gould, "The H and Q," p. 50.
xiv Wrote Larry King: L. King, "Bobby Thomson's 'Shot'," p. 16.
xiv Said Tallulah Bankhead: "Talullah: 'I'm So Happy'," p. 18.
xiv Said Dick Schaap: "The Shot Heard Round the World," HBO.
xiv 240,000 home runs: David Vincent, Society for American Baseball Research.

CHAPTER ONE

3 "Now do you understand": Lewis, et al. *Horace Walpole's Correspondence*, p. 408.
3 darkened in seconds: "Storm Ties Up," p. 1.
3 turned on lights: Ibid.
3 toppled a tree: Ibid.
3 hailstones big as: Ibid.
3 rocked Sheepshead Bay: "Storm Halts Traffic," p. 1.
3 temperature freefell: "Storm Ties Up," p. 1.
3 garbage cans afloat: Ibid.

3 eighteen inches of water: "Storm Halts Traffic," p. 1.

3 cold front in Canada: "Storm Ties Up," p. 1.

3 railroad porter: Associated Press, "Father of Baseball Great."

4 "On sunny summer Sunday": Rampersad, *Collected Works of Langston Hughes*, p. 64.

4 Mays renting the first floor: Willie Mays, interview, November 13, 2004.

4 three 34-ounce bats: Millstein, "'Natural Boy' of the Giants," p. SM16.

4 left its mark: Koppett, "Mays' Homer in 1st," p. 23.

4 "I never saw a fucking ball": Charles Einstein, interview, September 22, 2004. Several Giants players remembered this quote to reporter Charles Einstein the day after the Mays home run. Says Einstein, "There may be one 'fucking' that's out of place."

4 "Say hey!": Felker, "Mays Is Giants' Counter," p. 4.

4 even before his center fielder: Lewin, "Giants Call Up," p. 26.

4 "Every time a kid": Willie Mays, interview, March 26, 2002.

4 to wag behind his back: Ostler, "How Willie Mays," p. 70.

5 Dangling Thomson: Spink, "Cubs' Upsurge Tribute," p. 4.

5 Ted McGrew telegrammed: Emil Bavasi, interview, January 7, 2002.

5 "And a little child": Emil Bavasi, interview, January 7, 2002.

5 .944 fielding percentage: *www.baseball-reference.com.* Thomson would record four more shutouts before switching to third base, finishing 1951 with a .966 fielding percentage in the outfield.

5 they booed: K. Smith, "Bucs Top Giants," p. 26. AND K. Smith, "Long-Hitting Giants," p. 8.

5 his spikes pierced: Lauder, "New York Held," p. 23.

5 Colletti raised high: Tommy Colletti, interview, October 28, 2004. AND "Flying Pennant at PG," p. 1.

5 Anthony Palermo sewed: "Thompson Optioned to Ottawa," p. 14.

6 a group of NAACP lawyers: Cheryl Brown Henderson, interview, February 2004.

6 just one of the thirteen parents: Cheryl Brown Henderson, interview, February 2004.

6 an estimated .315: Hogan, *Shades of Glory,* p. 387. The statistics of Negro league baseball are grossly incomplete. *Shades of Glory* compiled all available box scores of league games and yet has records for just 710 Dandridge at-bats over eight seasons: 1933–1938, 1942 and 1944. (Missing are data for his entire 1949 season.)

6 an estimated .343: Baseball Library. *www.baseballlibrary.com/* The statistics of Mexican league baseball are grossly incomplete.

7 first black player: *Chicago Defender*, p. 15.

7 felt an acute pain: Beebe, "Dandridge Has Operation," p. 22.

7 Stoneham and Durocher had now: McCulley, "Henry Thompson Goes," p. C21.

7 ninety-nine members: "Red Sox–Giants Series Forecast," p. 4.

7 "A new era": Daley, "Opening a Second," p. 45.

8 ripped his team: Murray, "Giants Clubhouse Man," p. 46.

8 Durocher then stamped: Ibid.

8   a trail of Fabergé cologne: Laraine Day, interview, August 13, 2001.
8   Billie gave birth to a baby: Billie Spencer, interview, May 8, 2001.
8   a terrier named Briney Marlin: Laraine Day, interview, August 13, 2001.
8   Durocher always went straight home: Ibid.
8   baseball diamond etched: Ibid.

CHAPTER TWO

9   "For de little stealin' ": O'Neill, *The Emperor Jones*, p. 12.
9   "complete contradiction": Mann, *Baseball Confidential*, p. 67.
9   atop the kitchen table: Durocher, *Nice Guys Finish Last*, p. 17.
9   serving mass: Ibid., p. 19.
9   failed to recite: Mann, *Baseball Confidential*, p. 5.
9   the finger-glove: Ibid., p. 5.
9   George, an engineer: Durocher, *Nice Guys Finish Last*, p. 18.
9   eked out extra money: Eskenazi, *The Lip*, p. 19.
9   The $1.50 souvenirs: *Spalding Base Ball Guide*, p. 160.
9   at 50 School Street: Eskenazi, *The Lip*, p. 18.
9   there are no records: Ibid., p. 20.
10 shoot marbles then pool: Ibid., p. 20.
10 offering Durocher $30: Durocher, *Nice Guys Finish Last*, p. 26.
10 Durocher sat and tallied: Ibid.
10 battery manufacturer approached: Ibid.
10 Wico promised $57.50: Ibid.
10 $150 a month: Ibid., p. 30.
10 in the starting lineup: "Schwartz Is Hero," p. 1.
10 paid $7,000: Eskenazi, *The Lip*, p. 39.
10 on October 2, 1925: "Dykes Raps Out 5," p. 20.
10 $5,000: National Baseball Hall of Fame Library.
10 "Durocher's play,": Harrison, "Lazzeri's Big Blow," p. 18.
11 $5 argyle socks: Durocher, *Nice Guys Finish Last*, p. 51.
11 pearl-buttoned shirts: Ibid., p. 52.
11 delivered always from Sulka: Ibid., p. 51.
11 "Leo Durocher," noted: "Lots of Nerve," p. B3.
11 watched Jimmy Durante: Durocher, *Nice Guys Finish Last*, p. 52.
11 Bojangles Bill: Ibid., p. 51.
11 lots of showgirls: Ibid., p. 52.
11 headed to Scabouche's: Mann, *Baseball Confidential*, p. 20.
11 "Leo Durocher Day": Ibid., p. 9.
11 "the freshest and gamest": Ibid.
11 the Lip partied: Ibid., p. 10.
11 owed, for example, the Hotel: Durocher, *Nice Guys Finish Last*, p. 50.
11 to buy a Packard: Ibid., p. 49.
11 "The Yanks," reported: Wedge, "Leo Durocher Sent," p. 37.
12 a mess in Cincinnati: Mann, *Baseball Confidential*, p. 23.
12 in St. Louis great debts: Durocher, *Nice Guys Finish Last*, p. 56.
12 fleecing pitcher Kirby: Ibid., p. 223.

12 Murphy telephoned baseball commissioner: Kahn, *The Era*, p. 36. AND Roger Kahn, interview, July 27, 2004. Kahn reported that Bill Shea told him the story.

12 Father Vincent Powell: "C.Y.O. Turns Thumbs Down," p. 19.

12 freshly divorced starlet: "Laraine Day, Divorced," p. 1.

12 Durocher bellyached: Young, "Lippy Charges," p. 45.

12 "as a result": Durocher, *Nice Guys Finish Last*, p. 228.

12 beautiful in white gown: Mann, *Baseball Confidential*, p. 124.

12 1,500 diners applauded: Ibid.

12 a March night in Panama: Durocher, *Nice Guys Finish Last*, p. 178.

12 "I hear some of you": Ibid.

12 outfielder Dixie Walker: Years later, Walker told author Roger Kahn "it was the dumbest thing I did in all my life. . . . I am deeply sorry." (Kahn, *The Era*, p. 35.)

13 shipping his soiled shirts: Laraine Day, interview, August 13, 2001.

13 Rickey wrote on: Mann, *Baseball Confidential*, p. 158.

13 "I'm through": United Press, "Giants Lose No. 1," p. 9.

13 for perhaps the first time: Because there are not newspaper accounts of all such early games, it is impossible to know if the teams had met before.

13 October 21, 1845: *Brooklyn Eagle* photo caption: "A Great Match At Base-Ball This Afternoon," October 21, 1845, p. 2.

13 Knickerbocker Baseball Club: Chadwick, *Beadle's Dime Base-Ball Player (1860)*. The team codified its rules on September 23, 1845.

13 "the National game": "Base Ball," p. 268.

13 "Verily, Brooklyn is fast": "Brooklyn Base Ball," p. 245.

13 "If we are ahead": "Base Ball," p. 2.

13 "No other games": "The Base-Ball Field," p. 407.

14 a tall lineup and trolley dodgers: Sanborn, "Local Fans Must," p. C3. AND "Nickname of Giants," p. 11.

14 "Defeat from any": "One Game," p. 3.

14 "Tactics were": "Tricky Tactics," p. 1.

14 a botched signal: Kavanaugh and Macht, *Uncle Robbie*, p. 54.

14 alcohol-loosened: p. 53.

14 Giants 218, Dodgers 213: Dave Smith, *Retrosheet*.

15 "still in the league": Associated Press, "Dodgers After Giants'," p. A8.

15 three of New: The *New York Herald Tribune*, the *Daily News* and the *New York Evening Post*. The question asked of Terry that precipitated comment has long been attributed to the *New York Times* reporter Roscoe McGowen, but no papers credit him, and he himself doesn't mention his alleged role when on March 11, 1934, (page S5) he first mentions the quote.

15 "What has kept": Kahn, "Sixty Years of Feuding," p. 55

15 "the plump blond boys": Agee, "Brooklyn Is," p. 72.

15 Alfred Kazin played ball: Kazin, *A Walker in the City*, p. 86.

15 "through the outer parts of Brooklyn": "City Intelligence," p. 2.

15 "Dodger fans had every vulgarity": Kempton, "Back at the Polo Grounds," p. 46.

15 Robert Joyce shot: "Walks Into a Bar," p. 22.

15 "If Durocher keeps them": Parrott, "Stoneham Buries," p. 2.

16 Durocher whipped Stoneham: Dave Smith, *Retrosheet.*
16 fan named Fred Boysen: "Durocher Accused," p. 1.
16 Giant management decreed: "Leo Durocher Reinstated," p. 17.
16 eighty feet above center field: Lowry, *Green Cathedrals*, p. 196.

CHAPTER THREE

17 "The sailors come ashore": Mendelson, *W. H. Auden*, p. 197.
17 "Schenz can do everything": Garagiola and Quigley, *Baseball Is a Funny Game*, p. 46.
17 Wrote Joe Garagiola: Ibid.
17 "because he could run and holler": Article in a scrapbook of Susan Ehasz, missing publication details.
18 would one day be clocked: Haag, "Hank Schenz . . . A Dirt-Belly," p. 120. The article alleges that Cincinnati Red Evar Swanson set the record, 13.3 seconds, in 1929, but the Hall of Fame does not maintain such a record.
18 A broken thumb: Ward, "On Second Thought," p. 28.
18 ballplayer met bookkeeper: Wilda Simonton, interview, July 28, 2004.
18 "It was love at first sight": James Teaney, interview, July 28, 2004.
18 two seasons of Class D: From correspondence with Bill Francis: Schenz spent 1939 with Salem-Roanoke of the Virginia League and 1940 with Tarboro of the Coastal Plain League.
18 Betty put on a skirt and jacket: Wilda Simonton, interview, July 28, 2004.
18 "We used to call him 'Squeaky' ": Edward Wodzicki, interview, February 2002.
18 "Never says 'can't' ": This was written by an unnamed member of the Portsmouth organization and distributed in-house to each of the players. Courtesy of Susan Ehasz.
18 On September 24: Notice of Separation from U.S. Navy, courtesy of the Schenz family.
18 crew cut, camouflage and 20-millimeter: Phil Rizzuto, interview, December 2001.
18 "Schenz did his job well": Phil Rizzuto, interview, Fall 2000.
18 "Neither snow nor rain": The passage is from Book 8, Chapter 98, of Herodotus, and is the translation of architect Kendall himself. Schneider, "F.Y.I.," p. 2.
19 Schenz often recited them verbatim: Gloria Knapp, interview, June 4, 2001.
19 rated MAM 1C: Notice of Separation from U.S. Navy, courtesy of the Schenz family.
19 Nicknamed "Stamp": Haag, "Hank Schenz . . . A Dirt-Belly," p. 120.
19 "He did what all the ballplayers": James Schenz, interview, Fall 2000.
19 Upwards of 4,000: Bedingfield, *Baseball in World War II Europe*, introduction.
19 23 Norfolk at-bats: "Leading Yankee Slugger," p. 3.
19 On March 23, 1944: Gloria Knapp, interview, June 4, 2001.
19 "He drove like a postman": Ibid.
19 Next morning, Schenz: Ibid.
20 "If your dad says": James Schenz, interview, Fall 2000.

20 an 83-22-2 record: "Schenz Takes Hitting Honors," p. 5.

20 In 409 at-bats: Ibid.

20 "How come this sudden": Diehl, "Dealing it Out, p. 17.

20 boarding on October 13: Eddie Robinson, interview, December 27, 2001.

20 retrofitted President Lines cargo ship: Crissey, *Athletes Away*, p. 44.

20 lend their dogs: Allen, *Hawaii's War Years, 1941–1945*, p. 192.

20 makers of leis: Dye, *Hawai'i Chronicles III*, p. 49.

21 reconnoitering Pearl: Ibid., p. 107.

21 to plot the Formosa: Allen, *Hawaii's War Years, 1941–1945*, p. 187.

21 okayed smoking: Dye, *Hawai'i Chronicles III*, p. 161.

21 "Restoration Day": Ibid., p. 162.

21 faced the sea: Ibid., p. 168.

21 until 7:30 p.m.: Ibid., p. 167.

21 until eight: Ibid., p. 140.

21 pose for pictures: Ibid., p. 148.

21 amusement park: Ibid.

21 Pearl Harbor Submarine Base won: Crissey, *Athletes Away*, p. 58.

21 fifty-nine top players chosen: Ibid., p. 61.

21 450 ships docking: Allen, *Hawaii's War Years, 1941–1945*, p. 224.

21 some 253,000 troops: Ibid., p. 219.

21 a crowd of 22,000 servicemen: Crissey, *Athletes Away*, p. 63.

21 Schenz smacked a double: Ibid.

21 December 14, 1945: Notice of Separation from U.S. Navy, courtesy of the Schenz family.

22 2,116 fans: Effrat, "Cubs' 3-Run Eighth," p. 41.

22 umpire George Barr: Ibid.

22 Chicago swapped Schenz: "Schenz Shuffle," p. 23.

22 rated by New York scout: K. Smith, "Giants Land Schenz," p. 36.

22 "I can remember him sweeping": Joe Garagiola, interview, Fall 2000.

22 "Give me some": Nathan, *The McFarland Baseball Quotations Dictionary*, p. 149.

23 "Schenz, in all": "Holmes Sees Action," p. S2.

23 required thirty-day wait: In 1951, a team had to wait thirty days to re-release a player onto waivers if it was to collect the fee from his new team.

23 Schenz was in uniform: Uniform specifics courtesy of the Schenz family.

23 "the Little Giant": Charvat, " 'Pepper Pod' Schenz," p. 12.

23 "He'd wash our backs": Thomson, interview, November 19, 2000.

CHAPTER FOUR

24 "The player on the home": Potter, *The Theory and Practice of Gamesmanship*, p. 59.

24 handed the keys of his '47 Pontiac: Al Corwin, interviews, May 11, 2001, and June 5, 2001.

24 "That was about all I brought": Ibid.

24 Corwin, twenty-four, had grown up: Ibid., and June 5, 2001.

24 lightning lit the wet night: Ibid.

24 Corwin finally touched down: Ibid.

25 dialed WAdsworth 6-8160: Ibid.

25 the city's nearly 3.5 million: Cohn, *What A Year It Was! 1951*, p. 48.

25 was born: Pacini, "Remembering Gehrig," p. 26.

25 a little wagon: Ibid.

25 began operating the: Roberts, "A Boy Among Giants," p. 38.

25 the great Mel Ott: Ibid.

25 the average American annual income: Cohn, *What A Year It Was! 1951*, p. 46.

26 "I'm Al Corwin": Al Corwin, interview, June 5, 2001.

26 The Giant clubhouse: The description of the clubhouse that runs through page 29 was assembled through scores of interviews with people who spent considerable time in it, including Jerry Schwab, Eddie Logan, Roger Logan, Angelo Ambrosio, Chris Durocher, Laraine Day and a few dozen Giant players.

26 60 by 60 feet: Lowry, *Green Cathedrals*, p. 196.

26 painted bilious: "Some Marvels," p. M4.

26 going green in 1913: "More Yankees Sail," p. 11.

26 upper deck in 1922: "Kelly's Bat Leads," p. 27.

26 painted in 1948: McGowen, "Setting Improved," p. 36.

26 NO BETTING PERMITTED: Stein, *Under Coogan's Bluff*, p. 10.

26 two massage tables: Garreau, *Bat Boy of the Giants*, p. 168.

26 a handheld vibrating: Ibid.

26 a diathermy machine: Ibid.

27 packed ten dozen: Pacini, "Remembering Gehrig," p. 26.

27 Durocher kept the office: Description assembled from 1952 photographs courtesy of Chris Durocher.

27 mahogany desk: Richman, "Giant Manager Fears," p. 19.

27 a bar stocked: Durocher, *Nice Guys Finish Last*, p. 283.

27 forty-eight feet below: Lowry, *Green Cathedrals*, p. 198.

28 Five feet tall: Ibid.

28 sills eleven feet above field: Ibid.

28 no batted ball ever hit: Ibid., p. 200.

28 Logan handed him the smallest uniform: Al Corwin, interview, June 5, 2001.

28 the cover of *Time*: April 14, 1947, issue.

28 called Corwin to his office: Al Corwin, interview, June 5, 2001.

28 could see, just out the windows: Ibid.

28 the base-running boner: Baserunner Merkle did not touch second base after an Al Bridwell single on September 23, 1908.

28 fractured skull and death: A pitch from Carl Mays struck Chapman in the fifth inning on August 16, 1920.

28 the striking out consecutively: Hubbell struck out in succession Babe Ruth, Lou Gehrig, Jimmie Foxx, Al Simmons and Joe Cronin in the first two innings of the All-Star Game on July 10, 1934.

29 the speech by President Roosevelt: It was broadcast at the end of the seventh inning in a 1–1 game versus the Boston Braves.

29 "When your enemy": FDR Presidential Library and Museum. Said on May 27, 1941.

29 Neither did Bernard Doyle: McHarry and Lee, "Mystery Bullet," p. 3C.

29 vendors first hocked: Associated Press, "English-Born Creator," p. 1.
29 Jack Norworth wrote: Snyder, "Lagunan Still," p. OC1.
29 He would not take himself: Driscoll, "Pages From," p. A2.
29 home plate ump: Wedge, "Many Changes," p. 10B. Done on August 25, 1929.
29 a controversial home run: Hit by Red Harry Craft on July 15, 1939.
29 he convened his players: Kremenko, "Rookie Hurler," p. 16.
29 "He told": McCulley, "Giants Bazooka Cards," p. 57.
29 for $16 pheasant: Lait, *New York: Confidential!*, p. 48.
29 331 Manhattan: "Taverns," *New York City Classified Telephone Directory*, pp. 1685–86.
29 dope for sale: Lait, *New York: Confidential!*, p. 37.
29 where for $20: Ibid., p. 99.
29 slacks and a pastel: Rennie, "Durocher Puts Thomson," p. 17.
30 blow of a nose: Davis, *Lore and Legends of Baseball*, p. 152. AND Light, *The Cultural Encyclopedia of Baseball*, p. 671.
30 covering of a crotch: Lidz, "The Best Signs," p. 46.
30 direction of spit: Mentus, "Sign Language," p. 86.
30 In 1973, Joe Nossek: Joe Nossek, interview, February 5, 2002.
30 The Texas batter peered: Ibid.
30 "haven't the cerebral equipment": "He Needed," p. 36.
30 "Bunt, you meathead!": Gammons, "Sign Language," p. 80.
31 "Goddam it!" he yelled: Al Corwin, interview, Fall 2000.
31 "Win any way you can": Durocher, *Nice Guys Finish Last*, p. 1.
31 "He says a loyal Giant fan": Sal Yvars, interview, November 18, 2004.
31 "We've got to start": Al Corwin, interview, Fall 231.
31 Jules Loh: Loh, "It's Simple to Catch."
31 "Everyone talks about": Broeg, "Giants Stole," p. 16.
31 "The first-inning": Goddard, *All New Orioles Scorebook*, p. 15b.
32 "Who wants the signs?": Monte Irvin, interview, Fall 2000.
32 has just .13 seconds: Gutman, "The Physics," p. 74.
32 "Suppose he calls": Wes Westrum, interview, Fall 2000.
33 "You want the signs": Monte Irvin, interview, Fall 2000.
33 "You mean to tell me": Ibid.
33 Birdie Tebbetts had: Siegel, "Tigers Started," p. 30.
34 Enough of the team *did* want: Al Corwin, interview, January 2001.
34 digging trenches: McGowen, "Dodger Pitching Problem," p. 15.
34 its toll on the Midwest devastating: Cohn, *What A Year It Was! 1951*, p. 140.
34 "This rain is": Murray, "Rain Gives Lippy," p. 42.
34 "Rain Gives Lippy": *New York Post*, July 20, 1951, p. 42.

CHAPTER FIVE

35 "Early blue evening": Rampersad, *Collected Works of Langston Hughes*, p. 34.
35 "Baseball is in its infancy": Sanborn, "Local Fans Must," p. C3.
35 Elke and Isaac, were first cousins: Ina Chadwick, interview, July 7, 2001.

35 Moored in Poughkeepsie: "List or Manifest of Alien Immigrants for the Commissioner of Immigration." NARA.

35 boarded in Liverpool: Ibid.

35 two-masted: Bonsor, *North Atlantic Seaway*, Vol. 2, p. 762.

35 were spared disinfectant: "List or Manifest of Alien Immigrants for the Commissioner of Immigration." NARA.

35 a string of facts: Ibid.

36 (Likely it had been Czadwicz): Ina Chadwick, interview, July 7, 2001.

36 "What value does a game": Pollack and Mniewski, "Should Children," p. 4.

36 Cahan responded: Ibid.

36 at 120 Wallabout: "Thirteenth Census of the United States: 1910—Population." NARA.

36 Chadwick became the starting: *The High School Recorder*, pp. 33–36.

36 Afield he committed: Ibid.

36 the only student: *Red and Black*, p. 145.

37 "Captain Chadwick": Ibid.

37 Chadwick got kicked out: Harriet Mesulam, interview, November 28, 2000.

37 fresh and street-smart, Runyonesque: Harriet Mesulam and Helen Smith, interviews, July 3, 2001.

37 on October 29 took: "Amateurs Box," p. 15.

37 Chadwick was a linotype operator: Harriet Mesulam, interview, November 28, 2000.

37 On July 6, 1918: National Personnel Records Center and N.Y. State Archives.

37 Assigned to a medical: Ibid.

37 psychiatric wards and: Weed, *The Medical Department of the United States Army in the World War*, Vol. V, pp. 329–330.

37 "he stuffed dead bodies": Harriet Mesulam and Helen Smith, interviews, July 3, 2001.

37 647 Fox Street: National Personnel Records Center and N.Y. State Archives.

37 the men agreed to meet back: Harriet Mesulam and Helen Smith, interviews, July 3, 2001.

38 A bullet caught him: Ibid.

38 fell in love with Miriam Marblestone: Ibid.

38 as a stenographer: Helen Smith, interview, April 18, 2006. AND New York City Department of Records and Information Services, Marriage License, February 16, 1926.

38 On March 9, 1926: Certificate of Marriage, New York City Department of Records and Information Services, Certificate of Marriage, March 9, 1926.

38 480 Concord Avenue: "Fifteenth Census of the United States: 1930—Population Schedule." NARA. AND Harriet Mesulam and Helen Smith, interviews, July 3, 2001.

38 his Checker Model T: Photo of taxi courtesy of Harriet Mesulam, Chadwick's daughter.

38 the top half of: Sales brochure, 1933–34, Checker Taxi Corp.

39 two months after: Application for Account Number, Social Security Administration, September 9, 1937.

39 36 of them: "The Electric Light," *Boston Daily Globe*, p. 2.

39 just 90,000 candlepower: Ibid.

39 Jordan Marsh and R. H. White: "The Electric Light," *Boston Post*, p. 3.

39 first professional night game: "Muskogee Tramples," p. 10.

39 ten foot-candles of light: Pietrusza, *Lights On!*, p. 56.

39 "The night air": "Night Baseball," p. 4.

39 the National League voted: Drebinger, "Night Baseball on," p. 31.

40 616 1,500-watt lamps: Brands, "Initial Test," p. 3.

40 123,991 folks: Pietrusza, *Lights On!*, p. 117.

40 "Night baseball": "Giants Dispel," p. 37.

40 Dodger games aired: "Dodger Baseball," p. 29.

40 the 300,000 Brooklynites: Halberstam, *Sports on New York Radio*, p. 235.

40 "in the catbird seat": Smith, *Voices of the Game*, p. 46.

40 Chadwick often headed to the Bellmore: Willie Bly, interview, Winter 2002.

40 "We used to bring our own chocolate": Ibid.

41 "He was very animated": Bob Goldman, interview, July 16, 2001.

41 finagled for his big brother: Dr. Gerald Finkel, interview, December 7, 2000.

41 "This is to certify": Archives of the Joint Industry Board of the Electrical Industry.

41 abuzz with work: Duff, "Glamorizing a Trolley," p. 8.; Unver, "Idlewood Airport's," p. 4; Ebert, "Local 3 Men," p. 4.; AND "Waterside Powerhouse 1," p. 4.

41 "He would tell him where": Helen Smith, interview, March 16, 2002.

41 the union "was his life": Harriet Mesulam, interview, November 28, 2000.

42 "Suppose Hubbell": "Night Ball Dangers," p. 3.

42 the Giants finally announced: Drebinger, "Giants Will Play," p. 31.

42 roughly $135,000: Ibid.

42 Westinghouse Electric: Ibid.

42 enough to light: Patterson, "Giants' Lighting System," p. 25.

42 over Harrisburg: "Giants to Play 10," p. 67.

42 Belmont Iron Works: Drebinger, "Giants Will Play," p. 31.

42 only fastball: J. Smith, "Gumbert Faces," p. 52.

42 when play began: Cross, "New York Team's," p. 19.

42 "It was so bright": Cross, Ibid.

42 German submarines lurked: Baldwin, "U-Boats Off," p. 3.

43 had banned nighttime baseball: "Night Ball Is Assured," p. 11.

43 a wooden ladder, some twenty feet tall: Walter Carberry, interview, April 30, 2002.

43 step out onto the pebbled: Ibid.

43 "You had to have good thumbs": Ibid.

43 836 bulbs: Drebinger, "Giants Will Play," p. 31.

43 eight steel towers 150 feet: Ibid.

43 8.7 acres: "Polo Grounds Value," p. 42.

43 retreated to the stands: Harriet Mesulam, interview, July 3, 2001.

43 "Without me, no game": Ibid.

43 There were other pleasures as well: Harriet Mesulam and Helen Smith, interviews, July 3, 2001.

43 the empty lot on: Bernard Lomrantz, e-mail message, February 14, 2003.

43 captured in a silent home movie: Movie courtesy of Bernard Lomrantz.

43 mistaking for cheers: Bernard Lomrantz, e-mail message, February 14, 2003.

44 sat down at 4:30 p.m.: Letter courtesy of Helen Smith, daughter of Chadwick.

44 "He coughed every morning": Harriet Mesulam, interview, May 20, 2004.

44 brothers Chadwick welcomed: "Mayor Impelliteri," p. 1.

44 lighted the steel ball dropping: Bob Goldman, interview, March 16, 2002.

44 In 1951, Local 3 elected: Joe Jacobson, interview, July 17, 2001.

44 Abe had become: Margolies, "Bronx Acorn," p. 1.

44 "For these extras": Joe Jacobson, interview, July 17, 2001.

44 the union paid him: Payroll records from the Archives of the Joint Industry Board of the Electrical Industry.

44 had earned $388.80: Ibid.

45 "He would watch the banks of lights": Walter Carberry, interview, April 30, 2002.

45 the only pens: "Only Pen," p. 6. AND Burns, "Polo Grounds Glitters," p. B5.

45 "like cows": Angell, "Early Innings," p. 86.

45 an electrician of at best average ability: Joe Jacobson, interview, July 17, 2001.

45 the "J" on his union card carried a stigma: Ibid.

46 Carrying the few tools: The description of Chadwick's handiwork was assembled through several interviews with Walter Carberry and George Farrell, Jr., whom Chadwick told of his work, and with Dr. Gerald Finkel at the Local 3 electricians union, who diagrammed exactly how the work was done.

46 base plate: *Hawkins Electrical Guide Number 8*, p. 2378.

CHAPTER SIX

47 "The best mirror": Palmer, *The English Works of George Herbert*, p. 46.

47 he asked Tom Watson: McCulley, "Durocher Re-Signs," p. 26.

47 $50,000 richer: National Baseball Hall of Fame Library.

47 Franks was born: Herman Franks, interview, January 20, 2002.

47 Celeste Franch: Ibid.

47 Celeste and Edith divorced: Ibid.

48 Edith encouraged: Renzhofer, "Baseball Was," p. J4.

48 quickly at Pioneer Park: Mooney, "'Franks Park' Is," p. D1.

48 local mom and pops: McFadden, "Franks Gets Pilot," p. 19.

48 "Herman certainly needs": *Eastonia*, p. 45.

48 a cauliflower ear: Holtzman, "Hrabosky Slipping?," p. 17.

48 A smidge taller: Herman Franks, interview, January 20, 2002.

48 ninth native Utahan: Baseball-Reference.com. *www.baseball-reference.com.*

"Batters Born in Utah." Spencer Adams, Roy Castleton, Ed Heusser, Ray Jacobs, Newt Kimball, Red Peery, Gordon Slade, Lee Thompson.

48 for $25,000: Associated Press, "Herman Franks Sworn."

48 tying a major league: McGowen, "Dodgers Top Reds, p. 33. The NY Giants started the 1918 season 9-0.

48 *Times* ran a photo: Ibid.

48 "I varied them so much": Herman Franks, interview, December 17, 2000.

49 "They were trying": Ibid.

49 behind the plate that very: Associated Press, "Bears Start Hank."

49 Phelps was missing: "Brooklyn Catcher Insists," p. 12.

49 Durocher telephoned the catcher: Durocher, *Nice Guys Finish Last*, p. 60.

49 "I've had the misery": International News Service, "Babe Phelps Says," p. 16.

49 the stocky catcher had refused: "Giants to Open Series," p. 25.

49 not to catch against Pittsburgh: Creamer, *Baseball and Other Matters in 1941*, p. 179.

49 Two Brooklyn doctors: Ibid.

49 Durocher suspended Phelps: "Brooklyn Catcher Insists," p. 12.

49 a tag on the jaw: McGowen, "Reds' Five in Ninth," p. 22.

49 "could cuss, chew tobacco": Minter, "Risk Is," p. 2-JL.

50 35-ounce, 35-inch: Herman Franks, interview, January 20, 2002.

50 chewed hard: Ibid.

50 whiskey his preference: Golenbock, *BUMS*, p. 30.

50 a loner, had a bad temper: Ibid., p. 31.

51 Larry Goetz raised: AP photo in the *New York Post*, October 6, 1941, p. 15.

51 "He swung!": Mutual Broadcasting System, recording of game, October 5, 1941.

51 uniformed police: Drebinger, "Yanks Win in 9th," p. 21.

51 "It's an error for the catcher": Mutual Broadcasting System, recording of game, October 5, 1941.

51 89 degrees: "Mercury at 90," p. 1.

51 sat stunned: Drebinger, "Yanks Win in 9th," p. 21.

51 reliever Curt Davis: Ibid.

51 "there's a redheaded": Mutual Broadcasting System, recording of game, October 5, 1941.

51 bloodshot: Mitchell, "Most Incredible Break," p. 15.

51 "It was a great": McGowen, "Dodgers Stress Luck," p. 21.

51 "Series Goat": New York *Daily News* caption headline, October 6, 1941, p. 40.

51 "Owen Shoulders": *New York Times*, October 6, 1941, p. 21.

51 "Most Incredible": *New York Post*, October 6, 1941, p. 15.

52 returned, unsigned, his contract: "Franks Joins I.L.," p. 25.

52 more than a $50 raise: Herman Franks, interview, January 20, 2002.

52 applied for a commission: MacDonald, "Lip's Style," p. 3.

52 some 2,200 men: Ibid.

52 Franks entered the service: Associated Press, "Herman Franks Sworn."

52 There Franks sat: "MacPhail and Ticket," p. 21.

52 "Oh, they used to agitate": Edward Wodzicki, interview, February 2002.

52 spurning a large raise: "Mexican Offers Rejected," p. 34.

53 the only player-manager: McFadden, "Franks Gets Pilot," p. 29.

53 Lane fined him $25: United Press, "Dilatory Ballplayer," p. 36.

53 Lane fined him $50: "Lane Fines Franks," page unknown.

53 195 pounds: Herman Franks, interview, January 20, 2002.

53 bought forty-five acres in East Beach for $19,400: Herman Franks, interview, December 17, 2000.

53 "It was very nice": Herman Franks, interview, January 20, 2002.

54 "Leo was disgusted": Ibid.

54 had activated Franks: Effrat, "Giants, Conquered by Reds," p. 20.

54 had caught 141 games: www.baseball-reference.com.

54 the first hit off Bud: Murray, "Franks 'Revival' ", p. 39.

54 "He chugged down": Daley, "The New Giant," p. S2.

54 a welt throbbed: Murray, "Franks 'Revival'," p. 39.

54 the only player in baseball: Elias Sports Bureau, Inc.

54 "exhibited plenty of zip": K. Smith, "Giants Grab," p. 29.

54 "They were no-good": Golenbock, BUMS, p. 292.

55 At one a.m.: "Wife on Phone," p. 6.

55 "I am completely innocent": "Casey, Ex-Dodger," p. 18.

55 "I should've called time": Robinson, Pennants & Pinstripes, p. 71.

55 fill in as pitching coach: Effrat, "Pair of Grand Slams," p. 8.

55 Durocher subbed: Ibid.

55 parroting the question: Wes Westrum, interview, Fall 2000.

55 "Peanuts Lowery," Herman Franks: Cunningham, "Fine Art," p. D3.

56 "We decoded the German signs": Herman Franks, interview, Fall 2000.

CHAPTER SEVEN

57 "Can't hear with bawk": Joyce, Finnegans Wake, p. 215.

57 which Johnny Mize likened: Povich, "This Morning," July 14, 1948, p. 17.

57 founded Nieuw Haarlem: Riker, Harlem: Its Origin and Early Annals, p. 192.

57 tribes including the Wickquaskeek: Ibid., p. 187.

57 Richard Nicolls claiming: Ibid., pp. 252–253.

57 "doth and shall": Ibid., p. 272.

57 The first to privately own: Ibid., pp. 297–298, footnotes pp. 539–540, 559, 604–605.

57 "Division of the Common Lands": Ibid., pp. 604–605.

58 The two lots meandered: Ibid., p. 615.

58 passed for decades along Oblinus and Waldron heirs: Ibid., p. 615.

58 next belonged to a Jan Dykman: Ibid., p. 615.

58 John Watkins finished buying: Ibid., p. 520.

58 Watkins set sail for Wales: Heusser, The Forgotten General, p. 147.

58 wife Lydia, mindful of a husband: Ibid., p. 195.

58 "After leaving the falls": Steiner, Life and Correspondence of James McHenry, p. 21.

58 Dr. Samuel Watkins sold: Index of the City Register, Liber 557, p. 414.

58   Morgan in turn flipped: Ibid.
58   Harris, though, invested: "Interesting Developments," p. 1.
58   one William Lynch: "Real Estate," p. 8.
58   then ceded control: "Polo Grounds Transferred," p. 4.
58   in 1897 officially acquire: "Recorded Real," April 1, 1889, p. 10. AND
       "Recorded Real," December 24, 1897, p. 10.
58   Coogan and Lynch had wed: "Mrs. Coogan," p. 26.
58   mayoral bid failed: "Mrs. Coogan," p. 26.
58   "He was a practical": Bolton, *Washington Heights, Manhattan*, p. 103.
59   evicted by a city: "No Baseball on the," p. 8.
59   Staten Island: "A New Baseball," p. 3.
59   leasing the southern portion: Ibid.
59   John Day called his diamond: "The New Polo," p. 12.
59   leasing the northern half: Ward, "Baseballists Up," p. 2.
59   outcropping of mica: Bracker, "Memories of a Boyhood," p. S3.
59   free view: Ibid.
59   a "narrow, tantalizing wedge": Marx, with Barber, *Harpo Speaks . . .
       About New York*, p. 41.
59   "Dead-Head Hill": "The Giants Are at," p. 3.
59   "witnessed the game": "The Orange," p. 1.
59   the stands burned: "Polo Grounds Swept," p. 1.
59   $40,000: Sangree, "No More War," p. 27.
59   concrete footing: Herts, "Grand Stand," p. 457.
59   asbestos roof: J-M Asbestos Roofing ad. *Green's Fruit Grower*, p. 9.
59   telegraphs and telephones: Foster, "The Magnificent New," p. 102.
59   canvas sun shields: "Polo Grounds Ready," p. C5.
59   25,065 fannies: Brush, "The Evolution," p. 3.
59   Blue and gold: Foster, "The Magnificent New," p. 98.
59   Italian marble: Ibid.
59   eagles spread: Ibid.
59   eighty feet: Ibid.
59   bas-relief: Ibid.
59   "was the mightiest temple": Sangree, "No More War," p. 24.
60   "To a batter standing": Eig, *Luckiest Man*, p. 17.
60   "The mere age and squalor": Kempton, "Back at the Polo," p. 62.
60   extending an index finger: Andy Seminick, interview, July 2001.
60   a Wollensak trained on Howell's pink finger: John Jorgensen, interview, Fall
       2000.
60   "Whoever cut that hole": Al Gettel, interview, May 21, 2004.
60   THE GREATEST PITCHER: National Baseball Hall of Fame Library.
60   bronze on green concrete: Harrison, "Giants Break Even," p. 30. The
       plaque was unveiled on September 27, 1928.
60   "All is fair": Matthewson, *Pitching in a Pinch*, p. 143.
60   measured 35 millimeters: Roger Sinnott at *Sky & Telescope Magazine*
       examined the telescope.
60   optically perfect telescope: Ibid.
61   at least .2 inch: Ibid.

61 The *Sporting News*: Spink, *Baseball Register*, p. 149.
61 He had told Davey: Davey Williams, interview, Fall 2000.
61 "It was so loud": Al Corwin, interview, March 1, 2002.
61 "what was easiest to see": Al Corwin, interview, January 2001.
61 half-inch of field: Heinz, "Polo Grounds Has," p. 30.
61 paid Jimmy Slattery: Ibid.
61 3,000 cubic: Ibid.
61 a hybrid: Ibid.
61 just denied: Hynd, "Found," no page number.
61 Schwab stumbled: Ibid.
62 concrete blocks: King, "Giants Park Real," p. 17.
62 Stoneham said no: Hynd, "Found," no page number.
62 pale yellow: King, "Giants Park Real," p. 17.
62 discovered in 1946: True, "Ott Discovers," p. 38.
62 15 degrees cooler: Ibid.
62 sloped down 18 inches: Lowry, *Green Cathedrals*, p. 198.
62 Durocher could see only: Ibid.
63 the bowtied Irish umpire: Harry Wendelstedt, interview, March 4, 2002.
63 screamed: "BAAALLL!": Ibid.
63 "We thought the whole ballpark": Al Corwin, interview, Fall 2000.
63 Louis Kleppel who hawked novels: Nathaniel Kleppel, interview, July 2001.
63 a cabbie who always: Garagiola and Quigley, *Baseball Is a Funny Game*, p. 96.
63 a quartet of well-dressed women: Larry Jansen, interview, February 28, 2002.
63 Section 39 Solarium Club: "Solarium Club Formed," p. 7.
63 Section 5 Club: Effrat, "Giants, Dodgers, Yanks," p. 21.
63 Concourse Plaza: "Lockman Is Honored," p. 40.
63 "He can't hit": Daley, "Brave Dreams," p. 18.
63 Schenz's black-grain: The Schenz family showed me the telescope.
64 a four-pitch: L. Smith, "Redlegs Soft Touch," p. 11.
64 just the third time: Elias Sports Bureau, Inc. It also happened on May 28, 1950, and July 6, 1950.
64 iron loudspeakers: Stein, *Under Coogan's Bluff*, p. 2.
64 Giant Victory March: Tuckner, "Two Trumpets," p. 48.
65 WHAT YOU HEAR HERE: Garagiola and Quigley, *Baseball Is a Funny Game*, p. 24.
65 put on his Fabergé cologne and Patek Philippe watch: Laraine Day, interview, August 13, 2001.
65 stared down: Murray, "Far-Turn Switch," p. 4.
65 "There's one thing": Ibid.
65 was cheered by: King, "Life Lovely," p. 17.

CHAPTER EIGHT

66 "The great American game of baseball": Povich, "Sneaky A's," p. D1.
66 Judge Saul Strait sentenced: "Sentence Basket Fixer," p. F2.

66　The United States Military Academy: "Annapolis Has Code," p. 5.

66　signed into law: Laws of the General Assembly of the Commonwealth of Pennsylvania, pp. 1071–73.

66　"to be lost any game": Ibid., p. 1072.

66　owner Bill Veeck: Gutman, *Banana Bats and Ding-Dong Balls*, p. 99.

66　the Colorado Rockies: Marshall, "Rockies Turn to Environmental."

67　the bunts of Nellie: Piersall, "How the Home Team Cheats," p. 22.

67　"Ashburn's Ridge": Ibid.

67　before dawn on October 1 Jerry Schwab, interview, February 24, 2006.

67　"If you bore": Gutman, "The Physics," p. 74.

67　Tiger Norm Cash: Wulf, "Tricks of the Trade," p. 95.

67　a pitch may rotate: Gutman, "The Physics," p. 75.

67　as Durocher did regularly: Durocher, *Nice Guys Finish Last*, p. 3.

67　$a = (18\mu\rho v / d^2) f + g$: μ is the air viscosity, ρ is the ball density, v is the ball speed, d is the ball diameter and g is the acceleration of gravity.

67　"If the surface": Gutman, "The Physics," p. 77.

67　pitcher Ken Brett: Wojciechowski, "Baseball Cheating," p. 4C.

68　Joe Niekro: Associated Press, "Knuckleball": p. B6.

68　suspended catcher Angel Rodriguez: Barnes, "Rodriguez Handed," p. D1. Rodriguez played for the Class A Alexandria Dukes.

68　"Bootling information": R. Smith, "You're No Thief," p. 2.

68　"Any difference in the manner": Ward, *Base-Ball*, p. 49.

68　"as long as you saw the white": Yogi Berra, interview, March 10, 2002.

68　Del Baker noticed: Kernan, "There Is Spying," p. 104.

68　Westrum signaled the pitches: Wes Westrum, interview, Fall 2001. AND Marsh and Ehre, *Best Sports Stories*, p. 55.

69　folk games including stool-ball: Block, *Baseball Before We Knew It*, pp. 113, 124, 135. AND David Block, interview, March 26, 2005.

69　"There is nothing now": Longfellow, *Life of Henry Wadsworth Longfellow*, vol. 1, p. 51.

69　Alexander Cartwright Jr.: Kirsch, *The Creation of American Team Sports*, p. 57. AND Chadwick, *Beadle's Dime Base-Ball Player* (1860). Cartwright was among the founders of the Knickerbocker Base Ball Club that codified its rules on September 23,1845.

69　some 15 paces: *Revised Constitution, By-Laws and Rules of the Eagle Ball Club, Adopted 1854*, p. 9.

69　only a delivery swung at: Chadwick, *Beadle's Dime Base-Ball Player* (1860). Knickerbocker Base Ball Club Rules of 1845. Rule 11.

69　Roughly 10 to 15 feet: "Baseball in Newburgh," p. 108.

69　each pitch after it bounced: Ibid.

69　foul balls first landing: Chadwick, *Beadle's Dime Base-Ball Player (1860)*. Knickerbocker Base Ball Club Rules of 1845. Rule 8.

69　A third strike caught on one bounce: Ibid., Rule 11.

69　license to call strikes: By-Laws and Rules of the Hamilton Base Ball Club, p. 16. Rules adopted in 1858. Rule 37.

69　in 1863, balls too: Chadwick, *Beadle's Dime Base-Ball Player*, p. 13.

69　Candy Cummings, Phoney Martin: Spink, *The National Game*, pp. 128–129.

69   and Ben Hannegan: "Excelsior vs. Union," p. 356. Researcher Tom Shieber found this article, which notes the "twist" Hannegan imparted to his pitches.

69   permission to throw overhand: *Spalding's Official Base Ball Guide* (1884 season), p. 86. Rule 27. The words "with his hand passing below his shoulder" were removed, prior to the 1884 season, from description of the delivery of "a fair ball."

69   Beacon fires lit: Aeschylus, *The Oresteia*, p. 114.

69   the prophet Jeremiah: Jeremiah 6:1, *JPS Hebrew-English Tanakh*, p. 1020.

69   384-foot lighthouse: Clayton and Price, *The Seven Wonders of the Ancient World*, p. 155.

70   Greek historian Polybius: Woods, *A History of Tactical Communication*, pp. 6–7.

70   "one, if by land, and two, if by sea": Longfellow, "The Landlord's Tale," p. 362.

70   "the shot heard round": Ferguson, *The Norton Anthology of Poetry*, p. 850.

70   Benedictine monks vowed: Bruce, *Silence and Sign Language in Medieval Monasticism: The Cluniac Tradition (c. 900–1200)*, page number unavailable.

70   Mahé de la Bourdonnais: Woods, *A History of Tactical Communication*, p. 36.

70   1791, Claude Chappe: Ibid., p. 16.

70   Samuel Morse invented: Mabee, *The American Leonardo*, p. 151.

70   surgeon named Albert: Woods, *A History of Tactical Communication*, pp. 80–82.

70   "The catcher was also": "The Excelsior vs.," p. 3.

70   "All pitchers should follow": "The Sixth Rule," p. 2.

70   first to use the word *signal*: "An Interesting Game," p. 2.

70   "indicates by signs to the pitcher": "The Base-Ball Game," p. 1.

71   to pitch with both feet aground: Chadwick, *Beadle's Dime Base-Ball Player*, p. 13.

71   to remain mid-delivery: Ibid.

71   "Should the pitcher repeatedly fail": Ibid.

71   "This is 1867": "Irvington vs. Eureka," p. 45.

71   the right to request a high: "The Base Ball Convention," p. 285.

71   allowed to throw overhand: *Spalding's Official Base Ball Guide* (1884 season), Rule 27. p. 86.

71   no longer allowed the batter: The rule allowing batters to request the location of their pitch is absent in the *Spalding's Official Base Ball Guide* (1887 season).

71   four balls per walk: *Spalding's Official Base Ball Guide* (1889 season), Rule 44.

71   rubber set 60 feet, 6 inches: *Spalding's Official Base Ball Guide* (1893 season), Rule 5.

71   the infield fly rule: *Spalding's Official Base Ball Guide* (1895 season), Rule 45.

71   "The removal of certain": Ward, *Base-Ball*, p. 46.

71   "Every battery": Ibid., p. 53.

71   "Occasionally, say once an inning": Ibid., p. 52.

72   There is one thing I would: Harry Wright, letter to the editor, *New York Sunday Mercury*, March 27, 1870.

72   "He used the fingers": "American Association," p. 522.

72   "They give signs": "The National Game," p. 2.

72   "When he bats": "The Washington Ball," p. 2. Many have falsely cited Hoy as the father of baseball signals, a myth that researcher Bill Deane of SABR has soundly debunked.

72   every bit what Swiss linguist: Lehn, "Signs: Baseball's Hidden," (SABR conference, 2003).

72   "a linguistic system": Saussure, *The Course in General Linguistics*, pp. 118–19.

72   "The coacher": Ward, *Base-Ball*, p. 73.

72   "codes of this sort": Sangree, "The Strategy of," p. 511.

72   "Jim would crouch down": "By Reading Signs," p. 7.

72   "Upon the approach": Sangree, "The Strategy of," p. 510.

73   "Now it is almost": Ward, *Base-Ball*, p. 54.

73   James Tyng slipped: "Base-ball," *Harvard Crimson*, p. 56. AND Blanchard, *The H Book of Harvard Athletics 1852–1922*, p. 188.

73   "With the adoption": Sangree, "The Strategy of," p. 511.

73   "When a right-handed": Pfeffer, *Scientific Ball*, p. 18.

73   "Some years ago": Ward, *Base-Ball*, p. 54.

73   surrendered 36 runs: National Baseball Hall of Fame Library. Ward pitched June 9th, June 27th, August 10th and September 13th.

74   "The Brooklyns would have": "By Reading," p. 7.

74   a doubleheader on June 22: "Glory Enough," p. 4.

74   on May 1, 1876: In the "1876 boxscore scrapbook" in the National Baseball Hall of Fame Library. Uncovered by Bill Deane.

74   "made of several": "Base Ball Notes," p. 7.

74   "push his big gloved": "Tricks in," p. 6.

74   Pud Galvin took: "Base Ball Notes," August 14, 1889, p. 2.

74   "If the batter fails": *Spalding's Official Base Ball Guide* (1915 season), p. 29.

74   "Inside baseball was": MadDonald, "The Psychology of," pp. 188–89.

75   Arthur Irwin published: "News and Comment," January 25, 1896, p. 4.

75   "believes in signs": "Base-ball," p. 5.

75   Frank Selee went a step: Fullerton, "Wig-Wagging," p. 7.

75   "The signal system fails": "News and Comment," February 1, 1896, p. 4.

75   "The wolf, the snake": Traubel, *With Walt Whitman in Camden*, p. 145.

75   "The umpires objected": "The Referee," p. A1.

75   in the grandstand: Dryden, "Dryden Lays Bare," p. 14.

75   trained his glasses: Ibid.

75   He shared his discovery: Ibid.

75   "invested in a double": Ibid.

75   in the eighth window: Dryden, "Policemen Guard," p. 13.

76   If Murphy held: Ibid.

76   "Knowing that a curve": Dryden, "Dryden Lays Bare," p. 14.

76   rumors of a newspaper-holding: Ibid.

76   a copycat mole: "Ha! Ha! Pirates," p. 14.

76   "Hereafter it will": "Clever Murphy," p. 1.

76   "imparted a genial glow": Dryden, "Dryden Lays Bare," p. 14.

76   feeling with his feet: Dryden, "Morgan, Murphy Worked," p. 6.

76   "led to the introduction": Dryden, "Dryden Lays Bare," p. 14.

76   Arlie Latham, the Reds: Matthewson, *Pitching in a Pinch*, p. 145.

76   Corcoran charged out: Surprise, "Morgan Murphy's Signal," p. 10.

77   "Back to the mines": Ibid.

77   Dewey went into Manila: On May 1, 1898, Commodore George Dewey led the U.S. Navy to victory over Spain in the Battle of Manila Bay.

77   Ferdinand Abell: Dryden, "Another Victory," p. 13.

77   Dryden recommended: Ibid.

77   "The explanation that": "Rogers Knows Naught," p. 10.

77   relic of a traveling circus: Dryden, "Buzzer Out," p. 15.

77   "If it is fair": "Rogers Knows Naught," p. 10.

77   to change them too: Evers and Fullerton, *Touching Second*, p. 126.

77   "The success of any system": Purinton, "Baseball Technique," p. 209.

77   1906 graduate thesis: Ibid.

77   "Much depends upon": Sangree, "The Strategy of," p. 512.

77   "Two or three years ago": *Spalding Base Ball Guide, 1909*, p. 351.

78   Joe Cantillon, manager: Grillo, "That Scandal," p. 2.

78   on June 19: "Old Highlanders Used," p. 2. Recalling the game to the *Sporting News* forty-one years later, Street was unsure of the exact date. But his recollection squared perfectly with the June 19th game, one of three games Johnson won at New York in 1909.

78   Detroit manager Hughie: "Alleged 'Sign-Tipping'," p. 6.

78   Jennings dispatched pitcher Bill Donovan: Grillo, "That Scandal," p. 2.

78   Harry Tuthill, however, ambled over: Zuber, "Futile Protest," p. 6.

78   "There was a handle": Grillo, "That Scandal," p. 2.

78   that winter, Robert Hedges: Johnson, "The American League Holds," p. 6.

78   "There was no rule": Ibid.

78   that same "H" in the ad: Farrell, "An Old Scandal," p. 6.

78   some like the *New York Sun*: "Stallings Out," p. 8.

79   the $500 he offered: Johnson, "Offers Reward for," p. 3.

79   "The annual charges": Goewey, "Inconsistency and Its," p. 146.

79   "the practice of stealing": Fullerton, "The Right," p. 725.

79   "The reputation itself": Matthewson, *Pitching in a Pinch*, p. 150.

79   "Chief Bender, Danny": Spink, *Baseball Guide and Record Book*, p. 128.

79   "If a player is smart": Cobb, *Memories of Twenty Years in Baseball*, p. 83.

79   tutorials in magazines: See, for example, "Signals in Baseball," p. 240.

79   a 1916 short story: Claudy, "Tipped Hats," p. 8.

80   other "freak deliveries": *Spalding's Official Base Ball Guide* (1920 season), p. 23. Note on rule 30.

80   "Every team with a scoreboard": Hornsby and Surface, *My War with Baseball*, p. 162.

80   20 by 14: Lane, "How a Big," p. 317.
80   white numbered: Ibid.
80   "Not a lot of guys knew": Harold Manders, interview, December 2001.
80   "Life Lovely": King, "Life Lovely for Leo," p. 17.

CHAPTER NINE

81   "For 'tis the sport": Braunmuller, *Hamlet*, p. 96.
81   "Whoever this guy was": Al Corwin, interview, Fall 281.
81   "They bat the brains": Carver, "Say Dodgers," p. 21–P.
81   When Nat Chadwick slept around: Ina Chadwick, interview, July 1, 2001.
81   Some weekends, Chadwick subwayed: George Farrell, Jr., interview, November 2000.
82   he preened that the New York Giants: Ibid.
82   "Abe was definitely involved": Ibid.
82   "The electricians were proud": Walter Carberry, interview, Fall 2000.
82   Services ended at: "Van Arsdale's Mother," p. 1.
82   "He felt this weakness": Helen Smith, interview, November 28, 2000.
82   penciled in lower-case: Archives of the Joint Industry Board of the Electrical Industry. Payroll records.
83   Shirley Marblestone drove brother-in-law: Shirley Marblestone, interview, March 10, 2002.
83   named Walter Mersheimer: "Master Patient Index." Archives at Terence Cardinal Cooke Healthcare Center.
83   short, bushy-browed, tough: Carol and Werner Roeder, interviews, December 2001.
83   doctor had been adopted: Ibid.
83   he found not ulcers but tumors: Harriet Mesulam, interview, December 17, 2001.
83   its limestone base: "The Fifth Avenue," pp. 87–88.
83   Miriam told this to her two daughters: Ibid.
83   "God, you're all grown up": Ibid.
84   half the $50,000: National Baseball Hall of Fame Library.
84   "He was obsessed": Thomson, Heiman and Gutman, *The Giants Win the Pennant! The Giants Win the Pennant!*, pp. 76–7.
84   "Just stay close": Anderson, *Pennant Races*, p. 216.
84   "If the letter 'I'": Gross, "Speaking out," July 20, 1951, p. 16.
84   "Charlie's biggest problem": Herman Franks, interview, January 20, 2002.
84   "Leo," baited Dressen: Carl Erskine, interview, April 20, 2006.
85   after the game Dressen entered: Golenbock, *BUMS*, p. 301.
85   stood nearby at their lockers: Carl Erskine, interview, March 1, 2002.
85   "He said, 'Come on' ": Ibid.
85   "Palica and I didn't have": Ibid.
85   "Roll out the barrel!": Ibid.
85   "They were taunting": Whitey Lockman, interview, February 28, 2002.
85   "I'll put it this way": George Spencer, interview, February 28, 2002.
85   the league had ordered a brick wall built: Golenbock, *BUMS*, p. 302. AND Clem Labine, interview, April 20, 2006.

85 Mueller phoned his brother: Anderson, *Pennant Races*, p. 222.

85 quietly subletted: Crosby, "Faith, Prayer," pp. 54–55.

85 ten thousand viewers within fifty: Koppett, "25 Years Ago," p. 56.

85 "The Dodgers and Boston Braves: R. Smith, "View of Sport," p. 2.

86 "laying $1,200": Sylvester, "The Biggest Smash," p. 55.

86 brown shoes, brown slacks: Gross, "Speaking Out," August 29, 1951, p. 73.

86 "Maybe the National League": Sheehan, "Giants Defeat Dodgers," p. 20.

CHAPTER TEN

88 "He was but as the cuckoo": McEachern, *Henry IV*, p. 70.

88 had proven adept at decoding the signals: Al Corwin and Davey Williams, interviews, January 2001.

88 Durocher permanently left the dugout: K. Smith, "Giants Win, 7–2," p. 21.

88 The team largely stopped: Al Corwin, interview, Fall 2000.

88 "The guys who could hit": Ibid.

88 Salvador Anthony Yvars was born: Description of Yvars' upbringing assembled through interviews with Yvars and some family members.

89 "you went outside to take a crap": Sal Yvars, interview, March 14, 2002.

89 "Begonias, petunias, geraniums": Ibid.

89 "Somebody was paying me": Ibid.

90 batted above .500: Miller, "Yvars, Branca, Westchester," p. 31.

90 "a tall rugged specimen": "Kittyhawk .400," p. 5.

90 "I got the okay": Sal Yvars, interview.

90 "I took six and a half": Ibid.

91 "the best prospect ever developed": Fred Stafford, "Yvars Vastly Improved—Watters." Reporter Dispatch, February 1946.

91 "one of the most promising prospects": *The Union*, July 1946.

91 Bruno Betzel made Yvars: Yvars started a first time on August 2nd and then consistently beginning on August 8th.

91 thrown out 39 of 76: Daniel, "Detroit Escaped," p. 32.

91 Yvars squatted to receive: True, "Durocher and Yvars End," p. 28.

91 "Goddamit, Yvars," barked Durocher: Sal Yvars, interview, March 14, 2002.

92 "They're balls!": Ibid.

92 broke the middle finger: King, "Rookie Catcher," p. 34.

92 "I got the shin guard": Sal Yvars, interview, March 14, 2002.

92 But Yvars yelled: King, "Rookie Catcher," p. 34.

92 the only reason: King, Ibid.

92 scored 54 runs: "Indians-Giants Series," p. 43.

92 "he suddenly leaped into the box": Hall, "Yvars Hits Fan," p. 1.

92 after Koenig filed: "Insubordination Charge," p. 34.

92 Yvars refused to pay: Ibid.

93 "He'll never put": Associated Press, "Yvars Won't Pay."

93 "was such a patsy": K. Smith, "Giants Uncover Star," p. 9.

93 the Polo Grounds crowd: K. Smith, "Giants Blast," p. 24.

93 "Hey, Sal!" Yvars remembers one yelling: Sal Yvars, interview, March 14, 2002.

93 Owner handed catcher: Whelan, "August Special," p. D6.
94 "If Maglie makes": Kremenko, "Yvars Spark," p. 11.
94 "Come on! Bear down!": Sal Yvars, interview.
94 "I'd throw it back": Ibid.
94 three subpar throws: Down, "Yvars' Beef," p. 32.

CHAPTER ELEVEN

95 "we talked only about whether": Bukowski, *Dangling in the Tournefortia*, p. 45.
95 "For the Browns": Broeg, "Lots of Frosting," p. 1C.
95 Zack Taylor handed the ump: Ibid.
95 $100 a game: "Midget Story," p. 6.
95 errand boy: Ibid.
95 Jerry Sullivan: Overfield, "Small Wonders," p. 26.
96 several Yankees accuse: Epstein, "Yanks Caught with," p. 34.
96 the tenth time: Elias Sports Bureau, Inc.
96 "PARKS INFESTED": *The Sporting News* caption, September 5, 1951, p. 2.
96 Polo Grounds erupted: Roeder, "Fans Keep Eye," p. 2.
97 "The fine Italian arms": Young, "Branca 2-Hits," p. C20.
97 "Pitchers don't know": Golenbock, *BUMS*, p. 216.
97 "If the Dodgers blow": Burr, "Ralph Notches Second," p. 13.
97 "QUICK, THE OXYGEN!": *Brooklyn Eagle*, August 28, 1951, p. 13.
97 "It's only a dream": R Smith, "On the Profit," p. 22.
97 refused to change: Anderson, *Pennant Races*, p. 242.
97 Thomson made sure: Thomson, Heiman and Gutman, *The Giants Win the Pennant! The Giants Win the Pennant!*, p. 157.
98 to kick the foul side: Ibid.
98 Durocher carried with him: Kremenko, "Durocher Dances," p. 22.
98 Dark continued to use: Before the October 1st game, Rigney gave his glove to Dark.
98 "He's their lucky": *New York Post*, Auguts 21, 1951.
98 Four times in those 16 games: On August 19th, 21st and 24th, and in the first game of a doubleheader on August 27th.
98 Three more games: On August 15th and 22nd, and in the first game of a doubleheader on August 26th.
98 just one fewer late-inning: On May 25th, June 28th and July 6th, 7th and 24th.
98 "We get four runs ahead": Sal Yvars, interview, March 14, 2002.
98 began to sing in the shower: King, "Not That They," p. 35.
99 "I'm glad they're winning": Young, "Who's Afraid," p. C20.
99 had wrapped white tape: Buzzie Bavasi, interview, December 17, 2001.
99 Branca delivered one: Dave Smith, *Retrosheet*.
99 filling in for Dressen: Sheehan, "Triple Plays," p. S1.
100 "Charlie," Lavagetto said: Golenbock, *BUMS*, p. 281.
100 from Mike Kelley: Dressen, "Stealing Signs Is," p. 53.

100 "Charlie was great at": Sal Yvars, interview.

100 he instructed: Frank, "Will They Steal," p. 17.

100 "champion signal-stealers": Richman, "Durocher and Combs," p. 34.

100 "I know every": Gross, "Speaking Out," July 6, 1951, p. 50.

100 "His sense of timing": Durocher, *Nice Guys Finish Last*, p. 186.

101 "Joe McCarthy comes running": Bert Padell, interview, January 21, 2002.

101 "Take it easy.": Ibid.

101 "Bert," Stengel told his batboy: Ibid.

101 his roommate years earlier: Herman Franks, interview, Fall 2000.

101 "He ran over": Golenbock, *BUMS*, p. 281.

101 "Leo always wanted everyone": Al Corwin, interview, Fall 2001.

101 "Maglie . . . rode Newcombe . . . did Schenz": Mozley, "Barber's Vocals," p. 42.

101 garnered a Good Conduct: Notice of Separation from U.S. Navy, courtesy of the Schenz family.

101 Five players were ejected: K. Smith, "Belt Newcombe," p. 14.

101 ordered his remaining: Mozley, "Barber's Vocals," p. 42.

102 three minutes and three: Rosenthal, "Hearn Chalks Up," p. 13.

102 called time . . . "It's a boy!": "Mueller 'Pops'," p. 14.

102 six-pound son: Effrat, "Giants Again Crush," p. 17.

102 34.5 ounce bat: Anderson, *Pennant Races*, p. 223.

102 Twice they opened: Rosenthal, "Hearn Chalks Up," p. 13.

102 as Stoneham drank a scotch and soda: Buzzie Bavasi, interview, December 17, 2001.

102 "Would you like a drink": Buzzie Bavasi, interview, January 7, 2002.

102 "It wasn't much fun": Buzzie Bavasi, interview, December 17, 2001.

103 "Whatever [Durocher]": Golenbock, *BUMS*, p. 281.

103 and then Durocher had adopted: Durocher, *Nice Guys Finish Last*, p. 202.

103 The Polo Grounds was their playground: Description of the ballpark and the three boys assembled through interviews with Jerry Schwab, Eddie Logan, Chris Durocher and several others, including Tommy Colletti and Angelo Ambrosio.

103 Mays, for one, often roomed: Willie Mays, interview, March 26, 2002.

104 "He went with me": Ibid.

104 "There was always the talk": Chris Durocher, interview, March 7, 2002.

104 "Even at that age": Ibid., August 17, 2001.

104 a softball game: "Ball Game, Golf," p. 21.

104 Kleppel saw something: Roeder, "Straying Flock," p. 21. AND K. Smith, "Big Contrast," p. 11.

104 from the grippe: "Fever of 101," p. 30.

104 "I haven't felt well": McCulley, "Lippy Fears," p. 65.

105 just six players: "Official 1951," p. 17.

105 "I was more valuable giving the goddam signs": Sal Yvars, interview, March 14, 2002.

105 "What the fuck are you doing here?": Ibid.

105 "He says he's got a horse running": Ibid.

106 "Do what the fuck I tell you": Ibid.

106 Franks was clearly rusty: Murray, "Giants Beat Cubs," p. 38.

106 At 5:41 pm: *1951 Daily Racing Forum Chart Book*, chart #43816.

106 eight horses burst: Ibid.

107 down the homestretch: Mushnick, "A Few Giant," p. 51.

107 Chub Feeney fed the press poppycock: Down, "Yvars' Beef," p. 32.

107 "He has been": Murray, "Far-Turn Switch," p. 3.

107 "It's to be doubted": Daley, "No Joy," p. 34.

107 "What turned Thomson": Murray, "Far-Turn Switch," p. 3.

108 finger as hinge of 1951: Hurwitz, "Durocher Says," p. 18. AND Orr, "The Unpredictable Bobby," p. 60.

108 instead claim to: Hurwitz, "'Never Got Better,' " p. 18.

108 "I don't think particularly": Orr, "The Unpredictable Bobby," p. 60.

108 Chadwick read: Description of Chadwick assembled through several interviews with Helen Smith and Harriet Mesulam.

108 "What's happening to me?": Harriet Mesulam, interview, December 17, 2001.

108 Snider and Branca embodied: Dave Smith, *Retrosheet*.

109 playing golf: "Giants Will Keep Punching," p. 34.

109 A *Sporting News* headline: *The Sporting News*, September 26, 1951, p. 11.

109 gave Campanella $4,400 and Newcombe $3,600: Buzzie Bavasi, interview, January 7, 2002.

109 MANAGER OF THE: McGregory, *The Baseball Player*, p. 113.

109 a trophy given: "Major Flashes," October 3, 1951, p. 26.

109 "Luck is the residue": Daley, "What Makes," p. SM 22.

109 "the Creeping Terror": Corum, "The Creeping Terror," p. 20.

109 "like waiting for the doctor": Rosenfeld, *The Great Chase*, p. 172.

110 "THEY'RE TIED!": *New York Daily News*, September 29, 1951, back page.

111 toted too a tie: McGowen, "Brook 5–5 Tie," p. S1.

111 Chapter 136: "Use of Area," p. 8.

111 between stops in first: Elias Sports Bureau, Inc. It would be thirty years before another did. The 1981 Brewers, in a 162-game schedule, went 166 days.

111 a hepped-up Thomson: Newcombe, "Bobby Thomson: The Unwilling," p. 55.

111 at 3:35 p.m.: McGowen, "Dodgers, Giants Win," p. 26.

111 Bavasi had decided: Buzzie Bavasi, interview, January 7, 2002.

111 crowded about: "'Ulcers, Wonderful," p. 27.

111 Brooklyn won just one: Brooklyn won on September 19th and lost on August 23rd and 25th, and September 12th, 17th, 21st, 27th and 28th.

112 "They were having a hell": Herman Franks, interview, January 20, 2002.

112 Chub Feeney now called: Down, "Dodger Victory," p. 10.

112 "the Giants sat there,": Ibid.

112 "between Brooklyn and Philadelphia": Hemingway, *The Old Man and the Sea*, p. 16.

113 inspired Bernard Malamud: Protagonist Roy Hobbs is shot by a fan named Harriet Bird.

113 Leaning on coach: Young, "Robby HR," p. 21C.

113   Pennsylvania law: "Pennsylvania Law Ends," p. 15.

113   In 1794: Warrington, *The Fight for Sunday Baseball in Philadelphia*, philadelphiaathletics.org/history/sundaybaseball.html.

113   November 1933: Ibid.

114   never cared much for Jewish custom: Harriet Mesulam and Helen Smith, interviews, July 3, 2001.

114   the holy days the only days: Harriet Mesulam, interview, December 17, 2001.

114   "A demented Hollywood": Daley, "Achieving the Impossible," p. 28.

114   "the shot that could": Murray, "Hollywood Couldn't Have," p. 34.

115   "LEAVES FANS LIMP": *New York Times*, October 1, 1951, p. 1.

115   a joyous babysitter named Willette Bailey: Rachel Robinson, interview, May 2002.

115   Elizabeth Thomson prepared dinner: Thomson, interview, March 29, 2005.

CHAPTER TWELVE

116   Description of the lives of Thomson and Branca from birth until October 3, 1951, assembled from scores of interviews with the two men and dozens of their relatives and acquaintances. As elsewhere, I have cited separately all quotes, as well as those bits of information gotten from articles and books.

116   "Public opinion is a weak tyrant": *Walden*, p. 7.

116   ten minutes after: "Register of Births." Glasgow District.

116   forty-eight hours later: The Statue of Liberty–Ellis Island Foundation, Inc. *www.ellisisland.org*.

116   On December 9: "Army Form B. 2152. Short Service." Headquarters Scots Guard.

116   chaplain's letter: August 25, 1915, letter courtesy of the Thomson family.

116   training in Caterham: "Army Form B. 2152. Short Service." Headquarters Scots Guard.

116   on April 22: January 4, 1917, letter courtesy of the Thomson family.

116   on October 23: Archives of Headquarters Scots Guard.

117   the front lines: Ibid.

117   a squat man: Ibid.

117   6:20 a.m.: Ibid.

117   Yellow aerosol: Ibid.

117   February 17: Ibid.

117   tenement houses: Glenn Codere, e-mail message, September 10, 2002.

117   "less government in business": Harding, "Less Government," p. 25.

117   "very able, industrious": October 16, 1923, letter courtesy of the Thomson family.

117   16 knots: Mike Porter, e-mail message, August 23, 2002.

117   neither polygamist: The Statue of Liberty–Ellis Island Foundation, Inc. *www.ellisisland.org*. "James Thomson Passenger Record."

117   Dear Wee Ruby: Letter courtesy of the Thomson family.

118   January 6, 1926: Certificate of Birth, State of New York, Department of Health.

118   30,919 Italians, Jews: "Thirteenth Census of the United States: 1910—Population." NARA.

119   "At first the table": John Branca, interview, October 4, 2002.

119   the family consumed: Cribari, "The Distaff Side," p. 21.

120   "it was a lovely life": Rosemary Branca, interview, September 25, 2002.

120   passenger number 13: "List or Manifest of Alien Passengers for the United States Immigration Officer at Port of Arrival." SS *Caledonia*. National Archives.

120   Thomson tartan: Thomson showed me a Thomson-tartan tie.

120   toted: Courtesy of the Thomson family.

120   a 1,006-page bible: Jim Hicks, interview, February 10, 2003.

121   the money to buy: Thomson, Heiman and Gutman, *The Giants Win the Pennant! The Giants Win the Pennant!*, p. 48.

121   "We were," says Bobby: Thomson, interview, November 19, 2000.

121   "Stay in the background": Thomson, Heiman and Gutman, *The Giants Win the Pennant! The Giants Win the Pennant!*, p. 48.

121   "Do what's right": Thomson, interview, August 12, 2002.

121   "I just didn't have": Thomson, Heiman and Gutman, *The Giants Win the Pennant! The Giants Win the Pennant!*, p. 48.

121   Gillies Field: Gordon, "'. . . They Shoulda," p. B15.

122   "the cheapest meat you could get": Ruby Thomson Beatty, interview, Winter 2002.

122   "a little bit of awe": Ibid.

122   "He'd go down to the cellar": Thomson, interview, August 12, 2002.

123   "In this big family": John Branca, interview, October 4, 2002.

123   played for the Paramounts: Franko, *A Half Century of Making Men 1912–1962*, p. 80.

123   "I'd pitch five innings": Branca, interview, January 15, 2002.

123   "You sat down at the dinner table": John Branca, interview, October 4, 2002.

123   "My handwriting comes from": Branca, interview, January 15, 2002.

124   "He built houses": Ruby Thomson Beatty, interview, Winter 2002.

125   "She sang well, didn't she?": Ibid.

125   local sandlot teams: King, "The Flying Scot," p. 38. AND Thomson, Heiman and Gutman, *The Giants Win the Pennant! The Giants Win the Pennant!*, p. 49.

125   "I was just all baseball": Thomson, interview, September 5, 2002.

126   "There's a regular guy,": Ibid.

126   "He jumped out of": Ibid.

126   become superintendent: "James Thomson," p. 2.

126   failing three classes: Curtis High School report card, January 1939.

126   "I was the last one to ask": Ibid.

126   "Thomson, you got": Chandler, Oral History Project, University of Kentucky Libraries.

126   "never in front of me": Thomson, interview, September 5, 2002.

126   "[Bobby] was extremely quiet": Tommy Faucet, interview, March 2003.

127   "If he was in a group": Ralph DiStasio, interview, March 2003.

127 at 2 p.m.: "James Thomson," p. 2.

127 buried in plot 4399: The Moravian Cemetery.

127 "There was none of the weeping": Ruby Thomson Beatty, interview, Winter 2002.

127 "You know, the Scots": Thomson, interview, November 19, 2000.

127 Florence Exner was in his class: Fern Hack, interview, Winter 2002.

127 "He had the most beautiful": Ibid.

127 "I loved going over there": Ibid.

128 "I know your family": Branca, interview, January 15, 2002.

128 "God has a long": Branca, "Branca Recalls," p. 14.

128 severe growing pains: King, "The Flying Scot," p. 81.

128 batted .346: Phillips, "Six Curtis Players," p. 14.

129 "He used to say," remembers John: John Branca, interview, October 4, 2002.

129 Bender jotted a note: Branca, interview.

130 "His brother kept a tight rein": Danny Monahan, interview, March 2003.

130 "Whoo!" says Thomson: Thomson, interview, September 5, 2002.

130 "Haul ass, kid!": Ibid.

130 Mickey McConnell: Molter, *Famous American Athletes of Today*, p. 324. AND Thomson, Heiman and Gutman, *The Giants Win the Pennant! The Giants Win the Pennant!*, p. 50.

131 "That boy good!": "A Giant Fan," p. 3.

131 "was a very embarrassing thing": Thomson, interview, June 4, 2003.

131 inking on the outside stone: Thomson, Heiman and Gutman, *The Giants Win the Pennant! The Giants Win the Pennant!*, p. 51.

131 "It's difficult to think": Ibid.

131 "I got the ball over": Branca, interview.

132 thanks to a newspaperman: Newcombe, "Bobby Thomson: The Unwilling," p. 51.

132 "your severest critic": Thomson, interview, June 4, 2003.

132 Scot got drunk: Newcombe, "Bobby Thomson: The Unwilling," p. 52.

132 "Bub, didn't you": King, "The Flying Scot," p. 39.

132 "Gee," he said: Drees and Mullen, *Where Is He Now?*, 122.

133 "THIS BAT IS ROCKS' ": *Rocky Mount Telegram*, July 27, 1942, p. 6.

133 over the house: "Rocks Crush," p. 2.

133 3600 fans: "Bi-State Playoff," p. 9.

133 passed a hat: King, "The Flying Scot," p. 39.

133 he enlisted: "Personnel Qualifications Questionnaire," NARA.

133 Thomson chose: Ibid.

133 took a train: Ibid.

134 National Honor: "Mount Vernon Set," p. 10.

134 on May 1: "Personnel Qualifications Questionnaire," NARA.

134 "I got up to thirty-five": Thomson, interview.

134 "I'm playing around": Ibid.

134 On August 31: "Personnel Qualifications Questionnaire," NARA.

135 They were Class D Oilers: Billy DeMars, interview, Spring 2003.

135 picking up a new nickname: Ibid.

135 finished his second: "Personnel Qualifications Questionnaire," NARA.

135 converted that March: "Pre-Flight Cadets," p. 7.

135 awaited C.T.D.: "Personnel Qualifications Questionnaire," NARA.

135 turn the private: DuBois, "50 Years Ago," p. 7A.

135 little gray: "Eighty-Seventh College," p. 59.

135 "They hazed us": Thomson, interview.

135 bugle roused: "Eighty-Seventh College," p. 59.

135 class 43-C-12: "Flight 'E'," no page available.

135 the men ate: "Eighty-Seventh College," p. 59.

135 class began: Ibid.

135 from first aid: "Pre-Flight Cadets," p. 7.

135 "You see this?": Thomson, interview, June 4, 2003.

135 from reveille: "Eighty-Seventh College," p. 59.

135 taps at 2200: Ibid., p. 61.

135 face shaven: Dubois, "50 Years Ago," p. 7A.

136 "His glove was just so important": Daniel Reed, interview, August 30, 2003.

136 70 to 1: Dubois, "50 Years Ago," p. 7A.

136 "It will be necessary": "Investigation Into New," no page available.

136 "Lucy is a friend of mine!": LaVone Bergstrom, interview, September 6, 2003.

136 There in room 207 lived Millie Geistfeld: Ibid.

136 Raised on a farm in Lewisville: Nancy Huseby, interview, September 6, 2003.

137 "Bob was the epitome": LaVone Bergstrom, interview, September 8, 2003.

137 "this is the way God made me": Ibid.

137 "She really loved him": Ibid.

137 "It was my first situation": Thomson, interview, June 4, 2003.

137 a 178-pound: Golenbock, BUMS, p. 73.

137 Ten hours: "550 Air Cadets," p. 1.

138 dash from home: "Righty Swinger," p. 5.

138 "They said I jostled him": Thomson, interview, August 31, 2003.

138 "It was foolish": Ibid.

138 on February 12: "Lower Flight," page not numbered.

138 the sheen: "North Wind," page not numbered.

138 the sixteenth-of-an-inch: "New Notes," page not numbered.

138 "We're all standing out there": Thomson, interview, May 8, 2003.

139 "I didn't think I'd have": Thomson, interview.

139 April 22: Effrat, "Branca of N.Y.U.," p. S1.

139 one hour and forty-eight minutes: Ibid., p. S23.

139 another shutout: "N.Y.U. Routs," p. 17.

139 extended to 23: Effrat, "N.Y.U. Nine," p. S1.

139 seven straight: "Branca, Ex-Davis," p. 8.

139 finished 9–3: Ibid.

139 now a solid 205: Golenbock, BUMS, p. 73.

139 "If you found a jewel": John Branca, interview, October 4, 2002.

139 from 21,000 feet: McFarland, America's Pursuit of Precision Bombing, 1910–1945, p. 186.

140 "I do here": The Official National Museum of the United States Air Force.

140 He stood six: "Physical Examination for Flying," NARA.

140 "I'd lose my class": Thomson, interview, August 11, 2003.

141 "Are you superstitious?": Branca, interview, January 28, 2002.

141 "I was contrary": Ibid.

141 owing to world events: Blum, "Sports Comes to."

142 third-youngest Dodger: Holmes, LADugout.com. Chris Haughey and Gene Mauch were younger.

142 "I felt like I was walking": Branca, interview, May 2, 2005.

142 "a leopard hat and a scarf": Fern Hack, interview, Winter 2002.

143 eleven starts: McGowen, "Branca, Boy Behemoth," p. 366.

143 and one save: Saves did not become an official statistic until 1969. See Section 10.20 of the Official Rules of Major League Baseball.

143 ejected in July: "Strategie," p. 5.

143 "watching all the broads go by": Branca, interview, January 28, 2002.

143 Thomson graduated: "Form for Oath of Office," NARA.

143 a raise: "Officers' Pay, Allowance, and Mileage Voucher," NARA.

143 serial number: Ibid.

143 ordered him: Various military personnel records, NARA.

143 Sam Molnar at Lemoore loved baseball: Al Cutruzzula, interview, November 9, 2005.

143 "He used to play the tunes": Ibid.

143 " 'Bob, you've really improved' ": Thomson, interview, June 23, 2003.

143 "What did you *do* this winter?": Branca, interview, January 28, 2002.

143 "I was still a boy": Branca, interview, January 15, 2002.

144 *Cal McLish*: McGowen, "Branca, Boy Behemoth," p. 366.

144 "I can recall": McGowen, "Davis of Dodgers," p. 28.

144 3–1 pitch: J. Smith, "Cards Shade," p. 17C.

144 "I threw my glove": Thomson, interview, February 1, 2005.

145 Thomson paid: "Officers' Pay, Allowance, and Mileage Voucher," NARA.

145 a USO baseball tour: "Players Are Named," p. 26.

145 "Baseball people knew me": Thomson, interview, June 23, 2003.

145 Ben's Golden: King, "Declared Self," p. 3.

145 Devine, fifty, contacted: Newcombe, "Bobby Thomson: The Unwilling," p. 52.

145 returned to the U.S.: Steiger, "Dressen's Squad," p. 14.

145 the boy she called "wee Rab": Thomson, interview, August 12, 2002.

146 "The young Staten": "Team Will Leave," p. 18.

146 happy to tell: Powers, "The Powerhouse," March 4, 1946, p. 33.

146 "El Cheapo": Ibid., September 23, 1947, p. 47.

146 "Branch Rickey," wrote: Ibid., March 12, 1946, p. 41.

146 Four or five days: Gould, "Dodgers Have," p. 6.

146 panting after: Ibid.

146 "I'll hold out": Ibid.

146 his 3.04 ERA: Ibid.

146 "two of those": Ibid.

146 "Boys like Branca": Burr, "Dodger Holdouts," p. 11.

146 took the train: Burr, "Reiser, Branca," p. 11.

146   "I had just turned twenty": Branca, interview, January 28, 2002.

147   "I was mesmerized": Thomson, interview.

147   Higbe had reclaimed: Spink, "Lives Up to" p. 4.

147   "You can't," he snipped: Golenbock, *BUMS*, p. 85.

148   "I then stopped communication": Thomson, interview, June 4, 2003.

148   "BOBBY THOMSON'S HITTING": *Jersey Journal* headline: "Bobby Thomson's Hitting Lone Feature of Jerseys," July 27, 1946, p. 7.

148   "Each time Bobby": "Jerseys Continue," p. 11.

148   26 drives: "Cellar Dwellers," p. 13.

148   first autograph request: King, "The Flying Scot," p. 40.

148   headed to a local: Ibid.

148   the Scot bought: Ibid.

149   just a decoy: "Sport," p. 74.

149   "Sacrificial lamb my fucking ass!": Branca, interview, January 28, 2002.

149   "Keep thinking like that, kid": Ibid.

149   "I believed in myself.": Ibid.

149   recurring nightmare: Edelman, "Bobby Thomson: Safe," p. 54.

150   "Helps to get": Drebinger, "Bob Thomson, Scotland's," p. 379.

150   Less than 200,000 people: According to the U.S. Census, in 1950 there were 191,015 people living in Staten Island and 1,936,540 in Manhattan.

150   wooded and birded: Torrey, Place and Dickinson, *New York Walk Book*, pp. 14–15.

150   at 417 feet, the highest point: Ibid., p. 13.

150   newly planted Cape Cod beach grass: Ibid., p. 16.

150   "At the last moment,": Drebinger, "Bob Thomson, Scotland's," p. 380.

150   was picked off first: Chandler, Oral History Project, University of Kentucky Libraries.

151   resultant ad odd: Munsingwear advertisement. Munsingwear, Inc.

151   "To pitch like": Ibid.

151   in the seventy-five years of Major League baseball: The National Association began in 1871. Some cite 1876 as the start of MLB.

151   "It'll be Ralph": Drebinger, "Dodgers' Branca," p. 28.

151   Jimmy Carroll: Mockler, "Dyer Expects," p. 12.

151   megaphone-toting: "Spectaculars Find," p. 35.

151   had left his Rawlings: Felker, "Ticket Tornado," p. 9.

152   a dozen photographers, fifty writers: Rennie, "Cardinals Defeat," p. 1.

152   broadcasters from Cuba: "Spectaculars Find," p. 35.

152   clomping out: Cannon, "Jimmy Cannon Says," Octerber 2, 1946, p. 56.

152   "No comment!": Ibid.

152   edgy teammates bicker: Ibid., October 3, 1946, p. 48.

152   "They got a lot of flub hits": Branca, interview, July 23, 2003.

152   "The 20-year-old": Trimble, "Cardinals Rap," p. 63.

152   Thomson shared that he weighed: National Baseball Hall of Fame Library.

153   arranged for his: K. Smith, "Bob Thomson's Blows," p. 12.

153   "help me get": Drebinger, "Bob Thomson, Scotland's," p. 394.

153   "He had an easy": Victor Sacco, interview, June 2, 2003.

153   "Folks came to watch me throw": Thomson, interview, June 4, 2003.

153   "He found studying": Victor Sacco, interview, June 2, 2003.

153   "He wishes," explained his daughter Nancy: Nancy Mitchell, interview, April 24, 2003.

154   "I was starting to slip": Thomson, interview, June 4, 2003.

154   "If you leave school": Ibid.

154   semester grades: New York University, Office of the Registrar.

154   flown him to Cuba: "Branca Wins but," p. 33.

154   "That was a good excuse": Thomson, interview, June 4, 2003.

154   seven sextets: K. Smith, "Bob Thomson's Blows," p. 12.

154   rotating him: Huard, "Bobby Thomson: His," p. 91.

155   Ott asked Thomson: Ibid.

155   Ott now asked Gordon: Ibid.

155   very first home run: Simmons, "Heath's Four-Run," p. 17.

155   "It didn't bother me": Branca, interview, March 4, 2005.

155   "What's your name": Garreau, *Bat Boy of the Giants*, p. 49.

155   Player and batboy knelt: Ibid., p. 50.

156   Thomson reached for Garreau's hand: Ibid.

156   "Keep them that way": Ibid.

156   "Nice going, Bub!": Ibid., p. 52.

156   "Bobby Thomson," he wrote: Ibid.

156   "I thought the place": Cohen, "The Sports Parade," p. 19.

156   as always on days: McGowen, "Branca, Boy Behemoth," p. 365.

156   vaccinated the Giants: Burr, "Robinson Gets," p. 25.

157   low inside: Dave Smith, *Retrosheet*.

157   would drive upstate: Chandler, Oral History Project, University of Kentucky Libraries. AND Interview with Thomson, July 20, 2005.

158   second-to-last starting: Dave Smith, *Retrosheet*.

158   "Each pitch we were on tenterhooks": John Branca, interview, October 4, 2002.

158   "He would prepare the mail": Branca, interview, August 6, 2003.

158   1,500 fans: Franko, *A Half Century of Making Men 1912–1962*, p. 81.

158   scroll of thanks: Ibid.

158   his-and-his portable: Young, "Dodgers Rally," p. C18.

158   paying $3: "Branca-Karl Tribute," p. 1.

158   "There will be other": Franko, *A Half Century of Making Men 1912–1962*, p. 80.

159   a camera: Sheehan, "Mize Drives," p. S3.

159   Thomson had worried: Garreau, *Bat Boy of the Giants*, p. 157.

159   "my brother made up a speech": Thomson, interview, June 23, 2003.

159   note of thanks lay tucked: Garreau, *Bat Boy of the Giants*, p. 159.

159   waved his cap above his head: Ibid.

159   tipping his black cap in thanks six times: Ibid.

159   "Of the newcomers": Spink, "Big John," p. 2.

159   "JUNIOR THOMSON": *New York World-Telegram and Sun* headline: "Junior Thomson a New DiMag?," September 22, 1947, p. 12.

160   seven other pitchers: Sinins, *The Complete Baseball Encyclopedia*, originally released in 2000.

160   the very youngest: Elias Sports Bureau, Inc.

161   "There are times": Heinz, "Ralph Branca's Slow," p. 24.

161   cheered kindly: Rennie, "Yankees Beat Dodgers," p. 33.

161   Babe Ruth left: Daley, "Opening Day," p. 38.

161   "Suddenly, as if": Rennie, "Yankees Beat Dodgers," p. 1.

161   Rogers Hornsby: "First Game Gossip," p. 10.

161   "I was amazed": Bealmear, "Bucky Gambles," p. B8.

161   "How Ralph Branca ever": Wolf, "Sportraits," p. 14.

161   found Branca hunched: McGowen, "Branca Is Eager," p. 38.

161   "Do you feel": Ibid.

161   straightened his back: Ibid.

162   "I don't see": Ibid.

162   took on semipros: Lang, "World's Series," p. 16.

162   he answered "Working": Branca, interview, January 28, 2002.

162   homogenized Bond: Beckett Baseball Cards. *www.beckett.com.*

162   Tip Top Bread: Ibid.

162   "one of the most": McGowen, "Branca, Boy Behemoth," p. 365.

162   "one of the outstanding": Drebinger, "Bob Thomson, Scotland's," p. 380.

162   before 1,300: "1,300 See," p. 8.

162   left NYU to teach: "Stanky Opens, p. 22.

163   "Mount Vernon's pride": "Meet the Whirlwinds," p. 14.

163   "Branca Night": "Standards Upset," p. 8.

163   voted Rookie of the Year: Jackie Robinson won the award. In 151 games, he batted .297 with 175 hits, 125 runs scored and 29 stolen bases.

163   five Pasquel brothers: "Pasquel Fortune," p. 35.

163   to ban for five years: "Players Who Jumped," p. 41.

163   April 18, 1946: "Baseball Guild," p. 22.

163   Murphy sought to abolish: "Nats Get Bid," p. 12

163   Cincinnati offered: "Trade Winds," p. 17.

163   Ott now barred: King, "The Flying Scot," p. 38.

163   "The spectacle": Dawson, "Thomson Brought," p. 29.

164   All about strutted: McGowen, "Catcher, Last Holdout," p. 29.

164   "There are six": Heinz, "Ralph Branca's Slow," p. 24.

164   "What will happen": Baumgartner, "Can Branca Ride," p. 9.

164   "probably the most": Ibid.

164   "Will the blowups": Ibid.

164   crescent scar: Dawson, "Lockman, Thomson," p. 39.

165   as it retired: Associated Press, "Ott's No. 4," p. S1.

165   "All that counts now is Giants": Thomson, interview with Norman Macht, SABR, October 16, 1992.

165   uniform he borrowed: Dawson, "Giants Top Pirates," p. S2.

165   "never has impressed": Dawson, "Durocher, Outlining," p. 9.

165   celebrities Tony Martin: Thomson, Heiman and Gutman, *The Giants Win the Pennant! The Giants Win the Pennant!*, p. 65.

165   trainer Willie Schaeffer: Dawson, "Durocher, Outlining," p. 9.

166   "hurts every time": Burr, "Branca Adds," p. 8.

166   ankle swelled: McGowen, "Erskine Is Victor," p. 30.

166   delayed result: Ibid.
166   Swedish Hospital: McGowen, "Boston Holds," p. S1.
166   lanced the ankle: McGowen, "Dodgers Bow," p. 27.
166   shots of penicillin: McGowen, "Boston Holds," p. S1.
166   with shin guard: McGowen, "Borowy's 1-Hitter," p. 28.
166   "I'd really rather play center": King, "Thomson Blasts," p. 3.
166   Russ Meyer left: "Barnstorming Notes," p. 30.
167   "thrown together" in Cleveland: Branca, interview, June 11, 2002.
167   gone for tickets: "Leonard's Squad," p. 13.
167   pocketing on average: Thomson, Heiman and Gutman, *The Giants Win the Pennant! The Giants Win the Pennant!*, p. 65.
167   won 12–1: "Sisler's Nine," p. 12.
167   delighted the crowd: "'Shadow Baseball'," p. 9.
167   slugged home runs: Ibid.
168   "throwing beer cans": Thomson, interview, June 23, 2003.
168   removed Thomson's: "Major League Flashes," November 3, 1948, p. 21.
168   to Newport, Vermont: K. Smith, "Outfielder Has," p. 17.
168   Dutch Leonard: Brands, "Stratospheric Prices," p. 7.
168   offered Boston Thomson: Ruhl, "From the Ruhl," December 1, 1948, p. 20.
168   offered Pittsburgh Branca: "Branca for Westlake," p. 15.
168   third floor: "Majors Meet," p. 20.
168   "When Leo Durocher": Burr, "Anybody Want," p. 2.
168   the "mystery voice": Hand, "Branca Debuts," p. 12.
168   voice lessons: Ibid.
168   polite applause: Ibid.
169   MC Don Cummings: Ibid.
169   "And now": Ibid.
169   beads of sweat: Ibid.
169   paused from its: Ibid.
169   "How will": Ibid.
169   "I'd like to sing": Ibid.
169   not even once touching: Ibid.
169   confided in his audience: Ibid.
169   surrendered the stage: Ibid.
169   Thomson tripled: King, "Higbe's Ready," p. 28.
169   $40,000 for treatment: "Dodgers Take," p. 18.
169   fourteen men apart: Photo beside article. Daniel, "Ted's Catch High," p. 7.
170   "I needed a date": Branca, interview, January 28, 2002.
170   "She looked a lot like Katharine Hepburn": Branca, interview, July 23, 2003.
171   127th pitch: Drebinger, "Yanks Top Dodgers," p. 16.
171   was "most disconsolate": Lang, "Stengel Claims," p. 15.
171   sat alone: Mozley, "Mize Belted," p. C16.
171   "Just one more": Ibid.
172   "That's just the": Ibid.
172   "overpowering the Yankees.": Lang, "Stengel Claims," p. 15.

172   "terrific stuff": Ibid.

172   "There generally": Daley, "Gloom Over," p. 17.

172   "[They] never stuck in my craw": Branca, interview, July 23, 2003.

172   "Her family was steeped": Ibid.

172   Frank Scott: Litsky, "Frank Scott," p. B9.

172   "He's eaten Wheaties": Ad in *Senior Scholastic* magazine, September 28, 1949, p. 36.

172   "Chesterfields are tops": Chesterfield ad in *The Sporting News*, April 20, 1949, p. 56.

172   a dance number: "Rivals Dance," p. 8.

172   F Major: Simon and Ricardel, "The Brooklyn Dodgers Jump."

172   week of warbling: McGowan, "Branca Hit," p. 15.

172   "If Ralph Branca": "Go South," p. 65.

173   endorsing Buster Brown: Advertisement courtesy of the National Scouting Museum.

173   spent the winter: Ruhl, "From the Ruhl," January 11, 1950, p. 22.

173   Heeney Majeski: "Huge Crowd," p. 13.

173   telling *Sport*: King, "The Flying Scot," p. 40.

173   1,000 prints just $40: Ibid.

173   "Bobby's a Scotsman": Ted Rosen, interview, July 12, 2005.

173   Rosen was a friend: Ibid.

173   "I handled money for him": Ibid.

173   Thomson overstepping: "Bunts and Boots," April 19, 1950, p. 43.

173   second only to Musial: Kremenko, "Lockman, on Tip," p. 15.

174   88-degree: "23-Year High," p. 1.

174   clubhouse whimpering: Lang, "Second Guessers," p. 13.

174   "I never saw": Roeder, "One-Way Thomson," p. 14.

174   swung for an hour: Ibid.

174   "Hoot Mon," Alvin Dark confering: Thomson, interview, May 2, 2005.

175   undergoing an operation: McGowen, "Dressen Appointment," p. 52.

175   *New York Times* christened: Effrat, "Thomson Is Signed," p. 29.

175   removed his long khaki storm coat: Nancy Mitchell, interview, April 24, 2003.

175   "I was too naïve": Thomson, interview, June 4, 2003.

175   "Here we go running": Ibid.

175   "Can I call you?": Ibid.

176   "Bill was stuffy": Nancy Thomas, interview, April 28, 2003.

176   "This gal," he says. "Whoo!": Thomson, interview, August 11, 2003.

176   the biggest fall-off: Burnes, "Thomson Off," p. 10.

176   had asked Stoneham: Effrat, "Thomson Is Signed," p. 29.

176   every inning: "Giants' Radio Job," p. 42.

177   the team decided: "2 Pitching Mounts," p. 16.

177   left also to explain: McGowen, "Cox Hits," p. 48.

177   bout of pneumonia: McGowen, "Dodgers Trounce," p. 48.

177   his blood count: Thomson, "That Home Run," p. 68.

177   on a train bound: Orr, "The Unpredictable," p. 60.

177   some eighteen inches: Spink, "Barnstorming," p. 6.

178 "Hey!" Durocher yelled: Thomson, interview with Tom Harris, SABR September 26, 1993.

CHAPTER THIRTEEN

179 "Thy hour and thy harpoon": Melville, *Moby-Dick*, p. 637.

179 eating roast lamb: "Isnello Gives," p. 24.

179 Sharkey declared: "Sharkey Makes," p. 3.

179 Dressen's druthers: Fimrite, "Side By Side," p. 70. AND Buzzie Bavasi, interview, Fall 2001.

180 running belowground from New York: Sheldon Hochheiser, interview, January 2002.

180 radio transmitters and receivers were affixed: Ibid.

180 "almost awesome": Green, "The Eyes," p. 23.

180 sublet his apartment: Crosby, "Faith, Prayer," p. 55.

180 CBS in turn had no time: "Coast-to-Coast," p. 37.

180 American Tobacco: "TV Industry Plays," p. 29.

180 at 20 billion dollars: *Britannica Book of the Year*, p. 102.

180 On March 12: Hagerty, "Costello's Power," p. 1.

181 "What did you do": "Excerpts from Testimony," p. 28.

181 the hands of a don: Wolters, "Gambling Boss'," p. A8.

181 "It has everything": Block, "Kukla, Frank," p. 1.

181 "In eerie half-light": "Who's a Liar?," p. 22.

181 NBC inked Milton: "30-Year Contract," p. 41. AND Shales, "Replay on," p. B1.

181 "It will not solve": Cannon, "Jimmy Cannon Says," October 1, 1951, p. 34.

181 jotted two symbols: Roth scorecard, courtesy of the Roth family.

181 twelve-by-nineteen: Ibid.

181 Roth put down: Ibid.

182 BRASS RAIL.: Ibid.

182 counting backward: Stephan, "Allan Roth's True," 1993 SABR convention.

182 running back: Ibid.

182 December 16: Ibid.

182 "I didn't know what the hell": Esther Roth, interview, January 30, 2002.

182 Staller's performance: Stephan, "Allan Roth's True," 1993 SABR convention.

182 "It was fascinating": Esther Roth, interview, January 30, 2002.

182 on-base percentage: Rickey, "Goodbye to Some," p. 80.

182 "will accept": Ibid., p. 89.

182 met Roth at the Mont-Royal Hotel: Esther Roth, interview, January 30, 2002.

182 Lingering visa: Stephan, "Allan Roth's True," 1993 SABR convention.

183 good for $100 a week: Esther Roth, interview, January 30, 2002.

183 "Back then, my system": Thomson, Heiman and Gutman, *The Giants Win the Pennant! The Giants Win the Pennant!*, p. 171.

183 "I had one for": Ibid.

183 scribble it onto an index card: Esther Roth, interview, January 30, 2002.

183 his brown leather briefcase: Anderson, *Pennant Races*, p. 223.

183 "At that time": Esther Roth, interview, January 30, 2002.

183 wrote C. David Stephan: Stephan, "Allan Roth's True," 1993 SABR convention.

183 "When Walter took over": Buzzie Bavasi, interview, February 13, 2002.

183 Dressen did not want Roth: Ibid.

183 never having read a book: Kahn, *The Boys of Summer*, p. 150.

183 "Charlie won't pay attention": Buzzie Bavasi, interview, February 13, 2002.

184 Roth penciled: Roth scorecard, courtesy of the Roth family.

184 "twenty years older": Epstein, "Hearn Never," p. 27.

184 cell-blocks: Conklin, "Baseball Fever," p. 43.

184 military recruiting: "Leo's Little Giant," p. 1.

184 blood center: "Brooklyn Blood Center," p. 3.

184 *Daily Mirror* had its headline: *Daily Mirror* headline: "1 Game to Go for Giant Miracle," October 2, 1951, p. 3.

184 Angelo Ambrosio arrived: Angelo Ambrosio, interview, January 21, 2002.

184 he had work to do: Ibid.

185 "I heard it around": Ibid.

185 "He was someone you feared": Ibid.

185 Leonard, seventeen, was the Giant batboy: Jim Beattie, interview, February 26, 2004. AND Pat Leonard, interview, April 1, 2004.

185 he told friend Ed Goin about Herman Franks: Ed Goin, interview, March 25, 2004.

185 "He was our big celebrity": Jim Beattie, interview, February 26, 2004.

185 blocks of rosin to bang: Angelo Ambrosio, interview, January 21, 2002.

185 There were gloves to mend: Garreau, *Bat Boy of the Giants*, p. 39.

185 "Red, where's the": King, "The Dugout," p. 58.

185 Each trunk held ninety bats: Garreau, *Bat Boy of the Giants*, p. 25.

185 at the clubhouse by 10:30: Ibid., p. 36.

185 dragged two of them: Ibid., p. 16.

185 Jacobellis, thirty-one, knew: Marie Lippolis and Jules Warzybok, interviews, May 21, 2004.

186 "His caption read": Vern Shibla, interview, May 20, 2004.

186 "He was more talented": Paul Bereswill, interview, May 21, 2004.

186 an extra fifteen: "Extra Bat Practice," p. 33.

186 "You'd inhale those fumes": George Spencer, interview, February 28, 2002.

186 Schenz asked: Steiger, "Maglie vs. Newcombe," p. 53.

186 "Times Square assumed": Conklin, "Baseball Fever," p. 43.

186 600 Chesterfield cigarettes were on their way: Ernie Harwell, interview, May 2002.

187 "why Dressen isn't": Parker, "Durocher Gambles," p. 53.

187 "Jones is spitting": Trimble, "Chuck Howls," p. 90.

187 "He was a very vindictive person": Clem Labine, interview, February 28, 2002.

188 the battery switched: Epstein, "Jones Threw," p. 16.

188 The count went full: Clem Labine, interview, February 28, 2002.

188 a high school football pass: Ibid.

188 "It gave me so much pressure": Ibid.

188 to write in black: Baumgartner, "Chuck Calls," p. 3.

188 the poetry scrawled by Jerome David Salinger: Salinger, *The Catcher in the Rye*, p. 38.

188 Allie Caulfield: Ibid.

188 "If the ball's at": Clem Labine, interview, February 28, 2002.

188 "I was expecting": Lewin, "Ace in Hole," p. 16.

189 "It's just enough": Miller, "A Guy Named Schenz," page unknown.

189 When Schenz reached: Hugo, "Record Book," courtesy of Isabelle Hugo.

189 "As far as I can see,": Burr, "Jones Charged," p. 26.

189 "Labine pitched": Lewin, "Ace in Hole," p. 16.

189 "Many times, in": Berg, "Pitchers and," p. 287.

CHAPTER FOURTEEN

191 "No steel can enter": *Sochineniia*, p. 219.

191 John Steinbeck wrote: Steinbeck, *Journal of the Novel*, pp. vii, 163.

191 in a blue wing-back chair: Ibid., p. 8.

191 "getting my mental arm": Ibid., back cover.

191 "Today," he wrote: Ibid., p. 163.

191 three cents poorer: Harriet Mesulam, interview, December 17, 2001.

191 "This is it": Parker, "Durocher Gambles," p. 53.

191 did not even have the strength: Harriet Mesulam, interview, December 17, 2001.

191 Newcombe had shed six: Laney, "Stunned Crowd," p. 34.

191 Newcombe left his home: Don Newcombe, interview, March 1, 2002.

192 just eight times: Dave Smith, *Retrosheet*. New York played 157 games in 1908, and 158 games 1904, 1909 and 1917. Brooklyn played 157 games in 1933, 1939, 1941 and 1946. (Including its tie in Boston on May 12, Brooklyn played 158 games in 1951.)

192 spoke to the sportswriters: Harwell, "The Miracle of," p. 84.

192 loudspeakers serenading each: Roeder, "Reese Thigh," p. 39.

192 Dressen to Newcombe: Kahn, "The Day Bobby," p. 42.

192 Durocher to Maglie: Ibid.

192 a pre-noon nip: Bacon, *How Sweet It Is*, p. 102. It was author James Bacon, in his Gleason biography, *How Sweet It Is*, who first reported that Gleason, Sinatra and Shor attended the game together. Bacon told me on June 9, 2004, that the story was told to him by Sinatra and confirmed by Gleason. Laraine Day remembered to me on August 13, 2001, that she had sat near Sinatra during the game, and audiotape places Shor in the Giant clubhouse just after it. Bacon also wrote that J. Edgar Hoover had been seated at the game alongside Gleason, Sinatra and Shor. Newsprint confirms that Hoover was at Game One of the World Series. But he was not at the playoff. His daily log at the FBI shows that on October 3, 1951, he was at his Washington desk from 9:52 a.m. to 12:52 p.m., 1:40 p.m. to 3:10 p.m. and 4:32 to 4:35 p.m. (The log includes a record of those Hoover spoke to and met

with.) Furthermore, the appointment book of Charles Brannan shows that from 3:30 to 4 p.m., Hoover was in the Oval Office with President Truman. Hoover log courtesy of the FBI; Brannan log courtesy of the Truman Presidential Museum & Library.

192   Sinatra offered tickets: Bacon, *How Sweet It Is*, p. 102.

192   oak-plank floor: Anderson, "Toots Shor," p. 26.

192   a liquor-stocked: Bacon, *How Sweet It Is*, p. 103.

192   had been a barker: Archive of the Museum of Broadcast Communications. *www.museum.tv/archives/etv/H/htmlH/honeymooners/honeymooners.htm.*

192   restaurateur a bouncer: Anderson, "Toots Shor," p. 26.

192   arrested at twenty-three: Molotsky, "F.B.I. Releases," p. A21.

192   in twenty-six days allow: "Frank Sinatra," p. 30.

192   a live six-minute: Archive of the Museum of Broadcast Communications. *www.museum.tv/archives/etv/H/htmlH/honeymooners/honeymooners.htm.*

192   "Jackie guzzled booze": Bacon, *How Sweet It Is*, p. 103.

193   "I took advantage": Hemingway, *Misadventures of a Fly Fisherman*, p. 290.

193   word that Pauline Pfeiffer: Reynolds, *Hemingway: An Annotated Chronology*, p. 120.

193   "I wonder," says son Pat: Pat Hemingway, interview, December 1, 2003.

193   Schenz waved to his cousin: Robert Schenz, interview, February 27, 2002.

193   temperature was 71 degrees: "The Summary" (weather), October 4, 1951, p. 67.

193   at 5:35 a.m.: "The Summary" (weather), October 3, 1951, p. 67.

193   the *Daily News*: Trimble, "Chuck Howls," p. 90. AND "Assumed Sell-Out": *New York Times* headline, October 3, 1951, p. 43.

194   "SERIES OVERSUBSCRIBED": *New York Herald Tribune* headline, September 29, 1951, p. 12.

194   16.1 million: Thorn, Palmer and Gershman, *Total Baseball*, pp. 76–77.

194   was down 7.7 percent: Ibid.

194   Attendance had stagnated: Ibid.

194   Herbert Hoover would: McAuley, "Frick Shows," p. 11.

194   55.4 million: "Report of the Subcommittee on Study of Monopoly Power," p. 11.

194   two more than: In 1951, there were twelve football, ten basketball and four big league hockey teams.

194   "Baseball is a thousand": Ibid.

194   96 million: Eberly, "Replay It," p. 29.

195   WNBT and WPIX: "The New York City Television," p. 3.

195   "as nonchalantly as if": Roeder, "Reese Thigh," p. 39.

195   "Twenty years from now": Liberty Broadcasting Network, recording of game, October 3, 1951.

195   Six of the eventual: National Baseball Hall of Fame Library. Red Barber, Russ Hodges, Ernie Harwell, Vin Scully, Bob Prince and Harry Caray.

195   The press box clung: Description of broadcasters in press box from Ernie Harwell, interview, March 11, 2002.

195   Buck Canel and Felo Ramirez: Felo Remirez, interview, March 25, 2003.

195 black lenses of their Graflex: Jack Pokress, interview, April 30, 2002.

195 spring-loaded Eymos: Jack Balletti, interview, April 30, 2002.

196 the tin-ceilinged TV booth: Ernie Harwell, interview, April 26, 2002.

196 fifty-two NBC stations: "57 Video," p. D1.

196 short-sleeved yellow shirt: Pat Hodges, interview, May 8, 2002.

196 behind a hanging blanket: Hodges and Hirshberg, *My Giants*, p. 109.

196 Nat Allbright set to air: Nat Allbright and John Cooley, interviews, March 20, 2003.

196 ten All Star games: Baseball Almanac. *www.baseball-almanac.com.* Conlan: 1943, 1947, 1950; Goetz: 1939, 1946; Jorda: 1941, 1951; Stewart: 1936, 1940, 1948.

196 nine World Series: National Baseball Hall of Fame Library. Conlan: 1945, 1950; Goetz: 1941, 1947; Jorda: 1945, 1949; Stewart: 1937, 1943, 1948.

196 Stewart would be inducted: U.S. Hockey Hall of Fame. Inducted in 1982.

196 "First pitch of": Liberty Broadcasting Network, recording of game, October 3, 1951.

196 13–10 favorites: "Giants 13–10," p. 26.

196 losing record: He was 41–47 in six seasons.

197 did not snap: Daley, "Listening to," p. S2.

197 taught Maglie to tighten: Ibid.

197 265.05 feet: 184th Street and Fort Washington Blvd. Fort Washington/Bennett Park (Long Hill).

197 Henry Colletti yanked with his 137 pounds: Tommy Colletti, interview, October 28, 2004.

197 the number of TV sets: "The New York City Television," p. 3.

197 Dow Jones's . . . Belmont Park . . . New York Telephone Company: Conklin, "Baseball Fever," p. 43.

197 "I don't know why I wouldn't": Thomson, interview, November 2000.

197 "Thomson has now hit": R. Smith, "Last Chapter," p. 30.

198 "Outlined against a blue-gray": Rice, "Notre Dame's Cyclone," page 1.

198 "Now maybe Thomson": Kahn, "The Day Bobby," p. 44.

198 "We may have had": Liberty Broadcasting Network, recording of game, October 3, 1951.

198 "shielding his signs": Ibid.

199 Robinson called time: Laney, "Stunned Crowd," p. 34.

199 rubbed the arm with Capsulin: Golenbock, *BUMS*, p. 308.

199 "It burned so much": Branca, interview, February 20, 2002.

200 a quintet of pitchers: Al Corwin, interview, March 1, 2002.

200 up late the night before gargling Listerine: Pat Hodges, interview, May 8, 2002.

200 Hodges had first sat: Hodges and Hirshberg, *My Giants*, p. 23.

200 earned $20 a week: Ibid., p. 26.

200 assisted the great Yankee: Ibid., p. 45.

200 CBS TV Pabst Blue Ribbon: "Russ Hodges...," p. 46.

200 two years later $75,000: Ibid.

200 since 1903: Light, *The Cultural Encyclopedia of Baseball*, p. 798.

200 Dreyfuss donated: Ibid.

200   earmarked a minimum: Ibid., p. 799.

200    $5,737.95 went: Goodman, *The Little Red Book of Baseball*, p. 135.

201   the New York Stock Exchange stopped: Beginning on September 29, 1952, the market closed at 3:30 p.m.

201   Driven by metals: "Stocks Go Ahead," p. 51.

201   Dow Jones Industrial Average rose: Tara Lambert (*Wall Street Journal* Market Data Group), interview, December 22, 2003.

201   its highest close since 1930: Ibid.

201   "Boy," he said: Liberty Broadcasting Network, recording of game, October 3, 1951.

201   "If the game gets": Rosenfeld, *The Great Chase*, p. 49.

201   "How's he throwing?": Clem Labine, interview, February 28, 2002.

201   "dangerous," cautioned McClendon: Liberty Broadcasting Network, recording of game, October 3, 1951.

202   "He worked the shit out of me": Don Newcombe, interview, March 1, 2002.

202   "Don told Dressen: "Why Did Don," p. 27.

202   Some twenty-five reporters: Roeder, "The Shot Heard," *Phillies Present Famous Sports Moments*, p. 50. AND Jack Lang, interview, March 19, 2002.

202   Frank Bourgholtzer turned on a television: Frank Bourgholtzer, interview, August 14, 2002.

202   "I insisted that we watch": Ibid.

202   Genevieve Zeren appeared. "Press!": Genevieve Zeren, interview, August 2002.

202   a familiar gag: Montgomery, "D.C. Wash," p. 4.

202   transfixed by a game: "Bombshell Disrupts," p. 30.

202   "I'm serious": Montgomery, "D.C. Wash," p. 4.

202   And so at 3:20: Truman Presidential Museum & Library, October 3, 1951, press conference.

203   as Washington Republican Harry: Montgomery, "D.C. Wash," p. 4.

203   in Gatlinburg, Tennessee: "What Stalin's," p. 26.

203   "Compared with that": Ibid.

203   Facing the north: Donovan, "Truman's," p. 1.

203   "This won't take long": Truman Presidential Museum & Library. October 3, 1951, press conference.

203   White House official reporter Jack Romagna: Genevieve Zeren, interview, August 2002.

203   the press—Bourgholtzer: Truman Presidential Museum & Library, October 3, 1951, press conference.

203   "What about the rest? . . ." "Just a minute, Charlie!": Ibid.

203   a photograph of Ross: Donovan, "Truman's," p. 1.

203   "In spite of Soviet . . . for that effective": Truman Presidential Museum & Library. October 3, 1951, press conference.

204   President Truman: According to Truman's daily calendar, from 3:30 to 4 p.m. on October 3, 1951, he met with Attorney General J. Howard McGrath, Secretary of the Interior Oscar Chapman, Secretary of Agriculture Charles Bran-

nan, Director of Defense Mobilization Charles Wilson, Director of the Office of Price Stabilization Michael DiSalle and Director of the FBI J. Edgar Hoover. Truman log courtesy of Truman Presidential Museum & Library.

204   Truman three rooms over: Ibid., calendar.

204   discuss meat control: The log of Secretary of Agriculture Brannan specifies the subject of the meeting.

204   wire at 3:27 p.m.: "Joseph Stalin's," p. 27.

204   second atomic explosion: Podvig, *Russian Strategic Nuclear Forces*, p. 441. The first was on August 29, 1949.

204   six kilotons: Ibid.

204   share of its TV broadcast: "The New York City Television," p. 6.

204   the men half descended: Jack Lang, interview, March 19, 2002.

204   Pafko also had hypertension: Andy Pafko, interview, March 6, 2006.

205   "The Brooklyn fans were": Antoinette Yvars, interview, July 15, 2004.

205   "We wanted to beat the crowd": Yogi Berra, interview, March 10, 2002.

205   And so the men squeezed: Jack Lang, interview, March 19, 2002.

205   "He was sitting there": Ibid.

205   Old Gold cigarettes: Clem Labine, interview, February 28, 2002.

206   "You didn't smoke in uniform": Ibid.

206   "You could catch him in a rocking": Sal Yvars, interview.

206   the glove of Steve Lembo: Josie Limbo, interview, May 2002.

206   Brooklyn was home: Ibid.

206   "Don't shake yet": Haag, "Hank Schenz," p. 120.

206   "Piss on the fire": Heiman, Weiner and Gutman, *When the Cheering Stops*, p. 220.

206   Not once in baseball's: Dave Smith, *Retrosheet*. Among the 278 playoff and World Series games played prior to October 3, 1951, are five pennant playoff games that count as regular season games. There are ten such games among the 879 playoff and World Series games played after October 3, 1951.

206   Thomas Fitzgibbon: Thomas J. Fitzgibbon, letter, October 2001.

207   "You must have faith in St. Jude": Thomas Fitzgibbon, interview, October 2001.

207   In the Holbert home: Patrick Ledwith, e-mail message, May 6, 2004. AND George Ledwith, interview, May 11, 2004.

207   Morty Rothschild: Morty Rothschild, interview, February 2001.

207   "Who's ready?" he asked: Thomson, Heiman and Gutman, *The Giants Win the Pennant! The Giants Win the Pennant!*, p. 241.

207   "Branca was showing off": Green, *Forgotten Fields*, p. 148.

208   So did Art Suskind: Ernie Harwell, interview, April 26, 2002.

208   Western Electric microphone, model 632C: Ernie Harwell, interview, May 2002.

208   "That's Carl Erskine": Harwell, "The Miracle of," p. 87.

208   The cameras, RCA model TK11: George Hoover, interview, May 8, 2002.

208   "were four home runs": Musial, "Clem's Curve," p. 39.

208   Barber collapsed from ulcers: Halberstam, *Sports on New York Radio*, p. 237.

208   traded Harwell: Ibid.
208   "I'm okay," he told: Don Newcombe, interview.
208   "Now, a belt": Durocher, "How We Won," p. 85.
209   Girlfriend Pat Kannar: Pat Leonard, interview, April 1, 2004.
209   Adirondack model 302: National Baseball Hall of Fame and Museum.
209   The bat weighed: Ibid.
209   "Attention, press": Laney, "Stunned Crowd," p. 30.
209   John Webber had arranged: A. Smith, "There Is No," p. 12.
209   chef Walter Misbach: *Brooklyn Eagle* photo caption: "Instead of Turkey, They Ate Crow," October 4, 1951, p. 7.
209   cost: $20,000: A. Smith, "There Is No," p. 12.
209   Stoneham had left nephew: Dawson, "Game-Winning Homer," p. 42.
209   Tendons tore: Thomson, Heiman and Gutman, *The Giants Win the Pennant! The Giants Win the Pennant!*, p. 246.
209   The Lip knelt and touched: Don Mueller, interview, March 4, 2002.
209   pinch-run five men: Dave Smith, *Retrosheet*.
210   On December 17, 1945: *The 1951 Baseball Register*, p. 93.
210   He had cost $25,000: K. Smith, "Combination 'Feller," p. 14.
210   "could get $100,000": Meany, "The Mystery Man," p. 14.
210   "He sounded frantic": Thomson, Heiman and Gutman, *The Giants Win the Pennant! The Giants Win the Pennant!*, p. 241.
210   "Erskine just bounced": Clem Labine, interview.
210   a pitch he held across the seams: Carl Erskine, interview, March 1, 2002.
210   "I never had a problem": Ibid.
210   seventy-four feet behind home: Eskenazi, *The Lip*, p. 250. AND Lowry, *Green Cathedrals*, p. 196.
211   his hundredth pitch: Newcombe had thrown 65 strikes and 35 balls. Allan Roth data courtesy of Dave Smith, *Retrosheet*.
211   No Major League: Elias Sports Bureau, Inc. Previous to Newcombe, the last to throw at least 32 innings over eight days was Ken Raffensberger in 1949.
211   "This is too important": "Why Did Don," p. 27.
211   "The Dodgers have": WMCA, recording of game, October 3, 1951.
211   Off Branca: Dave Smith, *Retrosheet*.
211   Off Erskine: Ibid.
211   Thomson had faced each: Ibid.
211   "Who are you bringing": Conlan and Creamer, *Jocko*, p. 128.
211   patted Branca: Spink, "Boos Turned," p. 10.
211   "Hank Schenz returns": WMCA, recording of game, October 3, 1951.
212   turned to writer Tom Meany: Kritzer, "Biggest Day," p. 10.
212   shook his head: Rudd and Fischler, *The Sporting Life*, p. 105.
212   "Dressen didn't want": Thomson, Heiman and Gutman, *The Giants Win the Pennant! The Giants Win the Pennant!*, p. 171.
212   "It took ten days": Hand, "Branca Debuts," p. 12.
212   "Go get 'em, Ralph": Andy Pafko, interview, February 28, 2002.
212   walking down then up: Lowry, *Green Cathedrals*, p. 198.
213   "Go get 'em": Golenbock, *BUMS*, p. 308.
213   Branca slipped his left hand: Universal International News newsreel footage.

213   slapping three times: Ibid.
213   leather gloves touched: Ibid.
213   "Don't worry about it": Thomson, Heiman and Gutman, *The Giants Win the Pennant! The Giants Win the Pennant!*, p. 248.
213   Three times Branca: Dave Smith, *Retrosheet*. On July 26, 1950, August 17, 1950, and June 19, 1951.
213   Newcombe walked slowly: Universal International News newsreel footage.
213   took now Branca's jacket: Stanley Strull, interview, December 2000.
213   "Let's go get 'em": Ibid.
213   in 19 at-bats: Dave Smith, *Retrosheet*.
213   Mays had wilted: Ibid.
213   "Get him out": Kahn, "The Day Bobby," p. 52.
213   jangling 18 cents: Burr, "Dressen Keeps," p. 14.
214   "During that ninety feet": Thomson, interview, November 2000.
214   Durocher walked up to Thomson: Universal International News newsreel footage.
214   "Boy," he told: Bloom, "Thomson 'Was,' " p. 34.
214   Durocher slapped with his right: Universal International News newsreel footage.
214   His voice was hoarse: Hodges and Hirschberg, *My Giants*, p. 113.
214   "He'll be up": WMCA, recording of game, October 3, 1951.
214   "We had said," remembers Erskine: Carl Erskine, interview, March 1,2002.
214   Walker told Branca: Golenbock, *BUMS*, p. 303.
214   get ahead of Thomson: Kirby, "The Shot Heard," p. 29.
214   "What signs are we using?": Branca, interview, February 20, 2002.
214   Walker was partial: Ibid.
214   36.1 innings: Dave Smith, *Retrosheet*.
214   "Probably the best I felt": Branca, interview, February 20, 2002.
215   five playoff games: Prior to the first two games of the 1951 playoff, Brooklyn and St. Louis played two playoff games in 1946, and Cleveland and Boston played one in 1948.
215   "Why is it," Branca's brother: John Branca, interview.
215   Al Branca rose in his seat: Al Branca, interview, July 29, 2003.
215   section, row and seat: From the collection of Michael Santo.
215   eight practice throws: Spink, *Baseball Guide and Record Book 1951*, p. 583, MLB Rule 8.03.
215   "Isn't it nice": "Ralphie's Gopher," p. 73.
215   "My cleats fit like a glove": Thomson, interview, November 12, 2003.
215   the third-base side of the rubber: Branca, interview, November 21, 2005.
215   his 11-D black shoes: Branca, interview, February 20, 2002.
215   "Branca!" thought Thomson: Thomson, interview, November 2000,
215   both awakened that morning: Branca, "Branca: Diary," p. 7. AND Thomson, "Thomson: Diary," p. 6.
215   had eaten eggs: Ibid.
215   Both had left: Gallo, "Unforgettable," pp. 6–7.
216   "I didn't recognize the sequence": Whitey Lockman, interview, Fall 2000.
216   just the sixth time: Elias Sports Bureau, Inc. 1910: Philadelphia Athletics

and Cleveland; 1910: Boston and Cleveland; 1911: Cincinnati and St. Louis Cardinals; 1913: Philadelphia Phillies and New York Giants; 1944: Pittsburgh and St. Louis Cardinals.

216 "If I did nothing": Sal Yvars, interview, Fall 2000.

216 "Branca pitches and": WMGM, recording of game, October 3, 1951.

216 the latter now warming up too: Clem Labine, interview.

216 "Oh no!" shouted Erskine: Carl Erskine, interview, March 1, 2002.

216 "Nobody was tending": Don Mueller, interview, March 4, 2002.

216 The bespectacled clubhouse man had learned mid-game: Don Mueller, interview, March 4, 2002. AND Pacini, "Remembering Gehrig," p. 26.

216 Roth noted: Roth scorecard, courtesy of the Roth family.

217 "Answer us, God, answer us": *The Complete ArtScroll Siddur*, p. 243.

217 This Nota Schiller would: Nota Schiller, interview, April 19, 2004.

217 "Hail Mary, full of grace": Monks of Glenstal Abbey, *The Glenstal Book of Prayer*, p. 93.

217 Bavasi invoked the virgin mother: Buzzie Bavasi, interview, January 7, 2002.

217 So did Carl Bayuk: Carl Bayuk, letter to Thomson, October 1997. AND Beth Bayuk and Tom Bayuk, interviews, Spring 2003.

217 "If you hit a home": October 1997 letter from Carl Bayuk to Thomson, courtesy of Thomson.

217 "Please don't let it be": Mays with Sahadi, *Say Hey*, p. 15.

217 Carter, twenty-four, loved statistics: Estelle Kraysler, interview, April 2, 2004. AND Irwin Hundert, interview, April 4, 2004.

217 two baseball statistics: Jack Carter, letter to Jim Small at MLB, February 15, 1996. Courtesy of the Carter family.

217 vice president Feeney: Ibid.

218 "He was very excited": Estelle Kraysler, interview, April 2, 2004.

218 "He had to teach me": Ibid.

218 "when the Giants started": February 15, 1996, letter from Jack Carter to Jim Small at MLB, courtesy of the Carter family.

218 "Durocher changed the": Estelle Kraysler, interview, April 2, 2004.

218 in every slot: Dave Smith, *Retrosheet*.

218 collect three hits: Thomson, "Thomson: Diary," p. 6.

218 Robinson had: Branca, "They'll Never," p. 72.

218 white cotton bag: National Baseball Hall of Fame Library.

218 "Hartung down the": WMCA, recording of game, October 3, 1951.

219 the eye of a newsreel: Universal International News newsreel footage.

219 in his mouth half a stick: Thomson, interview, September 30, 2003.

219 "Of course!" says Thomson: Thomson, interview, November 2000.

219 "Branca throws": WMCA, recording of game, October 3, 1951.

219 rolling off at last touch: Branca, interview, February 20, 2002.

219 ninety-three miles: Branca, interview.

219 Thomson slightly lifted: Universal International News newsreel footage.

220 Walker raised his glove: Ibid.

220 "Get down!": Kahn, "The Day Bobby," p. 52.

220 Durocher called to Hartung: Durocher, *Nice Guys Finish Last*, p. 371.

220   "There's a long drive!": WMCA, recording of game, October 3, 1951.

220   "It's going to be!": Ibid.

220   lifting to his mouth: Clay Felker, interview, April 30, 2005.

220   "The Giants win the pennant!": WMCA, recording of game, October 3, 1951.

220   "Going, going, gone!": Liberty Broadcasting Network, recording of game, October 3, 1951.

220   "It is a home run!": WMGM, recording of game, October 3, 1951.

220   "*Los Gigantes*": Buck Canel rehashed the call on the October 3, 1951, World Series preview on the Mutual Broadcasting System.

221   "It's gone!": Ernie Harwell, interview, March 11, 2002.

221   204 home runs: SABR member John McCormack tracked where 131 of the 204 home runs landed. Picking up where he left off, I tracked all but six: May 13 Stanky, July 7 Stanky, July 7 Thompson, July 8 Mueller, July 15 Thomson, August 27 Stanky.

221   "The ball was hit so hard": Andy Pafko, interview, June 6, 2005.

221   Roth jotted: Roth scorecard, courtesy of the Roth family.

221   Charles Einstein turned now: Charles Einstein, interview, September 22, 2004.

221   "Exclamation point": Ibid.

221   "Oh my God": Halberstam, *Sports on New York Radio*, p. 240.

221   Clay Felker was statistician: Clay Felker, interview, Winter 2002.

221   "That's my boy!": Frank Bourgholtzer, interview, August 14, 2002.

221   Fitzgibbon screamed: Daley, "'Quarterback' of," p. 27.

222   "Bobby Thomson hits": WMCA, recording of game, October 3, 1951.

222   "We did it!": Kirby, "The Shot Heard," p. 31.

222   "It can't be!": Kahn, "The Day Bobby," p. 57.

222   "Oh, Pop!": Terry Seidler, interview, June 9, 2005.

222   "I can't believe it.": Harriet Mesulam, interview, November 28, 2000.

222   the Hurricane began to wave: Universal International News newsreel footage.

222   "Ohhh-ohhh!": WMCA, recording of game, October 3, 1951.

222   bent to grasp a rosin bag: Universal International News newsreel footage.

222   The white cotton bag skittered: Ibid.

222   Branca stuffed: Spink, "Boos Turned," p. 10.

223   loped for home, chuffing: Kiernan, *The Miracle at Coogan's Bluff*, p. 266.

223   Robinson turned: Bock, "Still Crazy," p. S6.

223   quickened hearts: Robert T. Knight (University of California at Berkeley professor of neuroscience), interview, April 13, 2005.

223   two of 34,320 hearts: Dawson, "Game-Winning Homer," p. 42.

223   "Mature people," wrote: Considine, "Thomson Authors," p. 32.

223   Bernard Davies dashed: National Baseball Hall of Fame Library. AND Michael Davies, interview, May 2002.

223   A man and woman: Kiernan, *The Miracle at Coogan's Bluff*, pp. 147–49. Author Thomas Kiernan relays in detail, over two-plus pages, the memories of two fans who witnessed the offending couple. Endless efforts to find these fans were fruitless. But after speaking with Kiernan, I am convinced

that the anecdote is at its core true and so I included here the barest mention of it.

223   long neck straining: Kirby, "The Shot Heard," p. 30.

223   Only little Chris Durocher: Chris Durocher, interview, August 17, 2001.

223   chewing gum: Crosby, "Faith, Prayer," p. 54.

223   "I know the great sorrow": Laraine Day, interview, August 13, 2001.

224   "It can't happen": King, "'53 Dodgers," p. 9.

224   Newcombe heard the stampede: Don Newcombe, interview, March 1, 2002.

224   "Home run," offered: Ibid.

224   Nat Allbright read the ticker: Nat Allbright, interview, March 20, 2003.

224   "It may go!": Ibid.

224   "I was," Franks explained: Renzhofer, "Baseball Was," p. J4.

CHAPTER FIFTEEN

227   "No matter where you sit": White, *Here Is New York*, p. 19.

227   Elizabeth dropped: Stern, "Bobby Takes Brooklyn," p. 30. AND *Daily Mirror* caption, "My Bobby Did It!," October 4, 1951, p. 1. Other papers reported that, nervous, she had turned off her TV and was making a Scotch dumpling when a neighbor delivered the news.

227   Rose Krobot fainted too: Charles Krobot, interview, July 6, 2002.

227   Dodger fan Philip: New York Department of Vital Statistics. AND Andrew Arbiter, interview, September 3, 2002. AND Cyril Greenhouse, interview, August 4, 2003.

227   Fred Fields, a boy: Fred Fields, e-mail message, January 31, 2001.

227   Atop a stairwell: Lyle Spatz, e-mail message, September 13, 2002.

227   Russ Hodges told Gerry Kremenko: Gerry Kremenko, interview, August 12, 2005.

228   Fedoras and straw hats: Plimpton, *The Cooperstown Symposium on Baseball and American Culture*, p. 27. AND George Plimpton, interview, February 2001.

228   Giant fan Bob Berggren: Fred Opper, interview, Spring 2003.

228   Larry Groff unable: Larry Groff, interview, May 28, 2005.

228   John Drebinger lost: Daley, "Sound Effects," p. 25.

228   Dodger fan Doris Kearns: Goodwin, *Wait Till Next Year*, p. 153.

228   "Gee whiz!": Bloom, "Thomson 'Was Feeling,' " p. 1.

228   One thousand feet over: Ron Littlefair, e-mail message, May 26, 2003.

228   Ron Littlefair sat at the stick: Ibid.

228   "Making final landing": Ibid.

228   a paper boy named: Paul Knatz, interview, June 2003.

228   In a Waldorf-Astoria suite: "Ball Game Gab," p. 2.

228   behind a meat counter: Anderson, "Nostaligia Time," p. D16. AND Fred Wilpon, interview, March 29, 2006.

228   Brooklyn basement on Crown: Lichtenstein, "The Home Run," p. D10. AND Grace Lichtenstein, interview, February 27, 2004.

228   Inside Coward's Shoes: Paul Hirsch, e-mail message, September 14, 2004.

229   In a radio studio in Guantanamo Bay: George Balamaci, interview, March 29, 2004.

229 Warren Buffett found: Warren Buffet, e-mail message, July 25, 2002.
229 Cub fan John Paul Stevens: John Paul Stevens, interview, September 17, 2002.
229 Harold Bloom halted: Harold Bloom, interview, February 2003.
229 Alan Greenspan, a Dodger fan: Alan Greenspan, e-mail message, August 21, 2002.
229 Red Sox announcer Curt Gowdy: Curt Gowdy, interview, November 29, 2004.
229 Hank Aaron, seventeen: Aaron, *I Had A Hammer*, p. 25. AND Hank Aaron, interview, February 12, 2003.
229 Thomson's heroics reached Gerald Ford: Gerald Ford, interview, August 5, 2002.
229 On the Q36 bus: Borsellino, "No Joy," p. 1B. AND Guy Cogan, interview, September 2001.
230 Sid Caesar, Carl Reiner, Mel Brooks, Neil Simon: Sid Caesar and Carl Reiner, interviews, August 21, 2002.
230 Milton Berle yelped: Buddy Arnold, interview, February 2003.
230 to pause a full: Montgomery, "D.C. Wash," p. 4.
230 A boy of twelve and a girl: Donald Millus, interview, May 20, 2005. AND Millus, *The Ebbets Field Knothole*, Chapter 21. *ww2.coastal.edu/millus/*.
230 "a very quiet if not": June 19, 2002, letter from Arthur Miller to the author.
230 "was screaming at two": Ibid.
230 "I was not any longer": Ibid.
230 bursts of flashbulb: R. Smith, "Last Chapter," p. 30.

CHAPTER SIXTEEN

231 "Man as the spectator": Niebuhr, *The Irony of American History*, p. 88.
231 Here Hodges lightly: Carl Erskine, interview, April 20, 2006. AND Fimrite, "Side by Side," p. 76.
231 skittered buttons: Kirby, "The Shot Heard," p. 31.
231 last bottles of bubbly: Golenbock, *BUMS*, p. 300.
231 He pitched his sweated blue cap: Branca, interview, February 20, 2002.
231 "There was nowhere to hide": Ibid.
231 "I don't believe": WMCA, recording of game, October 3, 1951.
232 silent over his mike: Ibid.
232 neared 40th Street: King, " 'I saw Dancing,' " p. 2.
232 "The screams became": Ibid.
232 the third floor of 24 Johnson: Dave Anderson, interview, March 2, 2004.
232 stood astride a stone: Ibid, AND "in My Brooklyn," Dave Anderson, interview, March 2, 2004.
232 The second child: Berkow, "Red Smith, Sports," p. 22.
232 ninety newspapers: Ibid.
233 "he was reading Red Smith": Hemingway, *Across the River and Into the Trees*, p. 166.
233 Just once before: The Boston Red Sox did so in 1948–49.
233 in suit, bow tie and fedora: Buzzie Bavasi, interview, September 17, 2003.
233 "We're a good club": Ibid.
233 told his players the same: Ibid.

233   O'Malley attempted to kid Cox: Berkow, "At 80," p. D5.

233   hold back tears: Kirby, "The Shot Heard," p. 31.

233   had Brooklyn's redoubt closed: Buzzie Bavasi, interview, September 17, 2003.

233   Just one man stood: Marsh and Ehre, *Best Sports Stories*, p. 16.

233   Barney Stein begging: Hamill, "The Gang Was," p. 4.

233   five feet tall: Bonnie Crosby, interview, September 21, 2003.

233   Speed Graphic: Barber, *The Rhubarb Patch*, p. 120, and Crosby interview.

233   The youngest of eleven children: Shirley Wershba, interview, September 21, 2003.

233   Strolling with his camera: Bonnie Crosby, interview, September 21, 2003.

233   he had risen before dawn: Ibid.

234   "I never saw such a lonely figure": Andy Pafko, interview, February 28, 2002.

234   "I'm never going to let baseball": Don Newcombe, interview, March 1, 2002.

234   never would he recall his slow walk: Branca, interview, February 20, 2002.

234   "I didn't give a shit": Ibid.

235   not one had: David Vincent, SABR. Thomson would hit 3 more game-ending homers.

235   giddy Buddy Kerr: Thomson, Heiman and Gutman, *The Giants Win the Pennant! The Giants Win the Pennant!*, p. 259. AND Thomson, interview, September 30, 2003.

235   offered Thomson $500: Ibid., p. 261.

235   "We want Thomson!": Bradley, "Thomson Says," p. 32.

235   a scrum of reporters: Dawson, "Scot Makes Light," p. 42.

235   "What do you have to say?": WMCA, recording of post-game interviews, October 3, 1951.

235   "I'm too upset to": Ibid.

235   "sagged against a pillar": Sinclair, "Winners Kiss," p. 31.

235   "Why are you crying": Fimrite, "Side by Side," p. 76.

235   "Damned if I know": Ibid.

236   "We want you to say hello!": WMCA, recording of post-game interviews, October 3, 1951.

236   "This is the greatest ball club": Ibid.

236   "the happiest moment of my life": Ibid.

236   "Did you fall down": Ibid.

236   "Did I fall down?": Ibid.

236   giving Mays his maiden nip: Willie Mays, interview, March 26, 2002. AND Hano, *Willie Mays*, p. 79.

236   sick at once: Lewin, "Scotch & Champagne!" p. 48.

236   Thomson too felt suddenly nauseous: Newcombe, "Bobby Thomson: The Unwilling," p. 56.

236   word reached Thomson: Dawson, "Scot Makes Light," p. 42.

236   two upraised arms: Lewin, "Scotch & Champagne!" p. 48.

236   "the most frenzied": Drebinger, "Giants Capture," p. 1.

237   Durocher throwing kisses: Feeney, "Miracle Team," p. 22.

237   "Why me?": Branca, interview.

237 Easier for the center fielder: Feeney, "Miracle Team," p. 23.

237 Robinson, Reese, Roe: Ibid.

237 "Nice going, Bobby": Clem Labine, interview.

237 stepped to a water: Rosenthal, "O'Malley Promises," p. 34.

237 pounding a fist: Grimsley, "Branca Tries," p. 13.

237 some fifteen minutes: Grimsley, "Branca Hot," p. 54.

237 "I'm too lucky": Biederman, "Branca 'Too Lucky'," p. 2.

237 Les Biederman: Ibid.

237 Will Grimsley was unstirred: Golenbock, *BUMS*, p. 308.

238 "What happened?" asked Grimsley: Branca, interview, February 20, 2002.

238 "Just leave me alone": Ibid. AND Golenbock, *BUMS*, p. 308.

238 "It wasn't a bad": Robinson, "'I Was Set," p. 15.

238 "I guess we weren't": McGowen, "O'Malley Puts Off," p. 43.

238 Branca held his large: Ibid.

238 "If I was a good": Dawson, "Scot Makes Light," p. 42.

238 told United Press: Thomson, "Around Bases," p. 23.

238 Milton Richman: "Most Famous Homer," p. 4B.

238 "Honest," Thomson said: "Better Hitter," p. 24.

238 hoisting him onto: Bradley, "Thomson Says," p. 32.

238 "It was a pitch": McCulley, "Thomson the Hero," p. 25.

239 tugboat whistles sounded: "Staten Island Joy," p. 44.

239 Angelo Lomangino heaved: Nick Lomangino, interview, September 28, 2004.

239 Salvatore Secino rushed: "'Giant' Celebrant," p. 1.

239 operator Grace Therkildsen: Spink, "Miss T?"," p. 8.

239 "She rode her": Bill Aquilino, interview, August 8, 2003.

239 last call at 4 a.m.: Breen, "Brooklyn's Famous," p. 2.

239 "Big, grown men were": Robinson, *The Home Run Heard 'Round the World*, p. 240.

239 a bar on Flatbush Avenue: Reynolds, *I, Willie Sutton*, p. 232.

239 "I don't think I've ever": Ibid., p. 233.

239 his sixth prison break: "Five Convicts," p. 11.

239 the FBI put Sutton: Federal Bureau of Investigation.

239 Sutton knew well: Reynolds, *I, Willie Sutton*, p. 233.

240 "I felt like going": Ibid.

240 "New cars, television": Dunnell, "Drama, Gripping," p. 16.

240 told him he was a victim: Branca, "They'll Never," p. 72.

240 "If it wasn't for you": Branca, interview, February 20, 2002.

240 $18,000 in tickets: Pacini, "Remembering Gehrig," p. 26.

240 "I never did get to see my sister": Ibid.

240 "He told me": Crosby, "Faith, Prayer," p. 54.

240 Antoinette Yvars, a happy wife: Antoinette Yvars, interview, July 15, 2004.

240 "I was right next to Ann": Ibid.

240 his Wilson shoes: National Baseball Hall of Fame Library and Museum.

240 an invigorating kiss: Thomson, Heiman and Gutman, *The Giants Win the Pennant! The Giants Win the Pennant!*, p. 261.

241 instructed his friend Al: Ibid., p. 262.

241 phoned John Mooney: Franks, "Franks: Giants' Promise," p. 29.

241 he told Mooney: Ibid.

241 "Branca had a good": Ibid.

241 "Maybe," he said: Ibid.

241 just one man remained: Branca, interview, February 20, 2002.

241 "to cool my body down": Ibid.

242 "Forget it, Ralph": Branca, "Branca Recalls," p. 1.

242 "Yes, Father": Ibid.

242 "The reason God": Ibid.

242 that jibed with scripture: Among the passages in the New Testament that express this sentiment are Romans 5:1–5, 2 Corinthians 1:3–7 and Letter to the Hebrews 10:32–37.

242 a TV at 449 Emerson Street: Al Talboy, interview, September 16, 2003.

242 Jack Bader walked: *Brooklyn Eagle* photo caption: "She Said It, And She Does," October 4, 1951, p. 7.

242 Patsy Esposito would find: Eskenazi, *A Sportswriter's Life*, p. 135. AND Gerald Eskenazi, interview, November 13, 2004.

243 a ponytailed girl: Arlene Thomas, letter to Thomson, July 21, 2002. AND Arlene Thomas, interview, January 9, 2004.

243 Pennsylvania telephone: Brown, "Thomson Home Run," p. 32. The telephone-exchange extended roughly from 25th to 43rd streets, west of either 5th Avenue or Avenue of the Americas.

243 *Herald Tribune* switchboard: Brown, "Thomson Home Run," p. 32.

243 "the worst event of my life": Jerry Stern, interview, November 5, 2003.

243 resolved to cross Brower: Kearns, *Wait Till Next Year*, p. 154.

243 "Robert's not feeling well.": Jim Bouton, interview.

243 Neither was Anne Prince: Prince, *Brooklyn's Dodgers*, p. ix. AND Carl Prince, interview, November 5, 2003.

243 Paul Daube's: Spink, "Boos Turned," p. 10.

243 rebroadcast of the game: "W-T&S Replay," p. 1.

243 a room stood: Kirby, "The Shot Heard," p. 31.

243 "Branca ate all right": Russell, "I'd Pick," p. 63.

243 A boy of eleven: Grange, *The City*, p. 58.

243 Shannon's Café: Brown, "Thomson Home Run," p. 32.

244 tables away from John and Elaine: Tom Guinzburg, interview, May 2002.

244 a party of four Durochers: Laraine Day, interview, August 13, 2001.

244 "Thank you very much, Frank": Mutual Broadcasting System, World Series preview, October 3, 1951.

244 If there has ever been: Ibid.

245 "There was," wrote the actress: Bankhead, *Tallulah: My Autobiography*, p. 20.

245 A trio of men: U.S. Air Force Project Blue Book. *www.bluebookarchive.org*.

245 "fantastic flying ball": United Press, "Flying Ball Seen," p. 1.

245 a three-tier headline: Universal International News newsreel footage.

245 "With one blast of his bat": Ibid.

245 Larry Goldberg discovered Russ Hodges: Larry Goldberg, interview, December 18, 2004.

245 a die cutter who weekly studied: Rudy Mancuso, interview, October 2001.

246   "When I heard the crack": Ibid.

246   an octagonal photographer: From the collection of Michael Santo.

246   in 1934: Farnsworth, "Frank Rino," p. 22.

246   heavyset: Ibid.

246   "supreme moment": Ibid.

246   his Speed Graphic steadied: Jerry Levine, Vic Delucia and Paul Rice, interviews, December 2, 2003.

246   beneath the glare of Pete Coutros: Pete Coutros, interview, December 13, 2003.

246   Coutros had joined the tabloid: Ibid.

247   with pen, ink: Bob Staake, interview, March 7, 2006.

247   Mullin drew a Giant: "Quick, Leo, the Bi-Carb," *New York World-Telegram and Sun* cartoon by Willard Mullin, October 2, 1951, p. 39.

247   rectangle of coquille board: Bob Staake, interview, March 7, 2006.

247   "The Little Miracle of": "Quick, Leo, the Bi-Carb," *New York World-Telegram and Sun* cartoon by Willard Mullin, October 2, 1951, p. 39.

247   Fern Hack sat down: Fern Hack, interview, Winter 2002.

247   This Fern wrote: Ibid.

247   Millie Martin would send: Nancy Huseby, interview, September 5, 2003.

247   stolen away midgame down: Thomson, Heiman and Gutman, *The Giants Win the Pennant! The Giants Win the Pennant!*, p. 84. AND Thomson, interview, September 30, 2003.

247   promised champagne: Ibid.

247   Thomson sang on air: A press release from Cunningham & Walsh, Inc., for Perry Como show, October 4, 1951.

247   hopped a cab: Newcombe, "Bobby Thomson: The," p. 56.

247   off at 9: Endress, "All Island," p. 2.

247   for some twenty-three minutes: Staten Island Ferry, NYC Department of Transportation.

247   sat alone on an upper deck: Thomson, interview, March 3, 2006.

247   down Bay Street: Gordon, "Thomson's Eye," p. D1.

247   "Bob," Jim asked: O'Connell, "The Man Who," p. 161.

248   into a station wagon: Endress, "All Island," p. 2.

248   in yellow dress: Ibid.

248   on her breast: Ibid.

248   a uniformed police band: Ibid., p. 1.

248   was a great thrill: Kenney, "His Mom's," p. 3.

248   "No matter what I": Ibid.

248   after eighty years: Most recognize the 1871 National Association season as the start of organized professional baseball.

248   85,000 major league games: Dave Smith, *Retrosheet*.

248   5.8 million at-bats: Thorn, Palmer and Gershman, *Total Baseball*.

248   Antonio Masse, born in Sorrento: Noel Moran, interview, July 6, 2002.

248   Ed Lucas, an ecstatic boy of twelve: Ed Lucas, interview, August 2002.

248   ate a steak: Endress, "All Island," p. 2.

248   careful before the snap: Thomson, Heiman and Gutman, *The Giants Win the Pennant! The Giants Win the Pennant!*, p. 262.

248   on West 57th: Michael Gray, interview, May 28, 2004.

248 finished at 10:56 p.m.: *Voice of America*, Daily Broadcast Content Report, October 3, 1951. NARA.

248 "We got a ballgame": Olderman, "Bobby Thomson Remembers," p. 12A.

248 A ringing phone: Miller, "Yankees Can't Awe," p. 38.

248 "We just got in": Ibid.

249 fallen eight degrees: "New York Records," p. 67.

249 "I knew I had done": Branca, "They'll Never," p. 72.

249 "Why," asked a: Ibid.

249 "Most of them": Ibid.

CHAPTER SEVENTEEN

250 "The task of an American writer": *The Journals of John Cheever*, p. 185.

250 "The score stood": Thayer, "Casey at," p. 4.

250 "And now the pitcher": Ibid.

250 strike out Roy Hobbs: A 1984 film adaptation of the novel ends instead with Hobbs hitting a home run.

250 "How in the hell": Fimrite, "Side by Side," p. 76.

251 "First came the most tumultuous": Associated Press, October 4, 1951.

251 "Even when Pearl": "Thomson's Homer Tops," p. 9.

251 "modern day version": Wolf, "Giants Gain," p. 1.

251 "as riotous a night": United Press, "'Tis a Braw," p. 1.

251 "the greatest bubble": Ogle, "Thomson's HR," p. 15.

251 "There Is No Joy": *Daily News* headline: "There Is No Joy in Flatbush," October 4, 1951, p. C3.

251 "a home run heard": "WHAT A FINISH," p. 32.

251 *Star Journal* concurred: *Long Island Star Journal* photo caption, October 4, 1951, p. 22.

251 *Journal American* hailed: Corum, "Thomson Blasts," p. 32.

251 the home run both: "Thomson Finished," p. 23.

251 two-page fifteen-inch: *Daily News* headline: "The Shot Heard 'Round the Baseball World," October 4, 1951, pp. 42–3.

251 "The Giants exploded": "WHAT A FINISH," p. 32.

251 wrote Grantland Rice: Rice, "End of Famous," p. 46.

251 "wore the kind of expressions": Schiff, "Brooklyn Kids," p. 5.

251 "JOSEPH STALIN'S BOMB": *New York Post* headline: "Joseph Stalin's Bomb, Bobby Thomson's Blast," October 4, 1951, p. 27.

251 "Any repercussions of": Ibid.

252 had the previous afternoon: Anders, *Forging the Atomic Shield*, p. 172.

252 at 9:19 a.m.: Podvig, *Russian Strategic Nuclear Forces*, p. 485.

252 "confirming the end": Tygiel, *Past Time*, p. 156.

252 "Did not receive": Anders, *Forging the Atomic Shield*, p. 172.

252 "ALL ISLAND JUBILANT": *Staten Island Advance* headline: "All Island Jubilant as Bobby Wins Game," October 4, 1951, p. 1.

252 "'TIS A BRAW": *Cleveland Press* headline: "'Tis a Braw, Bricht Nicht as Thomsonville Blows Cork," October 4, 1951, p. 1.

252 the entire back page: *New York Post* headline: "Ralph Branca 4:11 P.M. Oct. 3, 1951," October 4, 1951, p. 52.

252 earning Stein a $100: Hamill, "The Gang Was," p. 4.

252 "There were those": Wilcox, "'Wait'll Next," p. 2.

252 "I wanted to kill myself": Jim Borax, interview, May 13, 2005.

252 "Now it is done": R. Smith, "Last Chapter," p. 30.

253 "אין. סענסאציאנעלסטען ‏דעם‎": *Jewish Daily Forward*, p. 1. Translation: "The most sensational [victory] in the entire history of baseball."

253 "The finish was super": O'Meara, "The Passing," p. 54.

253 "Branca Apenas Pudo Hablar": Griffin, "Branca Apenas Pudo Hablar . . . ," p. 18. Translation: "Branca could barely speak."

253 "Los fanáticos": Considine, "Jonron de Thomson," p. 18. Translation: "The fanatical, incredible, stupendous Giants." The word "fanatical" should have read "fantastic." It was mistranslated from the article Bob Considine wrote for the International News Service.

253 "最終回の猛逆襲．": Nikkan Sports headline, p. 1. Translation: "A Ferocious Counter-Attack in the Final Inning: Tompuson's [sic] Dramatic Three-Run Homer."

253 atop Filipino swimming: *Manila Times* headline: "NY Giants Capture National League Title," October 5, 1951, p. 7.

253 "is America's most eligible": Oliver, "Don't Mention," p. 8.

253 ready before dawn to write: Steinbeck, *Journal of a Novel*, p. 164. AND Elaine Steinbeck, Jean Boone, Tom Guinzberg and Osborn Elliott, interviews, May 2002.

253 at his wooden drafting table: Steinbeck, *Journal of a Novel*, pp. vii, 6, 9, 35, 72, 131.

253 Set now at 5:30 a.m.: Ibid., p. 164.

253 "Baseball yesterday": Ibid.

253 created a fantasy league: Frank, "Writings That," p. E37.

253 "So we quickly find out": Kerouac, *On the Road*, pp. 252–253.

253 "When Bobby Thompson [sic]": Kerouac, "The Origins," p. 571.

253 eight-by-twelve: Sing Sing Correctional Facility.

253 A federal court had sentenced: Conklin, "Atom Spy," p. 1.

254 Prospects were slim: On October 13, 1952, the court declined to hear the appeal. And on June 19, 1953, after the court voted 6-2 (Justice Felix Frankfurter did not participate) to set aside a stay of execution granted by Justice William Douglas, Ethel and Julius Rosenberg were executed.

254 Harold Burton, careful: Burton diary, Library of Congress, Manuscript Division.

254 Pope Pius XII: Cianfarra, "Pope Sees Peril," p. 1.

254 inmate 110–649: Sing Sing Correctional Facility.

254 behind twelve steel bars: Ibid.

254 "Gloom of glooms": Meeropol, *The Rosenberg Letters*, p. 234. The Rosenberg Letters used with the permission of Michael and Robert Meeropol.

CHAPTER EIGHTEEN

255 "Toss'd and retoss'd": Homer, *The Odyssey*, p. 139.

255 little more than SASSAFRAS: Futrell, *USAF Historical Study No. 71*, p. 1.

255 Red Barber sought: Edwards, *Fridays with Red*, p. 114. Tape of that portion of Barber's call does not exist. But several listeners (including one who contacted Edwards) recall Barber mentioning the loss of U.S. lives in Korea.

255 the U.S. 24th Infantry: "Soldiers at Front," p. C2.

255 fourteen hours later: "Radio Schedule," p. 6. AND Associated Press, "Games Ruled," p. 24.

255 south of Kumsong: Hal Baker (Korean War Project), interview, November 23, 2005.

255 Eugene Istomin had come: Marta Casals Istomin, interview, February 19, 2004.

255 Concerto no. 14: Ibid.

256 The men had met: Ibid.

256 sat now together: Istomin, "Conversation with," p. SM59.

256 square writing table: Marta Casals Istomin, interview, February 19, 2004.

256 listening to Al Helfer: George Balamaci, interview, June 2, 2004.

256 "When the holocaust": Istomin, "Conversation with," p. SM59.

256 "What happened, my boy?": Ibid.

256 Jimmy Powers reporting: Powers, "The Powerhouse," October 8, 1951, p. 22.

256 auction house Lelands: Lelands, Inc. *www.Lelands.com.*

256 most recent to do so was Bill Moore: Bill Moore and Mike Heffner, interviews, March 30, 2005.

256 sold for $47,824: Lelands, Inc. *www.Lelands.com.*

256 Written on the Spalding: Ibid.

256 BOB THOMSON HOME RUN: Bill Moore and Mike Heffner, interviews, March 30, 2005.

256 author Thomas Kiernan: Kiernan, *The Miracle at Coogan's Bluff*, p. 146.

256 screenwriter Michael Sloane: Sloane, "Miracle at Coogan's Bluff," p. 113.

256 professor Bob Mitchell: Mitchell, "Once Upon a Fastball," p. 62.

256 novelist Don DeLillo: DeLillo, *Underworld*, p. 48.

257 Smith credibly claims: National Baseball Hall of Fame Library. Telephone Inquiry Record, August 9, 1991. AND John Lee Smith, interview, January 5, 2004.

257 Clearly visible in: Photo 4IV53K5F. *www.DailyNewsPix.com.*

257 "the birth of the": Santa Maria and Costello, *In the Shadows of the Diamond*, p. 84.

257 "religion, a cause": "Brooklyn Cowboy," p. 4.

257 Court and Montague: Chambers, "After 25 Years," p. 37.

257 a redhead with red eyes: Todd Merer, interview, July 11, 2004.

257 a school of stuffed: Snider and Gilbert, *The Duke of Flatbush*, p. 113.

257 "There were still some nice": Branca, interview, June 29, 2004.

257 only pitcher: "Uniform Numbers," p. 14. Three other players wore the number 13: Sibby Sisti, Eddie Pellagrini and Ted Beard.

257 black cat: *Brooklyn Eagle* photo caption: "Friday the Thirteenth," April 14, 1951, p. 6.

257 lost three of the six: Prior to the 1951 playoff, Brooklyn and St. Louis played two playoff games in 1946, and Cleveland and Boston played one in

1948. Branca had lost on October 1, 1946, October 1, 1951, and October 3, 1951.

257 turned triskaidekaphobe: Branca, "They'll Never," p. 72.

257 lose his license: Ruhl, "From the Ruhl," February 4, 1953, p. 14.

257 "They had wanted": Branca, "They'll Never," p. 72.

257 two men wearing .38: Ingraham, "Moretti, Gambler," p. 1.

258 ordered 80 cents: Ibid., p. 22.

258 The foursome moved: Ibid.

258 he prattled on: Associated Press, "Crime Probe," p. 15.

258 ascribed his loose lips: "Goodbye Willie," *www.crimelibrary.com*.

258 mafiosi who wished him offed: Bill Bonanno, interview, January 12, 2005.

258 But nineteen hours prior: There is no proof that the Mafia murdered Moretti because he welshed on bets. And Bill Bonanno, the son of crime boss Joseph Bonanno, told me that he did not think that was the case. But he is unsure. And to link the murder of a Mafia bookie to testimony he gave in December rather than to a big ballgame played hours before seems to me illogical.

258 the Marine Room: Kleinzahler, "Too Bad," p. 35.

258 had drawn heavy: Ingraham, "Moretti, Gambler," p. 1.

258 cream Packard convertible: Ibid., p. 22. AND Associated Press, "Gunmen Slay," p. 11.

258 near 11:20 a.m.: Ibid., Ingraham.

258 slapping Moretti on: Ibid.

258 "The pudgy, partly bald": Ibid., p. 1.

258 offered $15.50: "Giants Even," p. 19.

258 "was a climax built": Daley, "This Is," p. SM 78.

258 "World Series?": Winchell, "In New York," p. 4.

259 "The Yankees had already clinched": Don DeLillo, interview, April 30, 2004.

259 panjandrums J. Edgar: "Giants v. Yankees," p. 77.

259 some 140 million: "69,000,000 Heard," p. 21. AND "The World Series," p. 47. While the radio audience was estimated at 69 million, there were no official tallies of the TV audience. Viewership, however, of the 1952 World Series was estimated at 70 million. Given that the 1951 series was the first with a live national TV audience (and so generated incredible excitement), it seems fair to assume that viewership was of at least equal size to that of 1952.

259 Irvin stole home: October 4, 1951, Game One, first inning.

259 DiMaggio sent to left: October 8, 1951, Game Four, fifth inning.

259 Mays, Irvin and Thompson: October 4, 1951, Game One, first inning.

259 Mantle and DiMaggio: October 5, 1951, Game Two, fifth inning.

259 James and Louise Thompson named: Robert Thompson, interview, March 2003.

259 Belle, Harold and Rhoda: Plot owner file, Mount Ararat Cemetery records. AND "Philip Arbiter" (death notice), p. 4.

259 range J, plot 33: Mount Ararat Cemetery records.

259 the Giants did not use: Frank Mastro of International News Photos pho-

tographed pitcher Vic Raschi as he approached the clubhouse during the fifth inning of the third game of the World Series on October 6, 1951. The photo clearly shows that there is no person stationed behind the fourth window.

259   "They're roaming around": Sal Yvars, interview, July 15, 2004.

259   parceling their pennant: George Denman, letter, Sporting News Research Center. AND Richman, "Giant Manager," p. 19.

259   Herb Scharfman spotted the pitcher: Branca, interview, May 25, 2004.

260   "I thought it was pretty big": Thomson, interview, June 28, 2004.

260   Scharfman suggested that pitcher: Branca, interview, May 25, 2004.

260   "I was being a good guy": Branca, interview, June 29, 2004.

260   "THOMSON THE HERO, BRANCA THE GOAT": Daily News headline, October 4, 1951, p. 25C.

260   27 plays: Steve Gietschier, e-mail message, June 4, 2004.

260   "I wasn't very happy": Thomson, interview, June 28, 2004.

260   "He engineered a mad dash": Joe Diehl, "Claims Yvars Is Forgotten Man of the New York Giants." Date and publication missing from Yvars's scrapbook.

260   Yvars had broken: Kahn, The Era, p. 294.

261   34–21 in 55: Dave Smith, Retrosheet.

261   "Come on, Branca!": Hamburger, "4–3," p. 27.

261   "Wonder if he was posing": Effrat, "Durocher Received," p. 53.

261   Never before had the Scot: O'Connell, "The Man Who," p. 161.

261   picked up a bottle: Vecsey, "What's in," p. C3. AND Sal Yvars, interview, July 15, 2004.

261   "Sal was just never": Diehl, "Sal Yvars," p. 48.

261   phoned John Mooney: Franks, "Franks Blames," p. 31.

261   they flew west: Daily News photo caption: "Buttoned Lip," October 13, 1951, p. 1.

261   homecoming bash postponed: "Lip Won First," p. 8.

261   Shirley Marblestone drove: Shirley Marblestone, interview, March 10, 2002.

261   toiletries and slippers rounded: Harriet Mesulam, interview, July 27, 2004.

261   left of path seven: Certificate of Death, Bureau of Records and Statistics.

262   to disconnect: Winchell, "Walter Winchell . . . ," p. B11.

262   seven-word telegram: "Staten Island Joy," p. 44.

262   Thomsons wondering: United Press, "Bobby Thomson Disclaims."

262   fans $190,000: "Collins to Remain," p. 41.

262   "no alibis": From the collection of Donald Dewsbury.

262   Robert Wagner relented: Brown, "Thomson Home Run," p. 32.

262   bought up 930: Teague, "Pomp Is Planned," p. 41.

262   slathered its players with gifts: George Spencer, interview, June 10, 2004.

262   $156,957.46: George Denman, letter, Sporting News Research Center.

262   white lace: Ad for Woodbury Facial Soap. Family Circle, May 1952, p. 1.

262   "the happiest day of my life": Branca, interview, June 29, 2004.

262   Family Circle: Family Circle, May 1952, p. 1.

263   At 5:00 a.m.: Certificate of Death. Bureau of Records and Statistics.

263 in room 348: Ibid.

263 men from Local 3 who dug his grave: Harriet Mesulam, interview, November 28, 2000.

263 descendant from Brainsk: Certificate of Death, Bureau of Records and Statistics.

263 "He was a strong man": Helen Smith, interview, Fall 2000.

263 No one from the Giant organization: Harriet Mesulam, interview, July 27, 2004.

CHAPTER NINETEEN

264 "That day she put our heads together": Frost, "Tree at My," p. 187.

264 on February 21: "Baseball Asked," p. 16.

264 a Pulitzer Prize awarded: Award shared by John Robinson and Don Ultang of the *Des Moines Register and Tribune.*

264 the *Sporting News* innocently cropping: *The Sporting News,* October 10, 1951, p. 6.

264 "All I had to do": Munzel, "Base-Burglar," p. 6.

265 a thousand letters: Spink, "Mail Keeps," p. 6.

265 When days before: Thomson, "That Home Run," p. 68.

265 days before he: Dolan, "Four Runs," p. 20.

265 thirty-five letters per five hours: United Press, November 19, 1951.

265 triaged requests: Newcombe, "Bobby Thomson: The," p. 56.

265 Minneapolis: "Knife & Fork League," November 14, 1951, p. 20.

265 Buffalo: Kritzer, "Thomson Tale," p. 18.

265 Police Athletic: "Napp Tells," p. 19.

265 honorary cloth: "Testimonial for," p. 30.

265 Thomson rolled: "Thousands Cheer," p. 1.

265 Frank Merriwell come to life: Merriwell was the creation of Gilbert Patten, pen name Burt L. Standish. He first appeared in *Tip Top Weekly* magazine on April 18, 1896.

265 A twelve-car caravan: "Thousands Cheer," p. 2.

265 a tie: Ibid.

265 a suitcase: Ibid.

265 homemade cheer: Ibid., p. 1.

265 shook a thousand: Ibid., p. 2.

265 pet Dalmatian: Ibid.

265 Van Duzer: Ibid..

265 Highland Fling: Ibid.

265 a dinner dance: "Thomson Testimonial," p. 19.

265 1,400 homefolk: Ibid.

265 twenty-seven dignitaries: Testimonial Dinner Program.

265 Rabbi Millner: Ibid.

265 Giants spoke: Ibid.

265 the hero announcing: O'Regan, "Flying Scot," p. 21.

265 One man scheduled: Testimonial Dinner Program.

266 pitching instructor: "1,200 Youngsters," p. 41.

266   a haberdasher: Klein, "His Employer," p. 4.

266   800 Broad Street: Ibid.

266   "How about that": Branca, "They'll Never," p. 74.

266   "How do you go": Greenfeld, "A Life," p. 142.

266   showing up in: "Playoff Rivals," p. 22, "Sal Receives," p. 28.

266   did not in his address: Ibid.

266   *Sporting News* would: Povich,

266   the phrase "bye-bye baby": Crosby, "It's Wonderful," p. 21

266   "It's such a spontaneous": Bob Costas, interview, January 10, 2005.

266   Lou Weber had turned Hodges vinyl: Don Weber, interview, December 15, 2003. AND Ernie Harwell, interview, November 27, 2004.

266   contracted Gotham Recording: Ronny Buchman, interview, March 2003.

267   producer Bud Greenspan: Bud Greenspan, interview, February 24, 2003.

267   Tunney to Tchaikovsky: Talese, "Songs for Satters," p. X24. AND Bud Greenspan, interview, February 24, 2003. AND the 1955 "Columbia's New Year in Records."

267   "He said 'make believe'": Branca, interview, November 29, 2004.

267   Jean Curry turned to clothing: Michele Thomson, interview, November 14, 2005.

267   "We had Bobby Thomson pants": Ibid.

267   "unanimity such as the United": Felker, "Big Majority," p. 1.

267   "They talked over": Hamill, *A Drinking Life*, p. 150.

268   "The town loafers": Heimer, "My New York," p. 6.

268   first floor of 1901: Bill Shafer, interview, September 23, 2005.

268   "We massaged that": Ibid. AND Martin, *Nader*, p. 17.

268   "And then, Bobby": Joe Treneco cartoon, *Sport*, April 1952, p. 68.

268   "Reinhold Niebuhr was one": Elisabeth Sifton, interview, May 12, 2004.

268   "God, give us grace": Niebuhr, *The Book of a Thousand Prayers*, p. 153.

268   still pained Isaac Jaffe: Sports Night, "The Giants Win the Pennant, The Giants Win the Pennant," episode #33.

268   teacher Russell Handon would have caught: Rob Adams, interview, October 10, 2004.

268   Jackie Gleason ralphed: Bacon, *How Sweet It Is*, p. 103.

268   "Here is one": Ibid.

268   Toots Shor was: Drebinger, "That Home Run," p. 24.

268   70,000 times: Daniel, "32 Minutes," p. 20.

269   "criticized much too harshly": Spink, "Mail Keeps," p. 6.

269   adding years later: Durslag, "Don't Put," p. 14.

269   "get him out": Kahn, "The Day Bobby," p. 52.

269   "We fired Shotton": McGowen, "Dodger Rehiring," p. 6.

269   O'Malley not wishing: Kahn, *The Era*, p. 301.

269   "Most Courteous": "Chuck Gets," AP wire photo credit.

269   "Sukeforth," reported the AP: Associated Press, "Chuck and I," p. 18.

270   "absolutely perfect": Burton, "There's No," p. 68.

270   lawsuits filed this very spring: The suits were filed by Jim Prendergast in April, George Toolson in May and Walter Kowalski in June.

270   "What do you want?": Thomson, interview.

270   off Al Brazle: Dave Smith, *Retrosheet*. Hit August 25, 1951.
270   hanging now: "Old and New," p. 11.
270   grand ballroom: "Yank Hurler," p. 22.
270   "the premier social": Koppett, *The Rise and Fall of the Press Box*, p. 69.
270   would include props: Ibid.
270   jazz pianist: "Branca Socks," p. 16.
270   Branch Rickey would: Povich, "This Morning," February 5, 1952, p. 14.
270   Dressen as egomaniac: Rosenthal, "Branca Scores," p. 17.
270   Durocher as target: Povich, "This Morning," February 5, 1952, p. 14.
270   Arthur Mann: "Branca Socks," p. 16.
270   "Because of You": Ibid.
270   McLoughlin pointing: Rosenthal, "Branca Scores," p. 17.
270   Thomson aboard: Daniel, "Thomson, Branca Spark," p. 15.
270   "It was with": Ibid.
271   resting on easels: Rosenthal, "Branca Scores," p. 17.
271   high E-flat: Hammerstein and Wilkinson, "Because of You," Broadcast Music Inc.
271   ten-note: Ibid.
271   "*My fame is sure*": "Branca Socks," p. 16.
271   "*Because of you*": Ibid.
272   1,400 people: "Yank Hurler," p. 22.
272   "*One lonely bird*": "Branca Socks," p. 16.
272   Warren Giles crying: Talbot, "Sports Round-Up," p. 18.
272   "A great many": Ibid.
272   "even more vociferous": Daniel, "Thomson, Branca Spark," p. 15.
272   "the good winner": R. Smith, "Banca [sic] Still," p. 15.
272   "Baseball is one place": Dawidoff, "Hurts So Good," p. SM 14.
272    $500: Povich, "This Morning," p. C1.
272   "Branca's pitch": "Yank Hurler," p. 22.
273   "The world ended": Daley, "A Guy with," p. 34.
273   Norma King now answered: Clyde King, interview, November 6, 2003.
273   Audrey Hepburn and: *www.tvtome.com*. Episode #191.
273   13.6 million: Bowles, *A Thousand Sundays*, p. 49.
273    $500 given: Ruhl, "From the Ruhl," February 20, 1952 p. 14.
273   after Game Three: "On Television," p. 123.
273   "MOVE OVER BERLE": Mack, "Team of Destiny," p. 16.
273   "The Giants were": Ibid.
273   "'There he is.'": Murray, "Slugger 'May Be'," p. 4.
274   "I have to admit it": Ibid.
274   regimen was simple: Thomson, "That Home Run," p. 68.
274   "Ever since I came": Ibid., p. 26.
274   sixteen penciled: Grady, "A Chip Off," p. 8.
274   hopped in trench: *New York Times* photo: "Leaves for Spring Training," February 21, 1952, p. 33.
275   "I got hardened": "Branca Isn't," p. B6.
275   his first raise: National Baseball Hall of Fame Library. His salary rose from $15,000 to $17,500.

275   "Of all the": Squier, "On the Sport Trail," p. 11.

275   the only 2: On September 6, 1947, Walker Cooper hit one.

275   booed their own: Gellis, "Flock Rips," p. 36.

275   a red 12: Ruhl, "From the Ruhl," April 30, 1952, p. 14. The red numbers were new. Brooklyn had planned to unveil the uniforms in the 1951 World Series.

275   "The last thing": Thomson, Heiman and Gutman, *The Giants Win the Pennant! The Giants Win the Pennant!*, p. 267.

276   "I'd be kidding": Branca, "They'll Never," p. 11.

276   mention of both: Ibid., p. 72.

276   as John Updike wrote: Updike, "Hub Fans Bid," p. 128.

276   coccyx on Coke: Fimrite, "Side by Side," p. 77. AND Golenbock, *BUMS*, p. 309.

276   advice of team: McGowen, "X-Ray Shows," p. 7.

276   "Whatever the": Ibid.

276   "mental miseries": McGowen, "Dodgers' Heads," p. 9.

277   "This is an act": King, "'Braw Bobby," p. 13.

277   9 Down: Farrar, "Crossword Puzzle," p. 25.

277   "I'm glad I did": Rheingold advertisement. *New York Times*, June 30, 1952, p. 38.

277   "KER-RACK!": *Thrilling True Story of the Baseball GIANTS.*

277   "He said he had that telescope": John Jorgensen, interview, Fall 2000.

277   lay now unused in a leather sleeve: James Schenz, interview, Fall 2000.

277   Says Corwin, "the nucleus": Al Corwin, interview, Fall 2000.

277   sought to unload: "Sal Yvars' Trade," p. 22.

277   a kid pitcher: "Dodgers Recall," p. 20.

277   Erskine who now replaced: McGowen, "Brooks Win," p. 7.

278   "The evil that men do": Branca, interview, November 25, 2003.

278   on August 25: McGowen, "Upsurge in Bums'," p. 5.

278   The fans booed: McCulley, "Don't Boo," p. 89.

278   1,172,244 fans: "Musial Tops," p. 13.

278   record replayed in: Associated Press, "Greatest Thrill."

278   "Although Bobby is loathe": Newcombe, "Bobby Thomson: The," p. 49.

278   "I can't blame": Ibid., p. 57.

278   Warren Giles intervened: "Branca Eligible," p 23.

278   Phil Foster would call: Frommer, *New York City Baseball*, p. 170.

279   "Charlie wanted Black": Buzzie Bavasi, interview, November 29, 2004.

279   the third ballplayer: Baseball Almanac. *www.baseball-almanac.com*. The other two were Woody English on October 4, 1935, and Tuck Stainback on October 4, 1935.

279   Gerry Staley: Broeg, "Prizes by Stanky," p. 6.

279   Bob Rush: Murray, "Giants in Huddle," p. 33.

279   hip-deep in Barbara Benson: Thomson, Heiman and Gutman, *The Giants Win the Pennant! The Giants Win the Pennant!*, p. 84.

279   "His shyness," says daughter Nancy: Nancy Mitchell, interview, April 24, 2003.

279   "I decided it'd be easier": Thomson, interview, August 11, 2003.

279   permission of parents: Thomson, interview, February 1, 2005.
279   one day after: "Bobby Thomson Ejected," p. 27.
279   sent baseball $200: "Dressen's Reprimand," p. 9.
280   fingering instead: "Ralph Branca Fined," p. C1.
280   "What escapes me": Young, "If and Reverse," p. B3.
280   the Flennenheirmer: "Ralph Branca of Dodgers," p. 2.
280   offered Brooklyn: Ruhl, "From the Ruhl," May 6, 1953, p. 14.
280   mailed the compote: Graham, "Of Durocher," p. 23.
280   pinned freesia: Knorr, "Giant Star Wed," p. 1.
280   owing to the tax concerns: Nancy Mitchell, interview, April 24, 2003.
280   holiday trimmings: Knorr, "Giant Star Wed," p. 1.
280   twenty minutes: Ibid.
280   satin and seed: Ibid.
280   illusion veil: Ibid.
280   "The bride's": Ibid.
280   Mendelssohn then motorcade: Ibid., p. 8.
280   "You'd hear the golf clubs": Thomson, interview, November 8, 2004.
281   190 pounds: Drebinger, "Durocher in Doubt," p. 32.
281   Kathryn Murray: "Players on," p. 38.
281   opening of Ralph: "Ralph Branca of Dodgers," p. 2.
281   "From his local": Ibid.
281   "I was king shit": Sal Yvars, interview, November 18, 2004.
281   sold to St. Louis: "Cardinals Sell," p. 22.
281   "throwing as hard": McGowen, "Another Starters," p. 11.
281   "He told me I was swayback": Branca, interview, November 15, 2004.
281   asthma, toe fungus: "Bunts and Boots," March 11, 1953, p. 25.
281   a liner in practice: McGowen, "Campy, Snider," p. 15.
281   "Ailments, some real": Fraley, "Thomson's Homer."
281   "The validity": Ibid.
282   fifth metacarpal: Murray, "Lip Takes Two," p. 19.
282   from Robin Roberts: "First H.R.," p. 21.
282   a red wax Columbia record: 1953 record 806-PV.
282   "Baseball people sigh": Orr, "The Unpredictable," p. 21.
282   "Temperamentally, I think": Ibid.
282   for Herm Wehmeier: "Reports of Trades," p. 19.
282   "It could be thought": Lardner, "The Ways of," p. 71.
282   The pitcher simply felt: Drebinger, "Giants Overwhelm," p. 20.
283   Branca on waivers: "Major League Flashes," July 15, 1953, p. 39.
283   for $10,000: McGowen, "Branca Sold," p. 9.
283   the runway: McGowen, Ibid.
283   Ann cried: McGowen, Ibid.
283   "This is the greatest": United Press, "Branca's Move."
283   "the Giant players": Murray, "Irvin Bat," p. 15.
283   "of the curious": Lardner, "The Ways of," p. 71.
283   "Our lockers were together": Branca, interview, November 26, 2005.
283   "He was a helluva nice guy": Ted Gray, interview, November 26, 2005.
283   "The whole world got on him": Ibid.

284   trainer Jack Homel: Spoelstra, "Bengals Back," p. 18.

284   "It was almost": Grimsley, "Branca Tries," p. 13.

284   "The Giants is dead.": McGowen, "Campanella's 2 Home," p. S2.

284   voted the departed pitcher: "$8,280 for Yanks," p. 8.

284   Branca benched: "45,022 See," p. 18.

284   irreverent rumors: "Robinson-for-Thomson," p. 6.

284   seven pounds, ten ounces: "Girl to Bobby," p. S7.

284   Thomson returned home: Kremenko, "Scot Admits," p. 3.

284   "I'll never forget": Hurwitz, "'Never Got Better,'" p. 18.

284   in the same Waldorf: Drebinger, "Giants Trade," p. 1.

285   "Best of luck": "Thomson Assures Leo," p. 6.

285   "It was a fool": Drebinger, "Thomson Breaks," p. S1.

285   triple fracture: Ibid.

285   the current top 10: Roth, "Statistics Tell," p. 86.

286   for two months: The Giants obtained Rapp on July 1, 1951, and released him on August 28, 1951.

286   "We were having a couple": Ted Gray, interview, July 16, 2001.

CHAPTER TWENTY

289   "Then he filled up the hole": Graves, *The Greek Myths*, p. 283.

289   "I'll always be": Grimsley, "Branca Tries," p. 13.

289   "I thought it was something: Ted Gray, interview, July 16, 2001.

289   "He was downhearted": Ibid.

289   "We got to bed": Branca, interview, June 11, 2002.

290   "I think he just kind of shook": Ted Gray, interview, July 16, 2001.

290   "Guys gave you the needle": Thomson, interview, September 30, 2003.

290   led all baseball: Eck, "Thomson Led," p. 4.

290   "I know this," says Thomson: Thomson, interview, November 8, 2004.

290   "He was a chirpy Irishman": Thomson, interview, September 30, 2003.

290   "He'd bring it up": Ibid.

290   the very first pitch: Thisted, "Trailers Hold Back," p. 15.

290   "the most dramatic": "Bobby Got Special," p. 9.

291   "was a *perfect* pitch": Grimsley, "Branca Tries," p. 13.

291   "wrongs have a way": Branca, "Branca Recalls," p. 1.

291   the ranch house he and Ann rented: Del Reddy, interview, April 4, 2005.

291   a secret already confided: Branca, interview, February 23, 2005. AND John Branca, interview, April 30, 2005.

291   "'Sal, did this really happen?'": Sal Yvars, interview, July 15, 2004.

291   "from A to Z": Ibid.

291   "'Ralph, I was the messenger'": Sal Yvars, interview, February 16, 2005.

291   "I didn't feel guilty": Ibid.

291   "He didn't say too much": Ibid.

291   "It was my competitiveness": Branca, interview, February 23, 2005.

291   "I made a decision not": Branca, interview, December 28, 2000.

291   "I think I matured": Branca, interview, February 23, 2005.

292   5.80 ERA, highest: Spoelstra, "Weik Sent," p. 18.

292 "I threw every day for a week": Branca, interview, February 23, 2005.
292 "I called up Casey Stengel": Ibid.
292 Stengel had Ralph Houk: "Yanks Sign," p. 34.
292 "Even then, I didn't talk": Thomson, interview, November 19, 2000.
292 "As the year progressed": Al Corwin, interview, Fall 2000.
292 New York was 25–7: The team had been 13–8 at home through June 14th.
293 first cut: "Former Brook," p. 11.
293 his insurance company folding: Branca, interview, November 25, 2003.
293 Branca loitered: Effrat, "First-Sacker Fain," p. 46.
293 gave them free: Chapman, "Andy Pafko Still," p. 70.
293 was sick: Newcombe, "Bobby Thomson: The," p. 56.
293 North Water Street: Ibid., p. 50.
293 spokesman for Schlitz: "Four Braves," p. 27.
293 Optimist Club: "Thomson, Busy as," p. 35.
293 "is proving to be": Ibid.
293 Connecticut Little Leaguers: "Silverra Content," p. 28.
293 a guest on KEYD: "Church Sponsors," p. 14.
294 "It changed my personality": Branca, interview, June 11, 2002.
294 "I put it out of my mind": Thomson, interview, September 30, 2003.
294 "I've thought about this later": Thomson, interview, November 8, 2004.
294 he biked and rowed: Thisted, "Flying Scot Set," p. 22.
294 his first 15 innings: "Homer Snaps," p. 48.
294 eight of the first 19: "American Association," p. 34.
294 a loudmouthed fan in Omaha: Branca, interview, October 31, 2005.
294 teammates Alex Konikowski and Al Worthington: Ziegel, "Branca Takes
     Shot," p. 58. AND Branca, interview, October 31, 2005.
294 Andy Pafko turned: Andy Pafko, interview, February 28, 2002.
295 "Andy," he said: Ibid.
295 "That's history": Chapman, "Andy Pafko Still," p. 68.
295 "That's a tough": Drebinger, "Flying Scot to Land," p. 13.
295 "by nature, well suited": Newcombe, "Bobby Thomson: The," p. 50.
295 "I suppose I have been": Ibid.
295 "never was much tiger": Ibid.
295 "Not many .280": Ibid.
295 resigned from the club: "Posedel in New," p. 48.
296 became in July: Associated Press, "Yvars Lands," p. 18.
296 Schenz was let go: "Pitcher Al Widmar," p. D1.
296 forty-one days shy: Ford, "Schenz Remembers," p. 28.
296 "I was thinking of retiring": Branca, interview, March 14, 2005.
296 a horse-racing contest: Goodman, "SPORTalk," p. 10.
296 "A radio-TV": "Branca Eyeing," p. 22.
296 after a 6-for-33: Young, "Thomson Discards," p. 15.
296 a sporting goods: Young, "Big Klu," p. 27.
296 NBC aired: Daniel, "Too Much," p. 16.
296 "I fantasized that we'd changed": Branca, interview, November 25, 2003.
296 Bavasi signing Branca: "Brooklyn Again Signs," p. 35.
296 "He was a local boy": Buzzie Bavasi, interview, March 15, 2005.

296 "Scribes who thought": "Ralph Branca, Out of," p. 4.

297 "On the morning": Daley, "Return from," p. 32.

297 "How the muscles bulge": Nash, *You Can't Get There From Here*, p. 100.

297 "I was more nervous": Branca, interview, November 25, 2003.

297 One of just eighteen: Dave Smith, *Retrosheet*. Bud Byerly, Walker Cooper, Steve Gromek, Granny Hamner, George Kell, Jim Konstanty, Gene Mauch, Cal McLish, Eddie Miksis, Red Munger, Stan Musial, Ron Northey, Joe Nuxhall, Andy Pafko, Andy Seminick, Early Wynn, Eddie Yost.

297 applauded lustily: "Branca, in New," p. 27.

298 aboard the *Queen Mary*: "Major Flashes," December 26, 1956, p. 19.

298 The Coleys owned some 150 acres: Nancy Mitchell, interview, April 24, 2003. AND Nancy Thommes, interview, March 26, 2005.

298 a strong and self-sufficient man: Ibid.

298 "We were going to build houses": Thomson, interview, November 8, 2004.

298 slow screwball: McGowen, "Brooks Saddle," p. 26.

298 Branca lost: "Branca Gives Up," p. C4.

298 Of the 357 pitchers: Holmes, *LADugout.com*.

299 "I'd like to have": McGowen, "Valdes Triumphs," p. 25.

299 "It's tough to come": "Ralph Calls Quits," p. 33.

299 as many hits: Steve Gietschier. Thomson had one other 4-hit game as a Brave on June 25, 1956.

299 voted by scribes: "N.L. Pace-Setters," p. 2.

299 elected alternate: Thisted, "Route-Goers Lead," p. 14.

299 "All the luster": Thomson, interview with Tom Harris, SABR, September 26, 1993.

300 "When we go": O'Toole, "Giants Expect," p. 1.

300 he pointed: The *Sporting News* photo caption: "Where Historic Homer Was Hit," October 9, 1957, p. 16.

300 "All I could": Capaldo, "Braves Bury," p. 22.

300 E. B. White: White, "The Seven Steps," p. 37.

300 at 4:35 p.m.: Bracker, "Souvenir-Hunting Followers," p. 1.

300 leading on a dash: "Giants Leaving Baseball Field." Corbis.

300 tagged his metal: McDonald, "Marquard Recalls," p. 16.

300 whittled nubs: King, "Mob Scene," p. 16.

300 aimed a camera: Thomson, Heiman and Gutman, *The Giants Win the Pennant! The Giants Win the Pennant!*, p. 210.

CHAPTER TWENTY-ONE

301 "Sweet it is to remember labors": Petrarca, *Il Bucolicum Carmen*, p. 104.

301 Wrote Roger Angell: Angell, "Notes and Comment," p. 39.

301 "all-conclusive hit": Newcombe, "Bobby Thomson: The," p. 49.

302 Wrote the photographer: Cartier-Bresson, *The Decisive Moment*, Foreword.

302 "If we knew who had": Firestone, "Reticent Novelist," p. B2.

302 "a holy relic": Ibid.

302 "a talisman of history": Remnick, "Exile on Main," p. 44.

302 "Maybe it was the last time": DeLillo, *Underworld*, p. 94.

302   "[It] might have been": Sante, "Between Hell," p. 4.
302   turned cigarettes suspect: Norr, "Cancer by," pp. 7–8.
303   "If I wanted to destroy": "Have We Gone," p. 11.
303   "an experience of beauty": Grange, *The City*, p. 58.
303   "can be retrospectively": Sante, "Between Hell," p. 4.
303   "As we weigh the momentous": "Joseph Stalin's Bomb," p. 27.
303   "It is an icon": Congdon, "Permanent Things," p. 245.
303   "Bobby Thomson's home run": Cort, "The Fix," p. 329.
303   "the equivalent (in its sphere)": Dexter, "The Rhetoric of History," p. 380.
303   "Here was a reversal": Sahlins, *Apologies to Thucydides*, p. 130.
304   "So it is truly chutzpah": Ibid., p. 136.
304   Germany and Japan: "America: Policeman for the Third World?" Center for Defense Information.
304   author Russell Baker: Baker, "Fourteen Clues," p. SM108.
304   "Isn't it possible": DeLillo, *Underworld*, pp. 59–60.
304   "A sporting event": Istomin, "Conversations with," p. SM59.
304   "The wonderful purging": Barzun, *God's Country and Mine*, p. 151.
304   a goat awarded: Gray, "On the Etymology," pp. 60–63. Gray asserts that the etymology of tragedy is "goat song." He discusses five possible origins of the etymology: "The goat was a prize in early tragic contests...; there was a song of goats or goatmen . . . ; there was a song of men dressed in goat-skins . . . in honour of Dionysos . . . ; there was a song of men dressed in goat-skins . . . a survival of the archaic Greek dress . . . ; a goat was led by the chorus to be sacrificed. . . ."

CHAPTER TWENTY-TWO

305   "So set, before its echoes fade": Housman, "To an Athlete Dying Young," p. 13.
305   Hill and Knowlton had: Lieb, "Emphasis on Signs," p. 20.
305   the announcers alerted: Ibid.
305   sent for in February: "Giants Seek," p. 27.
305   Mutual Benefit: "Branca Becomes," p. 27.
305   sold from June through December: Branca, interview, November 25, 2003.
305   one million dollars: "Block Cited," p. 41.
306   dining Friday nights: Branca, interview, May 25, 2005.
306   enjoy barbecues: Wille, "Northbrook Takes Care," p. 17.
306   Little League: "Major League Flashes," August 28, 1957, p. 27.
306   Lions Club: "Knife & Fork League," November 6, 1957, p. 27.
306   a tire company: Ibid., February 12, 1958, p. 20.
306   at least $10,000: "Fans Still Hail," p. 18.
306   Queens housewife Harriet Mesulam: Harriet Mesulam, interview, March 10, 2005.
306   "We decided," says Thomson: Thomson, interview, February 1, 2005.
307   "I could see real estate": Thomson, interview, July 14, 2005.
307   he and Winkie paid $48,000: Thomson, interview, June 10, 2005.
307   Stratford Bowling: White, "From Hill," p. 35.

307 retired Wally Pipp: Daniel, "The Brat's," p. 9.

307 "Talking about it": Effrat, "Thomson Says He's," p. 18.

307 sweated semimonthly: Whitey Lockman, interview, January 25, 2005.

307 iron lung: "9000 Hear Graham," p. 8.

307 696,524 others: "Plea for Church," p. 1.

308 "Its work": "9308 Hear Graham," p. 8.

308 "My heart had pounded": Al Worthington, interview, September 12, 2002.

308 He had been a Methodist: Al Worthington, interview, May 18, 2005.

308 "If we continue to cheat": Ibid.

308 but ten players: "Thumper Tops," p. 4.

308 camel-hair coat: Talese, "Ebbets Field," p. 39.

308 The last and first: Ibid.

308 1,317 families: Ibid.

308 200 folks: Ibid.

308 auld acquaintance: Ibid.

308 "Ladies and gentlemen": Ibid.

308 a polite cheer: Ibid.

308 Two tons of: Ibid.

308 the phone to: Ibid.

309 pitch on July 17 from Early Wynn: Thomson flew out in the eighth inning of the second game of a doubleheader in Chicago.

309 23 of the 9,415: David Vincent, SABR.

309 hit his 264: Dave Smith, *Retrosheet.*

309 "I had to look": Skwar, "Thomson and Branca," p. D12.

309 "He would give up": Nancy Mitchell, interview, April 24, 2003.

310 "the established": Westvaco Corporation Records.

310 six-page report: Ibid.

310 "lack of business": Ibid.

310 "[Thomson] responds": Ibid.

310 salary $10,500: Ibid.

310 pulp of oak, sweet gum: Jeff Thomson, interview, June 15, 2005.

310 "He told me," says Patti: Patti Barnes, interview, July 23, 2003.

310 "That pitch gave me notoriety,": Branca, interview, May 25, 2005.

310 "For at least two": Eskenazi, "Branca Finds Thomson's," p. S3.

310 sold in 1960: Devaney, "15 Years Later," p. 89.

311 NYU offered him the job: "N.Y.U. Seeks Branca," p. 35.

311 to hold cement: Govlick, "Ex-Major League," p. 24.

311 the name on his business card: Thomson, interview, June 10, 2005.

311 "Paper bags," reflected: Devaney, "15 Years Later," p. 89.

311 forced nightly to sip: Thomson, interview, June 10, 2005.

311 endured an ectopic pregnancy: Nancy Mitchell, interview, October 8, 2003.

311 the couple decided now: Ibid.

311 Milwaukee filing: Associated Press, "Braves Protest," p. 45.

CHAPTER TWENTY-THREE

312 "I have only one eye": Southey, *The Life of Nelson*, p. 101.

312 "Danny," wrote once: Orr, "Danny Sees His," p. 3.

312 "You might say": Reichler, "'Spy' Tipped Thomson," p. 4C.
313 "If such a charge": Ibid.
313 "certainly would not": Ibid.
313 "the meaty portion": Angell, "Homeric Tales," p. 68.
313 co-host *Speaking of Sports*: Branca, interview, May 26, 2005.
314 "Larry came in to Cosell's office": Ibid., May 25, 2005.
314 a breezy Friday: "Weather Throughout," p. 95.
314 "It was so ingrained": Branca, interview, May 25, 2005.
314 "I said I knew about it": Ibid.
314 "Thomson didn't get": United Press International, "Thomson Homer Not," p. A3.
314 "I tried to brush": "Thomson Denies," p. 19.
314 "It positively isn't": Ibid.
314 "There are some things": Ibid.
314 "Show some character": Ibid.
314 the father of four fessing up: Thomson, interview, November 21, 2005.
314 "'You mean Leo Durocher'": Ibid., September 30, 2003.
314 Mays, Lockman, Westrum: Associated Press, "Stolen-Signal Charge," March 23, 1962.
314 "No, no, no": "Thomson Denies," p. 19.
314 "There was no buzzer": Daniel, "Ban Johnson Handed," p. 16.
315 "even if they are stolen": Young, "Signals and Spies," p. 45.
315 "this office cannot stress": Lebovitz, "Wigwam Enjoys," p. 18.
315 pitcher Spahn propose: Wolf, "'We have Proof,'" p. 8.
315 manager Tebbetts that: Ibid.
315 "the practice illegal": Daniel, "Frick Probes," p. 8.
315 Dick Young reported: Young, "Majors Ban," p. 134.
315 "Should a team": Ibid.
315 "Lying and stealing to us": Patti Barnes, interview, July 23, 2003.
315 "It was a question": Turan, "Mets' Fans Used," p. E1.
316 "Ralph Branca was there": Murray, "Back at the," p. 80.
316 "No responsible wire": McDonald," Signal Stealing Is," p. 10.
316 Little Patti Branca sat beside: Patti Barnes, interview, July 23, 2003.
316 "I heard 'bum, disgrace'": Ibid.
316 Dick Young, however, stopped Branca: Branca, interview, November 28, 2001.
316 "I'm not going to pose": "Ralph, Boy," p. 8.
317 "Uncomfortable," recalls Thomson: Thomson, interview, June 10, 2005.
317 Thomson shrugged: "Ralph, Boy," p. 8.
317 Branca threw to a Duke: Tuckner, "Branca Relives," p. S6.
317 "Nobody remembers that": Ibid.
317 2:00 p.m. when Jack Doscher: Ibid.
317 Durocher and Dressen replaced: Ibid.
317 "seemed sad as he": Ibid., p. S1.
317 A light rain: Ibid., p. 56.
317 old friends laughed: Young, "Young Ideas," p. 111.
317 Irvin told Thomson: Tuckner, "Branca Relives," p. S6.
317 Durocher pointed: Ibid.

317 "I just stayed up there": Thomson, interview, September 30, 2003.
318 "*Now* you get him": Young, "Young Ideas," p. 111.
318 Snider heaved a ball: Tuckner, "Branca Relives," p. S6.
318 "I was happy to get out": Thomson, interview, September 30, 2003.

CHAPTER TWENTY-FOUR

319 "There are, it is true": Levi, *The Drowned and the Saved*, p. 27.
319 seventeen straight: NBC, "Former Dodger Ace."
319 Branca led Arthur Levine: Hugh Downs, interview, Winter 2002. AND Norman Blumenthal, interview, June 15, 2005.
319 Fearful of a lawsuit: Ibid.
319 second game-show playoff: *Tic Tac Dough* had a playoff in 1959.
319 raft of prizes: NBC, "Former Dodger Ace."
319 "I have a running gag": Eskenazi, "Branca Finds Thomson's," p. S3.
319 "An hour after the game": Devaney, "15 Years Later," p. 45.
320 "taken years to live": "Ralph, Boy," p. 8.
320 Catcher Walker would tell daughter: Deborah Cogliano, interview, February 26, 2004.
320 Branca? A *fastball* pitcher?": Conlon and Creamer, *Jocko*, p. 128.
320 "That home run didn't": Devaney, "15 Years Later," p. 89.
320 1,548 pitches: Allan Roth data courtesy of Dave Smith, *Retrosheet.*
320 since June of 1948: Ibid. Missing from the data are 6.1 innings Branca threw in September 1950. The rest of that month, he threw just 277 pitches.
320 Thomson in 1955: Newcombe, "Bobby Thomson: The," p. 56.
320 Thomson in 1959: Oates, "Talking to Bobby," p. 2.
320 Thomson in 1986: Lupica, "Distant Replay," p. 19.
321 Thomson in 1991: Fimrite, "Side by Side," p. 75.
321 Thomson in 1996: Sargent, "Bobby Thomson, Giant," p. 9.
321 Thomson in 2000: Thomson, interview, November 19, 2000.
321 "I take credit": Sargent, "Bobby Thomson, Giant," p. 9.
321 "The team management": Berkow, "The 30-Year," p. 23.
321 losing in the limelight: Branca, interview, February 20, 2002.
321 "Every postseason game I started": Ibid.
321 "That idiot Alston": Branca, interview, July 15, 2005.
321 "It would not have been a home run": Ibid.
321 thirteen other ballparks: Shibe Park and Sportsman's Park were each home to two teams.
321 had it flown in Braves Field: Calculations of the flight of the ball in other parks courtesy of SABR member John Pastier.
322 from teammate Cal Abrams: Swirsky, *Baseball Letters*, p. 150.
322 to baseball memorabilia king Barry Halper: Barry Halper, interview, September 2000.
322 "ruined the baseball career": Frick and Graham, "Day Thomson Killed," p. 43-L.
322 "Down the stretch": Hano, *Willie Mays*, p. 74.
322 the maintenance man wiring: Tommy Colletti, interview, October 28, 2004.

322 New York writers: Ferdenzi, "Show-Stopper Skits," p. 10.
322 Dodger brass: Hunter, "O'Malley Host for Dinner," p. 17.
322 "Not enough money in it": Branca, interview, July 15, 2005.
322 head instructor: Kachline, "Kid Camps," p. 22.
322 year $13,000: Westvaco Corporation Records.
322 "Very well built": Saint and Stuart, *Twilight Teams*, p. 186.
323 oodles of chairs: Arnold, "Ah, Polo Grounds," p. 27.
323 Off to Closter: Lewis, "A Piece of," p. L-7.
323 Off to Cooperstown: National Baseball Hall of Fame Library.
323 120 red brick: Fried, "In the Shadow," p. R1.
323 "We are stabbed by": Angell, "Notes and Comment," p. 39.
323 Affixed to: Fried, "In the Shadow," p. R1.
323 paid by Schaefer beer $100: Alan Schuster, interview, July 9, 2005.
323 "Not too strong. Not too light": Thomson, interview, July 14, 2005.
323 income from Lehman: Ted Rosen, interview, July 12, 2005.
323 Winkie in her platinum: Nancy Mitchell, interview, July 10, 2005.
323 about her neck a gold "23": Ibid.
323 got just four: National Baseball Hall of Fame Library.
324 he left Mutual this same year: Branca, interview, April 8, 2005.
324 1966 dais among trucking: Devaney, "15 Years Later," p. 87.
324 "I was not very pleasant to him": Branca, interview, June 11, 2002.
324 "I would remember that as friendly": Thomson, interview, February 1, 2005.
324 Royal York: "Branca Found Loss," p. 36.
324 "Branca revealed": Ibid.
324 388 fans: Ibid.
324 Thomson followed: Ibid.
324 "a few of the things": Ibid.
324 "tremendous smash": Drebinger, "Giants' 4," p. S2.

CHAPTER TWENTY-FIVE

325 "Can two walk together": Amos 3:3, *The Bible: Authorized King James Version*, p. 1001.
325 a Watchung councilman skipped town: Richard Knies moved to Chicago during the summer of 1967.
325 Debates in Borough Hall: Thomson, interview, September 29, 2003.
325 edging opponent: "Watchung Elects," p. 36. AND Thomson and Richard Knies, interviews, September 29, 2005.
325 newly named: Ibid. The name change occurred on March 3, 1969.
325 his promotion: Westvaco Corporation Records.
325 throwing on a high school diamond: Greg O'Brien, interview, December 2, 2004.
325 "nobody asked me": Eisenberg, "Branca's Blessing," p. 23.
325 society of Jews: "B'nai B'rith," p. S2.
325 pitching to Branca: Koppett, "20 Years Later," p. S1.
325 "They're a more famous": Addie, "addie's atoms," p. 14.

325   "Maybe [Pancho]": Klein, "264 HRs," p. 7.

326   Richard Nixon welcomed: Kilpatrick, "Nixon to Broadcast," p. A4.

326   "I said, 'I don't like reading'": Thomson, interview, June 10, 2005.

326   the PBS television program: *The Way It Was,* "Dodgers-Giants Playoff," episode #1.

326   a Cub fan named Joel Schuster: Joel Schuster, interview, June 8, 2005.

326   Meir and Miriam Feder would mimic: Judy Feder, e-mail message, August 5, 2002.

326   "Every time I hear that": Marc Glassman, interview, July 20, 2005.

326   A Dodger fan named Jerry Stern: Jerry Stern, interview, November 5, 2003.

326   fields in Texas and California: Golenbock, *BUMS,* p. 309.

326   "Hey, Ralph": Ibid.

326   hit by Mike McCormick: McCormick homered on July 27, 1968, DiMaggio singled on August 10, 1968, and Mungo homered on July 24, 1965.

327   Branca, fifty, would not again play: Branca, interview, October 21, 2005.

327   Betsy Engelken wished husband Albert: Albert Engelken, interview, April 19, 2005.

327   Dodger fan Emil Lucev aimed: Emil Lucev, interview, June 14, 2003.

327   "an unhealed wound": Freundlich, *Reaching for the Stars,* p. 2.

327   "That home run never": Eisenberg, "Branca's Blessing," p. 23.

327   "Dago, if you wanted him": Branca, interview, March 14, 2005.

327   "For twenty-five years": Moran, "Reliving the Past," p. 49.

327   Sisler hit a home run: Golenbock, *BUMS,* p. 310.

328   "Is it true Ralph": "Your Question," p. 47.

328   "This is dedicated": New York Mets ad in *Daily News,* April 9, 1980, p. 52.

328   a merchant at Sherry-Lehmann: Branca, interview, October 21, 2005.

328   Section 50 classifying: New York State Civil Rights Law, Article 5, Section 50: "A person, firm or corporation that uses for advertising purposes, or for the purposes of trade, the name, portrait or picture of any living person without having first obtained the written consent of such person . . . is guilty of a misdemeanor."

328   word from new owner Wilpon: Ibid.

328   "I've lived with this": Berkow, "The 30-Year," p. 24.

328   *Goodbye, Bobby Thomson! Goodbye, John Wayne!*: Simon and Schuster, 1973.

328   *The Orange Air*: Charles Scribner's Sons, 1961. Author Roy Doliner cited Branca as the inspiration for protagonist Hank Easter. Roy Doliner, interview, Fall 2001.

328   Episode number 200: *M*A*S*H,* "A War for all Seasons," episode #200.

328   "it did seem to": Francis Ford Coppola, e-mail message, November 2, 2005.

328   "The Isotopes win": *The Simpsons,* "Dancin' Homer," Episode #18.

328   "the grand exclamation": Angell, "Homeric Tales," p. 68.

328   Michael Steinhardt to relay: Steinhardt, *No Bull,* p. 47. AND Michael Steinhardt, interview, September 21, 2005.

329   "never, repeat *never,* as dramatic": Pais, *A Tale of Two Continents,* p. 290.

329 Leroy Neiman: The 1991 painting was commissioned by Manufacturers Hanover Bank.

329 "Where were you": "Alligator in the Sky," p. 9.

329 humble apostle Peter: Rutler, The Church of Our Saviour. *www .oursaviournyc.org.*

329 Johann Ludwig Bach: Melamed, "Johan Ludwig," p. 1.

329 Grecian urn: Braiman, "John Keats' *Ode,*" *mrbraiman.home.att.net/keats .htm.*

329 "the philosophical equivalent": Branch, "New Frontiers," p. 47.

329 "Don't forget Bobby": Hockstader, "Witness Gives Scott," p. C1.

329 "there is always a future": Dorothy Rabinowitz, interview, December 5, 2005.

329 "Had Ralph Branca not thrown": Rudy Giuliani, interview, March 10, 2005.

329 "I really wish": Cerrone, "The 'Shot Heard'," p. 33.

329 "I sometimes wish": Frick and Graham, "Day Thomson Killed," p. 43-L.

329 "Honestly it was": Associated Press, "Brooklyn Welcomes."

329 "Perpetrator of": Westvaco Corporation Records.

329 "It's reared its ugly head": Thomson, interview, November 19, 2000.

329 "No," Thomson told: Gustkey, "Did Thomson Know," p. D11.

329 he had no desire to speak: Gustkey, "30 Years Later," p. D 11.

329 "talked about that day": Ibid.

329 "The Giants cheated": Gustkey, "Did Thomson Know," p. D11.

330 "If I was tipped": Ibid.

330 swung at a first: Dave Smith, *Retrosheet.* By way of comparison, in his 883 at-bats versus Brooklyn from 1947–1959, Thomson swung at 327 first pitches, or thirty-seven percent of the time. (Over that same span in Brooklyn's games, the league average was thirty-four percent.)

330 Durham owned a New Jersey sports: Ronald Durham, interview, Spring 2003.

330 "I didn't quite know": Madden, "Nostalgia Is," p. 12.

330 On December 27, 1983: Durham Associates contract, from the collection of Jerry Liebowitz.

330 "Guys had suitcases": Branca, interview, April 24, 2003.

330 as had done his aunt Rose: Branca, interview, January 15, 2002.

330 "They didn't have a meaningful": Ronald Durham, interview, Spring 2003.

331 "I said, 'Bob, these guys are making' ": Branca, interview, April 24, 2003.

331 upped their fee to two grand: Ibid.

331 slipped in a bathtub: Oates, "Talking to Bobby," p. 2.

331 five shows a year: Forman, "Fans Won't Let," p. 178.

331 integration of baseball: Irvin, *Nice Guys Finish First,* p. 125. In his autobiography, Monte Irvin singled out Thomson and Lockman as having embraced the black ballplayers. AND "Robbie Lauds," p. 21. AND McGowen, "Lead by 5½," p. S1. Branca embraced Jackie Robinson as he chased after a foul pop in 1947, a gesture Robinson often cited as significant.

331 "He was always sensitive": Thomson, interview, February 1, 2005.

331 "I got tired of man's inhumanity": Branca, interview, October 21, 2005.

331   reporter Mike Lupica: Lupica, "Distant Replay," p. 19.

331   "It's not about Thomson": DeLillo, *Underworld*, p. 97.

332   "[BAT] subconsciously might": Moran, "Reliving the Past," p. 49.

332   to infielder Bill Buckner: Branca, interview, October 31, 2005.

332   (and son-in-law) Bobby Valentine: Mary Valentine, interview, November 19, 2005.

332   "frequent and inevitable failures": Mandelbaum, *The Meaning of Sports*, p. 60.

332   "In *social memory*": Sahlins, *Apologies to Thucydides*, p. 158.

332   judge Harold Enten: Harold Enten, interview, November 8, 2004.

332   doctor Pete Paganussi: Fisher, "Sometimes One," p. B1.

332   "If you have": Karr, "This 50-Year-Old," p. A8.

332   "Two people came up to me": "Costas Coast to Coast," May 6, 1990.

332   "in the first row": Ibid.

332   "Dressen must've thought": Ibid.

333   "Leo sent Herman": Mushnick, "A Few Giant," p. 51.

333   "I wanted to tell": Sal Yvars, interview, July 15, 2004.

333   "No one believed it": Ibid.

333   Not Mushnick, says the reporter: Phil Mushnick, interview, November 4, 2005.

333   "If I'm ever asked": Herman Franks, interview, Fall 2000.

333   a guest of Ed Randall: *Ed Randall's Talking Baseball*, episode #187. Interviewed on October 29, 1991; aired throughout November 1991 on Prime Network.

333   "I saw him," says Thomson: Thomson, interview, January 8, 2004.

333   "He pulled me over": Carl Erskine, interview, July 23, 2004.

333   who four years prior: Rogers, "His Favorite Year," p. C2.

333   "Grab a poet who": Okrent, "The Boys of," p. 7.

334   "It was like pulling teeth": Bill Gutman, interview, November 4, 2005.

334   did not once bring up a telescope: Ibid.

334   "There has been speculation": Thomson, Heiman and Gutman, *The Giants Win the Pennant! The Giants Win the Pennant!*, p. 179.

334   Thomson did not read: Thomson, interview, January 2001.

334   "The book died because of him": Lee Heiman, interview, November 2000.

334   "Ralph appreciated that": O'Connell, "The Man Who," p. 161.

334   paid $10,000: "40 Years Later," p. B12.

334   Gore Vidal celebrated: Gore Vidal, interview, April 8, 2005.

334   in 1943 spurned the New York Giants: Vidal, *Palimpsest*, p. 23.

334   "the half of me": Ibid., p. 419.

334   Day the only of four exes: Michael Grilikhes, interview, November 11, 2005.

334   epigones gone on to manage: The 1951 Giant team alone saw Dark, Franks, Lockman, Rigney, Stanky and Westrum all become managers.

334   pallbearer Franks: Herman Franks, e-mail message, November 3, 2005.

335   "The Jerusalem Giants": Roth, *The Counterlife*, p. 94.

335   at Brown, UTEP: Yvonne Davies Tropp at Brown, and Travis Hartley Bennett at UTEP were both Class of 1953.

335   appeared in *Harper's* magazine: DeLillo, "Pafko at," pp. 35–70.

335   "some unrepeatable social": DeLillo, "The Power of," p. SM 60.

335   cruise: "It's a Long Way," p. C2.

335   fantasy camp: Cavanaugh, "New Sports-Fantasy," p. C16.

335   induction: Among MANY others, the Staten Island HOF inducted Thomson on December 3, 1995, and the Brooklyn Dodgers HOF inducted Branca on June 8, 1986.

335   honorary degree: Arenson, "Hostos Students," p. B6. Branca got his degree from Hostos Community College of the City University of New York.

335   post office and plebiscite: Schmid, "Post Office Announces."

335   eponymous . . . racehorse: Douglas Kass, interview, January 26, 2004. Douglas Kass named a yearling he bought in Bedminster, New Jersey, Kassa Branca.

335   Congress: New Jersey Congressman Bob Franks spoke of Thomson to the House of Representatives on September 20, 1994.

335   Carnegie Hall: "Baseball Blues" concert.

335   *Merriam-Webster's*: Webber and Feinsilber, *Merriam-Webster's Dictionary of Allusions*, p. 496.

335   It was January 1993: Nancy Mitchell, interview, November 5, 2005.

335   An August Red Cross: "Red Cross Golf," p. WC 18. Held on August 2, 1993.

336   "'You know who's here?'": Rod Gilbert, interview, October 23, 2005.

336   "Maybe once in fifty": Devaney, "15 Years Later," p. 87.

336   "He says to me in front": Rod Gilbert, interview, October 23, 2005.

336   "He's supposed to be a friend": Branca, interview, February 23, 2005.

336   "One of the great satisfactions": Thomson, interview with Norman Macht, SABR, October 16, 1992.

336   standing in the garden at Wilson: Thomson, interview, November 21, 2005.

337   each paid some $240,000: David Jurist, interview, November 22, 2005.

337   "We had to sign thousands": Branca, interview, April 24, 2003.

CHAPTER TWENTY-SIX

338   "These theories were": Mitton, *Conflict in the Cosmos*, p. 135.

338   "I have carried that": Davey Williams, interview, Fall 2000.

339   "The word 'stealing' ": Thomson, interview, November 2000.

339   "I'm tall and thin": Thomson, interview, November 16, 2000.

339   "I guess we were brought up": Thomson, interview, November 19, 2000.

339   "Suppose for a moment": Barbara Peters sermon, November 19, 2000, Wilson Memorial Union Church.

340   "I realized": Thomson, interview, November 19, 2000.

340   "you could almost": Ibid.

340   "It's all rationalizing": Ibid.

341   "He's sensitive and humble": Thomson, Heiman and Gutman, *The Giants Win the Pennant! The Giants Win the Pennant!*, p. 13.

341   "And remember," Jean concluded: Ibid., p. 46.

341   "I didn't want to look like": Branca, interview, December 28, 2000.

342 "it helps to be lucky": Thomson speaking on January 23, 2001.

342 "could love and really cherish": Branca speaking on January 23, 2001.

342 "I didn't enjoy being in his company": Thomson, interview, August 12, 2002.

342 "I guess I've been a jerk": Thomson, interview, November 19, 2000.

342 "I wasn't going to cry": Branca, interview, August 4, 2005.

342 "We've been together enough": Thomson, interview, November 19, 2000.

342 "I was just being too honest": Thomson, interview, January 26, 2001.

342 "You got me thinking serious": Ibid.

342 "It would take a little away": Ibid.

342 "My answer is no": Ibid.

343 postscript to a home run: *The Wall Street Journal*'s initial coverage was limited to a poorly punctuated blurb on October 4, 1951 (p. 1): "The New York Giants won the National League championship, defeating the Brooklyn Dodgers, 5 to 4 in the third game of the playoff series. Behind 4 to 2 in the ninth inning with one out, the Giant's third baseman Thomson smashed a home run with two men on base."

343 Branca sat in his rocking chair: Branca, interview, August 4, 2005.

343 "I just called him": "Mike and the Mad Dog," WFAN, February 1, 2001.

343 Branca asked if he had seen: Branca, interview, August 4, 2005.

343 "I guess you feel exonerated": Ibid.

343 testified on CNN: *Sports Tonight*, CNN, January 31, 2001.

343 "It's about as larcenous": Gordon, "Bobby Thomson: I," p. A1.

343 "It's as if the Nazis": "The Giants Steal," p. 14.

343 "Rightfully so, he feels that": "Mike and the Mad Dog," WFAN, February 1, 2001.

344 "Obviously it had to help us": Ibid.

344 "Signs at that moment?": Ibid..

344 "It's been brought up before": Ibid.

344 "I didn't feel good": Ibid.

344 "Ralph, uh, you know": Ibid.

344 Branca approached Thomson: Ben Walker, interview, April 19, 2005.

344 "Hiya, Hoot!": Walker, the Associated Press, February 4, 2001.

344 "They spoke alone, then turned": Ben Walker, interview, April 19, 2005.

345 "It's been a cleansing": Walker, the Associated Press, February 4, 2001.

EPILOGUE

347 Martin Arnold sought: Arnold, "The 'What-Ifs'," p. E3.

347 "No one except perhaps": Plimpton, *Home Run*, p. 7.

347 "The importance of protecting": Will, "A Season Spoiled," p. A23.

348 Brooklyn fan Joel Kramer: Joel Kramer, interview, January 31, 2001.

348 *Washington Post* reporter Thomas Bowsell: Boswell, "The Miracle," p. D1.

348 "Such equipment may": Marazzi, "Baseball Rules Corner," p. 87.

348 baseball commissioner since 1992: Having served as "acting commissioner" since 1992, Selig formally took the job in 1998.

348 no team had ever complained: Bud Selig, interview, July 29, 2005.

348 "they would be dealt with": Ibid.

348 "It's impossible to do today": Ken Singleton, interview, July 13, 2005.

348 "So did I know": Chuck Mitchell, "The Answer Is No," February 2001. Courtesy of Chuck Mitchell.

348 "Ralph Branca," it concluded: John Branca, "The Truth Shall Set Me Free," October 2002. Courtesy of John Branca.

348 "If you watch him swing": *The Shot Heard Round the World,* HBO.

348 "I'm proud to say": "Chat Wrap," ESPN, September 26, 2001.

349 "the most despicable": *Top 5 Reasons You Can't Blame,* November 1, 2005, ESPN. AND Swirsky, *Something to Write Home About,* p. 83.

349 "It's laughable": *The Shot Heard Round the World,* HBO.

349 "We've come apart": O'Connor, "Branca-Thomson Bond," p. C9.

349 "Bobby has had to live with a lie": Anderson, "A Fastball," p. D12.

349 the TV host thrice brought up: "The Early Show," October 2, 2001.

349 "To say I've got to live": Ibid.

349 Thomson to auction off: Thomson, interview, July 31, 2003.

349 "Now he doesn't see himself": Patti Barnes, interview, July 23, 2003.

349 "They'll never take away": "The Early Show," October 2, 2001.

350 "What I picked up in the museum": Frank McAveety speech, December 5, 2003.

350 signing nine straight weekends: Molly Ann Bracigliano, interview, November 28, 2005.

350 suing and settling: Maull, "Former Dodgers Pitcher." AND Branca, interview, May 2, 2005.

350 "Right now I'm more aware": Thomson, interview, February 1, 2005.

AUTHOR'S NOTE

352 "Summarizing the 1951 race": Kahn, *The Era,* p. 268.

355 "How did the New York Giants": Hexter, "The Rhetoric of History," p. 374.

355 "How to explain the overwhelming": Ibid., p. 379.

355 "confrontation with the riches of the event": Ibid., p. 380.

355 declared my article "scandalous": T. J. Quinn, February 4, 1002. Mr. Quinn later wrote me a gracious letter of apology.

355 one doctor used it: Ziegler and Goldfrank, *Emergency Doctor,* p. 110.

355 "You loosened my tongue": Branca, interview, February 1, 2001.

355 "I might have to be": Thomson, interview, November 8, 2004.

357 "I don't know anything": Herman Franks, interview, December 17, 2000.

357 gunfight in Korea: Berkow, "Now, a Stamp," p. C2.

357 "This whole book": Melville, *Moby-Dick,* p. 182.

BIBLIOGRAPHY

Aaron, Henry. *I Had a Hammer*. New York: HarperCollins, 1991.

Addie, Bob. "addie's atoms," *Sporting News*, June 1, 1974.

Aeschylus. *The Oresteia*. New York: Penguin, 1984.

Agee, James. "Brooklyn Is," *Esquire*, Vol. LXXX, No. 6, December 1968, 52–74, 180–81.

"Alleged 'Sign-Tipping'," *Sporting Life*, Vol. 54, No. 4, October 2, 1909.

Allen, Gwenfread E. *Hawaii's War Years, 1941–1945*. Westport, Conn.: Greenwood Press, 1971.

"Alligator in the Sky." iUniverse, Incorporated, 2005, 9–12.

"Amateurs Box For Free Trip to Fair," *New York Times*, October 30, 1915.

"America: Policeman for the Third World?" Center for Defense Information, Washington, D.C. Program #437. Original airdate June 2, 1991. Part of the television series "America's Defense Monitor."

"American Association," *New York Clipper*, October 30, 1886.

"American Association," *Sporting News*, May 11, 1955.

Anders, Roger M., ed. *Forging the Atomic Shield: Excerpts From the Office Diary of Gordon E. Dean*. Chapel Hill, N.C.: University of North Carolina Press, 1987.

Anderson, Dave. "A Fastball, a Swing and Forever," *New York Times*, October 1, 2001.

Anderson, Dave. "In My Brooklyn, There's Always Baseball," *New York Times*, June 24, 2001.

Anderson, Dave. "Nostalgia Time: The Selling of the Now-So-New Mets," *New York Times*, April 10, 1980.

Anderson, Dave. *Pennant Races: Baseball at its Best*. New York: Doubleday, 1994.

Anderson, Dave. "Toots Shor, 73, 'Saloonkeeper' and Host, Dies," *New York Times*, January 24, 1977.

Angell, Roger. "Early Innings," *New Yorker*, February 24, 1992. 84–92.

Angell, Roger. "Homeric Tales," *New Yorker*, May 27, 1991. 42–48.

Angell, Roger. "Notes and Comment," *New Yorker*, April 25, 1964.

"Annapolis Has Code Paralleling Point's," *New York Times*, August 4, 1951.

Archive of the Museum of Broadcast Communications.

Archives of the Joint Industry Board of the Electrical Industry. New York, New York.

Archives at Terence Cardinal Cooke Healthcare Center. New York, New York.

Arenson, Karen W. "Hostos Students Hear an Unusual Sound: Praise," *New York Times*, June 2, 1997.

"Army Form B. 2152. Short Service." Headquarters Scots Guard, London.

Arnold, Martin. "Ah, Polo Grounds, the Game Is Over," *New York Times*, April 11, 1964.

Arnold, Martin. "The 'What-Ifs' that Fascinate," *New York Times*, December 21, 2000.

Associated Press. "Bears Start Hank Borowy," April 17, 1941.

Associated Press. "Braves Protest 6–2 Loss to Cubs," *New York Times*, September 5, 1961.

Associated Press. "Brooklyn Welcomes the Best of Enemies," February 3, 1970.

Associated Press. "Casey, Ex-Dodger, Is Atlanta Suicide," *New York Times*, July 4, 1951.

Associated Press. "Chuck and I Are Friends—Sukeforth," Winnipeg Free Press, January 10, 1952.

Associated Press. "Crime Probe Hears Tobey Cry Against State Chiefs," *Washington Post*, December 14, 1950.

Associated Press. "Dodgers After Giants' Scalp," *Los Angeles Times*, January 27, 1934.

Associated Press. "English-Born Creator of Hot Dog Dies at 78," *Washington Post*, May 5, 1934.

Associated Press. "Father of Baseball Great Dies at 89," September 1, 1999.

Associated Press. "Games Ruled Not News, Troops Kept in Suspense," *New York Times*, October 6, 1951.

Associated Press. "Greatest Thrill of '51? Thomson Wins by Mile," January 13, 1952.

Associated Press. "Gunmen Slay Moretti, Crime Probe Witness," *Washington Post*, October 5, 1951.

Associated Press. "Herman Franks Sworn Into Navy," May 15, 1942.

Associated Press. "Knuckleball, Doctored Ball?," *New York Times*, August 4, 1987.

Associated Press. "Ott's No. 4 Uniform Retired by Giants," *New York Times*, July 18, 1948.

Associated Press. "Stolen-Signal Charge Untrue, Says Thomson," March 23, 1962.

Associated Press. "Yvars Lands a Job," *Washington Post*, July 6, 1955.

Associated Press. "Yvars Won't Pay Fine, Suspended Indefinitely," August 30, 1949.

Associated Press photo. "Series History in the Making," *New York Post*, October 6, 1941.

"Assumed Sell-Out Cuts Size of Crowd," *New York Times*, October 3, 1951.

Bacon, James. *How Sweet It Is: The Jackie Gleason Story.* New York: St. Martin's Press, 1986.

Baker, Russell. "Fourteen Clues to Washington News," *New York Times*, April 7, 1963.

Baldwin, Hanson W. "U-Boats Off Our Coasts," *New York Times*, January 16, 1942.

"Ball Game Gab," *Daily Variety*, October 4, 1951.

"Ball Game, Golf, Feasting Mark N.Y. Scribes' Outing," *Sporting News*, September 12, 1951.

Bankhead, Tallulah. *Tallulah: My Autobiography*. New York: Harper and Brothers Publishers, 1952.

Barber, Red. *The Rhubarb Patch: The Story of the Modern Brooklyn Dodgers*. New York: Simon and Schuster, 1954.

Barnes, Bart. "Rodriguez Handed 1-Year Suspension," *Washington Post*, February 2, 1982.

"Barnstorming Notes," *Sporting News*, October 20, 1948.

Barzun, Jacques. *God's Country and Mine*. New York: Vintage Books, 1954.

"Base Ball," *Brooklyn Eagle*, September 3, 1860.

"Base Ball," *New York Clipper*, December 13, 1856.

"Base Ball Notes," *Philadelphia Record*, July 5, 1884.

"Base Ball Notes," *Washington Post*, August 14, 1889.

"The Base Ball Convention," *New York Clipper*, December 10, 1870.

"Base-ball," *Harvard Crimson*, p. 56.

"The Base-Ball Field," *Spirit* 22, August 13, 1870.

"The Base-Ball Game at the Recreation Grounds," *Daily Alta California*, September 26, 1869.

"Baseball," *Sporting Life*, May 1, 1897.

Baseball Almanac. *www.baseball-almanac.com*.

"Baseball Asked to Restore Joe Jackson to Good Standing," *Washington Post*, February 22, 1951.

"Baseball Blues" concert, April 15, 1994. Carnegie Hall, New York, New York.

"Baseball Guild Will Investigate Reports of Player 'Intimidation'," *New York Times*, April 19, 1946.

Baseball Library. *www.baseballlibrary.com*.

"Baseball in Newburgh," *New York Clipper*, July 21, 1860.

Baseball Reference. *www.baseball-reference.com*.

Baumgartner, Stan. "Can Branca Ride Out '48 Jockeying?," *Sporting News*, November 26, 1947.

Baumgartner, Stan. "Chuck Calls T-U-R-N on Curver Labine," *Sporting News*, April 2, 1952.

Bealmear, Austin. "Bucky Gambles for Big Inning," *Washington Post*, October 1, 1947.

Beckett Baseball Cards. *www.beckett.com*.

Bedingfield, Gary. *Baseball in World War II Europe*. Charleston, S.C.: Arcadia Publishing, 1999.

Beebe, Bob. "Dandridge Has Operation, Lost Three Weeks," *Minneapolis Star*, July 16, 1951.

Berg, Moe. "Pitchers and Catchers," *Atlantic Monthly*, Vol. 168, Issue 3, September 1941, 281–88.

Berkow, Ira. "At 80, a Manager Keeps Going and Going and . . . ," *New York Times*, December 7, 2005.

Berkow, Ira. "Now, a Stamp to Be Sent 'Round the World," *New York Times*, April 8, 1998.

Berkow, Ira. "Red Smith, Sports Columnist Who Won Pulitzer, Dies at 76," *New York Times*, January 16, 1982.

Berkow, Ira. "The 30-Year Nemesis," *New York Times*, October 3, 1981.

"Better Hitter Would Have Let Pitch Go for Ball," *Staten Island Advance*, October 4, 1951.

The Bible: Authorized King James Version, Second Edition. New York: Oxford University Press, 1998.

Biederman, Les. "Branca 'Too Lucky in Love to Be Lucky at Everything'," *The All-Sports News*, Section Two of the *Sporting News*, January 2, 1952.

"Bi-State Playoff," *Sporting News*, September 17, 1942.

Blake, William. "The Ecchoing Green," in *The Complete Poetry and Prose of William Blake*. David V. Erdman, ed. New York: Anchor Books/Random House, 1988.

Blanchard, John A., ed. *The H Book of Harvard Athletics 1852–1922*. Cambridge, Mass.: Harvard Varsity Club, 1923. Printed by Harvard University Press.

"Block Cited by Insurance Co.," *Sporting News*, May 14, 1958.

Block, David. *Baseball Before We Knew It: A Search for the Roots of the Game*. Lincoln, Neb.: University of Nebraska Press, 2005.

Block, Hal. "Kukla, Frank & Kefauver [a review of the television show]," *Variety*, March 21, 1951.

Bloom, Dan. "Thomson 'Was Feeling Bad' When He Walloped 'Bad Ball'," *New York Herald Tribune*, October 4, 1951.

Blum, Romald, for the Associated Press. "Sports Comes to Standstill Following Terrorist Attacks," September 12, 2001.

"B'nai, B'rith Honors Stars of 7 Sports," *New York Times*, January 21, 1968.

"Bobby Got Special Hit for Fans," *Sporting News*, August 4, 1954.

"Bobby Thomson Ejected," *New York Times*, November 14, 1952.

Bock, Hal. "Still Crazy After All These Years," *Staten Island Advance*, September 30, 2001.

Bolton, Reginald Pelham. *Washington Heights, Manhattan: Its Eventful Past*. New York: The Dyckman Institute, 1924.

"Bombshell Disrupts TV Session at White House," *New York Daily Mirror*, October 4, 1951.

Bonsor, N.R.P. *North Atlantic Seaway*, Vol. 2, Newton Abbot, England: David & Charles, 1975.

Borsellino, Rob. "No Joy on Long Island After O'Malley Struck Out," *South Florida Sun–Sentinel*, August 28, 2001.

Boswell, Thomas. "The Miracle of Coogan's Bluff Tarnished," *Washington Post*, February 1, 2001.

Bowles, Jerry. *A Thousand Sundays: The Story of The Ed Sullivan Show*. New York: G. P. Putnam's Sons, 1980.

Bracker, Milton. "Memories of a Boyhood on Coogan's Bluff in Era of McGraw," *New York Times*, July 21, 1957.

Bracker, Milton. "Souvenir-Hunting Followers of Baseball Club Rip up Polo Grounds After Team Is Defeated There in its Final Game," *New York Times*, September, 30, 1957.

Bradley, Hugh. "Thomson Says Home Run Came From Bad Pitch," *New York Journal American*, October 3, 1951.

Braiman, Jay. "John Keats' *Ode on a Grecian Urn*," 2001. *http://mrbraiman .home.att.net/keats.htm*.

"Branca Becomes Insurance Agent," *Daily Argus* (NY), June 7, 1957.

"Branca Eligible for W.S.," *Sporting News*, September 10, 1952.

"Branca, Ex-Davis Star, Signaled by Brooklyn Dodgers; Hurler Joins Parent Club Today," *Daily Argus* (NY), June 7, 1944.

"Branca Eyeing Spot in Sports," *Sporting News*, October 5, 1955.

"Branca Found Loss of No. 13 Almost as Bad as Thomson Homer," *Globe and Mail* (Toronto), May 3, 1967.

"Branca Gives Up; Will Sell Insurance," *Washington Post*, March 29, 1957.

"Branca Isn't Brooding When He Predicts Winning 20 Games for Dodgers This Year," *Washington Post*, February 21, 1952.

"Branca-Karl Tribute Is Scheduled Aug. 13," *Daily Argus* (NY), June 20, 1947.

"Branca, in New Brook Bow, Hurls Two Shutout Innings," *Sporting News*, September 19, 1956.

Branca, Ralph, as told to Bill Gallo. "Branca: Diary of the Goat," *New York Daily News*, October 3, 1991.

Branca, Ralph, as told to John M. Ross. "They'll Never Forget," *Sport*, May 1952, 10–11, 72–74.

Branca, Ralph. "Branca Recalls Solace Priest Gave in 1951 After Thomson Homer," *Daily Argus* (NY), March 9, 1953.

"Branca Socks Home Run at Scribes' Shindig," *Sporting News*, February 13, 1952.

"Branca for Westlake, Plus 150 G's, Rejected by Bucs," *Sporting News*, December 22, 1948.

"Branca Wins but Higbe Loses," *New York Times*, October 14, 1946.

Branch, Taylor. "New Frontiers in American Philosophy," *New York Times*, August 14, 1977.

Brands, Edgar G. "Initial Test of Nocturnal Game at Cincinnati Proves its Practicability as Added Feature for Major Leagues," *Sporting News*, May 30, 1935.

Brands, E.G. "Stratospheric Prices Limit Big League Deals," *Sporting News*, December 22, 1948.

Braunmuller, A.R., ed. *Hamlet*. New York: Penguin Putnam, Inc., 2001.

Breen, Jay. "Brooklyn's Famouns Tree Now a Weeping Willow," *Long Island Star Journal*, October 4, 1951.

Britannica Book of the Year. Chicago: Encyclopedia Britannica, Inc., 1952.

Broeg, Bob. "Giants Stole Signals, But Not With Buzzer," *Sporting News*, April 14, 1962.

Broeg, Bob. "Lots of Frosting on Brownies' A.L. Birthday Cake, but Filling Turns Bitter with Two Defeats," *St. Louis Post–Dispatch*, August 20, 1951.

Broeg, Bob. "Prizes by Stanky to Spur Cardinals in Grapefruit Play," *Sporting News*, December 24, 1952.

Bronson, Eric, ed. *Baseball and Philosophy: Thinking Outside the Batter's Box*. Peru, Ill.: Open Court Publishing, 2004.

"Brooklyn Again Signs Brance, Victim of 1951 Play-Off Homer," *New York Times*, September 4, 1956.

"Brooklyn Base Ball Clubs," *Porter's Spirit* 2, June 20, 1857.

"Brooklyn Blood Center Gets 2 TV Sets to Show Playoffs," *Daily Mirror*, October 2, 1951.

"Brooklyn Catcher Insists He Is Ill," *New York Times*, June 14, 1941.

"Brooklyn Cowboy Runs Amok," *Sporting News*, July 21, 1938.

Brown, Harold. "Thomson Home Run Wipes Out $30,000 Dodger Victory Party," *New York Herald Tribune*, October 4, 1951.

Bruce, Scott G. *Silence and Sign Language in Medieval Monasticism: The Cluniac Tradition* (c. 900–1200). Cambridge, UK: Cambridge Studies in Medieval Life and Thought, 4th series, forthcoming (2007).

Brush, John T. "The Evolution of the Baseball Grandstand," *Baseball Magazine*, Vol. VIII, No. 6, April 1912, 1–3.

Bukowski, Charles. *Dangling in the Tournefortia*. Santa Barbara, Calif.: Black Sparrow Press, 1981.

"Bunts and Boots," *Sporting News*, March 11, 1953.

"Bunts and Boots," *Sporting News*, April 19, 1950.

Bureau of Records and Statistics. City of New York. New York, New York.

Burnes, Bob. "Thomson Off 100 Points," *Sporting News*, January 3, 1951.

Burns, Edward. "Polo Grounds Glitters, But It Isn't the Ideal Ball Park," *Chicago Daily Tribune*, June 27, 1937.

Burr, Harold. "Anybody Want a Catcher? Rickey Leaves Door Open," *Sporting News*, January 5, 1949.

Burr, Harold C. "Branca Adds Sore Arm to Dodger Pitching Woes," *Sporting News*, August 11, 1948.

Burr, Harold. "Dodger Holdouts May Yield After Coming Under Branch's Spell," *Brooklyn Eagle*, March 5, 1946.

Burr, Harold C. "Dressen Keeps Luck Coins," *New York World-Telegram and Sun*, October 1, 1951.

Burr, Harold. "Jones Charged With Wet Pitches," *Brooklyn Eagle*, October 3, 1951.

Burr, Harold. "Ralph Notches Second Shutout in Succession," *Brooklyn Eagle*, August 28, 1951.

Burr, Harold. "Reiser, Branca End Holdout Campaigns," *Brooklyn Eagle*, March 12, 1946.

Burr, Harold. "Robinson Gets 3 Hits Before Crowd of 53,091," *Brooklyn Eagle*, April 20, 1947.

Burton, Honorable Harold, copy of diary, October 3, 1951. Library of Congress, Manuscript Division.

Burton, Lewis. "There's No Manager Like Durocher," *Sport*, February 1952, 12–13,66–68.

By-Laws and Rules of the Hamilton Base Ball Club. Jersey City, N.J.: William R. Dunning, 1858.

"By Reading Signs," *Sporting News*, April 25, 1891.

Cannon, Jimmy. "Jimmy Cannon Says," *New York Post*, October 1, 1951.

Cannon, Jimmy. "Jimmy Cannon Says Defeat Stills Leo's Tongue," *New York Post*, October 2, 1946.

Cannon, Jimmy. "Jimmy Cannon Says Ego Kept Brooks Going," *New York Post*, October 3, 1946.

Capaldo, Chuck, for the Associated Press. Braves Bury 'Chokeup' Charges," *Sheboygan* (WI) *Press*, September 24, 1957.

"Cardinals Sell Catcher Yvars," *Washington Post*, December 4, 1954.

Cartier-Bresson, Henri. *The Decisive Moment: Photography by Henri Cartier-Bresson.* New York: Simon and Schuster, 1952.

Carver, Lawton. "Say Dodgers to Win by 20 Games," *Chicago Herald American,* July 21, 1951.

Cavanaugh, John. "New Sports-Fantasy Venture," *New York Times,* October 20, 1985.

"Cellar Dwellers Will Have Had Hand in Determining Outcome of Playoffs," *Jersey Journal,* September 9, 1946.

Cerrone, Rick. "The 'Shot Heard 'Round the World' Wasn't Always a Blessing for Ralph Branca," *Baseball Quarterly,* Summer 1977, 12, 32–33.

"Certificate of Birth." State of New York, Department of Health.

Chadwick, Henry, ed. *Beadle's Dime Base-Ball Player.* New York: Beadle and Company Publishers, 1864.

Chambers, Marcia. "After 25 Years, Thomson's Shot Is Still Painful," *New York Times,* October 3, 1976.

Chandler, A.B. "Happy." Oral History Project. University of Kentucky Libraries. Interview with Bobby Thomson. Conducted by William H, Marshall in Watchung, N.J. September 13, 1985.

Chapman, Lou. "Andy Pafko Still Remembers Shot Heard 'Round the World," *Baseball Digest,* November 1992, 68–73.

Charvat, Jack. "'Pepper Pod' Schenz Is Sparkplug of Tulsa Oilers," *Tulsa Tribune,* July 1, 1946.

The Chicago Defender (National Edition), March 19, 1949.

"Chuck Gets 'Cooperation' Award," AP photo credit. January 8, 1952.

"Church Sponsors Yuma Games," *Sporting News,* June 22, 1955.

Cianfarra, Camille M. "Pope Sees Peril of New War in Growing World Tensions," *New York Times,* October 1, 1951.

"City Intelligence," *Brooklyn Daily Eagle,* July 23, 1846.

Claudy, C.H., "Tipped Hats, Hitched Trousers," *The American Boy,* August 1916, 8–9.

Clayton, Peter A., and Martin J. Price. *The Seven Wonders of the Ancient World.* New York: Routledge, 1995.

"Clever Murphy," *Sporting Life,* Vol. 35, No. 2, March 31, 1900.

"Coast-to-Coast TV Carries Play-Off," *New York Times,* October 2, 1951.

Cobb, Ty. *Memories of Twenty Years in Baseball.* Edited by William R Cobb, Ph.D. Self-published.

Cohen, Leonard. "The Sports Parade," *New York Post,* April 19, 1947.

"Collins to Remain on Dodger Payroll," *New York Times,* February 3, 1952.

"Columbia's New Year in Records." Side 2. ZEP 36310.

The Complete ArtScroll Siddur. Brooklyn, N.Y.: Mesorah Publications, Ltd., 1984.

Congdon, Lee. "Permanent Things," *World & I,* June 1, 2002, 241–45.

Conklin, William R. "Atom Spy Couple Sentenced to Die; Aide Gets 30 Years," *New York Times,* April 6, 1951.

Conklin, William R. "Baseball Fever Grips City 3d Day," *New York Times,* October 3, 1951.

Conlan, Jocko, and Robert Creamer. *Jocko.* Philadelphia: J.B. Lippincott Company, 1967.

Considine, Bob. "Jonron de Thomson en el Noveno Dió el Pennant a los 'Gigantes'," *Diario de la Marina*, October 4, 1951.

Considine, Bob. "Thomson Authors Most Dramatic Episode in Baseball History," *Times-Picayune*, October 4, 1951.

Cort, David. "The Fix," *Commonweal*, January 4, 1952, 327–29.

Corum, Bill. "The Creeping Terror Keeps Flatbush Frantic," *New York Journal American*, September 25, 1951.

Corum, Bill. "Thomson Blasts Branca with 2 on to Down Brooks," *New York Journal American*, October 3, 1951.

"Costas Coast to Coast." Syndicated radio show. May 6, 1990.

Creamer, Robert W. *Baseball and Other Matters in 1941: A Celebration of the Best Baseball Season Ever—in the Year America Went to War*. Lincoln, Neb.: Bison Books, 2000.

Crepeau, Richard. *Baseball: America's Diamond Mind*. Lincoln, Neb.: Bison Books, 2000.

Cribari, Guido. "The Distaff Side of the Branca Story," *The Columns*, May 1952, 20–21, 35.

Crissey, Jr., Harrington E. *Athletes Away: A Selective Look at Professional Baseball Players in the Navy During World War II*. Philadelphia: Archway Press, 1984.

Crosby, Joan. "Faith, Prayer Helped Us Win Sobs Laraine," *Long Island Press*, October 4, 1951.

Crosby, John. "It's Wonderful at the Ball Game," *Washington Post*, September 8, 1951.

Cross, Harry. "New York Team's 5-Run Blast in Second Inning Routs Posedel," *Herald Tribune*, May 25, 1940.

Cunningham, Dave. "Fine Art of Sign Stealing Being Robbed of its History," *Long Beach Press–Telegram*, May 11, 1997.

Curtis High School Report Card. January 1939. Staten Island, New York.

"C.Y.O. Turns Thumbs Down on Durocher," *Chicago Daily Tribune*, March 1, 1947.

Daily Broadcast Content Report, Voice of America, October 3, 1951.

DailyNewsPix: the photo archive of the *New York Daily News*, *www.dailynewspix.com*.

Daley, Arthur. "Achieving the Impossible," *New York Times*, October 1, 1951.

Daley, Arthur. "Brave Dreams of the Braves," *New York Times*, March 8, 1948.

Daley, Arthur. "Gloom Over the Gowanus," *New York Times*, October 8, 1949.

Daley, Arthur. "A Guy with Class," *New York Times*, February 6, 1952.

Daley, Arthur. "Listening to the Barber," *New York Times*, May 25, 1952.

Daley, Arthur. "The New Giant Manager," *New York Times*, April 18, 1965.

Daley, Arthur. "No Joy in Flatbush," *New York Times*, October 2, 1951.

Daley, Arthur. "Opening a Second Front," *New York Times*, April 20, 1951.

Daley, Arthur. "Opening Day at the Stadium," *New York Times*, October 1, 1947.

Daley, Arthur. "'Quarterback' of the Baseball Team," *New York Times Magazine*, May 29, 1955, 20, 26–27.

Daley, Arthur. "Return from Oblivion," *New York Times*, September 5, 1956.

Daley, Arthur. "Sound Effects for a Historic Shot," *New York Times*, April 23, 1971.

Daley, Arthur. "This Is Baseball," *New York Times*, April 12, 1953.

Daley, Arthur. "What Makes a Great Batter," *New York Times*, April 18, 1948.

Daniel, Dan. "Ban Johnson Handed Spies Stiff Warning," *Sporting News*, April 4, 1962.

Daniel, Dan. "The Brat's Two-Bagger Drove in Beauty," *Sporting News*, August 19, 1959.

Daniel, Dan. "Detroit Escaped Dapper Hoax," *New York World-Telegram*, December 7, 1948.

Daniel, Dan. "Frick Probes 'Binocular' Charges," *Sporting News*, July 14, 1962.

Daniel, Dan. "Ted's Catch Highlight of All-Star Slugfest," *Sporting News*, July 20, 1949.

Daniel, Dan. "32 Minutes of Thrills in Series Film," *Sporting News*, January 7, 1953.

Daniel, Dan. "Thomson, Branca Spark N.Y. Writers' Show," *Sporting News*, February 13, 1952.

Daniel, Dan. "Too Much Hollywood, Too Little Major Leagues—and No Minors," *Sporting News*, April 25, 1956.

Davis, Mac. *Lore and Legends of Baseball*. New York: Lantern Press, 1953.

Dawidoff, Nicholas. "Hurts So Good," *New York Times*, August 26, 2001.

Dawson, James P. "Durocher, Outlining Giants' Plans, Will Experiment with Thomson in Infield," *New York Times*, July 17, 1948.

Dawson, James P. "Game-Winning Homer Wiped Out Stigma of Hero's Boner on Bases," *New York Times*, October 4, 1951.

Dawson, James P. "Giants Top Pirates with 2-Run 8th, 6–5, in Durocher Debut," *New York Times*, July 18, 1948.

Dawson, James P. "Lockman, Thomson to Play Tomorrow," *New York Times*, March 11, 1948.

Dawson, James P. "Thomson Brought Into Giants' Fold," *New York Times*, March 3, 1948.

Dawson, James P. "Scot Makes Light of Deciding Blow," *New York Times*, October 4, 1951.

Day, Laraine. *Day with the Giants*. Edited by Kyle Crichton. Garden City, N.Y.: Doubleday & Company, Inc., 1952.

DeLillo, Don. "Pafko at the Wall," *Harper's Magazine*, October 1992, 35–70.

DeLillo, Don. "The Power of History," *New York Times*, September 7, 1993.

DeLillo, Don. *Underworld*. New York: Scribner/Simon & Schuster, 1997.

Denman, George, MLB acting secretary-treasurer, October 15, 1951, letter. 1951 World Series clipping file, Sporting News Research Center. St. Louis, Missouri.

Devaney, John. "15 Years Later," *Sport*, October 1966, 44–47, 87–89.

Dickson, Paul. *The Hidden Language of Baseball: How Signs and Sign-Stealing Have Influenced the Course of Our National Pastime*. New York: Walker Publishing Company, Inc., 2003.

Diehl, Bill. "Dealing It Out," Norfolk (VA) *Ledger-Dispatch*, August 3, 1944.

Diehl, Joe. "Sal Yvars—Never Meant to Be a Hero," *Baseball Digest*, October–November 1961, 47–48.

"Dodger Baseball to be Broadcast," *New York Times*, December 7, 1938.

"Dodgers Recall Landrum; Hurled 8 Shutouts for Cats," *Sporting News*, August 6, 1952.

"Dodgers Take Round-Robin Baseball Game," *Long Island Daily Press*, July 12, 1949.

Dolan, Fred R. "Four Runs in Third Inning Give Big Leaguers Victory," *Herald News* (MA), October 15, 1951.

Doliner, Roy. *The Orange Air*. New York: Charles Scribner's Sons, 1961.

Donovan, Robert J. "Truman's Headline-Hunters," *Baltimore Sun*, July 29, 1951.

Down, Fred. "Dodger Victory Spoils Giants' Ride," *Newark Star-Ledger*, September 1, 1951.

Down, Fred. "Yvars' Beef Natural, but Leo Was Right Too, Says Feeney," *World-Telegram and Sun*, October 30, 1951.

Drebinger, John. "Bob Thomson, Scotland's Gift to Baseball," *Baseball Magazine*, Vol. LXXIX, No. 5, October 1947, 379–80, 394.

Drebinger, John. "Dodgers' Branca to Face Dickson or Pollet in First Play-Off Game Today," *New York Times*, October 1, 1946.

Drebinger, John. "Durocher in Doubt on Scot's Position," *New York Times*, January 29, 1953.

Drebinger, John. "Flying Scot to Land in Brooklyn Tomorrow," *New York Times*, April 30, 1955.

Drebinger, John. "Giants Capture Pennant, Beating Dodgers 5–4 in 9th on Thomson's 3-Run Homer," *New York Times*, October 4, 1951.

Drebinger, John. "Giants' 4 in Eighth Beat Pirates, 4–3," *New York Times*, June 12, 1949.

Drebinger, John. "Giants Overwhelm Dodgers with Sixteen Hits; Braves Divide with Cardinals," *New York Times*, July 6, 1953.

Drebinger, John. "Giants Trade Thomson to Braves; '51 Pennant Hero in 6-Player Deal," *New York Times*, February 2, 1954.

Drebinger, John. "Giants Will Play Night Baseball Here," *New York Times*, November 15, 1939.

Drebinger, John. "Night Baseball on Limited Scale Adopted Unanimously by National League," *New York Times*, December 13, 1934.

Drebinger, John. "That Home-Run Pitch to Thomson Returns on Film to Haunt Branca," *New York Times*, January 4, 1952.

Drebinger, John. "Thomson Breaks Ankle as Yankees Down Braves, 3–2," *New York Times*, March 14, 1954.

Drebinger, John. "Yanks Top Dodgers with 3-Run 9th, 4–3, for 2–1 Series Lead," *New York Times*, October 8, 1949.

Drebinger, John. "Yanks Win in 9th, Final 'Out' Turns Into 4-Run Rally," *New York Times*, October 6, 1941.

Drees, Jack and James C. Mullen. *Where Is He Now?: Sports Heroes of Yesterday—Revisited*. Middle Village, NY: Jonathan David Publishers, 1973.

Dressen, Chuck, as told to Al Hirshberg. "Stealing Signs Is My Business," *True*, March 1956, 26–27, 53–57.

"Dressen's Reprimand Tops Branca's List of '52 Woes," *Sporting News*, October 15, 1952.

Driscoll, Charles B. "Pages From a Journalist's Diary," *Washington Post*, January 1, 1939.

Dryden, Charles. "Another Victory for the Buzzer—Phillies," *North American*, October 2, 1900.

Dryden, Charles. "Buzzer Out of Order, Phillies Lost a Game," *North American*, October 3, 1900.

Dryden, Charles. "Dryden Lays Bare the Buzzer Secrets," *North American*, October 8, 1900.

Dryden, Charles. "Morgan, Murphy Worked the Buzzer and Gave Away Pitchers' Secrets," *North American*, September 19, 1900.

Dryden, Charles. "Policemen Guard the Poor Ball Players," *North American*, September 27, 1900.

DuBois, John. "50 Years Ago, Colleges Went to War," *St. Cloud* (MN) *Times*, May 31, 1993.

Duff, Austin. "Glamorizing a Trolley System," *Electrical Union World*, July 15, 1948.

Dunnell, Milt. "Drama, Gripping Suspense and Bobby Thomson," *Toronto Star*, October 4, 1951.

"Durocher Accused of Attacking Fan, Says He Merely Shoved an Ex-GI," *New York Times*, April 29, 1949.

Durocher, Leo. "How We Won the Pennant," *True Magazine*, February 1952, 43, 85–92.

Durocher, Leo, with Ed Linn. *Nice Guys Finish Last*. New York: Pocket Books, 1976.

Durslag, Melvin. "Don't Put the Blame on Branca," *Sporting News*, May 9, 1964.

Dye, Bob, ed. *Hawai'i Chronicles III: World War Two in Hawaii, From the Pages of the Paradise of the Pacific*. Honolulu: University of Hawaii Press, 2000.

"Dykes Raps Out 5 Safe Ones on 5 Pitched Balls," *New York Daily News*, October 2, 1925.

The Early Show, CBS. October 2, 2001.

Eastonia. East High yearbook. Salt Lake City, UT. 1931.

Eberly, Philip K. "Replay It Again, Sam," *New York Times*, October 9, 1971.

Ebert, John. "Local 3 Men Converting Movie Studios to NBC Television Station," *Electrical Union World*, February 15, 1949, 4–5.

Eck, Frank. "Thomson Led Majors as Second-Half Hitter," *Sporting News*, November 28, 1951.

Ed Randall's Talking Baseball. Episode #187.

Edelman, Rita. "Bobby Thomson: Safe at Home," *Newark Star Ledger*, June 3, 1987.

Edwards, Bob. *Fridays with Red: A Radio Friendship*. Riverside, N.J.: Simon and Schuster, 1993.

Effrat, Louis. "Branca of N.Y.U. Tops C.C.N.Y., 3–0," *New York Times*, April, 23, 1944.

Effrat, Louis. "Cubs' 3-Run Eighth Downs Giants, 4–3," *New York Times*, September 19, 1946.

Effrat, Louis. "Durocher Received Offer of Bribe Backed by Threats Through Mail," *New York Times*, October 11, 1951.

Effrat, Louis. "First-Sacker Fain Traded to Tigers," *New York Times*, December 7, 1954.

Effrat, Louis. "Giants Again Crush Dodgers and Move Within Five Games of League Leaders," *New York Times*, September 3, 1951.

Effrat, Louis. "Giants, Dodgers, Yanks Listed For Battles Under Arcs Tonight," *New York Times*, June 18, 1946.

Effrat, Louis. "Giants, Conquered by Reds, 10–3, Come Back to Gain 4–2 Triumph," *New York Times*, August 29, 1949.

Effrat, Louis. "N.Y.U. Nine Routs Brooklyn College," *New York Times*, April 30, 1944.

Effrat, Louis. "Pair of Grand Slams Helps Giants Rout Cards, 14–4, Regain 2d Place," *New York Times*, July 14, 1951.

Effrat, Louis. "Thomson Is Signed by Giants for 1951," *New York Times*, December 22, 1950.

Effrat, Louis. "Thomson Says He's No 'Has-Been'," *New York Times*, March 7, 1959.

Eig, Jonathan. *Luckiest Man: The Life and Death of Lou Gehrig.* New York: Simon & Schuster, 2005.

"$8,270 for Yanks, $6,178 to Brooks in Record Shares," *Sporting News*, October 14, 1953.

"Eighty-Seventh College Training Detachment," *The Sagatagan of 1944.* St. John's University yearbook.

Einstein, Charles. *Willie's Time.* New York: Lippincott, 1979.

Eisenberg, Dave. "Branca's Blessing in Disguise," *Sporting News*, September 13, 1969.

Elias Sports Bureau, Inc. New York, New York.

"The Electric Light," *Boston Daily Globe*, September 3, 1880.

"The Electric Light," *Boston Post*, September 3, 1880.

Endress, Erwin. "All Island Jubilant as Bobby Wins Game," *Staten Island Advance*, October 4, 1951.

Epstein, Ben. "Hearn Never Wins Big Ones, Eh? Ailing Campy Doubtful Today," *New York Daily Mirror*, October 2, 1951.

Epstein, Ben. "Jones Threw Spitter, All Came Out in Wash," *New York Daily Mirror*, October 3, 1951.

Epstein, Ben. "Yanks Caught with Signs Down, Accuse Indian Spy," *New York Daily Mirror*, August 24, 1951.

Eskenazi, Gerald. "Branca Finds Thomson's Wallop a 'Blessing in Disguise'," *New York Times*, October 2, 1966.

Eskenazi, Gerald. *The Lip.* New York: William Morrow and Company, Inc., 1993.

Eskenazi, Gerald. *A Sportswriter's Life: From the Desk of a* New York Times *Reporter.* Columbia, Mo.: University of Missouri Press, 2003.

Evers, John J., and Hugh S. Fullerton. *Touching Second: The Science of Baseball.* Mattituck, N.Y.: Amereon House, 1910.

"The Excelsior vs. Flour City Base Ball Clubs," *Rochester Evening Express*, July 9, 1860.

"Excelsior vs. Union," *Spirit of the Times*, August 9, 1862.

"Excerpts From Testimony on Second Day of Senate Crime Committee's Open Hearings in City," *New York Times*, March 14, 1951.

"Extra Bat Practice Didn't Help Mays," *New York Journal American*, October 3, 1951.

Falls, Joe. "Thomson's HR No. 1 for Drama." *Sporting News*, October 15, 1977.

"Fans Still Hail Thomson for Historic Homer," *Sporting News*, September 2, 1959.

Farnsworth, Marjorie. "Frank Rino of the J–A, a Famous Photographer," *New York Journal American*, August 23, 1965.

Farrar, Margaret, ed. "Crossword Puzzle," *New York Times*, June 18, 1952.

Farrell, Frank. "An Old Scandal Revived by Allegations of Unfair Tactics," *Sporting Life*, Vol. 55, No. 20, July 23, 1910.

Federal Bureau of Investigation. Washington, D.C.

Feeney, Charley. "Miracle Team Is in No Mood to Quit Now," *Long Island Star Journal*, October 4, 1951.

Felker, Carl T. "Big Majority Vote for Feat of Flying Scot," *The All-Sports News*, Section Two of the *Sporting News*, January 2, 1952.

Felker, Carl T. "Ticket Tornado Tosses Many Scalpers for Loss," *Sporting News*, October 9, 1946.

Felker, Clay. "Mays Is Giants' Counter Bid to Brooklyn's Negro Stars," *Sporting News*, August 15, 1951.

Ferdenzi, Til. "Show-Stopper Skits by Stan, Sandy Top N.Y. Writer Dinner," *Sporting News*, February 15, 1964.

Ferguson, Margaret, Mary Jo Salter, and Jon Stallworthy, eds. *The Norton Anthology of Poetry*. Fourth Edition. New York: W. W. Norton & Company, 1996.

"Fever of 101 Beds Lippy," *New York Journal American*, September 5, 1951.

"Fifteenth Census of the United States: 1930—Population Schedule." National Archives and Records Administration (NARA).

"The Fifth Avenue Hospital," *Architecture and Building*, Vol. LIV, No. 9, September 1922, 87–88 (plus unnumbered plates).

"57 Video, 740 Radio Stations to Carry Series," *Chicago Tribune*, October 4, 1951.

Fimrite, Ron. "Side By Side," *Sports Illustrated*, September 16, 1991, 66–77.

Firestone, David. "Reticent Novelist Talks Baseball, Not Books," *New York Times*, September 10, 1998.

"First Game Gossip," *Sporting News*, October 8, 1947.

"First H.R. by Thomson," *Sporting News*, April 22, 1953.

Fisher, Marc. "Sometimes One Homer Is Plenty," *Washington Post*, March 31, 2005.

"Five Convicts Break Prison; 3 Recaptured," *Chicago Daily Tribune*, February 11, 1947.

"550 Air Cadets Assigned to TC, St. Johns, Airport," *St. Cloud (MN) Daily Times*, February 17, 1943.

"Flight 'E' Graduates Saturday," *WIL–CO*, Vol. 2, No. 3, February 10, 1944.

"Flying Pennant at PG Tells Giants Result," *Grandstand Manager*, March 1952, Vol. II, No. 12: 1.

Folsom, Ed, ed. *Walt Whitman's Native Representations*. Cambridge, U.K.: Cambridge University Press, 1997.

Ford, Bill. "Schenz Remembers Baseball, Grimmly," *Cincinnati Enquirer*, April 9, 1980.

"Form for Oath of Office," October 21, 1945. NARA.

Forman, Ross. "Fans Won't Let Branca Forget 'The Shot'," *Sports Collectors Digest*, November 8, 1991.

"Former Brook Branca First to Go in Yankee Rebuilding," *Sporting News*, October 27, 1954.

"40 Years Later, Here's the Pitch," *New York Times*, October 3, 1991.

"45,022 See Jackie's Team in 15 Games," *Sporting News*, October 28, 1953.

Foster, Alan S. *Goodbye, Bobby Thomson! Goodbye, John Wayne!* New York: Simon & Schuster, 1973.

Foster, John. "The Magnificent New Polo Grounds," *Baseball Magazine*, Vol. VII, No. 6, October 1911, 6–8, 98–102.

"Four Braves Find It's Tough in 'Rubber Chicken' Circuit," *Sporting News*, December 29, 1954.

Fraley, Oscar for the *United Press*. "Thomson's Homer Seen Responsible for Branca's Ills."

Frank, Michael. "Writings That Defy Time's Toll," *New York Times*, April 26, 2002.

"Frank Sinatra Divorced," *New York Times*, October 31, 1951.

Frank, Stanley. "Will They Steal This Series?," *Saturday Evening Post*, October 2, 1937, 16–17, 73–74, 76.

Franklin D. Roosevelt Presidential Library and Museum. Hyde Park, New York. *www.fdrlibrary.marist.edu/052741/html*.

Franko, Dr. Alfred M. *A Half Century of Making Men 1912–1962: The Human Story of the Boys Club of Mount Vernon.* Self-published in Mount Vernon, N.Y., year unknown.

Franks, Herman, as told via telephone to John Mooney. "Franks Blames Rizzuto for Giant Series Lost," *Salt Lake Tribune*, October 11, 1951.

Franks, Herman, as told via telephone to John Mooney. "Franks: Giants' Promise to Lip to Won Game," *Salt Lake Tribune*, October 4, 1951.

"Franks Joins I.L. Club—Until Draft," *Salt Lake Tribune*, March 28, 1942.

Freundlich, Larry, ed. *Reaching for the Stars: A Celebration of Italian Americans in Major League Baseball.* New York: Ballantine Books, 2003.

Frick, Ford, and Frank Graham. "Day Thomson Killed Frick," *New York Journal American*, March 19, 1961.

Fried, Joseph P. "In the Shadow of Coogan's Bluff, New Era Begins," *New York Times*, October 29, 1967.

Frommer, Harvey. *New York City Baseball: The Last Golden Age, 1947–1957.* Madison, Wisc.: The University of Wisconsin Press, 2004.

Frost, Robert. "Tree at My Window," in *Robert Frost's Poems*. New York: St. Martin's, 2002.

Fullerton, Hugh S. "The Right and Wrong of Baseball," *American Magazine*, October 1911.

Fullerton, Hugh S. "Wig-Wagging in Baseball," *American Legion Weekly*, July 22, 1921, 7–8, 21–22.

Futrell, Robert F. *USAF Historical Study No. 71: United States Air Force Operations in the Korean Conflict, 25 June—1 July 1952.* Department of the Air Force, USAF Historical Division. July 1, 1952.

Gallo, Bill. "Unforgettable & Unforgiving," *New York Daily News*, October 3, 1991.

Gammons, Peter. "Sign Language," *Sports Illustrated*, April 15, 1991, 74–78, 80.

Garagiola, Joe, and Martin Quigley. *Baseball Is a Funny Game*. Philadelphia: J. B. Lippincott Company, 1960.

Garreau, Garth. *Bat Boy of the Giants*. New York: Comet Books, 1949.

Gellis, Ike. "Flock Rips Giants; Nats Blank Yanks," *New York Post*, April 20, 1952.

Gelman, Eli. "Historic Baseball Moment Remembered," *The Montclarion*, October 4, 2001.

"'Giant' Celebrant Can't See Effigy Through the 'Haze'," *Long Island Star Journal*, October 4, 1951.

"A Giant Fan, He Passed Up Dodgers," *Sporting News*, December 14, 1949.

"The Giants Are at Home," *New York Times*, July 9, 1889.

"Giants Dispel Polo Grounds Gloom," *New York Sun*, November 15, 1939.

"Giants Even Bet Odds," *Salt Lake Tribune*, October 8, 1951.

"Giants to Keep Punching, Just in Case," *New York World-Telegram and Sun*, September 20, 1951.

"Giants Leaving Baseball Field." Corbis Stock Photography and Pictures. U1141188.

"Giants to Open Series Today with Dodgers," *Chicago Daily Tribune*, February 28, 1941.

"Giants to Play 10 Night Tilts," *New York Daily News*, November 15, 1939.

"Giants Radio Job to Aro," *New York Times*, March 29, 1951.

"Giants Seek Streamlining," *New York Times*, December 31, 1957.

"The Giants Steal the Pennant!," *Chicago Tribune*, February 2, 2001.

"Giants 13–10 Choice Over Brooks Today," *Brooklyn Eagle*, October 3, 1951.

"Giants v. Yankees," *Time*, October 15, 1951, 77–78.

"Girl to Bobby Thomsons," *New York Times*, November 1, 1953.

"Glory Enough for One Day," *Boston Herald*, June 23, 1889.

Goddard, Joe. *All New Orioles Scorebook*, 3rd Edition. Baltimore: Stadia Operations, 1980.

Godley, A.D., Trans. *Herodotus*, Vol. 4, Book 8, Verse 98. Cambridge, Mass.: Harvard University Press, 1924.

Goewey, Ed. A., "Inconsistency and Its Relation to Various Sports," *Leslie's Weekly*, August 11, 1910.

Goldblatt, Andrew. *The Giants and the Dodgers: Four Cities, Two Teams, One Rivalry*. Jefferson, N.C.: McFarland & Company, Inc., 2003.

Golenbock, Peter. *BUMS: An Oral History of the Brooklyn Dodgers*. Chicago: Contemporary Books, 2000.

"Goodbye Willie, Hello Strife." Court TV's Crime Library. *www.crimelibrary.com*.

Goodman, Irv. "SPORTalk," *Sport*, May 1956, 8–10.

Goodman, Lester R., ed. *The Little Red Book of Major League Baseball*. New York: Munro Elias Baseball Bureau, Inc., 1952.

Goodwin, Doris Kearns. *Wait Till Next Year: A Memoir*. New York: Simon & Schuster, 1997.

"Go South with Ralph Branca," *Sport*, March 1950, 65–68.

Gordon, Cormac. "Bobby Thomson: I Didn't Steal Pennant," *Staten Island Advance*, February 1, 2001.

Gordon, Cormac. "'. . . They Shoulda Named a Town After Him'," *Staten Island Advance*, November 2, 1997.

Gordon, Cormac. "Thomson's Eye Still on the Ball," *Staten Island Advance*, October 4, 2001.

Gould, Ben. "Dodgers Have Tough Holdout in Branca," *Brooklyn Eagle*, February 23, 1946.

Gould, Stephen Jay. "The H and Q of Baseball" *New York Review of Books*, October 24, 1991, 47–52.

Govlick, George. "Ex-Major League Star Thomson Is Now Man in Gray Tweed Suit," *Courier News*, April 17, 1961.

Grady, Al. "A Chip Off the Old Cobb," *Iowa City Press-Citizen*, March 29, 1952.

Graham, Frank. "Of Durocher and Thomson," *New York Journal American*, January 29, 1953.

Graham, Frank, Jr. *Great Pennant Races of the Major Leagues*. New York: Random House, 1967.

Grange, Joseph. *The City: An Urban Cosmology*. Albany: State University of New York Press, 1999.

Graves, Robert, Trans. *The Greek Myths*. Combined Edition. New York: Penguin Books, 1992.

Gray, Louis H. "On the Etymology of Tragedia," *The Classical Quarterly*, Vol. 6, No. 1, January 1912, 60–63.

"A Great Match At Base Ball—This Afternoon" [photo caption], *Brooklyn Eagle*, October 21, 1845.

Green, Abel. "The Eyes on the World," *Variety*, September 12, 1951.

Green, Paul. *Forgotten Fields*. Waupaca, Wisc.: Parker Publications, 1984.

Greenfeld, Karl Taro. "A Life After Wide Right," *Sports Illustrated*, July 12, 2004, 140–54.

Griffin, John, for United Press. "Branca Apenas Pudo Hablar . . . ," *El Universal*, October 4, 1951.

Grillo, J. Ed. "That Scandal," *Sporting Life*, Vol. 54, No. 8, October 30, 1909.

Grimsley, Will. "Branca Hot in Bullpen—But Flock Quickly Chilled," *Long Island Press*, October 4, 1951.

Grimsley, Will. "Branca Tries to Forget with Tigers," *Pacific Stars & Stripes*, August 10, 1953.

Gross, Milton. "Speaking Out," *New York Post*, July 6, 1951.

Gross, Milton. "Speaking Out," *New York Post*, July 20, 1951.

Gross, Milton. "Speaking Out," *New York Post*, August 29, 1951.

Gustkey, Earl. "Did Thomson Know What Was Coming?," *Los Angeles Times*, October 3, 1981.

Gustkey, Earl. "30 Years Later, It's a Shot That Some Still Find Hard to Swallow," *Los Angeles Times*, October 3, 1981.

Gutman, Dan. *Banana Bats and Ding-Dong Balls*. New York: Macmillan, 1995.

Gutman, Dan. "The Physics of Foul Play," *Discover*, April 1988, 70–77.

"Ha! Ha! Pirates Ring into the Buzzer Game," *Philadelphia Inquirer*, September 30, 1900.

Haag, Ken. "Hank Schenz . . . A 'Dirt-Belly Rascal' in Saints Flannels," *Sports Collectors Digest*, June 19, 1992, 120–21.

Hagerty, James A. "Costello's Power in Politics, Crime Shown at Hearing," *New York Times*, March 13, 1951.

Halberstam, David. *The Fifties*. New York: Fawcett Columbine/Ballantine Books, 1994.

Halberstam, David J. *Sports on New York Radio*. New York: McGraw-Hill, 1999.

Hall, Halsey. "Yvars Hits Fan in Baseball Row," *Minneapolis Morning Tribune*, July 16, 1949.

Ham, Eldon L. *Larceny & Old Leather: The Mischievous Legacy of Major League Baseball*. Chicago: Academy Chicago Publishers, 2005.

Hamburger, Philip. "4–3," *New Yorker*, October 20, 1951, 26–27.

Hamill, Pete. *A Drinking Life: A Memoir*. Boston: Deidre Enterprises, 1994.

Hamill, Pete. "The Gang Was All There for Barney," *New York Post*, September 19, 1988.

Hammerstein, Arthur, and Dudley Wilkinson [words and music]. "Because of You," Broadcast Music Incorporated, 1940. New York, New York.

Hand, Jack. "Branca Debuts as Crooner on the Theater Circuit," *Long Island Press*, January 25, 1949.

Hano, Arnold. *Willie Mays*. New York: Tempo Books/Grosset & Dunlap, 1966.

Harding, Warren G. "Less Government in Business and More Business in Government," *World's Work*, Vol. XLI, No. 1, November 1920.

Hardy, James D. *The New York Giants Baseball Club: The Growth of a Team and a Sport, 1870 to 1900*. Jefferson, N.C.: McFarland & Company, Inc., 1996.

Harrison, James R. "Giants Break Even; Now Trail by Game," *New York Times*, September 28, 1928.

Harrison, James R. "Lazzeri's Big Blow Halts Browns, 4–3," *New York Times*, June 15, 1928.

Harwell, Ernie. "The Miracle of Coogan's Bluff." Chapter 8 in *Voices of Sport*. New York: Grossett & Dunlap, 1971.

"Have We Gone Soft?" *New Republic*, February 15, 1960, 11–15.

Hawkins Electrical Guide Number 8. New York: Theo Audel & Co., 1917.

Headquarters Scots Guard, London.

Heiman, Lee, Dave Weiner, and Bill Gutman. *When the Cheering Stops: Ex-Major Leaguers Talk About Their Game and Their Lives*. New York: Macmillan Publishing Company, 1990.

Heimer, Mel. "My New York," *Bedford* (PA) *Gazette*, October 24, 1951.

Heinz, W.C. "Polo Grounds Has Face Lift," *New York Sun*, October 18, 1945.

Heinz, W.C. "Ralph Branca's Slow Note," *New York Sun*, January 27, 1949.

Hemingway, Ernest. *Across the River and Into the Trees*. New York: Charles Scribner's Sons, 1950.

Hemingway, Ernest. *The Old Man and the Sea*. New York: Penguin Books, 1973.

Hemingway, Jack. *Misadventures of a Fly Fisherman*. New York: McGraw-Hill, 1987.

"He Needed an Interpreter," *Baseball Digest*, February 1944, 36.

Herts, Henry B. "Grand Stand for the Polo Grounds," *Architecture and Building*, Vol. XLIV, No. 11, November 1912, 457–59.

Heusser, Albert. *The Forgotten General: Robert Erskine, F.R.S. (1735–1788)*. Paterson, N.J.: The Benjamin Franklin Press, 1928.

Hexter, J.H. "The Rhetoric of History," in *The International Encyclopedia of the Social Sciences*, Vol. 6, New York: Macmillan & The Free Press, 1968, 368–94.

The High School Recorder. Boys High (Brooklyn, New York): March 1913.

Hockstader, Lee. "Witness Gives Scott an Alibi," *Washington Post*, February 12, 1988.

Hodges, Russ, and Al Hirshberg. *My Giants*. Garden City, N.Y.: Doubleday & Company, Inc., 1963.

Hogan, Lawrence D. *Shades of Glory: The Negro Leagues and the Story of African-American Baseball*. With a Foreword by Jules Tygiel. Washington, D.C.: National Geographic, 2006.

"Holmes Sees Action," *New York Times*, July 1, 1951.

Holmes, Tot. *www.LADugout.com*.

Holtzman, Jerome. "Hrabosky Slipping?," *Sporting News*, July 23, 1977.

Homer. *The Odyssey*. Translated by Alexander Pope. Whitefish, Mont.: Kessinger Publishing, 2004.

"Homer Snaps Branca's Skein," *Sporting News*, April 13, 1955.

Hornsby, Rogers, and Bill Surface. *My War with Baseball*. New York: Coward-McCann, 1962.

Housman, A. E. "To an Athlete Dying Young," in *A Shropshire Lad*. Mineola, N.Y.: Dover Publications, Inc., 1990.

Huard, Kevin. "Bobby Thomson: His Dramatic Shot Will Be Remembered Forever," *Sports Collectors Digest*, April 5, 1991, 90–92.

"Huge Crowd Honors Baseball Star at Testimonial Dinner," *Staten Island Advance*, January 24, 1949.

Hugo, Bill. "Record Book," *Reds Alert*.

Hunter, Bob. "O'Malley Host for Dinner, Day's Outing in Bahamas," *Sporting News*, March 16, 1963.

Hurwitz, Hy. "Durocher Says He Would Have Walked Thomson," *Boston Daily Globe*, October 4, 1951.

Hurwitz, Hy. "'Never Got Better Surprise'—Lip; Sees Koslo Good Bet Vs. Yank Lefties," *Boston Daily Globe*, October 4, 1951.

Hynd, Noel. "FOUND: CHARMING 2BR, 1BTH APT, IN THE LEFTFIELD STANDS, POLO GROUNDS," *Sports Illustrated*, October 20, 1986.

Index of the City Register. Recorder of Deeds and Mortgages. Transfer of Block 2107 from Samuel Watkins to Matthew Morgan. March 29, 1844. Liber 557, p. 414.

"Indians-Giants Series," *Sporting News*, April 27, 1949.

Ingraham, Joseph C. "Moretti, Gambler, Slain by 4 Gunmen in New Jersey Café," *New York Times*, October 5, 1951.

"Insubordination Charge Brings Yvars Suspension," *Sporting News*, September 7, 1949.

"Interesting Developments," *New York Daily Times*, December 20, 1856.

"An Interesting Game in Williamsburgh," *Brooklyn Eagle*, August 24, 1863.

International News Service. "Babe Phelps Says 'Misery' Has Him; Boss Seeks a Deal," *Washington Post*, June 14, 1941.

"Investigation Into New Rumor Reveals Unusual Situation," *WIL–CO*, Vol. 2, No. 3, February 10, 1944.

Irvin, Monte, with James A. Riley. *Nice Guys Finish First*. New York: Carroll & Graf Publishers, Inc., 1996.

"Irvington vs. Eureka," *New York Clipper*, May 18, 1867.

"Isnello Gives Impy Festive Homecoming," *New York Daily News*, October 1, 1951.

Istomin, Eugene. "Conversations with 'Fingers'," *New York Times*, October 9, 1977.

"It's a Long Way From Coogan's Bluff," *New York Times*, May 18, 1992.

"James Thomson," obituary, *Staten Island Advance*, July 3, 1940.

"Jerseys Continue to Flash Inconsistent Performances," *Jersey Journal*, August 5, 1946.

J-M Asbestos Roofing ad. *Green's Fruit Grocer*, March 1912.

Johnson, Ban. "The American League Holds Its Winter Meeting Also in New York, and Transacts Its Business As Usual, With Neatness and Dispatch," *Sporting Life*, Vol. 54, No. 16, December 25, 1909.

Johnson, Ban. "Offers Reward for Evidence of 'Signal Tipping' in New York," *Sporting Life*, Vol. 55, No. 21, July 30, 1910.

"Joseph Stalin's Bomb, Bobby Thomson's Blast," *New York Post*, October 4, 1951.

The Journals of John Cheever. New York: Alfred A. Knopf, 1991.

Joyce, James. *Finnegans Wake*. New York: Penguin Books, 1999.

JPS Hebrew-English Tanakh, Second Edition. Philadelphia: Jewish Publication Society, 2000.

Kachline, Clifford. "Kid Camps Mushrooming Across Map," *Sporting News*, August 18, 1962.

Kahn, Roger. *Boys of Summer*. New York: Perennial Library, 1987.

Kahn, Roger. "The Day Bobby Hit the Home Run," *Sports Illustrated*, October 10, 1960, 40–59.

Kahn, Roger. *The Era*. New York: Ticknor & Fields, 1993.

Kahn, Roger. "Sixty Years of Feuding: How the Giants and Dodgers Got That Way," *Sport*, January 1958, 53–62.

Karr, Albert R. "This 50-Year-Old Sees His Idol as Last of the Sports Heroes— How a Home Run Hit in 1951 Has Engaged the Life of One Albert Engelken," *Wall Street Journal*, October 27, 1989.

Kavanaugh, Jack, and Norman Macht. *Uncle Robbie*. Cleveland, Ohio: Society for American Baseball Research, 1999.

Kazin, Alfred. *A Walker in the City*. New York: Harvest/Harcourt Brace Jovanovich, 1951.

Keene, Kerry. *1951: When Giants Played the Game*. Champagne, Ill.: Sports Publishing L.L.C., 2001.

"Kelly's Bat Leads Giants to Victory," *New York Times*, April 9, 1922.

Kempton, Murray. "Back at the Polo Grounds," *Sport*, August 1962, 44–47, 80–81.

Kenney, Jerry. "His Mom's 'Happiest Moment'," *New York Daily News*, October 4, 1951.

Kernan, Kevin. "There Is Spying in Baseball," *New York Post*, February 11, 2001.

Kerouac, Jack. *On the Road*. New York: Penguin Books, 1991.

Kerouac, Jack. "The Origins of the Beat Generation," in *The Portable Jack Kerouac*, edited by Ann Charters. New York: Penguin Books, 1996, 565–72.

Kiernan, Thomas. *The Miracle at Coogan's Bluff*. Boston: Crowell-Collier Publishing Co., 1975.

Kilpatrick, Carroll. "Nixon to Broadcast Crime, Drug Talk," *Washington Post*, October 14, 1972.

King, Joe. "'Braw Bobby at Bat' Smash Hit in Revival," *Sporting News*, June 25, 1952.

King, Joe. "Declared Self to Leo, Won Outfield Post," *Sporting News*, December 14, 1949.

King, Joe. "The Dugout," *Sport*, October 1951, 36–39, 58.

King, Joe. "'53 Dodgers Best of Five Winners, Says Reese," *Sporting News*, September 30, 1953.

King, Joe. "The Flying Scot of the Giants," *Sport*, May 1950, 38–40, 81.

King, Joe. "Giants Park Real Home for Schwabs Since '46," *Sporting News*, October 9, 1957.

King, Joe. "Higbe's Ready—Beats Dodgers, Ties Yankees," *New York World-Telegram*, July 12, 1949.

King, Joe. "'I Saw Danciing in Streets—on Cars and Ledges, Too'," *The All-Sports News*, Section Two of the *Sporting News*, January 2, 1952.

King, Joe. "Life Lovely for Leo 'Neath Harlem Moon," *New York World-Telegram and Sun*, July 21, 1951.

King, Joe. "Mob Scene Marks Polo Grounds Wake," *Sporting News*, October 9, 1957.

King, Joe. "Not That They Were Worried, Mind You, Bums Just Feel Better," *New York World-Telegram and Sun*, August 29, 1951.

King, Joe. "Rookie Catcher Catches Leo's Just Wrath," *New York World-Telegram*, March 30, 1949.

King, Joe. "Thomson Blasts Bad Breaks to Stardom," *Sporting News*, December 14, 1949.

King, Larry. "Bobby Thomson's 'Shot' Still Leaves a Scar," *Diamond Magazine*, June 1993.

Kipling, Rudyard. "If," in *The Collected Poems of Rudyard Kipling*. Ware, England: Wordsworth Editions, 1994.

Kirby, Gene. "The Shot Heard Again," *Sports Heritage*, Vol. 1, No. 5, September/October 1987, 27–31.

Kirsch, George B. *The Creation of American Team Sports*. Chicago: University of Illinois Press, 1989.

"Kittyhawk .400 Hitter Makes With the Flowers," *Post Script* (OH), Vol. 1, No. 13, May 26, 1945.

Klein, Willie. "His Employer Features Yogi in Ads," *Sporting News*, November 21, 1951.

Klein, Willie. "264 HRs, but Thomson Only Hears about THE One," *Newark Star-Ledger*, section 5, September 12, 1971.

Kleinzahler, Augus. "Too Bad about Mrs[sic] Ferri," *London Review of Books*, September 20, 2001.

"Knife & Fork League," *Sporting News*, November 14, 1951.

"Knife & Fork League," *Sporting News*, November 6, 1957.

"Knife & Fork League," *Sporting News*, February 12, 1958.

Knorr, Barbara. "Giant Star Wed in New Dorp to New Jersey Girl," *Staten Island Advance*, December 29, 1952.

Koppett, Leonard. "Mays' Homer in 1st Averts Shutout for New York; Gettel Yields 2 Blows in 7 Innings of Relief," *New York Herald Tribune*, May 29, 1951.

Koppett, Leonard. *The Rise and Fall of the Press Box*. Toronto: Sport Media Publishing, Inc., 2003.

Koppett, Leonard. "20 Years Later: It's Branca at Bat, Thomson Pitching," *New York Times*, August 1, 1971.

Koppett, Leonard. "25 Years Ago, Giants Kindled Flames of 'Miracle'," *New York Times*, August 11, 1976.

Kremenko, Barney. "Durocher Dances While Radio Plays Dodger Dirge," *New York Journal American*, September 28, 1951.

Kremenko, Barney. "Lockman, on Tip From Ott, Pegging with More Accuracy," *Sporting News*, April 5, 1950.

Kremenko, Barney. "Rookie Hurler May Solve Leo's Quest for Stamina," *New York Journal American*, July 20, 1951.

Kremenko, Barney. "Scot Admits Tiff with the Lip After Being Accused of 'Loafing'," *Sporting News*, February 10, 1954.

Kremenko, Barney. "Yvars Spark," *New York Journal American*, July 21, 1951.

Kritzer, Cy. "Biggest Day of '60? When Pittsburgh Went Berserk!," *The All-Sports News*, Section Two of the *Sporting News*, January 4, 1961.

Kritzer, Cy. "Thomson Tale of Flag Homer Makes Hit with Buffalo Fans," *Sporting News*, November 21, 1951.

Lait, Jack, and Lee Mortimer. *New York: Confidential! The Lowdown on Its Bright Life*, 1951 Edition. New York: Dell Publishing Company, Inc., 1948.

Lane, F.C. "How a Big League Score Board is Operated," *Baseball Magazine*, Vol. XXV, No. 1, June 1920, 315–17, 353.

"Lane Fines Franks," *New York World-Telegram*, August 1, 1947.

Laney, Al. "Stunned Crowd, Unable to Cheer at First, Stays in Park for Hour," *New York Herald Tribune*, October 4, 1951.

Lang, Jack. "Second Guessers Blame Stock for Dodgers' Loss," *Long Island Press*, October 2, 1950.

Lang, Jack. "Stengel Claims Homers Didn't Unsteady Page," *Long Island Press*, October 8, 1949.

Lang, Jack. "World's Series Stars Bums to Bushwick Club," *Sporting News*, October 22, 1947.

"Laraine Day, Divorced, to Wed Durocher Today," *Los Angeles Times*, January 21, 1947.

Lardner, John. "The Ways of Shell Shock," *Newsweek*, August 3, 1953.

Lauder, Bill. "New York Held to 4 Scattered Hits by Hiller," *New York Herald Tribune*, July 19, 1951.

Laws of the General Assembly of the Commonwealth of Pennsylvania, Session of 1951. Harrisburg, Pennsylvania.

"Leading Yankee Slugger in 1942 Does It For NTS," *Norfolk* (VA) *Seabag*, September 18, 1943.

Lebovitz, Hal. "Wigwan Enjoys Heap Big Laugh Over Spy Letter," *Sporting News*, September 20, 1961.

Lehn, William A. "Signs: Baseball's Hidden Language." Lecture at SABR conference, Denver, Colorado, July 7, 2003.

Lelands.com. Lelands, Inc. Seaford, New York.

"Leo Durocher Reinstated By Chandler," *Washington Post*, May 4, 1949.

"Leonard's Squad Set for Thursday," *Illinois State Register*, October 15, 1948.

"Leo's Little Giant Takes Warmup Pitches Too," *New York World-Telegram and Sun*, October 3, 1951.

Levi, Primo. *The Drowned and the Saved*. New York: Random House, 1989.

Lewin, Leonard. "Ace in Hole Is Lippy's Trump in Final Hand," *New York Daily Mirror*, October 3, 1951.

Lewin, Leonard. "Giants Call Up Mays," *New York Daily Mirror*, May 25, 1951.

Lewin, Leonard. "Scotch & Champagne!," *New York Daily Mirror*, October 4, 1951.

Lewis, Martin S., et al., eds. *Horace Walpole's Correspondence*, 48 vols. New Haven, Conn.: Yale University Press, 1937–83. Vol. 20: 408.

Lewis, Raphael. "A Piece of Baseball Lore Fades to Black," *Bergen County* (NJ) *Record*, May 13, 1998.

Liberty Broadcasting Network.

Lichtenstein, Grace. "The Home Run That Broke a Girl's Heart," *New York Times*, October 1, 2001.

Lidz, Franz. "The Best Signs of the Times," *Sports Illustrated*, July 19, 1982, 46–47.

Lieb, Frederick G. "Emphasis on Signs Whets Series Fans' Interest in Strategy," *Sporting News*, October 16, 1957.

Light, Jonathan. *The Cultural Encyclopedia of Baseball*. Jefferson, N.C.: McFarland & Company, Inc., 1997.

"Lip Won First Game Toss," *Sporting News*, October 10, 1951.

"List or Manifest of Alien Immigrants for the Commissioner of Immigration." NARA.

"List or Manifest of Alien Passengers for the United States Immigration Officer at Port of Arrival." *S.S. "Caledonia."* National Archives—Northeast Region. New York, New York.

Litsky, Frank. "Frank Scott, 80, Baseball's First Player Agent," *New York Times*, June 30, 1998.

"Lockman Is Honored," *New York Times*, May 6, 1953.

Loh, Jules, and Bill Gilbert. "It's Simple to Catch Signs, Say Spy-Glass Reporters." Unpublished (written for the *Sporting News*).

Longfellow, Henry Wadsworth. "The Landlord's Tale: Paul Revere's Ride," in *Henry Wadsworth Longfellow: Poems and Other Writing*. New York: Library of America, 2000, 362–65.

Longfellow, Samuel, ed. *Life of Henry Wadsworth Longfellow with Extracts from His Journals and Correspondence*, 2 vols. Boston: Ticknor, 1886.

"Lots of Nerve," *Los Angeles Times*, August 14, 1928.

"Lower Flight Has Command," *WIL–CO*, Vol. 2, No. 3, February 24, 1944.

Lowry, Philip J. *Green Cathedrals: The Ultimate Celebration of All 273 Major League and Negro League Ballparks Past and Present.* Reading, Mass.: Addison-Wesley, 1992.

Lupica, Mike. "Distant Replay," *Daily News Magazine*, September 28, 1986, 14–17, 19, 30.

Mabee, Carleton. *The American Leonardo: A Life of Samuel F. B. Morse*, Revised Edition. Fleischmanns, N.Y.: Purpole Mountain Press, Ltd., 2000.

MacDonald, Arthur. "The Psychology of Baseball," *Scientific American*, August 28, 1915.

MacDonald, Jack. "Lip's Style Rubbed Off on Pilot Franks," *Sporting News*, October 24, 1964.

Mack, Gene. "Team of Destiny" [cartoon title], *Boston Daily Globe*, October 4, 1951.

"MacPhail and Ticket Specs Draw in Latest Skirmish," *New York World-Telegram*, June 16, 1942.

Madden, Bill. "Nostalgia Is Key Ingredient," *Sporting News*, February 6, 1984.

"Major Flashes," *Sporting News*, November 3, 1948.

"Major Flashes," *Sporting News*, October 3, 1951.

"Major Flashes," *Sporting News*, December 26, 1956.

"Major League Flashes," *Sporting News*, July 15, 1953.

"Major League Flashes," *Sporting News*, August 28, 1957.

"Majors Meet in Chicago Three Days, Dec. 13–15," *Sporting News*, December 1, 1948.

Mandelbaum, Michael. *The Meaning of Sports: Why Americans Watch Baseball, Football, and Basketball, and What They See When They Do.* New York: PublicAffairs, 2004.

Mann, Arthur. *Baseball Confidential: Secret History of the War Among Chandler, Durocher, MacPhail, and Rickey.* New York: David McKay Company, Inc., 1951.

Marazzi, Rich. "Baseball Rules Corner—How Baseball Teams Steal Signs from Each Other in the Past and Present," *Baseball Digest*, Vol. 60, No. 6, June 2001, 86–88.

Margolies, S. "Bronx Acorn Installation," *Electrical Union World*, February 15, 1950.

Marsh, Irving T., and Edward Ehre, eds. *Best Sports Stories, 1952 Edition: A Panorama of the 1951 Sports Year.* New York: E. P. Dutton & Co., Inc., 1952.

Marsh, Irving. "Thomson's Homer Tops Sport Thrills," *The All-Sports News*, Section Two of the *Sporting News*, January 2, 1952.

Marshall, John, for the *Associated Press*. "Rockies Turn to Environmental Chamber to Keep Balls From Flying out of Coors Field," May 8, 2002.

Marshall, William. *Baseball's Pivotal Era, 1945–1951.* Lexington, Ky.: The University Press of Kentucky, 1999.

Martin, Justin. *Nader: Crusader, Spoiler, Icon.* Cambridge, Mass.: Perseus Publishing, 2002.

Marx, Harpo, with Rowland Barber. *Harpo Speaks . . . About New York.* New York: The Little Bookroom, 2001.

M*A*S*H. Episode #200: "A War for all Seasons." Original airdate December 29, 1980.

Matthewson, Christy. *Pitching in a Pinch, or, Baseball from the Inside.* New York: Grosset & Dunlap, 1912.

Maull, Samuel, for the Associated Press. "Former Dodgers Pitcher Branca Sues Over Baseball Trading Cards," April 29, 2005.

"Mayor Impelliteri Addresses Our Meeting," *Electrical Union World,* November 15, 1950.

Mays, Willie with Low Sahadi. *Say Hey: The Autobiography of Willie Mays.* New York: Simon and Schuster, 1988.

McAuley, Ed. "Frick Shows Punch in Talk at Cleveland," *Sporting News,* November 21, 1951.

McAveety, Frank. Speech at the induction ceremony of the Scottish Sports Hall of Fame. Museum of Scotland, Edinburgh. December 5, 2003.

McCulley, Jim. "Don't Boo Our Bobby, He Won '51 Flag—Leo," *New York Daily News,* August 17, 1952.

McCulley, Jim. "Durocher Re-Signs With Giants for '52," *New York Daily News,* July 21, 1951.

McCulley, Jim. "Giants Bazooka Cards, 13–3," *New York Daily News,* 2nd Ed., July 21, 1950.

McCulley, Jim. "Henry Thompson Goes to Ottawa," *New York Daily News,* July 19, 1951.

McCulley, Jim. "Lippy Fears P4 Time Booby Trap to Flag," *New York Daily News,* September 18, 1951.

McCulley, Jim. "Thomson the Hero, Branca the Goat in Big Payoff," *New York Daily News,* October 4, 1951.

McDonald, Jack. "Marquard Recalls His Record Streak as Giants Say Goodbye," *Sporting News,* October 9, 1957.

McDonald, Jack. "Signal Stealing Is an Overrated Trick," *San Francisco News–Call Bulletin,* March 24, 1962.

McEachern, Claire, ed. *Henry IV, Part I.* New York: Penguin Putnam, 2000.

McFadden, Ed. "Franks Gets Pilot Position in AA," *Salt Lake Tribune,* January 11, 1947.

McFarland, Stephen L. *America's Pursuit of Precision Bombing, 1910–1945.* Washington, D.C.: Smithsonian Institution Press, 1995.

McGowan, Lloyd. "Branca Hit as Warbler in Montreal," *Sporting News,* November 16, 1949.

McGowen, Roscoe. "Another Starter First on Chuck's Man-Wanted List," *Sporting News,* February 18, 1953.

McGowen, Roscoe. "Borowy's 1-Hitter Blanks Brooks, 3–0," *New York Times,* September 1, 1948.

McGowen, Roscoe. "Boston Holds Lead," *New York Times,* August 22, 1948.

McGowen, Roscoe. "Branca, Boy Behemoth of the Brooks," *Baseball Magazine,* Vol. LXXIX, No. 5, October 1947, 365–66.

McGowen, Roscoe. "Branca Is Eager for Another Try," *New York Times,* October 1, 1947.

McGowen, Roscoe. "Branca Sold to Tigers, Wife Sheds Tears as They Tell Dodgers Goodbye," *Sporting News,* July 22, 1953.

McGowen, Roscoe. "Brook 5–5 Tie Ends in 13th at Boston," *New York Times,* May 13, 1951.

McGowen, Roscoe. "Brooks Saddle Workhorse Darnell for Bull-Pen Duty," *Sporting News*, February 20, 1957.

McGowen, Roscoe. "Brooks Win in 10th on Pafko Homer, 6–3," *New York Times*, August 9, 1952.

McGowen, Roscoe. "Campanella's 2 Home Runs Help Vanquish Redlegs, 7–4," *New York Times*, August 9, 1953.

McGowen, Roscoe. "Campy, Snider and Gilliam Good for What Ails Brooks," *Sporting News*, May 13, 1953.

McGowen, Roscoe. "Catcher, Last Holdout, Capitulates After Talk With Rickey—Reese, Stanky and Branca Arrive at Trujillo Camp," *New York Times*, March 3, 1948.

McGowen, Roscoe. "Cox Hits Grand-Slam Four-Bagger as Brooks Overcome Pirates, 11–4," *New York Times*, May 24, 1951.

McGowen, Roscoe. "Davis of Dodgers Trips Phillies, 8–2," *New York Times*, April 18, 1945.

McGowen, Roscoe. "Dodger Pitching Problem Solved When Rain Puts Off Pirate Games," *New York Times*, July 20, 1951.

McGowen, Roscoe. "Dodger Rehiring of Dressen Starts Rumors Spinning," *Sporting News*, November 6, 1957.

McGowen, Roscoe. "Dodgers Bow to Braves in 14th and Fall to Third Place," *New York Times*, August 24, 1948.

McGowen, Roscoe. "Dodgers, Giants Win, End Regular Season in Tie, Start Flag Play-Off Today," *New York Times*, October 1, 1951.

McGowen, Roscoe. "Dodgers' Heads Spin Over $500,000 Tag Put on Spahn," *Sporting News*, December 17, 1952.

McGowen, Roscoe. "Dodgers Stress Luck of Rivals," *New York Times*, October 6, 1941.

McGowen, Roscoe. "Dodgers Top Reds for 9th in Row, 3–0," *New York Times*, May 1, 1940.

McGowen, Roscoe. "Dodgers Trounce Greensboro, 13–3," *New York Times*, April 11, 1951.

McGowen, Roscoe. "Dressen Appointment as Manager to Succeed Burt Shotton Expected," *New York Times*, November 28, 1950.

McGowen, Roscoe. "Erskine Is Victor Over Phils, 10 to 1," *New York Times*, August 18, 1948.

McGowen, Roscoe. "Lead by 5½ Games," *New York Times*, September 14, 1947.

McGowen, Roscoe. "O'Malley Puts Off Talk on Manager," *New York Times*, October 4, 1951.

McGowen, Roscoe. "Reds' Five in Ninth Halt Brooklyn, 5–4," *New York Times*, July 23, 1941.

McGowen, Roscoe. "Setting Improved, Giants Unchanged," *New York Times*, April 21, 1948.

McGowen, Roscoe. "Upsurge in Bums' Hurling Brightens Skies in the West," *Sporting News*, August 27, 1952.

McGowen, Roscoe. "Valdes Triumphs in Relief, 8 to 3," *New York Times*, March 29, 1957.

McGowen, Roscoe. "X-Ray Shows Broken Digit; Campy's Hand Put in Cast," *Sporting News*, July 30, 1952.

McGregory, Paul M. *The Baseball Player: An Economic Study.* Washington, D.C.: Public Affairs Press, 1956.

McHarry, Charles, and Henry Lee. "Mystery Bullet Kills Fan at Giants Game," *New York Daily News*, July 5, 1950.

Meany, Tom. "The Mystery Man," *New York World-Telegram*, Dec. 12, 1945.

Meeropol, Michael, ed. *The Rosenberg Letters: A Complete Edition of the Prison Correspondence of Julius and Ethel Rosenberg.* New York: Garland Publishing, Inc., 1994.

"Meet the Whirlwinds," *Daily Argus* (NY), November 25, 1947.

Melamed, Daniel R., Editor. "Johann Ludwig Back: Motets," *Embellishments: A Newsletter About Recent Researches*, Summer 2001.

Melville, Herman. *Moby-Dick.* New York: Barnes & Noble Classics, 2003.

Mendelson, Edward, ed. *W. H. Auden: Selected Poems.* New Edition. New York: Vintage, 1979.

Mentus, Ron. "Sign Language: Baseball's Silent Strategy Code," *Baseball Digest*, September 1984, 84–86.

"Mercury at 90 Sets a Second Fall Heat Mark," *New York Herald Tribune*, October 6, 1941.

"Mexican Offers Rejected by Four Dodgers," *New York World-Telegram*, March 27, 1946.

"Midget Story Given New Twist by Veeck," *Sporting News*, August 29, 1951.

"Mike and the Mad Dog," WFAN radio show. February 1, 2001.

Miller, Lou. "A Guy Named Schenz Aids Giant Drive, Too," *New York World-Telegram and Sun*, October 2, 1951.

Miller, Lou. "Yankees Can't Awe Thomson," *New York World-Telegram and Sun*, October 4, 1951.

Miller, Lou. "Yvars, Branca Westchester Finalists," *New York World-Telegram*, June 24, 1942.

Millstein, Gilbert. "'Natural Boy' of the Giants," *New York Times*, July 11, 1954.

Millus, Donald. *The Ebbets Field Keyhole. ww2.coastal.edu/millus/.* Self-published.

Minter, Jim. "Risk Is No Surprise to Sportswriters," *Atlanta Journal–Constitution*, June 22, 2000.

Mitchell, Bob. *Once Upon a Fastball.* New York: Kensington Publishing Corp, 2008.

Mitchell, Jerry. "Most Incredible Break in Baseball!" *New York Post*, Oct. 6, 1941.

Mitton, Simon. *Conflict in the Cosmos: Fred Hoyle's Life in Science.* Washington, D.C.: Joseph Henry Press, 2005.

Mockler, Stan. "Dyer Expects Playoff Series to Go the Limit," *Long Island Press*, October 1, 1946.

Molotsky, Irvin. "F.B.I. Releases its Sinatra File, with Tidbits Old and New," *New York Times*, December 9, 1998.

Molter, Harry. *Famous Athletes of Today.* Boston: L.C. Page, 1953.

Monks of Glenstal Abbey. *The Glenstal Book of Prayer: A Benedictine Prayer Book.* Collegeville, Minn.: The Liturgical Press, 2001.

Montgomery, Ruth. "D.C. Wash," *New York Daily News*, October 6, 1951.

Mooney, John. "'Franks Park' Is His No. 1 Honor," *Salt Lake Tribune*, July 18, 1989.

Moran, Malcolm. "Reliving the Past With a Purpose," *New York Times*, February 7, 1987.

The Moravian Cemetery. Staten Island, New York.

"More Yankees Sail," *New York Times*, March 1, 1913.

"Most Famous Homer Hit 20 Years Ago Today," *Times Recorder* (OH), October 3, 1971.

Mount Ararat Cemetery records. North Lindenhurst, New York.

"Mount Vernon Set to Honor Branca, Karl Tomorrow," *Daily Argus* (NY), August 12, 1947.

Mozley, Dana. "Barber's Vocals Shave Newcombe Too Close," *New York Daily News*, September 3, 1951.

Mozley, Dana. "Mize Belted One He Wasn't Supposed to Hit," *New York Daily News*, October 8, 1949.

"Mrs. Coogan Dies; Large Landholder," *New York Times*, December 19, 1947.

"Mueller 'Pops' Into Record Book on Homer in 8th," *New York Daily Mirror*, September 3, 1951.

Munsingwear, Inc. Minneapolis, Minnesota.

Munzel, Edgar. "Base-Burglar Minnie Steals How in 90-Second Speech," *Sporting News*, January 23, 1952.

Murray, Arch, "Far-Turn Switch Turns Bobby Into Star," *Sporting News*, September 19, 1951.

Murray, Arch. "Franks 'Revival' Revives Giants," *New York Post*, August 29, 1949.

Murray, Arch. "Giants Beat Cubs, 5–2; Westrum Suspended," *New York Post*, September 16, 1951.

Murray, Arch. "Giants Clubhouse Man Gets the Rap for Upsetting Spencer," *New York Post*, July 19, 1951.

Murray, Arch. "Giants in Huddle Over Mound Help," *Sporting News*, October 15, 1952.

Murray, Arch. "Hollywood Couldn't Have Done It Better for Jackie," *New York Post*, October 1, 1951.

Murray, Arch. "Irvin Bat Thunder Backs Warning of Giants' Flagstorm," *Sporting News*, July 22, 1953.

Murray, Arch. "Lip Takes Two in the Chin; Army Won't Release Mays, Injury Sidelines Thomson," *Sporting News*, March 25, 1953.

Murray, Arch. "Rain Gives Lippy Chance to Reassemble Hill Staff," *New York Post*, July 20, 1951.

Murray, Arch. "Slugger 'May B Working Out by July': Thomson Shifted to Outfield to Plug Gap," *Sporting News*, April 9, 1952.

Murray, Arch. "Twenty-One at Twenty-One," *Baseball Digest*, Vol. 7, No. 1, January 1948, 57–63.

Mushnick, Phil. "A Few Giant Tales," *New York Post*, August 29, 1990.

Musial, Stan. "Clem's Curve Caught Stan's Eye," *New York World-Telegram and Sun*, October 3, 1951.

"Musial Tops Poll for 2nd Year in Row," *Sporting News*, July 9, 1952.

"Muskogee Tramples Locals in One Big Inning to Win, 13–3," *Independence* (KS) *Daily Reporter*, April 29, 1930.

Mutual Broadcasting System.

"Napp Tells of Umps' Duties," *Sporting News*, November 14, 1951.

Nash, Ogden. *You Can't Get There From Here*. Boston: Little, Brown and Company, 1957.

Nathan, David. *The McFarland Baseball Quotations Dictionary*. Jefferson, N.C.: McFarland & Company, Inc., 2000.

National Baseball Hall of Fame Library. Cooperstown, New York.

"The National Game," *Washington Post*, May 17, 1885.

National Personnel Records Center and New York State Archives.

National Scouting Museum. Irving, Texas.

"Nats Get Bid from Baseball Guild Without Enthusiasm," *Washington Post*, May 9, 1946.

NBC, "Former Dodger Ace Ralph Branca Pitches Right Answers to Set Record for Consecutive Victories on 'Concentration'," press release, August 22, 1961.

"A New Baseball Field," *New York Times*, June 22, 1889.

Newcombe, Jack. "Bobby Thomson: The Unwilling Hero," *Sport*, May 1955, 49–57.

"The New Polo Grounds," *Chicago Tribune*, June 30, 1889.

"News and Comment," *Sporting Life*, Vol. 26, No. 18, January 25, 1896.

"News and Comment," *Sporting Life*, Vol. 26, No. 19, February 1, 1896.

"News Notes/Note from Santa Ana," *WIL–CO*, Vol. 2, No. 4, March 16, 1944.

New York City Classified Telephone Directory. New York Telephone Company, November 1950.

New York City Department of Records and Information Services. New York, New York.

New York Department of Vital Statistics. New York, New York.

"The New York City Television Audience: Oct. 1–8, 1951." American Research Bureau, Inc., Washington, D.C.

"New York Records," *New York Times*, October 4, 1951.

"Nickname of Giants," letters to the sports editor, *New York Times*, February 22, 1936.

Niebuhr, Reinhold. *The Book of a Thousand Prayers*, Second Edition. Compiled by Angela Ashwin. Grand Rapids, Mich.: Zondervan, 2002.

Niebuhr, Reinhold. *The Irony of American History*. New York: Charles Scribner's Sons, 1952.

"Night Ball Dangers Steer Giants Away," *Sporting News*, December 27, 1934.

"Night Ball Is Assured for New York," *Washington Post*, January 25, 1944.

"Night Baseball," *Sporting News*, January 16, 1930.

"9000 Hear Graham Tell of Trinity," *San Francisco Chronicle*, June 4, 1958.

1951 Daily Racing Forum Chart Book. New York, New York, January 1952. Chart #43816.

"N.L. Pace-Setters Picked by Scribes," *Sporting News*, March 30, 1955.

"No Baseball on the Polo Grounds," *New York Times*, March 28, 1889.

Norr, R. "Cancer by the Dozen," *Reader's Digest*, December 1952, 7–8.

"North Wind Moves Cadet Sport Program Indoors," *WIL–CO*, Vol. 2, No. 3, October 28, 1943.

"N.Y.U. Routs Stevens, 9–0," *New York Times*, April 27, 1944.

"N.Y.U. Seeks Branca as Coach," *New York Times*, May 19, 1961.

Oates, Bob. "Talking to Bobby Thomson," *Los Angeles Examiner*, Section 1, Part D, July 26, 1959.

O'Connell, T. S. "The Man Who Fired 'The Shot Heard Round the World' Had an All-Star Career That Seems Largely Overlooked," *Sports Collectors Digest*, July 1, 1994, 161–64.

O'Connor, Ian. "Branca-Thomson Bond as Strong as in '51," *USA Today*, September 28, 2001.

Office of the Registar. New York University, School of Education. New York, New York.

"Officers' Pay, Allowance, and Mileage Voucher." War Department. October 21, 1945. NARA.

The Official National Museum of the United States Air Force. Wright-Patterson Air Force Base, Ohio.

"Official 1951 National League Bat Records," *Sporting News*, December 19, 1951.

Ogle, Jim. "Thomson's HR Nails Flag, 5–4," *Newark* (NJ) *Star-Ledger*, October 4, 1951.

Okrent, Daniel. "The Boys of Spring," *New York Times Book Review*, April 6, 1986.

"Old Highlanders Used Fence-Hole Signaler," *Sporting News*, August 9, 1950.

"Old and New Illustrations of N.Y.–Brooklyn Rivalry," *Sporting News*, May 14, 1952.

Olderman, Murray. "Bobby Thomson Remembers," *Burlington* (NC) *Times-News*, October 6, 1971.

Oliver, Frank. "Don't Mention His Name in Brooklyn," *Scottish Daily Record* (Glasgow, Scotland), October 5, 1951.

O'Meara, Bay. "The Passing Sport Show," *Montreal Star*, October 4, 1951.

O'Neill, Eugene. *The Emperor Jones.* New York: Vintage Books, 1972.

"On Television This Week," *New York Times*, October 7, 1951.

"One Game for Brooklyn," *New York Times*, October 19, 1889.

"1,300 See Whirlwinds Top Gothams," *Daily Argus* (NY), November 29, 1947.

"1,200 Youngsters State Baseball Studies Here," *New York Times*, November 6, 1951.

"Only Pen on Playing Field," *Sporting News*, May 16, 1956.

"The Orange Above the Blue," *New York Times*, December 1, 1893.

O'Regan, Paddy. "Flying Scot Given All-Day Fling of Festivities on Staten Island," *Sporting News*, December 19, 1951.

Orr, Jack. "Danny Sees His Deal as 'Luck of Irish'," *Sporting News*, January 20, 1954.

Orr, Jack. "The Unpredictable Bobby Thomson," *Sport*, June 1953, 20–21, 60–61.

Ostler, Scott. "How Willie Mays 'Called the Shots' for Giants," *Baseball Digest*, July 1989, 69–71.

O'Toole, Thomas. "Giants Expect 1,000% Profits Rise in Shift to San Francisco," *Wall Street Journal*, August 8, 1957.

Overfield, Joe. "Small Wonders," *Bisongram*, April 1991, 26–27.

Pacini, Le. "Remembering Gehrig, Willie and the Babe," *California Living Magazine*, April 19, 1981, 26–30.

Pais, Abraham. *A Tale of Two Continents: The Life of a Physicist in a Turbulent World*. Princeton, N.J.: Princeton University Press, 1997.

Palmer, George Herbert. *The English Works of George Herbert, Newly Arranged and Annotated and Considered in Relation to His Life*, Vol. 2. Boston; Houghton Mifflin, 1905.

Parker, Dan. "Durocher Gambles on Pitching and Loses," *New York Daily Mirror, Early Edition*, October 3, 1951.

Parrott, Harold. "Stoneham Buries Ax—In McPhail's Neck," *Brooklyn Eagle*, "Beat the Giants" supplemental section, July 8, 1939.

"Pasquel Fortune of $60,000,000 Supports Mexican Baseball Fight," *New York Times*, April 5, 1946.

Patterson, Arthur E. "Giants' Lighting System Will Be Nation's Best for Night Baseball," *New York Herald Tribune*, November 15, 1939.

"Pennsylvania Law Ends 7 P.M. Baseball Curfew," *New York Times*, July 31, 1959.

Pepper, Al. *Mendoza's Heroes: Fifty Batters Below .200*. Clifton, Va.: Pocol Press, 2002.

"Personnel Qualifications Questionnaire." November 25, 1944. NARA.

Petrarca, Francesco. *Il Bucolicum Carmen*. Edited by Tonino T. Matucci. Pisa: Giardini, 1970.

Pfeffer, N. Fred. *Scientific Ball*. Chicago: N. Fred Pfeffer, Publisher, 1889.

"Philip Arbiter," *Amityville Record*, October 11, 1951.

Phillips, Gene. "Six Curtis Players Make First Team; Holder and Peterson Named Pitchers," *Staten Island Advance*, June 10, 1941.

"Physical Examination for Flying," October 11, 1944. NARA.

Piersall, Jimmy. "How the Home Team Cheats," *Baseball Monthly*, May 1962, 21–23, 61–62.

Pietrusza, David. *Lights On!: The Wild Century-Long Saga of Night Baseball*. Lanham, Md.: Scarecrow Press, Inc., 1997.

"Pitcher Al Widmar to Manage Tulsa in 1956," *Chicago Daily Tribune*, September 29, 1955.

"Players Are Named for Tour of Pacific," *New York Times*, November 16, 1945.

"Players on Arthur Murray TV," *Sporting News*, May 6, 1953.

"Players Who Jumped Contracts Ruled Automatically Suspended," *New York Times*, April 17, 1946.

"Playoff Rivals Branca and Thomson Meet Again at Dinner for Sal Yvars," *Sporting News*, November 28, 1951.

"Plea for Church Revival Ends Graham's Crusade," *San Francisco Chronicle*, June 16, 1958.

Plimpton, George. *The Cooperstown Symposium on Baseball and American Culture, 2001*. Editor William M. Simons. Series editor Alvin L. Hall. Jefferson, N.C.: McFarland & Company, Inc., 2002.

Plimpton, George, ed. *Home Run*. Orlando, Fl.: Harcourt, Inc., 2001.

Podvig, Pavel, ed. *Russian Strategic Nuclear Forces*. Cambridge, Mass.: MIT Press, 2001.

Pollack, Chana, and Myra Mniewski, trans. "Should Children Play Baseball?" *Jewish Daily Forward*, August 6, 1903.

"Polo Grounds Ready," *New York Times*, June 25, 1911.

"Polo Grounds Swept by Fire," *New York Times*, April 14, 1911.

"Polo Grounds Transferred," *New York Times*, December 29, 1897.

"Polo Grounds Value Slashed," *New York Sun*, December 12, 1940.

"Posedel in New Post," *New York Times*, November 6, 1958.

Potter, Stephen. *The Theory and Practice of Gamesmanship: or, The Art of Winning Games Without Actually Cheating*. Wakefield, R.I.: Moyer Bell, 1947.

Povich, Shirley. "Sneaky A's Job Bench," *Washington Post*, October 20, 1972.

Povich, Shirley. "This Morning," *Washington Post*, April 18, 1948.

Povich, Shirley. "This Morning with Shirley Povich," *Washington Post*, January 7, 1952.

Povich, Shirley. "This Morning with Shirley Povich," *Washington Post*, February 5, 1952.

Povich, Shirley. "This Morning with Shirley Povich," *Washington Post*, February 24, 1952.

Powers, Jimmy. "The Powerhouse," *New York Daily News*, March 4, 1946.

Powers, Jimmy. "The Powerhouse," *New York Daily News*, March 12, 1946.

Powers, Jimmy. "The Powerhouse," *New York Daily News*, September 23, 1947.

Powers, Jimmy. "The Powerhouse," *New York Daily News*, October 8, 1951.

"Pre-Flight Cadets Arrive at Teachers College Today," *St. Cloud* (MN) *Daily Times*, March 1, 1943.

Prince, Carl E. *Brooklyn's Dodgers: The Bums, The Borough, and the Best of Baseball 1947–1957*. New York: Oxford University Press, 1996.

Purinton, Royce D. "Baseball Technique," *American Physical Education Review*, Vol. 12, No. 1, June 1907, 132–43.

Purinton, Royce D. "Baseball Technique," *American Physical Education Review*, Vol. 8, issue 4, April 1908, 209–13.

"Radio Schedule/ F E N Korea," *Pacific Stars & Stripes*, October 3, 1951.

"Ralph, Boy, Forget It," *Sports Illustrated*, July 23, 1962.

"Ralph Branca of Dodgers Opens Insurance Firm Here," *Daily Argus* (NY), March 7, 1953.

"Ralph Branca Fined $200 for Heckling," *Los Angeles Times*, October 9, 1952.

"Ralph Branca, Out of Game for Year, Back with Brooks," *Sporting News*, September 12, 1956.

"Ralph Calls Quits to Career," *Sporting News*, April 10, 1957.

"Ralphie's Gopher Stuns His Fiancee," *New York Daily News*, October 4, 1951.

Rampersad, Arnold, ed. *Collected Works of Langston Hughes: The Poems 1951–1967*, Vol. 3. Columbia, Mo.: University of Missouri Press, 2001.

"Real Estate—Friday, April 30," *New York Times*, May 1, 1858.

"Recorded Real Estate Transfers," *New York Times*, April 1, 1889.

"Recorded Real Estate Transfers," *New York Times*, December 24, 1897.

Red and Black. Yearbook of Boys High. Brooklyn, New York, 1914.

"Red Cross Golf," *New York Times*, August 1, 1993.

"Red Sox–Giants Series Forecast in Poll of Writers," *Sporting News*, April 18, 1951.

"The Referee," *Chicago Daily Tribune*, April 14, 1907.

"Register of Births." Glasgow District, Scotland.

Remnick, David. "Exile on Main," *New Yorker*, September 15, 1997. 68–84.

Rennie, Rud. "Cardinals Defeat Dodgers, 4–2, in Opener of Pennant Play-Off," *New York Herald Tribune*, October 2, 1946.

Rennie, Rud. "Durocher Puts Thomson on 3d After Thompson Disappoints," *New York Herald Tribune*, July 20, 1951.

Rennie, Rud. "Yankees Beat Dodgers, 5–3, Before 73,365," *New York Herald Tribune*, October 1, 1947.

Renzhofer, Martin. "Baseball Was His Business," *Salt Lake Tribune*, February 18, 1996.

"Report of the Subcommittee on Study of Monopoly Power of the Committee on the Judiciary Pursuant to H. R. 95," Organized Baseball. Union Calendar No. 632. May 27, 1952.

"Reports of Trades Multiply as June 15 Deadline Nears," *Sporting News*, June 10, 1953.

Retrosheet. Newark, Delaware.

Revised Constitution, By-Laws and Rules of the Eagle Ball Club, Adopted 1854. New York: Oliver & Brother/Steam Job Printers, 1854.

Reynolds, Michael. *Hemingway: An Annotated Chronology.* Detroit, Mich.: Omnigraphics, Inc. 1991.

Reynolds, Quentin. *I, Willie Sutton.* New York: Farrar, Straus, and Young, 1953.

Rheingold advertisement. New York, New York. Appeared in *New York Times*, June 30, 1952.

Rice, Grantland. "End of Famous 53 Days," *New York Daily Mirror*, October 4, 1951.

Rice, Grantland. "Notre Dame's Cyclone Beats Army, 13–7," *New York Herald Tribune*, October 19, 1924.

Richman, Milton. "Durocher and Combs Best Signal Stealers," *New York Post*, August 27, 1950.

Richman, Milton. "Giant Manager Fears Delay May Hurt," *Salt Lake Tribune*, October 8, 1951.

Rickey, Branch. "Goodbye to Some Old Baseball Ideas," *Life*, August 2, 1954, 78–83, 89.

"Righty Swinger Bobby Timed at 3.3 as Bunter," *Sporting News*, February 4, 1953.

Riker, James. *Harlem: Its Origins and Early Annals.* New York: 1881. Printed for the author.

"Rivals Dance to Dodger Music—Fans Will, Too," *Sporting News*, June 22, 1949.

"Robbie Lauds Dyer, Branca for Helping Him as Rookie," *Sporting News*, February 11, 1953.

Roberts, Ssgt. Mike, HQ AFOSI. "A Boy Among Giants," *Airman Magazine*, October 1977, Vol. XXI, No. 10, 37–39.

Robinson, Orlo. "'I Was Set for Pitch,' Gloats Thomson," *Newark Star-Ledger*, October 4, 1951.

Robinson, Ray. *The Home Run Heard 'Round the World.* New York: Harper-Collins, 1991.

Robinson, Ray. *Pennants & Pinstripes.* New York: Viking Studio, 2002.

"Robinson-for-Thomson Deal Only a Rumor in Brooklyn," *Sporting News,* November 25, 1953.

"Rocks Crush Tobs 11–4 Series Finals," *Wilson* (NC) *Daily Times,* September 12, 1942.

Roeder, Bill. "Fans Keep Eye on Giants and Ear on Dodgers," *Sporting News,* September 5, 1951.

Roeder, Bill. "One-Way Thomson Needs New Road Map," *New York World-Telegram,* September 9, 1950.

Roeder, Bill. "Reese Thigh Taped and Sprayed, He's Got the Sympathy Aches," *New York World-Telegram and Sun,* October 3, 1951.

Roeder, Bill. "The Shot Heard 'Round the World." in *Phillies Present Famous Sports Moments.* New York: Associated Features, 1959, 50–52.

Roeder, Bill. "Straying Flock Led Back to Promised Land by Preacher," *New York Daily Mirror,* September 15, 1951.

"Rogers Knows Naught," *Philadelphia Inquirer,* October 1, 1900.

Rogers, Thomas. "His Favorite Year" ("World Series Specials"), *New York Times,* October 20, 1986.

Rosen, Charley. *Scandals of '51: How the Gamblers Almost Killed College Basketball.* New York: Seven Stories Press, 1999.

Rosenfeld, Harvey. *The Great Chase: The Dodgers-Giants Pennant Race of 1951.* Jefferson, N.C.: McFaland & Company, Inc., 1992.

Rosenthal, Harold. "Branca Scores with Thomson on Big Hit at Writers' Dinner," *New York Herald Tribune,* February 4, 1952.

Rosenthal, Harold. "Hearn Chalks Up 14th Victory As He Holds Brooklyn to 6 Hits," *New York Herald Tribune,* September 3, 1951.

Rosenthal, Harold. "O'Malley Promises to Make Statement After World Series," *New York Herald Tribune,* October 4, 1951.

Roth, Allan. "Statistics Tell the Story," *Sport,* June 1954.

Roth, Philip. *The Counterlife.* New York: Vintage Books, 1996.

Rudd, Irving, and Stan Fischler. *The Sporting Life: The Duke and Jackie, Pee Wee, Razor Phil, Ali, Mushky Jackson, and Me.* New York: St. Martin's Press, 1990.

Ruhl, Oscar. "From the Ruhl Book," *Sporting News,* December 1, 1948.

Ruhl, Oscar. "From the Ruhl Book," *Sporting News,* January 11, 1950.

Ruhl, Oscar. "From the Ruhl Book," *Sporting News,* February 20, 1952.

Ruhl, Oscar. "From the Ruhl Book," *Sporting News,* April 30, 1952.

Ruhl, Oscar. "From the Ruhl Book," *Sporting News,* February 4, 1953.

Ruhl, Oscar. "From the Ruhl Book," *Sporting News,* May 6, 1953.

Russell, Fred. "I'd Pick Branca Again," *Baseball Digest,* May 1952, 63–64.

"Russ Hodges . . . Voice of the Giants," *Look Magazine,* Vol. 15, June 19, 1951.

Rutler, Rev. George W. Sermon at The Church of Our Saviour. New York, New York.

Sahlins, Marshall David. *Apologies to Thucydides.* Chicago: The University of Chicago Press, 2004.

Saint, Jeffrey, and John Stuart. *Twilight Teams.* Somerville, N.J.: Sark Publishing, 2000.

"Sal Receives Bond, Gifts at Dinner," *Reporter Dispatch,* November 19, 1951.

"Sal Yvars' Trade to Chisox Botched," *Washington Post,* May 7, 1952.

Salinger, J. D. *The Catcher in the Rye.* Boston: Little, Brown and Company, 1991.

Sanborn, I. E. "Local Fans Must Be Patient," *Chicago Daily Tribune*, January 2, 1910.

Sangree, Allan. "No More War in Baseball, Part II," *Baseball Magazine*, Vol. VII, No. 5, September 1911, 21–29.

Sangree, Allan. "The Strategy of the Ball Field," *Everybody's Magazine*, October 1906, 509–16.

Santa Maria, Michael, and James Costello. *In the Shadows of the Diamond: Hard Times in the National Pastime.* Dubuque, Iowa: The Elysian Fields Press, 1992.

Sante, Luc. "Between Hell and History," *New York Review of Books*, November 6, 1997.

Sargent, Jim. "Bobby Thomson, Giant Hero," *Oldtyme Baseball News*, Vol. 7, Issue 6.

Saussure, Ferdinand de, Charles Bally, and Albert Sechehaye, eds. Roy Harris, trans. *The Course in General Linguistics.* London: Duckworth, 1983.

"Schenz Shuffle Leaves 26 Bums, One Still to Go," *New York World-Telegram*, May 17, 1949.

"Schenz Takes Hitting Honors," *Norfolk* (VA) *Seabag*, September 16, 1944.

Schiff, Bennett. "Brooklyn Kids Weep for Fallen Idols," *New York Post*, October 4, 1951.

Schmid, Randolph E. for the *Associated Press.* "Post Office Announces Stamps to Commemorate the '50s," April 1, 1998.

Schneider, Daniel B. "F.Y.I.," *New York Times*, section 13, June 22, 1997.

"Schwartz Is Hero as Hartford Opens by Beating Bears," *Hartford* (CT) *Courant*, April 23, 1925.

"Sentence Basket Fixer Sollazzo, Players, Today," *Chicago Daily Tribune*, November 15, 1951.

"'Shadow Baseball' Appeals to Fans; Cards Nip Sox 20–11," *Johnson City* (TN) *Press Chronicle*, October 19, 1948.

Shales, Tom. "Replay on Mr. Television," *Washington Post*, November 11, 1974.

"Sharkey Makes It Baseball Week in New York," *New York Daily Mirror*, October 2, 1951.

Sheehan, Joseph M. "Giants Defeat Dodgers Again, Cut Lead to 9½ Games; Yankees Win," *New York Times*, August 17, 1951.

Sheehan, Joseph M. "Mize Drives No. 50 as Giants Triumph Over Phillies, 5–3," *New York Times*, September 21, 1947.

Sheehan, Joseph M. "Triple Play Helps," *New York Times*, September 2, 1951.

The Shot Heard Round the World, HBO, July 11, 2001.

Siegel, Arthur. "Tigers Started Stealing Signs with Binoculars," *Boston Traveler*, August 23, 1950.

"Signals in Baseball," *Youth's Companion*, May 5, 1910.

"Silverra Content as Stand-In," *Sporting News*, December 8, 1954.

Simmons, Harry. "Heath's Four-Run Homer Completes Majors' 'Firsts'," *Sporting News*, May 7, 1947.

Simon, George T. (lyrics) and Joe Ricardel (music). "The Brooklyn Dodgers Jump." Bars Music Publishing Corp. New York, New York. 1949.

Simons, William M., ed. *The Cooperstown Symposium on Baseball and American Culture, 2001*. Jefferson, N.C.: McFarland & Company, Inc., 2002.

The Simpsons. Episode #18: "Dancin' Homer." Original airdate November 8, 1990.

Sinclair, Ed. "Winners Kiss, Hug Mates in Big Mob Scene," *New York Herald Tribune*, October 4, 1951.

Sing Sing Correctional Facility. New York State Department of Correctional Services.

Sinins, Lee. *The Complete Baseball Encyclopedia*. (computer software) Sabermetric Baseball Encyclopedia. Originally released in 2000.

"Sisler's Nine Downs Locals by 12–1 Count," *Illinois State Register*, October 15, 1948.

"The Sixth Rule of the Game," *Brooklyn Eagle*, July 13, 1864.

"69,000,000 Heard Series by Radio, Mutual Reports," *Sporting News*, October 31, 1951.

Skwar, Don. "Thomson and Branca: 25 Years Later," *Daily Record*, October 3, 1976.

Sloane, Michael. "Miracle at Coogan's Bluff." Unpublished screenplay.

Smith, Art. "There Is No Joy in Flatbush," *Daily News*, October 4, 1951.

Smith, Curt. *Voices of the Game*, Revised Edition. New York: Simon & Schuster, 1982.

Smith, Jack. "Cards Shade Dodgers, 2–1, on Kurowski's HR," *New York Daily News*, August 15, 1945.

Smith, Jack. "Gumbert Faces Posedel in First PG Night Game," *New York Daily News*, May 24, 1940.

Smith, Ken. "Belt Newcombe, Cut Deficit to 5; Mueller Poles 2, Ties Record," *New York Daily Mirror*, September 3, 1951.

Smith, Ken. "Big Contrast Between Giant '37 Champs, '51 Runners-Up," *Sporting News*, September 26, 1951.

Smith, Ken. "Bob Thomson's Blows Bracing Giant Thunder," *Sporting News*, June 18, 1947.

Smith, Ken. "Bucs Top Giants, 7–6, in 12, Kayo Sal in 7th," *New York Daily Mirror*, July 16, 1951.

Smith, Ken. "Combination 'Feller and Ruth,' Still in Army, Bought by Giants," *Sporting News*, December 20, 1945.

Smith, Ken. "Giants Blast Dodgers, 15–9; Ott, Weintraub Wallop Two," *New York Daily Mirror*, June 13, 1944.

Smith, Ken. "Giants Grab 2nd, 4–2 After Bowing to Reds' Wehmeier in Opener," *New York Daily Mirror*, August 29, 1949.

Smith, Ken. "Giants Land Schenz, 2d Sacker, from Bucs," *New York Daily Mirror*, July 1, 1951.

Smith, Ken. "Giants Uncover Star at Third in Thomson," *Sporting News*, August 15, 1951.

Smith, Ken. "Giants Win, 7–2; Hearn's 15th," *New York Daily Mirror*, September 15, 1951.

Smith, Ken. "Long-Hitting Giants Get Short Pitching," *Sporting News*, July 25, 1951.

Smith, Ken. "Outfielder Has Scar Tissue Removed from Ankle, Operations Re-Sewn," *Sporting News*, December 8, 1948.

Smith, Lou. "Redlegs Soft Touch for Giants of Lippy," *Cincinnati Enquirer*, July 21, 1951.

Smith, Red. "Banca [sic] Still Smiles and Even Can Sing," *Washington Post*, February 5, 1952.

Smith, Red. "Last Chapter," *New York Herald Tribune*, October 4, 1951.

Smith, Red. "On the Profit Side," *New York Herald Tribune*, August 28, 1951.

Smith, Red. "View of Sport," *New York Herald Tribune*, Section 3, August 12, 1951.

Smith, Red. "You're No Thief Stealing Signs," *New York Herald Tribune*, August 6, 1950.

Snider, Duke, and Bill Gilbert. *The Duke of Flatbush*. New York: Citadel Press, 2002.

Snyder, Clyde, "Lagunan Still Thrills to Baseball's Anthem," *Los Angeles Times*, April 13, 1958.

Sochineniia, 2 vols. Moscow: Khudozh, 1990.

Society for American Baseball Research. Cleveland, Ohio.

"Solarium Club Formed by PG Fans," *Grandstand Manager*, April 1951, 1, 7.

"Soldiers at Front Hear World Series," *Los Angeles Times*, October 8, 1951.

"Some Marvels of Pitching," *Washington Post*, June 12, 1910.

Southey, Robert. *The Life of Nelson*. New York: Maynard, Merrill, & Company, 1896.

Spalding's Official Base Ball Guide (1884 season). Chicago: A.G. Spalding and Bros., 1884.

Spalding's Official Base Ball Guide (1889 season). Chicago: A.G. Spalding and Bros., 1889.

Spalding's Official Base Ball Guide (1893 season). Chicago: A.G. Spalding and Bros., 1893.

Spalding's Official Base Ball Guide (1895 season). New York: American Sports Publishing Company, 1895.

Spalding's Official Base Ball Guide (1915 season). New York: American Sports Publishing Company, 1915.

Spalding's Official Base Ball Guide (1920 season). New York: American Sports Publishing Company, 1920.

"Spectaculars Find Day Is a Sad One," *New York Times*, October 2, 1946.

Spink, Alfred H. *The National Game*, 2nd Edition. St. Louis, Mo.: The National Game Publishing Company, 1911.

Spink, J.G. Taylor. "Barnstorming Big Mistake," *Sporting News*, January 16, 1952.

Spink, J.G. Taylor, Compiler. *Baseball Guide and Record Book 1951*. St. Louis: Charles C. Spink & Son, 1951.

Spink, J.G. Taylor, Compiler. *Baseball Register*. St. Louis: Charles C. Spink & Son, Publishers, 1951.

Spink, J.G. Taylor. "Big John Keeps Swinging and Grinning," *Sporting News*, September 10, 1947.

Spink, J.G. Taylor. "Boos Turned to 'Buck-Ups' for Branca," *Sporting News*, January 30, 1952.

Spink, J.G. Taylor. "Cubs Upsurge Tribute to Wid," *Sporting News*, June 11, 1952.

Spink, J.G. Taylor. "Lives Up to B.B. Name," *Sporting News*, July 3, 1946.

Spink, J.G. Taylor. "Mail Keeps Piling Up for Thomson," *Sporting News*, January 16, 1952.

Spink, J.G. Taylor. "Miss T? She's Visiting Cheryl Elizabeth," *Sporting News*, May 23, 1956.

Spoelstra, Watson. "Bengals Back in the Black as '53 Ends in Bright Note," *Sporting News*, December 30, 1953.

Spoelstra, Watson. "Weik Sent to Little Rock; Branca Released," *Sporting News*, July 21, 1954.

"Sport," *Time*, September 23, 1946, 74–76.

Sports Night. Episode #33: "The Giants Win the Pennant, The Giants Win the Pennant." Original airdate January 11, 2000.

"Sports Tonight," CNN. January 31, 2001.

Squier, Hal J. "On the Sport Trail with Hal J. Squier," *Staten Island Advance*, January 8, 1952.

"Stallings Out, Chase In," *New York Sun*, September 22, 1910.

"Standards Upset Forum 61–60 in a Thriller," *Daily Argus* (NY), February 14, 1948.

"Stanky Opens Free School," *Sporting News*, January 28, 1948.

Staten Island Ferry, New York City Department of Transportation. New York, New York.

"Staten Island Joy at Record Heights," *New York Times*, October 4, 1951.

Staten Island Museum. Staten Island, New York.

The Statue of Liberty–Ellis Island Foundation, Inc. *www.ellisisland.org*.

Steiger, Gus. "Dressen's Squard Won 17 and Lost Only 5 Games on Tour," *Sporting News*, January 31, 1946.

Steiger, Gus. "Maglie vs. Newcombe in Flag Fray," *New York Daily Mirror*, October 3, 1951.

Stephan, C. David. "Allan Roth's True Discovery of Sabermetrics Revealed, With Others' 'Bells 'n' Whistles'." Lecture at 1993 SABR convention, San Diego, California.

Stein, Fred. *Under Coogan's Bluff: A Fan's Recollections of the New York Giants Under Terry and Ott*. Self-published, 1978.

Steinbeck, John. *Journal of a Novel: The East of Eden Letters*. New York: Penguin Books, 1990.

Steiner, Bernard C. *Life and Correspondence of James McHenry*. Cleveland, Ohio: Burrows Bros. Co., 1907.

Steinhardt, Michael. *No Bull: My Life In and Out of Markets*. New York: Wily & Sons, Inc., 2001.

Stern, Seymour. "Bobby Takes Brooklyn Off Map, Puts Staten Island On," *Daily Mirror*, October 4, 1951.

"Stocks Go Ahead Third Day in Row," *New York Times*, October 4, 1951.

"Storm Ties Up IRT in Brooklyn," *New York Journal American*, July 19, 1851.

"Storm Halts Traffic, IRT Trains Here," *Brooklyn Eagle*, July 19, 1951.

"Strategie Checkmate," *Sporting News*, August 3, 1944.

Sullivan, "Ted." *Humorous Stories of the Ball Field: A Complete History of the Game and Its Exponents*. Chicago: M. A. Donohue & Company, 1903.

"The Summary," *New York Times*, October 3, 1951.

"The Summary," *New York Times*, October 4, 1951.

Surprise, Archie W. A. "Morgan Murphy's Signal Service Exposed at Last," *Philadelphia Inquirer*, September 18, 1900.

Swirsky, Seth. *Baseball Letters: A Fan's Correspondence with His Heroes*. New York: Kodansha America, Inc., 1996.

Swirsky, Seth. *Something to Write Home About: Great Baseball Memories in Letters to a Fan*. New York: Crown Publishers, 2003.

Sylvester, Robert. "The Biggest Smash," *New York Daily News*, June 1, 1971.

Talbot, Gayle. "Sports Round-Up," *Ironwood* (MI) *Daily Globe*, February 6, 1952.

Talese, Gay. "Ebbets Field Goes on the Scrap Pile," *New York Times*, February 24, 1960.

Talese, Gay. "Songs for Swatters, Hosannas for Halfbacks," *New York Times*, March 22, 1959.

"Tallulah: 'I'm So Happy I Don't Make Sense'," *Boston Daily Globe*, October 4, 1951.

Teague, Robert L. "Pomp Is Planned at Polo Grounds," *New York Times*, April 13, 1962.

"Team Will Leave Jacksonville Tonight for Return to Jersey City," *Jersey Journal*, April 11, 1946.

Testimonial Dinner Program. New Dorp Rolladium. Staten Island, New York. December 6, 1951.

"Testimonial for Thomson," *Sporting News*, December 5, 1951.

Thayer, Ernest (pen name Phin). "Casey at the Bat," *Daily Examiner*, June 3, 1888.

"Thirteenth Census of the United States: 1910—Population." NARA.

"30-Year Contract Is Signed by Berle," *New York Times*, March 19, 1951.

Thisted, Red. "Flying Scot Set to Soar Once More," *Sporting News*, January 5, 1955.

Thisted, Red. "Route-Goers Lead Braves Back on Road," *Sporting News*, July 20, 1955.

Thisted, Red. "Trailers Hold Back Braves to Slow Pace," *Sporting News*, July 21, 1954.

"Thompson Optioned to Ottawa by Giants," *New York Daily Mirror*, July 19, 1951.

"Thomson Assures Leo He Regrets to Leave Giants," *Sporting News*, February 24, 1954.

Thomson, Bobby, as told to Bill Gallo. "Thomson: Diary of the Hero," *New York Daily News*, October 3, 1991.

Thomson, Bobby, as told to the United Press. "Around Bases on a P.G. Cloud," *Brooklyn Eagle*, October 4, 1951.

Thomson, Bobby, with Lee Heiman and Bill Gutman. *The Giants Win the Pennant! The Giants Win the Pennant!* New York: Citadel Press, 2001.

Thomson, Bobby. "That Home Run Saved Me!," *Sport*, April 1952, 26–27, 68–69.

"Thomson, Busy as Speaker, Sees Braves One, Two, Three," *Sporting News,* December 1, 1954.

"Thomson Denies Secret Signal Led to Pennant-Winning Homer," *New York Times,* March 24, 1962.

"Thomson Finished with 100 RBI's," *Staten Island Advance,* October 4, 1951.

"Thomson Testimonial Huge Success at S.I. Rolladium," *Staten Island Advance,* December 7, 1951.

Thorn, John, Pete Palmer, and Michael Gershman, eds., with Matthew Silverman, Sean Lahman, and Greg Spira. *Total Baseball,* Seventh Edition. Kingston, N.Y.: Total Sports Publishing, 2001.

Thornley, Stew. *Land of the Giants: New York's Polo Grounds.* Philadelphia: Temple University Press, 2000.

"Thousands Cheer Bobby Thomson on Triumphal Islandwide Tour," *Staten Island Advance,* December 7, 1951.

Thrilling True Story of the Baseball GIANTS. Greenwich, Conn.: Fawcett Publications, Inc., 1952.

"Thumper Tops Mileage Marathon—He's 41, Year Older Than Wynn," *Sporting News,* March 9, 1960.

Top 5 Reasons You Can't Blame, ESPN, November 1, 2005.

Torrey, Raymond, Frank Place, Jr., and Robert L. Dickinson. *New York Walk Book.* Third Edition. New York: The American Geographical Society, 1951.

"Trade Winds Fall to Whisper Among Miami Palm Trees," *Sporting News,* December 10, 1947.

Traubel, Horace. Edited by Gertrude Traubel. *With Walt Whitman in Camden,* Volume 5. Carbondale, Ill.: Southern Illinois University Press, 1964.

"Tricks in Base Ball," *Sporting News,* January 21, 1893.

"Tricky Tactics," *Brooklyn Eagle,* June 3, 1890.

Trimble, Joe. "Cardinals Rap Dodgers, 4–2, in First Playoff," *Daily News,* October 2, 1946.

Trimble, Joe. "Chuck Howls 'Spitter!' at Jones' Trick Pitch," *Daily News,* October 3, 1951.

True, Frank C. "Durocher and Yvars End Row," *New York Sun,* March 21, 1949.

True, Frank C. "Ott Discovers 'Cooler" for Pitchers," *New York Sun,* April 18, 1946.

Truman Presidential Museum & Library. Independence, Missouri.

Tuckner, Howard M. "Branca Relives a Mournful Day," *New York Times,* July 15, 1962.

Tuckner, Howard M. "Two Trumpets and a Trombone Sound Dirge in Empty Ballpark, *New York Times,* September 30, 1957.

Turan, Kenneth. "Mets' Fan Used to Choke, but Not on Laughter," *Washington Post,* October 10, 1969.

"TV Industry Plays Ball in N.Y. Playoff on Dodgers-Giants," *Variety,* October 3, 1951.

TV Tome. *www.tvtome.com.* Episode #191: "Toast of the Town," aired February 10, 1952.

"23-Year High of 87° Due to Crash Today," *Brooklyn Eagle,* October 2, 1951.

"2 Pitching Mounts in Each Bullpen Asked by Dodgers," *Sporting News,* May 30, 1951.

Twombly, Wells. "Arguments Rage for 20 Years." *Sporting News*, May 8, 1971.

Tygiel, Jules. *Past Time: Baseball as History.* New York: Oxford University Press, 2000.

"'Ulcers, Wonderful Ulcers,' Says Pafko, Summing Up Effects of Giant-Dodger Finish," *New York Times*, October 1, 1951.

"Uniform Numbers Range from 1 to 59," *Sporting News*, May 9, 1951.

United Press. "Bobby Thomson Disclaims Credit for Giants Victory," November 19, 1951.

United Press. "Branca's Move to Tigers Pleases Ex-Bum Hurler," July 12, 1953.

United Press. "Dilatory Ballplayer Fined for Arguing," *New York World-Telegram*, May 27, 1947.

United Press. "Flying Ball Seen in N.Y.," *Montreal Star*, October 3, 1951, late edition.

United Press. "Giants Lose No. 1 Fan, Indignant Over Shift," *New York Times*, July 17, 1948.

United Press. "'Tis a Braw, Bricht Nicht as Thomsonville Blows Cork," *Cleveland Press*, October 4, 1951.

United Press International. "Thomson Homer Not on 'Steal,' Says Branca," *Los Angeles Times*, March 24, 1962.

United States Hockey Hall of Fame. Eveleth, Minnesota.

Universal International News.

Unver, George. "Idlewood Airport's Anti-Fog Lights," *Electrical Union World*, February 1, 1949.

Updike, John. "Hub Fans Bid Kid Adieu," *New Yorker*, October 22, 1960, 109–31.

U.S. Air Force Project Blue Book. Air Intelligence Information Report, October 3, 1951. *www.bluebookarchive.org.*

"Use of Area Complicates Sunday Curfew in Boston," *Sporting News*, May 2, 1951.

"Van Arsdale's Mother Dies," *Electrical Union World*, August 1, 1951.

Vecsey, George. "What's in a Name?," *New York Times*, July 2, 1984.

Vidal, Gore. *Palimpsest: A Memoir.* New York: Penguin Books, 1995.

Voice of America, Daily Broadcast Content Report, October 3, 1951. NARA.

Walden: The Writings of Henry D. Thoreau. Princeton, N.J.: Princeton University Press, 2004.

"Walks Into a Bar, Kills 1, Wounds 1," *New York Times*, July 13, 1938.

Walker, Ben, for the Associated Press. February 4, 2001.

Ward, Alan. "On Second Thought," *Oakland Tribune*, May 13, 1952.

Ward, John Montgomery. *Base-Ball: How to Become a Player with the Origin, History, and Explanation of the Game.* Cleveland: Society for American Baseball Research, 1993.

Ward, John M. "Baseballists Up in Arms: A League Composed of Brotherhood Players May Now Be Formed," *New York World*, September 21, 1889.

Warrington, Bob. *The Fight for Sunday Baseball in Philadelphia. philadelphiaath letics.org/history/sundaybaseball.html.* Philadelphia Athletics Society, Inc., 2001.

"The Washington Ball Club," *Washington DC Evening Star*, April 7, 1888.

"Watchung Elects GOP Councilman," *Courier News*, November 8, 1967.

"Waterside Powerhouse 1," *Electrical Union World*, November 1, 1948.

The Way It Was. Episode #1: "Dodgers-Giants Playoff." Original airdate October 3, 1974.

"Weather Throughout the Nation and Abroad," *New York Times*, March 25, 1962.

Webber, Elizabeth, and Mike Feinsilber. *Merriam-Webster's Dictionary of Allusions*. Springfield, Mass.: Merriam-Webster, 1999.

Wedge, Will. "Leo Durocher Sent to Reds," *New York Sun*, February 6, 1930.

Wedge, Will. "Many Changes in Appurtenances and Dress of Game Since 1849." *Sporting News*, May 21, 1936.

Weed, Lieut. Col. Frank W., M.C., U.S. Army. (Prepared under the direction of Maj. Gen. M. W. Ireland, M.D., Surgeon General of the Army.) *The Medical Department of the United States Army in the World War*, Vol. V. Washington, D.C.: Government Printing Office, 1923. 323–62.

Westvaco Corporation Records. Library and Archives, Forest History Society. Durham, North Carolina.

"WHAT A FINISH," *New York Times*, October 4, 1951.

"What Stalin's A-Bomb Means to the West and Its Defense," *Newsweek*, October 15, 1951, 20–29.

Whelan, Tom. "August Special to Sal Yvars," *Reporter Dispatch*, August 7, 1977.

White, E. B. *Here Is New York*. New York: The Little Bookroom, 1999.

White, E. B. "The Seven Steps to Heaven," *New Yorker*, September 7, 1957. 32–37.

White, G. Edward. *Creating the National Pastime: Baseball Transforms Itself, 1903–1953*. Princeton, N.J.: Princeton University Press, 1996.

White, Jr., Gordon S. "From Hill to Lanes," *New York Times*, July 14, 1959.

Wilson Memorial Union Church, Watchung, New Jersey.

"Who's a Liar?," *Life*, April 2, 1951.

"Why Did Don Newcombe Leave Playoff? His Arm Was Dead, Robinson Explains," *Sporting News*, October 17, 1951.

"Wife on Phone As Hugh Casey Ends His Life," *New York Herald Tribune*, July 4, 1951.

Wilcox, Edwin. "'Wait'll Next Year,' Weep B'klyn Fans," *New York Daily Mirror*, October 4, 1951.

Will, George F. "A Season Spoiled," *Washington Post*, February 8, 2001.

Wille, Lois. "Northbrook Takes Care of Its Thomsons," *Chicago Daily News*, July 26, 1958.

Williams, Jonathan. "Paying Respects." *New York Times*, December 19, 1976.

Winchell, Walter. "In New York," *Washington Post*, October 7, 1951.

Winchell, Walter. "Walter Winchell . . . of New York," *Washington Post*, November 6, 1951.

Wojciechowski, Gene. "Baseball Cheating: A Spitting Image," *Press & Sun-Bulletin* (NY), August 7, 1990.

Wolf, Al. "Giants Gain Series Spot with 5–4 Win," *Los Angeles Times*, October 4, 1951.

Wolf, Al. "Sportraits," *Los Angeles Times*, October 5, 1947.

Wolf, Bob. "'We Have Proof of Sign Thefts,' Tebbetts Claims," *Sporting News*, July 14, 1962.

Wolters, Larry. "Gambling Boss' Hands Betray His Fears to TV," *Chicago Daily Tribune*, March 14, 1951.

Woods, David. *A History of Tactical Communications Techniques*. Orlando: The Martin Co., 1965.

"The World Series Stare," *Life*, October 20, 1952, 47–48, 50, 53.

"W-T&S Replay of Today's Game, Tune in WMGM—7 P.M.," *New York World-Telegram and Sun*, October 3, 1951.

Wulf, Steve. "Ticks of the Trade," *Sports Illustrated*, September 13, 1981, 92–108.

"Yank Hurler Gets Mercer Memorial," *New York Times*, February 4, 1952.

"Yanks Sign Ralph Branca; Enos Back on Active List," *Sporting News*, July 28, 1954.

Young, Dick. "Big Klu Swings at 116 Miles Per Hour," *Sporting News*, July 11, 1956.

Young, Dick. "Branca 2-Hits Bucs 5–0; Furillo, Robby Homer," *New York Daily News*, August 28, 1951.

Young, Dick. "Dodgers Rally Twice to Down Braves, 10–5," *Daily Argus* (NY), August 14, 1947.

Young, Dick. "If and Reverse," *New York Daily News*, October 9, 1952.

Young, Dick. "Lippy Charges MacPhail Entertains Gamblers," *New York Daily News*, March 10, 1947.

Young, Dick. "Majors Ban Mechanical Pilfering of Enemy Signs," *New York Daily News*, April 1, 1962.

Young, Dick. "Robby HR Cops in 14th," *New York Daily News*, October 1, 1951.

Young, Dick. "Signals and Spies," *Sports Illustrated*, July 2, 1956.

Young, Dick. "Thomson Discards 'Unlucky' Number," *Sporting News*, June 13, 1956.

Young, Dick. "Who's Afraid of the Giants? Dodgers Aren't—Much," *New York Daily News*, August 29, 1951.

Young, Dick. "Young Ideas," *New York Daily News*, July 15, 1962.

"Your Question, Please," *Sporting News*, July 15, 1985.

Ziegel, Vic. "Branca Takes Shot at Giants Pitches in On Sign Scam," *New York Daily News*, July 11, 2001.

Ziegler, Edward, and Lewis Goldfrank. *Emergency Doctor*. New York: Ballantine Books, 1988.

Zuber, Chas. H. "Futile Protest," *Sporting Life*, Vol. 54, No. 4, October 2, 1909.

INDEX